Public Finance
IN THEORY AND PRACTICE

Holley H. Ulbrich
Clemson University

THOMSON
SOUTH-WESTERN

Australia · Canada · Mexico · Singapore · Spain · United Kingdom · United States

THOMSON

SOUTH-WESTERN

inance in Theory and Practice

Holley H. Ulbrich

Vice President/Team Director:
Michael P. Roche

Publisher:
Mike Mercier

Acquisitions Editor:
Mike Worls

Developmental Editor:
Bob Sandman

Marketing Manager:
Janet Hennies

Production Editor:
Margaret M. Bril

Editorial Assistant:
Sarah Curtis

Manufacturing Coordinator:
Sandee Milewski

Production House:
Buuji, Inc.

Printer:
World Color
Taunton, Massachusetts 02780

Design Project Manager:
Rik Moore

Internal Design:
Rik Moore

Cover Designer:
Rik Moore

Cover Image:
©PhotoDisc, Inc.

Photography Manager:
Rik Moore

Photo Researcher:
Rik Moore

Library of Congress Cataloging-
in-Publication Data

Ulbrich, Holley H.
  Public finance : in theory
and practice / Holley Hewitt
Ulbrich.
    p. cm.
  Includes bibliographical
references and index.
  ISBN 0-324-01660-3
(alk. paper)
    1. Finance, Public.   I.
Title: Public finance in theory
and practice. II. Title.

HJ141 .U43 2003
336—dc21
                    2001057724

BRIEF CONTENTS

CONTENTS

iv

PREFACE

Despite the rhetoric of value-free economics, economists themselves in fact espouse particular sets of values in all of the roles they play. Sometimes they articulate those values and make them explicit. Prefaces are one of the places where those values are likely to be set forth.

Those of us who are writers of economics textbooks are teachers, authors, and economists with a special interest in a particular field. In each of those capacities we hold a philosophy, a set of values, a way of being in the world. A textbook will reflect a philosophy of teaching, a philosophy about textbooks, and a philosophical approach to the particular field that is the subject of both teaching and textbook.

As a teacher, I have found over 30 years that economics, and particularly the economic way of thinking, is absorbed slowly and with frequent repetition. One of the values that has emerged from that experience is my firm belief that too much theory and too little application or institutional content leaves the student floundering without having integrated that theory into his or her way of being in the world, without any empirical or institutional content. On the other hand (a favorite expression of economists), too little theory leaves the student with no mental framework in which to process new encounters with experience and institutions by applying the theory.

Like many students, I was originally attracted to economics as a way to make the world a better place, a tool for public policy that would result in better, more thoughtful, more conscious choices about human interactions in the economic sphere. I wanted my learning experience to provide me not only with a set of analytical tools but also a lot of practice in applying them to concrete situations in real-world settings.

For new faculty in particular, coming directly from graduate school where they have just absorbed a great deal of economic theory and have not yet had the opportunity to accumulate the "stories" that make theory come alive, it is tempting to teach undergraduates in ways that tip the balance heavily toward theory. Older faculty often lean toward the other end of the spectrum, toward the stories, the particularities within which the theory is embedded and applied. This textbook tries to strike a balance to ensure that students acquire the basic analytical tools of public sector economics and learn to apply them in multiple institutional contexts—federal, state, local, and frequently, in the context of another nation or culture.

Consciously thinking about the appropriate balance of theory, applications, and institutions represents the economic way of thinking about learning, choosing a mix of learning and topics that lies along the middle of the production possibilities frontier.

As a textbook writer, I face the basic economic problem of scarcity and choice within each chapter and in the book as a whole. The scarcity is not only the economy of page space but also the economy of reader attention. How much theory can be absorbed in a given chapter, and which theoretical models or topics should be included? Which of the many applications should be there? How much institutional and historical context—data, events, structures of governments, processes—does the student need in order to understand how theory plays out in a cultural, historical, and institutional context?

Ten years ago I was part of a U.S. mission to Bulgaria to help local government officials understand the role that they would play in a market system. Like many people who go abroad to "help," I learned more than I taught, and I learned as much about my own society as about theirs because I could view it from the vantage point of a society that had been organized differently and through the eyes of people who wanted to borrow from our way of doing things without becoming a copy of the American way. I admitted our failings in child care and health care. I explained the great diversity of state and local taxes and fees, beach access, and alcohol regulations. I had to assure them that the market could do as well as the government in ensuring that grocery stores had bread and milk, and that economic freedom was not the same as anarchy. I wanted to share some of that cross-cultural insight with students both in teaching and in textbook writing.

That desire to embed theory in both applications and societal contexts has led to two important dimensions of this book. The first is that state and local government are present throughout the book, not just at the end as has been the custom in many previous public sector textbooks. Not only is a lot of the action in the public sector at the state and local level right now, but also these "laboratories of federalism" provide some of the necessary diversity of cultural context in which theory and applications are played out. The second is that there are a number of boxed features scattered throughout the text that describe how a particular tax, or program, or issue plays out in a different country or group of countries. From the upward flow of revenue from local to central government in China, to the nature of federalism in Switzerland, to the difference between English-style and French-style property tax systems, understanding that there are other ways to do these things helps us better understand the choices that the United States has made in these areas.

As an economist who has for 30 years specialized in questions of public sector economics, with particular emphasis on state and local issues, I have developed a philosophy of the public sector that is neither the optimistic view in which I was trained in the golden days of the mid-1960s nor the cynical pessimism about government that has since emerged. There are, after all, many necessary parts of life that the market cannot adequately supply. As Jefferson said, it is for that reason ". . . that governments are instituted among men [*sic*]"—to assist us in our individual and collective experience of ". . . life, liberty, and the pursuit of happiness."

But unlike Jefferson, I live in postmodern society, a pluralistic world with no simple either–or, right–wrong, yes–no answers, with substantial doubts about the existence of objective truth, and with a growing recognition of the many dimensions of power and powerlessness. In this postmodern society, as in the modern society that dominated the last two centuries, government is still an important resource. It can be, and often is, a tool to correct the injustices of unfettered private self-interest. It can also be captured by those same private self-interests and used on their own behalf. Government can be reactive, responding to one problem at a time. Or it can be visionary, proactive, ensuring that the needs and interests of future generations are included in our current policies. Government can be a part of the problem—or part of the solution. Government can appear to be a monolith, as it was to a large degree in Eastern Europe prior to 1990, or it can be a complex blend of independent governments at multiple levels approaching similar problems in different ways or different problems in similar ways. Much of the time government is all of these things at once.

It has been my goal as a teacher, a researcher, a policy analyst, and a textbook writer to help others to understand how government works, how government works well, and how it fails. Such understanding is an important foundation for ensuring that this tool is used to promote the ideals reflected in the Declaration of Independence and goals set forth in the preamble to the constitution (". . . to establish justice, ensure domestic tranquillity, provide for the common defense, promote the general welfare, and secure the blessings of liberty to ourselves and our posterity.") These are still valid ideals and goals in the 21st century.

Even when only one name is listed on the cover, no author works alone. I am grateful to those who taught me public finance as a student—Philip Taylor and Dorothy Goodwin—and to the many colleagues with whom I continued my public sector education at Clemson University and elsewhere, including Ralph Byrns, Jim Hite, Rodney Mabry, Ryan Amacher, Hugh Macaulay, Susannah Calkins, Daphne Kenyon, Harry Miley, Randy Martin, Jon Pierce, and John Shannon. I appreciate the shared learning experience with many students, undergraduate and graduate, over the years, especially Ellen Saltzman, who now works with me at the Strom Thurmond Institute. My editor, Bob Sandman, provided wise guidance, counsel, and encouragement. A number of anonymous reviewers made excellent suggestions. My husband Carlton, not an economist, patiently did multiple drafts of all the diagrams. Ellen Reneke, a long-time friend and library staffer in agricultural economics at Clemson University, provided research support. It takes a village to write a textbook. This is my village.

ACKNOWLEDGMENTS

I am grateful to the following reviewers who provided comments on the manuscript for this textbook.

Alan S. Caniglia
Franklin & Marshall College

Don Cole
Drew University

F. Trenery Dolbear, Jr.
Brandeis University

Gerald Fox
High Point University

Roger S. Hewett
Drake University

Robert M. McNab
Naval Postgraduate School

Donald M. Peppard
Connecticut College

Tony Popp
New Mexico State University

Jonathan Sandy
University of San Diego

Paul Seidenstat
Temple University

Holley Ulbrich
Clemson, South Carolina

ABOUT THE AUTHOR

Holley Hewitt Ulbrich is Alumni Distinguished Professor Emerita at Clemson University and a Senior Fellow at the Strom Thurmond Institute at Clemson and the Center for Governmental Studies at the University of South Carolina. She holds a PhD in economics from the University of Connecticut. The author of five textbooks and well known as a consultant to state and local government agencies, she has had a considerable amount of experience in public finance at the local, state, national, and even international level, including service on an Agency for International Development mission to Bulgaria and teaching short courses in taxation and public finance at the World Bank. Dr. Ulbrich worked as a policy analyst for the U.S. Advisory Commission on Intergovernmental Relations during 1984–1985, where she wrote a widely cited analysis of the taxation of interstate mail order sales as well as two monographs on local taxes, one on local sales taxes and one on local income taxes. She continues to work as a consultant on public finance issues to a number of state agencies and public interest organizations.

GOVERNMENT AND THE MARKET

From before recorded history, governments have been instituted among humans. Some, like the American government, in the words of the Declaration of Independence, "derive their just powers from the consent of the governed. . . ." Others exist by force of arms, or tradition, or external imposition, or other sources of power. Very small societies often manage with relatively little government. But once societies become large, complex, and technologically sophisticated, the need arises for a referee, a rule setter, an authority for resolving disputes. Governments are called into being to provide a way to reconcile the needs of the individual for autonomy and freedom with the need for citizens to find ways to work together to address common concerns, managed shared resources, and resolve the boundary problems that separate one household from another. However limited its original mandate, however—and in the United States, the original mandate, the Articles of Confederation, was very limited indeed—sooner or later the role of government begins to expand. Much thought and discussion goes into determining what government should be permitted to do when intruding on an essentially private society that is largely governed by individual choice.

The paragraph above describes a distinctly American view of government. Most Americans consider this individualistic interpretation of the role of government as the intruder into primarily market and private decisions to be natural, or at least the norm. In fact, in some nations there is no such persistent division of spheres of activity into primary (market) and secondary (government). These countries have a fluctuating mix of public and private activity, with the roles determined on an *ad hoc* basis. The nations of Western Europe

and many countries in Latin America in particular have shifted from time to time between a larger public role and a larger private role as they attempt to balance competing goals of equity and efficiency, individual security and work incentives, public infrastructure and private capital.

Still other societies are even now going through a public-versus-private sorting-out process in reverse. In these societies, including the former Soviet Union and Eastern Europe, the challenge has been to transition from a system in which the community took precedence over the individual to one that provides a much larger sphere for private, individual decisions. It is a slow and confusing road to travel in going from a society in which government managed almost all economic activity to an alternative economic system in which individuals, markets, and private voluntary associations play important roles in organizing economic activity. Watching the experience of Eastern and Central Europe at a distance makes it clear that there is no single "right" balance between individual and community, public and private, government and the market. Different societies can and do settle at different points along the continuum from minimum government, maximum market/private sector to the opposite extreme.

Like other branches of economics, public finance or public sector economics combines a body of theory with a set of institutions to describe, analyze, and interpret the workings of government in a predominantly private economy. The theory is more or less universal, but it is implemented differently in different institutional contexts. Policies that work for a small, homogeneous, highly centralized nation or highly competitive markets may have very different effects in another nation that is larger, heterogeneous, decentralized, or characterized by a lot of private market power. To provide an institutional setting in which to explore public finance theory, this book assumes the institutions of the U.S. economy, because that is the set of institutions most familiar to readers of this book. However, all of us need to stretch our minds to include consideration of outside perspectives. Many of the chapters in this book have boxed features in which one of the questions or issues raised in the chapter is viewed through the filter of another country's history and institutions.

The three chapters in Part 1 address some fundamental issues about government that provide the background for a closer examination of the revenue and expenditure dimensions of public sector activity. While the first chapter reviews basic understandings about the division of responsibility between governments and markets, Chapters 2 and 3 resolve more around the political economy of the public sector, blending financial considerations from economics with structural issues that might more properly be considered to fall in the realm of political science. This institutional context is very important for understanding what *is*, rather than what *could* or *should be*, an essential part of one's education as a policy economist.

CHAPTER 1

GOVERNMENT IN A MARKET SYSTEM

Once students get past their introductory course in economics, they may find that whatever university or college they attend offers a fairly standard package of upper division courses in economics. This package almost always includes intermediate macroeconomics, intermediate microeconomics, statistics and/or econometrics, money and banking, and labor economics. Note that even in this short list there are several courses in which the government plays a central role. One is macroeconomics, and another is money and banking, two courses taken by most economics majors. Students may also have an opportunity to take courses in government and business, environmental economics, economic development, urban economics, public choice, and, of course, **public finance** or **public sector economics.** All of these courses devote a significant part of the material to the role of government in that particular area. How much overlap is there between these fields? What parts of the role of government in a market system are included in a course in public sector economics and which are reserved for other courses? The answer to that question has evolved considerably in the last few decades.

One of the great figures of 20th-century public finance, Richard Musgrave, divided the economic role of government into allocation, distribution, and stabilization. **Allocation** refers to anything the government does that affects the mixture (quantity and quality) of goods and services that the economy produces, from direct government production to regulation to tax incentives

to penalties for illegal activities. **Distribution** refers to anything the government does that affects the distribution of income and wealth. Just about everything the government does, from locating roads to tax cuts to school vouchers and college scholarships to mortgage insurance guarantees, affects the distribution of income and wealth. Finally, **stabilization** refers to those government actions that influence the overall level of employment, output, and prices. To do justice to all of those aspects of government involvement in the economy would require several volumes and span several courses, so courses and textbooks in public sector economics or public finance have over time set some boundaries that have narrowed the subject matter somewhat.

Although the name *public sector economics* has been displacing *public finance* as the preferred title of the field, the older title of public finance does have an advantage in defining the scope. The "finance" in public finance refers to the taxing, spending, and budgeting activities of government, so any activities of the government that are not primarily budget-related (particularly regulatory activities) are usually left to other courses. A second way in which public finance/public sector economics narrowed its scope in the last two decades was to assign the stabilization function to courses in macroeconomics and money and banking, along with government policies that encourage or retard economic growth. So technically speaking, a course in public sector economics or public finance is really a course in the microeconomics of public finance. Except for some discussion of the size and management of the public debt and deficits/surpluses, stabilization is largely absent from public finance courses and textbooks. This narrower definition, tying public finance to microeconomics and to budget-centered issues of taxing and spending, provided the central focus for the economic subdiscipline of public finance for several decades.

More recently, as public finance has evolved into public sector economics, the scope of the field has broadened beyond the components of the budget.[1] The use of taxes, fees, and charges as instruments to achieve social or regulatory objectives has led to much more analysis of issues in public sector pricing, such as the design of congestion fees and effluent charges, demand measurement for public goods, Lindahl pricing, and other topics that will be addressed in later chapters. The relatively new field of public choice that has developed during the last 30 years has also exerted considerable influence on economists' understanding of how decisions are made in the public sector. **Public choice** is a partially separate field of economics that analyzes the behavior of elected officials and bureaucrats in the public sector and explores the policy implications of government failure. Sometimes public choice appears in the course catalog as a component of public sector economics; other times, public choice commands a separate course of its own.

1. For an extended discussion of the development of the field of public economics or public sector economics, see Jacques Dreze, "Forty Years of Public Economics: A Personal Perspective," *Journal of Economic Perspectives*, 9(2) (Spring 1995): 111–130.

GOVERNMENT AND THE MARKET

Although economies can be designed with very diverse spheres for the public and private sectors, the market system has become the dominant form of economic organization at the beginning of the 21st century. While some things governments do are quite similar to what markets do, some fundamental differences between markets and governments will be explored more fully in later chapters. Two central differences between market processes and government processes, however, should be noted at the beginning. In the market, citizens vote with dollars. Unequal incomes make for very different abilities to make purchases in the market. In most markets, furthermore, buyers all pay the same price but may consume different quantities of goods and services. With government, citizens vote with—votes. (They also try to influence legislators in other ways—with letters, phone calls, paid lobbyists, and campaign contributions.) Each citizen has one and only one vote. And when governments provide services financed with taxes, citizens all pay different prices yet have the option to consume the same quantity of goods and services. Clearly, some citizens will be happier with market processes and outcomes, others with government processes and outcomes—or the same citizen may be happier with markets for some services and government for others.

Government as Rule-Maker and Referee

A market system is based on private ownership of the means of production: land, labor, capital, and enterprise. The use of those resources and the products that those resources are used to produce are bought and sold in the marketplace. To engage in exchange or negotiate contracts with strangers or over long distances or time periods, buyers and sellers need some assurances that the seller really owns what is being sold, that buyers know what rights are being conveyed with purchase, and that contracts are enforceable. A market system requires a clear definition of property rights and a guarantee that those rights are protected. The government, from before recorded history, has been the creator, protector, definer, interpreter, and enforcer of property rights. The government-provided system of courts and law enforcement is there to ensure that people who owe money can be compelled to pay, that sellers are liable for defective products, that the car you bought was really owned by the seller, or that the title to the lot you sold did (or did not) include mineral or water rights.

Because of the central importance of property rights in a market system, the rule-making and rule-enforcing function of government is its primary economic responsibility. These rules include the Constitution, laws, and the interpretation of the laws by the executive branch, the courts, and the various administrative agencies. When people fail to abide by some kinds of rules set by the government, they can be arrested and charged with crimes against the state, ranging from illegal parking to high treason. People can also be charged with crimes against other individuals, such as murder, theft, embezzlement, and assault. But the government also establishes rules and procedures for resolving disputes between private individuals over such matters as ownership of property, trespass, enforcement of contracts, and divorce. There are also courts and enforcement procedures for such civil matters. (The word *civil,* derived from the Latin *civis* or "citizen," refers to cases between private citizens, including corporations as well as individuals.)

Another significant, if somewhat nebulous, role for government in an essentially market society is as the creator of an economic and social framework. Should courtrooms have the Ten Commandments on the wall, or should cities allow nativity scenes at Christmas on public property? Can states impose sales taxes on interstate commerce? Does free speech extend to pornography on the Internet? What role should the federal government play in ensuring a connective network of airports, highways, seaports, and other means of transportation? Who sets the rules for engaging in international commerce? Where does money (currency and coins) come from and who ensures that it will be accepted as legal tender? Some of these roles fall outside the domain of economics, but the provision of public infrastructure (roads, dams, national parks, etc.) and the management of the monetary system and foreign commerce are historically roles assigned to the federal government by the Constitution.

Markets and Efficiency

In a market system, private individuals and organizations (including corporations) make most of the economic decisions in pursuit of their own self-interest. The widespread preference for markets as the decision-making tool is grounded in microeconomic theory. Microeconomics demonstrates that under ideal conditions, the market will be more efficient than any alternative system. **Economic efficiency** is measured by the quantity and variety of goods and services that its members produce, consume, and distribute out of their limited available resources. The market is more efficient than any other method for discerning what combination of goods and services people want and delivering that combination. The market is more efficient in ensuring that goods are produced at the lowest possible resource cost and sold at the lowest possible price. The market is more efficient at rewarding those who heed market signals and punishing those who pay no attention. If efficiency in the use of scarce resources is a primary objective, the market is the ideal tool to achieve that goal.

In its strongest form, this ideal efficient outcome of markets is referred to as **Pareto optimality.** An economic situation of production or distribution or both is Pareto optimal when it is not possible to make at least one person better off without making one or more persons worse off. All prices are equal to marginal cost, all products are being produced with the most efficient resource mix, all inputs are paid the value of their marginal product, and all consumers have allocated their budgets so that the satisfaction that they receive from the last unit of each goods purchased is just equal to the price, which is in turn equal to the marginal cost of producing it. Costs and prices reflect social as well as private costs. In such a Pareto-optimal world, there would be little need for government.

Government, Efficiency, and Equity

Because a perfectly functioning market system would lead to a Pareto-optimal allocation of resources, such a system would limit government's role to those functions that the market cannot perform at all. The list is surprisingly short. Almost all of the activities that people have come to associate with government—providing for defense, controlling the money supply, ensuring law enforcement, building highways, and educating the next generation, for example—can be and have been produced privately by either nonprofit or for-profit firms at some time. Private security guards can protect life and property. Hired mercenaries can defend citizens from foreign enemies. Private toll roads were the norm in colonial New England and continue to exist along public highways in some places. Scrip in company towns in the 19th and early 20th centuries served as private money. Private schools continue to educate large numbers of students. Is there anything the market cannot do? That is, is there any essential, indispensable function for government in a market system?

It is true that just about every function of government can be, or has been, performed by private groups, but often the market does not perform those functions very satisfactorily or even very efficiently. Why? Perhaps one or more of the ideal market conditions needed to ensure efficiency (or Pareto optimality) do not hold. Students should recall from earlier courses what those conditions are, because they are the assumptions that underlie the perfectly competitive model:

- Large numbers of individuals and firms,
- Little or no concentration of market power,
- Perfect information, free mobility of resources and products, and
- No spillover effects in either production or consumption so that private and social costs and benefits are the same.

When any of these assumptions are violated, there is a likelihood of market failure. When the market delivers less than satisfactory outcomes, a case can be made for turning to government for improved results. Chapter 4 will explore the role for government in identifying and addressing these kinds of **market failure.**

A second reason for calling in the government is that the objective function—that is, the desired goals and objectives of economic activity—may include additional considerations besides economic efficiency. Most often, those additional considerations involve **equity,** or some agreed-on notion of fairness in the distribution of the costs and benefits of government among groups of citizens at the current time, or between present and future generations. Equity between members of the same generation or between successive generations is very difficult to define in a way that will result in broad agreement. Despite the difficulty of defining equity, however, it has been a central concern of philosophers of the public sector since Plato's *Republic* more than 2,000 years ago gave central place to justice in the design of the perfect society.

Government Response to Market Failure

When the market fails to produce desired goods and services, or to produce them in sufficient quantity/quality, or when it produces undesirable goods and services, or produces too much of goods with harmful spillovers, then governments may intervene to try to restore production to something closer to optimal levels. The government has a number of tools at its disposal to encourage or discourage production of particular goods and services:

1. Subsidies (reducing seller costs or net price paid by the buyer, e.g., subsidizing higher education with grants to students and/or to colleges and universities) can encourage private production or consumption of goods and services with broad public benefits.[2]
2. Tax incentives (e.g., tax deductions for educational expenditures or charitable contributions) can encourage private production/consumption of specified goods and services that are believed to provide broad public benefits.
3. Guarantees can reduce risk (e.g., disaster insurance, crop insurance, mortgage loan guarantees, student loan guarantees, bank deposit insurance) and thus encourage private production/consumption of specified goods and services.
4. Penalties can be levied in the form of taxes, charges, or fines, for excessive production of goods or services that are believed to impose costs on others.
5. Mandates can require production/consumption of a particular good or service (e.g., seat belts in cars, safety helmets on motorcycles).
6. Laws and regulations can forbid production/consumption of a particular good or service (e.g., cocaine, tobacco, or pornography to people under age 18, prostitution outside of Nevada).
7. Public production can provide certain products and services (e.g., national defense, law enforcement).
8. Private production with public financing can provide certain products and services.

---

2. The issue of public benefits and costs associated with private consumption is discussed in Chapter 4.

PRODUCTION, PROVISION, AND PRIVATIZATION

The first seven of the preceding options will appear in later chapters as policy options available for addressing various issues. The eighth option of private production on contract with the government is addressed in this chapter. This issue has particularly captured the public's attention in the United States and around the world since the early 1980s. Together with widespread disillusionment about the ability of government to intervene effectively, the **privatization** movement spread rapidly from country to country as nations reassessed the roles of the public and private sectors. Privatization, which means assigning more of the responsibility for certain kinds of production to the market or the private sector, goes directly to the heart of the debate over the role of government in relation to the market.

The allocation function of government, as defined by Musgrave, refers to efforts to influence the composition of output through taxing, spending, and regulatory tools. One option for ensuring a supply of public and quasi-public goods, such as lighthouses, money (currency), national defense, a court system, prisons, and highways, is for the government to produce those goods and services itself. A second option is to contract with a private firm to produce the goods or services. That contract can range all the way from using private suppliers of inputs (e.g., buying airplanes for the military or copiers for congressional staff) to total control, as when private contractors take over entire public school systems or prisons. **Public provision** is a broader concept than public production; public provision means that government finances a service with public revenue either by producing the service itself or by contracting the actual production or delivery of the good or service to a private firm.

The shift of many areas of government provision from public production to contracts with private producers (privatization) is not just an American phenomenon. The United Kingdom actually led the way with the sale of many public enterprises including steel and auto companies, electric and telephone monopolies, and housing owned by local governments (council housing), which was sold to the occupants on very favorable terms. Privatization has been a popular movement in many developing countries as well. In the United States, many of the experiments with privatization have been at the state and local level, including private management of garbage collection, prisons, fire protection, and even public schools.[3]

The advantages of privatization are numerous. Governments, particularly state and local governments, are generalists who must produce many kinds of services; private firms can specialize. Private firms are often more flexible in responding to changes in demand, because they are not burdened by civil service

3. For a good discussion of recent experience with privatization at the state and local level, see Arnold H. Raphaelson, ed., *Restructuring State and Local Services: Ideas, Proposals, and Experiments* (Westport, CT: Praeger Publishers, 1998).

A CASE STUDY IN PRIVATIZATION: PRISON REALTY CORPORATION

One of the "services" of government that most citizens would prefer not to experience is that of being a prisoner in a state prison or local jail. With truth-in-sentencing laws resulting in longer times served, and more convictions for drug-related offenses, America's prison population is booming; in fact, it is growing faster than the ability of states to build and staff prisons. In 1983, two entrepreneurs in Nashville saw an economic opportunity in prisons, founding the Corrections Corporation of America (CCA) to build and operate prisons under contract to the federal and state governments.[1] The founders of the new company thought that it would be possible to build prisons cheaper and faster than the government could without procurement red tape, and operate them more cheaply because there would be no unions or civil service to contend with. By 1999, when CCA merged with Prison Realty Trust to form Prison Realty Corporation, it was managing 79 facilities in three countries with almost 70,000 beds.[2]

The successes and failures of this privatization venture are a good case study of the hazards and benefits of privatization. States, which are among the principal customers for such services, found that their management headaches did not go away when they contracted out the building and operation of prisons. Complaints have been made about mistreatment of boys in a South Carolina juvenile facility, violence in an Ohio CCA prison, and, most commonly, importation of "undesirable" prisoners from other states. Problems have arisen when prison employees have had to deal with prison riots and escapes, which are law enforcement functions involving the use of force that are normally reserved for the public sector. States find that prisoners, sometimes high-risk ones, are being transferred to their prisons from other states, raising thorny problems of jurisdiction in the case of escapes.[3] And accusations have been made that private prison firms "skim" the most docile prisoners and transfer the difficult ones to state prisons, which holds down their costs but drives up the cost of the remaining state-operated facilities.

On the other hand, there are satisfied customers like Bent County, Colorado, which sold its correctional facility to CCA in 1998. Bent County is pleased to receive a per diem payment of $2

rules for their workers. For small local governments, privatization reduces the variety of activities and employees that have to be overseen by a small staff and a part-time, volunteer elected board or council. Local monopolies in the public sector have to compete with or be replaced by private firms that are often in competition with each other for contracts with multiple governments, forcing them to offer quality service at a low price. Privatization may make it easier to share or pool services with nearby towns or counties when one private supplier may be able to serve them all at a lower average cost because of economies of scale. In some parts of the country, privatization has enabled producers to bypass work rules and seniority rights that stood in the way of greater productivity. For all of these reasons, many of the privatization efforts undertaken thus far have resulted in significant gains in productivity and lower costs.

But privatization is not costless. Competition is key; replacing a monopoly public agency with a monopoly private supplier is unlikely to result in substantial benefits. Public employees are also at risk and will fight privatization unless they are given some protection or reassurance during the tran-

(CONTINUED)

per prisoner, property tax revenues from the privately owned facility, and immediate revenue from the sale of the facility that the county can put into a much-needed new jail.[4]

Eric Barnes, writing in *The Nation*, cites a study by the General Accounting Office, which is a federal agency that examines issues of efficiency in many areas of government. The General Accounting Office summarized the research on private prisons in 1996: "These studies do not offer substantial evidence that savings have occurred." In Tennessee, for example, the saving was only 1% over state operation.[5] Where savings do occur, it is often from constructing prisons in such a way that prisoners can be monitored more easily with video cameras and fewer guards, economizing on labor costs. Barnes argues:

The same economic logic that motivates companies to run prisons more efficiently also encourages them to cut corners at the expense of workers, prisoners and the public. Private prisons essentially mirror the cost cutting practices of health maintenance organizations. Companies receive a guaranteed fee for each prisoner, regard-

less of the actual costs. Every dime they don't spend on food or medical care or training for guards is a dime they can pocket.[6]

CCA and its successor, Prison Realty Corporation, have to face competition and assume the risks of failure. Other firms have entered the prison industry, so Prison Realty does not have a monopoly. Furthermore, states still operate their own facilities and are free to terminate contracts if dissatisfied. Because most of the prison employees are local, a state could simply install its own administrator, keep on the local staff, and transfer ownership and management fairly quickly if a problem arose. With these forms of market discipline, and with the steady growth in the numbers of beds, prisons, and contracts with private firms, privatization of prisons in the United States could be judged a qualified success.

1. *Forbes*, October 26, 1992, p. 14.
2. PR Newswire, January 4, 1999, p. 1680.
3. Eric Barnes, "Private Prisons," *The Nation*, January 5, 1998, pp. 11–18.
4. Knight-Ridder/Tribune Business News, May 31, 1998.
5. Barnes, "Private Prisons," p. 12.
6. *Ibid*, p. 14.

sition. Many governments have committed to a no-layoff policy, with public employment declining gradually as workers quit or retire. Others have insisted that private producers give hiring preference to former city workers. Some services do not lend themselves to private production as well as others. Questions have been raised about the authority of private firms to deal with violent criminals in high-risk prisons, or about too much focus on measurable outcomes in privately run contract schools. Nevertheless, privatization has resulted in some significant cost savings and some creative new approaches to the provision of public services.

EFFICIENCY AND INEFFICIENCY IN THE PUBLIC SECTOR

When governments intervene to correct market failure, they may create new forms of inefficiency and inequity that are equal to or even greater than the inefficiencies and/or inequities they were intended to address. These risks are not just theoretical. Certain characteristics of government, even the best designed governmental systems, make them prone to **government failure.** Like market failure, government failure means that intervention by government results in less than optimal or efficient outcomes—outcomes that are sometimes even less efficient or desirable than the unsatisfactory outcomes these interventions were intended to correct.

Government workers and agencies are not normally disciplined by the competition of the marketplace as private firms are. They are not motivated by profit or threatened with the fear of losses that keeps private firms on their toes. Government workers often have more job security than workers in the private sector and consequently have less incentive to please their "customers." Government procurement practices are designed to circumvent graft and corruption and are often cumbersome and inefficient, resulting in the government paying more for its purchases than would a private sector firm. Although the Pentagon traditionally gets the most press for overpriced hammers and toilet seats, the same kind of cost overruns occur in other agencies as well. Even a well-intentioned government finds it difficult to determine exactly what the public wants and what price the public is willing to pay for shared goods and public services. Chapter 5 addresses the problem of government failure.

ORGANIZATION OF THE BOOK

This book is divided into four major sections. Part 1, the first three chapters, addresses foundation issues of the nature of public sector economics, the structure of government from an economic perspective, and the measurement of government activity. The four chapters in Part 2 address the central theoretical questions in public sector economics related to demand for public goods and goods with externalities, decision processes, the effect of government on the distribution of income, and the role of competition, monopoly, and mobility in public finance. This section provides the foundation for addressing efficiency and equity questions in both the revenue and expenditure sides of government.

Part 3 consists of seven chapters addressing the revenue side of government—the theory and implementation issues involved in designing a revenue system and a closer look at the three major tax families (income, sales, and property) as well as revenue from fees and charges and intergovernmental grants.

The five chapters in Part 4 take a closer look at government spending, including budgeting and debt and an analysis of the determinants of expenditure and related issues in four major spending areas: education, infrastructure, social security and welfare, and health care. An epilogue offers a prognosis for the future of federal, state, and local government in a national and world economy that is evolving and changing at a rapid pace.

Throughout this book, it is important to emphasize that government includes all levels of government—federal, state, and local. Their respective roles have changed greatly in just the past two decades. Much more of the "action" in terms of service delivery and revenue raising is now concentrated at the state and local level. The next two chapters will develop some perspectives on the historic and emerging roles of each level of government and the magnitude of their revenues and spending.

Students in the United States often understandably think that the way things are done in their country (and often in their home state as well) is "the way it is." In fact, in many respects government in the United States is quite different from much of the rest of the world. Unlike the United States, the majority of countries rely heavily on a value-added tax[4] as a major revenue source for the central government. The United States relies more heavily on laws and less on regulations for environmental protection than most of the nations of Western Europe. And, of course, this country is one of the rare industrial nations without some kind of comprehensive national health insurance.

The United States is also one of a handful of countries with a federal form of government (Canada, Germany, Switzerland, and Australia are among the others). A federal form has three levels of government and some independent sphere of authority for the middle tier of states (United States, Australia), cantons (Switzerland), provinces (Canada), or Länder (Germany). The vast majority of nations only have two really functional levels of government, central and local. (Federal and unitary structures and their economic implications are discussed in Chapter 2.)

Because one of the best ways to understand your own country is to look at it through someone else's eyes, some of the public finance practices from other nations will be introduced from time to time in future chapters. These other experiences will serve as a reminder that economic theory and policy analysis rarely produce a single solution to a particular question or problem, but rather a number of possible solutions with different attributes. Different nations might reasonably make different choices that are more suited to their size, income levels, history, and preferences. It is important to recognize and investigate such alternatives.

---

4. See Chapter 11 for a discussion of the value-added tax.

SUMMARY

In the United States and some other countries, the economy is regarded as largely a private matter with government intervening where needed. 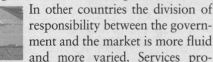 In other countries the division of responsibility between the government and the market is more fluid and more varied. Services provided by the private sector are often produced or provided by the public sector elsewhere.

Public finance or public sector economics combines a body of theory with a set of institutions to describe, analyze, and interpret the workings of government in a predominantly private economy. Public finance courses generally focus on microeconomic and budget-centered issues of taxing and spending. In terms of Musgrave's classification of allocation, distribution, and stabilization, public finance focuses mainly on allocation and somewhat on redistribution, leaving stabilization to other branches of economics. In recent years, two major areas of expansion in public finance have been issues of public sector pricing and the influential, relatively new area of public choice. Public choice analyzes the behavior of elected officials and bureaucrats in the public sector and explores the policy implications of government failure.

Fundamental differences between markets and governments include the expression of preference through voting rather than buying or spending, and the fact that citizens pay different prices but all have the option to consume the same quantity of public services. In the market, citizens usually pay the same prices and choose to consume different quantities. The most basic function of government in a market system is to act as a referee in defining and enforcing property rights, because market systems are based on private property.

For most economic activity, well-functioning markets are more efficient than government, bringing the economy closer to the ideal of Pareto optimality. Markets will achieve this peak efficiency if they are competitive, have large numbers of individuals and firms, perfect information, free mobility of resources and products, and no spillover effects. If any of these conditions do not hold, the market will fail, and it may be desirable for the government to correct such market failure. Government may also be called on to intervene if there is a general perception that the outcomes of market processes are inequitable, that is, that the distribution of income is unacceptable.

Possible tools for the government to use in correcting market failure are subsidies, tax incentives, guarantees, penalties (including tax penalties), mandates or prohibitions of certain items, public production, or private production with public financing. In the last two decades there has been a strong move toward privatization, or assigning more of the responsibility for certain kinds of production to the market or the private sector, often retaining public financing. Privatization often can increase efficiency and reduce costs.

Privatization has been a response to the problem of government failure, in which government interventions may cause new forms of inefficiency and inequity that are equal to or even greater than the inefficiencies and inequities they were intended to address. Government workers and agencies are not disciplined by competition or motivated by profit; they have more job security than workers in the private sector and less incentive to satisfy their "customers." Safeguards in government procurement to reduce graft and corruption are cumbersome and often result in the government paying too much for its purchases. It is more difficult for government than private firms to get clear signals of what consumers/citizens want because of the lack of market prices.

This book is divided into four major sections: foundation issues, decision-making processes, taxes and revenue sources, and expenditure analysis. Issues are examined at all levels of government throughout the book. Examples of practices and issues from other countries offer reminders that the way that the economics of

public finance works in practice in the United States is the result of an encounter of a general theory with a specific history and set of institutions. Differences between countries reflect the same theory at work in different cultures with different histories, resources, and values.

KEY TERMS AND CONCEPTS

public finance, 3
public sector economics, 3
allocation, 3
distribution, 4
stabilization, 4

public choice, 4
economic efficiency, 6
Pareto optimality, 6
market failure, 7
equity, 8

privatization, 9
public provision, 9
government failure, 12

DISCUSSION QUESTIONS

1. Which of the following services traditionally provided by government do you think would be good candidates for privatization? Why or why not?
   a. Fire protection
   b. Preschool education
   c. Rescues at sea
   d. Highway construction and maintenance
2. The government has been actively involved in providing flood insurance to people along rivers and coasts who are at risk from floods and hurricanes, along with efforts to reduce potential damage and discourage building in the highest risk areas. Why do you think the private sector failed to meet this need? Do you see any risks in government intervention in this area?

3. Suppose that your local government is trying to decide whether to commit additional funds to more police protection (more patrols) or more tennis courts. In what way is this an efficiency question? In what way might it be an equity question?
4. Assume that studies have demonstrated that your state is lagging in economic development because too few students go on to postsecondary education, whether technical or academic. Review the list of eight tools for responding to market failure and suggest how each is or could be used to address this problem.

CHAPTER 2

THE STRUCTURE OF GOVERNMENTS

Before analyzing the economic role of government, it would be helpful to have a clearer picture of the public sector in general and specifically in the United States. We can describe governments in two useful ways. One descriptor is structural—the number of governments, their sizes, their relationships to one another, and their areas of authority and responsibility. The other descriptor is financial—the amount of money flowing through governments and the sources and uses of those funds. This chapter explores the structural aspect of the public sector, while Chapter 3 describes the financial dimensions. Structure is particularly important in the United States because of the sharing of responsibility between the federal, state, and local levels of government.

At first glance, studying the structure of governments may seem more like political science than economics. However, structure is just one of several areas in which these two disciplines overlap. Larger governments may enjoy economies of scale. Some of the spillover effects (both positive and negative) that smaller governments create for their neighbors and do not take into account in their decisions will be internal to a larger, more regional government. For example, industrial wastes from Community A may affect the water supply in Community B, but if they are part of a larger regional government that is responsible for the entire watershed, the decisions about effluents and water treatment are internal to the larger sized government. On the other hand, if there are more, smaller governments, it may be easier for citizens to match their

preferences for taxes and services to a particular community and to make their voices heard, so that public officials have some measure of demand. Multiple state and local governments introduce some competition into what would otherwise be monopoly government. These issues of scale economies, spillover effects, accommodating diversity, the benefits of competition, and expressing demand for public services are economic in nature. The economic response to these issues cannot be separated from the institutional framework of the structure of governments.

ORGANIZING PUBLIC SERVICE DELIVERY

Delivery of public services within the public sector can be organized in many ways. In some countries, especially smaller countries but some larger ones as well, the central government plays the primary role in supplying everything from roads and prisons to health care and education. Local governments may have limited powers to raise and spend revenues, often under rules set by the central government. Sometimes, as in China, local governments are responsible for raising the revenue and sending it to the central government, which keeps most of it and sends a small amount back. All of these arrangements involving multilevel government are aspects of **fiscal federalism,** which describes the ways in which revenues and responsibilities are divided, assigned, or shared among different levels of government within a given country.[1]

Throughout history, there has been an unending search for balance between central authority and local diversity and flexibility in deciding which level of government should collect what kinds of revenues and carry out what kinds of service provision. Likewise, there has been a search for the balance between central control and local autonomy. There is no single right answer for all countries and all times, or for all kinds of revenues and services. Small, homogeneous countries like Bulgaria, Sri Lanka, Taiwan, or Costa Rica can function fairly well with a strong central government, local governments with limited autonomy, and selective delegation of powers and responsibilities. Large and culturally heterogeneous countries like Russia, Canada, India, Brazil, and the United States have to provide services to populations that are much more diverse in terms of incomes, cultures, languages, climates, and rural/urban mix. The way in which the Education Ministry in Paris works to control a highly standardized French public school system would not work in Canada, where harsh weather inside the Arctic Circle, one French-speaking province, a multiethnic population,

---

1. The word *fiscal* describes anything that relates to the treasury or finances of government. *Fisc,* or the public treasury, is the English form of the Latin word *fiscus,* which was originally a woven basket or money basket used by tax collectors.

and very lightly populated areas on the prairies create different educational needs in different provinces.

Depending on the revenue sources used, one level of government may have an advantage over another in its ability to raise funds. That advantage may derive from economies of scale in collecting taxes, or from a degree of monopoly power that makes it difficult to avoid the tax by moving property, purchases, or production activity to another location. In the United States, the federal government has generally enjoyed such an advantage. In other countries, particularly developing countries, raising revenue is most successful at the local level, where personal knowledge of individuals' assets and income and direct personal contact play an important role in tax collection. On the spending side, some services are highly local in their benefits (streetlights), others national (defense), while still others have both a national and a local aspect (roads and highways, environmental protection, higher education) with the effects of policies and programs spilling over from one jurisdiction to another.

Various countries and even states within a country make different choices about the assignment of both revenue sources and service responsibilities. Education through high school is a national function in France, a primarily state function in Hawaii, a primarily local function in New Hampshire. The sales tax, in the form of a value-added tax, is a central government tax in most of Europe and Latin America, while in the form of a retail sales tax it is the exclusive possession of state and local governments in the United States.

MULTIPLE LEVELS OF GOVERNMENT

In the 1997 *Census of Governments,* the United States had 87,510 governments.[2] Citizens paid taxes and received services from federal, state, and territorial governments, counties and parishes, cities, towns, townships, school districts, and special districts. Fortunately, individual American citizens only have to deal with a small subset of those 87,510 governments. All citizens are served by the federal government, their state or territorial government, and a county, parish, or township government (Table 2–1). In some states, there is a separate school district. Some citizens are also served by the government of a city or town if they live inside an incorporated municipality, or perhaps one or more special districts. So the average citizen deals with at least three and perhaps as many as six or seven governments, a rather large number. In other countries, the average citizen may deal with only two governments, the central and the local government.

---

2. Including the District of Columbia and the five territories—Puerto Rico, American Samoa, Guam, Virgin Islands, and Northern Mariana Islands—brings the total to 87,510.

Table 2–1
Governments
in the United States,
1997 Census

Level/Type	Number
Federal	1
States and District of Columbia	51
Territorial	5
Counties/parishes	3,043
Cities/towns/townships	36,001
School districts	13,726
Special districts	34,683
TOTAL	87,510

*Territorial governments include Puerto Rico, American Samoa, Virgin Islands, and Northern Mariana Islands.

The optimal number of governments, particularly the number of levels of government, depends both on the size (population and land area) of the country and the kinds of diversity (cultural, linguistic, climatic, etc.) that government is trying to accommodate. It also depends on the nation's particular history as well as its cultural values such as the balance between uniformity and diversity or direct and representative democracy.

Gains and Losses from Centralization

The size of a government can be measured in at least three ways. One measure is land area—the number of square miles under its control. A second measure is population—the number of residents from whom revenues can be extracted and to whom services must be provided (and who want to have their voices heard by elected officials!). The third measure, which is discussed in the next chapter, is its level of fiscal activity—how much revenue it takes in, how many dollars it spends, how much it owns in the way of public sector capital, and how much debt it has accumulated.

Once a nation's boundaries are defined, its land area is more or less fixed (subject to reclamation, erosion, and other natural forces). Its population may grow due to natural increase or immigration, and its economic activity may grow because of conscious choices by its citizens or public officials. But there is also a set of choices to be made about smaller governments that take responsibility for some subset of that total nation, whether it is a rural village or the state of California. How big (or small) should those second- and third-tier governments be? Do they all need to be about the same size, or is it necessary (or desirable) to have different sizes? And, most important, which revenue sources and which service responsibilities should be retained by the central government, and which should be delegated or assigned to state or local governments?

Different countries, again, make different choices about **centralization,** or concentration of authority and responsibility at higher levels or in larger governmental units. A highly centralized governmental structure is one that concentrates much of the authority, power, decision making, and tax collection at a higher level of government. When lower levels of government enjoy more autonomy, authority, and independent sources of revenue, the system is more decentralized.

Advantages of Centralization

The principal economic advantage of centralization is that the level and variety of public services that each citizen receives do not depend on whether that person lives in a rich state or a poor state, a wealthy suburb or an urban ghetto or a dying prairie town. All citizens are entitled to roughly the same quality of education and other major public services. Rich communities pay more in taxes than poor communities (or states), so there is indirect redistribution between rich and poor communities (as well as individuals) when they pay different amounts according to ability to pay but receive pretty much the same services.

A second economic advantage of centralization is that some services have substantial economies of scale; that is, the average cost curve continues to decline with a larger population or service area up to a very large number. Economies of scale have been found in such services as water, sewer, and garbage collection. In the case of fire protection, economies of scale are found up to populations of 400,000.

A third economic advantage of centralizing at least some services has to do with capturing spillover benefits or taking the negative effects of spillovers into account. If citizens of Oklahoma were providing their own defense against foreign enemies, they would inadvertently also be providing some protection to Texans. But Oklahoma would have no way to force the Texans to pay for those benefits, so those benefits would not be taken into account in Oklahoma's decision about how much defense to provide. (The problem of deciding how much of a public good to provide is discussed in Chapter 4.) Likewise, if Georgia draws too much water from the Savannah River, it will affect the water supply and the recreational use of the river by downstream cities on the opposite bank in South Carolina. Spillovers of benefits (or cost) of activities from one jurisdiction to another mean that some beneficiaries are not made to pay and some people who are negatively affected by certain decisions have no voice. By having the largest possible jurisdiction, more of the affected parties (both those who benefit and those who incur costs) are included in paying their fair share as well as in making their voices heard.

Finally, centralization is one way to prevent competition among states from limiting the advantages of a large national market for goods and services, capital, and labor. When workers and owners of firms know that they will pay the same taxes and receive pretty much the same services regardless of where they are located in the country, their location decisions will not be distorted. They will make decisions based on such economically relevant factors as access to markets, availability of complementary resources (business services, suppliers, raw materials, water, inexpensive land, climate), and personal preferences. Buyers of goods and services will not seek out the state with the lowest sales tax, but will look for the best deal wherever it can be found (including the cost of transportation and search time). We will look more closely at these issues of interstate competition in Chapter 7.

Advantages of Decentralization

Decentralization has at least three advantages that must be weighed against the advantages of centralization. The first is that decentralization is better suited to accommodating diversity. Different groups of citizens have different needs, preferences, and desires. Spending on highways may be more important to Montana than to Delaware, where the distances are short and there are fewer miles of highway per resident. Heat assistance in the winter may be crucial to survival for the poorest citizens of Maine and Minnesota, but help with fans, air conditioning, or other defenses against extreme heat may be more important to their low-income counterparts in Arizona or Mississippi. Homelessness is a largely urban problem, while transportation is more likely to be a major need for rural areas. Citizens also have different service demands. Some communities may be more interested in public recreation, others in public transportation, still others in quality public schools. By allowing citizens to make different choices in different communities, it is possible to accommodate, if not individual preferences, then at least smaller group preferences.

Second, and closely related, is the positive value of competition, which weighs in on behalf of both centralization and decentralization. If communities offer different service (and tax) mixes, citizens can migrate to those communities that most mirror their preferences, a phenomenon that does indeed occur. Some citizens may opt for high-service communities even if that means high taxes, others for less of both. Seniors may choose retirement communities that offer more recreational amenities and services to the elderly but spend little on public schools. Creating relatively homogeneous communities in terms of these kinds of preferences increases citizen satisfaction. (This issue will be discussed in Chapter 7 in connection with the Tiebout hypothesis.) Mobile citizens also are better able to communicate their preferences clearly to elected officials. The threat of losing more affluent residents and the taxes they pay forces local public officials to be more sensitive to the needs and preferences of current and potential residents.

Third, and also closely related, is the value of innovation and experimentation. Many features of the welfare reform programs of the late 1990s were adapted from experimental programs developed in Massachusetts, Wisconsin, and other states. It is less costly to experiment and fail in one state than in all 50. States (or cantons, or provinces, or Länder) can serve as laboratories of federalism, with the good ideas propagated or even adopted by the central government and the unsuccessful ideas discarded without the high cost of trying them out everywhere. States also learn from each other. The Georgia lottery, drawing on criticism of how lottery-based education financing was handled in other states such as New York and Florida, was carefully designed to segregate lottery funds for some specific educational purposes, providing a new model that other states could copy. Georgia, in turn, benefited from being one of the later states to implement a lottery, so that it could learn from the successes as well as the mistakes of others.

These same arguments for and against centralization play out again at lower levels of government, in debates over state versus local control of education or prisons or highways. At the local level, the argument about centralization translates into a question of optimal size for a city or county.[3] How much land area can a local government effectively serve? (In parts of the South in the 19th century, this answer was often given: A county seat needs to be no more than a day's drive by horse and buggy round-trip from the farthest point in the county.) How many citizens can it effectively listen and respond to? How big, in land area and/or population, does a city have to be to enjoy economies of scale in its service provision?

If a city (or county) is too small, the benefits of the services it offers or the costs of its activities (pollution, congestion) are likely to spill over to adjacent cities or counties, to people who have no voice and pay no taxes. But as it grows larger, the population within a city is likely to become increasingly diverse, and it is harder for elected officials to find a tax/service mix that will satisfy those very different preferences. Finding a satisfactory size means weighing these two opposing considerations.

Counties usually have fixed boundaries. Whether they are the "right" size or not, their land areas rarely change, and their populations change only through births, deaths, and migration. Cities, however, can expand through annexation of unincorporated areas as well. When cities look to expand, or when citizens of outlying areas are consulted about being annexed, both parties need to weigh these costs and benefits. What is the value/cost of the services provided? How much tax burden/revenue can be expected of new households? Can the city get so large that it begins to experience diseconomies of scale, that is, an inability to manage the level and diversity of functions it has to carry out? These questions are discussed further a little later in this chapter and again in Chapter 4, which addresses the economic implications of voter mobility.

---

3. Counties are the most common form of general-purpose local governments that include all citizens, as opposed to school districts (which are special purpose, providing only one service) or cities/towns, which only include those residents that choose to live inside the corporate limits of the city. In Louisiana the equivalent of a county is a parish. In New England and some other states, the township is roughly equivalent to the county in terms of functions performed for all citizens, urban or rural.

DESIGNING A FEDERAL STRUCTURE

Weighing all of these considerations, each nation must address three important questions about the structure of government:

1. How many levels of government will there be?
2. How much autonomy will each level have?
3. To what degree will functions and revenue sources be separated by levels of government, and to what degree will they overlap and require coordination?

How many levels? This question is usually the easiest of the three to resolve because the answer is rarely one, usually either two or three, and almost never more than three, although there may be several coexisting or overlapping governments at the local level. Small, fairly homogeneous countries can manage with two levels—central and local. There may be regional divisions for administrative purposes, but most functions can be satisfactorily designated as either local (few spillovers to the rest of the country, amenable to local control, lack of uniformity is not a problem, services can be financed through local revenue sources) or central (requiring a uniform national program, affecting all citizens equally, and requiring a financial contribution from all segments of the country). Switzerland is one of the rare examples of a small (but ethnically and linguistically diverse) nation that is genuinely federal in its structure, with the four cantons exercising considerable independent authority.

Countries with multiple levels of government, particularly where the middle level is genuinely separate and somewhat independent rather than just a convenient administrative division, were often formed by the union of those middle levels to form a larger whole. Such was the case in the United States and Germany, both of which wrote constitutions specifying a federal structure with substantial state autonomy. (Australia and Canada have a somewhat different history because of their long status as part of the British Commonwealth, but they too deliberately wrote federal constitutions.) These countries face a greater challenge in determining which level of government does what.

Larger nations tend to adopt some modified federal system and smaller nations tends to have two major levels, central and local. Countries with only central and local governments are referred to as *unitary states*.

How much autonomy? Some countries that appear to be federal are really less so than they appear, because the middle level (state or province) has relatively little independent authority and serves largely as an administrative division of the central government. If there is a constitution (which most modern nations have), it usually spells out some division of

THE ORIGINAL FEDERALISTS

When the United States joined 13 formerly independent British colonies into a federal country, they had at least one precedent to guide them. One of the oldest modern nations to come into being as a federation is Switzerland, founded in 1291 as the Swiss Federation, or *Confoederatio Helvetica*. Switzerland, a nation of less than 7 million people, has four official languages (French, German, Italian, and Romansch). Its diversity of ethnic backgrounds at the crossroads of Europe is one of the main reasons that Switzerland, despite its small size, is organized as a federal rather than a unitary government. It has also been a model of political stability and economic prosperity, and has been remarkably successful in insulating itself from the wars that swirled about it in the 20th century.

The Swiss central government, the confederation or *Eidgenossenschaft,* is responsible for protection of the country and its citizens, postal services, the monetary system, telephone and telecommunications, transportation, the military, customs, and diplomatic relations. The 23 *Kantone* (cantons, or states) are responsible for education,

cantonal roads (state highways), and social institutions. Each canton is in turn divided into *Bezirke* or districts, which are responsible for education and judicature. *Bezirke* are roughly equivalent to counties in the United States. Each district includes a number of *Gemeinden,* or municipalities, 3,000 of them altogether, ranging from *dorfs* (villages) of less than 10,000 citizens to large *Stadts* (towns) like Zurich. Municipalities provide local services (electricity, water, fire and police protection), local roads, and schools. Taxes vary significantly from municipality to municipality as they do in the United States.

Some of the federal states created after Switzerland have had difficulty holding their unions together, as evidenced by the American Civil War and the secessionist movement in Canada's Quebec province. Switzerland holds out hope that a federation of very diverse states cannot only come together but survive for many centuries as a workable compromise between local autonomy, regional differences, and national interests.

responsibilities. In Germany, the Länder exercise authority both in the second chamber of the national legislature and in their separate spheres of responsibility, particularly education and culture. In Canada, all authority not granted to the provinces is reserved to the central government, whereas in the U.S. Constitution (Article X), all powers not delegated to the central government are reserved to the states. Ironically, in practice Canada has seen a gradual shift of authority to the provinces, whereas until recently power gravitated toward Washington, D.C. in the United States rather than to the 50 state capitals.

There are two keys to autonomy for state and local governments. One is access to independent revenue sources, so that the state and local governments are not primarily dependent on the central government to collect and dispense funds. The other is some defined independent sphere(s) of service provision. For example, state governments might be assigned exclusive authority (and responsibility) to regulate banks and insurance companies, or to provide highways and public education. Constitutional provisions that either permit state governments or forbid the central government from certain activities provide the strongest safeguards for state autonomy. Until the Sixteenth Amendment was ratified in 1913, the U.S. federal government was prohibited from collecting direct taxes, which in practice meant it could not use an income tax, leaving that field open to state governments to use if they chose. (Most states did not adopt income taxes, however, until after the federal government had come to rely on this tax.) The Sixteen Amendment broadened the base of revenue sources the federal government could tap and laid the foundation for an expansion of its powers and responsibilities relative to state governments in the 20th century.

As new kinds of government activities develop, the process of sorting out who does what continues to evolve. Ideally, provision for a particular service or use of a particular revenue source would be assigned to that level of government for which it was most suited in terms of scale economies, internalizing potential spillovers, competitive effects, and other considerations. In practice, such sorting out has rarely been done on the basis of economic efficiency. The assignment of general (retail) sales taxes to state and local governments, for example, was not a deliberate act but an accidental result of a sudden need for a new revenue source by states during the Great Depression.

Separation, Overlap, and Autonomy It is difficult to find a country that does not assign responsibility to the central government for foreign affairs, national defense, international commerce, fiscal policy, and issuing currency. Beyond that limited consensus, countries show considerable diversity on both the revenue and spending sides. Sales taxes are primarily state and local taxes in the United States, but are much more often national (as value-added taxes) in most other countries. Education and health care are national responsibilities in many countries, but much more of a state and local responsibility in the United States.

Although it appears to be easier to divide up responsibilities (e.g., defense is national, education is state, police is local) than to share them between levels of government, in practice assignment of functions is never that clear-cut. For example, police are primarily local in the United States, but the effects of criminal activity spill over from one community to another, and some kinds of police activity enjoy significant economies of scale. Every state has some kind of state bureau of investigation or law enforcement division and a state highway patrol. But some crimes, like treason, espionage, and kidnapping, are federal crimes. Even for state crimes coordination is required in terms of access to records and investigative resources. Unlike many other nations, the United States does not have a genuinely national police force, but it does have the Federal Bureau of Investigation, which works closely with state and local police on cases that require their assistance and that call for federal intervention as well as pursuing cases involving federal crimes on their own.

Similar overlap occurs in most government functions. Even national defense is complemented by state national guard units that are under the control of state governors, who can call them out in emergencies. Banks, insurance companies, and public utilities are subject to a mix of state and federal regulation. National parks are supplemented by a second tier of state parks and recreation areas. Interstate highways are a joint federal–state undertaking that link state and local roads into a national network.

The chief advantage of a clear separation of responsibilities is the ability to offer better accountability to citizens or voters. If services are good and taxes are low, they know who deserves the credit. Citizens vote to retain the incumbents or they choose to move into local communities that have proven to be well run. If services are bad and taxes are high, they can boot the rascals out or move to a better managed locale. These signals of voter satisfaction or dissatisfaction are important for providing direction to public officials. When services and revenue sources are commingled, however—partly federal, partly state, partly local—it is more difficult to assign credit or blame.

We do see that sharing responsibilities across levels of government does have some advantages. Suppose, for example, that most of the benefit of education in the lower grades accrues to the locality where the students live. They stay in the area and become adult workers and citizens, and the quality of both the public and private sector is enhanced when they are better educated. But some of them, inevitably, move elsewhere. The benefits of their education accrue to other jurisdictions. If every jurisdiction spent the same, and there was no migration or balanced migration, the costs incurred in educating young people would be roughly balanced by the benefits received from educated adult workers and citizens, whether locally raised or migrating in. But these conditions rarely hold. Some of the benefits of educating young people in Nebraska accrue to Missouri when they are lured away by the bright lights of St. Louis. And certainly the benefits of educating children in Albany, Georgia, are likely to bear fruit in the magnet city of Atlanta, which attracts young workers from all over the Southeast. So the cost of educating those young people should be primarily local, but also shared by those other areas of the state or nation that benefit from the service. Some of the general mechanisms for sharing are discussed in more detail in Chapter 14 (and in the specific case of education, Chapter 16).

Finally, state governments and especially local governments differ greatly in their ability to generate revenues to finance public services. If citizens are entitled to a certain basic level of public services wherever they live by virtue of being part of one nation, then state and federal governments will have to redistribute resources toward low-income communities in order to ensure that level of services. The conceptual dimensions of redistribution are addressed in Chapter 6, and the practical implementation in Chapters 17 and 18. The division of responsibility for welfare in particular has just been through a major change that is explored in detail in Chapter 18.

COMMUNICATION BETWEEN GOVERNMENTS

When responsibilities are commingled between states (or provinces) and the central government, it is necessary to have some formal mechanisms of communication and some way of resolving where the ultimate decision-making power rests when conflict arises. The federal government in the United States frequently uses mandates or requirements attached to grants to state governments in order to impose its preferences on state governments. Highway funds have been held hostage to agreeing to federal preferences on speed limits. Funds to assist public schools or colleges and universities come with obligations to accommodate students with disabilities, practice nondiscrimination in admissions, and provide equity between men's and women's sports programs. States can refuse to comply, but the dollar price may be steep.

What tools do states have in return when they want to force the federal government to act (or stop acting) in a particular way? One tool that has been used recently and fairly effectively is the lawsuit. When Congress failed to act on tobacco and gun control in the late 1990s, states took the initiative in the former case and municipalities in the latter. States argued that tobacco-related illnesses were imposing major costs on state governments for Medicaid and other health care programs, which gave them the standing they needed to take the cigarette manufacturers to court. Similarly, municipalities argued that guns were creating significant additional costs in public safety and corrections and sued firearms manufacturers to recover some of those losses.

THE STATE–LOCAL RELATIONSHIP

The relationship between a state and its local governments is quite different from that between the federal and state governments in the United States. Although the existence of states is specified by the U.S. Constitution, along with some indication of their powers and the procedures for admitting new states to the union, there is no mention of local governments. Each state makes its own rules, and while there are many similarities between states in the form and sphere of local government, there are also some striking differences.

Home Rule

Home rule refers to the degree of autonomy or independence that local governments enjoy in making all kinds of decisions. In public finance, a particularly important dimension of the state–local relationship that varies greatly from state to state is local **fiscal autonomy**. Fiscal autonomy refers to the degree of freedom that a city, county, or school district has to set its own property tax rate, use nonproperty tax revenue sources, and decide what quantity and variety of services to offer. Most states have some involvement in the administration of the property tax, particularly in overseeing the assessment process and determining what kinds of property should be subject to the tax. In 17 states, the state determines different assessment rates[4] for different classes of property (residential, commercial, agricultural, etc.) that are subject to the local property tax. Many states also determine what properties will be exempt, and some states compensate local governments for the lost revenue. Local governments usually have a high degree of freedom in setting the tax rate or mill rate, although in the 1980s and 1990s many state governments imposed some limits on increases in property tax millage in response to taxpayer protests.

The state may specify other revenue sources (including permissible rates) that local governments are allowed to use, which often include local income taxes, local sales taxes, fees, business licenses, and accommodations taxes (taxes on motels, hotels, and other short-term rentals). Or states may give local governments (most often just cities) free rein in tapping revenue sources, or least limit their direction to a list of revenue sources that local governments *may* not use, leaving them free to explore those sources that are not forbidden.

On the spending side, the state may specify certain kinds and levels of spending to a surprisingly fine degree, for example, how many minutes to spend on biology each week in the seventh grade, what grade of paving material to use on the highway, or how many square feet of space to provide in a circuit judge's courtroom. These specific directives are known as *mandates*. When these spending responsibilities come without the money to pay for implementing them, they are known as unfunded mandates, fighting words to most local public officials. Some states are much more controlling of local spending than others. In some cases the state spells out what kinds of services a city or county may provide, in other cases which ones they are not to provide.

A more indirect way in which state governments influence local government activity is through revenue sharing and state grants to local governments. Local governments derive about one-third of their revenue on average from state grants and state shared revenues, some of the funds with specific spending directives attached, some going into the local general fund to be spent according to local directives.

Structure of Local Government

In general, states are divided into counties, parishes (Louisiana), or townships (mostly in the northeast). The important feature of this kind of local government is that every part of the state is located in a county, parish, or town-

---

4. The assessment rate is the percentage of the market value of taxable property that is used as the base for calculating the tax. The mill rate is the tax rate expressed as 1/1000th of a dollar. The mill (or mil) is an old English coin worth 1/10 of a cent. The details of property tax administration are spelled out in Chapter 12.

ship. Counties and their counterparts in other states almost always rely heavily on the property tax for revenue and usually have responsibilities for highways, law enforcement, and a variety of other functions. They may or may not also have responsibility for schools. In some states, counties are primarily regional agents of state government, while in other states they have significant independent authority. In urban areas in some states it is possible for a county (or counties) to merge with its primary city or cities to form a single metropolitan government that carries out both municipal and county functions and exercises the powers of both.

The other universal form of local government is the city or town, which differs from a county or parish or township in having defined boundaries that can be changed by annexation. Unlike counties, cities and towns do not include the entire landscape; many citizens live in unincorporated areas or "out in the county" without enjoying or paying for municipal services. A city is more like a club, which citizens join by buying or renting residential property inside the city limits or by being annexed to an existing city. Cities are also heavy users of property taxes as a revenue source, although they tend to be more diversified in their revenue sources than counties. Because residents of cities and towns are packed into less land area than those in counties and rural areas, many of their service demands are related to density: more traffic management, solid waste collection services, more police patrols, sidewalks and street lights. Cities and towns are responsible for schools in some states, while in other states school districts are separate from both cities and counties.

Creation and Growth of Cities

One major way in which states differ in their treatment of cities relates to the process of forming or expanding cities. Cities come into being through incorporation and expand through annexation or consolidation (the former being the addition of unincorporated areas to the city, the latter a merger with another city). Residents of suburbs reap benefits from being close to the city but often contribute little if anything to the cost of maintaining that city. In other words, cities generate spillover benefits or positive externalities for their neighbors.[5] Also, citizens in unincorporated areas may rely more heavily on county services (such as the sheriff or county recreation programs) than those in the city, who have municipal services. But in many states people living outside city limits pay the same county taxes as city-dwellers and no city taxes—a situation that seems very unfair to those living inside city limits, a clear case of "free riding."

Incorporation is very easy in some states and difficult in others. States often may impose requirements of population size, density, or tax base on

---

5. Externalities and free riding, which should be familiar from your principles course, are discussed in detail in Chapter 4.

incorporation in order to ensure that a city will be viable, that is, able to support the provision of basic municipal services out of its revenue base. Incorporation may involve petitions, votes, or other procedures specified by the state.

Annexation, likewise, is usually governed by state rules. In some states, such as North Carolina, annexation is relatively easy, done largely at the initiative of the annexing city, often despite protests from the areas being annexed. These liberal annexation laws have made it easy for cities like Charlotte, Asheville, and Greensboro to grow and expand by taking in their growing suburbs, whether or not those suburbs want to become part of the city. In other states, such as Connecticut, annexation is more difficult. Connecticut's older cities like Hartford and Waterbury have seen suburbs spring up around them that use the city as a commercial and service center but contribute little to its revenues.

Both incorporation and annexation involve important economic issues of balancing costs and benefits. From the city's point of view, do additional citizens add more to revenue than they do to cost? From the viewpoint of those being annexed, does the value of the services provided by the city justify the additional taxes they will have to pay and the additional regulations (like no open burning or keeping dogs on leashes) with which they will have to comply? Economists would expect there to be some optimal size for a city that precisely balances the marginal cost (broadly defined) of adding another citizen with the marginal revenue that citizen generates. This question is explored further in Chapter 7.

Trends in State–Local Relationships

For most states, the role of local governments and the degree of autonomy they enjoy are embedded in the constitution, although it can still evolve over time. Protests against the property tax have involved legislatures in a number of states in exerting greater control over local property taxes than was true 10 or 20 years ago. States are understandably reluctant in many cases to turn too much control over to local governments because they know that they are responsible for their local governments. Exerting some control in the name of fiscal responsibility is one way in which states protect themselves against the financial risk of a municipal (or county) bankruptcy. Financial risk is not the only problem. Court cases such as *Serrano v. Priest* have made it clear that the state has the responsibility for providing essentially equal education for all of its citizens, regardless of whether states control public education directly or delegate much of the power and responsibility to cities, counties, or school districts. Consequently, states have been forced to devise programs that redistribute funds between different parts of the state, directly or indirectly, to ensure at least minimum standards of educational quality in all school districts. (The difficult challenges of managing education financing to address this problem are discussed in Chapter 16.)

HOG FARMS, NIMBY, AND LOCAL GOVERNMENTS

State government officials often complain that Washington intervenes in their affairs to tell them how to manage their environment, educate their children, spend their tax dollars, and locate their highways. Sometimes these interventions come from federal regulators, sometimes from federal courts, and occasionally as strings attached to federal grant funds. In any case, these actions mean that the values of the federal government supersede those of state officials. State officials, understandably, complain loudly when such mandates arrive from Washington. But these same state officials are likely to treat their local governments the same way. Case in point: location of hog farms, waste sites, and other unattractive facilities that state governments may want to attract but local governments want somewhere else, a situation known as *NIMBY*—not in my backyard.

Recent experience in Iowa, Utah, North Carolina, and South Carolina over the location of large, industrial-style hog farms has provided an interesting case study not only in the management of spillover effects but also, for purposes of this chapter, in state–local relations. These "factory" farms have been displacing small, diversified family operations in the production of pork for America's tables, resulting in problems of odor and of spillage of hog waste into nearby streams. For the state, a hog farm or a hazardous waste disposal site is a source of public revenue and private jobs, two very important goals. Often the site chosen is in a rural area with relatively few residents and high unemployment. But residents in the area may have other priorities, like preserving property values and quality of life. Both hog farms and hazardous waste sites create serious environmental risks, particularly for water quality. If the smell of hog farms was not bad enough, a major spill of hog waste in the New River in eastern North Carolina in 1997 alerted many communities to the potential costs of having a hog farm for a neighbor. Ham and pork for America's tables have to be raised somewhere. Is there a suitable site, or a suitable way of raising hogs, that can satisfy all of these competing concerns?

Growth of hog farming has been more rapid in North Carolina than in any other state; the state's hog population grew from 2.6 million in 1987 to 9.7 million by the end of 1998.[1] These hogs produce 19 million tons of waste a year, concentrated in the state's environmentally sensitive eastern coastal plain. Initially the hog farmers were successful in winning the support of the state legislature, but the tide turned when sewage spills created serious environmental problems near the state's coast. An alliance of the federal Environmental Protection Agency, outraged local citizens and environmental groups such as the American Canoe Association demanded, and won, a moratorium on further expansion of hog farming in the state in August 1997 that was extended to September 1999 while the state pondered its options. At the same time, the legislature put stronger state inspection and control requirements on hog farms and granted counties the authority to use zoning to control the influx of hog farms.[2]

The interesting questions for the economist thinking about division of governmental responsibilities are these: Which government is in charge here? Does the state have a right to impose its priorities—jobs and tax revenues—on residents of local communities with different priorities? Can local governments protect themselves with zoning or denial of water rights or discriminatory taxation or other methods from having the state attract undesirable industries into their backyards? And which citizens get to decide, the local citizens most heavily impacted or the citizens of the state as a whole, most of them far away from the smell of the hog farms, the truckloads of hazardous wastes along their roads, and the risks to the community's future? Whose costs get weighed against whose benefits? Often the costs fall heavily on one group while the benefits accrue to another. These kinds of difficult questions lie at the heart of designing and maintaining a federal system that is responsive to the needs and values of all citizens.

1. Bob Williams, "Hog Count Hits High in N. C.," *The News and Observer on the Web,* December 30, 1998.
2. Joseph Neff, "House Passes Curbs on Hog Farms, " *The News and Observer on the Web,* April 30, 1997.

EVOLUTION OF FISCAL FEDERALISM IN THE UNITED STATES

Immediately after the American Revolution, representatives of the 13 states (formerly colonies) gathered to write a document that set the parameters for their fiscal constitution. That document was the Articles of Confederation, which only survived eight years before being replaced by the Constitution that is still in effect today. The Articles of Confederation reflected a strong desire to retain state sovereignty among the 13 independent and somewhat quarrelsome former colonies. Consequently, it assigned most power to the states and envisioned only a limited coordinating role for the central government.

The Constitution

The Constitution adopted in 1789 and still in effect today created a much stronger central government than the Articles of Confederation, while still reserving some spheres of independent sovereignty to states. One of the major goals of the Constitution was to create a common market, in which states could not restrict commerce between its residents and residents of other states, as specified in the very significant interstate commerce clause. The common market created in the U.S. Constitution has served as a model for groups of nations (most notably the European Union) that were seeking to create a single large market. Like the United States, such common markets sometimes involve a single currency; more often, the emphasis is on free movement of goods and resources in order to enjoy the economic benefits of both competition and economies of scale. An important function of the federal government under this new Constitution was to safeguard that unified national market from state efforts to insulate local businesses and interests from the rigors of the larger marketplace.

Expansion of the Federal Role

Over time, the federal role gradually expanded. Early on, some of that expansion was driven by healthy surpluses in the federal treasury during the 1820s and early 1830s with ample funds from Western land sales and tariffs on imported goods. The federal government turned some of those surpluses back to states to spend, but rejected proposals to spend it on public works or other new undertakings at the federal level. This period also saw considerable testing of the tensions between the supporters of a strong central government and the states' rights movement under the leadership of John C. Calhoun. Calhoun proposed that a state that did not approve of a federal law (specifically, the high tariffs passed in 1828) could refuse to enforce them (specifically, in the port of Charleston in his home state of South Carolina). This view, called the Nullification Doctrine, was a precursor of the Civil War that erupted three decades later. It represented a significant challenge to the notion of a unified national market in a country that was made up of 13 former colonies with very different sectional interests: the manufacturing-oriented, protectionist Northeast versus the slavery-based, export-oriented plantation agriculture of the South.

The states' rights movement was considerably weakened by the defeat of the South in the Civil War. Over time, the federal government's role gradually expanded into other areas. Among these expansions of the federal role were the creation of the National Banking System (1863), which invaded the area of banking supervision previously reserved to states, and the land-grant college program (1881), which created a federal role in higher education. The alphabet soup of regulatory commissions of the early 20th century—the Interstate Commerce Commission, Federal Trade Commission, Federal Communications Commission—marked another expansion of the federal role, often invading state regulatory territory. Finally, the Great Depression of the 1930s marked a high point in federal involvement in programs previously left to states, including provision for the poor and the elderly (welfare and Social Security) as well as an even more expanded federal role in ensuring the safety of the banking system.

New Federal Roles in the Late 20th Century

Soon after World War II the federal role expanded in three new directions. One was the development of the interstate highway system, a landmark contribution to a unified national market. The interstate highway system, dating from the 1950s, created a coordinated highway network in which states, traditionally responsible for roads, found themselves as junior partners in a federally financed highway system.

A second expansion was a greatly enhanced role for federal grants to states and cities to encourage development of new programs and services. Federal grants both enabled and enticed state and local governments into undertaking programs in education, urban renewal, municipal water and sewer systems, low-income housing, recreation, and other areas that might never have come into being without the federal carrot dangling before the noses of elected officials. (The economics of intergovernmental grants is explored in Chapter 14.) When the grants dwindled in later years, states and cities found themselves with an aging infrastructure for which they would have to find maintenance and replacement funds.

The third expansion was an increase in social and environmental regulation. This expansion involved both legislation (Clean Water Act, Clean Air Act, Endangered Species Act, Americans with Disabilities Act) and new agencies (Consumer Product Safety Commission, Occupational Safety and Health Administration, Environmental Protection Agency), which further "trespassed" on what had been considered a state role. These laws and their implementation by growing Washington bureaucracies placed constraints on citizens and business firms as well as state and local governments, resulting in increased anger and hostility toward Washington as the balance of power began to tip heavily toward the central government.

The 1960s also saw a brief experiment in direct dealings between the federal government and local governments (especially cities and counties). At that time, the dominant view in Washington was that state capitals were captive to rural and suburban interests and unresponsive to the evolving needs of cities—especially large urban centers. After a series of court decisions forced states to reapportion their legislatures on the principle of one person, one vote, state legislatures began to mirror the population distribution of their respective states more closely. The earlier justification for direct federal intervention in urban affairs became less viable. Federal aid to local governments diminished, although federal aid remains a modest but important local revenue source today.

Rethinking the Federal Role

The process of "rebalancing federalism," or shifting power to the states, actually began in the 1950s, as the Eisenhower administration began to search (unsuccessfully) for ways to turn back revenue sources and responsibilities to states. Federal grants to state and local governments peaked in 1978 and began to decline under President Reagan. Deregulation also began during the Carter administration in the late 1970s and expanded in scope during the 1980s, most notably the deregulation of banks and airlines.

The fiscal federalism watchword for the last two decades of the 20th century was **devolution,** a newly coined word to describe the deliberate shifting of responsibilities (and sometimes the revenues to carry them out) from the federal to the state and/or local level. Devolution reflected at least four interrelated factors that contributed to a "sea change" in American politics. First was a concern about the growing federal budget deficit. Second, particularly in the 1980s, was a desire to limit the growth of government at all levels (but especially the central level). Third, reengineering and other tactics that became popular as a means for businesses to become more efficient encouraged elected officials to search for more market-like mechanisms (such as competition) to make government service delivery more efficient and responsive. Finally, and perhaps most important, people were greatly disillusioned by the high costs and limited results of some of the ambitious federal programs of the 1960s and early 1970s.

The biggest experiment in devolution to date has been the welfare system. Aid to Families with Dependent Children (AFDC), the central program of what is popularly known as welfare, was created in 1935 to give states some relief from the burden of providing for the poor during the Great Depression. Over 60 years, this program had become a shared federal–state–local program with a blend of funding, regulations, and procedures at all three levels. In 1995 Congress renamed the program Temporary Assistance to Needy Families (TANF) and turned it back to the states to administer, with some remaining federal funding and strong guidelines aimed at getting people off welfare and into productive employment with assistance in job search, training, transportation, and child care to make the transition. This particular devolution actually marked a success of sorts for the theory that states provide a laboratory of federalism in which experiments can be conducted, with the successful ones transplanted to other states. It was the success of some state programs (particularly in Massachusetts and Wisconsin) in welfare-to-work, or workfare programs, that provided much of the rationale for devolving welfare programs to the states

SUMMARY

The structure of governments, or the number of governments, the number of levels and types, and the sizes, responsibility, and autonomy of each level or type are the essence of the institutional framework within which public economics operates. The choice of a structure involves such economic concerns as scale economies, internalizing externalities, measuring demand, and the benefits of intergovernmental competition. The appropriate choice of structure will depend on the country—its size, diversity, values, culture, and level of economic development. The United States is one of a relatively small number of countries with a federal structure, consisting of three levels with a significant amount of independent authority at the middle (state) level.

Governments come in many sizes. Within a country, the second and third tiers can be split into states, cities, towns, counties, parishes, townships, and school districts of greatly varying populations and land areas. Larger or more centralized governments may enjoy greater economies of scale and be able to include most of the beneficiaries of their services within the taxing jurisdiction (internalize externalities). A large, centralized government will be able to offer the same level of services to all citizens and control destructive competition by lower levels of government seeking to lure businesses or high-income residents. However, decentralization allows for diversity of citizen preferences, beneficial competition, and innovation and experimentation.

The three fundamental questions that a structure of governments must address are how many levels of government, how much autonomy to allow each level, and to what degree functions and revenue sources will be separated or coordinated between levels of government. Most countries have either two or three levels. Autonomy means that lower levels of government must have some independent revenue sources and some separate service responsibilities. While some responsibilities are clearly assigned to certain levels of government in the United States, overlap occurs between levels of government in most areas. Separation of responsibilities makes it easier to ensure accountability, but sharing of responsibilities makes it easier to assign the cost to those who benefit from the services. Also, different levels of government have different abilities to raise revenue, which may not match up to their service responsibilities.

At the local level, states in the United States are divided into counties, parishes, or townships, sometimes into separate school districts; and some citizens live inside corporate cities or towns, others outside. In some states, local governments enjoy a high degree of independence in raising revenues and providing services, while in other states local governments are more closely monitored and regulated by the state. Counties are created by the state and cover the entire state, while cities are created by incorporation and grow by annexation. The expansion of cities poses questions of balancing costs and benefits both for the city and its current residents and for those who are to be annexed.

The structure of governments in the United States, which began as a very weak federation under the Articles of Confederation (1781), was strengthened considerably by the adoption of a Constitution (1789) that gave the central government important powers to create a single unified market. The federal role expanded steadily throughout the 19th century, particularly after the Civil War stilled the voice of the states' rights movement. The regulatory commissions of the early 20th century and the expansion of the federal government to cope with the Great Depression led to further centralization of government activity. Federal grants to state and local government led to a peak in central government activity and control in the period from 1950 to the mid-1970s, after which the pendulum swung back toward a greater role for state and local governments. Under the rubric of devolution, federal aid to state and local governments has been reduced and some responsibilities, notably welfare, have been turned back to the states.

KEY TERMS AND CONCEPTS

fiscal federalism, 17
centralization, 19
home rule, 27

fiscal autonomy, 27
devolution, 34

DISCUSSION QUESTIONS

1. Is your state's structure of state and local government highly centralized compared to other states? How would you measure the degree of centralization?
2. What are the principal services provided by your local government? How much of the benefits accrue to strictly local residents, and how much to visitors and others? Who should pay for those services?
3. What might be the benefits and costs to existing residents in expanding the size of your city? To those being annexed? Based on your analysis, do you think it should it be easy or difficult for cities to annex the surrounding areas?

4. Which of the following government services seems most suited to national or central rather than local provision? Why?
   a. Environmental protection
   b. Public welfare (aid to the poor)
   c. Lighthouses
   d. Inoculations for preschool children
5. While local governments are supposedly "closest to the people" and therefore more responsive than state or federal governments, in the last 25 years state governments have imposed increasing restrictions on the ability of local governments to raise taxes and borrow money. Would it be appropriate for state governments to put such restrictions on local governments? Why or why not?

CHAPTER 3

MEASURING THE SIZE AND SCOPE OF GOVERNMENT

For two decades, one of the most popular whipping boys among Americans has been "big government." But just how big is government? What kind of a indicators can be used to measure it? The full economic impact of government is hard to measure. Regulations affect the quality and cost of everything people buy from meat inspection and food labels to the safety of automobiles and baby cribs. The government is involved in the rate of pay that people earn, the safety conditions of their workplaces, and the freedom of expression on the airwaves they listen to and the newspapers they read. Although these impacts are important, in public sector economics the efforts to measure government are focused mainly on the fiscal or budgetary dimensions.

Here are some of the questions most frequently asked by policy makers, politicians, and interested citizens who are trying to get a handle on the size of government: How much money does "the government" collect, and what do they do with it? Where does the money come from? How much comes from taxes, and how much from other sources? How much of it is collected and spent by each level of government? And how do these answers compare to what government was doing last year, 10 years ago, half a century ago? How does what *our* government (federal, state, or local) is doing compare to what other governments in other countries, states, counties, or cities are doing?

Answers to these questions can be mined from a rich source of descriptive data, the U.S. Bureau of the Census. The Bureau of the Census collects financial data on governments from a variety of sources. Other good sources of current and historical fiscal data are the annual *Economic Report of the President* and the monthly periodical *Survey of Current Business*, issued by the U.S. Department of Commerce.

THE CHALLENGE OF COMPARISONS

Numbers in isolation are meaningless. The fact, for example, that state and local governments spent $295 billion on public education in 1997 does not provide much information unless it is combined with a few more facts. How many pupils did that account for; that is, how much was spent per pupil? The answer to that question would give a little sense of educational quality. Is per-pupil spending increasing or decreasing over time? Is that measurement before or after adjusting for inflation? That answer may help citizens decide whether it is poor administration or inadequate resources that are the source of poor performance by their children in readings, math, and standardized tests. How much did the average citizen have to pay in taxes to support the public schools? What percentage of his or her income did it take to pay for education, and is that percentage rising or falling over time? Those answers may help determine how burdensome it is to support public education, and whether that burden is increasing or decreasing. How does this state's, or school district's, spending compare to that of other states or school districts? This comparison is always of great interest, because taxpayers in districts that spend more expect to see better results in terms of learning, graduation rates, and SAT scores. How unequal is the spending between rich states and poor states, or rich districts and poor districts? This question is of interest to policy makers who want to ensure that a child's chances of getting a decent education are not unduly affected by geography. How does education spending in the United States per pupil, or as a percentage of GDP, or as a percentage of total government spending compare to what other nations spend? This answer may help policy makers to grapple with differences in academic performance by comparing inputs and seeing to what extent they are connected with outputs.

Population Growth and Inflation

Comparative numbers must be used with caution. The most obvious caution is to be careful with comparisons over time, because these figures have to be adjusted for inflation and for increases (or decreases) in population. The inflation adjustment is sometimes done using the Consumer Price Index or the GDP deflator, but a more accurate adjustment calls for using the GDP deflator for the government sector, which is available in the *Survey of Current Business*. Adjusting for inflation ensures that you are comparing the same amount of real resources in different years. An indirect method of adjusting for inflation is to compare the growth of revenues or spending to the growth of personal income, since both are affected similarly by inflation.

Adjustment for increases in population can be done directly, by putting all figures in per capita terms, or indirectly, by expressing data for all years as a percentage of personal income or of GDP. Because income or GDP grows with population, either method will make some correction for population growth. The direct method of computing per capita values makes a far more precise correction, because personal income is subject to fluctuations over the course of economic expansions or recessions.

Differences in Income, Wealth, or Special Conditions

Comparisons of national, state, or local governments with each other during the same year suffer from a different set of hazards. Suppose that you were told that State A collected only $520 per capita in income taxes while state B collected $750 in the same year. What could you conclude? Less than you might think. It may appear that State B has higher income tax rates, but it may just have a higher per capita income. A poor state will raise less money per capita with the same tax at the same rates than a wealthier state. Suppose, instead, taxes are compared as a percentage of personal income; in State A income taxes took 4% of personal income, while in State B they took only 3.5%. Now are taxes higher in State A? You can answer yes with a little more confidence in this case. State A may have higher tax rates, or perhaps it has smaller households, or an income that is more unequally distributed. State B may have low income taxes but high sales or property taxes, so that the overall tax burden is not particularly low. Finally, like Alaska and Texas, State B may enjoy substantial revenues from mineral extraction that fall largely on nonresidents and do not burden its own citizens.

Per capita figures are useful in comparing states (or nations or cities) with similar incomes in the same year. Per capita measures offer a reasonable indication of what government costs and what government provides in the way of services to the average resident. Percentage of income figures are better for making comparisons within a state or nation and between states and nations over time, because both the numerator and the denominator are affected equally by inflation, and because population growth is highly correlated with income growth. Thus, the percentage of income figure is not distorted by inflation and is much less sensitive to population growth. However, tax revenues as a percentage of income figures are very sensitive to fluctuations in income and output. During a recession, the percentage of income going to taxes and public services will rise just because the denominator (personal

income) is falling, while during rapid expansion the percentage of income passing through government is likely to fall even though governments are collecting and spending more.[1]

Incomplete Data

A final hazard of comparisons is that of incompleteness. Many of the international sources only report central government data. This problem makes
international comparisons more difficult. In unitary countries, with no middle level, per capita spending may be relatively higher because the central
government is responsible for functions carried out by two levels of government in federal countries, only one of which is reported. Likewise, in comparing states (or provinces), it is important to include both state and local
revenues and spending in the comparison, because some states are more fis-
cally centralized than others and different states divide spending responsibilities differently.

FEDERAL GOVERNMENT REVENUES AND SPENDING

Most of the revenues and spending of the federal government pass through
the government budget, which takes effect on October 1 each year. Federal
fiscal years are referred to by the ending date: for example, fiscal year (FY)
2001 refers to the 12-month period that ends September 30, 2001. Of the off-
budget funds, the most significant are the Social Security Trust Fund and the
Medicare Trust Fund. When these off-budget funds are lumped together with
the budgeted funds, the result is called the **unified budget.** The unified budget is the most important one for purposes of fiscal policy; the deficit or surplus reported each year refers to the unified budget, including the revenues
and expenditures of the trust funds.[2] However, the debates in Congress and
in the executive branch about changing tax laws, raising or lowering taxes,
and how to allocate the federal revenues among various spending priorities
refer to the budget approved by Congress and signed by the president each
year. This legislated budget does not include the trust funds.

Trends in Federal Revenue: Levels and Composition

In FY2000, the federal government took in $2,025 billion in revenue, of which
$1,544 billion was on budget and $481 billion was off budget. This unified
budget figure represented 20.2% of GDP in 2000—15.4% on budget and

---

1. Yet another method of interstate comparison is the measure of fiscal capacity, described in an appendix to
this chapter.
2. Social Security is discussed in Chapter 18.

4.8% in the trust funds. Individual income taxes are the mainstay of the federal budget, contributing $1,004 billion or 50% of the unified budget total (Figure 3–1). Corporate income taxes contributed another $207 billion. Social insurance and retirement receipts that went into the general treasury fund rather than the trust funds accounted for $167 billion, and excise taxes on gasoline, cigarettes, automobile tires, and other items contributed $69 billion. These four revenue sources accounted for 95% of all federal on-budget revenue. Estate and gift taxes, customs receipts from tariffs on imported goods, fees and charges for federal services, and miscellaneous minor items make up the remaining 5% of federal revenue.

Table 3–1 summarizes the federal government's unified budget revenue. Overall federal revenues have grown at a rate of 5.8% per year since 1989, and on-budget revenues only 2.8% a year over the same time period, while personal income grew at an average rate of 5.8% per year. In other words, federal revenues overall have kept pace with income growth, but outside of the trust funds being fed by an army of working baby boomers, federal revenues have actually lagged behind growth of personal income.

Has the Federal government been taking an increasing share of the nation's income over time? The answer to this question is not affected by the rate of inflation, because both federal revenue and GDP (or national income) are measured in current dollars. The answer is yes, if you go back far enough. But in the period since World War II the federal government's share of the economy's income has been relatively stable, and the on-budget share has actually declined. In 1930, at the start of the Great Depression, the government collected 4.1% of GDP in taxes and other revenues. That share rose only slightly until World War II. The government collected a record high 20.9% of GDP in 1944—a number never again equaled, although current collections come close.

Table 3–1
Federal Government
Revenue, FY2000

	Dollars (in billions)	Per Capita
On-budget revenues	$1,544	$5,437
Individual income taxes	1,004	3,535
Corporate income taxes	207	729
Social insurance/retirement	167	588
Excise taxes	69	243
Other	97	342
Trust fund revenue		
Social Security Trust Fund	481	1,704
TOTAL unified budget	$2,025	$7,130

Source: *Economic Report of the President 2001* (Washington, DC: Government Printing Office, 2001).

Since that time, the federal government's revenue as a percent of GDP has ranged from a low of 14.4% in 1950 to a high of 20.1% in 2000, with most years in the 17% to 19% range. Off-budget receipts for the Social Security and, later, Medicare Trust Funds were less than 1% of GDP until 1950, when they began a slow but steady upward trend with increasing employment and wages plus higher payroll tax rates. In 2000, trust fund revenues accounted for almost a third of federal revenue and 6.4% of GDP.

Once the effect of increases in Social Security and Medicare revenue is removed, there is relatively little growth in government revenue as a share of GDP. On-budget receipts as a share of GDP were actually lower in recent years than they were in the 1950s and 1960s. In 2000, the share of GDP going into the federal budget (excluding trust funds) was 15.3%, which was lower than the typical share for the 1970s and 1980s. Instead, real growth in government has been occurring in the state and local sector (see below).

The mixture of federal government revenue sources (shown in Figure 3–1 for FY2000) has changed relatively little also. Individual income taxes have accounted for 40% to 50% of all federal revenue in every year but four for more than half a century.[3] Corporate income taxes have shown a steady decline in their share of the total from more than 20% in the 1950s and 1960s to 13% currently. Corporate income taxes are also much more sensitive to fluctuations in economic activity, so there are greater swings in receipts from year to year. There is also a steady downward trend reflecting changes in the tax code that reduce tax burdens on corporations. Excise taxes were cut sharply in the 1960s and have been a declining share of revenue since that time; currently there are only 3% of the unified budget.

Trends in Federal Spending

Spending figures do not even come close to matching revenue figures on an annual basis because the federal government, unlike most state and local governments, is not obligated to balance its budget.[4] For most of the last half of the 20th century, until the very end, the federal government's spending consistently exceeded its revenue. In 2000, federal government spending came to $1,788 billion, of which $1,457 billion was on budget and the remainder off budget. With a remarkable surplus of $237 billion, federal spending in 2000 only accounted for 7.8% of GDP, the smallest share since 1974. (The peak year in the last half century was 1983, at 23.6%.)

There are many ways to sort federal spending: by cabinet department or agency, by direct spending or by grants and transfers. Three major categories in the unified budget accounted for 89% of federal spending in 2000: national

3. In 1949 and 1950 the share dropped to just under 40%; in 1982 and 1983, it rose to 48.2% and 48.1%, respectively.
4. Actually, spending and revenue figures often do not match even in states and cities that operate under a balanced budget requirement. Unexpected surpluses and deficits can occur, or revenues can be carried over from a previous year to be spent in later years.

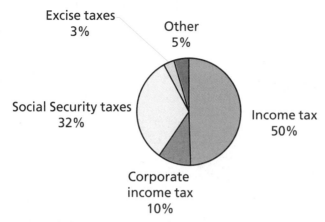

defense, human services including Social Security benefits, and net interest. Figure 3–2 shows federal spending patterns for FY2000, and Table 3–2 shows the dollar figures for total and per capita federal spending by category.

Although the revenue mix has been relatively stable, the makeup of federal spending has changed dramatically in the last half century. Defense spending has been particularly volatile. In 1950 (after World War II but early in the Korean War), national defense was 32% of the federal budget and 5% of GDP. It rose sharply during the Korean War and remained over 40% of federal spending (and 7% to 10% of GDP) until 1971, when it began to decline. By 1980, defense spending had fallen to 23% of the federal budget and 5% of GDP. President Reagan emphasized rebuilding defense in the last decade of the Cold War, and defense spending surged to 28% of the budget (1987) and more than 6% of GDP before starting a steady decline to a 17% share of federal outlays and a 3% share of GDP in 2000.

Human resources is a broad category that has come to be dominated by more than $400 billion in Social Security benefits as the largest single item. Income security (welfare), Medicare, and health are the other major items in this largest budget category, which also includes education, training, employment, social services, and veterans' programs. Even in 1950 this category made up one-third of the budget, with veterans' benefits (mostly from World War II) accounting for the largest share of the spending. By 1956 Social Security surpassed veterans' benefits and has been the dominant share ever since. Income security, or welfare, has also shown steady growth, but less rapidly than Social Security; with recent reforms its growth should be much slower in the future. Medicare joined this budget category in 1965 and has grown extremely rapidly, with projected continued rapid growth in the next 20 years as the baby boomer generation approaches age 65.

The growth in the human resource category reflects a shift in the role of the federal government from being primarily a producer/provider of services

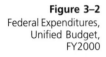

Figure 3–2
Federal Expenditures,
Unified Budget,
FY2000

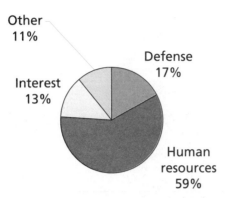

Other
11%

Defense
17%

Interest
13%

Human
resources
59%

Table 3–2
Federal Government
Spending, FY2000

	Dollars (in billions)	Per Capita
On-budget revenues	$1,457	$5,204
National defense	294	1,050
Human services	668	2,386
Net interest	223	796
Other functions	241	860
Offsetting receipts*	−43	
Trust fund spending	331	1,182
TOTAL federal spending	$1,788	$6,386

*Revenues from fees, fines, and other sources that go directly to the agency rather than the Treasury.

to being primarily a guarantor of income security through **transfer payments.**
Transfer payments collect taxes from citizens and give them to selected groups
of citizens, not in payment for services but because they are believed to be
needy, deserving, or entitled to such payments (including payments of Social
Security benefits to retired workers who have contributed to the system).
Transfer payments are considered in more detail in Chapters 5 and 18.

Net interest is determined by two factors: the growth of the government
debt and the prevailing market interest rates. As the economy and the budget
"grew into" managing the accumulated debt from World War II, the share of
the budget going to net interest fell from 11% in 1950 to the 6% to 8% range.
This decline reversed in 1979, when high interest rates and increasing deficits
drove its share upward to over 14% in 1988 and 15% in 1995 before it began to decline again with lower deficits and the emerging surpluses, as well
as lower interest rates.

Finally, there is the category of other expenditures, which includes most
of what we think of as the primary activities of government, but which account for only about 5% of the budget: infrastructure, international affairs,

science, space and technology, agriculture, administration of justice, and general government. These functions claim about 1% to 2% of GDP but have declined in relative importance with the rising share of the budget that goes to transfer payments.

Overall, federal spending other than transfer payments, adjusted for inflation, has declined during recent years. According to the *Survey of Current Business*,[5] the quantity index for federal government purchases (i.e., adjusted for inflation) was 111 in 1989 and only 102 in 1999. For state and local governments, however, the same quantity index rose from 84 to 112 during the same period. The devolution described in Chapter 2 is certainly reflected in changed spending patterns

Trends in Federal Debt and Deficits

As you have undoubtedly noticed, the 1990s saw a dramatic shift in a long-term trend in federal government borrowing and the growth of the national debt, with the first unified budget surplus in almost 40 years appearing in 1998. By 2000, that surplus had risen to $150 billion. In 1999 and 2000 both the on-budget balance and the unified budget balance showed surpluses, with about two-thirds of the surplus coming from the Social Security Trust Fund. This pattern is expected to hold more or less through the first decade of this century until the baby boomers (those born between 1946 and 1964) begin to retire in large numbers. At that point, the Social Security Trust Funds will begin to present the IOUs to the Treasury that have been collecting for several decades, and it will be necessary to run larger on-budget surpluses in order to redeem those IOUs. Figure 3–3 shows the trends from 1980 to 2000 in unified budget revenue and expenditures, with the gap between them measuring the deficit or surplus.

STATE AND LOCAL REVENUE AND EXPENDITURES

State and local governments have a very different mix of revenue sources and spending obligations than that of the federal government, as is appropriate in a federal system. While most of the federal government's revenue comes from individual income taxes and Social Security taxes, state and local governments rely on a fairly even mix of income taxes, retail sales taxes, and property taxes. Like the federal government, state and local governments also receive some revenue from corporate income taxes and excise taxes, but unlike the federal government, they receive substantial and increasing revenue from fees and charges of various kinds ranging from dog tags to business licenses to highway tolls. On the spending side, education and welfare are the big ticket items,

5. *Survey of Current Business* (Washington, DC: U.S. Department of Commerce, August 2000), p. 128.

Figure 3–3
Federal Unified
Budget Revenues
and Expenditures,
1980–2000

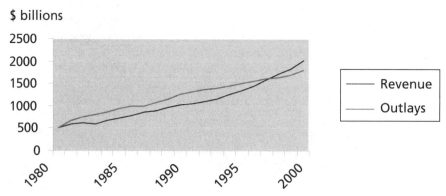

with substantial outlays for health and hospitals, highways, and law enforcement and corrections.

Patterns of revenue and spending vary greatly from state to state. Forty-five states and the District of Columbia have retail sales taxes, 41 have broad-based individual income taxes, and 1 state—New Hampshire—has neither. Excise taxes on tobacco are very high in the northeast, but very low in the tobacco-growing states of North Carolina, South Carolina, Virginia, and Kentucky. Lotteries are now a minor but significant source of revenue in a majority of states, a significant change since the first state (New Hampshire) adopted its lottery in 1964. Spending patterns tend to be a little more uniform, since there is fairly widespread agreement that the state, in partnership with local governments, has major responsibilities for education, highways, law enforcement, and public health. But even in these categories great variations are observed in per capita spending from state to state as well as within states.[6]

State Revenue

Table 3–3 and Figure 3–4 summarize state revenue patterns. Note that states distinguish between total revenue, general revenue, and own-source revenues. **Total revenue** includes the earnings of state operated enterprises such as public utilities, liquor stores, and insurance trust funds. **General revenue** includes intergovernmental revenue—revenue from other governments, federal to state, state to local, federal to local, sometimes even interlocal—as well as **own-source revenues,** which are those raised by that particular level of government by imposing taxes, fees, and charges. The pie chart of Figure 3–4 makes it quite clear that sales (both general and selective) and individual income taxes are the main revenue sources of state governments. Government enterprises

6. The appendix to this chapter describes an alternative way of making state-to-state comparisons called the representative tax (or revenue) system.

Table 3–3
State Revenue,
FY1998–1999

	Dollars (in billions)	Per Capita
State revenue		
TOTAL	$1,153	$4,233
General revenue	906	3,319
Intergovernmental	254	930
Own-source	652	2,388
General sales taxes	164	601
Selective sales taxes	75	275
License taxes	14	51
Individual income taxes	173	634
Corporate income taxes	31	114
Other taxes	43	158
Current charges/fees	152	557
Miscellaneous	73	267

Source: *Census of Governments, 1999* (Washington, DC: U.S. Census Bureau, 1999).

Figure 3–4
State General
Revenue,
1998–1999

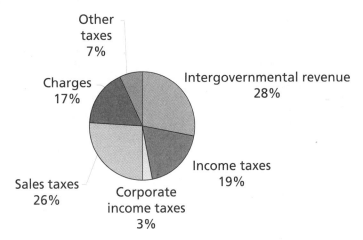

include insurance trust funds as well as state liquor stores and other enterprises. Intergovernmental revenue also remains a significant source for states at more than one-quarter of general revenue.

Great diversity exists among the states in taxes and in services. Tax collections per capita, for example, ranged from nearly $3,000 in Connecticut to less than $900 in New Hampshire in 1999. The significant differences in the mix of taxes used, the quality and variety of services provided, and the division of revenue collections and expenditure responsibilities between state and local governments make comparisons very difficult.

States experienced strong revenue growth during the 1990s, enabling many of them to reduce taxes while expanding the quality and variety of services. Beginning in 2001, however, a number of states saw revenue and revenue forecasts leveling off, making it difficult to maintain real spending per capita (i.e., responding to population growth and inflation) out of a slow-growing revenue pool.

Local Revenue

Table 3–4 and Figure 3–5 present a summary of local government revenue in the United States in 1997. (There are longer lags in collecting local government data than state data). As you can see, local governments depend even

Table 3–4
Local Government Revenue, 1998–1999

	Dollars (in billions)	Per Capita
TOTAL revenue	$952	$3,487
General revenue	906	3,318
Intergovernmental	254	1,195
Own-source	652	1,871
Property taxes	228	835
Sales/excise taxes	51	187
Individual income taxes	17	62
Corporate income taxes	1	4
Other taxes	15	55
Charges	196	718
Miscellaneous	64	234

Source: Census of Governments, 1999 (Washington, DC: U. S. Census Bureau, 1999).

Figure 3–5
Local Government General Revenue, 1998–1999

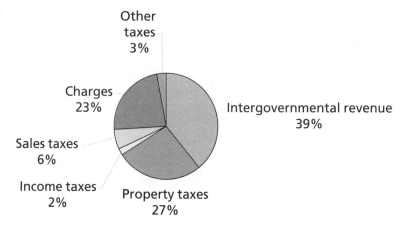

more heavily on intergovernmental funds (more than one-third of general revenue) than states. Most of these local funds originate at the state level, although some come from the federal government. Property taxes and charges (and miscellaneous) provide 65% of local own-source revenue, with the rest coming from a variety of smaller sources.

Retail sales taxes and individual income taxes are clearly the workhorses of state government, whereas local governments rely primarily on property taxes, intergovernmental aid, and charges. The low figures for local sales and income taxes reflect both very low rates (typically 1% for both taxes) and the limited number of local governments that use such taxes.

State and Local Expenditures

Education is a substantial component of state and local spending, accounting for 13% of state general expenditures and 38% of local spending, which includes state aid to local governments for education. Public welfare has historically been a significant spending area for states also, although it has begun to decline as a result of welfare reform in the late 1990s. State and local governments share responsibilities in many areas but particularly highways, with the state paying about two-thirds of highway costs and local governments the other one-third. In public safety (police, fire, correction), local governments spend nearly as much as state governments. Parks and recreation and sewer and solid waste management are primarily local expenses. Within education, states assume most of the responsibility for higher education and share responsibility for the public schools.

State expenditures are described in Table 3–5 and Figure 3–6. As you can see, education and social services account for half of state spending, with the other major areas being intergovernmental and interest on debt. Local expenditures are described in Table 3–6 and Figure 3–7.

Table 3–5
State Expenditures,
FY1998–1999

	Dollars (in billions)	Per Capita
TOTAL state expenditures	$998	$3656
Intergovernmental	305	1,117
Direct	693	2,538
Education and libraries	127	462
Social services/income support	240	879
Transportation	58	212
Public Safety	44	161
Government administration	32	117
Interest on general debt	28	103
Other	164	604

Source: *Census of Governments 1999* (Washington, DC: U.S. Census Bureau, 1999).

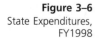

Figure 3–6
State Expenditures,
FY1998

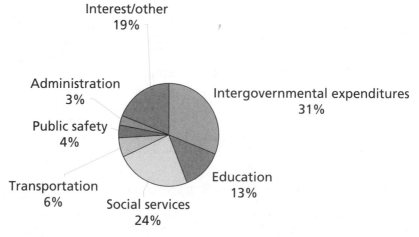

Interest/other
19%

Administration
3%

Public safety
4%

Transportation
6%

Social services
24%

Intergovernmental expenditures
31%

Education
13%

Table 3–6
Local Government
1998–1999

	Dollars (in billions)	Per Capita
TOTAL local expenditures	$939	$3446
Intergovernmental	10	37
Direct	929	3,403
Education	357	1,308
Social services	98	359
Transportation	51	187
Police/fire/corrections	85	311
Sewer/solid waste	40	147
Government administration	44	161
Interest on debt	40	147
All other	214	784

Source: *Census of Governments 1999* (Washington, DC: U.S. Census Bureau, 1999).

HOW BIG SHOULD GOVERNMENT BE?

The 1980s and 1990s saw an extended debate in the United States over the size and growth of government, a debate that can be viewed as a search for "right-sizing." How much government—how much tax burden, how much in the way of services, how much borrowing—is "enough"? This question goes beyond the kinds of taxes used and the kinds of spending decisions made, or the mix of revenue sources and outlays, to the issue of overall size. If government's share grows, the share of the private sector shrinks, and the private sector offers significant advantages in terms of greater efficiency and respon-

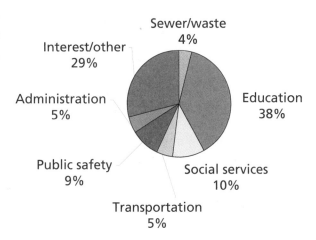

Sewer/waste
4%

Interest/other
29%

Administration
5%

Education
38%

Public safety
9%

Social services
10%

Transportation
5%

siveness. So the issue of size of government is an important topic of debate
for Americans, one with few easy answers. Efforts to impose constitutional
or statutory limits on the size and growth of government at all levels are a response to such concerns about efficiency, responsiveness, and uncontrolled
growth.

How can we measure how much government is enough? The ideal measure would be the level of satisfaction of the representative citizen with his or
her tax burdens relative to services received. If the marginal value of the last
unit of government services is just equal to the pain of parting with the last few
dollars of tax money to pay for that service, then the level of government activity is optimal. However, there is no good way to make such measurements.
Elections give some very rough and general guidance to the level of citizen satisfaction or dissatisfaction, but often noneconomic issues dominate political
races, or the choices are not clear enough for voters to send an unambiguous
message. So it becomes necessary to use some less satisfactory indicators. One
measure is how fast government is growing, absolutely and relative to population or GDP. Another way is to compare the size of government in the United
States, per capita or as a share of GDP, to the size of government in other nations, especially other nations at similar levels of economic development.

Share of GDP

As we have seen, the federal government's share of GDP has been relatively
stable, particularly on the revenue side. State and local revenue and spending
as a share of GDP have grown considerably during the last half century, from
6% to 7% in the 1950s and early 1960s to more than 10% in the 1970s.
That growth leveled off in the late 1970s, but has picked up again since the
mid-1980s in spite of deliberate efforts to limit the growth of government
through tax and expenditure limitations.

International Comparisons

A second possible indicator of the size of government is a comparison with other industrial nations. The World Bank groups the United States with 25 other nations as high-income countries, ranging from Portugal to the United Arab Emirates. Excluding the four nations that are very small and/or oil-based (Kuwait, Hong Kong, Singapore, United Arab Emirates), a "peer group" of 21 countries remains within which the United States can reasonably be compared. In 1994, according to the *World Development Report,* central government tax receipts in these 21 countries ranged from 17.8% of GDP (Japan) to 44.7% (Netherlands), and total revenue from 20% of GDP (Japan, United States) to 48.5% (Netherlands). The United States was second lowest in tax revenue at 18.5% and tied with Japan for lowest in total revenue at 20%. Similarly, on the spending side, the share of GDP ranged from 23% in the United States to 52.9% in the Netherlands.

Table 3–7 summarizes revenue and spending by some of these 21 central governments as a share of GDP for 1998. Note, however, that three of the countries with exceptionally low ratios of revenue and spending to GDP are federal countries: the United States, Switzerland, and Australia. In the United

Table 3–7
Comparative Central Government Revenue and Spending as Percent of GDP, 1998

Country	Revenue as Percent of GDP	Spending as Percent of GDP
Switzerland*	23.7%	28.0%
Norway	34.1%	39.2%
United States*	21.8%	21.0%
Germany*	31.7%	33.5%
Austria	37.3%	41.5%
Sweden	40.3%	42.8%
France	41.8%	46.6%
Belgium	44.0%	46.6%
Netherlands	45.7%	47.8%
Italy	41.5%	44.6%
Finland	32.0%	35.3%
United Kingdom	38.3%	37.8%
Australia*	24.5%	24.6%
Israel	42.2%	48.1%
Ireland	33.2%	35.4%
Spain	30.1%	36.1%
New Zealand	34.2%	33.4%
Portugal	35.7%	40.8%

Countries are ranked by per capita income, highest to lowest. Canada and Japan are not included because of lack of recent data. Figures include both tax and nontax revenues, current and capital spending.
*Federal country.
Source: *World Development Report 2000/1* (Washington, DC: World Bank, 2001), pp. 300–301

States, 10.8% of all revenue in 1994 was raised by state and local governments, which would increase the U.S. revenue/GDP ratio to 30.8%. Similar adjustment would be likely for other federal countries, including Germany, but such corrections would still place government in the United States toward the lower end of the size spectrum.

The inclusion of state and local governments (which are particularly important in the United States) raises the 1998 U.S. revenue figure to 29.2% of GDP. This percentage is considerably higher than the federal-only figure but still below the percentage of GDP going to central government revenue in 16 of the other 17 industrial nations. Both of the peer nations—Switzerland and Australia—that report lower shares of GDP going to the central government are also federal countries with substantial state and local sectors. In both cases, their central government revenue was higher than U.S. central government revenue. It is fairly clear from these data (and the patterns do not vary greatly from year to year) that by any measure the United States has a lower share of economic activity passing through its public sector than most other industrial nations.

What does this comparison mean? Probably not too much. It means that Americans have chosen to produce or provide a larger share of what they consume through the market or through private, voluntary groups. Health care, for example, is almost universally run through government in these other nations, but the private sector still dominates the provision and financing of health care in the United States. Services to low-income households are more likely to be provided by private voluntary organizations in the United States. A significant number of American students are served by private schools from prekindergarten through college. These differences represent a combination of conscious choices and historical patterns for Americans. There is no "right" share for government, but it is clear that proponents of smaller government will have to base their arguments on something other than international comparisons.

WHAT MAKES GOVERNMENT GROW?

The dramatic growth of government, and especially state and local spending, in the last half century not only sparked discussion of what size is optimal but also led to a search for explanations about what made it grow. Is it some insatiable monster—a Leviathan[7] that will continue to demand larger and larger shares of the economic pie unless it is somehow constrained? And if so, why? Is government growing in response to citizen demand for more services? Is it growing because elected officials and bureaucrats like to create programs

---

7. The description of government as Leviathan, a monster mentioned in the Bible, was popularized by Nobel Prize-winning economist James Buchanan but originated with 17th century British philosopher Thomas Hobbes. The Leviathan debate is reviewed in Chapter 5.

that they can control and are able to sneak them by an inattentive public? Is it growing because the revenue system continues to generate rapid growth of revenues to state and local governments that legislators choose to spend rather than return in the form of tax cuts? Is some of the growth reflective of the fee-for-service approach to many public services in which beneficiaries pay to use public campgrounds, boat launches, roads, and other services? At the federal level, has the absence of a meaningful budget constraint (the ability to run deficits at will) allowed runaway growth of federal spending? Let's consider each of these explanations in turn.

Citizen Demand

At least at the state and local level, some of the spending does seem to be demand-driven. Back in the 1950s, economist John Kenneth Galbraith crafted a memorable and often quoted description of an imbalance between private consumption and the public infrastructure and services to go with it in *The Affluent Society:*

The family which takes its mauve and cerise, air-conditioned, power steered and power-braked automobile out for a tour passes through cities that are badly paved, made hideous by litter, blighted buildings, billboards, and posts for wires that should long since have been put underground. They pass into a countryside that has been rendered largely invisible by commercial art. . . . They picnic on exquisitely packaged food from a portable icebox by a polluted stream and go on to spend the night at a park, which is a menace to public health and morals. Just before dozing off on an air mattress, beneath a nylon tent, amid the stench of decaying refuse, they may reflect vaguely on the unevenness of their blessings.[8]

Galbraith might not have written that paragraph in the 1990s, when billboards are more restricted, newer communities have underground utilities, pollution is more tightly controlled, and better efforts are being made to dispose of trash, although the complaints about the conditions of roads and blighted buildings still has some validity. As consumers become more affluent, they do expect better infrastructure and better public services, whether it is recreation, better schools, roads, trash collection, or law enforcement. Some citizens retreat to gated communities and private schools and purchase these services privately, but many citizens pressure state and local governments to provide more and better public services to complement their higher standard of private consumption. Often they are willing to pay for those services at least partly through fees, which are one of the faster growing components of state and local revenues.

At the federal level, much of the growth is driven by two very popular programs, Social Security and Medicare. National defense spending rose

8. John Kenneth Galbraith, *The Affluent Society,* 2nd ed. (Boston: Houghton Mifflin, 1968), p. 223.

sharply during the Reagan years but has declined since the end of the Cold War, and most of the growth in the 1990s is concentrated in those two areas. Thus, while citizen demand is not likely to be the whole explanation, it certainly plays some role, particularly for federal transfer payments and local public services.

Bureaucracy-Driven Demand

Public choice economists developed this explanation as a factor in government growth. Combine the desire of elected officials to get themselves re-elected by enacting popular programs and getting "pork barrel" projects for their districts with the desire of government bureaucrats to keep their jobs and enhance their power and prestige by the growth of their agencies, and it is easy to see that the forces for growth are strong. Apathetic citizens, knowing that their individual votes have little impact, are a weak constraint against these pressures. Some of the models that attempt to explain why citizens get more government than they might consciously choose are described in Chapters 4 and 5.

Elastic Revenue Sources

Yet a third explanation for government growth is that at least some of the revenue sources in place at all three levels—federal, state, and local—have been able to generate a steady growth of revenue that is faster than population growth and faster than personal income growth, most of the time without requiring an increase in tax rates. The automatic growth of revenues, keyed to the growth of the tax base (income, spending, and wealth), could lead to an automatic and uncontrolled growth of the public sector without a conscious decision about how much of economic activity citizens want to have run through or managed by government.

The problem of growth driven by elastic revenue sources is that the income elasticity also holds when there is a slowdown in economic activity. If elected officials, especially at the state level, have been using revenue growth to fund programs that will require future annual appropriations, or want to enable permanent cuts in tax rates or other recurring tax breaks, then they run the risk of sudden budget shortfalls. A number of states, including Texas and Florida, had that experience in preparing budgets for the 2001–2002 fiscal year after about eight years of impressive revenue growth that had funded both tax cuts and increased state expenditures.

Fee for Service

Increasingly, governments at all levels, but especially state and local, have shifted some of the responsibility of paying for government services to those who benefit directly from those services. Whether it is building inspection fees, access to parks, airports paid for with fees from both airlines and passengers, highway tolls, trash pickup fees, or recreation charges, citizens have come to expect that many services provided by government will be funded partly through taxes and partly through user fees. These fees, which are discussed in detail in Chapter 13, have made it possible for government to provide some services that are unprofitable for the private sector to undertake but desirable from the social standpoint. Such fee-financed services represent at least part of the expanded size and scope of government activity.

Lack of a Budget Constraint

During the 1980s and early 1990s, the fact that Congress could pass unbalanced budgets and run deficits without any meaningful constraints was considered the primary culprit in growth of federal spending. After several unsuccessful attempts to legislate a budget constraint in the 1980s, a combination of steady economic growth, declining inflation and interest rates, and bipartisan agreements to hold the line on spending brought the budget under control at the end of the 20th century. The 1990s did not see a significant slowdown in government growth, but at least expenditure growth was limited until it finally matched the revenue available to pay for it.

Lack of a budget constraint may have explained federal spending growth, but not growth in state and local spending, which is almost always subject to a balanced budget requirement. In 49 states and the District of Columbia, a balanced budget is required by law. For local governments, the balanced budget is a practical issue of limited ability to borrow to fund operating deficits over more than a year or two at a time.

CONSTRAINING THE GROWTH OF GOVERNMENT

The rapid growth of federal, state, and local spending in the 1960s and 1970s led to a variety of efforts to put some reins on rising public budgets. While the Gramm–Rudman Act was the best known effort at the federal level, many states followed suit. Typically these state **tax and expenditure limitations (TELs)** put a limit on spending growth, holding budgeted spending growth to the same rate as growth of income or population. Others attempted to limit revenue growth.

At the local level, the focus was on limiting the growth of the property tax. The best known of these efforts was the Jarvis–Gann Amendment in California, passed in 1978 and better known as Proposition 13. Proposition 13 put limits on the growth of property taxes in California, which had been rising rapidly during the inflation-fueled housing boom of the 1970s. Other states soon followed—Proposition 2½ in Massachusetts, for example. Some states, such as Michigan and South Carolina, attempted to shift the burden

THE TRIM EXPERIENCE IN PRINCE GEORGE'S COUNTY

Prince George's County, Maryland, is a very large county lying just to the east of the District of Columbia. In 1978, during the great wave of tax and expenditure limitations, Prince George's County passed one of the most restrictive spending limits in the country. While other states and counties were limiting tax rates, or annual rates of revenue growth or spending growth, or tying budgetary growth to population or personal income, Prince George's County went a step further. The TRIM proposition, which passed in November 1978, put a ceiling on the total tax dollars that the county could collect.

The District of Columbia has five adjoining counties, two in Maryland, three in Virginia. For lower to middle income families trying to move out of the district and into the suburbs, Prince George's County, which shares a very long eastern border with the district, has long been the most affordable. After the TRIM proposition passed, county population continued to grow at a very rapid rate, and county officials found that they were having to serve more people, and pay higher prices for labor and materials as a result of inflation, without additional dollars. It was an untenable situation. Class sizes grew larger, and so did potholes. Police response time became longer and longer. Finally, in 1984 there was an organized revolt against the impossible limitations on county government. A well-orchestrated campaign, complete with bumper stickers, billboards, meetings at public schools, and distribution of flyers at Metro stops, persuaded the citizens of Prince George's County to reverse themselves and repeal the TRIM amendment.

The important lesson in this experience is that an overly restrictive TEL can be worse than none at all, making it impossible for government to do its job. One of the basic skills that you learn as an economist-in-training is to balance costs and benefits, to know how far is far enough, or in the words of Gilbert and Sullivan, to make the punishment fit the crime. Making marginal adjustments, fine-tuning, balancing opposing needs and concerns is the bread-and-butter of economics. An economist, asked to design an appropriate constraint on the growth of government in Prince George's County, would have been much more likely to have limited its rate of growth to that required to maintain real per capita spending, that is, a rate that reflects inflation and increases in population. This limitation would ensure that real per capita spending and services would not decline steadily under the double hammer of inflation and population growth. Instead of seesawing between an intolerable restriction followed by no restriction at all, the county would have had a workable constraint on growth of government

of school financing away from the property tax and more toward state revenue sources like sales and income taxes. A few states even tried to abolish the property tax, but were hard-pressed to find an adequate substitute for funding local governments. The TEL movement peaked in 1984, with no major new legislated TELs since that time. Some of the more restrictive TELs have had unfortunate repercussions, as discussed in the boxed material. In California, the quality of schools and local public services was initially maintained with an infusion of state funds, but as state budgets became tighter, local governments ran into serious revenue shortfalls and citizens began to experience crowded classrooms, aging infrastructures, crowded public facilities, and more potholes.

SUMMARY

The size of government is measured by revenues, spending, deficits, and debt. To make valid comparisons between time periods, or between states, cities, and countries, various adjustments can be made. These adjustments may include correcting for inflation, dividing by population (per capita), or expressing revenue or spending relative to GDP or personal income. In comparisons among countries, it is important to consider that central government figures may understate total spending in federal countries. In comparisons among states, it is important to consider combined state–local figures, since the division of revenues and responsibilities varies from state to state.

Federal revenues and spending are presented both in the regular budget and in the trust fund account, the total of both accounts is called the unified budget. Reported deficits usually refer to the unified budget. Total federal revenue has been growing at about the same rate as personal income, more slowly if the trust funds are not included. Federal revenue as a share of GDP has been relatively stable during the last 50 years. The individual income tax and Social Security taxes are the main sources of federal revenue.

The composition of federal spending has changed dramatically in the last 50 years with a decline in defense spending more than offset by transfer payments, especially for Social Security. Interest payments have also claimed a larger share because of many years of budget deficits and borrowing. Major categories of federal spending are national defense, human resources, physical resources, interest on debt, and other. Because spending has consistently exceeded revenues for most of the last 50 years (until very recently), there has been steady growth in the national debt, both that held by the public and that held by government agencies.

State and local governments have a very different mix of revenue sources and spending obligations than that of the federal government. States rely heavily on income and sales taxes, local governments on property taxes and state aid, and both on fees and charges of various kinds. Education and welfare are the main spending categories, along with health and hospitals, highways, and law enforcement and corrections. Patterns of revenue and spending vary greatly from state to state. Comparisons of revenues or expenditures between states generally are made using per capita figures to adjust for very different populations, or as a percentage of income.

There is no simple way to measure the "right" size of government. Indicators might include how fast government is growing, absolutely and relative to population and/or GDP, or comparisons of the size of our government to the size of government in other nations at similar levels of economic development. In the United States, the federal government's share of GDP has been relatively stable, particularly on the revenue side. State and local revenue and spending as a share of GDP have grown considerably during the last half century. International comparisons find the United States near the bottom in share of GDP passing through the government relative to other developed industrial countries. These differences, however, do not mean that government in the United States is too small; they represent a combination of conscious choices and historical patterns for Americans.

Reasons why government might grow rapidly include citizen demand, bureaucracy behavior, elastic revenue sources, increased use of fees and charges, and at the federal level, lack of an effective budget constraint.

Efforts to contain government growth at the state and local level are known as tax and expenditure limitations such as Proposition 13 in California. Some TELs have had a negative impact on the quality of local public services. The TEL movement peaked in the mid-1980s as a method to control the growth of government.

KEY TERMS AND CONCEPTS

fiscal year, 40
unified budget, 40
transfer payments, 44
total revenue, 46
general revenue, 46

own-source revenue
  (state), 46
tax and spending limitations
  (TELs), 56

DISCUSSION QUESTIONS

1. Suppose you are employed by a politician who is getting ready to make a speech, and he asks you to tell him how fast government has been growing in your state. What kind of answer would make growth look slowest? What kind would make it look fastest? What kind of answer would be the most honest representation of actual growth?

2. Using the *Survey of Current Business* or the *Economic Report of the President,* find answers to the following questions:
    a. What was the federal budget deficit or surplus in 2001? In 2002?
    b. How much did spending for highways by state and local governments increase between 1990 and 2000 before and after adjusting for inflation? What happened to per capita spending for highways?
    c. Which states were highest and lowest in per capita property taxes? Were they the same states that were highest and lowest in property taxes as a percent of personal income? If not, explain the difference.
    d. What has happened to federal defense spending—total, inflation-adjusted, and per capita—since the early 1980s?

3. What factors might explain the great diversity in government spending as a share of GDP among industrial nations?

4. If you worked for a congressional committee that was considering an across-the-board tax cut, what kinds of aggregate revenue and spending and debt data, both for the United States and for other countries, might you muster in support of the tax cut? What kinds of data might you use to argue against it?

Interstate Comparisons: Fiscal Capacity and Fiscal Need

Suppose that you, as an interested citizen, are attending a political debate in which one candidate claims that your state's taxes are much higher than its neighboring states and he plans to reduce them substantially if elected. The opponent cites figures to prove that your state is in fact a low tax state and that tax cuts would further reduce the ability of the state to fund needed public services, especially education. This scenario is far from hypothetical; it happens on a regular basis. As a student of public finance, how do you sort out these claims?

First, make sure that both candidates are talking about the overall level of taxation (or even revenue, which includes fees and charges as well as taxes), rather than just zeroing on one particular tax. Sales taxes may be high in your state because property taxes are low and the sales tax funds the schools, or perhaps because you live in one of the nine states without a broad-based income tax. If a particular tax is high, then perhaps its role in the revenue system needs to be reconsidered, but that's a different matter from the level of the overall tax burden.

Second, any such comparisons need to be made with combined state and local taxes or revenue, because different states divide up responsibilities and revenue sources in various ways. Connecticut has traditionally had low state taxes but high property taxes because the property tax pays a larger share of the public education bill. Other states may fund more of education, highways, or law enforcement at the state level and thus have lower local (mostly property) taxes.

After resolving these two problems, what is the best way to compare taxes, and specifically the tax burden on citizens, among states? As already noted, references to per capita taxes are misleading because the same tax will raise less per capita in a low-income state than a high-income state. Taxes as a share of personal income come a little closer to providing a meaningful comparison. However, there is one important difference between states that is not captured by this measure. You may notice that Alaska has exceptionally high revenue both per capita and as a percent of income, but a careful look at the specific familiar taxes (sales, income, property) shows no sales tax (except for some local sales taxes), no state income tax, and no property tax. Where does the money come from? Oil! Some states, especially Alaska and Texas, have much greater ability to extract tax revenues from nonresidents than others. The process of shifting the tax burden to nonresidents is called tax exporting. Two of the major opportunities for tax exporting are natural resources (gas, oil, minerals) and tourism. States capture revenues from out-of-state buyers of depletable mineral resources mainly through severance taxes, and from tourists through accommodations taxes, amusement taxes, gambling taxes, and sales taxes.

To account for these differences in the ability of states to tax outsiders, the U.S. Advisory Commission on Intergovernmental Relations developed a standardized measure based on the Representative Tax System (RTS), later expanded to the Representative Revenue System (RRS). RTS and RRS created a hypothetical "average" tax and revenue system using 27 used state and local revenue sources at national average rates and "typical" structures (food exemption from the sales tax, typical deductions/exemptions on income tax, etc.). The large number of taxes reflects many specific excise taxes on items such as gasoline, tobacco, and alcohol.

Once this hypothetical structure was created, it was applied to the tax base in each state: retail sales for the sales tax, cigarette sales for cigarette taxes, personal income for the income tax, and so forth. That calculation determined the amount of revenue a state could raise per capita if it used all possible revenue sources at national average rates and with typical exclusions and exemptions. This measure, expressed as a percentage of the national average, referred to as *fiscal capacity*. For example, a state with a fiscal capacity of 85 would be able to raise per capita revenue of 85% of the national average if it used that standardized revenue system.

A second measure then compared that per capita potential revenue figure to actual per capita collections, again expressed as a percentage. This second measure was called *fiscal effort*, because it measured how hard the state was trying to raise revenue—the percentage of what it could collect against what it was actually collecting. A state like Mississippi might score very low on fiscal capacity because of low personal income, yet high on fiscal effort because it was collecting a high share of its potential relative to other states.

These two measures provide a different and useful perspective on the concept of high and low tax revenue states. Table 3–8 gives the fiscal capacity and fiscal effort measures for the 50 states and the District of Columbia in 1996. As you can see, some states are high in both capacity and effort, particularly in the Northeast (New York, Connecticut, Massachusetts, Delaware, New Jersey, and the District of Columbia). Other states, especially in the South, are low in both capacity and effort—Alabama, Arkansas, Louisiana, and South Carolina, among others. A few states, such as Alaska, Colorado, and Hawaii, enjoy the luxury of high capacity and low effort, because relatively low tax rates yield more than adequate revenue, a result of tax revenues from tourism and/or mineral extraction. Finally, some states, such as Rhode Island and Wisconsin, have below-average capacity and are attempting to maintain a high level of services by taxing that capacity more heavily than average.

The third column in Table 3–8 presents yet another useful comparative measure on the expenditure side, the *fiscal need* index. Developed by Robert Rafuse of the U.S. Treasury in the late 1980s, this measure has been refined and updated by Robert Tannewald at the Boston Federal Reserve. This index attempts to compare states on the basis of the workload facing govern-

State	(1) Fiscal Capacity	(2) Fiscal Effort	(3) Fiscal Need	(4) Fiscal Comfort
Alabama	83	83	104	79
Alaska	127	116	102	124
Arizona	94	93	105	90
Arkansas	81	92	100	81
California	103	101	110	94
Colorado	114	82	90	126
Connecticut	129	115	102	126
Delaware	121	90	89	135
District of Columbia	126	141	126	100
Florida	100	90	96	104
Georgia	96	96	104	92
Hawaii	120	104	90	134
Idaho	90	92	100	90
Illinois	110	97	101	109
Indiana	97	88	92	104
Iowa	97	98	89	105
Kansas	96	99	95	101
Kentucky	84	99	101	83
Louisiana	88	86	109	81
Maine	89	113	88	100
Maryland	108	100	95	113
Massachusetts	116	104	93	126
Michigan	98	100	101	97
Minnesota	107	113	94	113
Mississippi	72	102	110	65
Missouri	97	87	92	105

(continues)

ments. While some spending is proportional to population, the 1986 Rafuse study identified six functions for which the level of spending is influenced by state-specific factors other than income or demand and population: elementary and secondary education, higher education, public welfare, health and hospitals, highways, and police and corrections, which account for more than two-thirds of total state and local spending. Such factors as vehicle miles traveled, poverty rate, and age distribution of the population (particularly the percent of school-age children, for education needs, and elderly, for Medicaid expenses) are important components of the fiscal need calculation. The fiscal need index is also expressed as a percent of the U.S. average. Because it only reflects a few additional factors besides population, the variation in the fiscal need index is much smaller than the variation in the tax capacity index. While fiscal capacity ranges from 141 in Nevada to 72 in Mississippi,

State	(1) Fiscal Capacity	(2) Fiscal Effort	(3) Fiscal Need	(4) Fiscal Comfort
Montana	99	79	98	101
Nebraska	99	99	88	112
Nevada	141	73	94	150
New Hampshire	118	74	84	141
New Jersey	116	114	96	122
New Mexico	85	102	115	74
New York	109	141	104	105
North Carolina	92	94	95	97
North Dakota	97	89	96	101
Ohio	96	100	97	99
Oklahoma	84	92	104	80
Oregon	103	85	91	113
Pennsylvania	95	102	93	102
Rhode Island	91	117	89	102
South Carolina	85	89	101	85
South Dakota	95	79	96	100
Tennessee	92	79	102	90
Texas	91	90	108	86
Utah	92	89	95	97
Vermont	99	100	90	111
Virginia	101	89	96	105
Washington	104	104	95	109
West Virginia	78	99	100	78
Wisconsin	97	117	89	109
Wyoming	127	74	101	126

Source: Robert Tannewald, "Fiscal Disparities Among the States Revisited," *New England Economic Review,*
July/August 1999, pp. 3–25.

the fiscal need index ranges from 126 in the District of Columbia to 88 in Nebraska.

Finally, both Rafuse and Tannewald computed a simple index of *fiscal comfort*—the ratio of fiscal capacity to fiscal need—by dividing the first (column 1) by the second (column 3). This index, which measures how easily a state can meet its service needs with its available resources, is given in column 4 of Table 3–8. This index also shows a wide range from 150 in Nevada, which enjoys an excellent tourism- and mineral-based tax base and a small population, a low poverty rate, and relatively few road miles and students, to Mississippi (65), with few tax resources, a high poverty rate, and a high percentage of both school-age children and senior citizens.

DISCUSSION QUESTION

A1. Use Table 3–8 to find the indexes for fiscal capacity, fiscal effort, fiscal need, and fiscal comfort for your state and three neighboring states. How does your state compare? What factors do you think influence your state's tax capacity and fiscal need? Based on this information, would you argue that your state is a high, low, or average tax state? Explain your answer.

PART 2

THEORETICAL FOUNDATIONS

Efficiency and equity are the two central concerns of market economics. These issues also inform the evaluation of the performance of the public sector. The profit motive, self-interest, and the constraints of competition do very well at ensuring efficiency in the private sector for most economic activity, although the equity of market outcomes is often questioned. What forces are working toward efficiency and equity in the public sector? What kinds of institutions can be created that will make efficient or equitable outcomes more likely? What role does competition play in making government more efficient, and how do the actions of government impact on competition in the private sphere?

The first chapter in Part 2 explores the efficiency dimension of providing the optimal level of public and quasi-public goods and making the optimal interventions in the case of privately produced goods with strong negative or positive externalities. Chapter 5 addresses some of the challenges in making decisions in the public sector. Chapter 6 explores equity issues, and Chapter 7 looks at the role of government in promoting or constraining competition both within the public sector and the private sector and between public and private sectors.

CHAPTER 4

EFFICIENCY: PUBLIC GOODS AND EXTERNALITIES

Efficiency is the major achievement that the market has to offer. The market is, as a general rule, very good at allocating resources to their "highest and best" uses and distributing output to those who desire it the most, as measured by the prices people are willing to pay. The market is good at ensuring that, under favorable conditions, goods and services will be produced at the lowest possible resource costs, and that changes in consumer preferences or resource availability will call forth a rapid response in terms of input or output combinations.

The relationship between government and efficiency in a market economy has several aspects. One connection is that the government is expected to ensure that the conditions under which the market operates are indeed favorable to efficiency, particularly in terms of competition (an issue addressed in Chapter 7). A second connection is that the government itself should strive for some of the same kinds of efficiency as the private sector in terms of cost and desired output mix. This efficiency issue is addressed in Chapter 5. A third relationship lies in the rationale for government production of goods and services, namely, that there are certain kinds of goods and services demanded by consumers/citizens that the market fails to produce in the right quantities or sometimes fails to produce at all. It is this kind of efficiency that is the subject of this chapter.

PUBLIC GOODS, PRIVATE GOODS, AND GOODS WITH EXTERNALITIES

n casual use, the term *public goods and services* is used to describe whatever it is that governments provide, from streetlights to defense to a system of courts. Economists, however, use the term **public goods** in a more precise sense to describe goods (or more often, services) that have two key characteristics: **nonrivalry** in consumption and **nonexcludability**. These two characteristics must both be present in significant degree for something to qualify as a public good.

Nonrivalry

A good that is nonrival in consumption can be consumed by any number of people simultaneously, without diminishing the amount available to be consumed by others. A beautiful sunset is a pure public good. A pair of shoes is a private good; if you are wearing them, no one else can use them at the same time. Between shoes and sunsets lies a whole spectrum of nearly private and nearly public goods. At the public end of the spectrum are national defense and lighthouses, because the same army and the same lighthouse that affords you protection can simultaneously protect others without in any way diminishing your safety. Note that nonrivalry does not mean that all consumers value the public good equally, only that they share consumption in a noncompetitive way. Nearer to the private end of the spectrum in rivalry are such traditional publicly produced services as garbage pickup and early childhood education. As more consumers are added, the frequency of pickups or the attention to the individual child is likely to diminish. It has probably occurred to you that some things that share this nonrivalry characteristic would not be described as "good," that is, desirable. There are also "public bads"—environmental deterioration, blight, or crime that makes large areas unsafe at night. In fact, many activities of the public sector can be viewed not so much as the provision of public goods, but as the elimination of public bads. This problem in semantics is easy to address; the elimination or reduction in a public bad can be defined as a public good. Improved environmental quality, neighborhood revitalization, and increased public safety would be the obverse of the public bads.

Nonexcludability

The second dimension of publicness is nonexcludability. This term describes the inability to keep people, specifically nonpayers, from consuming the good or service. A sunset and a lighthouse also qualify on this criterion, because it is difficult to locate and collect payment from all those who benefit. National defense suffers from the same problem. If Ms. Smith did not pay any taxes, it would be very difficult for the government to single her out as an acceptable target for enemy forces to attack, because she did not pay for protection, without endangering her neighbors as well.

Exclusion is not a matter of possible/not possible, but of cost relative to benefits. If the cost of excluding a nonpayer is low relative to the payment that would be received, then it makes sense to undertake the effort to exclude. In many parts of the United States, for example, public recreation areas charge a fee with a gatekeeper during peak seasons (when the revenue generated exceeds the cost of collection) and allow free admission during the off-season, when the receipts would not cover the cost of staffing the gatehouse.

It is the problem of excluding nonpayers rather than nonrivalry that is often the determining factor in calling for public production. When innovations in technology or just more imaginative solutions reduce the cost of excluding nonpayers, it becomes possible to shift some activities from the public sector to the private sector. For example, it is much cheaper to have automatic tollbooths or subway entries than it is to staff them with human toll collectors. An electronic readable device on cars that records their highway use and collects payments by electronic funds transfer is another new exclusion technology. Likewise, new methods of identification such as voiceprints and handprints can bypass the human gatekeeper in ensuring access only to those who are entitled by membership and contribution.

As new techniques develop, some of them will make exclusion more difficult rather than easier. The Napster case in 2000 involved a technology that made it difficult for owners of intellectual property rights to charge users because they could not exclude them from access to other people's recordings of their music. A previously excludable private good lost some of the essential quality that made private production profitable, a quality that was eventually restored by court action.

Balancing probabilities with penalties is another useful exclusion technique. Parking regulations or beach access restrictions can be enforced with infrequent checks but high fines for violation. The higher fines and less frequent enforcement will have a similar effect on compliance, as do lower fines with more frequent checks because the expected cost of violation will be similar. The expected cost of illegal or expired parking is equal to the probability of being caught multiplied by the amount of the penalty or fine. A low probability of being caught such as 5%, can be combined with a high penalty, say, $200, so that the expected cost of illegal parking or accessing a restricted beach is $10 ($.05 \times \$200$). The same expected cost of $10 could be the result of frequent patrols that raise the probability of being caught to 50% but only impose a $20 fine. But the combination of low probability (less enforcement effort) and a high fine for violation greatly reduces the cost of excluding nonpayers.

Free Riding and Public Goods

The primary reason why it is difficult to rely on the market to produce public goods is the free-rider problem. The term **free rider** comes from the labor union movement. Labor unions produce a limited public good. They negotiate on behalf of all the workers in their plant or trade group, and nonunion workers benefit from those negotiations whether or not they pay their union dues. There is an obvious incentive to obtain the benefits without paying. If a large number of people decide to free ride, not enough dues will be paid to keep the union going, nor will it have enough members to make the union a recognized bargaining agent.

In the case of a public good, free riding means that there will not be enough payers to cover the costs of private for-profit firms undertaking production. Because it is easy to consume while avoiding payment, many users would refuse to pay, and a private firm could not recover its costs. Where the number of users/residents is large, free riders know that the availability of the public good is largely independent of their small contribution to its cost. One person reasoning this way will gain the benefit of having the public good and not bearing any of the cost. Large numbers of people reasoning this way will make it impossible to finance the public good, and it will not come into being. It is for this reason that goods and services with both very low rivalry *and* very low excludability are usually provided through the public sector and paid for with compulsory taxes.

Some Qualifications

Just because something meets the two tests of publicness does not mean that it is, or should be, produced in the public sector. Some public goods are not "produced" in the economic sense, such as integrity, but are nevertheless essential for the workings of markets and for the general health of society. Each of us benefits from the integrity of others, from the dependability of their word and their promises. Integrity is nonrival and nonexcludable. Other public goods are produced by private nonprofit organizations. Medical research, for example, is often funded and carried out by private nonprofit organizations using voluntary contributions, and the results benefit many people who did not contribute. Finally, as we noted in Chapter 1, public provision is not the same as public production. A significant amount of national defense, a public good, is produced by private contractors in the United States and other countries.

IDENTIFYING PUBLIC GOODS

The biggest difficulty in distinguishing public goods from private goods is that both of the defining characteristics of public goods exist in varying degrees, making it hard to draw a clear dividing line between pure public goods, pure private goods, and goods with varying degrees of publicness. Very few public goods, like a sunset, exist in a pure form where consumption is totally nonrival and exclusion virtually impossible. Likewise, relatively few private goods

FREE RIDING AND STREETLIGHTS—A TRUE STORY

On the outskirts of the small town of Clemson, South Carolina, in the 1960s, there were few sidewalks and even fewer streetlights. These outskirts were fairly densely populated but not a part of the nearby small town. The only local government was the county, but the county did not provide streetlights, which were regarded as a municipal (city) service. Some citizens took the initiative to pay the electric company $30 a year for a streetlight, but most fumbled along in the dark with flashlights. As a result, walking at night was a chancy venture, although it was not the crime rate that citizens worried about. It was ditches and potholes that threatened pedestrians after dark.

In one particular neighborhood, Mrs. G. had undertaken to have a streetlight installed in front of her house, and some of her neighbors, when they remembered, would chip in toward the $30 annual payment. But many did not chip in, because they knew that the streetlight would shine whether they kicked in or not, and it was easier to free ride on Mrs. G's public-spiritedness. Unfortunately, the free riders were in the majority, and streetlights were few and far between. One dark Halloween night one of Mrs. G's neighbors took his little daughter out to trick-or-treat. With only the light of a flashlight to see by, the little girl fell in a ditch filled with burning leaves and burned her hand—an accident that could have been prevented with a few well-placed streetlights.

The next year, this neighborhood along with many others was annexed into the city. One of the first actions of the city council of the enlarged community was to extend the public provision of streetlights throughout the city, paid for with taxes. Free riders could no longer free ride, children had a little more protection from ditches and burning leaves, and even strangers to the city could bask in the glow of streetlights as they sought to find addresses in the subdivisions around the city.

Although this story may sound like an edifying moral tale for the ears of little children, it is based on an actual incident. A streetlight is a local public good. Most of its benefits accrue to local residents, especially within neighborhoods, but people travel from one neighborhood to another, so the benefits of a streetlight are shared throughout the city. It is easy to free ride if streetlights are privately provided, difficult to exclude nonpayers from benefiting from the light. A streetlight is largely nonrival in consumption; it shines on the rich and poor, payers and nonpayers alike. It has the two defining attributes of a public good that suggest that private provision will be difficult at best. Because most of the benefits accrue to local residents rather than visitors passing through, a streetlight is a local public good. Nonrival in consumption and highly nonexcludable, streetlights are a clear candidate for local public production.

Was the level of streetlight production optimal (marginal social cost = marginal social benefit) after this intervention? Perhaps, perhaps not. It is fairly clear that before government intervention, the level of streetlight production was below optimal, but whether the after-intervention level of production was still below optimal, optimal, or beyond optimal is difficult to determine. Depending on whether government intervention moved the output level closer to the optimum or beyond the optimum, the effect of intervention could have increased or decreased economic efficiency.

And what about equity? Was pricing perfectly allocated among taxpayers? Probably not. Some taxpayers go out at night frequently, others not at all. Pedestrians value streetlights more than automobile passengers, families with children more than those without. The streetlights were funded with property taxes, which base the tax price on the value of property owned, which is not perfectly correlated with demand for streetlights. Thus, an imperfect private outcome was replaced with an imperfect government intervention.

are totally rival and excludable, because most consumption (and production) has at least some shared aspects. Your consumption of a T-shirt with a provocative slogan has an impact on those you encounter. Once you put the T-shirt on, it is difficult to exclude passersby from seeing it, whether you want them to or not. The smell of your burger, the sound of your motorcycle, the sight of your answers on a test all impact those who share your company on a given day. You may seek out an isolated corner in which to eat the burger, put a muffler on your motorcycle, or cover your test paper, but exclusion is not costless even for these essentially private goods.

Figure 4-1 categorizes some common goods and services on two axes. The horizontal axis ranges from highly excludable (to the left of the origin) to virtually impossible to exclude. The vertical axis ranges from the highly nonrival in consumption (at the top) to the highly rival (at the bottom). Goods and services in the northeast quadrant are, to varying degrees, public goods. Those in the southwest quadrant are mostly private goods. Those in the northwest quadrant are "club goods" or **local public goods,** jointly consumed by club members or residents but easily kept from nonmembers or nonresidents. Club goods are nonrival but excludable. This quadrant also includes **congestible goods,** which are nonrival in consumption until capacity is approached. Once that point is reached, competition for parking spaces, seats on the subway, or space on the freeway makes congestible goods rival in consumption.

Figure 4–1
Classifying Goods
and Services
by Rivalry
and Excludability

Weak rivalry

Club goods/local public goods	**Public goods**
Outdoor concerts	Sunset
Public buildings	Lighthouse, streetlights
Movie (in theater)	Defense
Public parks, recreational facilities	Environmental quality
Libraries	Lakes, rivers
Indoor concerts	Television
Limited access highways	
Beaches/beach access	
Police and fire protection	
Recreation facilities	
Parking spaces	

High excludability - **Low excludability**

Houses, cars	Education
Food, clothing	Garbage pickup
Personal services (haircuts,	Local roads
medical care)	Sewer service
Private goods	**Goods with externalities**

High rivalry

Public Goods versus Private Goods

The northeast and southwest quadrants of Figure 4–1 are the most clear-cut in terms of distinction. (The southeast quadrant, goods with externalities, is discussed later in the chapter.) Goods and services in which one person's consumption is not diminished by sharing it with another (low rivalry) and where exclusion is difficult or costly (low excludability) are clearly public goods. If a private producer attempts to produce such goods, she will find that she cannot easily keep nonpayers from sharing in that consumption. Nor is there any good economic reason to exclude them, since consumption is noncompetitive. Goods and services with high rivalry and excludability (southwest quadrant), in contrast, lend themselves readily to market production and distribution. Consumers are readily identified and can be excluded for nonpayment, and consumption is competitive.

Demand, Price, and Level of Output

Figures 4–2 and 4–3 illustrates the differences in demand for public and private goods in a society of only two individuals (or, more realistically, two groups of individuals), A and B. In Figure 4–2, which represents private goods with high rivalry and high excludability, the demand curves of A (D_A) and B (D_B) are added horizontally to create a market demand curve. The combined curve, D_T, has a kink in it, because it runs along B's demand curve until the price is low enough so that A enters the market. Beyond that kink, the points on the combined demand curve are added by choosing a price (any price) and adding the quantity demanded by A at that price to the quantity demanded by B at that price. The intersection of that market demand curve with the supply or marginal cost (MC) curve determines the equilibrium price P_1 and the equilibrium quantity Q_T. The total quantity is divided between A and B on the basis of the quantity each wishes to purchase at market price P_1, which is Q_A for person A and Q_B for person B.[1]

However, in Figure 4–3, for a public good with low rivalry and low excludability, the situation is quite different. Because these goods are nonrival in nature, the amount available for A to consume is always the same as the amount available to B, even if they benefit from it to greater or lesser degree. If A has an army with 100,000 soldiers so does B, even if B is a pacifist and totally opposed to war. If A has a lighthouse and 20 traffic lights, so does B, even if B does not own a ship or a car. In this case, what can vary is not the quantity each person consumes (as for private goods) but rather the marginal benefit to each consumer and (with appropriate price discrimination) the prices paid by the two consumers of this shared good. In fact, there is a quantity for which A's marginal benefit is zero—she doesn't want more at any price—and only B is willing to pay a positive price. This quantity creates the "kink" in

---

1. The appendix to this chapter expresses the same concepts in terms of equations.

Figure 4–2
Market Demand and
Optimal Output for
Private Goods

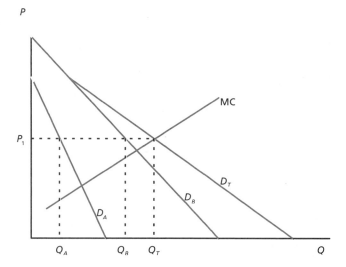

Figure 4–3
Demand, Supply,
and Equilibrium in
the Market for a
Public Good

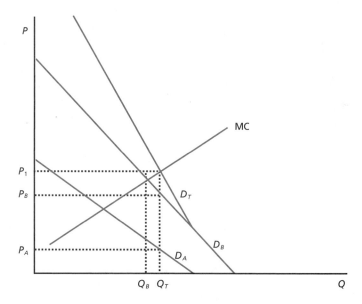

the total demand curve, beyond which the only demand for more units of the
public good comes from B. Think about national defense, for example. Consumer A may want just enough defense spending to protect us from a "traditional" war fought with armies and navies, whereas consumer B may want
a much higher level of protection such as what the "Star Wars" missile shield

might provide. Consumer A is not willing to contribute a single dollar toward the missile shield.

Because of the peculiar nature of public goods, their demand curves are added vertically rather than horizontally. For private goods, you add demand curves by choosing a price and adding the quantities that A and B want to consume at that price. For public goods, the quantity consumed is the same for both A and B, but the prices that A and B are willing to pay are different, because they value the public good differently. In Figure 4–3, B's demand for this particular public good is much stronger than A's, as indicated by the higher prices B is willing to pay for any given quantity.

The question that Figure 4–3 answers is how to set marginal benefit (measured by the prices A and B are willing to pay) equal to marginal cost (the MC curve) in order to determine the optimal amount of the public good to produce. That optimum occurs at Q_T, with a price of P_1. Person A is willing to pay only P_A, while person B is willing to pay a much higher price P_B.

Who Pays for Public Goods?

Two problems are readily apparent in the situation shown in Figure 4–3. First of all, there is the challenge of determining A's and B's valuations of the public good so that each can be charged the appropriate price. When a good is not directly sold to an individual in the marketplace, producers have to guess at how much is desired at various alternative prices. Second, and closely related, is the problem of getting to the optimal quantity when it is not possible to exclude nonpayers or free riders. It is very likely (in the absence of any intervention) that A will choose to pay nothing and just enjoy the benefits of the public good that B chooses for his or her own consumption, since that would still be a generous plenty (by A's standards) of Q_B. Person A has every incentive to be a free rider in this instance. Ensuring production of the optimal amount and assigning payment to beneficiaries is much more difficult when citizens have widely different demand curves for a public good.

In Figure 4–3, the appropriate prices to charge are P_A for person A and P_B for person B. These prices, representing the marginal benefit to each consumer, are called **Lindahl prices**. Optimality requires not only that total marginal benefit (measured by the combined demand curve) be equal to marginal cost, but also that the **marginal tax price** paid by each citizen be equal to the marginal benefit received.

Price discrimination by means of Lindahl prices make it more likely that the public sector will produce the optimal amount of the public good. If all citizens paid the same price, then in Figure 4–3 each person would pay a price of $P_T/2$. Person A would complain about high taxes for too much of a public good that she does not care that much about, and B would complain about too little (but probably not about his taxes being too low). To placate A, production would be reduced so that each person would pay the lower price A is willing to pay. The result would be a level of production that is less than optimal in terms of marginal benefit and marginal costs.

Implementing Lindahl prices for most public goods is quite difficult, because public goods are usually financed through broad-based taxes such as income, sales, and property taxes. Suppose, for example, that the city of Smallville has decided to build a public park and finance it through an increase in the property tax levied on the value of property in the city. The marginal tax price is the amount of additional tax a particular citizen has to pay in order to finance this park. In Smallville, the new park costs an amount P, which is financed by a property tax at rate $t = P/V$ on all the value of the property (V) in the community. If the nth taxpayer owns property with a value of v_n, then the marginal tax price facing the nth taxpayer for another unit of the public good is

$$\text{MTP} = P/V \times v_n = t \times v_n .$$

For example, suppose that the park costs \$500,000, and the value of all property in town is \$200 million. A park would require a tax rate of \$500,000/\$200,000,000, or 0.25%. If you are taxpayer n, and you own a house worth \$75,000, your share of the cost of the park is 0.25% of \$75,000, or \$187.50. It is this value that the citizen compares to the additional benefit of having the park in deciding whether or not to encourage or discourage public officials from building the park. Sometimes citizens get to vote directly on additional tax levies, but more often public officials must make these decisions with limited information about how citizen preferences match up with cost shares in new ventures. The decision may be made on the basis of rough proxies, such as assuming that the desire for public parks rises with income and that the value of property owned is a good proxy for income. Or officials may focus on balancing the tax burden and service demands of the median voter, as discussed in the next chapter.

If there is reason to believe that demand for a public good, like national defense, is similar from one household to another, then a tax that collects the same amount from each household is an appropriate funding mechanism from the perspective of efficiency. (Equity may be another matter.) If demand is closely related to income, as it might be for education or cultural facilities, then a proportional tax that rises as income rises would be a suitable way to raise the revenue, giving a reasonable approximation to matching tax prices to benefits.

In a few cases, those who benefit most are a definable subset of the population who can be assigned their share of the cost through a **benefit tax.** Taxes on gasoline to finance highway construction and maintenance ensure that those who drive more (using the highways more and causing more wear and tear) pay a larger share of the cost through gasoline taxes. Special assessment on property taxes for improvements that only benefit one part of the community ensure that those who benefit are the ones who pay. The property tax in general, because it pays for services whose value is linked to the value of property (police protection, garbage collection, sidewalks, fire protection, etc.), has some claim to being a benefit tax.

In general, the challenge to governments in attempting to implement Lindahl pricing is twofold. The first challenge is to measure or estimate differences in demand from different individuals or groups within the population. The second challenge is to devise ways of collecting revenue that approximate those Lindahl prices for different segments of the population. Some public goods lend themselves more easily than others to such a strategy. If a lighthouse benefits primarily commercial fishing boats, then a property tax or other levy that applied only to boats would ensure that those who obtained most of the benefit would incur most or all of the cost.

Local Public Goods, Club Goods, and Congestible Goods

Free riding is much less problematic in small groups—clubs, small towns, and neighborhood associations, for example. With small numbers, one person's contribution of time, money, or votes does make a difference to the outcome. Participation or nonparticipation becomes visible and personal, making free riding more difficult. The northwest quadrant of Figure 4–1 identifies some of these local public goods and club goods, which are characterized by low rivalry but also by lower costs or fewer obstacles to excluding nonpayers than public goods.[2]

Any time it is possible to enclose the good or service and put a ticket-taker, a tollbooth, a security guard, or a passcode at the entryway at a moderate cost, the free-riding problem can be overcome. The key to payment in such cases, however, is not usually a per-use charge. Instead, these local public goods, club goods, or congestible goods are often financed by a membership fee or local tax that entitles the user to access the facility or service. Examples include a municipal swimming pool, a county library with a library card, or a beach with a membership sticker or local-resident sticker or nonresident pass displayed in the car. The single payment for unlimited access reflects the nonrival characteristic of local public goods, while at the same time identifying beneficiaries and assigning the cost of construction, maintenance, and operations to those who choose to use the facility. (Often local government will assume that most residents will choose to use the facility to some degree and simply pay for the facility with taxes, issue identification cards to local residents, and only charge nonresidents.) Because the marginal cost of

2. Extensive literature is available on the theory of clubs, or private voluntary associations for the production of shared goods, such as churches, tennis and sailing clubs, and neighborhood associations. Most of what has been written on this subject draws inspiration from the classic article by James Buchanan, "An Economic Theory of Clubs, *Economica*, 32(5), (February 1965):1–14. Local governments, especially cities, have many characteristics in common with such clubs. For a thorough summary of some of the earlier literature on local public goods, see David King, *Fiscal Tiers* (London: George Allen and Unwin, 1984).

an additional user or an additional use is equal or close to zero, users should be encouraged to use the good or service up to the point where the marginal benefit is equal or close to zero. Users will only expand their consumption to that point if the price of an additional swim in the pool or day at the beach is zero. Thus, the flat membership fee with no per-use charge is both efficient and equitable.

Many of the goods and services listed in the northwest quadrant of Figure 4–1 are *congestible goods*. A congestible good is one for which consumption is nonrival up to a point at which crowding begins to diminish the enjoyment of all users. Beyond that point, the good becomes more rival in nature and more like a private good. While local public goods and club goods are usually produced by local governments or private associations such as neighborhood associations, sailing clubs, and nonprofit groups, congestible goods can be found in all three producing sectors—public agencies, private for-profit firms, and private nonprofit, voluntary organizations.

A highway, an outdoor concert series, a library, a beach, and downtown parking are all congestible goods. All of them have periods of low demand and peak demand depending on the time of day, the season of the year, or the reputation of the concert performer. For those low-demand periods, as noted earlier, it may be less expensive to allow free usage than to incur the cost of a gatekeeper to collect admission. The problem of when to exclude nonpayers and what price to charge to discourage congestion is illustrated in Figure 4–4.

Up to a point (about where D_2 crosses the MC curve), additional users create only a very low and constant marginal cost (sometimes even zero); so low that it may not be worth the trouble to try to collect a payment from them. Parking in a downtown area with lots of empty spaces, riders on a

Figure 4–4
Supply, Demand, and Price for a Congestible Good

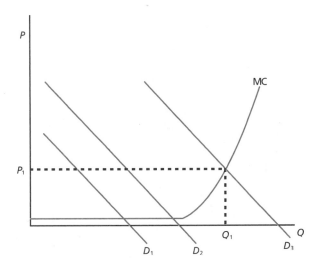

nearly empty subway train, drivers on a largely vacant stretch of highway, extra listeners at a lightly attended outdoor concert all impose very low marginal costs either on other users or in wear-and-tear damage or other marginal costs on the supplier. But at periods of peak demand, additional users require extra cars on the subway train, cause congestion and accidents on the Beltway, or compete for scarce parking spaces. In this case, there are at least five reasons why the producer should be charging a peak-period fee:

1. The fee rations a scarce good among competing users, ensuring that the parking space, the spot in the subway car, or the space on the highway goes to the person who values it the most.
2. Revenue collected relative to the cost of collecting it rises sharply, so that it is worth incurring the cost of posting a gatekeeper to enforce payment and exclude nonpayers.
3. Additional users or would-be users—drivers, parkers, riders—are imposing significant costs on others in terms of congestion and delay.
4. In the absence of a fee, public demand would pressure the authorities in charge of the facility to expand the available "slots" up to the point where the demand curve crosses the horizontal axis, that is, up to the point where marginal benefit is equal to the zero price.
5. The price difference for congestion and noncongestion times offers an incentive for some would-be users to consider alternate times, alternative routes, or other substitutions, thus reducing peak-load demand and pressure to expand capacity.

Thus, a two-part pricing schedule is appropriate for congestible goods, and is widely observed in differential tolls on highways and rates on subways for peak periods and off-peak periods, as well as periods when parking is charged (weekdays) and periods when it is free (weekends, Sundays). This pricing strategy has a parallel in price discrimination in the private sector, where differential pricing for matinee and evening movie seats and afternoon and evening bowling offer an example of congestion or peak-period pricing. The strategy of making the service free during periods of low demand and charging only during periods of higher demand is appropriate when the marginal cost of another user is essentially zero during off-peak periods.

If the marginal cost is high enough to justify the cost of paying a gatekeeper to exclude nonpayers, then an alternative strategy is one borrowed from utility pricing called the **two-part tariff**.[3] The two-part tariff can be used to describe a variety of charges based on a written schedule. Typically, the manager sets a charge for users with two components, one for membership or access and one for each actual use. For example, a boat may be docked at a marina for an annual charge for boat storage and a small dock fee for each time the owner actually uses the dock. Or the boat owner may

3. You may associate the term *tariff* with a tax on imports, but in its more general use it can be used to describe a variety of charges based on a written schedule.

have an annual pass to a city park that entitles her to free entry, with an extra charge if she wants to use any services like the volleyball court or the tennis court or the pool. The fixed fee is intended to ration the available capacity among a limited number of persons with the right of access, while the per-use charge covers the variable costs of cleanup, maintenance, or other services that are positively related to the number of times the facility is actually used.

EXTERNALITIES

Finally, the southeast quadrant of Figure 4–1 includes a sampling of goods and services that create **externalities,** or spillover effects. Externalities are costs imposed on third parties or benefits received by third parties outside the market transaction, costs that they cannot impose on their creators or benefits for which they are not charged. Externalities can result from either production or consumption.[4] Consumption (production) externalities occur when a second person is affected by your consumption (production) of a good or service, either positively or negatively, even though that person (or often, many persons) is not a party to the transaction leading to your consumption (production). Typically, when positive externalities arise in either consumption or production, it is very difficult to exclude nonpayers from receiving those benefits.

Both consumption and production externalities can also be negative. Examples include overcrowding on local roads, poorly maintained yards and houses that detract from the neighborhood and property values, sewage discharge into waterways that affect downstream residents, and litter discarded along the sides of highways. The reduction of negative externalities poses similar challenges to the enhancement of positive externalities.

An important characteristic of externalities, positive or negative, consumption or production, is that they are reciprocal in nature. A firm may impose externalities on its neighborhood residents by creating traffic congestion or odors. On the other hand, its neighbors' demands for less traffic or aroma may be seen as imposing costs on the firm. Costs arise regardless of whether there is more or less traffic or more or less smell. The real question is who bears the costs (or reaps the benefits, in the case of positive externalities). Much of the debate about externalities is about the distribution of costs and benefits. The economist's concern is to distribute the costs and benefits in ways that move production toward the level at which marginal cost is equal to marginal benefit, when all costs and benefits are taken into

---

4. A third class of externalities, pecuniary externalities, deals with financial effects, which are not an issue in this discussion. This section focuses on the two more familiar categories of production and consumption externalities.

account. As we will see, that objective can be achieved in many different ways.

Positive Externalities

A child's education not only benefits the child and her family but also other people in the community. Others in the community benefit from being a part of a more educated, productive community. Educated citizens are more productive, more informed citizens, and more likely to have a taste for consumer goods and services (upscale restaurants, bookstores, concert halls, etc.) that require a critical mass of educated citizens to support them. Similarly, when your neighbor's garbage is collected regularly, your health risk is reduced and the value of your property is enhanced. When a streetlight is located half a block from your house, paid for by the resident there, you can walk in greater safety at night. When one family remodels its home or landscapes the yard attractively, benefits accrue particularly to neighbors but also to those who walk or drive through the neighborhood.

Figure 4–5 illustrates the situations of positive externalities, also known as social benefits. Note that the curve labeled MSB (marginal social benefit) looks very similar to the demand curve for one of the two individuals in the case of a public good. **Marginal social benefit** is a measure of the value of positive externalities at various levels of output or consumption. In both cases, the benefits are added vertically rather than horizontally, because the same quantity of output that produces a given level of private benefits will also generate social benefits. However, in the case of positive externalities, the demand curve D_A represents the direct beneficiary or beneficiaries, while

Figure 4–5
Optimal Output for a Good with Positive Externalities

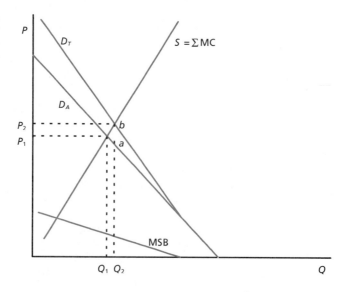

MSB represents marginal social benefits to all of those who are indirect beneficiaries of the purchase of the same quantities of this good with positive spillover effects. Most of the benefits accrue to the direct buyers and most of the cost rightly should fall on them in a world that is both efficient and equitable.

The problem associated with the private production and sale of goods with positive externalities is that these private transactions do not reflect social benefits. Because those who benefit are not easily excluded from the spillover effects of Person A's consumption, they can free ride rather than contribute to its purchase. Without the contribution ab from those enjoying social benefits, the sole force in the market on the demand side is D_A, and the quantity purchased will be Q_1 at a price of P_1—both of which are lower than the socially optimal quantity Q_2 and price P_2. The appropriate price to charge the primary user or direct customers is measured on the graph by the vertical distance Q_2a. The appropriate contribution per unit from all the would-be free riders who experience social benefits (or positive externalities) is measured by the distance ab.

The fact that there are external benefits does not necessarily mean underproduction will occur. If most of the benefits are private, and social benefits are small relative to private benefits, the total benefit curve may intersect the marginal cost curve at a point below where social benefits "kick in" (the kink in Figure 4–5). Postgraduate education is an example of a good with substantial private benefits (particularly for MBAs and law and medical students) so that subsidy is not necessary in order to produce the socially optimum level of output.

When intervention is needed, however, the question is how to fill in the ab gap. Setting appropriate prices, taxes, subsidies, and fees so as to distribute the burden of payment efficiently and equitably while giving the appropriate amount of encouragement to production of goods with positive externalities is a significant challenge of public sector economics. Some of the appropriate techniques are considered in Chapters 8 and 13.

You should note that the choice of a method to move from Q_2 to Q_1 will have significant effects on the distribution of income and wealth. Among the common methods of addressing positive externalities are public (tax-financed) production or public subsidies of private production. Public production will distribute the cost among all taxpayers even though the benefits accrue primarily to a smaller subset of principal users, whether the good is education, parks, or garbage pickup. Heavier users will enjoy benefits in excess of their costs, whereas light users or nonusers who only get external benefits are likely to pay more in taxes than the benefits they receive. Public subsidies for private production are a little more successfully targeted, in that the primary consumers still pay the bulk of the cost, and the subsidy from general tax revenues only covers the difference between private and social benefits. But the distribution of the tax burden may be very different from the distribution of the external benefits.

Negative Externalities

Figure 4–6 illustrates negative externalities, or external social costs. External social costs can result from either production or consumption. Second-hand smoke from cigars and cigarettes are examples of consumption externalities, while water pollution from factory effluent would be a production externality. Figure 4–6 illustrates a production externality. Because production externalities are on the cost side of the supply–demand relationship, they affect the supply curve. The additive process is the same, but the interpretation and the outcome are different. When goods are produced and sold (and consumed), the seller's supply curve (or marginal cost curve) only reflects the explicit costs that he or she has to pay in order to produce the good. If costs fall on others because the production (or consumption) of the good creates noise, pollution, hazards, or other social costs, market forces will not take those external effects into account in determining the equilibrium price (P_1) and the quantity (Q_1). In the absence of intervention, producers and consumers will strike a bargain at a price that is too low and a quantity that is too high, because they have failed to take into account all the costs of producing the good, including the social costs.

Social costs are taken into account by adding the cost of the spillover effects to the cost of raw materials, labor, capital, and other inputs to the firm's marginal cost/supply curve. Spillover effects are measured graphically on the **marginal social cost** (MSC) curve, which shows the value of negative externalities experienced by all parties at various levels of production or consumption. These curves are added vertically because the combined cost is the

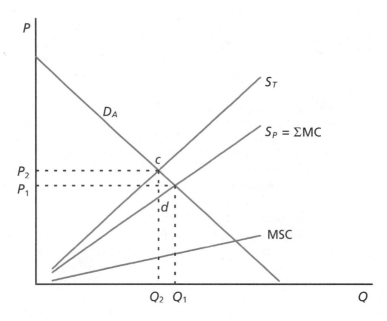

Figure 4–6
Optimal Output
for a Good
with Negative
Externalities

sum of two kinds of costs for the same quantity of output. If social costs are reflected in the supply curve, consumers will face higher prices and choose a smaller quantity, so that the equilibrium will occur at the higher equilibrium price P_2 and the lower equilibrium quantity Q_2. Somehow the additional cost cd has to be reflected in the costs incurred by the producer so that it will be reflected in the market price, a process known as **internalizing externalities.**

Many techniques are available for internalizing externalities. Regulations can force producers to use methods of production that increase worker or product safety, reduce emissions, effluents, or noise, or reduce costs in other ways. In recent years, however, there has been increased reliance on market-like mechanisms of fees, fines, taxes, and charges that are set so as to shift the cost curve to S_T, internalizing the externalities and moving market choices toward the socially optimal level of output

How are the externalities internalized? Most commonly, a tax, fee, or effluent charge is used in the case of air emissions or water effluents. If the amount of the fee per unit can be set at a value approximately equal to cd in Figure 4–6, then production of the externality-causing good or service will be reduced to the socially optimal level. Effluent charges have been used for many years in France, Germany, and the Netherlands in order to ensure acceptable levels of water quality.[5] Their use in the United States is more recent.

An alternative approach to analyzing negative externalities is to focus on the externality itself rather than the good whose production or consumption creates the externality. Whether the externality is pollution, congestion, noise, beauty, ambience, or the sound of beautiful music, this approach focuses only on the marginal social cost and marginal private benefit of creating or experiencing the externality. In both cases, unless the externalities are extremely severe in their social costs, the optimal level of a negative externality is not likely to be zero, because zero externalities would also shut down the production and consumption of desirable goods and services.

Creative Solutions

Determining the optimal level of public good production and allocating the cost appropriately among users is a real challenge to public officials. So is measuring externalities and designing and executing appropriate interventions to move output to the appropriate level and assign the costs to beneficiaries to the extent possible. In the 1950s and 1960s, the standard response to this form of market failure was for the government to produce public goods or goods with substantial positive externalities. For negative externalities, the response was to regulate, forbid, or restrict the production of those externalities, either directly (limits on discharges into the air or water,

5. Robert W. Hahn, "Economic Prescriptions for Environmental Problems: How the Patient Followed the Doctor's Orders," *Journal of Economic Perspectives* (Spring 1989): 95–114.

or example) or through limits on the production and consumption of goods that cause negative externalities (safety regulations, restrictions on access to alcohol, etc.).

In recent decades, much attention has been given to identifying existing mechanisms for providing public goods and correcting externalities as well as devising new techniques. One simple approach discussed earlier in this chapter is to reduce the cost of exclusion, which makes private production feasible. Here are some other techniques that have evolved in the last few decades:

- Assignment of property rights (the Coase theorem),
- Tax incentives and vouchers,
- Educational/informational programs to encourage or discourage certain types of production,
- Development of markets in permits for emissions, and
- Shifting production from federal or state government to local government (devolution) or to nonprofit providers for goods that are nonrival in consumption.

Property Rights and the Coase Theorem

The Coase theorem, developed by Nobel Prize winner Ronald Coase, suggests that some externality problems could be resolved through assignment of property rights. Specifically, this theorem says that, where small numbers of participants are involved, property rights can assigned to one of the parties for a contested resource (such as the use of a lake or waterway), and subsequent negotiations will result in the socially optimal use of the resource. This outcome is independent of which of the two parties is given the property right, although the distributional effects can be an important consideration.[6]

For example, suppose that an industrial firm and a group of nature lovers are interested in using a small lake, the former for discharging wastes, the latter for swimming, boating, and fishing. These two uses are not compatible. Which is the best and highest use of the lake? If it is assumed that both parties have enough resources to express their effective demand, then the lake should be used by the party who is willing to pay the highest price for the use of the lake. Suppose that the industrial firm is assigned the right to use the lake as it sees fit. The group of nature lovers could make the firm an offer to restrict its effluent below a certain level that would make the lake still usable for recreation. If the cost of disposing of its effluent in another way was less than the amount offered by the nature lovers, the industrial firm would agree, and the lake would be used for fishing, boating, and swimming.

Suppose, conversely, that the right to control the use of the lake was assigned to the nature lovers group. The industrial firm could approach them

---

6. Ronald Coase, "The Problem of Social Cost," *Journal of Law and Economics 3* (October 1960): 1–44.

with an offer of a price at which a given amount of effluent could be discharged into the lake. If that amount is sufficient for the nature lovers to either restore the lake to their desired use or make satisfactory other arrangements for their outdoor recreation, then the lake will be used for industrial discharge. If not, it will be used for recreation. The cost always falls on the group that did not receive the initial distribution of property rights, so the distribution of costs and benefits is very different, but the outcome in terms of the use of the resource is the same in both instances.

The Coase theorem obviously applies only to cases where there are relatively few affected parties. However, it has considerable potential for resolving local disputes or neighborhood conflicts if the equity issue can be addressed. The great advantage of this approach is that it forces participants to reveal their demand or preferences by bidding for the use of the contested resource. However, as the affected parties increase in number there is still a potential for free riding. If you are a nature lover and it appears that your side will win by bidding the rights away from the industrial plant, you can remain quiet, hoping that you will get to use the lake for recreation without having to contribute. In some cases exclusion mechanisms exist that limit the use of the contested resource to those who paid, in other cases exclusion is difficult. But certainly a Coase solution is one recourse for addressing some problems of externalities.

Tax Incentives and Vouchers

Tax incentives (deductions, exclusions, or credits, usually on the income tax) and vouchers are two techniques used to encourage the production and consumption of goods that generate positive externalities. In both cases, these instruments are intended to roughly approximate the value of the marginal social benefits in order to increase consumption of such desirable goods and services as education, beautification, energy-efficient housing, and private social welfare agencies (through the charitable deduction). The value of the tax revenue foregone in order to promote certain kinds of production or consumption is known as a **tax expenditure**, which is discussed further in Chapter 8. **Vouchers** (typically for housing, education, or health care services) allow individuals to purchase those goods or services free or at a reduced price. (Education vouchers are discussed in Chapter 16.) The service provider redeems the vouchers for payment from the government that issued them.

The appeal of these two techniques is that the decision about whether and how much to consume and what supplier to patronize is transferred from the government to the consumer. By utilizing the private sector, there is more opportunity for competition, which may hold down costs and make suppliers more responsive to consumers. The drawback is that both methods can be somewhat inefficient in terms of the amount of consumption that they stimulate per tax dollar spent, relative to the amount of spending for those purposes that would have taken place without the incentive or voucher. The tax credit or voucher goes to all consumers who qualify, including a

THE GARBAGE DILEMMA

One of the biggest problems facing local governments is the collection and disposal of household solid waste. Environmental regulations to protect groundwater from leaking out of landfills have made it expensive to build landfills, and land at a convenient location for disposal is hard to find, especially since very few people want a landfill sited in their backyards. By the 1990s, local governments had begun to recognize that, while solid waste (including its shadow companion, litter) was an unavoidable negative externality in a consumer society, the production of solid waste appeared to be exceeding the socially optimal level. Faced with the unpleasant prospect of raising local taxes, local officials felt that the savings in collection and disposal costs by reducing solid waste going into the landfill would exceed the inconvenience, higher prices, restricted choices, or other negative incentives that citizens would have to endure.

The "old" style of dealing with negative externalities would have been a regulatory approach that simply limited the amount of waste a household could have picked up and imposed severe penalties on other forms of disposal (like drop-ping it by the side of the road). But that approach would have penalized large households or households with children. Instead, local governments adopted a mixed bag of carrots and sticks designed to reduce household wastes, often under pressure from their state governments to meet specific targets. Recycling programs, including educational efforts and programs to make it easier and more convenient (like curbside pickup and convenient collection stations), succeeded in reducing the amount of trash that found its way into the landfill. Some local governments even made money reselling recyclables!

Pay-as-you-throw programs were another incentive system, in which garbage had to be put out in bags purchased only from the local government. The more bags you put out, the more you paid. Sorted recyclables, however, were picked up at no charge. Although results have been mixed, this blend of recycling incentives and higher marginal cost of more waste has been widely adopted across the country. It may not have resulted in the optimal level of trash, but the pile of garbage has at least been reduced, a move in the correct direction.

substantial number of those who would have made the purchase without the incentive. Targeted vouchers or tax breaks, limited to those below a certain income level, above a certain family size or age, or other criteria, may reduce this inefficiency.

Shifting the Demand Curve

Yet another approach to encouraging the consumption of goods with positive externalities, such as education, is to attempt to stimulate a stronger preference for those goods through educational and informational methods. Likewise, it is possible to discourage the consumption of goods with negative externalities—alcohol, cigarettes, tobacco—through advertising and educational campaigns. Shifting the private demand for goods with positive externalities to the right and those with negative externalities to the left can reduce the relative importance of social costs and/or social benefits in determining the optimal level of output and make the private market output closer to the optimal level.

Marketable Emission Permits

Frustration with the rigidity of regulatory approaches to environmental quality has led to the development of a market in permits for emissions and other methods of allowing firms or groups of firms to allocate the "right to pollute" based on market forces. If the ultimate goal is a certain level of air quality or water quality, or a target maximum level of emissions, that goal can be attained in many ways. Some sources can be reduced more cheaply than others. By using markets to allocate a limited number of emission permits, the goal will be attained more efficiently than by regulations that do not differentiate between pollution sources that can reduce emissions easily and others that can only do it at high cost.

Other Providers

Finally, in some cases the most efficient method of providing a public good may be to locate production elsewhere with central government financing. It is often easier to monitor exclusion of nonpayers, determine citizen preferences, and/or prevent free riding at the local level, which is one of the rationales for devolution of responsibilities from central to state governments and from state to local governments. In some cases, the responsibility is shifted to the nonprofit sector—churches, private schools, YMCAs, or civic groups—which offers similar advantages. The Head Start program for preschool children is provided primarily through the private nonprofit sector.

SUMMARY

The public sector faces the same challenges of efficiency and equity as the private sector. Governments take responsibility for producing those goods that the private sector fails to produce or to produce in an optimal amount because of the free-rider problem, which refers to how difficult it is to exclude nonpayers from consumption.

Public goods are characterized by nonrivalry in consumption and nonexcludability of those who do not pay. There are few pure cases of public goods, but many goods with little rivalry and great difficulty in exclusion exist.

All goods can be classified according to the degree of rivalry and excludability into four classes. Low rivalry, low excludability goods are public goods; high rivalry, high excludability goods are private goods; low rivalry, high excludability goods are local public goods or club goods; and high rivalry, low excludability goods are those that create positive or negative externalities. Externalities are spillover effects from consumption or production that fall on third parties.

For public goods, demand is added vertically rather than horizontally to determine the optimum quantity. When each person pays the price that reflects his marginal benefit, he is being charged Lindahl prices. In the absence of government intervention, the market will produce too little of the public good and charge a price that is too low for optimality. Optimality requires not only that total marginal benefit (measured by the combined demand curve) be equal to marginal cost, but also that the marginal tax price paid by each citizen be equal to the marginal benefit received. The marginal tax price is the citizen's share of the additional taxes required to pay for the public good.

A local public good or a club good is shared by members of a group or community on the basis of shared membership. Free riding is avoided because the good is excludable. Payment is made by membership fees or local taxes with a gatekeeper to restrict access to members or local residents, usually with little or no charge for each particular use. Congestible goods are a special case of local public goods (or private or club goods) in which the marginal cost is very low up to a capacity point at which the marginal cost of additional users begins to rise sharply. For congestible goods, a fee per use is assessed during periods of peak demand in order to ration a scarce good among competing users, charge for costs imposed by new users on other users, restrain demand for additional capacity, and encourage substitution. Often it is only during peak periods that the revenue collected is enough to justify employing a gatekeeper.

Goods that create positive externalities or marginal social benefits to someone other than the buyer will be underproduced by the market in the absence of intervention. To determine the optimal quantity and price, private demand and marginal social benefits are added vertically. Goods that create negative externalities or marginal social costs to someone other than the producer or consumer will be overproduced by the market in the absence of intervention. To determine the optimal quantity and price, marginal social costs are added vertically to the supply or marginal private cost curve. Possible forms of intervention include public production, taxes, subsidies, and regulations.

Evolving forms of correction for externalities and underproduction of public goods include many alternatives to the traditional regulation or public production approaches. These other solutions include reducing the cost of exclusion, which makes private production feasible, assignment of property rights, use of tax incentives and vouchers, educational/informational programs to encourage or discourage certain types of production, the development of markets in permits for emissions, and shifting from federal or state government to local government (devolution) or nonprofit providers for goods that are nonrival in consumption. Assignment of property rights where the number of parties affected is small, according to the Coase theorem, will result in an optimal allocation of resources regardless of which party receives the initial assignment of property rights.

KEY TERMS AND CONCEPTS

efficiency, 66
public goods, 67
nonrivalry, 67
nonexcludability, 67
free rider, 68
local public goods, 71

congestible goods, 71
Lindahl prices, 74
marginal tax price, 74
benefit tax, 75
two-part tariff, 78
externality, 79

marginal social benefit, 80
marginal social cost, 82
internalizing externalities, 83
tax expenditure, 85
vouchers, 85

DISCUSSION QUESTIONS

1. Figure 4–6 shows the solution to a problem of a negative production externality. In the case of negative consumption externalities, consumers would buy too much because they failed to take into account the costs their consumption imposes on others. This kind of externality is illustrated with demand curves rather than supply curves. Redraw Figure 4–6 to illustrate a negative consumption externality and find the socially optimal level of consumption and the amount of tax or penalty needed to bring it about.

2. Suggest at least two appropriate ways to address each of the following kinds of externality problems:
   a. Noise pollution from a neighbor who insists on mowing his lawn at 7 a.m. Sunday morning
   b. Rundown houses that reduce property values
   c. Overcrowding on a public beach
   d. Underinvestment in postsecondary education
   e. Higher health costs for everyone to cover indigent care for newborns because mothers in low-income families fail to get adequate prenatal care
   f. Accidents due to driving under the influence of alcohol

3. Suppose that you live in a small, self-contained neighborhood that has a neighborhood association. The association automatically counts all property owners in the neighborhood as voting members. The association owns a vacant lot, and the members are evenly divided about its use. One group wants to leave it undeveloped as green space, a quiet buffer against outside noises; the other group wants to develop it into a picnic area and a playground for the children. You, as president of the association, have to help them find a solution. How might the Coase theorem help you work through this problem?

4. In what ways might tax breaks and vouchers be preferable to direct public production of preschool education? In what ways might they be less satisfactory?

The Mathematics of Private Goods, Public Goods, and Goods with Externalities

Private Goods

The mathematical determination of the price and quantity in a market with (for simplicity) just two consumers or groups of consumers is as follows. The expressions

$$Q_a{}^x = f_a(P^x) \text{ and } Q_b{}^x = f_b(P^x) \tag{4-1}$$

represent the quantities of good x that persons a and b will purchase at various alternative prices. In the private sector, the market demand curve is simply the horizontal (quantity) sum of these two demand curves:

$$Q_m = Q_a{}^x + Q_b{}^x = f_a(P^x) + f_b(P^x) \ . \tag{4-2}$$

For example, consider two linear demand curves for good x for persons A and B:

$$Q_A{}^x = A_0 - a_1 P^x \text{ and } Q_B{}^x = B_0 - b_1 P^x \ , \tag{4-3}$$

which sum to

$$Q_M{}^x = Q_A{}^x + Q_B{}^x = A_0 - a_1 P^x + B_0 - b_1 P^x = (A_0 + B_0) - (a_1 + b_1) P^x \ . \tag{4-4}$$

This equation can be solved for price as a function of quantity:

$$P^x = \frac{(A_0 + B_0) - Q_M{}^x}{(a_1 + b_1)} \tag{4-5}$$

The market supply curve is the marginal cost curve, also expressed with price as a function of quantity:

$$MC = P^x = C_0 + c_1 Q_M{}^x \ . \tag{4-6}$$

These two equations can be solved for the unique equilibrium values of P^x and $Q_M{}^x$ expressed in terms of the six parameters A_0, B_0, and C_0 and a_1, b_1, and c_1 . Once P^x is determined, consumers A and B can substitute that value into their demand curves to determine their individual shares of the total market purchases of good x. Each consumer pays the same price and chooses a quantity for which his or her marginal benefit, as reflected in the demand curve, is equal to the price of the good.

Public Goods

Mathematically, the public goods problem is similar to the private goods one just explained, except that in this case the solution is for a market-clearing quantity, and different prices are paid by the two buyers. Let A and B, as before, have demand curves

$$Q^x = A_0 - a_1 P_a{}^x \quad \text{and} \quad Q^x = B_0 - b_1 P_b{}^x \; , \tag{4-7}$$

which must be inverted before adding them to get the sum of the prices that the two buyers will pay:

$$P_a{}^x = \frac{A_0 - Q^x}{a_1} \quad \text{and} \quad P_a{}^x = \frac{B_0 - Q^x}{b_1} \; . \tag{4-8}$$

Since the price paid is the sum of the contributions of A and B,

$$\begin{aligned} P^x = P_A{}^x + P_B{}^x &= A_0/a_1 - (1/a_1)Q^x + B_0/b_1 - (1/b_1)Q^x \\ &= (A_0/a_1 + B_0/b_1) - (1/a_1 + 1/b_1)\, Q^x \; . \end{aligned} \tag{4-9}$$

This equation can be rewritten so that the shared quantity Q^x is expressed as a function of the price and the parameters or constants A_0, B_0, a_1, and b_1:

$$Q^x = \frac{(A_0/a_1 + B_0/b_1) - P^x}{(1/a_1 + 1/b_1)} \; . \tag{4-10}$$

The supply curve (or marginal cost curve) for the good,

$$MC = P^x = C_0 + c_1 Q^x \; , \tag{4-11}$$

must also be rewritten with Q^x as a function of price:

$$Q^x = -C_0/c_1 + (1/c_1)P^x \; . \tag{4-12}$$

Equations (4–10) and (4–12) can be solved to find P^x, which can then be plugged into either equation to determine Q^x. The two equations (4–10) and (4–12) will yield unique equilibrium values for Q^x and P^x that can be expressed in terms of the six parameters A_0, B_0, and C_0 and a_1, b_1, and c_1. This value of Q^x can then be substituted back in the demand equations of Eq. (4–8) to determine the (different) prices that A and B are willing to pay for that quantity of the shared good. Q^x is optimal because the marginal benefit (A's plus B's) is equal to the marginal cost at that quantity.

Externalities

Mathematically, the solution to this problem of negative externalities is again similar to that for public goods, except that it is the marginal cost or supply curve that involves adding prices or costs rather than the demand curve.

$$Q^x = C_0 + c_1 P_c^x \text{ and } Q^x = D_0 + d_1 P_d^x \,, \tag{4-13}$$

where P_c and P_d represent, respectively, the private costs and the social costs being borne by bystanders to the transaction. Again, these two equations must be rewritten before adding them to get the sum of the costs incurred in the production of this product:

$$P_c^x = \frac{Q^x - C_0}{c_1} \text{ and } P_d^x = \frac{D_0 - Q^x}{d_1} \,. \tag{4-14}$$

Because the total cost, including social cost, is the sum of the cost paid by the firm (P_c) and the cost imposed on others (P_d), along a supply curve that fully reflects both private and social costs the price will be

$$P^x = P_c^x + P_d^x = -C_0/c_1 + (1/c_1)Q^x + D_0/d_1 - (1/d_1)Q^x$$

$$= (-C_0/c_1 + D_0/d_1) + (1/c_1 - 1/d_1)\, Q^x \,. \tag{4-15}$$

This equation can be rewritten so that the quantity Q^x, is expressed as a function of the price/cost and the parameters or constants C_0, D_0, c_1, and d_1:

$$Q^x = \frac{P^x + (C_0/c_1 - D_0/d_1)}{(1/c_1 + 1/d_1)} \,. \tag{4-16}$$

The demand curve for this product is a normal market demand curve of the form

$$Q^x = A_0 - a_1 P^x \tag{4-17}$$

Once again, there is a supply curve with quantity supplied expressed in terms of the full-cost price P^x and a normal market demand curve in which quantity demanded is expressed as a function of the same price. Elimination of quantity between these two equations gives a unique solution for the value of P^x in terms of the parameters A_0, C_0, D_0 and a_1, c_1, and d_1. This value can then be substituted back in either equation to determine the socially optimal level of output, which corresponds to Q_2 at a price of P_2 in Figure 4–6.

    The solution to determine the equilibrium price and quantity for a good with positive externalities and the appropriate division of the price between the direct purchasers and those who receive spillover benefits is quite similar to the public good problem described in Eqs. (4–7) to (4–12). This computation is left as an exercise for the reader.

CHAPTER 5

DECISION MAKING IN THE PUBLIC SECTOR

The theoretical principles of public sector economics discussed in the previous chapter may have implied that determining the amount of public production to undertake and assigning the burden of payment is an exact science. Nothing could be further from the truth. In the last three decades an extensive economic literature has grown up attesting to the problems of government failure and the challenges of making good decisions in the public sector. Much of this literature crosses the boundary between economics and political science in order to look at the interaction between the institutions of government, the self-interested behavior of individuals in both the public and private sectors, and market or quasi-market forces. The intersection of markets, self-interested individuals, and governments determines what government produces, directly or indirectly, and how the burden of paying for that production is distributed.

This chapter has two purposes: (1) to explore how decisions are made in the public sector and how that process is similar to and different from the private sector, and (2) to explore some of the dimensions of and possible remedies for the problem of government failure. More applied techniques of public sector decision making, such as budgeting and cost benefit analysis, are discussed in Chapter 15.

DIFFERENCES BETWEEN THE PUBLIC AND PRIVATE SECTORS

Some of the differences between the public and private sectors that affect decision making were visible in the previous chapter. There are four important differences between the private sector and the public sector that can make the public sector less efficient and less responsive than the market:

1. Unlike the market, the public sector has no clear residual claimant for the surplus or deficit (profit or loss), so the incentives facing public officials are different from those facing managers in private for-profit firms.
2. Much of public sector production is for collective rather than individual consumption, so clear price signals are lacking.
3. It is difficult to get "consumers" (citizens) to clearly reveal their preferences.
4. It is more difficult to measure and value output in the public sector.

These four interconnected properties of public sector production, taken together, often result in poor communication from citizens and lack of responsiveness from public officials and bureaucrats. When government officials either do not know or do not care what citizens want, we are faced with the problem of **government failure.** If market failure means that the market fails to provide the socially optimal level and combination of output, government failure in turn means that intervention designed to correct market failure can either fail to provide better results or actually provide worse results than the private market. To understand government failure, we need to look more carefully at the four unique features of government production identified above.

Lack of a Residual Claimant

The presence of a **residual claimant** — a person or group that is entitled to what is left over from revenue after costs have been paid—is an important part of what makes the private market work. In a privately owned company, the hope of profit or fear of loss puts pressure on entrepreneurs, owners, and managers to improve their responsiveness to consumers and their efficiency in using resources. If their prices or costs are too high or their product is of poor quality or not responsive to changing consumer tastes, those bad decisions will be reflected in the company's bottom line. In a company whose stock is publicly traded, the pressure for profit comes from stockholders (especially large stockholders or institutional investors), who are likely to throw out the management if performance is poor. Or the pressure may come from other companies who seek to acquire a firm when its stock is cheap because of poor past performance in the hope that they can shape it up and resell it at a profit.

Bureaucrats and Incentives

Public sector managers, along with managers of nonprofit organizations, rarely have such clear-cut measures of success or failure or such immediate and direct pressures for efficient performance as managers of private firms. The only stockholders are the citizens, and their interest, knowledge, and involvement is generally very diffused. Public agencies do not usually sell their product or services; their revenue stream comes from appropriations and is not tied directly to product quality, output levels, or customer satisfaction. If an agency runs a surplus, its budget is likely to be cut the following year, leading to is a powerful incentive to spend it all before the end of the fiscal year!

Obviously, there are exceptions. City water and sewer managers, state park operators, port authorities, the postal service, and other public agencies that sell their services directly to customers have to be somewhat attuned to customer needs, preferences, and complaints. But as a general rule, customers of the government—better known as citizens—find it more difficult to communicate effectively with or enforce responsiveness from their suppliers of defense, law enforcement, and highways than their private sector suppliers of food, clothing, entertainment, and other goods.

William Niskanen and other public choice economists have developed economic models of the behavior of bureaucrats that reflect this different environment.[1] **Public choice** is the area of economics (and political science) that addresses the processes by which decisions are made in the public sector. Typically, these public choice models begin by exploring the self-interested behavior of the bureaucrat. Because the bureaucrat cannot enhance his or her well-being by making profits, Niskanen assumes that self-interested behavior will take the form of seeking more power and influence, perks and compensation, and opportunities for advancement in the bureaucracy. Such motivations would lead the bureaucrat to try to maximize his or her budget, number of employees, sphere of influence, and level of activity. Chances for success are greater when the "boss" is a large number of citizens with relatively little interest in any particular agency and no good channels of protest. The result is likely to be uncontrolled growth of government.

Other public choice economists, most notably James Buchanan, borrowed from 16th century British philosopher Thomas Hobbes the name **Leviathan** for this tendency toward excessive growth of government. Leviathan, which was originally the name of a Babylonian sea monster, describes a monster—in this case, a monster that gobbles up resources and threatens our economic well-being. The debate over whether government is a Leviathan and what steps can be taken to bring it under control has been going on for several decades.

1. William A. Niskanen, Jr., *Bureaucracy and Public Economics* 2nd ed (1996), Edward Elgae Publishing.

Citizens and Rational Ignorance

But isn't the citizen the residual claimant—the one who benefits from any increases in efficiency? Yes, theoretically, but in practice, citizens often find that the costs of asserting their claims exceed the benefits. Citizens will free ride on others. They may count on the Sierra Club, the Heritage Foundation, the League of Women Votes, or other organized think tanks and citizen interest groups to do their work for them. As a result, not enough information is conveyed from citizens to government; that is, information, which is itself a public good, is underproduced.

The idea that effective communication about the size and scope of government activity is lacking follows logically from the self-interested behavior of citizens/voters. Citizens are more likely to get involved in the political process—vote, lobby, make campaign contributions, even run for office—when they are affected immediately and substantially by a policy decision. Citizens for whom the effect of a proposed policy is modest or inconsequential are much less likely to get involved, because the cost of their efforts is greater than the benefits they will receive. The economist's model of self-interested behavior suggests that a democratic society is likely to suffer from voter apathy. More recently, public choice economists have labeled the intentional lack of effort and involvement by voters by an even more descriptive label, **rational ignorance.**

Voters not only choose not to participate but also to avoid making the effort to acquire the information needed to participate intelligently in the political process. Rational ignorance is a choice based on weighing the costs of acquiring and acting on relevant information versus the expected benefits. Most people, consciously or not, choose to be rationally ignorant about many aspects of their lives from purchasing pencils to knowing the ingredients of foods to auto safety. In some cases, they are engaging in a form of free-riding behavior, assuming that enough other consumers have checked the prices of pencils, the crash safety reports on cars, and the fat content of food. Alternatively, they may be assuming that monitoring by government agencies is at least ensuring auto and food safety. But in both public and private decisions, citizens make a choice about the amount of effort to invest in acquiring and processing information about all kinds of decisions. For public sector decisions, the benefit to an individual citizen/voter from being better informed is often very small relative to the cost or effort.

Rational ignorance has been a very fruitful hypothesis in explaining some forms of government failure. Rational ignorance makes it more likely that a policy with overall costs that exceed benefits can nevertheless be enacted if the benefits are immediate and concentrated on a small number of citizens, while the costs are either delayed or diffused thinly among a large number of citizens. A new missile system is of immediate interest to defense contractors, their employees, and the communities in which their facilities are located. With 300 million Americans, even a $3 billion price tag comes to only $10 per citizen, hardly enough for most people to go to the effort of becoming informed and writing their members of Congress. Even if the sum of the costs exceeds the value of the benefits, such a policy is likely to win simply because the intensity of preference among the few big gainers swamps the apathy of the many small losers.

Is there no hope that public policy will ever reflect citizen preferences? Fortunately, some forces counter the harmful effects of rational ignorance. In many cases, countercoalitions evolve whose members' feelings or valuations are equally intense in the opposite direction. The anti-missile coalition, for example, could include groups trying to divert military funding to other projects as well as pacifists and even groups covertly supported by foreign governments. Whatever the issue, there is always the potential to mobilize a group strongly in favor and a group strongly opposed and to pit them against one another in a battle for money and votes fought with letters, lobbyists, position papers, and campaign contributions. The outcome may fall short of optimal, but the clash of coalitions will push the outcome toward the middle rather than the extremes.

Collective versus Individual Consumption

The problems associated with collective rather than individual consumption of certain goods was addressed in Chapter 4. If goods are collectively consumed but excludable, it is still possible to measure demand, charge users, and exclude nonpayers in order to prevent free riding. The challenge is how to apportion the cost among the users. The most common solution is to charge a single price for access to the collective good, and let all those who value it at least that much have access to it. But this solution is likely to be inefficient. If the price is greater than zero while the marginal cost of another user is zero, the amount consumed will fall short of the optimal level. Potential users will be excluded even though the cost of serving more users is zero. When nonexcludability is added to the mix, it is virtually impossible for the public sector to target users and charge them appropriate Lindahl prices.[2]

Lack of Revealed Preference

Because pure public goods are nonexcludable as well as nonrival in consumption, citizens have no incentive to truthfully reveal their preferences. Suppose citizens think that the price they will be expected to pay individually will be based on the value they admit the good has for them, that is, their marginal benefit. Then they will have an incentive to hide their true demand in order to increase their opportunity to free ride. The result will be a vertical sum of expressed benefits that is less than the actual benefits if people were truthful, and output will be less than the socially optimal amount.

---

2. The use of fees and charges for information as well as for rationing purposes is discussed in Chapter 13

In private transactions, citizens reveal their preferences by the prices they are willing to pay and the quantities they choose to purchase. In the public sector, even if voters choose to be truthful, they still must send these signals through indirect methods: voting, lobbying, responding to polls, and campaign contributions. None of these methods is very effective. Voting is aimed primarily at choosing candidates who represent the voter, and each candidate represents a "package" or positions rather than a specific choice about a new missile system or single-payer health care. Lobbying represents the most intense preferences, but rarely the most numerous—the vocal minority is heard, but the silent majority is not. Polls are sometimes a useful technique, but it is difficult to elicit clear responses to complex questions about resource allocation by this method. Campaign contributions, like lobbying, give a louder voice to the minority who benefit most directly.

Measuring and Valuing Output

Finally, most of the services provided in the public sector are financed partially or entirely from taxes or general revenue rather than by a payment from the user. This lack of direct payment makes it difficult to measure and value output. How much would people have purchased if they were confronted with a price and a choice? That question is difficult to answer for goods and services with a strong element of collective consumption or for goods with substantial social benefits.

Three measures of production in the public sector are used for various purposes. One is inputs, or the cost of producing goods and services in the public sector. This is the set of numbers that is used to value public sector output in the national income accounts. It does not measure consumption or the value of that production to citizens.

These inputs are used to produce intermediate and final outputs. Intermediate outputs measure activities—such as streets patrolled, student attendance, park visitors, or prison inmate days. Intermediate outputs cannot be priced and valued either, because they are not sold, but they at least provide a quantitative measure for comparison purposes. For example, one state can be compared to another in terms of prison expenditures per prison inmate day to see if costs are unusually high or low for some reason.

Final outputs represent what citizens want—educated children, safety, clean water, a prompt and responsive police and fire department, a reasonable travel time and travel access between locations. These final outputs represent the purpose of public sector production, but they are also the most difficult to measure. Water quality is testable. Students' test scores are at least a partial indicator of what the public schools are doing, as are employer satisfaction surveys of the performance of graduates of public high schools and technical colleges. Insurance ratings give some measure of the quality of a local government's fire department. But all of these measures are just indicators of performance that cannot be added in the way that prices and quantities in the private sector can be added. Evidence of satisfaction or dissatisfaction with public production is difficult to obtain and interpret, making it even more difficult for policy makers to make good choices about how to allocate public sector resources.

VOTING AND PUBLIC CHOICE

Citizens have many means at their disposal for trying to influence or convey their desires to public officials. They can lobby, individually or as part of organized interest groups, write letters, provide information, offer persuasive arguments, and help draft legislation. They can make campaign contributions. Running for public office is very expensive, especially at the federal level, and politicians are inclined to listen more closely to those big contributors whose resources they will need to tap in the next election.

Because voting is the most widely available method for influencing public officials, economists have paid a great deal of attention to voting: why people vote, how people vote, how different voting schema influence outcomes, and how voting might be better designed to convey more precise information. The study of voting is one of several areas where economists and political scientists meet. The classic study of the economic dimensions of voting and voting systems is Buchanan and Tullock's *The Calculus of Consent*, which provided a foundation for many later studies of the role of voting in public sector decision making.[3]

One Person, One Vote

Voting is usually done on the basis of one person, one vote, whether it is to elect a mayor or member of Congress or to pass a referendum or vote on a new ordinance in a city council. This system has the attraction of equality among citizens. People "voting" with dollars on what goods and services to produce in the private sector have very unequal amounts of dollars with which to vote. In the public sector, however, each citizen is endowed with exactly the same amount of voting power, although income inequality still means unequal ability to influence the political process through lobbying and campaign contributions. However, equal numbers of votes do not necessarily produce "better" outcomes. People with equal voting rights often have different intensities of preferences, but those people who feel more strongly cannot buy an extra vote to cast. The most they can do is to try to influence the outcome with campaign contributions and/or efforts to convince others to vote the same way.

---

3. James Buchanan and Gordon Tullock, *The Calculus of Consent* (Ann Arbor, MI: University of Michigan Press 1962).

Winner-Take-All versus Proportional Representation

Another common feature at all levels of American government is the single-member district, in which voters select a single person for each office. Whether the winner gets most of the votes or a bare 50% plus one, that candidate gets the prize and the person supported by a minority of up to 49+% has no voice. Even in many local elections where multiple members of a school board or a city council are being elected, it is common to have candidates run for a designated seat, forcing voters to constrain their choices to selecting from a subset of the total field for each seat. That is, there may be 12 candidates for six seats, but the voter cannot choose their top 6 candidates. Instead, each seat pits one of the 12 candidates against a specific alternative. For some seats the voter might like both candidates, for other seats neither.

A single-member district system has advantages and drawbacks in terms of successful communication of voter preferences in the public sector. In this system, all elected officials have defined constituencies to which they are somewhat accountable. However, the resulting collection of elected officials may not adequately represent voter preferences. Suppose, for example, that the vote in a certain congressional district is 51% for the Democratic candidate and 49% for the Republican. The resulting representation for that district is 100% Democratic and 0% Republican. In an extreme case, if the same thing happened in all 435 congressional districts, the House of Representatives would have 435 Democrats and no Republicans, even though a House that matched citizen preferences would contain 222 Democrats and 213 Republicans.

In some public bodies in this country and in many other countries, particularly those with multiple political parties, a given district will have several representatives rather than just one, and the seats in each district will be allocated in proportion to the vote for the various parties. Such a system is one method of providing **proportional representation,** or a legislative body whose composition reflects the percentage vote for each party. Alternatively, a pool of candidates may run for several seats on a school board or city council. A city council election might have 12 candidates for four seats, with the slots going to the highest vote-getters. This system also allows voters to register their preferences a little more precisely at the expense of having a clear one-on-one link of each representative to a particular district.

Inconsistent Results and the Voting Paradox

Either/or, up/down, yes/no voting takes place on issues as well as candidates, and with similar ambiguous results. One famous demonstration of how such bilateral/polar choices give dubious results was spelled out by Nobel Prize-winning economist Kenneth Arrow. Arrow posed an interesting challenge to public sector decision making by way of voting, namely, that in a group of three or more options there may be no clear-cut first choice—a demonstration known as the **voting paradox.** Consider the simplified situation shown in Table 5–1 involving three voters (or equal-sized groups of voters) contemplating

Group/Option	Children's Park	Fire Station	Road Improvements
A	1	2	3
B	2	3	1
C	3	1	2

Table 5–1
The Voting Paradox

three options for spending $1 million in Central City, USA, with their preference ranking for the three options.

Suppose that voters are asked to choose between the children's park and the fire station. A and B vote for the park, C for the fire station, and the park wins. Suppose, however, that the choice is between the park and the potholes. Voters B and C vote for road improvements, A for the park, and the potholes win. Finally, suppose voters get to choose between the fire station and road improvements. Voters A and C vote for the fire station and B for the road improvements. It appears that the park is preferred to the fire station, the fire station is preferred to the road improvements, and the road improvements are preferred to the park! You may have learned in either mathematics or logic that such a rank ordering violates the transitivity principle, which states that if A > B and B > C (or in this case, A is preferred to B and B is preferred to C), then A > C (A is preferred to C).

What this example points to is how difficult it is to make efficient and responsive public sector decisions through simple voting. The problem with simple yes/no, either/or voting is that there is no way of measuring the intensity of those preferences. Voter A may strongly prefer a park to any alternative. Voter B may weight the park and road improvements almost equally with no interest in a fire station. Voter C may be largely indifferent with all three options being moderately attractive but the fire station just barely edging out the other two on his preference scale. A simple yes/no, either/or vote does not convey the same wealth of information as prices offered and accepted, quantities bought and sold in the private marketplace.

The second lesson in this model is the importance of controlling the agenda. If the city manager's preference is for the park, she will make sure that it is matched against the fire station in the budget deliberations, while the road improvements are not listed among the options. By excluding certain choices from the set under consideration, there appears to be a clear preference among voters or the city council for the park option when in fact the outcome would be different if the choices were paired differently.

Other Voting Systems

In addition to proportional representation, a number of alternative voting systems can be used to attempt to glean more information from the ballots cast. One is ranked voting, as discussed in the accompanying boxed material. A

A SIMPLE RANKED VOTING SCHEME

Suppose that your city elects all six of its council members at large rather than from single-member districts. One method of electing them is to allow voters to vote for up to six of the numerous candidates and declare the six candidates with the most votes elected. More often, the rule will require that winners receive a majority of votes cast and calls for a runoff if less than a majority results. Because many voters will cast votes for only one or two candidates, this system is very likely to result in a runoff election. Ranked voting prevents runoffs and gives a slightly stronger measure of voter preference between alternatives.

In ranked voting, voters are asked to rank the candidates from first down as far on the list as they choose to go. If there are 15 candidates, a voter may choose to rank only 1 or 2 or all 15. Assume that 200 votes are cast. First-place ballots are counted; if any candidate receives a majority of first-place votes (101), he or she is declared elected. Second-place votes are then counted for the remaining candidates, and if any candidate receives a majority of first- plus second-place votes, he or she is elected. The process continues until the required number of candidates is elected.

Ranked voting is a hybrid between the simple one-person, one-vote system (or a system in which voters can choose as many candidates as there are slots to be filled) and the more complex system of distributive voting described in the text. It provides more information than "vote for three" because a first-place vote is worth more than a second- or third-place vote. A voter can more clearly distinguish between candidates according to how closely they reflect his or her values and what kinds of agendas they have promised to pursue. Any voting system that allows the voter to convey more precise information improves the ability of public officials to hear what voters are trying to say.

second is a scheme, popular among economists, in which each voter gets a certain number of votes that can be allocated any way the voter likes—all on one candidate or spread among several candidates. A voter may have 10 votes to spread among 15 candidates for five slots. A voter with a really intense preference for one candidate may put all 10 votes on that person; another voter with five preferred candidates may put 2 votes on each; a third voter may put 4 votes on her first choice, 3 on the second, 2 on the third, and 1 on the fourth. While this voting scheme does not offer as clear a signaling method as the market, voters can convey more information about their preference rankings and preference intensities with such a system.

A system of single-member districts, widely used in the United States for everything from city councils and school boards to the U.S. House of Representatives, offers both advantages and disadvantages in terms of providing opportunities for voters to express their values, needs, and preferences through the act of voting. If there are two candidates in the district (the usual situation), they may offer a clear-cut choice in terms of values, priorities, and agendas. Residents know where and how to find their one allotted representative, and find that person to be more responsive to a clearly defined set of constituents. But each voter gets to vote for or influence only one of the 6 or 12 or 435 members of the legislative body. The choices the voter confronts in a single district may be unsatisfactory; with only two candidates (the most common situation) in the running, the voter may have to select the less unacceptable of two candidates who really do not reflect his needs, wants, and preferences. Legislators from single-member districts tend to be particularly attuned to the needs and preferences of their own districts, often at the expense of the larger view of the national (or state or citywide) interest.

PARTIES AND PLATFORMS

While many countries have multiple political parties and form coalition governments, the United States has historically had two major parties and a series of minor ones that have had relatively little impact. Parties have platforms, which are sets of positions on a variety of policy issues ranging from abortion and school choice to tax reform and trade policy. With only two major parties, each party must design its platform to appeal to a broad spectrum of voters. Voters, in turn, have to buy package deals—much like going to the supermarket and being offered your choice between two prefilled grocery carts with a different mix of foods in each. A two-party system is a classic case of the **duopoly** model in microeconomic theory, which is a special case of oligopoly with only two suppliers. A number of models of duopoly are seen in the economic literature, but one in particular is relevant to the political system.

Consider the owner of two mobile refreshment stands along a mile of beachfront. The sole owner would locate them strategically one-fourth of a mile from each end of the mile-long stretch. But suppose that, tired of operating two refreshment stands, the owner sold one of his franchises to a competitor. Now there is a duopoly—a market supplied by only two firms. The refreshment stand on the north end of the beach has the exclusive custom of all the surfers to the north of her stand; the only way to increase patronage is to move toward the middle and capture more customers to the south. The owner of the refreshment stand on the south end reasons the same way. Over time, the two migrate to the center, side by side. So do political parties, when there are only two, very close to the center of the distribution of preferences among citizens. These two parties are both trying to capture to populous center while holding on to their fringes in each direction who have no viable alternative. Both are in search of the median voter.

MEDIAN VOTER MODEL

If government cannot be precise in assigning costs and benefits to citizens, and if voting is a clumsy form of communication, what is a usable substitute? One useful model of how communication occurs, one with good predictive power in terms of the behavior of both citizens and politicians, is based on the

PARLIAMENTARY SYSTEMS AND MULTIPLE PARTIES

The United States is somewhat unique in the Western world in its form of government, in which the executive and legislative branches are clearly separated not only in powers but also in the electoral process. Much more common is a parliamentary system, in which voters elect a legislature (usually with more than two parties), and the dominant party or coalition of parties chooses the prime minister and the cabinet from among their own number. Most of the countries of Europe as well as Canada and Australia have their own versions of a parliamentary system, but in general, parliamentary systems blur the lines between the legislative and executive branches. The prime minister and the cabinet ministers are also members of the parliament or central legislative body.

Parties play a more important role in a parliamentary system than they do in the American system, where the individual candidate is often more important than the party, and the president, who chooses the executive branch (cabinet) leadership, is elected independently. One consequence of this diminished party role is that after the election, party discipline is much weaker in the American system than in most parliamentary systems. As a result, while presidents generally try to carry out their platforms, members of Congress have less obligation to try to implement their party's platform, weakening some of the links between platforms, voters, and what government actually does.

Another important difference between systems is that the American system is more adversarial than the typical parliamentary system. In a parliamentary system the executive and legislative branches are generally singing the same tune, while the minority party (in Britain, Her Majesty's loyal opposition) is the source of questions, conflict, and dissent. In the American system, the party conflicts are overlaid with and intertwined with the conflict between the executive and legislative branches. The adversarial system provides more points of entry for people trying to influence either legislation or bureaucratic decision making, and thus may facilitate the process of communication between voters and public officials.

A third difference between most parliamentary systems and the American system is the timing of elections. In the U.S. system, elections occur at regular intervals at all levels, federal, state, and local. Typically governors serve for four years, state legislators and members of Congress for two years, U.S. senators for six years. There is an election on the first Tuesday after the first Monday in November in every even-numbered year. In a parliamentary system, elections are called on short notice, and the campaigns are much shorter and more intense. This system may reduce the impact of campaign contributions and media advertising relative to voting on the final outcome.

For economists, the important question is whether a parliamentary system improves or weakens communication between voters and those who make decisions about government taxing, spending, and other economic activities. In any system where legislators are elected by single-member districts, they are likely to be more sensitive to the preferences of their voters than to the general electorate. Because those electorates are smaller, the voice of the median voter within each district may be heard more clearly. Members of Congress also have to run for reelection every other year, more often than in most other national assemblies. Both of these factors increase the sensitivity of elected officials to the median voter.

Also, in the American system the president wields considerable power from an independent base because he (or she) is elected independently of the legislative body. The checks and balances in the separation of powers in the U.S. Constitution may be a weak substitute for the market discipline of competition, but they do mean that Congress has somewhat less power for good or for ill than its counterparts in other countries.

concept of the median voter. The **median voter** is not the median citizen or resident. Public officials are responsive primarily to those who participate in the political process. They vote, they contribute to campaigns, they lobby, they write letters. The median voter, then, is the person right at the center of the distribution of preferences among that subset of people who will actually go to the polls and who must therefore be courted by politicians seeking election. The median voter does not necessarily (in fact, probably does not) have a median income or a median family size. Younger people, both single and married with children, are less likely to vote and therefore are underrepresented in determining the preferences of the median voter. The median voter represents a different person or collection of persons on different issues.

The median voter is also a moving target. People's preferences change as their incomes change, as they have children, as children grow up, as they retire. Preferences also change in response to external stimuli of both information and persuasion. Another source of change is the influence of different cohorts of people born in different decades as they move into the voting population. The "young-old" (ages 60 to 70) of the current decade were born during the Great Depression and grew up in the 1940s, periods of economic and social and political upheaval. The baby boomers, a very large cohort born between 1946 and 1964, began to exert influence through their parents from the time they were born. From the late 1970s until well into the 21st century, the boomers have been and will continue to be a dominant share of the voting population. They now range in age from the late-30s to late-50s, and are particularly concerned about issues that impact their lives, ranging from child care to health care to retirement and the future of Social Security.

Distribution of Preferences

This notion of a distribution of preferences rather than an either/or, yes/no, polar choice mirrors what occurs in the private sector, where people choose houses of different sizes, clothing in various quantities and qualities, and trade off between hamburger and steak, beef and chicken. In the public sector, the choice is often not simply park/no park, but what kind, what size, what location, and how much to spend on improvements and facilities.

You are probably familiar with the normal distribution—also known as "the curve" when it comes to grading student performance. If people's preferences are normally distributed, as in Figures 5–1 and 5–2, then most people are clustered around the middle of the distribution. The vertical axis, $F(x)$, measures the number of people whose preference lies at that point on the horizontal axis. The median voter is the person who lies at the peak of the distribution, that is, at x-bar. The horizontal axis may represent the quantity of the public good in dollars, space, or capacity, or it may represent some other measurable attribute of the public good. In Figures 5–1 and 5–2, the horizontal axis represents dollars spent on park acquisition and improvements.

Figure 5–1
Normal Distribution
of Citizen
Preferences
for Park Spending

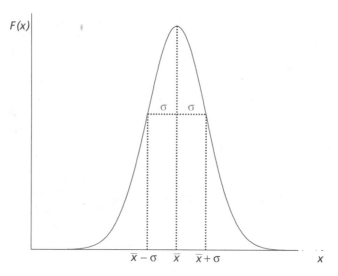

Figure 5–2
Normal Distribution
of Citizen
Preferences
for Park Spending
with a Larger
Standard Deviation
than Figure 5–1

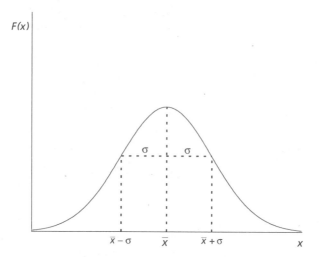

There are a few people at one end of the distribution who want very little spending on parks, and a few on the other end who want a lot, but most voters are clustered toward the middle, balancing their tax burden and their desire for parks.

To be elected and reelected, public officials need the support of at least 50% of the voters. The easiest way to get that support is to concentrate on that large block of voters that lie within one standard deviation (sigma) of either side of the mean. In a normal distribution, the mean plus or minus one standard deviation will include about two-thirds of all voters, a solid majority. So a key element in the signaling of preferences from voters to politicians and bureaucrats is to pinpoint that center of the distribution and aim close to it. Politicians will attempt to locate the median voter through polling, focus groups, meetings with constituents, and other methods. Voters who are outside that center of the distribution will attempt to muddy the waters through letter-writing campaigns, turning up in large numbers at meetings, and other methods. The purpose of all this activity is to convince elected officials that the mean of the distribution is in fact quite far to the right (or left) of where it actually is.

Normal distributions may be fairly sharply peaked with a small standard deviation, as in Figure 5–1, or rather flat with a large standard deviation, as in Figure 5–2. In Figure 5–1, it is easy for politicians to obtain a stable majority of support for the middle-of-the road position, because so many voters are tightly clustered around the mean. In Figure 5–2, however, the majority will include more voters whose preferences are somewhat farther from the mean and who will be more dissatisfied with the outcome—too much or too little spending on parks.

Other Distributions

Not all preferences are distributed according to the normal distribution, or bell-shaped curve. Figures 5–3 and 5–4 show two of the many possible alternative distributions. Figure 5–3 is a one tailed distribution with a peak near the origin, known as a Poisson distribution. Again, the x-axis represents desired spending on parks, while the vertical axis represents the percentage of all citizens wanting to spend a particular amount. This distribution of preferences suggests that most citizens want to spend very little on parks. There is a tail to the right of people who strongly support spending on parks, but the strong majority is clustered closer to the origin.

Figure 5–4, which shows a real challenge to politicians, is one that often occurs—a bimodal distribution. In this case the median voter lies between the peaks. One peak consists of a large and vocal group of voters who want very little spending on parks (clustered around spending level x_1). The other peak reflects a second, equally large and vocal group, who wants more parks, bigger parks, better parks (clustered around spending level x_2). Satisfying the median voter, who is at x_3, will leave the great majority of the population dissatisfied. This situation has occurred in disputes over public school spending in areas with large populations of retirees. In at least one instance, steps had to be taken to exclude a retirement community from the school district in order to pass a bond referendum to meet the urgent demands of families with children.

With a bimodal distribution, it is difficult to find satisfactory compromises. Campaigns to change tastes and preferences (often disguised as "educational" campaigns) are often focused on issues for which the distribution

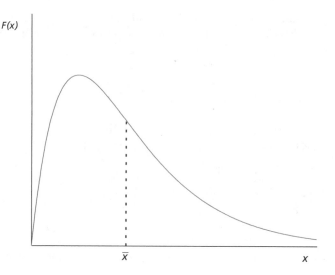

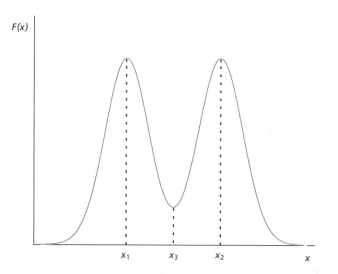

of voter preferences is bimodal. Sometimes these campaigns center around finding common ground. Other times they are addressed at moving a critical mass of voters from one group to the other to create a working majority clustered around one of the two poles. Still a third strategy is to refocus the question. Instead of park spending, the issue might be cast as recreational opportunities for all age groups of which park spending is a subset. Alternatively, the parks might be tied into a plan for green space, which would enhance the attractiveness of the community and increase property values appealing to citizens not interested in the parks for recreational purposes. Each time the question is redefined, citizens will distribute themselves a little differently along the continuum.

If the distribution of preferences is normal, and the government manages to satisfy the preferences of the median voter, would the results pass the test of economic efficiency or Pareto optimality? Probably not. Recall that the efficiency test in microeconomic theory requires that the marginal tax price paid by the buyer be equal to the marginal benefit received from the last unit of the public good. But in a society in which income is distributed unequally, the median voter is likely to have less than the median income. If tax prices are allocated (as they most often are) in proportion to income, then the marginal tax price for the median voter is less than it is for the citizen/voter with the median income. If the median voter and the person with the median income have the same preferences, the median voter will demand a higher level of public production/provision of services than the citizen with the median income, because his or her marginal tax price is lower.

Taken by itself, this model implies that government production or provision of goods will in general exceed the socially optimal level. Of course, if wealthier citizens are able to impress elected officials more strongly with their preferences because of their campaign contributions or hired lobbyists, they could turn the tide in the opposite direction. Alternatively, if the demand for public services rises with income levels, then the person with the median income will have a higher marginal tax price but will also demand a higher quantity of public services than the median voter.

ADDRESSING THE PROBLEM OF GOVERNMENT FAILURE

The insights of public choice economics during the last 35 years have made it clear that government intervention in cases of market failure will not always improve outcomes and may, in fact, result in less efficient allocation of resources. Most of that error results in excess production of public goods and other government services relative to the socially optimal level, either because of the problem just described, or because of the incentives facing politicians and bureaucrats, or because of rational ignorance on the part of voters.

This conclusion does not mean that government should be eliminated in favor of anarchy. Rather, public choice economics, combined with practical innovations in the 1980s and 1990s, has pointed out some ways in which government's role in the economy can be made both more constructive and less inefficient. Among the proposed and actual strategies for increasing the efficiency and responsiveness of government decision making are privatization and devolution (discussed in Chapter 2), balancing rules versus discretion, and direct citizen participation in decision making via town meetings, initiatives, and referenda. All of these strategies involve either increasing the use of market incentives or providing more effective channels of citizen participation or both.

Privatization

The many privatization initiatives of the last 20 years, discussed in Chapter 2, are one response to government failure. From the Great Depression of the 1930s through the late 1970s, in both the size and scope of government activity at all levels expanded significantly. Some of the activities undertaken by government lend themselves to private production or at least private provision. For those activities, there is an opportunity to use the beneficial effects of market prices, competition, and the profit motive to ensure that suppliers are listening to their customers in more effective ways than bureaucrats and politicians are able (or willing) to do.

Devolution

Devolution is another trend of the last 20 years that was discussed in Chapter 2. Devolution means shifting responsibility for providing (and sometimes financing) certain government activities from the central government to state and/or local governments. Where no significant externalities are involved (with costs or benefits spilling over to adjacent jurisdictions), there can be some real increases in efficiency from placing the provision and financing of services at the lowest possible level of government.

These gains come from two sources. First of all, with smaller numbers, less rational ignorance and free riding on the revealed preferences of others will occur. One person's participation or failure to participate, whether in voting or in contributing to the cost of a local public good, will make a measurable difference. It is also easier for citizens to convey their opinions and preferences (lower signaling costs).

Second, the availability of small, competing jurisdictions makes it more likely that preferences will be more homogeneous within those local jurisdictions. People will be attracted to communities offering the mix and level of services that they prefer, a point discussed further in Chapter 7. The distribution of tastes and preferences tends to look more like Figure 5–1 than Figure 5–2 for smaller communities where people have had an opportunity to select from several residential locations offering alternative features, including local tax levels and services. There will be fewer citizens whose preferred packages of public services are far from the mean. In any normal distribution of preferences, the mean plus and minus one standard deviation will always contain about two-thirds of the citizens, but the size of the standard deviation (i.e., the degree to which the not-quite-average citizen is dissatisfied) will be much smaller.

Rules versus Discretion

Yet another response to government failure is to limit the discretionary authority of both elected officials (politicians) and appointed or civil service government workers (bureaucrats). Many rules have been passed that tie the hands of judges (truth in sentencing), future legislatures and city councils (tax and expenditure limitations), regulatory agencies (the ban on cancer-causing substances), and the executive branch (requiring 49 of the 50 governors to submit a balanced budget). When the federal budget deficit was large, there was considerable pressure to add an amendment to the U.S. Constitution requiring a balanced budget. This proposal has faded as the budget has returned to balance in the 21st century.

The advantage of rules is that they offer certainty for the citizen, the business firm, and the politician. Rules make it easier to make difficult or unpopular decisions, pointing to the rule as limiting one's ability to make the decision being sought. Rules make it harder for big contributors or organized lobbies to use the government for their own purposes. Rules can be effective in slowing the growth of government beyond the optimal level.

The drawback of rules is that they make no allowance for special circumstances. Jails are full of first-time drug offenders caught in the wave of mandatory sentencing laws. Improved ability to detect carcinogens has made the congressional ban on cancer-causing substances a formidable barrier to development of new pharmaceuticals and processed foods. An unbalanced budget as a temporary measure might be the wisest policy in a catastrophe, a war, or a major depression. Economists would like to see the costs and benefits weighed for every question to achieve a balance at the margin. Rules rarely allow such balancing processes to happen.

Citizen Decision Making

Finally, places still exist where citizens are directly involved in making decisions—about legislation, about budgets, about rules. One form of direct citizen decision making is the town meeting, still popular in New England's small towns but also used in other places. Annual (or special) town meetings may approve the budget, approve ordinances, and take other actions, leaving the local governing body (the city council or board of selectmen) to run the town's affairs between meetings. The use of town meetings has not increased, but it does provide an effective channel of communication between voters and elected officials in a small town setting.

The other form of citizen decision making that is in fairly widespread use is initiative and referendum, both of which have seen increased use in recent decades. **Initiatives** place issues on the ballot at the request of a group of citizens, usually with some minimum number of signatures. Initiative is not an option in every state, and only a few states use it freely. California's numerous citizen initiatives have dealt with such hot-button issues as secondhand smoke, ending affirmative action, and most famous of all, Proposition 13, which limited the property taxes. **Referenda** are questions referred to the voters by the state legislature or local governing body. Referenda frequently deal with such fundamental questions as a change in the form of government or the state constitution or with bond issues, although less weighty matters can appear on the ballot as well. Some referenda are binding, others advisory. In a system of representative government, most decisions are still made by politicians and bureaucrats, but initiative and referenda do offer an alternative form of expression for citizen preferences.

SUMMARY

Significant differences between the public and private sectors include the lack of a residual claimant, collective rather than individual  consumption of much of its production, difficulty getting "consumers" (citizens) to clearly reveal their preferences, and the difficulty of measuring and valuing public sector output. Incentives for politicians, bureaucrats, and citizens lead to excessive government spending and poor signals about citizen preferences or demand. When government production/provision of goods and services deviates substantially from the socially optimal level and mixture, government failure occurs.

The existence of a residual claimant to any surplus provides a measure of success or failure and/or a monetary system of reward and punishment that is the driving force for self-interested individuals in the private sector to be responsive to the preferences of their customers. In the public sector, self-interested behavior by politicians and bureaucrats is likely to take the form of seeking more power and influence, perks and compensation, and opportunities for advancement in the bureaucracy. Such motivations would lead the bureaucrat to try to maximize his or her budget, number of employees, sphere of influence, and level of activity. The result is likely to be uncontrolled growth of government.

The self-interested behavior of voters tends to result in low participation in the political system, including voting, because of rational ignorance. Rational ignorance means that the payoff for participation is low relative to the cost or effort. Voters only get involved if they have a direct, immediate, personal interest at stake, which means that a lot of lobbying goes on to seek beneficial outcomes. The result of this behavior is that government actions are likely to benefit the few at the expense of the many, often with overall costs exceeding overall benefits. Sometimes countervailing forces will check this tendency as lobbyists on opposite sides of an issue force the outcome toward the middle. Signals are also unclear because of collective consumption and the opportunity to free ride. Voters may conceal their true preferences in order to escape paying for a good that they hope to be able to consume without contributing. Public sector output is difficult to value because it is not bought and sold at market prices like private sector output.

While citizens have unequal amounts to spend in the private marketplace, in theory they are all equal in the political marketplace because of the principle of one person, one vote. In practice, unequal incomes translate into unequal impact in the political marketplace because wealthier voters can influence an election through lobbying and campaign contributions. In addition, the one-person, one-vote system does not take into account the different intensity of preferences among voters. Single-member districts and winner-take-all systems also limit the ability to translate voter preferences into a representative elected body.

In voting on either issues or candidates, voters may not have clear-cut preferred alternatives. The Arrow impossibility theorem demonstrates that it is possible for each of three or more alternatives to be selected depending on the way they are paired in an either/or choice. This theorem not only points to the difficulty of making such choices for collective consumption but also highlights the role of agenda-setting in determining outcomes.

A two-party system shares some of the characteristics of duopoly in the private sector in that both parties aim at the center of the distribution of voters and offer very similar platforms and programs.

The median voter model offers an explanation of how politicians seek voter support in their positions on issues and their votes on legislation. The median voter is the one at the center of a distribution of tastes and preferences of those who are actually likely to vote, a subset of the larger population. If tastes and preferences are distributed normally, two-thirds of voters will lie within one standard deviation of the mean, so finding and satisfying the center of that distribution greatly enhances the likelihood of election. A normal distribution with a high peak and a small standard deviation makes it easier to satisfy a majority of voters than one with a low peak and a large standard deviation.

Preferences may not be normally distributed. Two of the many alternative distributions are the Poisson distribution and the bimodal distribution. The Poisson distribution has only one "tail" and a mean that is fairly close to the origin. The bimodal distribution represents a real challenge to politicians because voters are clumped together in two widely separated groups with few of them occupying the middle ground.

Government failure cannot be eliminated without eliminating government, but there are some possible partial solutions to the problem of government failure. These include privatization and devolution, imposing rules rather than allowing politicians and bureaucrats wide discretion in their decision making, and expanding the role of citizen participation in decisions to include town meetings, initiative, and referenda.

KEY TERMS AND CONCEPTS

government failure, 94	rational ignorance, 96	duopoly, 103
residual claimant, 94	proportional representation,	median voter, 105
public choice, 95	100	initiative, 111
Leviathan, 95	voting paradox, 100	referendum, 111

DISCUSSION QUESTIONS

1. Suppose that your class has the opportunity to vote on the format of an exam. The options are multiple choice, essay, or a combination of the two. Suggest at least two voting schemes that would be used to make this decision and evaluate the advantages and drawbacks of each.

2. You are an elected official who is up for reelection. How is your strategy likely to differ for the four different preference distributions in the median voter graphs in this chapter (steep normal, flat normal, Poisson, and bimodal)?

3. Why and how is government likely to fail? What can citizens (or writers of constitutions, or even politicians) do to minimize government failure?
4. What happens to the voting paradox when there are more than three choices and/or more voters or voting groups? Try a simple experiment. Add to the table of preferences (Table 5–1 in the text) a fourth choice, new school buses, with the same three voters or groups of voters.

   Is there now a clear dominant choice or a clear rejection, that is, one choice that loses in any pairwise comparison? What do you think would happen if you increased the number of voters while holding the array of choices the same?

5. Return now to the original example of Table 5–1 with just three blocks of voters and three spending choices. Suppose that, instead of giving each voter an opportunity to rank the choices, we gave each of them 10 votes to spread among the options. (This is a method of voting very popular with economists, because it mimics the price system.) The preferences of A, B, and C are given below in terms of how many "votes" they will spend on each choice. Now is there a clearly preferred choice? What is it? Why is that choice preferred? Whose preferences are dominating the decision?

Table supplement for question 4.

Group/Option	Children's Park	Fire Station	Road Improvements	School Buses
A	1	2	3	4
B	2	3	4	1
C	3	4	1	2

Table supplement for question 5.

Group/Option	Children's Park	Fire Station	Road Improvements
A	5	3	2
B	2	1	7
C	1	6	3

CHAPTER 6

EQUITY AND INCOME DISTRIBUTION

For economists, the two desired outcomes of market and government processes are efficiency and equity. The last few chapters have concentrated heavily on efficiency, or the allocation of resources among competing uses so as to obtain a given level of output (or utility, or satisfaction) at the least cost. Alternatively, efficiency can be defined as getting the most (output, value, utility, satisfaction) out of available resources.

Equity is a different matter. Whereas efficiency falls somewhat short of being a purely objective concept, equity is unquestionably much more normative in nature. Equity means "fairness" in the distribution of wealth, income, and resources. Equity does not mean simple equality; but in a society in which those economic aggregates are distributed very unequally, a movement toward less inequality is generally interpreted as a move in the direction of equity. Such movements can occur through market forces, private voluntary redistribution, or government, but the major player in redistribution is usually government.

GOVERNMENT AND REDISTRIBUTION

Redistribution through government does not simply consist of taking money in the form of taxes from the rich and giving it either in cash or in services to the poor. Everything the government does is redistributive, and much of that redistribution does not benefit the poor and

needy. Corporate welfare, tax breaks for the rich, and tax structures that favor the voting majority in the middle class are among those other types of redistribution.

Think about any government program and ask yourself who pays for it and who benefits from it. Rarely do the two match up one for one, except in the case of a fee-for-service operation, such as Amtrak or the U. S. Postal Service (and even these services are not without redistributive effects). Suppose, for example, that the Corps of Engineers develops a new flood control/power/recreational lake facility in Missouri. The initial cost is paid for with federal funds, and the operating costs are shared between federal funding, state funding, revenues from the electricity wholesaler, and user fees from those who use the lake for recreation. Where is the redistribution? Taxes come from citizens across the United States and are distributed unequally according to various measures of ability to pay (income, family size, wages, etc.). Benefits go to local landowners, who realize increased property values (especially along the lakefront) and reduced flood risk; to power customers, who may experience lower costs per kilowatt hour; and to recreational users, most of whom live in Missouri. But not everyone who lives in Missouri benefits equally. Missourians who fish and swim and sail for recreation benefit more than those who hunt and bowl and play video games. Residents of Missouri who live closer to the lake benefit more than those farther away. Residents of Missouri (and of surrounding states) who get electricity from this source benefit more if they happen to use electricity for heating instead of oil or natural gas. Even in this relatively simple case, the distribution of costs and benefits is complex and difficult to track.

Redistribution is not limited to taxing and spending programs. Regulatory actions also redistribute income and wealth among citizens. Remember the controversy over logging the habitat of the endangered spotted owl in the Pacific Northwest? Who gained and who lost (besides the spotted owls)? Loggers lost directly in terms of jobs. New home prices rose with the higher prices for lumber, affecting the construction industry as well as would-be home buyers. As new homes became more expensive, they pulled up the values of existing homes as well. Higher real estate values generated more commissions for realtors and more property tax dollars for local governments. Environmentalists gained in terms of achieving their desire to protect not only spotted owls but also old-growth forests. Lawyers, as they often do, gained because of the demand for their services in extensive litigation.

Because government is such a powerful tool for redistributing income and wealth, small, well-organized groups are tempted to use government for that purpose. Lobbying, campaign contributions, and media campaigns are often directed at pressuring either legislators or bureaucrats to make decisions that redistribute income or wealth in favor of particular groups. Being able to identify and quantify these redistributive effects is an important part of the function of a public policy analyst. This chapter, however, focuses on a subset of the redistributive activities of government for which the primary purpose is to create a more equitable distribution of income, resources, and opportunities.

CONCEPTS OF EQUITY

Economists find it difficult to formulate an acceptable definition of distributional equity because such a definition would require interpersonal comparisons of utility. Ideally, a tax and expenditure system would require equal sacrifice, not of dollars, but of utility from each citizen in order to support shared public services. If A is very poor and B is very rich, it seems reasonable that a smaller contribution from A and a larger contribution from B would meet this standard of equal sacrifice.

To simplify the equity question, suppose that, instead of taking $2 from A and $1 from B to finance a public service that A and B can share equally, the government simply takes a dollar from A and gives it to B. Is equity (and social welfare) increased, decreased, or unchanged by this action? If A is rich and B is poor, a typical response is that equity has increased, and that in the opposite case equity would have decreased. But to arrive at that judgment implies some comparison of the marginal utility of income (or wealth) between persons A and B. To make such comparisons, some assumptions have to be made about whether income or wealth as a whole (as distinct from a particular kind of consumption) is subject to diminishing marginal utility, and whether the marginal utility declines at similar or different rates for different people. If the marginal utility of income declines as income rises, and does so at about the same rate for everyone, then a transfer from A to B would indeed increase utility, because the gain to B would be greater than the loss to A. But what if income or wealth is not subject to diminishing marginal utility? Or suppose that A, while wealthier, also has a greater capacity to enjoy income due to her cultured tastes, while B is an ascetic with limited needs and wants. A's greater capacity for enjoying income could mean that the utility she sacrifices is greater than the utility B gains. In either case, nothing can be said about net gains and losses in utility to society as a whole.

Equity is a central issue in public sector economics and in public policy. It is at the heart of almost all economic policy debates. Is there a way out of this impasse that might make it possible to define equity? This question has engaged some of the best minds in economics in the last two centuries, resulting in some creative if not always definitive answers.

Horizontal Equity

One partial answer to the dilemma of defining and measuring equity is the concept of **horizontal equity**, which means treating people alike if they are in the same or similar economic situations—making them pay the same taxes and providing them with the same public services. Implicit in the notion of horizontal equity is an assumption that people's capacity to enjoy income is similar, at least within a given range of incomes.

Economic situation is not simply income. It could include the concept of permanent or lifetime income rather than simply current annual income. It might take into account wealth, family size, age, or special circumstances such as disability or chronic health problems. As a result, a generally accepted measure of horizontal equity can be difficult to find. Instead, it is defined differently in specific contexts; charges for admission to national parks are by the carload, all income up to a certain level is taxed at the same rate, all children are entitled to 12 years of free public schooling. Much of the complexity in the federal income tax arises from attempts to define equal economic situations for purposes of horizontal equity.

Vertical Equity

A second and even more challenging concept of equity is **vertical equity.** Vertical equity means treating people differently according to the differences in their income, wealth, or other measure of need or ability to pay. Vertical equity appears in many different contexts. Progressive income taxes, discussed in Chapter 10, are often justified on the basis of some concept of vertical equity. Vertical equity is also reflected in the use of **means testing** for many public programs, including free or reduced price school lunches, subsidized housing, and Medicaid. (Tax relief at the state and local levels is also means tested in many cases.) Means testing refers to determining eligibility for a public program or service on the basis of having an income that is less than some threshold level. Often the threshold is a cutoff point in a means-tested program. Subsidized child care, for example, might be available to households with incomes up to 150% of the poverty level. Once the family reaches that level, it is no longer eligible. Other programs gradually reduce the benefits as family income gets higher, and at the threshold level the benefit finally reaches zero.

One difficulty with using vertical equity as a guide to public policy is in measurement. How unequal should the treatment of people be in relation to their unequal ability to pay? In a famous work on the progressive income tax, McCullough argues that once we depart from the notion of proportionality in taxation ". . . we are at sea without rudder or compass."[1] Does having twice as much income mean twice as much ability to pay taxes or three times as much? Does a family of four with an income of less than $15,000 deserve food stamps, but the same family should no longer be entitled when its income reaches $15,001? The use of cutoff income levels as a tool for vertical equity creates notches in eligibility for benefits or services that create new inequities between those just under the notch and those just over the notch. Attempting to determine vertical equity also raises the seri-

---

1. J. R. McCullough, *Treatise on the Principles and Practical Influence of Taxation and the Funding System* p. 142 (1845). Quoted in Walter J. Blum and Harold Calven, *The Uneasy Case for Progressive Taxation,* (Chicago: Phoenix Books and University of Chicago Press, 1953), p. 45.

ous problems discussed earlier that are associated with interpersonal comparisons of utility.

Compensation Principle

Finally, a third route out of the thicket of interpersonal comparisons of utility lies in the theory of the second best and the compensation principle. Recall from Chapter 1 that Pareto optimality is a state in which no change can be made that makes some people better off without making at least one person worse off. Strictly interpreted, the concept of Pareto optimality is heavily loaded in favor of the status quo. Most policy proposals—tax cuts, highway programs, sentencing guidelines, or almost anything you can imagine—involve both winners and losers. A criterion of Pareto optimality would rule out such changes. The inability to make interpersonal comparisons of utility makes it very difficult to justify any policy change for which there are losers as well as gainers. Pareto optimality becomes a strong endorsement of the status quo, whatever that status quo happens to be.

Recognizing this problem, economists have searched for some criteria for policy decisions where Pareto optimality is not attainable. These criteria provide a guide to making "second-best" decisions. One of the most useful criteria is the **compensation principle**,[2] which offers a rough guide to choosing between alternative policies on the basis of which one does more to increase social welfare. The principle goes something like this: If, in moving from state A to state B, the gainers from the move can compensate the losers for their losses and still be better off, then the move is desirable from the standpoint of total social welfare. Conversely, if those who lose by moving from state A to state B can bribe the gainers not to make the change and still have some welfare gain remaining, then the change should not be made.

Note that the compensation does not actually have to be paid. Payment is a political rather than a theoretical question, whether the "bribe" is actually either required to get legislation passed (or other change approved) or desirable from the standpoint of income distribution (e.g., gainers are rich, losers are poor). And even if compensation is used, it does not necessarily have to be in cash. When the nuclear plant for processing nuclear weapons materials in Barnwell County, South Carolina, was built in the 1970s, the federal government helped to build a new town and relocate the people in the small town of Ellington to that new site. This action recognized a need to compensate for the cost imposed on the citizens of Ellington in order to have the land area needed for the facility.

The compensation principle has been particularly visible in trade policy. The gradual reduction of barriers to international trade benefited consumers and exporters at the expense of workers and owners in import-competing industries, and they were compensated with trade adjustment assistance as well

---

2. Also known as the Kaldor criterion after the British economist who formulated this concept.

as gradual implementation of policy changes. (Gradualism in implementing new policies, giving those affected time to adjust, is one form that the compensation principle takes.) But almost any proposal for spending or changing the tax rules or siting a new prison or building a new highway creates both winners and losers. There is always an opportunity to negotiate compensation for at least some of the losers as a condition for persuading politicians to vote for such legislation.

Coase Theorem Revisited: Efficiency Challenges Equity

Equity questions also arise in the recent trend toward seeking market-based solutions to conflicts by assigning property rights. The Coase theorem was introduced in Chapter 4 as a method of attaining efficiency, but its implications for equity are at least as important as its usefulness in promoting efficient outcomes. As Nobel Prize–winning economist Ronald Coase[3] has ably demonstrated, the outcome of a conflict over how certain resources are to be used is likely to be the same regardless of which of the conflicting parties is initially assigned the property rights. There will, however, be major differences in the distribution of income and wealth.

Suppose, for example, that the common property in dispute is a small lake. The property adjacent to the lake is owned by 10 private homeowners and one factory. The homeowners' association wants to use the lake for boating, swimming, and fishing, while the factory wants to use the lake as a source of water for its operations and a way to dispose of industrial wastes at a point beyond that intake. The latter use is in conflict with the desires of homeowners. The government could intervene in this dispute in a regulatory fashion by restricting the rights of either or both parties, or it could simply assign property rights to either the factory owner or the 10 homeowners and let market forces resolve the dispute. If the property rights to the lake are assigned to the factory owner, he or she will use the lake for disposal purposes. But if the value of the lake for recreation is high enough for the 10 residential property owners to band together and bribe the factory owner to find another method of waste disposal, the lake will be used for recreation.

Conversely, if the right to determine the use of the lake is assigned to the residential property owners' association, it will be used for recreation, unless its value to the factory owner for disposal purposes is so high that he or she can pay the homeowners' association to take their recreation elsewhere. In either case, the use of the lake will go to the party that values it the most. The only difference between assigning rights to residents versus the factory owner is the distribution of wealth between the two parties, because the one who receives the initial property rights either gets to control the use of the lake or gets paid to have it used otherwise.

---

3. Ronald Coase, "The Problem of Social Cost," *Journal of Law and Economics,* 3 (October 1960): 1–44.

Once property rights are assigned, the Coase theorem states that the property in dispute will tend toward its highest and best use as valued by market prices as long as the number of parties involved is small enough. But even though the outcome of assigning property rights is likely to be efficient, it is not necessarily perceived as equitable, because the conflicting parties do not have equal resources with which to bid for the use of the disputed property. When the government addresses conflicts over use of resources by assigning property rights, it is important to take such equity considerations into account.

EQUITY, ADMINISTRATIVE EFFICIENCY, AND INCENTIVES

Although some economists and policy makers want little or no intentional redistribution of income through government, there appears to be some degree of social consensus that at least some aid to designated groups (such as the elderly, abandoned children, or people with disabilities) is a desirable activity for government to undertake. Once it is agreed that it is appropriate for the government to undertake some direct redistribution, then the challenge becomes one of finding a way to do so with maximum efficiency. Efficiency in redistribution can mean several different things. One aspect of efficiency is targeting aid to those who "deserve" it, with minimal expenditures for administration and minimal diversion of revenues to those who are perceived as "undeserving" (including those who obtain assistance via fraud or misrepresentation). Those two qualifications may be mutually exclusive. If the goal is to minimize administration, then the limited resources for oversight may make it difficult to exclude the undeserving. If an extensive cross-checking system is created to root out fraud and abuse, then administrative costs will be much higher.

Efficiency, Administrative Cost, and Fraud

The two most successful programs of redistribution in terms of minimizing both fraud and misrepresentation while operating with very low overhead expense are the Social Security system and the Earned Income Tax Credit on the federal income tax. The success of Social Security rests on two important features: near-universal participation and no means testing. Near universal participation means that Social Security enrollment is simple and automatic. Much of the burden of getting revenue into the system with the accompanying documentation falls on employers and the self-employed. For the pension part of Social Security, the only test is a simple one of age and years of participation in the system, both of which are easy to verify. The disability part of Social Security is another matter altogether, because eligibility rests on a complex screening system to verify the nature and extent of the disability. In the case of the Earned Income Tax Credit, the tests are again fairly simple and straightforward because they rely on the information provided for income tax purposes. Other forms of income transfers, such as Aid to Families with Dependent Children, housing vouchers, and food stamps, require a complex verification process to determine eligibility and are much more complex to administer. Most of that complexity is a result of efforts to prevent fraud.

It is quite possible that for some kinds of redistribution the cost of monitoring to prevent fraud would be greater than the cost saving. That is, it could very well be cheaper to operate a system that is 90% fraud proof and allow 10% to get away with cheating, because the benefits paid to that 10% would cost less than the additional monitoring effort required to screen cheaters out. That argument may be valid in the short run, but in the long run the negative effects on the system as a whole outweigh the short-run cost savings from tolerating a certain amount of fraud and abuse. It does not take long for rational, calculating people to figure out how to "game" the system for their own benefit if the risk is perceived as low (because of lack of monitoring) and the payoff high. In the long run, a system that is vulnerable to fraud and abuse because of inadequate safeguards will attract cheaters. This long-run effect will not only increase costs but also decrease faith in and support for the system of redistribution.

Efficiency and Work Incentives

Another important efficiency issue in redistribution is the work (and investment and entrepreneurial risk) disincentive effects on both those who "contribute" the tax monies and those who receive the aid. The tax wedge between the gross earnings of the worker, investor, and entrepreneur and the after-tax earnings can result in a diminution of effort below the optimal level. The combined effect of state and federal income taxes and Social Security taxes can push the marginal tax rate on a highly productive worker above 40%, discouraging overtime, freelancing, moonlighting, or other forms of extra effort.

When redistribution of one's earnings to others reduces the return to work or investment effort, many rational, calculating members of society will respond by making less effort than they would otherwise have done. They will substitute leisure, which is not taxed, for income from working, which is taxed. Figure 6–1 shows a representative citizen balancing the choices between work and leisure. With no taxes on earnings (line A_1B), this individual would choose OX_1 of earnings and OY_1 of leisure. If a tax is placed on earnings while leisure is untaxed, the budget line rotates to A_2B. The worker is forced to accept less of both earnings and leisure, but the drop in earnings (to OX_2) is greater than the drop in leisure (OY_1). If the tax became severe enough (A_3B), the worker might respond by increasing leisure to OY_1 at the expense of earnings (now only OX_3).[4]

---

4. As an exercise, you should try to separate the income and substitution effects of the tax on income and leisure. The income effect is measured by drawing a line parallel to A_1B but tangent to the lower indifference curve that is tangent to A_2B or A_3B. The combination chosen with this budget line represents the income effect. The further changes to the income/leisure combination represent the substitution effect.

Figure 6–1
Income, Leisure,
and Taxation

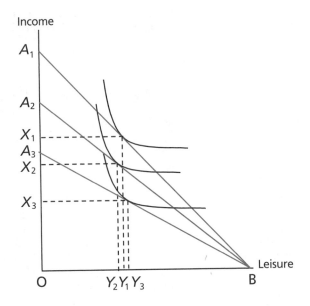

The availability of public assistance, and the likelihood of losing that assistance when moving into paid employment, can also create disincentive effects on the recipient side. In the past, prior to welfare reform, recipients of aid who compared the returns to working 40 hours a week at the minimum wage or slightly above, after adjusting for the costs of working (child care, transportation, etc.) and the loss of benefits, might well have concluded that there would be little or no increase in economic well-being as a result of entering the workforce. Welfare reform addressed some of these challenges by providing support services and delaying the cutoff of benefits to those who do enter the labor force, while at the same time imposing time limits on benefits and other penalties on those who do not respond to work opportunities. These issues, which affect both support for and design of any redistributive programs, are addressed in greater detail in Chapter 18.

MARKETS, POVERTY, AND INEQUALITY

While markets get high marks for efficiency, they do not perform as well on most measures of equity. The distribution of income and wealth that results purely from market processes tends to be highly unequal. Most societies expect their governments to make at least some effort to address that inequality, with a focus on the alleviation of poverty and its effects rather than on simply reducing inequality by taking from the rich and giving to the poor in

MEASURING INEQUALITY

The United States and Other Nations

Although alleviating poverty has been a primary focus of government policy in redistribution, the government also faces important questions about the overall distribution of income. The most widely used measure of income distribution is the Lorenz curve, which shows the cumulative percentages of income accruing to various percentages of the population. Usually the population is sorted into quintiles, or fifths, so the graph shows the percent of income received by the lowest fifth (20%), the lowest two-fifths (40%), and so forth (Figure A). If income were distributed with complete equality, the Lorenz curve would be the straight line from the origin (at zero on the southwest corner) to the northeast corner of the box. The greater the deviation of the actual curve from that straight line, the greater the degree of inequality. To provide a numerical comparison, the area between the diagonal line and the curve is divided by the total area of the lower half of the diagram (below the diagonal). This number is called a *Gini coefficient*.

In Figure A, which shows the U.S. income distribution in 1999, the lowest 20% of the population receives only 3.7% of the income; the lowest 40%, 12.7% of income; and the lowest 60%, 27.7%, leaving 72.3% for the top 40% and 49.3% for the top 20%. Inequality has actually in-

creased in the United States during the last three decades, particularly in the shares of the lowest 20% and the top 5%.

The Lorenz curve is particularly useful as a comparative tool in measuring changes in income distribution over time and differences in income distribution between different countries. Figure B shows a comparison of the distribution of income in the United States, the United Kingdom, and Germany in the late 1980s.[1] In comparison with 14 European countries reported, the United States had a higher degree of inequality, with a Gini coefficient of 0.341. The United Kingdom, Ireland, Switzerland, Italy, Portugal, Spain, and Ireland were all close to that level with Gini ratios ranging from 0.304 in the United Kingdom to 0.33 in Ireland. The other seven nations all had Gini ratios under 0.30, with Sweden the lowest at 0.22, indicating a higher degree of income equality.[2]

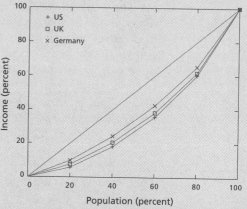

Income Distribution in the United States, United Kingdom, and Germany in the 1980s

[1]Data and Gini coefficients are from A. B. Atkinson, "Income Distribution in Europe and the United States," *Oxford Review of Economic Policy*, 12(1) (1996), pp. 15–21.
[2]Note that Lorenz curves from different nations or different time periods may cross, making it difficult to compare them on a strictly visual basis. The Gini coefficient is helpful, but keep in mind that it does not distinguish clearly between, for example, a transfer from the rich to the poor, from the middle class to the poor, or from the rich to the middle class; all three would give a smaller Gini coefficient, but the equity implications are different.

U.S. Income Distribution in 1999

some form. Musgrave's schema described in Chapter 1 lists the functions of government as allocation, distribution, and stabilization. Relieving poverty is the primary intentional component of the distribution function. (Governments also redistribute both intentionally and unintentionally in ways that do not relieve poverty, as discussed above.) This redistribution takes place through a variety of means, but primarily through the tax system and through income security programs to the poor, the elderly, people with disabilities, and other target groups.

POVERTY IN THE UNITED STATES

In 1999 the official poverty rate in the United States was 11.8%, a modest decline from the 13.5% at the beginning of the decade. About 32 million people were classed as below the poverty threshold of $17,029 a year in income for a family of four (or other thresholds for single persons or families of varying size). Despite a robust economy and low unemployment rates, the poverty rate remained stubbornly steady. The highest poverty rate was for children (19.9% of those under 18 years of age, and 21.6% of those under 6 years of age, were poor in 1997), while the lowest rate was for those aged 65 and over (10.5%).[5]

Through the last three decades of Aid to Families with Dependent Children, food stamps, Supplemental Security Income, housing programs, and, most recently, welfare reform, the poverty rate at the end of that period had declined only modestly. The poverty figures include a significant number of households where there was at least one year-round, full-time worker (about one in six) or where there was at least some work effort. The lack of a high school diploma affected the employment opportunities of more than 40% of poor households.

The "Deserving Poor"

Some economists regard poverty as a form of market failure, or at least some kinds of poverty. When poverty results from intentional choices—to be a starving artist, to drop out of the labor force and do nothing—then there is no particular need or justification for providing assistance. To do so would weaken the incentives to work and contribute to society that lie at the heart of a market-driven economy. The concern about poverty deals, rather, with four groups of people who do not fare well under a pure market economy. Some people are unable to work because they are too old, or disabled in some way. A second group suffers from lack of access to jobs because of their location, or lack of access to transportation or child care. Recent reforms in the

---

5. U.S. Census Bureau, The Official Statistics, *Poverty in the United States: 1997*, September 9, 1998, p. v–vi and A-3.

welfare system, discussed in more detail in Chapter 18, have addressed some of the problems represented by the second category, while Social Security (also addressed in Chapter 18) is intended to protect the elderly and those with disabilities. The third and fourth groups, however, account for a great deal of poverty among children. For the most part, poor children live in poor families with adults who fall into one of the following categories:

- Those who work but who lack the skills, training, or experience to earn a wage that will pull them and their families above the poverty level. The responsibility for addressing this source of poverty falls heavily on the states in such programs as school-to-work, TechPrep, technical and community colleges, job training programs for industries, and other activities that link economic development with getting people ready to fully participate in the labor force.
- Those with special circumstances such as health or family size or special responsibilities to care for dependents (e.g., aging parents, family members with disabilities) that make it possible either to work or to maintain an above-poverty standard of living on their earnings, even though such earnings might be adequate under more normal circumstances.[6] The primary policy response to this source of poverty is the Earned Income Tax Credit (see Chapter 10). A second form of response has been direct provision or services such as health care and children's services of various kinds.

Interdependence, Externalities, and Market Failure

In what sense does this kind of poverty constitute market failure? One argument offered for classifying these cases as a form of market failure is that the existence of poverty among some individuals reduces the well-being of others (because of empathy with the suffering of others) and therefore has the same kinds of spillover effects as water pollution, noise, litter, or other familiar negative externalities.

A second argument is along these lines: Even if one is not motivated by empathy, poverty can be considered as diminishing the quality of life of the community. Poverty may breed drugs, illegitimacy, blight, crime, and other social ills that impact on more prosperous households. Children of the poor may attend some of the same public schools as children of the middle class and rich. Poor children who lack basic health care and skills may grow up to be unproductive workers or dependents on society. A little prevention or correction of these social ills will benefit others besides the target population. This is a different type of externality argument that still treats the consequences of poverty as a form of market failure.

---

6. An excellent critique of the failure of American society to address the needs of dependent persons and particularly of dependency workers (paid or unpaid) who care for them is Eva Feder Kittay's *Love's Labor: Essays on Women, Equality and Dependency* (New York: Routledge, 1999).

Social Safety Net as a Public Good

Yet a third argument is that there is an insurance element in having social safety nets that catch those who suffer from economic reversals outside their control. There is some notion that "this could happen to me as well, and I would like to ensure the existence of a social safety net in case I should ever happen to need one." Some kinds of insurance lend themselves better to private provision than others. Least suited to purely private (unsubsidized, nonmandatory) insurance are disasters that strike unexpectedly at identifiable target groups, such as floods, hurricanes, earthquakes—or unemployment, prolonged illness, or disability. Those most at risk are often willing to buy insurance, but the premiums are prohibitively high because of the high probability of loss. Those least at risk see no need for the insurance and opt out of the pool, leaving only the high-risk applicants.

If those applicants are not only high risk but also low income, as they often are in the case of unemployment or disability, the private market will not be able to resolve their need for a social safety net with private insurance. (You may want to think of the high-risk group and the low-risk group in terms of the bimodal distribution described in Chapter 5, with the median insurable person falling in between the two peaks in terms of risk or probability of unemployment or disability.) For this reason, social insurance (discussed in Chapter 18) has been one of the fastest growing categories of government activity in the United States and other nations in the last century. Because the market fails to provide insurance against these types of hazards, the argument can be made that the absence of such a market constitutes a form of market failure, and the provision of this service has some attributes of a public good.

Redistribution and Free-Riding Behavior

Few people will argue against any redistribution, but it is often argued that redistribution should be funded by voluntary contributions rather than mandatory through taxation by the government. Some voluntary redistribution occurs through churches, nonprofit agencies, and individual charities, which modifies the distribution of income and wealth determined by market forces. If voluntary redistribution were sufficient to bring about an acceptable reduction in poverty or inequality, no government intervention would be needed. But is it possible to rely on individual decisions to ensure that the total amount of redistribution is socially optimal? Probably not. It is too easy to free ride on the charity of others, even more so in larger communities than in smaller ones where your failure to contribute is more likely to be noticed.

If Mrs. Jones is a widow with six children and unable to work because of a lack of child care, lack of opportunity, and health problems, most people would feel charitably disposed toward her and the six children. But because their contribution would likely be a very small part of the total required to address this problem, they are likely to free ride, feeling that the amount

RAWLS' THEORY OF JUSTICE

Equity, fairness, and justice are all closely intertwined. Justice may be thought of as more structural in nature, the rules of society that determine the rights, privileges, and obligations as well as the opportunities, income, and wealth that each of us is entitled to as a member of society. In his landmark 1971 book *A Theory of Justice,* John Rawls set forth a theoretical model for how those rules might be developed for a particular society.[1] In his more recent work, *Political Liberalism,* Rawls answers some of his critics and extends his model.[2] The rules that Rawls developed in both of these works that are of particular concern to public sector economics are those that pertain to distribution of resources, including income and wealth.

Suppose you were given the charge to design a system to distribute opportunities, resources, and rewards among workers and nonworkers, old and young, productive and unproductive, skilled and unskilled, without any prior knowledge of where you will find yourself in the system you have designed. Rawls described this decision framework in his earlier work as the **veil of ignorance.** The reader is asked to think about how to design a system of incentives and rewards without knowing where he or she will be located in the system once it is in place. Needless to say, the outcome of such a thought experiment is usually a system of rules and practices that provides more protection for those who find themselves most disadvantaged in a market system—those with few skills, little education, or other handicaps that affect their productivity. In particular, Rawls suggests that the rules of society that result from such an experiment are likely to reflect the "maximin principle" from game theory. The maximin principle is short for maximizing the value of the worst (minimum) outcome in the system.

In his later work, Rawls attempted to extend his theory to address the specific challenge of a

society of pluralism. Markets are particularly efficient in addressing the diverse material needs of a pluralistic society, but the challenge Rawls attempted to address is that different values among different groups make it difficult to develop an agreed-on set of rules by which society should operate. Those different values among different groups are described by Rawls as "reasonable comprehensive doctrines." Rawls suggested that it would be necessary to identify the areas of agreement or overlapping consensus among those competing comprehensive doctrines (of the goals of society, or the nature of the good), and to base the rules for distribution of society's income, wealth, and opportunities on those areas of agreement. Among the areas of agreement that Rawls thought might emerge from such a process are some basic personal liberties guaranteed to all, and a set of rules that guaranteed equality of opportunity in competing for public offices and positions with different rewards. In addition, Rawls believed (as in his earlier work) that any rules that allowed inequality in income and wealth must be designed so as to be of the greatest benefit to the least advantaged members of society.

While Rawls' philosophical system is more general than the specific distributional issues of concern to a modified market economy, it does raise some interesting questions about the existing distribution of income and wealth as well as the distribution of the increases in income and wealth that result from innovation, risk-taking, skill improvements, and other factors. These actions result in increased output per worker in a firm (micro) or economic growth (macro). How much of the additional income and wealth should go to those responsible for creating it as an efficiency incentive and how much should be shared with fellow workers and owners (micro) or with others in the economy (macro)? Rawls' notion of the veil of ignorance is also a useful way of thinking about proposals to modify reward and incentive systems for such groups as those retired on Social Security or welfare recipients being encouraged (or pressured) to find paid employment.

[1]John Rawls, *A Theory of Justice* (Cambridge, MA: Belknap Press/Harvard University Press, 1971).
[2]John Rawls, *Political Liberalism* (New York: Columbia University Press, 1993).

of aid going to Mrs. Jones will not be significantly altered by their small share of the total required. If everyone reasons this way, Mrs. Jones is out of luck. In very small communities, shirking one's due share of the obligation is too visible and has too much impact on the outcome to allow free riding to dominate. But in a highly mobile society, and a society in which most people live in large urban areas where the poor and needy are often less directly visible, free riding is likely to dominate. With free riding, the amount of private voluntary redistribution will fall short of the socially optimum level.

BALANCING DONOR GOALS AND RECIPIENT NEEDS

Donors—taxpayers in the case of public redistribution—may have different goals and objectives from recipients. Both groups vote, lobby, and exercise political influence in various ways. In general, donors are more interested in creating equality of opportunity and in making sure that funds are spent in particular ways, while recipients are more interested in equality of results and in having some flexibility in how the resources that come their way are used.

Equality of Opportunity versus Equality of Results

Beyond the earlier debates over whether there should be any governmental redistribution at all, a secondary debate among both economists and policy makers considered whether the goal of any intentional redistribution should focus on equality of opportunity or equality of results. **Equality of opportunity**—providing education, health care and other services that allow people to develop into and remain productive, contributing adults—is a philosophy more in accord with a market system. For a large share of the population, equality of opportunity efforts represent the primary form of redistribution, especially in the form of free, compulsory public education and low-cost, state-sponsored postsecondary education and training programs. These services are available to all, more or less irrespective of ability to pay. Even access to postsecondary education is heavily subsidized with Pell grants, low-cost student loans, and federal (and state) funded work-study opportunities. In other countries, including Canada and Western Europe, the extent of such services is much greater, including health care and day care for preschool children.

Equality of results emphasizes reducing disparities in income and direct alleviation of poverty immediately, rather than emphasizing "investing" in poor people. The difference in strategy is captured in the old proverb "Give a man a fish, he can eat for a day; teach a man to fish, he can eat for a lifetime." Often the need is too immediate and direct to be addressed by longer term strategies of education and training. In general, equality of results as an antipoverty strategy has become less popular in the United States in the last few decades. One component of equality of results in the United States and elsewhere is the progressive income tax, which takes a larger share of income in taxes from higher income households than from lower income ones. Since World War II, when the top bracket on the income tax rose to 98% during the war, Congress has enacted a series of reductions in federal income tax rates across the board, but particularly at the top, making the system less progressive. (Income taxes are discussed in Chapter 10.) Features such as the earned income credit and larger personal exemptions have also favored lower income households, although a variety of specialized tax breaks have also reduced tax burdens on middle and upper income taxpayers. The other programs that aim at equality of results are payments, direct or indirect, to low-income households in the form of cash, food stamps, housing subsidies, and other forms of income support. Social Security has been particularly successful in reducing poverty among the elderly.

In Kind or In Cash?

A second issue that is often viewed differently by donors and recipients is the form that redistribution takes. Recipients prefer cash, which gives them more flexibility in how they use the funds. Donors, however, are often looking for specific outcomes and want to impose their preferences rather than those of recipients on the use of funds. Donors may want to see the money earmarked for food, housing, child care, or health services. The easiest way to earmark funds is to provide the services directly rather than cash payments. Health clinics and education programs are examples of direct service provision.

A second substitute for cash, increasingly popular in recent years, is a **voucher.** Vouchers are written claims, issued by the government, that can be exchanged for housing, education, food (food stamps), or other designated uses. The voucher is presented to the seller as the equivalent of cash, but only for the specific designated use. Vouchers are not supposed to be converted into cash which can then be spent on other purposes. (One of the great controversies in the food stamp program has been the ease with which they can be converted into cash for nonfood purchases.) Although in-kind payments may satisfy donor (or taxpayer or legislator) preferences about how funds are spent, they are usually much more costly to implement than cash payments.

RESPONSIBILITY FOR REDISTRIBUTION

Assuming that a consensus exists for some kind of redistribution to designated groups, the next question is whether that redistribution should be the responsibility of the central government, state (or provincial) government, or local government. Or should it be shared between them? Until the 1930s, addressing poverty in the United States was primarily a responsibility of local governments, with workhouses for families with employable members and "outdoor relief" (outside of poorhouses or workhouses) for widows and orphans. Private charity took care of some problems. With the advent of the Great Depression, first local and later state governments were overwhelmed with the magnitude of the problem of poverty resulting from widespread unemployment. A major part of the New Deal was a series of programs designed to relieve poverty among the aged, those with disabilities, widows with small children, and the unemployed. (Most of these programs are discussed in Chapter 18.) Even in the 1930s, however, state and local governments continued to have a role in poverty relief. Federal aid consisted primarily of cash payments to the poor with some state matching funds. The required match varied from state to state depending on income and poverty levels in each state.

These programs continued to exist, expand, and evolve until 1996 when welfare reform significantly reduced this kind of federal aid to individuals mediated through state social service agencies.

The case for centralization of redistribution rests on competition among states. If one state offers more attractive benefits to persons in need than another, it risks becoming a haven for migration of those persons. Faced with the threat of attracting the needy and overburdening the welfare system, states will reduce their benefit levels below what they would offer in the absence of migration. Uniform national standards (adjusted for differences in the cost of living) remove that incentive to migrate between states in search of better benefits.

The case for localization rests on the arguments offered earlier for why poverty might be regarded as market failure. Both the empathy and the social blight arguments for poverty relief suggest that the benefits from relieving poverty are very local in nature. In addition, there is the need to monitor eligibility and control fraud, which is much easier to do effectively at the local community level. Despite repeated efforts to sort out responsibilities and assign responsibilities for poverty relief to a particular level of government, it is—as it has been since the Great Depression—a shared function of federal, state, and local governments.

REDISTRIBUTION AMONG GOVERNMENTS

Redistribution is not limited to individuals. State and local governments have similar responsibilities and demands but very different resources for meeting those demands. Local governments are more limited than state governments in their ability to raise revenue, state governments more so than the central government. These two kinds of inequality lead to redistribution of revenues between levels of government, between states, and between local governments within a state in order to provide a better match between needs and resources. Redistribution between levels of government in order to match revenues with responsibilities is known as **vertical equalization;** redistribution among governments at the same level in order to ensure citizens of equal access to services regardless of the wealth of their communities is known as **horizontal equalization.**

Vertical equalization can go either up or down. In China and in Russia and Eastern Europe before the revolution, revenue was collected locally and sent to the central government. In the United States and many Western countries, the pattern is normally the reverse. Funds collected by the central government are shared with state and local governments, and some of the funds collected by state governments are redistributed to local governments. However, the funds rarely return to state or local governments in proportion to the revenue originating in each place, so some horizontal redistribution occurs between states and between local governments in the process. If that kind of redistribution also reduces the inequality between states or between local governments, then horizontal equalization is also occurring.

General Revenue Sharing

The most famous experiment in vertical equalization in the United States was conceived in 1964 by President Johnson's Council of Economic Advisers, put into effect in the early 1970s under President Nixon, and eliminated during the early 1980s as a budget-cutting move during the Reagan administration. That experiment was known as **General Revenue Sharing.** Unlike various categorical and block grants (discussed in Chapter 14), General Revenue Sharing was apportioned to state and local governments on a formula basis (partly population, partly other factors) and could be spent for any appropriate public purpose.

The idea was born during a time period when it was anticipated that the highly productive federal income tax would generate rapidly increasing amounts of revenue for the federal treasury. One possible response to this surplus, of course, could have been to cut tax rates. However, economists were concerned about the growing responsibilities of state and local government and what they perceived as their more limited ability to raise funds (compared to the federal government), for two reasons. First, they relied on less elastic revenue sources, such as sales and property taxes. Second, interstate and interlocal competition for desirable residents, commercial facilities, and industry limited their ability to increase tax rates. If the needs were at the state and local level, but the revenue raising ability was greater at the federal level, General Revenue Sharing seemed like the perfect answer.

It wasn't. Successive cuts in federal income tax rates, the war in Vietnam, a sluggish economy in most of the 1970s, and growing federal budget deficits took the steam out of that budget surplus argument for General Revenue Sharing. General Revenue Sharing to state governments was eliminated in 1982 and to local governments three years later. Federal funds to state and local government reverted to the more familiar form of grants-in-aid for programs and projects. In the dozen years the program was in effect, federal tax cuts and dismal economic conditions meant that the surpluses that were supposed to support General Revenue Sharing did not materialize. The mood in Washington shifted to an expectation that state and local governments could decide for themselves the level of services they wanted to provide and raise the tax monies to pay for it.

A significant part of the problem for politicians was that Congress took the heat for the taxes they collected while state and local governments took the credit for the services they provided, financed out of federal tax monies through General Revenue Sharing. There was too much "disconnect" between the pain of taxes and the pleasure of receiving services that reduced accountability for state and local public officials.

State Aid to Local Governments

In 1997, local governments across the country received an average of 38.4% of general revenue from higher levels of government, of which 3.9% was federal and 34.5% was from the parent state.[7] On the surface, state aid to local governments—counties, cities, school districts—has some similarities to General Revenue Sharing (with a much longer history). But, in fact, there is an important difference. States have considerable autonomy in the U.S. federal system, while local governments are created by and dependent on their state governments. Court decisions, particularly related to education funding (see Chapter 16), have forced states to play an increasingly important role in ensuring that the quality of a child's education is not too heavily dependent on the wealth of the school district in which that child resides. Increasingly, the burden of paying for public education (kindergarten through grade 12) has been shifting to the state level. States also often mandate that county or municipal governments offer certain services or meet certain standards, and there is pressure on states to fund those mandates so as not to overburden smaller or poorer communities with limited taxable wealth.

A third factor in justifying state aid is the extremely competitive situation facing local governments in attracting or retaining both residents and commercial/industrial taxpayers. No local government can afford to let either its tax rates or its service quality (especially schools) get too far out of line with its neighbors. Yet a city or county or school district with very little taxable wealth requires a much higher tax rate to generate the same amount of rev-

7. State aid to local governments is addressed in more detail in Chapter 14. While much more current data are available for the federal government and for state governments, local government data trickle into the aggregate data system much more slowly, usually with a lag of four to five years from the end of the fiscal year (June 30), for collection, processing, and distribution through state and federal channels.

enue and provide the same quality of public services as a wealthy neighbor. To protect poorer communities from the consequences of the tax competition game, states either partially fund certain local services or redistribute tax revenues from wealthier to poorer areas.

SUMMARY

Government is inherently redistributive; every action, whether taxing, spending, or regulating, changes the distribution of income and wealth. Because government is  such a powerful tool for redistributing income and wealth, organized groups attempt (and often succeed) at using government for that purpose.

This chapter addresses redistribution to create a more equitable distribution of income, resources, and opportunities. There are many different concepts of distributional equity. The problem of defining and measuring equity results from the difficulty of making interpersonal comparisons of utility. Horizontal equity means treating people alike if they are in the same or similar economic situations. Vertical equity means treating people differently according to the differences in their income, wealth, or other measure of need or ability to pay.

Most changes in public policy involve gains and losses to different groups, redistributing income and wealth. Redistribution complicates the issue of evaluating policy alternatives. The compensation principle offers a guide to incorporating redistributional effects into policy evaluation. According to the compensation principle, when policy changes from State A to State B, if the gainers from the move can compensate the losers for their losses and still be better off (or the losers cannot bribe the gainers to avoid the change and still have some net gain), then the move is desirable from the

standpoint of total social welfare. Whether compensation should actually be paid is a political rather than an economic question.

Another equity challenge arises from the conflict between efficiency and equity in attempting to rely more on the market for resolving conflicts by assigning property rights. According to the Coase theorem, the outcome of a conflict over use of resources is likely to be the same regardless of which of the conflicting parties is initially assigned the property rights. However, the distributional effects will be very different. Efficiency is also an issue in the process of distribution, because efficiency in redistribution means targeting aid to those who "deserve" it, with minimal expenditures for administration and minimal diversion of revenues to those who are perceived as "undeserving." These two aspects of efficiency are in conflict because the cost of excluding those who seek to defraud the system can be very high.

In the United States the poverty rate was 13.3% in 1997, or about 36 million people, a rate that had held steady for many years. Some economists regard certain types of poverty as a form of market failure. In a market system, where income is based on contributions to the economy, four factors contribute to poverty: inability to work because of age (too young or too old), having a disability, or lack of access to jobs; workers who lack the skills, training, or experience to earn an adequate wage; and special circumstances such as health, family size, or obligations that make it impossible to maintain an above-poverty standard of living on their earnings. Poverty is sometimes classed as market failure because (1) the existence of poverty among some individuals reduces the well-being of others; (2) poverty can be considered as diminishing the quality of life of the community because it breeds drugs, illegitimacy, blight, crime, and other social ills that impact on more prosperous households; (3) there is a public good insurance element in having social safety nets that catch those who suffer from economic reversals outside their control; and (4) private redistribution will be less than adequate because of free-riding behavior.

Redistribution can be aimed at equality of opportunity or equality of results and can be done either in cash or in kind. Equality of opportunity—providing education, health care and other services that allow people to develop into and remain productive, contributing adults—is a philosophy more in accord with a market system. Equality of results, aimed at immediate and direct relief of poverty, emphasizes reducing disparities in income and is less popular in the United States, particularly in the last few decades. The progressive income tax, food stamps, housing subsidies, and Social Security are examples of programs based on equality of results.

Redistribution also takes place between governments. Redistribution between levels of government in order to match revenues with responsibilities is vertical equalization; redistribution among governments at the same level in order to ensure citizens equal access to services regardless of the wealth of their communities is known as horizontal equalization. Both processes take place from federal to state and local and from state to local governments in the United States. General Revenue Sharing was the most famous experiment in vertical equalization in recent decades. States play an important role in redistribution between richer and poorer local communities both through paying directly for services (such as education), funding services that the state wants provided at the local level, and reducing tax-based competition for residents and industry between local governments.

Good arguments can be made both for centralizing and for localizing redistribution. The case for centralization rests on competition among states, with beneficiaries migrating to states with the most generous benefits. Uniform national standards remove that incentive to migrate. The case for localization rests on the empathy and social blight arguments for poverty as market failure, with both of these factors being very local in nature. It is also easier to monitor eligibility and control fraud at the local community level. As a result, poverty programs are a shared function of federal, state, and local governments in the United States.

KEY TERMS AND CONCEPTS

horizontal equity, 117
vertical equity, 118
means testing, 118
compensation principle, 119

veil of ignorance, 128
equality of opportunity, 129
equality of results, 129
voucher, 130

vertical equalization, 132
horizontal equalization, 132
General Revenue Sharing, 132

DISCUSSION QUESTIONS

1. Try a Rawls-type thought experiment like the one described in the boxed section based on his *Theory of Justice*. Consider a situation in which a group of employees at a plant all receive the same pay. An outside efficiency expert concludes that if five employees at key points in the process work harder than the others, output can increase by a significant percentage. Should those five workers be paid more? How much more? Should they get all the increase in the company's net income since they created it, or should it be at least partly shared with other workers? What considerations influenced your answer?

2. How might either the Coase theorem or the compensation principle help in the following situations?

   a. One neighbor in a subdivision who does not maintain her property and makes it less attractive to everyone else and reduces adjacent property values

   b. Conflict between those who want more streetlights for safety and those who like dark streets at night so the light does not keep them awake

   c. Access to a limited supply of potable water that households want to use but that farmers would like to have for irrigation

   d. Allocating an unexpected increase in local government revenue for street improvements

3. What are some of the ways in which states can engage in horizontal equalization between cities and counties? What criteria might they use for distributing funds and resources? What are the advantages and disadvantages of each of the following methods?

   a. Direct state provision of certain services

   b. Sending money to local governments to provide the same services, with relatively more per capita going to cities and counties with a smaller tax base or a higher percentage of poor people

   c. Sending the same amount per capita to all cities and counties to provide the same services

4. What are the efficiency, equity, and administrative advantages and disadvantages of a means-testing system that phases out eligibility as household income approaches a certain limit instead of just saying that every household below that limit is eligible and those above it are not?

CHAPTER 7

COMPETITION AND GOVERNMENT

In a market system at its best, the forces of self-interest combined with the constraint of competition will tend to allocate resources in a way that is socially optimal or, at a minimum, economically efficient. Productive resources will be combined in the least cost way to produce the products and services that consumers want the most, all guided by signals of price and profit. Competition is the force that compels individuals and firms to respond to market signals in order to attract and retain buyers for what they have to sell. Firms with monopoly power are somewhat less responsive to consumers, because they are not likely to lose many customers or sales regardless of how they behave; that is, they face a relatively inelastic demand curve.

Because competition is so central to the workings of a market system, public finance must consider the relationship between competition and government in a market economy. That role takes many forms: government actions to encourage or constrain competition, competition between governments, competition among private firms in supplying products and services to the government as buyer, and the frequent cases when both government and private producers (for-profit and nonprofit) are supplying similar services to overlapping clienteles. In an increasingly global economy, even competition in the public sector has an international dimension. The tax, service, and regulatory choices of governments affect decisions that both firms and citizens, here and abroad, make about where to locate their production activities or residences.

GOVERNMENT INFLUENCE ON COMPETITION

Because competition is an important factor in making private markets serve the general interest, governments attempt to encourage or promote competition within the private sector. Sometimes, intentionally or not, government actions have the less desirable effect of discouraging or preventing competition.

Encouraging Competition

Governments (especially the U.S. government) have two primary tools with which to promote competition and restrain the excesses of monopoly. One tool is antitrust law, which defines and imposes penalties for behavior by firms that is intended to limit or destroy competition. Entire courses and volumes of case law are devoted to this aspect of government's attempts to promote competition by thwarting attempts to destroy, buy out, or otherwise eliminate competitors. The other tool has been a variety of regulatory agencies empowered to curb the excesses of monopolies that are not within the reach of the antitrust laws. Historically, these regulated monopolies have included telecommunications, banking, railroads, trucking, airlines, and electric power providers.

In the 1980s and 1990s, much of this regulatory apparatus was dismantled, at least partly in response to two lines of research pursued by economists. First, there is usually enough **workable competition.** The competitors who generate workable competition may be firms in related industries or workable competition may come about as the result of new technology. In either case, its main feature is to offer consumers some alternative suppliers or products in order to restrain most of the excesses of what generally proves to be only temporary monopoly power. Second, regulatory agencies tend to develop cozy relationships over time with the industries that they regulate, thwarting the intent of oversight. Expertise in the workings of some technologically and financially sophisticated firms often lies primarily in the industry itself, so regulatory agencies are staffed by people who come from the regulated industry. As a result, the **capture theory of regulation** says that these agencies will come to regulate their industries largely for the benefit of the industries themselves rather than their customers, who are underrepresented in the regulatory process.

In recent decades, more emphasis has been placed on positive approaches to encouraging competition. Some of these approaches include

- Facilitating technology transfer (particularly from universities and government laboratories),
- Small business development,
- Business incubators,
- Pooled risk management, and

- Other services that enable new firms to get a start against established competition with some hope of survival.

These strategies, used more at the state and local rather than the national level in the United States, concentrate on developing competition and competitors rather than constraining or punishing large and powerful firms. While both kinds of methods are still in use, the preference has shifted to the latter approach. In part, this shift is a response to rapid development of new technologies in the last two decades (especially computer-based technologies). New technologies have made it possible for new firms to overtake and outrun stodgy established firms and for stodgy established firms to make a comeback and develop new life when faced with sudden competition.

Discouraging Competition

People who invest in physical or human capital have no trouble establishing their property rights to that investment in order to try to earn a fair rate of return. However, for people who invest in intellectual or artistic creations (works of art, books, songs, inventions, or designs), protecting property rights is a major challenge. Governments offer creators of such valuable products and services some degree of protection through patents, trademarks, and copyrights. These protections allow the creator to sue those who copy or appropriate their work without permission (e.g., recording a song someone else has copyrighted) as a way of asserting their property rights and earning a return on their investment. However, patents, trademarks, and copyrights also create some degree of monopoly power for their owners.

To avoid creating long-term monopolies, these intellectual property rights have finite lifetimes. Eventually they expire. But while their owners possess the exclusive right to sing, print, produce, or copy their own work, they are protected from potential competition. They may earn monopoly profits, be insensitive to customer needs, and become lazy and inefficient. Every government in a market system has to weigh the trade-offs between ensuring that people have an incentive to invent, innovate, and create and the risk of encouraging small, inefficient, unresponsive monopolies. In fact, this debate goes beyond national borders; some of the touchiest issues in trade negotiations in recent years have centered on protection of intellectual property rights from foreign bootlegging, copycatting, or duplicating of music, movies, and books.

A second effect that government has, indirectly, on competition in the private sector is through its procurement practices. Government purchasing, especially at the federal level, favors large firms, because the paperwork is complex, the volume of the order is often very large, and larger firms are just more connected to the information network through which information about planned government purchases is disseminated. The most visible examples of problems in government purchasing have been found in defense procurement, where a network of Defense Department officials and defense contractors developed long-term, reciprocally beneficial relationships that were often costly to the public. The $600 toilet seats and the $91 screws purchased by the Pentagon are part of American economic folklore, but they really happened.

A third, indirect but significant effect that government has on competition has to do with the paperwork burden that firms incur in complying with a host of regulations, such as environmental, disability access, gender equity, and worker safety rules. All firms have to comply with the same rules (sometimes very small firms are exempt). But the cost of compliance is much higher for small firms as a percentage of their employment, production, or sales. Because these compliance costs will raise the average or unit cost more for a small firm than a large one, regulations have the effect of putting small firms at a competitive disadvantage.

Finally, governments have historically been the sole supplier of certain kinds of services because the market was so limited and the economies of scale so substantial that only one firm—or perhaps none—could profitably serve the market. Public transportation, rural electricity, and solid waste collection and disposal have all been in government hands (and still are in many cases) because the alternative was either a private monopoly or no supplier of the service at all—services that were considered desirable as merit goods or goods with positive externalities but not able to generate a profit as an inducement for a private supplier. These roles for government have diminished at the federal and state levels since the 1950s, but continue to be important at the local level. Some of these activities have been privatized, as described in Chapter 1, but many bus and transit services, electrical utilities, and other services are still operated by local governments.

COMPETITION BETWEEN GOVERNMENT AND PRIVATE FIRMS

One of the defining characteristics of government is that it possesses certain kinds of monopoly power. At a minimum, governments have a monopoly on the lawful use of force, which is reserved to the police or sheriff. Other exclusive rights are also reserved to the government. In the U.S. Constitution, monopoly powers of the federal government include coining and printing money (now shared with a private banking system), police and military powers, and control over foreign commerce. When the government has monopoly power over the legal use of force, it is able to compel citizens to submit to its demands. Those demands include payment of taxes, compliance with the speed limit, registering for the military draft, attending school until age 16, and smoking only in designated places. When a government agency has the exclusive right to provide services such as putting mail into private mailboxes, it cannot force people to use its services but it can prevent others from supplying similar services. That government agency (the post office in this case) is less constrained by competition from Federal Express or United Parcel Service. As a result it will be less sensitive to customer concerns and less likely to try to be more efficient, to keep prices down, and to provide better services.

In many areas, government agencies compete both directly and indirectly with private firms, both for-profit and nonprofit. The direct competition takes place when certain services, such as education, recreation, transportation, and health care, are offered by both public and private agencies. Indirect competition simply means that many government activities could also be undertaken by private suppliers, in which case the threat of lost jobs and loss of power and prestige can have the same effect as direct competition on bureaucrats and government workers. The threat of competition forces government agencies to be more efficient, responsive, and accountable if they think that service provision might be turned over to a private supplier. Many privatization ventures in provision of local public services have had precisely this effect, with the public provider competing with (and sometimes winning out over) private providers of fire service or garbage collection. Osborne and Gaebler, in their widely read study of efficiency and innovation in government *Reinventing Government,* describe at least one instance where city sanitation workers lost in district-by-district contract competition to provided garbage collection services, only to win them back one by one through determined efforts by both workers and management.[1]

Should Government Compete?

On the other hand, when government is expected to compete directly with private suppliers of some services (education, for example), what happens to those social benefits or public goods aspects of the service that justified public involvement in the first place? It is inevitable that in a competitive situation with private suppliers, government agencies will adopt some of the values and operating styles of those private firms. Politicians often run on a platform that promises to "make government run more like a business." It is not entirely clear what that slogan means. If it means more emphasis on accountability, efficiency, and responsiveness, then there is almost always room for improvement in those areas. Although accountability, efficiency, and responsiveness are not always that easy to accomplish in an environment of weak signals from citizens, bureaucratic incentives, and requirements to ensure equity that challenge most government programs, that does not mean that more effort should not be expended in those directions.

But what if that slogan means, instead, that the primary goal of public agencies should be market share, revenue maximization, short-run profitability, and going after those clientele most easily served and satisfied—all goals common to private firms? Might these alternative goals not defeat the purposes of providing public goods and goods with positive social benefits while constraining negative social benefits and ensuring some degree of equity in the

---

1. David Osborne and Ted Gaebler, *Reinventing Government: How the Entrepreneurial Spirit Is Transforming the Public Sector* (New York: Plume Books, 1993).

distribution of cost and services? In that case, perhaps running government like a business may not be such a desirable goal. Consider, for example, the National Park Service, which operates U.S. national parks, national forests, and national monuments. The National Park Service is in some sense in competition with Disneyland, other amusement parks, and other kinds of outdoor recreation. In fact, there has been political pressure at some of the more popular national parks to make them "more like Disneyland." If the Park Service is forced to focus on generating more revenue, the result is likely to be more congestion, higher fees, and more ready access by the public. These outcomes may conflict with other, publicly determined goals of park management, such as wildlife conservation and preservation of fragile environments.

While government agencies and business firms have some common challenges, methods, and characteristics, often they are quite different in mission and purpose. The similarities and differences will vary greatly from one agency to another. The appropriate standards for evaluating their performance may likewise be very different.

Competing in the Labor Market

Government also competes with private firms in the resource market, especially the labor market. Private firms and governments at all levels compete in the labor market for the same pool of available workers. The package offered by government (at least at the state and federal level) tends to be different. Often the wage scale is less attractive, but there is much more job security, often more opportunity for advancement, and frequently more generous benefits, particularly sick leave and annual leave. Private firms vary greatly, but they tend to rely heavily on salary as an incentive rather than job security or benefits. In areas where the government is a major employer, the job attributes it offers to its workers will spill over to private firms who may have to offer more benefits or leave time in order to compete.

Even at the local level, in large cities like New York or Los Angeles, competition between the government and other major employers affects the total cost of labor, labor turnover, and the kinds of workers each side can attract. In boom times, when private employers offer attractive salary packages and even bonuses, it becomes increasingly difficult for public agencies to staff some of their positions, particularly in more professional jobs. In leaner times, however, government workers are grateful for their job stability while private sector workers experience more short hours or unemployment.

Competition for Resources within Government

All government agencies have to compete for resources, because government, like households and firms, faces a budget constraint. The budget constraint is strongest for local governments, who usually must balance their budgets and

COMPETITION IN POSTAL SERVICES

The U.S. Constitution created a postal monopoly for the federal government, a practice common in other nations, particularly Great Britain. Only the Post Office could perform certain services, of which the most notable was the delivery of first-class mail. The arguments for a public role in mail delivery are a mix of positive externalities and "merit goods." The positive externalities rest with the social benefits of ready, rapid, and inexpensive universal access to a medium of communication. The merit goods argument, which is also applied to food, basic housing, and health care, is that certain services should be available to all regardless of ability to pay. Access to some form of communication is sometimes assigned to the category of merit goods.

Until 1970, postal service was represented in a cabinet department headed by the postmaster general. In major legislation in 1970, the Post Office became the U.S. Postal Service, outside the cabinet, strongly encouraged to be self-supporting, and largely self-governing, although postal rate changes still required congressional approval. Now the U.S. Postal Service (USPS), along with its counterparts in the rest of the world, is in the throes of major changes in its competitive situation.

The USPS is a very large operation that processes 40% of the world's mail. It handles 107 billion pieces of first-class mail each year, collected at 312,000 mail collection boxes and 38,019 post offices and delivered to 130 million delivery points by 234,033 mail carriers. But increasingly, it is facing competition from Federal Express, United Parcel Service, and the Internet for different parts of its service package. Mail is now only one way to deliver a message, and not always the fastest or most effective. Is it time to eliminate the postal monopoly over the delivery of first-class mail, or even do away with the USPS entirely?

Other countries have explored the gamut of possible solutions, with reforms ranging from closer monitoring of universal service to limiting the postal monopoly, privatizing postal services, and expanding postal service into new and related markets. In general, the private goal of a postal service would be profit maximization, while the public goal would be the provision of universal service that is of high quality (speed and dependability), accessibility, and price. One concern is that complete privatization might leave some higher cost markets unserved or underserved, thus undermining the goal of accessible and affordable universal service.

Finland in 1991 and Sweden in 1993 abolished the public postal monopoly on mail delivery, while Germany is scheduled to do so in 2002, with auctions of some Deutsche Post shares (the government will retain a 50% stake for an extended period). The Netherlands and Argentina have both privatized their postal services. The Dutch sold it to a private supplier with some terms specified for quality, cost, and accessibility, while Argentina created a semi-independent entity with more commercial freedom but still government owned. Japan, the next largest mail deliverer after the United States, still has an extensive government-owned monopoly somewhat similar to that of the U.S. Postal Service.

The postal issue is a classic case of technological innovation undermining monopoly by creating newer and more satisfactory substitutes for the goods or services provided by the monopoly. The invasion of some parts of the postal service's market by private suppliers of overnight mail services and package delivery has challenged the USPS for several decades now. E-mail, faxes, and electronic funds transfer in banking have all cut into the demand for first-class mail services. While some of the more radical changes in Europe and elsewhere are not yet on the agenda for the United States, your friendly neighborhood post office is likely to see sweeping changes in its operating rules and its competitive situation in the near future.

have limited ability to raise taxes or tap new revenue sources. It is still strong at the state level, because states also have to balance budgets and are concerned about competition for residents and business firms, which limits their ability to raise taxes. The budget constraint is weakest at the federal level, although in the 1990s strong pressure to eliminate the budget deficit had the effect of imposing a budget constraint. Once an effective budget constraint is in place, more funds for one project or agency mean less for another. From the citizens' standpoint, this kind of budgetary pressure is a healthy force, requiring agencies to justify their budget requests and demonstrate that their project or program is more beneficial or cost effective than others. Zero-based budgeting, discussed in Chapter 15, has a very similar effect.

FISCAL SURPLUS, FISCAL IMPACT, AND ECONOMIC IMPACT

Competition by nations, states, and local governments for industry and jobs, high-income residents, and attractive commercial developments is based on three important considerations: fiscal surplus, fiscal impact, and economic impact. **Fiscal surplus** measures the cost–benefit calculations made by the industry, potential resident or commercial developer in terms of taxes, fees, and public services. **Fiscal impact** measures the opposite side of the coin, looking at taxes and fees generated and public services demanded from the government's point of view. **Economic impact** is the broadest of the three measures, looking at the total change in economic activity in terms of income, employment, and wealth creation.

Fiscal Surplus or Deficit

Any citizen who is considering moving from one state to another or one city or county to another within a state will take into account the fiscal surplus or deficit in each of the alternative locations. The concept is simple: Just add up the value of services received, and subtract the value of taxes paid (including any fees or other nontax obligations).[2]

If the difference is positive, the taxpayer has a fiscal surplus; if negative, a fiscal deficit. Notice that while taxes are easy to measure, the value of services received is highly subjective, so that two taxpayers with the same tax burden may have different fiscal surpluses because they value services differently. Families with school age children often enjoy a big difference in the size of the surplus over childless families for whom non-school services or lower taxes are more important.

---

2. Mathematically, the fiscal surplus for the ith individual in the jth location is given by $FS_{ij} = \Sigma SV_{ij} - \Sigma T_{ij}$ where FS is fiscal surplus, SV is the value of services received from governments, and T represents taxes, including fees and other forms of nontax obligations.

Taxpayers can generally gather information about tax burdens and service quality from realtors, local public officials, prospective employers, and other sources so that they can compare the package of taxes and services. Often local governments distribute that kind of information to visitors and prospective residents, presenting their tax/service package as attractively as possible in order to get the most desirable residential–commercial–industrial mix.

Fiscal Impact

Fiscal impact represents the opposite side of the coin, subtracting service costs from revenues to determine whether the impact of new residents, commercial developments, or industry is a net addition to or a drain on local and state public sector resources. The government compares the cost of providing services for the additional resident to the amount of revenue that resident would be expected to generate. If the new resident or firm will generate more revenue to the government than the cost of providing the additional services, the fiscal impact is positive.[3]

The revenue side is the easier part of the computation. The cost of serving an additional household may vary greatly according to its size, income level, and location. In-fill developments that put homes on vacant lots are usually less expensive to serve than new homes built in more isolated locations where the cost of running services (roads, utilities, streetlights, police and fire protection, trash pickup, etc.) to the location will be much higher per household. High-density housing, such as apartment complexes, can be less expensive to serve with transportation, streetlights, and trash pickup, but often generate much higher demand for police protection and recreation services. Industry is usually attractive to local governments not only because it provides jobs but also because it tends to have lower service demands than households. Commercial development lies somewhere in between. Because the most expensive local public service is education, mobile home parks with their many children and low tax revenue per household are often actively discouraged by local governments.

Determination of fiscal surplus and fiscal impact is not a zero-sum game, although there are some trade-offs. It is possible for both calculations to be positive. The revenue side may be the same from both the citizen and government view, but there is no reason that the value of services to residents and firms has to be equal to the cost of providing it. If the value that the citizens place on the service is higher than the cost of producing it, then citizens can have a fiscal surplus even while the local government has a positive fiscal impact. In the case of a pure public good, where adding another user does

---

3. The mathematical formula is quite similar to that for determining the fiscal surplus, with fiscal surplus (FS) replaced by fiscal impact (FI) and the value of services (SV) replaced by the estimated additional service costs (SC): $FI_{ij} = \Sigma T_{ij} - \Sigma SC_{ij}$.

not diminish the amount available to existing users, the service cost of an extra resident is zero while the value of the service remains positive. The government can afford to offer this taxpayer a favorable tax service package because an extra resident will result in a revenue increase, yet expenditures will
remain unchanged.

Economic Impact

The third and broadest measure of the three is economic impact. Economic
impact measures not only the effect on/of the public sector but also the impact on the private economy from adding new firms or residents. The key to
creating a positive economic impact is some external source of private revenue, which may come from selling goods and services to nonresidents (like
an industry or a tourist attraction) or from attracting residents that have a
source of income from outside the local economy (such as pensions or sales
of goods and services to outsiders). Even services that are heavily local in nature, such as health care facilities, can generate that kind of outside income
if they draw on a broad region for their clientele.

If industry is broadly defined to include a retirement industry, a tourism
industry, a health care industry as well as more traditional manufacturing and
service industries that serve a regional, national, or even international clientele, then those industries are part of a locality's export base. *Export* refers
to out of the region, not necessarily out of the country; something that brings
in revenue from outside the region, creates jobs in doing so, and thus offers
an income base on which to develop a local economy. The local economy,
which usually has a narrower market, provides groceries, recreation, health
care, legal services, clothing, and other goods and services to local residents.
Some of the income derived from exporting is used to purchase goods and
services produced outside the local economy.

The computation of economic impact is complex, but the intuition underlying it is simple. Suppose a local economy has two employers, one making kayaks and one making auto carpet out of recycled materials. Together
those two industries employ 500 workers with an annual payroll of $20 mil-
lion and the purchase of materials and supplies from the local economy adds
another $5 million annually. Economic impact would translate that initial im-
pact into secondary sales and jobs as employees in the two firms patronize
local hairdressers, grocery stores, optometrists, and bowling alleys. Those
firms, in turn, generate wages that are spent in the local economy. Those who
work in those local secondary firms, in turn, spend much (but rarely all) of
their extra income on local purchases.

If this description sounds like the multiplier concept that you learned in
principles of macroeconomics, you are on the right track. Export industries—
local firms that sell primarily to buyers outside the local market—are said to
have **multiplier effects** on the local economy in terms of the additional spending and job creation that result from their payroll. Multipliers vary greatly

from one industry or another, but numbers in the range of two to three are fairly common. Communities need export industries in order to acquire the resources to pay for imports, that is, to make purchases of goods and services produced outside the immediate locality. A manufacturing industry is one way to have that multiplier effect, but so are medical centers, commercial/cultural centers, resource-based industries (timber, agriculture, oil and gas, minerals), or a "mailbox economy" of retirees receiving pensions and Social Security checks from elsewhere.

INTERSTATE COMPETITION AND TAX/SERVICE INCENTIVES

States are in competition with one another for industry and high-income residents. Every state would like to attract or develop high-quality employers who pay good wages, pay lots of taxes, demand relatively few services, respect the environment, and in general enhance the quality of life in the state. States also like to attract or retain residents who are relatively prosperous, paying generous amounts of taxes, demanding relatively few services, and being good community citizens. In other words, states are looking to create positive fiscal impacts. To do so, however, they must lure these residents and firms with both special amenities and tax/service packages that are competitive with other locations, not merely positive fiscal surplus.

Most states have some amenities to market that will be attractive to some segment of mobile firms and individuals. Those amenities may include beaches, lakes, and mountains; urban centers with cultural and sports attractions; special recreational facilities; lots of flat, inexpensive land; a good water supply; good highway access and location convenient to major markets; and good weather or climate. States have become very adept at identifying and marketing these amenities.

To balance the desire for a positive fiscal impact with the firm's (or citizen's) search for fiscal surplus, states increasingly are turning to negotiated agreements with business firms, which is a form of price discrimination. The value of the tax/service package (which is often heavily weighted with tax breaks, but is likely to include some services as well) will be worked out with the firm based on how much competition there is for that firm and how desirable it is to the state or locality. How much investment will it make? How long will it stay? How many jobs will it create? Is it likely to attract related firms? What kind of reputation does it have in terms of being a good employer and in terms of protecting the environment? Will workers have an opportunity to learn new skills and enhance their earnings? Is the firm likely to be an eyesore and an environmental nuisance, or will it be an attractive addition to the community? In a rapidly growing area with low unemployment, economic developers and local officials may be concerned about pressures on infrastructure, congestion, and other costs of expanding the housing supply or the industrial base. Depending on the answers to these questions, a state or local government may or may not choose to aggressively court a firm with specific offers that enhance the firm's fiscal surplus.

The variety of inducements offered by state and local governments is end-less. Most states and local governments offer some kind of tax savings on corporate income tax and property tax. Firms often receive credits against corporate income tax for job training and job creation, for example. Property tax savings can take the form of accelerated depreciation of plant and equipment, negotiated fees in lieu of taxes, lower assessment rates, lower property tax (mill) rates, or state ownership of the site to keep it off the tax rolls. Firms may also be given special treatment with respect to sales tax on business purchases. On the expenditure side, firms may be promised a variety of special services, such as site preparation, worker training at state expense, road improvements, enhanced fire service, and access to water and sewer on favorable terms.

These inducements often have a high up-front cost, but pay off to the state in terms of both economic and fiscal impact over a long period. Because of this difference in time frames, some states have taken steps to protect themselves from the possibility that a firm will be induced to come, take advantage of the tax breaks and services, and then move on to another state. While many firms build large, expensive physical plants that have a long useful life-time, others require relatively little capital investment and can easily pick up and relocate. Because of this risk, some states or local governments have included in their agreements with new or expanding firms who receive such inducements a provision known as a **clawback.** A clawback provision requires repayment of certain benefits if the firm does not stay in that location for some minimum period of time or fulfill the terms of the agreement in terms of dollars invested and jobs created.

INTERLOCAL COMPETITION AND THE TIEBOUT HYPOTHESIS

Even more intense than the competition between states for residents and industry is the competition between local governments for high-income residents, commercial facilities of various kinds, industry, and even state institutions (colleges, prisons, hospitals). Tax differences do factor into the choice of a state location for both mobile individuals and firms, although they are rarely at the top of the list. Within a state, however, the individual or firm will zero in on a particular region, perhaps because of its interstate highway access, training facilities, labor availability, or other factors. Within that region, there are likely to be a variety of suitable locations. The fiscal surplus offered by competing cities, counties/townships, or school districts is often an important consideration in pinpointing a site on which to build a house, an industrial facility, a shopping center, or a recreational facility. Making those choices, moving between localities because of the relative attractiveness of the tax and service packages, is called "voting with one's feet."

Tiebout Hypothesis

The classic description of the workings of interlocal competition was that of regional economist Charles Tiebout in 1956.[4] The **Tiebout hypothesis** has been one of the most fruitful ideas in regional economics in that it has led to considerable empirical testing as well as further refinements of our understanding of locational decisions and capitalization of the fiscal surplus into the prices of land and homes.

Tiebout's basic concept was quite simple. It was based on the assumption that both workers and firms not only engage in the usual informed, self-interested decision-making processes that lie at the heart of economics, but also that workers and firms are mobile. They can move to one community to another, or if relocating in a particular region, they can choose from several competing communities that offer alternative tax and service packages. Communities, in turn, are trying to attain some optimal population in order to reach an efficient size that will minimize the average cost of providing public services.

Under these circumstances, people will tend to cluster in communities in which tastes and preferences for public services and taxes are relatively homogeneous. There will be high-, low-, and medium-service (and tax) communities from which to select. This model suggests a monopolistically competitive model of many similar communities differentiated by the offerings of the public sector as well as other amenities that influence people's locational choices. It also accords with what is observed in the real world. Real estate agents consistently note that the questions about a community always zero in on taxes and school quality as two key decision factors—and schools are generally the largest and most expensive local public service. Firms, likewise, take into account both taxes and those public services that are important to them (such as transportation and fire protection) in choosing between alternative locations.

Not all communities are in an intense Tiebout-type competitive situation. Some are too isolated. Others have attractions (such as the state capitol, access to the ocean, or location at the intersection of two interstate highways) that dilute the importance of the fiscal package. But in the suburbs of large cities, or in areas where many small to medium-sized cities are clustered together, the Tiebout hypothesis suggests that mobility gives voters much more voice and clout in the decisions of the local public sector. The threat of losing residents or commercial and industrial facilities because of mobility is a powerful device for getting the attention of politicians and bureaucrats, much

4. Charles M. Tiebout, "A Pure Theory of Local Expenditures," *Journal of Political Economy,* 64 (October 1956): 416–424.

more powerful than was suggested in Chapter 5, where demand was being voiced by a fixed/given group of immobile voters.

Homogeneous Communities?

The Tiebout hypothesis suggests that market-type forces will result in communities that are relatively homogeneous in terms of preferences for public services and the willingness to pay for them. Will these communities also be homogeneous in terms of income? They might, because tastes for public services are likely to be related to income levels. But other factors are at work, particularly the attraction of being a low-income resident in a high-income community.

Remember, for local governments the property tax is usually the primary source of local revenue. Thus, the tax burden one must bear in a community will be related to the value of taxable property one owns—a house for many families, and perhaps one or two cars. But the service level is the same for everyone in the community. People who own less taxable property (smaller houses, older cars) will have larger fiscal surpluses than those who live in more expensive houses or drive newer, pricier cars. No one will want to be the biggest property owner in town, especially a town with high service levels. So communities that raise their taxes too high, or communities that have only a few high-value properties and a large number of low- to medium-value properties, face a threat of losing some of their wealthier residents. As those residents depart, they sell their houses at depressed prices, because prospective buyers are deterred by the high tax burden associated with that house. When the price falls, so does the tax burden.

Higher income residents are likely to seek out communities that are homogeneous not only in taste for public services but also in income levels and housing values so that their fiscal surpluses are not diminished by having to support services for occupants of lower valued homes. Thus, one conclusion of the Tiebout hypothesis is that there may be some tendency for communities to become segregated by income levels.

At the other end of the scale, a high-service community might be very attractive to someone looking to buy a small, inexpensive house, because the tax burden will be relatively small, both in comparison to services received and in comparison to the average tax burden on residents. Demand for a limited supply of such houses will drive up their price and their value for tax purposes.

So this high-service community is likely to attract residents seeking smaller, lower valued homes and discourage those looking for larger and more upscale residences. But in the process, the tax burden on smaller houses rises and that on larger houses falls, reducing some of the disparity in the fiscal surplus enjoyed by residents with very different housing choices. These market-like forces mitigate the inflow and outflow of residents attracted to or driven off by relative tax burdens.

Fiscal Capitalization

The process by which present and future fiscal surpluses are reflected in the prices of houses is called **fiscal capitalization.** Capitalization refers to the process by which a stream of future income flows or expected costs is incorporated into the present value of an asset, in this case a house or other real estate. Recall that the present value of any series of future payments, positive or negative, is the sum of the discounted value of each of those future payments. If, for example, in the sixth year from now the tax bill is expected to be $500, and the interest rate used is 6%, then the present value of the tax liability in six years is $500/(1.06)^6$, which works out to $352.49. The present value of future tax liabilities is given by the present value formula

$$PV = \Sigma FV_i/(1 + r)^i \ ,$$

where PV is present value, FV is future value, r is the interest rate, and i is the number of years.

If the tax bill will be $500 per year for the next 10 years, then the present value of 10 years of tax liabilities is $500 × [1/1.06 + 1/(1.06)2 + (1/1.06)3 + . . . + (1/1.06)10]$, or $3,680, which is the amount that one would have to set aside right now at 6% interest in order to make that total of $5,000 in future tax payments at a rate of $500 a year.

The same calculation can be made for the value of public services in future years. They may be the same, or they may be different. Perhaps the household will only have children in schools for some of those years. Perhaps they are presently using wells and septic tanks and live off a gravel road, but have assurances of city water, city sewer, and paved roads in the near future. Combining the calculations yields the present value of future taxes and services. If one of those factors changes, the present value will increase or decrease. If the fiscal surplus on a property increases, the value of the property should increase by the same amount, other things being equal. If the fiscal surplus decreases, either because the expected future tax burden increases or the expected value of services decreases, the value of the property should decline, other things being equal. The change in the stream of future obligations and benefits is incorporated into the value of the property, or capitalized.

An important implication of fiscal capitalization is that any changes in taxes or service levels impact primarily those who own the property at the time, not future owners. If, for example, a tax increase in Smallville results in a decline in the fiscal surplus associated with residences in that town relative to neighboring towns, housing prices will decline. Current owners not only have to pay the higher taxes, but if they attempt to escape them by relocating, they will find that the (lower) price they receive for their property will reflect the higher tax burdens. The next buyer will have to pay the higher taxes, but he or she will also be able to purchase the house at a lower price that reflects that disadvantage.

Fiscal Zoning

Another implication of the Tiebout hypothesis is that cities and even counties can attempt to defend themselves against some of the undesirable effects of citizen mobility through zoning designed to limit in-migration of low-tax, high-service demand residents. When zoning regulations set high minimum lot sizes or minimum square footage requirements in order to protect the value of the fiscal surplus of established and higher income residents, they are engaging in **fiscal zoning.** Lower income households cannot move in and buy or build small houses to enjoy larger fiscal surpluses at the expense of high tax burdens on larger, more valuable properties. Again, the result of fiscal zoning tends to be communities that are homogeneous not only in tastes and preferences but also in income and wealth.

INTERNATIONAL COMPETITION AND GOVERNMENT

Local and state governments are not the only ones to find that competition for residents and businesses constrains their choices and actions. In a global economy, national governments—even very large national governments like that of the United States—find that competition with other nations puts constraints on their monopoly power. If labor costs get too high relative to those of other nations, as they have in Germany and Sweden, their firms start building new plants abroad. If environmental restrictions limit the ability of firms to choose cheaper production and waste disposal options, these firms may seek a location in a country that is not quite as particular about environmental protection. If one nation levies high taxes on business firms, there is always another nation ready to welcome those firms with lighter tax burdens.

In the past, a significant source of monopoly power for governments was the international immobility of labor and capital between nations. If the factors of production tended not to move, then the only source of competition between national governments was the movement of goods, which governments could restrict with tariffs, quotas, and other regulations. As markets for labor, capital, and goods have become truly global, the power of a single government to impose stricter regulations, maintain a welfare state, raise taxes, or allow strong labor unions to drive up the cost of wages and benefits has been greatly weakened. As a consequence, regulations (especially environmental and health and safety regulations), taxes, and labor market conditions tend to move toward the lowest common denominator. And that lowest common denominator may be lower than what would have been chosen if governments and even citizens could have joined together in a conscious decision. Just as the mobility of Americans between states has put downward pressure on the level of social services and welfare benefits offered to poor citizens, so likewise has international competition put the same kinds of downward pressure in other areas of governmental activity.

Those powers have always been weak for smaller nations with more open borders. Honduras, Sri Lanka, Portugal, and Uruguay have always recognized that they are the nation-state equivalent of perfect competitors on the international scene. They are price takers; they cannot impose more stringent restrictions or higher taxes than other nations without suffering an exodus of capital and skilled labor and finding it difficult to market their products internationally. A few small countries, particularly those with oil or other mineral resources, have some degree of monopoly power to insulate them from the pressures of the global marketplace.

The creation of multinational markets with quasigovernmental authorities such as the European Union and the North American Free Trade Agreement can be seen as a response to the threat of diminished governmental power through globalization. If a single government has lost much of its monopoly power, perhaps it can regain or retain some power by joining with other nations to become one of several oligopolists or "price leaders" in a global society made up largely of very small to moderate-sized nations. Large nations or coalitions of nations have considerable influence in international negotiations on such issues as working conditions, environmental regulations, fishing rights, and protection of intellectual property rights.

SUMMARY

Competition is a central feature of a market economy that makes it more likely that the pursuit of self-interest will result in socially desirable outcomes. Government affects competition in many ways and is itself subject to competition from the private sector, from other governments, and from within the government sector itself.

Historically, the U.S. government has used antitrust laws and regulatory agencies to restrain the excesses of monopoly. More recently, governments have been more proactive in promoting competition through such means as facilitating technology transfer (particularly from universities and government laboratories), small business development, business incubators, and assistance with risk management. Rapidly changing technology makes it less likely that monopolies will persist over long periods. Government also discourages competition through policies to protect intellectual property rights and through procurement practices and regulatory requirements that favor larger firms over smaller ones.

When government agencies compete with private firms, gains may be realized in terms of efficiency and responsiveness, but also costs in terms of changing the goals and objectives of the public agency or program. Governments compete with private firms not only in the provision of services but also in the labor market. Government jobs often pay less but generally offer better fringe benefits and job security. Different agencies within government also compete for limited budgetary resources.

States, cities, and counties compete for residents and business firms to locate or remain in their area by offering them attractive tax/

service packages. Fiscal surplus measures the cost–benefit calculations made by the industry, potential resident, or commercial developer in terms of taxes, fees, and public services. Fiscal surplus is the value of services received less taxes and fees paid from the perspective of the taxpayer. Fiscal impact measures the opposite side of the coin, looking at taxes and fees generated and the cost of public services supplied from the government's point of view. The citizens' combined fiscal surpluses and the government's fiscal impact can both be positive as long as the value of services received exceeds their cost of production.

Economic impact is the broadest of the three impact measures. It measures the total change in economic activity in terms of income, employment, and wealth creation, including secondary or multiplier effects on local economic activity.

States compete with one another for high-income residents and attractive industrial and service firms by offering tax breaks or services such as worker training and infrastructure. Often the up-front cost is high but the long-run payoff in fiscal and economic impact is expected to be positive. Some states have instituted clawback requirements that make firms repay some of the costs of benefits provided if they do not remain in the state for some specified length of time.

The fiscal surplus offered by competing cities, counties/townships, or school districts is often an important consideration for individuals and firms when choosing a location. The Tiebout hypothesis suggests that, if workers and firms are mobile and make self-interested choices, they will select a community that offers the most attractive fiscal package. Communities are trying to attain some optimal population in order to reach an efficient size that will minimize the average cost of providing public services. Under these circumstances, people will tend to cluster in communities in

which tastes and preferences for public services and taxes are relatively homogeneous.

Lower income residents tend to migrate to wealthier communities and purchase smaller homes with lower property tax burdens in order to enjoy larger fiscal surpluses. Higher income residents will seek communities with higher average home sizes and income levels in order to avoid having to subsidize the public service consumption of less affluent families. This migration will tend to drive up the prices of small homes in more affluent communities and depress the prices of large homes in communities with a concentration of smaller homes and less affluent residents.

The process by which changes in taxes or service levels are translated through fiscal surplus into appreciation or depreciation in home prices is called tax capitalization. One consequence of tax capitalization is that the wealth effect of a change in tax or service levels falls on those who owned property at the time of the change and not on subsequent owners.

Fiscal zoning is an attempt to protect the interests of higher income (and property-owning) residents by restricting the ability to construct smaller homes for less affluent families. Fiscal zoning creates relatively homogeneous communities, generally of higher income residents.

International competition puts some constraints on the monopoly power of central governments. Central governments in small countries have relatively little ability to make independent choices about wages and working conditions, environmental and health regulations, tax levels, or other policies that might inhibit their ability to attract and retain desirable residents and business activities. Even in the United States, global competition has limited the ability of the government to impose strong environmental or health and safety regulations and is a consideration in tax and labor policies.

KEY TERMS AND CONCEPTS

workable competition, 138
capture theory of regulation, 138
fiscal surplus (deficit), 144

fiscal impact, 144
economic impact, 144
multiplier effects, 146
clawback, 148

Tiebout hypothesis, 149
fiscal capitalization, 151
fiscal zoning, 152

DISCUSSION QUESTIONS

1. In what ways is competition between state governments (or local governments) beneficial to citizens and firms? In what ways might it be harmful?
2. In which of the following kinds of new development do you think that fiscal impact on local government is likely to be negative, as opposed to moderately or even highly positive? Why? What strategies are implied from the perspective of local government in order to minimize adverse fiscal impacts?
   a. Mobile home parks with large number of children
   b. Upscale residential communities for wealthy retirees
   c. Low-density suburbs of moderate-priced households on fairly large lots, with lots of open space
   d. A large, dense commercial district with shops, restaurants, and service firms
   e. An industrial park with light, high-tech industry
   f. A hog farm (see "Hog Farms, NIMBY, and Local Governments", Chapter 2)
3. Proponents of making it easier for students to attend private schools contend that one of the benefits of subsidizing private school tuition is that the competition will force public schools to shape up. Opponents argue that public schools create social benefits in terms of building community and

shared values, and also that the private schools will (and do) "siphon off" the easy-to-teach students (higher income, two-parent families, no physical or emotional problems, etc.) and leave the public schools with the higher cost, harder to serve population that makes it difficult to compete effectively in terms of cost and student performance. Evaluate this argument in terms of the costs and benefits of competition for public agencies and the externalities argument for public production.

4. The 2001 case against Napster as a way of sharing copyrighted music has pointed out the problems of protecting intellectual property rights in order to allow the creators to benefit from their work. (Check www.napster.com for details.) In what ways does this decision increase or decrease competition and/or incentives in the market for recorded music?

5. Suppose that your local government is thinking about offering substantial property tax relief as an inducement for a firm employing 100 workers to locate in the community. How might that decision affect your fiscal surplus (or deficit) as a resident? As the owner of a local restaurant? Under what circumstances might the economic impact outweigh the fiscal impact?

PART 3

FUNDING GOVERNMENT: TAXES, FEES, AND GRANTS

The next seven chapters address the revenue side of government, the funds to pay for public programs, the distribution of the burden of paying for government, and the use of revenue instruments as means toward specific policy ends. The primary revenue source for government is taxes, which are the focus of the next five chapters, two on the theory and practice of tax system design and three on the primary kinds of taxes on income, sales, and property. The final two chapters in this section examine two other important revenue sources, fees and charges and intergovernmental grants.

According to Justice Oliver Wendell Holmes, taxes are the price we pay for a civilized society. That dictum still leaves room to argue over whether the taxes are too high relative to the amount of civilization that citizens want or need or actually receive in return. It does mean that taxes are an inevitable part of living in society. Given the necessity of taxes, the economist's task is to provide some guidance in designing a tax system that minimizes the undesired side effects of collecting them (efficiency) and apportions the burden in some way that satisfies the equity concerns discussed in Chapter 6.

Although taxes are still the primary form of revenue for governments at all levels, they are not the only source. Fees and charges, discussed in Chapter 13, are a second and increasingly important way of paying for services that have some advantages in terms of both efficiency and equity. For state and local governments, intergovernmental grants also represent an important supplement to own-source revenues, a subject addressed in Chapter 14.

CHAPTER 8

PRINCIPLES OF TAXATION 1: EFFICIENCY AND EQUITY ISSUES

Given the need to raise revenues to fund the activities of government, economists are tasked with figuring out how to design a revenue system that is both efficient (minimizing distortions in household and business decisions) and equitable (distributing the burden fairly). Figuring out how to best raise revenue has been a central concern of economists at least since Adam Smith devoted an entire book, *The Wealth of Nations* (1776), to "the revenue of the sovereign," including his famous dictum that the taxes one pays should be "proportional to the revenue enjoyed under the protection of the state." David Ricardo, an important 19th century figure in the history of microeconomic theory, titled his most famous book *Principles of Political Economy and Taxation*. Until the latter half of the 20th century, courses in the public sector were aptly named public finance, because they concentrated so heavily on the revenue side of the public sector to the neglect of the equally important decisions on the expenditure side. Today the balance has shifted, but an understanding of the principles of tax design, both theoretical and applied, is still a central part of the study of public sector economics.

EFFICIENCY ISSUES IN TAX DESIGN

A tax is said to be efficient if it does not change any of the economic decisions that firms and households would have made in the absence of the tax. Very few taxes can meet that high standard

of efficiency. A **poll tax,** which is a flat charge per person or per household, is one of the few taxes that does not distort economic decisions. The burden of a poll tax does not change with changes in location, work effort, consumption spending, wealth, or any of the other factors that affect one's tax liability for income, sales, property, excise, and estate taxes. The poll tax is rarely used in modern industrial nations (it was briefly introduced in Great Britain during the 1980s and then repealed) because it is extremely regressive; that is, it takes a much higher percentage of income from the poor than the rich. But the poll tax does provide a useful standard of nondistortion against which the effects of other taxes can be measured.

Consumer Surplus and Excess Burden

An analytical tool that is useful in evaluating the distorting effect of taxes and their impact on consumer welfare is the concept of consumer surplus. This concept may be familiar to you from an earlier course. Recall that each point on the demand curve measures the amount consumers are willing to pay for a particular quantity of a good. But in most cases, all consumers pay the same price, the market price, even though for many consumers (or many units purchased) the price they would have been willing to pay is higher.

Figure 8-1 is the demand curve for bread for an individual consumer. If Q_1 is one loaf, and Q_2 is two loaves, then this consumer would be willing to pay P_1 for the first loaf and P_2 for the second loaf. When she goes to the store and finds that the actual price is P_2, she buys two loaves. The "extra utility" she receives for getting the first loaf at price P_2 when it was worth P_1 to her is called **consumer surplus.** Consumer surplus for a quantity Q_2 is the difference between the entire area under the demand curve, $OABQ_2$, and the amount actually paid, which is rectangle OP_2BQ_2 (price times quantity). The consumer surplus associated with purchasing a quantity Q_2 is triangle P_2AC, the difference between the area under the demand curve up to quantity Q_2 and the amount that consumers must pay to purchase the good.

Anything that changes the price paid will also alter the amount of consumer surplus received. A rightward shift in supply will lower the price and increase consumer surplus, whereas a leftward shift will raise the price and reduce consumer surplus. Imposing a tax will also have the effect of reducing consumer surplus.

Taxes are generally represented graphically as either **shadow demand curves** or shadow supply curves. The word *shadow* is intended to convey that the second demand or supply curve does not represent a shift in the original curve, but rather a wedge between the demand curve as perceived by the buyer and the demand curve as perceived by the seller. In Figure 8–2, an excise tax is imposed on the purchase of lightbulbs in the amount of AE per lightbulb, the vertical distance between demand curve D_1 and demand curve D_T. The demand curve for lightbulbs from the consumer's perspective is unchanged, but from

Figure 8–1
Measuring
Consumer Surplus

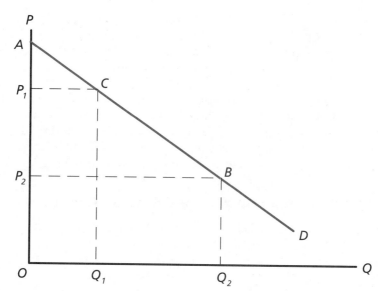

the supplier's perspective the demand curve D_T represents average revenue net of excise tax. As a result, consumers pay a higher price, buy fewer lightbulbs, and experience a loss of consumer surplus measured by area P_1P_TAB.

Where does the consumer surplus go? Some of it (rectangle P_1P_TAC) goes to the government in tax revenue. Total tax revenue is actually the larger rectangle P_2P_TAE, with the rest of the tax revenue coming from the producer (see below). So this transfer is not necessarily undesirable, because the additional government services paid for with that tax revenue may compensate consumers for their loss of utility in consuming lightbulbs. But a little piece of consumer surplus is lost to consumers and not transferred to the government, triangle ABC. This loss is known as **excess burden** in a context of taxation, but is more generally referred to as **deadweight loss**. This excess burden or deadweight loss represents a decline in consumer surplus and consumer welfare that does not get transferred to firms or to government but is lost entirely. It represents an interaction between the higher price and the decline in quantity purchased and consumed. The rectangle of consumer surplus transferred to government only captures the effect of the higher price paid on the smaller quantity.

Triangle ABC, however, only captures part of the excess burden of taxation. A similar loss accrues to producers as long as supply is not perfectly elastic. In Figure 8–2, producers also suffer a loss in their surplus of revenue over marginal or variable costs (which may or may not be profit). When quantity declines from Q_2 to Q_1, producers lose revenue measured by the difference between rectangles OP_1BQ_1 and OP_2EQ_2. The area below the supply curve, Q_2EBQ_1, represents a reduction in marginal or variable costs because

Figure 8–2
Excess Burden
of an Excise Tax
on Lightbulbs

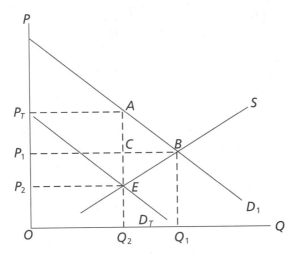

of the reduced production, and rectangle P_2P_1CE is transferred to the government as tax revenue. Producers also lose the value of triangle CBE above the supply curve, a loss of producers' surplus that is comparable to the loss of consumer surplus. Both triangles ABC and CBE are also known as *Harberger triangles*, named for the economist who first analyzed them in detail.

The triangles in Figure 8–2 are very important both analytically and in practice. Different tax rates or levels or different elasticities of supply or demand will result in triangles of different sizes and shapes that represent larger or smaller deadweight losses, or in the case of taxes, excess burden. One of the objectives of good tax and revenue system design is to minimize the excess burden represented by the Harberger triangles. The concrete, intuitive meaning behind these triangles is the forced adjustment in consumption (or sometimes production) patterns as a result of the tax, which generates a loss of consumer welfare over and above the transfer of resources from the consumer to the government.

Shifting, Incidence, and Price Elasticity

If you refer back to Figure 8–2, you will notice another interesting point about the effect of taxes. In that diagram, the price paid by the buyer rose, *but it rose by less than the amount of the tax*. And if you look again, you will notice in that figure a price P_2 where D_T crosses the supply curve. P_2 is the price received by the seller, which is lower than the equilibrium market price P_1 that had prevailed prior to the tax. So part of the tax reflects a lower net price to the seller. The total revenue collected by the government from this tax is measured by rectangle P_2P_TAE, of which P_1P_TAC comes from the buyer in the form of higher prices paid and P_1P_2CE comes from the seller in the form of lower net price received.

It does not matter whether the law says that the tax must be paid by the seller or the buyer. Economic factors, primarily price elasticities of demand and supply, determine the division of the tax burden between the two parties. Responsibility for collecting and remitting the tax may initially fall on the seller, as it does for most sales taxes. But if the seller is able to pass part of that tax on to the buyer in the form of higher prices, then there is **shifting** of part of the tax burden. The place where the burden ultimately falls, or the division of the tax burden between the parties involved, is known as tax **incidence**.

To illustrate what determines the division of the tax burden, consider Figure 8–3, which shows a tax imposed on a commodity in completely inelastic supply—perhaps land, or tickets to a concert where seating is limited and cannot be expanded. In this case, the entire burden of the tax falls on the seller, because the seller is unable to adjust the quantity at all. Because buyers demand Q_1 at a price P_1, nothing has changed to make buyers feel any differently. The entire tax burden $P_T P_1 AC$ falls on the seller in the form of reduced net revenue. Note, too, that there is no excess burden or Harberger triangle in this case, because there is no quantity change.

Needless to say, it is very tempting for policy makers to look for situations like that in Figure 8–3 to provide a revenue source. In the 19th century, economist Henry George reasoned that the most useful and appropriate tax would be a single tax on land (not improvements, such as buildings) because land was fixed in supply, and the tax would cause no distortions in behavior or deadweight loss. In recent years, Henry George's ideas are again being considered in designing the property tax in some parts of the United States and Canada. For example, more of the value of the property may be assigned to the land value and less to the buildings or other improvements, so as not to discourage improvements. More often, taxes are imposed on goods where the supply is highly if not perfectly inelastic, because the resulting excess burden triangle will be smaller than it would be for a more elastic supply curve.

Figure 8–4 illustrates the effects of imposing an excise tax on a product with relatively inelastic demand, such as cigarettes, alcohol, or gasoline. Note that in Figure 8–4, the share of the tax revenue $P_T P_1 AE$ that falls on the buyer ($P_1 P_T AC$) is much larger than the share falling on the seller ($P_1 P_2 CE$). Why? Because the seller is more able to alter his behavior in response to the tax, cutting back on production from Q_1 to Q_2. But because consumers are unwilling or unable to shift to substitute products, competition among buyers for the reduced quantity drives the price up to P_T. Typical items in this category are drugs (both illegal and prescription), salt, and water, all of which have very inelastic demand curves until the price gets well out of its familiar range.

Ad Valorem Taxes

All of the illustrations thus far show a fairly simple type of tax, called a **specific tax**, which is imposed on the basis of some quantity measure—units, volume, or weight. A tax of 50 cents on a pack of cigarettes, $1 a gallon on

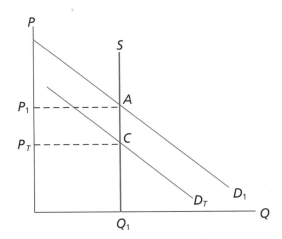

Figure 8–3
Tax Incidence
with Completely
Inelastic Supply

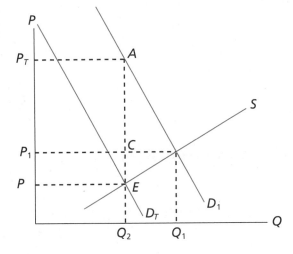

Figure 8–4
Tax Burdens
with Inelastic
Demand

wine, or 20 cents a pound on imported cashew nuts would be examples of a specific tax. Much more common are *ad valorem* **taxes,** which (as their name suggests) are imposed as a percentage of the price or value. State retail sales taxes are *ad valorem* taxes imposed at rates ranging from 3% to 8% of the value of the item sold. Many excise taxes, such as those on telephone service and automobile tires, are *ad valorem* taxes. The property tax is also an *ad valorem* tax, because it applies a mill rate (a mill is a tenth of a cent) to the assessed value of the property.

For a specific tax, the shadow demand curve is parallel to the original demand curve. The distance between them measures the tax per unit. For an *ad valorem* tax, the distance between the two curves changes with the price, and the "tax wedge" gets larger and larger as the price gets higher. Figure 8–5

Figure 8–5
An *Ad Valorem* Tax

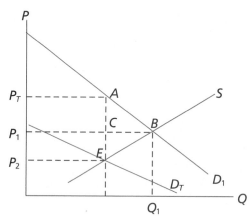

illustrates the effects of an *ad valorem* tax on price, quantity, tax revenue, and division of the tax burden between buyer and seller. As a result of the tax, the price paid by the buyer rises from P_1 to P_T and price received by the seller falls from P_1 to P_2. Total government revenue, as before, is P_2P_TAE, of which P_1P_TAC comes from the buyer in the form of higher prices paid and P_2P_1CE comes from the seller in the form of lower net price received. Excess burden or deadweight loss is measured by triangle ABC for consumers and triangle BCE for producers or sellers.

Effect of Taxes on Work Effort

The taxes whose effects are illustrated in Figures 8–1 to 8–5 include various kinds of sales taxes. They can also be applied to some kinds of income tax deductions, because an expenditure that is tax deductible has a lower effective price than one that is not deductible (see Chapter 10). A different analytical approach is needed to assess the general efficiency effects of an income tax, which is illustrated in Figure 8–6. This figure, which can be used to analyze a variety of taxes besides income taxes, shows an indifference map that describes an individual's preferences between various combinations of two desirable activities, in this case income and leisure.

Assume that the person being taxed on figure 8–6 can earn $15 an hour. Putting all waking hours (7×16, or 112) into work would result in an income of $1,680 a week and zero hours of leisure. On the opposite axis, a choice of zero working hours would result in no income and 112 hours of leisure (not including sleep). Faced with the time constraint and the rate of pay, this individual chooses point A, which reflects 47 hours of work and 65 hours of leisure with an income of $705 a week. Any other choice would put this person on a lower indifference curve, implying a lower level of satisfaction or utility.

Now introduce a payroll tax as a percentage of earnings. The intercept with the horizontal axis does not change, because leisure is not taxed. But

Figure 8–6
Effects of a Payroll
Tax

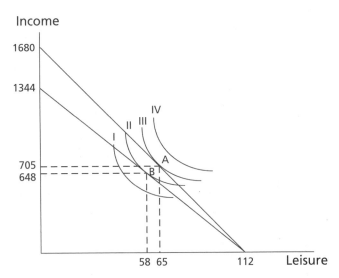

every hour of work now nets $12 instead of $15 because of the tax. The maximum weekly earnings drop to $1,344, the new intercept on the vertical axis. Faced with this new "budget" constraint, this worker adjusts his/her behavior, selecting point B, which represents only 58 hours of leisure and income of only $648 after taxes. This individual experiences both an income effect (the tax reduces income) and a substitution effect (leisure is now cheaper in terms of income foregone) that affects his or her work behavior. Different preferences, reflected in a different shape for the indifference curve, might have actually resulted in fewer work hours and more leisure.

There is no easy way to design an income tax that avoids distorting the work/leisure choice. The same analysis can be applied to consumption and saving, where a tax on purchases makes saving less expensive than consuming, or to other choices between taxable and nontaxable options. As long as a tax is not truly universal, it will tip the balance for at least some individuals toward the decision or activity that is not subject to tax. Only a poll tax, which cannot be evaded by rearranging one's work, spending, owning, or other decisions, is neutral among consumer choices.

Tax Incidence Revisited

Regardless of how the tax law is written, or who writes the check for the tax due, all taxes are ultimately paid by households in one form or another. A given tax, such as a retail sales tax, can be shifted forward to the consumer or can be absorbed by the seller. But even if a tax is absorbed by the seller, the impact does not end there, because the seller is merely an intermediary for workers, suppliers, and owners—often stockholders. The share of the tax paid by the seller has to come out of the earnings of one or more of those groups. It may result in lower wages for workers, lower dividends for stockholders, lower profits in the case of a privately owned firm, or even lower payments to providers of inputs, depending on the degree of competition in each of the relevant markets. The group of households on whom the tax falls is likely to be different when more of the tax falls on the seller than when more is shifted forward to the buyers, but the burden still falls on households in one or more of their incarnations as consumers, workers, or owners.

Locational Effects

Another set of choices that is influenced by taxes, as noted in Chapter 7, is locational decisions—where to site a new factory, open a restaurant, or buy or build a home. The kinds of taxes imposed, the rates, the coverage, and other features will impact differently on homeowners than on owners of commercial or industrial property. Even within the same category (such as homeowners), the impact of various taxes will be different. Younger households with children might be more sensitive to differences in the sales tax on tangible goods (the typical state retail sales tax), whereas older households may be hit harder by property taxes as their taxable wealth increases while their purchases of tangible goods decline. Among commercial establishments, some will generate more tax liabilities than others out of any given tax code. In any case, it is important to note that householders and firms weigh relative rather than absolute tax burdens and tax burdens in relation to the service package offered in making location decisions.

Multiple Tax Bases and Excess Burden

Every tax but the poll tax causes some kind of excess burden. Because the poll tax is very unsatisfactory on equity grounds, public officials are forced to employ other tax instruments that distort people's choices. From the perspective of efficiency, is it better to employ just one distortionary tax at a fairly high rate, or several such taxes, each at a low rate? Which one will cause less loss of consumer welfare, that is, which excess burden triangle will have the smallest area? The answer to this question is basically a proposition in geometry. For simplicity, consider a case where supply is perfectly elastic, so that the price paid by the consumer is equal to the full amount of the tax, as shown in Figure 8–7.

Recall that the area of a right triangle is one-half the base times the height. The height of the excess burden triangle is the increase in price as a result of the tax. If the tax is *ad valorem*, and t is the tax rate, then the area of an excess burden triangle is measured as

$$ABC = \tfrac{1}{2}t \times P_1 \times (Q_1 - Q_T) , \qquad\qquad (8\text{-}1)$$

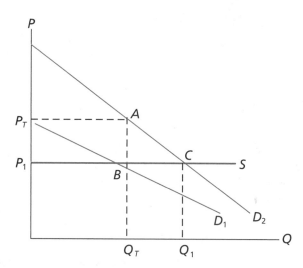

Figure 8–7
Tax Rate and Excess
Burden

The change in Q depends on the tax rate t, with the exact amount of the change being the result of elasticity. Elasticity, ε, is equal to the percentage change in quantity divided by the percentage change in price:

$$\varepsilon = \frac{t\,/(P_1+P_T)}{(Q_1 - Q_T)/(Q_1 + Q_T)} \tag{8-2}$$

Solving Eq. (8–2 for $Q_T - Q_1$,

$$Q_T - Q_1 = \frac{t \times (Q_T + Q_1)}{\varepsilon \times P_1 \times (1 + t)} \tag{8-3}$$

Substituting this expression into Eq. 8–1 gives

$$ABC = \frac{\tfrac{1}{2}t^2 P_1 \times (Q_T + Q_1)}{\varepsilon \times (P_T + P_1)} \tag{8-4}$$

Given the initial price and quantity, Eq. (8–4) conveys a very important insight. The size of the excess burden triangle, or the "waste" that takes place in transferring revenue to the government, depends on two factors. The excess burden is inversely dependent on the elasticity of demand (the greater the elasticity, the smaller the excess burden). But excess burden increases directly in proportion to, not just the tax rate, but the *square* of the tax rate. From the same starting point and on the same demand curve, the size of the excess burden increases with the square of the tax rate. Doubling the tax rate will quadruple the excess burden or deadweight loss.

This bit of theory has important implications for tax policy. First, it suggests that taxes should be imposed to the extent possible on items for which demand is relatively inelastic. The instinctive response to that observation is to think of addictive substances (alcohol, tobacco, heroin) or inexpensive necessities (flour, salt). That is one possible choice. But another response is suggested by the fact that elasticity is lower when there are few substitutes. The easiest way to design a tax where the possibility of substitution is minimal is to make the base as broad as possible. A retail sales tax has a broader base than an excise tax, because consumers have fewer possibilities for substitution. A retail sales tax that includes services as well as goods (see Chapter 11) will be less distorting than one that only taxes tangible goods. An income tax that includes income from investments will result in less distortion in behavior than a payroll tax that only covers wages.

Second, and equally important, Eq. 8–4 suggests that the distortions caused by a tax are very sensitive to changes in the tax rate, and that very high rates cause substantially greater distortions in people's decisions and greater excess burden over and above the revenue collected. The fact that the excess burden rises with the square of the rate is an important caution in tax design. To avoid extremely high rates for a particular tax, governments usually resort to more than one broad-based tax combined with a variety of specialty taxes on particular products or services. States like Florida and Tennessee that do not have a broad-based income tax are forced to make more intensive use of sales and property taxes. A high sales tax rate results in a lot of cross-border shopping in a state like Tennessee, which borders seven other states.

Tax Rates, Elasticity, and Base Erosion

A tax on any kind of spending has two effects: It raises the price and reduces the quantity. In raising price, the tax will increase revenue, but in reducing quantity, or eroding the tax base, it will reduce revenue. The same kind of effects can be observed in the case of taxes on income or on assets. Is there some point at which the second effect, or base erosion, dominates the first, so that an increase in the tax rate will reduce tax revenue rather than increase it? This is the question to which economist Arthur Laffer sketched out an answer on a napkin in the form of his famous diagram, the **Laffer curve** (Figure 8–8).

Laffer expressed this concern very simply. At a zero tax rate, there is no tax revenue. At a 100% tax rate, taxable economic activity is pointless, so there will be no tax base and there will again be no revenue. Between those extremes, the tax system will generate revenue, but there are trade-offs between the revenue-increasing and revenue-decreasing effects of higher rates. Not all of these effects are capturable in a simple algebraic or graphic model. If tax rates get high enough, people will resort to barter or tax evasion; they will go underground, reduce their work effort, leave the country, buy abroad. Under these circumstances, a reduction in tax rates (such as from 60% to 50% in Figure 8–8) might actually generate more revenue (R_2) rather than less (R_1).

Figure 8–8
A Laffer Curve

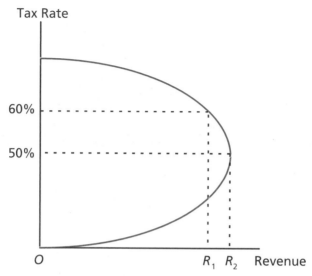

Laffer's ideas were very popular during the Reagan administration in the early 1980s, although little empirical evidence is available about just how high a tax rate must be in order to cause the revenue function to turn backward. But the insight behind the Laffer curve offers a useful caution. Moving up the demand curve, eventually even the most inelastic demand curve enters an elastic range in which buyers become more and more sensitive to price increases. The author of this textbook was asked a similar question by a state legislator who wanted to know how high the sales tax rate would have to be to generate enough revenue to eliminate the property tax. The answer was that no such sales tax rate existed, because as the rate rose, people would have more and more incentive to avoid or evade the sales tax—cross-border shopping, catalog shopping, internet shopping, collusion with sellers to hide transactions, or just plain reductions in spending.

Using Taxes to Alter Decisions

Although in general the goal of tax design is to minimize the distortions in people's decisions, taxes can also be used to deliberately alter decisions because of the positive and negative externalities associated with certain kinds of individual decisions. Taxes on alcohol, cigarettes, and gambling are intended in part to discourage consumption of those products, all of which have negative externalities of one kind or another associated with them. The same is true of taxes or charges on pollution that are tied to the volume of emissions, in order to discourage socially undesirable activities. Some tax

expenditures[1] or tax subsidies of various kinds are designed to encourage activities with social benefits, such as giving to charity, investing in one's own
education, or becoming a homeowner (which presumably creates more stable
communities). Finally, certain tax subsidies or tax expenditures are intended
to benefit one group of taxpayers in preference to others, which is intentional
redistribution of income or wealth.

Some taxes are more effective tools for altering decisions than others. For
a subsidy or tax expenditure, an effective tax tool will target the population
or activity fairly narrowly without losing more revenue than is needed to accomplish the objective. How much encouragement do people need to buy a
house, and how many of them would do so anyway in the absence of the deductibility of mortgage interest and property taxes? Would people continue
to borrow to pay for their education even if the interest on student loans were
not tax deductible? How much has that borrowing increased since the deduction became available in 1999, relative to the amount of borrowing that
would have occurred without the tax break? Does the tax deductibility of
charitable contributions really affect the amount people give, and does it go
to causes that really fit the criterion of creating social benefits?

Figure 8–9 illustrates this dilemma. Supply curve S_1 represents annual supply of houses in the absence of a tax subsidy, and S_2 represents perceived or
shadow supply with the tax subsidy. The demand curve D_1 faces a relatively
inelastic housing supply S_1, resulting in an initial equilibrium of P_1, Q_1. Now
a new tax law permits all new homebuyers to deduct the interest on their
mortgages.[2] What happens? The gross price of homes rises to P_2, but the net
price (net of the capitalized value of future tax savings from the interest deduction) declines to P_S. Housing purchases increase modestly from Q_1 to Q_2.
The cost to the government over the lifetime of the mortgages taken out in
the current year is measured by the rectangle $P_S P_2 AB$. (Again, because the diagram shows demand and supply for an asset, this rectangle measures the present value of future tax revenue losses as a result of this subsidy.) The increase
in consumer surplus is measured by quadrilateral $P_1 P_2 AC$. Clearly the revenue loss is greater than the increase in consumer surplus.

Short-Run versus Long-Run Effects

The diagrammatic approach emphasizes immediate effects of changes in tax
rates or tax structures on decisions. But remember, elasticities are always

---

1. See Chapter 9. Determining the size of the optimal tax or subsidy was discussed in Chapter 4.
2. Note that Figure 8–9 shows a best case scenario, where the tax law only applies to new purchases. If the
new tax break were to be extended to all homeowners, including those who had already purchased the homes
and were making monthly mortgage payments, the initial tax cost would be much higher than that indicated
on the diagram, because the diagram only measures the flow of home purchases, not the stock of existing
owned and mortgaged dwellings. Over time, as those who owned homes at the time the tax law changed paid
off mortgages or bought newer houses and acquired new mortgages, the annual cost of the tax deduction would
be about the same whether or not existing homeowners were initially included.

Figure 8–9
Demand for
Housing and
a Tax Subsidy

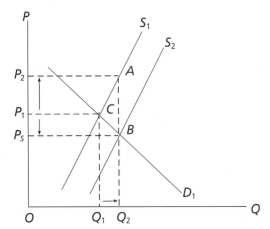

greater in the long run, once contracts expire or people have had a chance to gather information and consider alternatives. A tax that raises a substantial amount of revenue the first year or two may slack off after people have found ways to evade, avoid, or reduce the burden of the tax by a change in spending, working, investing, or locational choices.

Figure 8–10 illustrates this situation with a specific tax on soft drinks. The short-run demand curves with and without the tax are D_S and D_{ST}, and the long-run demand curves are D_L and D_{LT}. The greater elasticity in the long run reflects the opportunity to change to other kinds of beverages that are not subject to the tax, or to buy them out of state where the tax is not imposed. Note that in the short run the decline in quantity is very small (Q_1 to Q_2), but in the long run there is a further decline to Q_3. With the smaller base, revenue shrinks. Because the elasticity is greater and the decline in quantity larger, while the price change is the same, the deadweight loss to consumers is also greater in the long run (triangle *EFG*).

EQUITY ISSUES IN TAX DESIGN

Equity is at least as important as efficiency, sometimes more so to policy makers, when designing and reforming tax systems. Every change in the tax base, tax rates, or tax rules alters the distribution of the tax burden among taxpayers. Substantial lobbying effort is expended on tax breaks for particular firms, individuals, or activities. Efforts to redistribute the burden, whether in the interests of greater equity or in response to lobbying by particular interests, are the source of much of the complexity in the tax system, especially the income tax.

Figure 8–10
Short- and Long-
Run Tax Effects

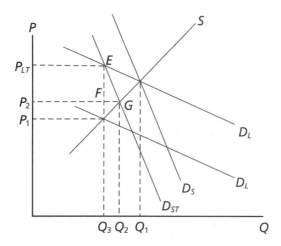

Measures of Ability to Pay

The most widely used criterion for tax fairness is called **ability to pay.** Ability to pay as a determinant of one's tax burden implies that those who have more resources than others can and should make a larger contribution toward the cost of government and public services. (Contrast this notion with the poll tax, where everyone makes an equal contribution regardless of ability to pay.) How is ability to pay measured? The simplest measure is income—the amount of revenue flowing through the household in a month or a year. A second measure is consumption or spending, and a third measure is assets or property owned. These three measures are the bases for the principal tax revenue sources in the U.S. economy and most other places as well—the income tax, some form of sales or consumption tax, and the property tax. (Inheritance and estate taxes are also based on assets.) We will have more to say about the problems of measuring ability to pay for each tax when we examine the various kinds of taxes in Chapters 10 through 12.

Some of these measures of ability to pay are more accessible to the tax collector than others. Consumption is the easiest measure to track because it involves transactions in the marketplace that can be tapped at the point of sale. Some income, particularly wage and salary income, is easy to track through payroll records, but other forms of income—self-employment earnings, interest and dividends, profits from proprietary businesses, capital gains—are much harder to uncover. Assets are the most challenging tax base of all. Few tax systems attempt to be broadly inclusive of all assets (household furnishings, stocks, bonds, jewelry, works of art) and just focus on certain kinds of property, most commonly as real estate, automobiles, and boats.

When direct information is not available, proxies are sometimes used. In Turkey tax collectors have assessed income taxes based on "lifestyle indicators"—occupation, number of horses owned, size of house, and so forth. Lacking market values for real property that was rarely sold, 19th century British tax collectors estimated the value of property on the basis of such easily determined factors as the number of windows. Even today, in a much more monetized economy with high turnover of real property, assessing real property (land and buildings) for tax purposes is the most challenging of all tax measurements to undertake.

Benefit Principle

A second principle of taxation is the **benefit principle.** Unlike ability to pay, the benefit principle links the tax obligation to the value of the services received in exchange. Adam Smith argued that a proportional income tax is, in fact, a sort of benefit tax, because the tax payment would be ". . . proportional to the revenue enjoyed under the protection of the state." The state's social, legal, and economic framework makes it possible to earn and keep one's income, and the value of those services can be assumed to be proportional to that income. The same argument has been made for the property tax as a benefit tax. Most local services (except for education) are fairly directly related to property. Police protection, fire protection, roads, streetlights, and garbage pickup are the most obvious examples. A case could be made that the value of those services to property rises with the value of the property being served or protected.

In general, however, the benefit principle is invoked for some highly specialized taxes where a clear relationship exists between the user of the taxed good or service and the user of the public service that the tax is used to finance. The best known example of a benefit tax is the tax on gasoline, which is earmarked for highway construction and maintenance. Those who purchase more gasoline either drive more miles or drive heavier, less fuel-efficient cars, but in either case they cause more wear and tear on the roads. Those who drive less do not have to subsidize those who drive a lot, and those who drive smaller, more fuel-efficient cars do not have to subsidize those who drive gas guzzlers.

Relatively few taxes lend themselves to benefit principle implementation like the tax on gasoline. More recently, the benefit principle has been expressed in the increased use of fees and charges for government services ranging from marriage licenses to health clinics to libraries to public parks. The fee usually does not cover the full cost of the service, but it does shift more of the burden of paying for the service to users rather than taxpayers in general. The search for an appropriate balance between tax financing and fees for services is discussed in Chapter 13.

Horizontal and Vertical Equity Revisited

Chapter 6 raised the question of defining equity between households with equal ability to pay (horizontal equity) and households with unequal ability to pay (vertical equity). Such equity issues are central to tax design. If taxes

THE MARRIAGE TAX

A chronic problem in U.S. federal income taxation has been to find an equitable way to treat single persons, married persons, and heads of households (those who are not married but have at least one dependent living with them). The problem arises from the progressive rates structure, where increases in income tax are subject to a higher rate on the last dollars earned. If everyone is treated as a single person, can married persons split their income and land in a lower tax bracket? Do households of two or more persons enjoy economies of scale that leave singles disadvantaged? Are two-earner married couples the tax equivalent of one-earner married couples, considering all the costs of earning a second income? Does the present progressive income tax discourage one partner in a marriage, usually but not always the wife, from working because the tax bite on the second income is so much higher? Should couples who live together be treated the same as those who are actually married? In a word, does the tax law unfairly discriminate against one or more of these groups of people in favor of another?

This example is multiplied many times over in other parts of the individual income tax code as well as in all other federal, state, and local taxes that people pay. But the marriage issue has been the most challenging to unravel. Many couples pay a marriage penalty, while others receive a marriage subsidy. It is not the intent of the tax law to encourage and reward some people for marrying, while discouraging and penalizing others. But at least one recent study suggests that two-earner families with children are statistically likely to incur substantial marriage penalties, while one-earner families receive a marriage subsidy.[1]

Where does the penalty/subsidy come from? It is the result of the combined effect of a progressive rate structure and a flat exclusion of a certain base amount. Consider the following simple example. Prior to 2001 the federal tax structure had five rates, but the great majority of taxpayers only encountered two, 15% and 28%. (In 2001 a new bottom-bracket rate of 10% was introduced.) In addition, the standard deduction and personal exemption excluded about $6,000 of income for a single person and $11,000 for a married couple.

To illustrate the problem, assume for simplicity that the 15% rate applied to the first $30,000 of income and the 28% to income over that level. What would be the tax burdens on a single person with an income of $60,000, a one-earner couple with an income of $60,000, and a two-earner couple with a combined income of $60,000? The answers are $11,220 for the single person, $9,820 for both married couples filing joint returns. But if the second married couple divorced (and each earns $30,000), their combined tax bill would decline to $7,200. This system would favor singles and one-earner married couples over two-earner couples. However, a system that offers a break to two-earner couples by allowing them to file separately as singles will have the effect of discriminating against one-earner married couples.

The history of the controversy over how to tax married couples goes back to 1948 and to the difference between community property states (in

are perceived as unfair, there will be constant pressure to adjust the mix, and each adjustment of the mix changes the distribution of the tax burden and sparks further protests. Both the income tax (see boxed material) and the property tax have been subjected to such serial complaints and redistribution of the burden in recent decades. Homeowners have protested their property tax burdens in many states, persuading legislators to shift the burden to industrial, commercial, rental, and personal property. Industry has also sought tax relief by threatening local governments with the loss of jobs and income if the industry moves or shuts down. In South Carolina, such relief to industry and

(CONTINUED)

the West and Southwest, including California) and the rest of the country. In community property states, all income and all assets are considered to be the equal property of both spouses, regardless of who earned the income or acquired the asset. In those states, married couples could file separate federal income tax returns and each claim half the income for tax purposes, even though it was all earned by only one of the partners in the marriage. With progressive tax rates (and tax rates were very progressive and very high in the 1940s), income splitting saved a significant amount of taxes for residents of community property states. But the majority of Americans did not live in community property states and could not take advantage of income splitting. Residents of other states raised two challenges: (1) The federal government could not impose different tax liabilities based solely on the state of residence and (2) the tax law discriminated against what was then considered the norm, the single-earner household. (Married couples who both worked could file two returns based on their separate earnings, then and now.) The result of litigation on this issue was the creation of the joint tax return.

The 2001 change in the tax law has the effect of gradually extending the community property principle to everyone. Earnings by married couples, whether with one earner or two, are taxed at rates that are equivalent to two single persons by doubling the sizes of the tax brackets and the standard deduction for married filers compared to single filers. This solution will probably hold for a while.

Unfortunately, the problem of defining equity among two-earner couples, one-earner couples, single persons, and heads of households has refused to be resolved in an acceptable manner for any length of time. Now that married couples can essentially split their income regardless of whether it was earned by one or both, the high earner with a spouse pays lower taxes than a single person with the same income. Two-earner couples pay the same tax as a one-earner couple with the same income even though they incurred higher (nondeductible) costs of earning that income in terms of commuting costs and foregone leisure. And people who maintained households for dependents, whose economic situation was similar to that of married couples, did not get the same tax advantage.

Every major reform of the federal income tax since 1948, including the 2001 change, has tackled this problem with different approaches. In the 1980s, a short-lived two-earner tax credit was applied to the second income. The 2001 change, once it has been phased in, does not completely eliminate the marriage penalty, especially in higher income brackets, although it does reduce it somewhat. When it comes to equity and a progressive income tax, no legislation is going to satisfy enough people long enough to become a permanent solution.

1. James Alm and Leslie A. Whittington, "The rise and Fall and Rise . . . of the Marriage Tax," *National Tax Journal*, XLIX(4) (December 1996): 571–589.

homeowners was followed by demands for relief from property taxes on automobiles.

Regressive, Proportional, and Progressive Taxation

Although designing tax systems for equity is a highly normative issue, there are some positive ways of at least measuring the impact of alternative tax structures on different groups. The central equity issue is almost always framed as one of tax burdens relative to income. Once the distribution of the tax burden for alternative tax systems is clearly understood, a tax structure can be developed (or reformed) that represents some consensus about how the tax burden should be distributed across income classes. Within the context of that tax system, the narrower issues of equity like the one just posed can be addressed as a matter of fine-tuning the tax system.

Regardless of whether the actual base of the revenue source is expenditures (such as the retail sales tax), assets (such as the property tax), income (income or payroll taxes), some specialized economic activity (excise taxes or severance taxes), or actual use of government services (fees and charges), the measure used to compute this burden is to calculate the burden as a percentage of income. Taxes and tax/revenue systems are then classified as regressive, proportional, or progressive according to whether that percentage decreases, remains the same, or increases as income rises.

A **regressive tax** takes a smaller percentage of income as income rises. A poll tax is the ultimate regressive tax, because it is a flat fee per person. A poll tax of $100 a year represents 2% of income for a person earning $5,000 a year, dropping to 1% at $10,000, 0.1% at $100,000, and continuing to decline as income rises. Retail sales taxes are regressive because they generally do not cover services, and the consumption of services becomes a larger share of total spending as income rises. Retail sales taxes are also regressive because they only tax spending; saving is exempt, and saving rises as income rises. Because the base of the retail sales tax does not increase at the same rate as the increase in income, it is regressive. (We will explore this issue further in Chapter 11.) Some excise taxes are regressive, while others are not, depending on how consumption patterns for cigarettes, gasoline, alcohol, and other items subject to excise taxes vary with income.

A **proportional tax** takes a constant fraction of income as income rises. It is difficult to find examples of truly proportional taxes in the U.S. tax system. A payroll tax such as the Social Security tax or many local income taxes (such as those used by cities in Ohio and counties in Maryland) appears to be proportional because they take a constant fraction of income with no exemptions or deductions. However, these kinds of taxes exclude other kinds of income such as interest and dividends, which tend to go mainly to higher income families. Social Security taxes are collected only on wages and salaries, not nonwage income, and even then the tax is limited to a wage and salary ceiling that is adjusted each year. Consequently, all of these taxes that appear to be proportional are at least moderately regressive. Some states, such as Illinois, have simple, flat income taxes that take a constant percentage of all income (not just payroll or wage and salary) without any deductions or exemptions. These taxes are correctly classified as proportional.

The quotation from Adam Smith earlier in this chapter appears to support the notion of proportional taxation (". . . proportional to the revenue enjoyed under the protection of the state. . . ."). Much of the support for replacing the federal income tax with some variant of a flat tax in recent years was based on the perception that a proportional tax is fair in a way that a regressive or progressive tax is not. Even the proposed flat tax, however, was not purely proportional, because it exempted some base amount of income (making it progressive, as explained below), and also because at least some versions exempted capital gains and investment income, making the flat tax more regressive.

A **progressive tax** takes an increasing percentage of income as income rises. A tax can be made progressive in two fairly simple ways. One is to tax items that are consumed much more heavily by higher income households, such as jewelry, new cars, air travel or yachts (an experiment in the first Bush administration that was quickly abandoned). A more systematic approach is to design an income tax that exempts a certain amount for each person or household (like the personal exemption and standard deduction in the U.S. federal income tax). Consider a 10% income tax that exempts the first $20,000 in income for each person. Then the tax burden would look like Table 8–1. As you can see, as incomes get very large the tax as a percent of income gets closer and closer to 10%. Many state income taxes follow this mildly progressive pattern.

The progressivity of such an income tax with a baseline exemption can be enhanced by the use of graduated rates. In Table 8–1, in addition to exempting the first $20,000 of income, perhaps the tax rate could be 10% for the next $30,000 and 20% for income above that level—a simple two-rate tax system. If we apply that structure to Table 8–1, we get a different pattern of progressivity as shown in Table 8–2. Note that at incomes of $50,000 and above, the tax computation is a little more difficult, because income has to be segmented into parts taxed at different rates. At $100,000, for example, $20,000 is taxed at a rate of zero, $30,000 at a rate of 10%, and the last $50,000 at a rate of 20%. The degree of progressivity is the same at lower incomes but rises sharply at higher incomes.

The primary theoretical justification for a progressive rather than a proportional tax system rests on two concepts: equal sacrifice and the diminishing marginal utility of income. If all citizens have equal access to public services (some of which they may not choose to use), then there is some equity justification for asking citizens to make equal sacrifices in order to provide

Table 8-1
A Simple Progressive Income Tax

Gross Income	Taxable Income	Tax	Tax as % of Income
$10,000	0	0	0
$20,000	0	0	0
$30,000	$10,000	$1,000	3.3%
$40,000	$20,000	$2,000	5.0%
$50,000	$30,000	$3,000	6.0%
$100,000	$80,000	$8,000	8.0%
$500,000	$480,000	$48,000	9.6%

Gross Income	Taxable Income	Tax	Tax as % of Income
$10,000	0	0	0
$20,000	0	0	0
$30,000	$10,000	$1,000	3.3%
$40,000	$20,000	$2,000	5.0%
$50,000	$30,000	$3,000	6.0%
$100,000	$80,000	$13,000	13.0%
$500,000	$480,000	$93,000	18.6%

those services. But what is an equal sacrifice? A poll tax takes the same number of dollars from each citizen but is a much larger share of income for the poor than the rich. Is that an equal sacrifice? Is an equal percentage of income from all (a proportional tax) fair? Or is it possible that giving up a dollar is less painful to a rich person than a poor one because of diminishing marginal utility of income?

Diminishing marginal utility of income suggests that as a person gets richer the needs/wants being met by the additional income are less urgent or add less to total utility than those met by earlier dollars, which go to food, clothing, shelter, and other basic needs. Wealthier persons may spend their dollars on culture, or gambling, or fancier homes or expensive clothes or even contributions to charity, choices that they would not have made on a lower income and which must therefore be of lower priority, value—or utility.

This concept is visualized in Figure 8–11. The marginal utility function for income, MU_V indicates that the gain in utility (*AEFB*) in moving from income *A* to income *B* is much greater than the gain in utility (*CHID*) in moving from income *C* to income *D*, even though the increased number of dollars is the same in both cases. If the gain in utility is smaller in moving from *C* to *D* than from *A* to *B*, then the loss in utility (and particularly the deadweight loss, *HIJ* versus *GEF*) will be smaller when taxes move someone's income from *D* to *C* than when income is reduced from *B* to *A*. If individuals are similar in their capacity to enjoy income, so that their marginal utility schedules for income are similar, then the utility loss from an equal tax would be greater for a poor person than a rich one. This argument of diminishing marginal utility is often used to argue against regressive taxation, where an equal dollar sacrifice translates into a greater utility loss. It is used with somewhat less conviction to argue for progressive rather than proportional taxation.

There are more pragmatic grounds for having at least some progressive taxes in the tax system. First, such taxes can raise substantial amounts of revenue. Second, it is inevitable that some taxes in the system will be regressive. It is very difficult to design a structure of sales taxes, for example, that is not at least moderately regressive. Having at least one progressive tax in the system may create some balance that moves the overall tax structure toward the equity measure that is easiest to defend, proportionality. On the negative side,

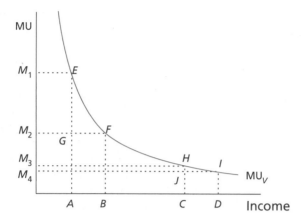

Figure 8–11
Diminishing Marginal Utility of Income

high marginal rates will cause greater distortion in decisions by those subject to those rates, and they may often respond by devoting more effort to tax avoidance or evasion than to productive work in order to increase their after-tax income.

Particular taxes may be inequitable along many lines, not just regressive. They may discriminate against (or for) singles versus married couples, home-owners versus renters, older people versus young families, wage earners versus self-employed persons. But other parts of the tax system may compensate for those weaknesses, tilting the equity back toward the center. Any tax and any proposed tax change need to be viewed in the context of the overall tax system.

SUMMARY

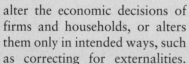

The theoretical issues in tax design can be classed as issues of efficiency and issues of equity. A tax is said to be efficient if it does not alter the economic decisions of firms and households, or alters them only in intended ways, such as correcting for externalities. Taxes reduce consumer surplus, or the difference between what individuals pay for their purchases and their value or utility. Some of the consumer surplus is transferred to the government to finance public services, but some portion of it (the deadweight loss, excess burden, or Harberger triangle) is just lost. That loss is the efficiency cost of collecting taxes. The size of the loss rises with the square of the tax rate.

The burden of a tax on consumption or spending is apportioned between the buyer and seller differently depending on the elasticities of supply and demand. If demand is relatively inelastic, more of the burden falls on the buyer in the form of higher prices paid, while if supply is relatively inelastic, more of the burden falls on the seller in the form of lower net price received. The allocation of the burden is referred to as incidence. Shifting refers to the change in incidence from the party originally responsible for collecting and remitting the tax to another party.

Tax shifting and incidence and measurement of excess burden can be represented with shadow demand curves. The shadow demand curve for a specific tax (one based on volume, weight, or quantity) is parallel to the regular demand curve, while the shadow demand for an *ad valorem* tax (percentage of price) will be flatter than the regular demand curve because the difference widens as the price gets higher. The vertical distance between the two curves is the amount of the tax.

The excess burden triangle increases in proportion to the square of the tax rate and is inversely related to the elasticities of demand and supply. The net effect of a tax increase on revenue is the outcome of the higher rate itself (positive) and the resulting erosion of the tax base (negative). If the rate is high enough, further increases could reduce rather than increase revenue.

Income and payroll taxes distort the income–leisure trade-off. In some cases work effort may increase to maintain income; in other cases work effort may decrease as the opportunity cost of leisure declines.

All taxes ultimately fall on households in one way or another as consumers, workers, stockholders, and owners of business firms. Tax subsidies and tax expenditures are intended to alter people's decisions in order to correct externalities, encourage desirable activities, and in some cases, to redistribute income. Short-run effects of tax changes are often different (more revenue, less base erosion) than long-run effects because long-run elasticities of demand are greater.

Equity in tax design involves both horizontal and vertical equity, both of which are difficult to define or measure. Equity in a tax system is based on two principles, ability to pay and the benefit principle. The ability to pay criterion favors a proportional tax over either regressive or progressive taxes, which take (respectively) smaller and smaller or larger and larger shares of one's income as income rises. However, a system with multiple revenue sources can and probably will include a mixture of regressive, proportional, and progressive taxes. The important measure is the equity of the revenue structure rather than a particular tax or fee.

A complementary equity principle that is useful in some circumstances is the benefit principle, which attempts to assign tax/fee burdens in proportion to the intensity of use of the public service that is being financed from that revenue source. An example is a gasoline tax. Fees that cover part of the cost of public services are also based on the benefit principle.

An income tax can be progressive even with just one rate if there is a base amount exempt from the tax. The arguments for progressive taxation are (1) diminishing marginal utility of income and the principle of equal sacrifice and (2) as a balancing component of a revenue system that also includes regressive elements.

KEY TERMS AND CONCEPTS

poll tax, 159
consumer surplus, 159
shadow demand (supply) curve, 159
excess burden, 160
deadweight loss, 160

shifting (of tax burden), 162
incidence, 162
specific tax, 162
ad valorem tax, 163
Laffer curve, 168
ability to pay, 172

benefit principle, 173
regressive tax, 176
proportional tax, 176
progressive tax, 177

DISCUSSION QUESTIONS

1. Tax incidence can be measured with shadow supply curves instead of shadow demand curves. When a tax is imposed, it can be visualized with a shadow supply curve S_T, which lies above and to the left of the original supply curve. Using that information, analyze both a specific tax on gasoline and an *ad valorem* tax on gasoline and determine the new price and quantity and the division of the tax burden between buyer and seller. Do you think your conclusions would be any different if you used a shadow demand curve instead of a shadow supply curve? Why or why not?

2. Suppose that you work for the state legislature's Ways and Means Committee. The committee is searching for a way to pay for beachfront improvements along the coast, which is visited by both residents and nonresidents in large numbers. Taking into account equity as well as efficiency considerations, come up with a mixture of at least three revenue sources to finance these improvements. Justify your choices.

3. Supply and demand analysis can also be used to think about other kinds of taxes, such as the payroll tax. The payroll tax in the United States is legally shared equally between the employer and the employee, each paying 7.6% of wages. Using graphs, analyze the incidence and excess burden of this tax under each of these conditions:
   a. Labor supply is perfectly elastic.
   b. Both labor supply and demand are highly elastic.
   c. Labor supply is relatively inelastic, labor demand is relatively elastic.
   d. Labor supply is relatively elastic, labor demand is relatively inelastic.

4. A state legislator asks you to figure out how to eliminate the property tax and replace the lost revenue with a higher sales tax. Both the sales tax and the property tax currently provide about 25% of total state and local revenue. She wants to know how high the sales rate would have to be. What arguments would you use to persuade her that this is not such a good idea, using the concept of elasticity, Figure 8–10, and Eq. (8–4) in your answer.

5. Which of the following taxes do you think would cause the larger deadweight loss? Why?
   a. A poll tax or a sales tax
   b. A sales tax on both services and goods or a sales tax only on goods
   c. An income tax only on interest and dividends or an income tax on income from all sources
   d. A tax on soft drinks or a tax on all beverages

CHAPTER 9

PRINCIPLES OF TAXATION 2: PRACTICAL PROBLEMS IN TAX DESIGN

Armed with the theoretical considerations in tax system design from Chapter 8, what else do policy makers need to consider? This chapter addresses some of the more pragmatic considerations that enter into the design of a revenue system as well as some of the implementation issues faced when making changes to that system.

The criteria developed here and in Chapter 8 will be applied in subsequent chapters to the four broad groups of related revenue sources: income taxes, consumption/sales taxes, wealth/property taxes, and fees and charges. Within each of these four groups there are broad-based taxes, such as the federal individual income tax and the retail sales tax, as well as narrow taxes with limited bases, such as some state taxes on interest and dividend income or excise taxes on tobacco and alcohol. Table 9–1 identifies the principal taxes and nontax revenue sources within each of these four groups. Not all criteria are relevant to a particular tax or revenue source. The goal of tax policy is to create a revenue system with desirable attributes even if not every individual component scores high on all or most of those attributes.

CRITERIA FOR TAX/REVENUE SYSTEM DESIGN

Taxes and nontax revenue sources have a number of different attributes. Chapter 8 made it clear that different revenue sources have different impacts on taxpayer economic decisions (efficiency

Table 9-1
Major Revenue
Sources for Federal,
State, and Local
Governments

	Used by
Income Taxes	
Individual income taxes*	F, S, L
Payroll taxes	F, S, L
Corporate income taxes	F, S, L
Business licenses**	L
Consumption/Sales Taxes	
Value-added taxes	(not used in United States)
Gross receipts taxes	S
Retail sales taxes	S, L
Excise/selective sales taxes†	F, S, L
Tariffs/import duties	F
Wealth/Property Taxes	
Real estate taxes	S, L
Personal property taxes	S, L
Poll taxes	(not used in United States)
Inheritance taxes	S
Estate taxes	F
Fees and Charges (Nontax revenues)	
Licenses	F, S, L
Franchise fees	F, S, L
Permits	F, S, L
Service charges	F, S, L
Penalties/fines	F, S, L
Earnings on investments	F, S, L

*Including both broad-based income taxes and those that only tax passive income (interest, dividends, rents, and royalties).
**Business licenses that are based on gross receipts or net receipts (sometimes by class of business) should be considered a form of income tax.
†Imposed on such diverse bases as alcohol, tobacco, telephone service, gasoline, automobile tires, gambling revenues, accommodations, air flight departures, rental cars, amusements/admissions, and so forth.

effects) and on the distribution of income and wealth (equity effects). Some taxes generate more revenue than others. Some are sensitive to economic growth and inflation, while others are not. Some revenue sources are stable, others volatile. Some are readily apparent to taxpayers, while others are hidden. Some taxes are complicated or expensive to collect or to pay, while others are not. Finally, taxes are used as a competitive tool by nations, states, and local governments, with different taxes having different competitive effects. Different taxes or revenue sources will score higher on some of these criteria and lower on others. A good tax system will use a mix of taxes with different desired characteristics.

Efficiency and Equity

Chapter 8 was largely devoted to an analysis of the theory of taxation from both an efficiency and an equity perspective. Taxes that minimize unintended distortions of economic decisions in the private sector while steering taxpayers toward desired choices involving externalities are the foundation of a good revenue system. Designing taxes that achieve both equity (ability to pay and benefit principle) and revenue objectives is also important to creating a good revenue system. Recognizing that all revenue sources have weaknesses in terms of both equity and efficiency, Chapter 8 led to the logical conclusion that a good revenue system relies on a diversity of sources. As additional criteria are developed, bear in mind that the criteria of efficiency and equity remain at the top of the list in selecting and designing both taxes and nontax revenue sources.

Adequacy

A revenue system has to generate adequate funds to pay for the desired level of public services. **Adequacy** is a tricky concept, because revenue and services are not clearly linked. Unlike private markets, public revenues and expenditures do not have a one-to-one correspondence in the form of payment for goods sold or services rendered. Some kinds of revenue systems could generate too much revenue relative to the optimal level and mix of public services to be funded. Legislators awash in funds are rarely without pet projects to fund, and they will respond to a revenue windfall with additional spending, although sometimes they do respond to rapid revenue growth with tax cuts. The fear that the revenue system would prove "too adequate" drove many of the tax and expenditure limitations enacted in the 1970s and 1980s, and that was the foundation for the huge 2001 federal income tax reduction. At other times, revenue can fall short of the amount needed to fund basic services at the desired level. After many years of revenue increases, a number of states found themselves back in the era of tight budgets, looming deficits, and program cuts in 2001 and beyond.

In general, a revenue system needs to provide revenue growth that at least matches the increase in population and in the costs of inputs into providing public goods and services. The system may also need to keep pace with real income growth, because demand for public services as a complement to private consumption can be expected to increase as the standard of living rises.

Unlike other attributes, adequacy is more a property of a revenue system as a whole than of a particular tax or revenue source. But some taxes (or revenue sources) contribute more to adequacy than others. At least one tax with a broad base—income, retail sales, or property—is an essential part of the revenue system for each level of government in order to ensure adequacy. In most cases, states and their local governments use all three. Those states that attempt to rely on only two of those three (or in the case of New Hampshire, only one) find it difficult to fund public services and are forced to use fairly high rates for the broad-based taxes they do collect. (Alaska is an exception because of other unusual revenue sources.) Five states have no retail sales tax: Delaware, New Hampshire, Montana, Oregon, and Alaska. Nine states do not have a full-scale personal income tax. In the absence of a broad-based income tax, Tennessee has leaned heavily on a very high rate for its retail sales tax. Florida tried to compensate for its lack of an income tax in the 1990s with an unsuccessful attempt to broaden the base of the retail sales tax to include many services. Texas, also with no state income tax, has found it very difficult to equalize revenue among school districts because schools in that state rely primarily on local property tax funding, and the property tax base is distributed very unevenly among districts.

Specialty taxes—accommodations, admissions, severance, alcohol, gasoline—make a contribution to adequacy. But with a few exceptions (accommodations taxes for major tourism destination cities, royalties and severance taxes in mineral-rich states) these more narrowly based taxes score low on the adequacy criterion.

Ensuring and defending adequacy means that legislators must be sensitive to the dangers of base erosion. Adding exemptions to the sales tax, increasing deductions on the income tax, and using corporate income tax breaks to lure industry all exact a cost in terms of not just current revenue adequacy but also future revenue flows.

Stability

Some of the revenue sources in the overall system need to offer a cushion of **stability,** particularly for state and local governments that must balance their budgets annually through recessions as well as periods of prosperity. Stability means that the revenue flow is not unduly sensitive to fluctuations in economic activity.

Stability is not as important a criterion for the central government, which can run deficits during recessions and surpluses during prosperous years (although the U.S. government has only recently returned to that historic pattern after 30 years of sizable deficits). But most state governments are required to balance their budgets by statute or constitutional law, and local governments have little leeway in running deficits. For local governments, an important positive attribute of the property tax is its stability. For the two major state taxes, the appropriate measure of stability is the short-run income elasticity of the tax base. That is, does the tax base fluctuate more than, less than, or about the same as fluctuations in gross state product or state personal income? The base of the state individual income tax is either personal taxable income, for which the short-run tax elasticity is 1.164, or adjusted gross income, with an elasticity of 0.970.[1] These two estimates

---

1. These estimates are from Russell S. Sobol and Randall G. Holcombe, "Measuring the Growth and Variability of Tax Bases," *National Tax Journal,* Vol. XLIX(4) (December 1996): pp. 535–552.

THE NEW HAMPSHIRE STORY

Only two states use neither a broad-based personal income tax nor a retail sales tax. Alaska, which ranks first among the 50 states in both total and general revenue, both per capita and as a percentage of income, is a special exception. Its uniqueness stems from its vast area, small population, immense earnings on mineral resources, and Federal payments of various kinds. Alaska actually has a reverse income tax for permanent residents. Payments are sent out each year from surplus funds after providing necessary public services to the state's 500,000 residents.

Unlike Alaska, New Hampshire has no special sources of funds. Fiscal conservatism, Yankee thriftiness, and a strong antitax mentality have made New Hampshire the only state in the lower 48 to get along thus far without either a retail sales tax or a broad-based income tax. But that uniqueness is under fire, in part due to steady in-migration, and may be about to change.

How has New Hampshire managed to provide public services thus far without the two workhorses of state tax systems, income and retail sales taxes? First, the state spends less. The state ranks 50th in both total revenue and general revenue as a percent of personal income. New Hampshire ranks higher than 50th in per capita spending because it enjoys a relatively high per capita income, but its 1998 state per capita total revenue of $3,384 and general revenue of $2,504 were both well below the U.S. averages of $4,062 and $3,206, respectively.

To compensate for the lack of a retail sales tax or a broad-based income tax, New Hampshire has leaned harder on the property tax as well as other specialized revenue sources. At $1,160 per capita in 1996, New Hampshire ranked first in per capita property taxes. New Hampshire was the first state to institute a lottery in this century, starting in 1964, and also generates substantial revenue from state-operated liquor stores and a variety of excise taxes. Court tests have upheld challenges to a 1999 statewide property tax for aid to schools, which transfers funds from about 50 wealthy communities to other, poorer locations.

But all good things are likely to come to an end. In the 1999, 2000, and 2001 sessions of the legislature, efforts were made to institute a state income tax. Because heavy reliance on the property tax to pay for education results in inequities in school funding, a court case has forced the state to consider alternatives. Remedying this problem is estimated to require between $650 million and $1 billion in new funding. While legislators considered a statewide property tax, video gambling, and additional excise taxes, an income tax also had considerable support. It is likely that within the next decade both Alaska and New Hampshire will bow to the need for a second broad-based tax, as other states with more generous public services and fewer unique revenue sources concluded many years ago.

suggest that the base of the income tax fluctuates at about the same rate or slightly more so than underlying total income. Revenue from an income tax that is indexed, like the U.S. federal income tax and many state income taxes, will fluctuate less in proportion to changes in personal income than one that is not.

However, if the tax rate structure has any progressivity to it, the revenue will fluctuate more than the tax base even with indexing for two reasons. First, as real incomes rise, people will find themselves in higher tax brackets during expansions; when real incomes decline, they will be in lower tax brackets during recession. Second, the exempt amount (personal exemptions and standard deductions), even after indexing, becomes a smaller proportion of total personal or adjusted gross income during expansions and a larger proportion during recessions.

Retail sales have a short-term income elasticity of 1.039. For those states that do not tax food, the income elasticity of nonfood retail sales is 1.377.[2] These numbers mean that a 1% increase in personal income will generate a 1.039% increase in retail sales tax revenue in general, or a 1.377% increase in states that do not tax food. These elasticities imply that the retail sales tax tracks short-term income fluctuations pretty closely if food is taxed, but will vary much more over the course of recessions and expansions in states where food is not subject to sales tax. The commonsense explanation for this greater fluctuation in states that do not tax food is that the nonfood part of the tax base is more volatile. Some purchases of consumer durables (appliances, cars, furniture) and nondurables (housewares, clothing) can be postponed during times of unemployment or economic uncertainty. These items play a larger role as sources of sales tax revenue, particularly when food is not included in the tax base.

The corporate income tax, which is a substantial revenue source in some states, is extremely sensitive to fluctuations in income because profit or net corporate income is very sensitive to recessions and expansions. The short-run elasticity of corporate taxable income is estimated at 3.562, meaning that a 1% change in income results in more than a 3% change in corporate net income.

Stability has a price. A tax or revenue source that is stable over the business cycle tends to be unresponsive to growth in population, income, or the price level (inflation). For this reason, a stable tax is an important component of the revenue mix, but it needs to be balanced with other taxes that are more responsive. Some taxes, like the retail sales tax, lie toward the middle of the spectrum of these two opposing attributes. The retail sales tax is more stable than the individual income tax at both the state and national level but is moderately sensitive to income growth and somewhat more sensitive to population growth and inflation.

Sensitivity to Growth and Inflation

The mirror image of stability is sensitivity to growth and inflation, which allows government revenues and expenditures to keep pace with changing costs and needs. Growth has three different components: (1) population growth, (2) income growth, and (3) inflation. To understand the interaction between these three types of growth, imagine a community of 1,000 people with a total personal income of $12 million, which comes to $12,000 per capita. Suppose that in this year personal income has risen to $15 million, a 25% increase.

2. *Ibid.*

Population has increased to 1,100, and the price level has risen by 8%. What are the components of that growth?

Do not be tempted to think of this question as one of simple addition. Suppose that over some period, personal income is up by 25%. Population has risen by 10%, and prices by 8%, leaving the other 7% of personal income growth as real growth in per capita income. Finding the answer by simple addition may be approximately correct if all the numbers are small, but not in this case. Table 9–2 shows how to break down that increase into its components. Note that the steps in the table take place sequentially such that personal income is first divided by population and then by the price index (1.00 for the first year, 1.08 for the second year, to show 8% inflation). This sequence leads to a more accurate result than does addition. Particularly over long time periods, or during periods of rapid population growth or high inflation rates, trying to add (or subtract) the various elements of growth will give increasingly inaccurate results.

Growth needs to be separated into these three components before evaluating the sensitivity of revenue sources to growth for two reasons. First, some revenue sources are sensitive (or not) only to inflation, or only to population, or (more rarely) only to real income growth. Second, demands for public expenditures react differently to each of these three components of nominal income growth.

As the population grows, revenue needs to grow in order to finance the additional services required by a growing population, although the correspondence is not necessarily one to one. Population growth may involve scale economies in the provision of some services, so that revenue does not need to grow quite as fast as population. The additional revenue required to serve a growing population also depends on where the new residents are located (infill versus new development, rural versus urban, isolated versus clustered in subdivisions), what the age distribution of the new residents is, and whether there is a concentration of special needs populations. California, Texas, and Florida have incurred high expenditure demands because their borders are major points of entry for immigrant workers, which places above-average demands on school systems and social services. Any population growth in young families will create demand for more spending on the largest component of local government expense, public education. Older citizens typically have lower service demands.

It is more difficult to find clear links between growth of population and growth on the revenue side of the ledger. Retail sales tend to be tied to population growth, particularly at younger ages, that is, a high birth rate will increase retail sales more than an influx of retirees. The residential and commercial components of the property tax base reflect population growth, but in some cases the quality (and therefore taxable value) of the property will grow faster than population if new developments are upscale. In other cases those values will grow more slowly if, for example, an area experiences mushrooming mobile home parks and low-income housing develop-

Table 9-2 Decomposing Income Growth	Year 1 (Population: 1,000)	Year 2 (Population: 1,100)	Year 3
Personal income	$12,000,000	$15,000,000	25.0%
Per capita income	$12,000	$13,636	13.6%
Per capita income adjusted for inflation (8%)	$12,000	$12,626	5.2%

ments. In this case, the income of the new residents will be the deciding factor as to whether property tax revenue grows faster than, more slowly than, or at about the same pace as population. The same is true, obviously, of income tax revenue.

Inflation also impacts both the expenditure and revenue sides of government budgets. Inflation drives up the cost of providing public services. The revenue side is more complicated. Prolonged periods of inflation result in increased demands for real property, especially houses and undeveloped land, as an inflation hedge (because their values tend to rise at least as fast as the general price level). Property values tend to rise more rapidly than the overall inflation rate, increasing property tax revenues faster than the rate of inflation, as they did most notably in California in the 1970s, resulting in the property tax revolt. Until the federal income tax code and most state income taxes were indexed for inflation (mostly in the mid-1980s), revenues from income taxes also tended to grow very rapidly during periods of inflation.[3] With indexing, inflation has little or no effect on individual income tax revenues, although growth in real income does increase revenue. Retail sales tax revenue tracks the inflation rate fairly closely if the inflation is spread broadly over the full range of goods and services. When inflation is largely concentrated in such items as health care and housing, both of which are not subject to retail sales taxes, then sales tax revenue is more likely to lag behind the rate of inflation.

Real income (income adjusted for inflation) grows with population but also independently. During the 1960s through 1990s, the average rate of real growth of personal income has been about 2.5% a year, and the average rate of growth of real per capita income has been about 1.4% a year. If real per capita income grows, revenue will increase from all major and most minor sources because spending, income, and property values will all increase. Real income growth will also result in increased demand for government services.

Economists Sobol and Holcombe have also measured the sensitivity of the bases for the major state taxes to long-term income growth (which reflects all three kinds of growth, population, inflation, and real income). Personal

3. Indexing in the U.S. income tax system refers to the annual adjustment of the personal exemption and the standard deduction, described in Chapter 10 by the same percentage as the increase in the price index.

taxable income has a long-run elasticity of 1.215, and adjusted gross income a long-run elasticity of 0.945, again tracking income to some degree but perhaps growing a little faster than income. Retail sales tax elasticity is quite low over the longer time frame with an elasticity of 0.66 (0.701 when food is excluded), and so is corporate taxable income (elasticity = 0.670).[4] States that rely solely on sales taxes are at a disadvantage when trying to generate revenue to keep pace with long-term growth of population, inflation, and the demand for public services associated with real income growth.

Visibility

One of the more controversial attributes of a tax or tax system is **visibility,** or how obvious the amount of tax being paid is to taxpayers and others. Value-added taxes (see Chapter 11) are typically low visibility because they are reflected in the quoted prices of goods, while retail sales taxes are much more visible because they are added to the quoted price at the time of purchase. However, people are not very aware of how much they pay annually in retail sales taxes because this type of tax is collected frequently and in small amounts. The painful visibility of income taxes, likewise, is reduced by weekly or monthly withholding. Property taxes, in contrast, are extremely visible because they are usually collected in a lump sum once a year. In parts of the country where town meetings are held to vote on the local budget and the tax rate, taxes are also highly visible.

Is visibility desirable? It depends on one's perspective. Those who think that government is too large prefer that taxes be highly visible so that the pain of paying taxes will be weighed carefully against the benefits from government services, especially at the margin. Others argue that, because many government services are low visibility, taxes should be equally low in visibility in order to avoid limiting the size and scope of government activity to a level that is less than optimal. In practice, the mix of taxes and revenue sources in the system ranges from high visibility (property taxes) to moderate visibility (sales taxes, payroll taxes) to low visibility (excise taxes included in the price). Likewise, government services range from high visibility (road repairs, trash pickup, schools) to moderate visibility (national defense, parks, prisons) to low visibility (building inspection, financial administration).

Taxes can be made more visible in a variety of ways. Referenda, usually on bond issues for schools and other capital expenses, give taxpayers a chance to directly weigh an increase in taxes against an increase in services. Stating the retail sales tax separately from the price, a practice in most states with retail sales taxes, makes it more visible. Posting the excise tax on the pump at gas stations is another way to try to make consumers more aware of how much of what they pay is for the product itself and how much is tax.

---

4. Sobol and Holcombe, "Measuring the Growth." (op. cit.)

Collection and Compliance Costs

In addition to the excess burden discussed in Chapter 8, there is an even more direct cost of transferring revenue from taxpayers to governments that does not get transferred into increased government services. To collect taxes, bureaucracies must be created to interpret the tax laws and ensure that taxes are collected. The cost of printing forms, processing and auditing returns, and assessing tax liabilities is the **collection cost.**

Taxpayers also incur costs in addition to the excess burden. They have to keep records, fill out forms, go through audits, and pay tax accountants to make sure that they are in compliance. These costs that fall on the taxpayers are called **compliance costs.** Some taxes are costly to administer but not to comply with, like the property tax, while others are burdensome on both the tax collector and the taxpayer, like the individual income tax. In some cases, compliance costs fall on third parties, such as employers who must keep the records and file the returns for Social Security taxes or retailers who must collect and remit the retail sales tax.

The remaining tariffs imposed by the federal government probably win the "prize" in terms of collection costs, because they cost more to administer than they generate in revenue. However, these residual tariffs are not designed to raise revenue, but to protect certain industries from foreign competition. In the early days of the nation, the tariff was a primary source of federal government revenue. Today's collection costs are only high relative to the small amount of revenue generated. If politicians chose to impose more and higher tariffs, as the United States did prior to 1934, then the collection costs would be a relatively small percentage of the amount of revenue generated.

Although compliance costs for property taxes are low, these taxes are quite expensive to administer because of the need to assess the market value of a variety of assets, and to handle disputes and appeals over the values assigned. Being the property tax assessor is one of the more frustrating tasks in local government!

A few rules of thumb can provide some guidance in reducing these costs. As a general rule, it is cheaper in terms of collection costs to administer a tax centrally rather than locally, because each local government will need its own staff. Substantial economies of scale in tax administration result in counties collecting property taxes on behalf of municipalities and states collecting and distributing local sales taxes on behalf of their cities and counties. It is also less expensive to administer a broad-based income tax than one with many exemptions, exclusions, adjustments, and deductions. For retail sales taxes, it is less costly to administer and to comply with a tax that is broad based in terms of tangible goods, because neither the tax collector nor the retailer has to worry much about separating taxable from nontaxable sales. On the other hand, expanding the tax to include services increases the costs of both collection and compliance because of the large number of very small firms that have to be included in the process.

TARGETING INDIVIDUALS, FIRMS, PRODUCTS, AND SERVICES

Some taxes in the system, and features within those taxes, score poorly on several, most, or sometimes all of the criteria just listed. For example, consider the exemption of food from the retail sales tax; about two-thirds of the states with retail sales taxes exempt food, and this number is increasing.[5] Eliminating food from the base means that the retail sales tax produces less revenue (reducing adequacy) and is less stable over the course of the business cycle. A retail sales tax without food in the base is also more costly to comply with and to collect, because the retailer (and the tax collector) must carefully distinguish between taxable and exempt items. Although the food exemption is touted as a way to help the poor, and it does appear to make the sales tax less regressive, it is a relatively inefficient equity tool, because the tax savings go to all income levels, not just the poor.

So why is the exemption so popular? In part this exemption is used because taxing food is highly visible, which makes the exemptions small contribution to equity more visible and hence more politically popular. This exemption is also in part a response to the notion of basic rights to food and shelter regardless of ability to pay, an important cultural norm that may override the rather arid principles of good tax design. Almost every tax has some anomalies of this sort that transcend economic considerations in the name of some other purpose, value, or interest group.

Some provisions in the tax law are intentionally designed to encourage or discourage specific kinds of consumption or production activities. Taxes on alcohol and tobacco, also known as sumptuary taxes, are intended to discourage the consumption of harmful substances (and there is still a strong constituency to add marijuana to the list as a legal but taxed-and-discouraged substance). Taxes on emissions of various kinds that reduce the quality of air or water are intended to correct negative externalities. Tax breaks for energy-efficiency retrofitting are still a part of the federal tax code.

TAX EXPENDITURES

When provisions are inserted into the tax law to exempt certain taxpayers, organizations, or activities from taxation, or to reduce their tax burden relative to others, a measurable loss of revenue results. (The loss of revenue depends on the tax rate, the amount of the activity prior to the exemption, and the responsiveness of the activity to the stimulus of the tax break.) That rev-

---

5. Historically, most of the states that tax food are in the South, but in just the last few years the South has seen a movement to eliminate food from the sales tax base. Georgia and Louisiana have removed the sales tax on food, and North Carolina is in the process of reducing it.

enue foregone is more or less equivalent to a direct expenditure on the exempted good or service and is thus known as a **tax expenditure.**

Many tax expenditures favor charitable organizations. These nonprofit firms that meet certain tests (mainly not using their funds for lobbying purposes) are often exempt from paying state sales taxes and local property taxes, and contributions to such organizations are deductible for federal and many state income tax purposes. Their net income is considered "surplus" rather than a taxable "profit" and is not subject to income taxes at any level. The revenue lost from the federal income tax deduction for charitable contributions alone was estimated at $26 billion in 2000.

At the federal level, a list of tax expenditures has been included in the budget beginning with the Congressional Budget Act of 1974. These tax expenditures run to hundreds of billions of dollars, with the largest share coming from the federal income tax. The top-ranked categories are employee fringe benefits: exclusion of pension contributions and earnings in employer plans ($84 billion in 2000) and employer contributions to medical insurance and medical care ($78 billion). The 15 largest tax expenditures in the income tax accounted for revenue loss of more than $500 billion in the 2000 budget forecast. In addition to the two fringe benefit items, the top 15 tax expenditures included deductions for mortgage interest, state and local taxes, and charitable contributions; treatment of capital gains and accelerated depreciation; and exclusion of municipal bond interest, IRA contributions, and Social Security benefits from income.

Tax expenditures have both advantages and drawbacks in comparison to either direct expenditures as a means of furthering a particular social goal. Tax expenditures are less visible and thus easier to enact, which is both an advantage and a drawback. They are less likely to come up for annual review. Because they create demand in the private sector for delivery of services, they develop strong lobbying constituencies. Consider, for example, how banks, home builders, and realtors defend the mortgage interest deduction.[6] They can be put into effect more quickly than direct expenditures and do not create an administrative bureaucracy, although they do increase the cost of tax administration. Finally, they create tax relief for activities that were already ongoing or would have been undertaken anyway, so that their marginal impact in offering incentives requires a fairly high expenditure over the total range of the target activity to achieve an often modest increase or decrease. For example, how much additional home ownership is there as a result of the mortgage interest deduction, and how much tax revenue did it cost to provide that relief both to those who required an incentive and those who did not? Rather than encourage home ownership, did the tax incentive merely make it possible for many home buyers to buy larger and more expensive homes than they would otherwise have

6. For a thorough analysis of the pros and cons of tax expenditures, see Christopher Howard, "Testing the Tools Approach: Tax Expenditures Versus Direct Expenditures," *Public Administration Review,* 55(5) (September–October 1995): pp. 439–447.

chosen? Perhaps it would be more efficient to target particular populations through a direct subsidy, such as a voucher or a mortgage guarantee. Tax expenditures remain a very popular policy tool, but they are not always the best way to attain a particular goal at the lowest possible cost.

IMPLEMENTING AND RESISTING CHANGE

In any area of public policy the appropriate pace and amount of change is a source of debate. There are always plenty of sound bites to avoid change: "If it ain't broke, don't fix it," "The best is the enemy of the good," "Better the devil you know than the one you haven't met," etc. But there are also some important economic principles related to the stability of the tax code and the pace at which changes are implemented. Stability of the tax law and the revenue it generates is of important economic and political value. Gradualism can be an issue on the expenditure side as well. Changes in Social Security are often phased in so that people currently retired or about to retire do not feel the full impact, while younger people have more time to adjust their financial planning. The notion of Pareto optimality, or at least the compensation principle, may well be better served by gradual rather than immediate implementation.

Value of Stable Tax Rules

The tax code represents a part of the operating rules of a city, county, state, or nation, along with other structures and institutions such as contract law and penalties for misdemeanors and the right to attend public schools. People make decisions and commitments based on the current tax code and the expectation that those tax rules will continue into the future. They buy houses with 30-year mortgages, expecting to be able to deduct the mortgage interest and property taxes on their federal and state income tax returns, and they calculate how much house they can afford based on that expectation. They choose to invest in municipal bonds (which pay lower interest, but the interest is tax exempt) or in stocks that offer more hope of capital gains than dividends, based on current tax treatment of municipal bond interest, dividends, and capital gains. Firms build plants in particular locations based on certain assumptions about local property and state corporate income taxes, some of which are contractual arrangements between the government and the firm, others of which are subject to change without notice.

When the rules change, windfall gains and losses happen. Eliminating the deduction for local property taxes would result in a decline in the price of houses. The decline would vary from one section of the country to another and be greater for more expensive houses (both because their property taxes are higher and because, in a higher tax bracket, the value of the lost exemption was greater). A rate increase, a lost deduction, a broadening of the tax base all change the rules to which taxpayers have become accustomed and that were factored into their financial planning. For this reason, the federal income tax code only undergoes major revisions about every 10 years, although smaller changes are made almost every year. Even if the tax code is imperfect, or inequitable, it is not clear that the gains from frequent alteration outweigh the cost of adjustments falling on taxpayers who made decisions on the basis of existing tax rules.

Frequent changes in the tax law result in other costs as well. The period from 1986 to 1998 witnessed 6,493 changes in the federal income tax law. All of these changes have made it more difficult and expensive for the Internal Revenue Service to administer the tax code and for taxpayers to understand the rules. More than half of U.S. taxpayers now pay someone else to compute their tax returns for them, a sign of both increased complexity and frequent change.

Gradual or Rapid Implementation

The impact of a change in the tax rules can be mitigated by phasing it in, or delaying its implementation. Gradual implementation in changing tax policy or indeed in changing any policy has advantages, as noted above, but good arguments can also be made for making changes quickly and decisively. If the change in the tax rules was undertaken in order to raise more revenue and the change is implemented gradually, revenue will come in more slowly, and the total amount of revenue increase will be smaller by missing the immediate/ short-run effect when elasticities are very low. If the tax change was proposed in order to mitigate an inequity or provide desired incentives or disincentives, the gradual or delayed implementation will mean that citizens have to live with a less optimal situation in terms of either efficiency or equity for a longer period of time. Finally, tax changes should be no different from changes that take place suddenly in the market. The signals of impending change are always there well in advance, whether the change is in market interest rates or federal income tax indexing. Quick changes induce faster responses, and dynamic change is both a benefit and a cost of a market system.

What are the advantages of gradual or phased implementation of tax changes? The main advantage is an offshoot of the value of stability itself, discussed above. If taxpayers cannot have stability in the tax rules that affect their economic and financial decisions, the next best thing is to have enough time to prepare for and adapt to changes in those rules. In that way they can better shield themselves from the potential negative impact or position themselves better to experience a positive impact from a change in, say, the tax treatment of out-of-state purchases, sales tax exemptions, income tax treatment of capital gains, or changes in allowable income tax deductions. By giving taxpayers advance notice, they can act to mitigate some of the windfall redistribution of income, wealth, and tax burdens resulting from a change in the tax rules.

INTERSTATE TAX ISSUES

At the state level, efficiency and equity take on additional dimensions. In addition to the efficiency and equity dimensions of a tax discussed earlier, which apply to taxes at all levels of government, state and local governments also have to consider equity and efficiency in a competitive context. Will this change in the tax law affect decisions about locating a business, shopping out of state, choosing where to retire? Those are efficiency aspects of state (and local) taxation. How should the burden of taxation be apportioned equitably among business firms and individuals, in-state and out-of-state buyers and sellers, as well as rich and poor? How will those equity decisions affect the competitive status of this state, city, or county?

Efficiency and Interstate Competition

Interstate competition for industrial and residential location can both enhance and reduce economic efficiency. Some of the benefits of competition apply to states as well as to private firms. If states are forced to be more efficient in the provision of services in order to hold down taxes while satisfying residents' demands, then interstate competition is efficiency enhancing. Interstate competition places some important constraints on the actions of legislators and city councils to reinforce the voters' efforts to make them responsive in terms of both taxes and services.

However, interstate competition can also push governments from beyond optimal to below optimal levels of taxes and spending in attempting to make government lean and fiscal surpluses attractive to newcomers. Given the rational ignorance of most voters, and the short-term time horizon of most elected officials, success in holding down taxes and attracting industry and jobs may be more visible and more influential in voting decisions than in longer term decisions about maintaining infrastructure and providing quality public services. This argument is particularly relevant when evaluating economic development incentives.[7]

Equity and Interstate Competition

How does interstate competition to lure high-income residents and attractive industries affect the equity of the revenue structure? Tax incentives, whether for retirees (usually income and property tax relief) or industry (most often corporate income and property tax breaks), shift the burden of taxation to other groups. Some of that increased burden may fall on existing industry, including commercial and service firms. Often the tax burden falls more heav-

---

7. For a discussion of this issue, see William F. Fox and David Mayes, "Are Economic Development Incentives Too Large?" (pp. 203–209), and Douglas Woodward, "Assessing Economic Development Incentives: Lessons from BMW" (pp. 210–215), *Proceedings of the 86th Annual Conference* (Washington, DC: National Tax Association, 1994).

ORIGIN AND DESTINATION PRINCIPLES

Many individuals and firms engage in economic activities that cross state or national lines. Firms have multiple plants and buy inputs and sell their products throughout the country and beyond. Individuals may live in one state and work in another, and almost always will make some of their purchases out of state, either directly when they travel or indirectly through catalogs or the Internet. Because states have different tax bases and rates, these transactions across state lines create problems for the taxpayer and the tax collector.

For most state income taxes, the preferred solution is to apportion income according to the state(s) in which it was earned. The challenging questions occur most often in the case of sales taxes, particularly the retail sales tax imposed by 45 states and the District of Columbia. Most states consider the retail sales tax to be an obligation of the buyer, but it is collected as a matter of convenience by the seller, who may be located in another state. The same issue arose in the formation of the European Union; all six of the original member countries agreed to reform their various kinds of sales taxes into a value-added tax (discussed in Chapter 11), eventually at a uniform rate. If both buyer and seller are in the same state or country, there is no problem. But what if the seller is in one place and the buyer is in another? Which state or nation gets the revenue, and whose rate and structure apply—that of the seller (the origin principle) or that of the buyer (the destination principle)?

Two economic questions are involved in a choice between the origin and destination principle. The first economic question is where the actual economic incidence of the tax falls, that is, whether the primary effect is to raise the price paid by the buyer or to reduce the price paid by the seller. If the incidence is primarily on the buyer, then it seems appropriate that the revenues accrue to the state or nation where the buyer re-

sides. The buyer will then benefit from the services that those taxes finance. If the seller bears more of the burden, perhaps the state or nation of the seller is entitled to the revenue. In the case of a broad-based retail sales tax or value-added tax, demand is quite inelastic (because there is limited opportunity for substitution), so most of the incidence falls on the buyer, which tilts the balance toward the destination principle.

The second question is more subtle. If the state of origin is also the place of production, then one might consider state and local services—roads, police and fire protection, and so on—as inputs to the production process. In that case, one could argue that the state in which the product is produced is entitled to at least some share of the revenue.

In general, however, the incidence consideration has dominated the discussion of where to impose and collect the tax. Both the value-added tax in the European Union and retail sales taxes in the United States are imposed and collected on a destination basis.

The choice of an origin or destination principle is not merely a theoretical issue. A number of Supreme Court cases have wrestled with this question from a legal as well as an economic standpoint. States have created a complement to the retail sales tax, called a **use tax,** to ensure that their states' residents have a legal obligation to pay tax on out-of-state purchases that they bring into the state by car, truck, mail, or other delivery systems that bypass the local tax-collecting retail merchant. With the rapid growth of Internet sales, the revenue loss from being unable to require vendors to collect retail sales taxes of destination states has become an important national issue in the United States (see boxed feature later in chapter). The revenue losses that result from collecting sales taxes on the destination rather than the origin principle are substantial and growing.

ily on the state's least mobile residents, who are likely to be lower to middle-income groups. Alternatively, the quality of public services may decline as the increase in residents and firms to be served is not matched with an increase in revenue to pay for the additional services. In that case, the burden of

TAXATION OF INTERSTATE MAIL-ORDER SALES

No single issue captures all of the applied issues in tax design in the modern postindustrial economy better than the tax treatment of interstate mail-order sales. The retail sales tax is a destination principle tax. Tax (the use tax, a companion to the sales tax for out-of-state purchases) is owed by the buyer to the buyer's state. It is normally, but not always, collected from the seller. However, a series of Supreme Court cases, most notably *National Bellas Hess v. State of Illinois* (1967) ruled that a state cannot compel an out-of-state firm to collect and remit sales taxes on purchases by its residents unless the firm has some tangible link to that state. Known in legal terms as *nexus,* that connection may be a warehouse, a resident sales office, a retail outlet, a catalog store, or some other kinds of physical presence. The nexus requirement was originally based on the due process and interstate commerce clauses of the Constitution. A 1994 decision in the case of *Quill v. North Dakota,* however, determined that only the interstate commerce issue was valid, opening the door for remedial legislation by Congress, which has authority over interstate commerce. Thus far, Congress has not acted, primarily because the pres-

sure from organized mail-order retailers has been more effective and better funded than the less organized efforts of state revenue officers and competing Main Street merchants—an object lesson in the public choice principles set forth in Chapter 5.

National firms like J.C. Penney with catalog operations have nexus in most states. Some major catalog firms have gone to great lengths to avoid creating nexus in any state except the one from which they operate, even avoiding 800 phone numbers as a possible indicator of intent to sell in the destination state that could be construed as nexus. States have therefore had either to attempt to establish nexus, develop voluntary agreements, try to collect from the buyer, or forgo substantial amounts of revenue. A recent estimate by the General Accounting Office for state sales tax revenue losses from all remote sales (catalog, Internet, and other) for 2003 was from $2.5 to $20.4 billion, or 2% to 5% of state sales tax revenue.[1]

From an efficiency standpoint, this tax advantage for the mail-order firm distorts consumer decisions in favor of catalog shopping rather than in-state malls or Main Street merchants. From an equity standpoint, the nexus rule discriminates ar-

providing such tax incentives falls on the existing population as a whole, both individual and industrial/commercial.

Tax Exporting

State and local governments (and sometimes national governments as well) are always alert to opportunities to shift the burden of paying for government to nonresidents, also known as **tax exporting.** The theoretical justification for such shifting is that nonresidents benefit from services that the state provides but make little if any contribution toward the cost—the externalities argument in Chapter 4. States that attract large numbers of tourists, for example, incur high costs for extra infrastructure, police and fire protection, solid waste disposal, and public recreational facilities for a transient and seasonal population. These states can use accommodations taxes, admissions taxes, and special fees of various kinds to recoup some of that cost.

The pragmatic justification for tax exporting is that residents are more likely to vote than nonresidents. If some of the pain of paying for public ser-

(CONTINUED)

bitrarily between classes of consumers by how they choose to shop. Additionally, as shoppers shift to tax-free catalog shopping in the long run, states will see more base erosion and revenue loss. Based on the criteria developed in this chapter and the previous one, it would be desirable for states to be allowed to collect retail sales taxes on all mail-order purchases. From a practical standpoint, higher collection and compliance costs might justify exempting smaller mail-order firms from collecting the tax. Proposed legislation, stalled for more than 15 years in Congress, offered a sales threshold below which firms would not be required to collect the tax.

In the last few years, the arguments over catalog sales have paled in comparison to the tax debate brewing as a result of the phenomenal growth of Internet retailing. Congress created a national commission to study the taxation of Internet sales, which at present is under a moratorium that prevents states from collecting from Internet firms without nexus. The electronic commerce lobby has exerted political pressure to extend the moratorium indefinitely. Representatives of state and local governments, recognizing

the threat not only to sales tax revenue but to their state retail establishments, have attempted to offer some compromises to simplify compliance costs. The most likely proposal will result in a uniform state sales tax base and a single rate for each state, combining the multiple local rates in some way, in order to greatly reduce compliance costs for vendors.

Taxation of mail-order and Internet sales is a useful case study in policy analysis. It blends legal (nexus, due process, interstate commerce), political (the power of organized lobbyists, federal–state relations), and economic (efficiency, equity, and collection and compliance costs) dimensions. From the standpoint of state revenue officers, however, it represents more than 30 years of frustrated efforts to protect their retail sales tax bases and provide a level playing field between their own in-state retailers and their out-of-state competitors. With Internet shopping growing rapidly, the biggest challenges are still ahead.

1. General Accounting Office, *Sales Taxes: Electronic Commerce Growth Presents Challenges; Revenue Losses Are Uncertain* (Washington, DC: Government Printing Office, June 2000).

vices can be shifted from likely voters to those who have no voice or vote, politicians will have a more contented citizenry and will be more likely to be reelected. Public choice theory plays an important role in explaining the preference for tax exporting!

The opportunities for tax exporting are usually fairly limited. For most goods and services, a single state is in a highly competitive situation and is a price taker. The exceptions occur where a state (or a city or county) has some limited degree of monopoly power. Monopoly power comes from two sources. One is access to unique or exceptionally attractive tourist/business destinations—large cities, beaches, national parks, ski areas. The other is natural resources such as oil, natural gas, coal, or various minerals. Taxes aimed at tourists and business travelers are very popular in states such as Florida and Hawaii. Natural resource extraction is usually subject to a specific levy called a **severance tax,** which is successfully shifted forward to the buyer because there are few good alternatives. Wyoming, Texas, and Louisiana are among the states that make good use of severance taxes as a revenue source.

TAXATION IN A GLOBAL ECONOMY

State and local governments are not the only ones that are constrained by competition in designing revenue structures that are attractive and acceptable. Even national governments have to take into consideration the effects of their tax structures on decisions by firms and individuals about where they live and work, where they locate their businesses and invest their financial assets, and where they make their purchases and sales. Firms, resources, and individuals are increasingly mobile, particularly in the electronic age.

The taxation of corporate net income has been a hotly contested issue. Firms tend to locate their headquarters where the terms of taxation are most favorable. Ships register in Liberia because of favorable tax considerations. Wealthy jet-setters choose their citizenship according to where their income tax burdens will be lowest. Some kinds of taxes on goods are rebated on export (value-added taxes in particular), which may give an advantage to exporters from nations that rely more heavily on value-added than on income taxation.

Different tax structures will be more attractive to some firms, some citizens, or some investors. Nations that are interested in attracting multinational firms and financial investors will structure their tax packages with the goal of offering an attractive fiscal surplus, sometimes at the expense of some fraction of their own citizens. The same kinds of positive and negative effects of fiscal competition that states experience also apply to nations, particularly small nations but increasingly even large countries like Canada and the United States.

SUMMARY

In addition to equity and efficiency, other considerations are reflected in the design of a good tax/revenue system. These other criteria in-clude adequacy, visibility, stability, sensitivity to growth and inflation, visibility, and collection and compliance costs.

Adequacy means generating enough (but not too much) revenue in order to fund the desired level of public services. Generally, governments need at least one broad-based tax in order to provide adequate revenue, and most U.S. state and local governments combined rely on three—individual income tax, retail sales tax, and real and personal property tax. At least some major components of the revenue system should also have the attribute of stability, so that revenue will not be unduly sensitive to fluctuations in the level of economic activity. Some major components also need to be responsive to economic growth, which reflects increases in population, the price level (inflation), and real income growth. All three of these components result in increased costs of providing public services, but different revenue sources have different degrees of sensitivity to the three components of growth.

A tax is visible if taxpayers are highly aware of the tax's existence and how much they are paying. Increased visibility is associated with increased tax resistance. Visibility is a positive attribute if it contributes to restraining excess growth of government, a negative attribute if it restrains government spending to below the optimal level.

Stability is measured by the short-term income elasticities of the tax bases. Responsiveness to growth is measured by long-term income elasticities. Generally, income taxes are less stable and more responsive to growth than retail sales taxes.

In addition to excess burden, collecting taxes creates other costs. Collection costs are the administrative expenses that governments incur in collecting taxes. Compliance costs are those that fall on the taxpayer—record keeping, filling out forms, and related costs. Taxes can be high in collection but not compliance costs, or high in compliance but not collection costs, or high or low in both.

Some taxes are part of the system not because of their high score on the various criteria but because they serve to promote or discourage certain kinds of economic activity. One technique for targeting desired activities is tax expenditures, which exempt or exclude certain kinds of activities, income, or wealth from taxation. Tax expenditures are an alternative to direct expenditures that involve significant reduction in revenue collections.

Costs are associated with frequent or rapid changes in tax rules. People make decisions based on existing tax rules and experience windfall gains or losses resulting from sudden or unexpected changes in tax laws. Making changes less frequent, or phasing in changes gradually in some cases, can reduce these windfall gains or losses and make it easier for individuals to plan.

State and local tax systems raise additional issues of efficiency and equity in a competitive environment where governments are attempting to attract industry and higher income residents. The competitive situation may force taxes or services below the socially optimal level, or it may provide a useful constraint on the growth of government. It may also redistribute the tax burden toward existing firms and residents or toward those who are least mobile. States also attempt to shift part of their tax burden to nonresidents through tax exporting, which is achieved mainly through taxes on tourists and natural resources.

National governments must also take the revenue structures of other nations into account in designing their own revenue system. Like state governments, national governments are in competition for export markets, high-income residents, industry and jobs, and investment dollars in an increasingly global environment where workers, residents, firms, and financial resources are highly mobile.

KEY TERMS AND CONCEPTS

adequacy, 184
stability, 185
visibility, 190

collection costs, 191
compliance costs, 191
tax expenditure, 193

use tax, 197
tax exporting, 198
severance tax, 199

DISCUSSION QUESTIONS

1. Take a look at the tax structure of your state in comparison to neighboring states and the U.S. average. In what ways is it similar? In what ways is it different?

2. How would you compare the distribution of the tax burden among two or more states? How would you decide how to rank those states in terms of equity?

3. Why do you think Alaska and New Hampshire chose to consider adopting an income tax rather than a sales tax as a way to increase state revenue? What strengths and weaknesses does each tax have for those states in terms of the criteria developed in this chapter?

4. Some economists have argued for a balanced state–local revenue structure in which the "big three" (sales, property, and income taxes) account for the bulk of the revenue, with a relatively minor role for excise taxes and fees and charges. How would you defend (or criticize) that model in terms of the criteria in this chapter?

5. A legislator would like to introduce a new tax on automobile repair services that would be used to pay for accident prevention and emergency services. This proposal is appealing in terms of the benefit principle, but automobile repair services are carried out by many small service providers and funded largely through insurance payments. Armed with these considerations, evaluate this proposal in terms of the criteria in both this chapter and Chapter 8.

CHAPTER 10

TAXES ON INCOME

Every April 15 there are gatherings at post offices across the country to observe one of the rites of spring: the last minute filing of federal income tax returns. Many post offices stay open until midnight so that procrastinating taxpayers can get that crucial April 15 postmark on their tax returns and avoid penalties for late filing. Other taxpayers are mailing a much thinner packet that contains a request for an extension, some because of special circumstances, others because they want to delay the costs in time and irritation required to pull together the necessary records, make the calculations, and fill out the forms. An increasing number of Americans (56% in a 1999 Associated Press poll[1]), baffled and intimidated by the complexity of the federal income tax, have turned the whole problem over to their accountants or professional tax preparers. Having filed, some taxpayers wait for a refund, others for questions or revisions from the Internal Revenue Service, or in less than 2% of returns, the dreaded audit.

The income tax is the largest—but one of the newest—sources of federal revenue. In the early years, the new nation funded its federal government largely with land sales and tariff revenues. The two largest sources of federal revenue today, the individual income tax and the Social Security payroll tax, are 20th-century innovations. The income tax actually required a constitutional amendment, the 16th, passed in 1913, because the original Constitution forbade direct taxation.

1. Curt Anderson, "More Tax Law Changes Sought Amid Complaints of Complexity," *The Greenville News*, June 1, 1999, p. 7B.

he term *income tax* registers in most people's minds as the individual in-come tax, but several other kinds of taxes are also based directly on income. The Social Security payroll tax and other payroll taxes are also income taxes, as is the corporate income tax. Many local business license taxes are income taxes because they are based on the firm's gross receipts, or income.

Unlike most other countries, the U.S. relies almost exclusively on income taxes to fund its central government. In addition, 41 states and more than 4,000 local governments also depend on individual income taxes as a source of revenue. Table 10–1 summarizes the role of individual and corporate in-come taxes and Social Security taxes as revenue sources at the federal, state, and local levels.

WHY TAX INCOME?

To modern Americans who have lived with the income tax for most of the 20th century, this question may sound strange. But income is notoriously tricky to discover, track, and define. It is easier to hide from the tax collec-tor than many other kinds of tax bases. For most of human history, taxes have been collected where "tax handles" can be found—a visible asset, a trans-action, a border crossing. Property taxes, poll taxes, sales and excise taxes, and tariffs or tolls have a much longer history than income taxes. Even to-day, the United States is unique among modern industrial nations in its high dependence on income and payroll taxes as a source of both central govern-ment and regional government revenues.

In other countries, sales taxes (particularly value-added taxes, described in Chapter 11) play a much bigger revenue role. In many cases, the choice of sales rather than income tax as the primary revenue source reflected a high degree of noncompliance with the income tax. Income taxes depend heavily on the voluntary cooperation of taxpayers and employers, backed by threats of audit and penalties for at least some tax cheaters. Remember, Al Capone was not sent to jail for his many other alleged criminal activities, but for in-come tax evasion!

If, however, the government is able to generate the paper trail necessary to administer an income tax, this tax has certain significant advantages. It can be a highly productive revenue source. Progressive income taxes are the only major federal or state revenue source with an elasticity greater than 1, that is, for which a 1% increase in income leads to more than a 1% increase in tax revenue. This tax lends itself to fine-tuning both in terms of equity and in terms of achieving social goals of encouraging desirable activities. It gen-erates a regular flow of revenue to the government through withholding, unlike the property tax, which comes in all at once for most local govern-ments. It even provides information that enables tax collectors to do a better job of enforcement on other taxes.

	Percent of Revenue
Federal (2000)	
Individual income tax	48.6%
Corporate income tax	9.8%
Social Security payroll tax	33.2%
TOTAL, federal income taxes	91.6%

	Percent of Own-Source Revenue
State and local (1998–1999)	
Individual income tax	16.3%
Corporate income tax	2.9%
TOTAL, state and local taxes	19.2%

Source: U.S. Census Bureau.

Although a number of taxes fall under the heading of income tax, most of this chapter is devoted to the federal income tax and its counterparts at the state and local levels. Corporate income taxes also get some attention here, although they are a much more modest and declining source of public revenue, especially at the state level. Payroll taxes for Social Security are addressed briefly here and again in Chapter 18 in connection with other Social Security issues.

MEASURING INCOME FOR TAX PURPOSES

You may have an intuitive sense of what income is—that flow of money into your checkbook and your wallet that enables you to pay the bills and make purchases. That's a start, but it is not good enough. Some of that flow may be scholarships or gifts from parents or others, which is not considered income for tax purposes. Some of the flow may come from the sale of assets—shares of stock, a used car, or a home. To the extent that you sold that asset for more than you paid for it, the difference may be considered income (capital gains), but the recovery of the purchase price is not income, even though it does generate funds with which to pay bills and make purchases.

Recall from your principles course the distinction between stocks and flows. Wealth is a stock of assets, income a flow. Taxes on wealth, chiefly property taxes, are covered in a later chapter. Income taxes are based on a flow. But there are several important relationships between the stock of wealth in a household and the flow of income. First, wealth or assets generate income. Second, any flow of income into the household must by definition either be consumed or saved, and any consumption or saving must be financed by an inflow of revenue from earnings, income from capital (interest, dividends, rents, and royalties), gifts, asset appreciation, or increased debt.[2] So one possible definition of a household's income is the change in a household's net wealth over the course of a year plus consumption spending. This definition would incorporate all flows into the household less any new debt incurred, because any increase in debt reduces the household's net wealth.

This definition of income is broader than most governments would choose to use as a base for an income tax, but it does provide a starting point from which adjustments can be made. Adjustments are made (and criticized) primarily for three reasons: efficiency, equity, and costs of collection/compliance. Policy makers have to bear in mind that any exclusion of categories of income from the base will reduce the base and either reduce potential revenue or require a higher tax rate to achieve the same revenue.

EFFICIENCY ISSUES IN INCOME TAXATION

As Chapter 8 demonstrated, taxing income but not leisure is the fundamental source of distortions in choice that results from any form of income taxation. An income tax will have a substitution effect that leads to replacing taxed working hours with untaxed leisure time, and an income effect because it now requires more working hours to earn the same take-home pay. Different taxpayers will react differently to the imposition of income taxes, but all of them will see some distortion of their choices relative to what they would have done in the absence of an income tax.

Creating exclusions or favoring certain sources of income over others provides an incentive to arrange one's sources of income so as to minimize the tax liability. If dividends are taxable and capital gains are not, there is an incentive for taxpayers to encourage firms in which they hold stock to focus on creating capital gains in the form of higher stock prices instead of distributing net earnings of the corporation in the form of (taxable) dividends. If earnings from student jobs are taxable but scholarships are not, then colleges and students will favor a student aid mix that is higher in scholarship money than in paid on-campus jobs, even though the latter may be more desirable in terms of valuable student learning experiences. If some financial assets receive highly favorable tax treatment (such as municipal bonds or tax-deferred annuities), funds will flow into those assets at the expense of other assets with higher pretax returns.

These distortions of household decisions in response to tax rules are among the most important efficiency effects of income taxation. If efficiency were the only goal, the tax code would use the broadest possible base for the

---

2. Income from unincorporated businesses, both proprietorships and partnerships, is treated as individual income for tax purposes in the United States.

income tax in order to minimize such changes in behavior. Such a broad base would also make it possible to collect the same revenue with lower rates, reducing those distortions in income–leisure choices that rise with the square of the tax rate.

The broadest possible base, however, is a difficult standard to maintain when the tax collector must deal with actual flows of revenue through households. Some kinds of income create greater challenges in tracking and collecting than others. Consider, for example, increases in the market value of assets owned by households, better known as capital gains. Should those gains be considered taxable income each year because they increase household wealth, even if the asset is not sold and no actual cash flow is generated with which to pay taxes? If such unrealized capital gains were taxed, then the income tax collector would be forced to get into the business of assessing the value of household assets (including real estate), and the cost of administering the income tax would rise astronomically. But if capital gains on assets are excluded from taxable income until the assets are sold (thus dodging the assessment problem), then there is a "lumping" of income in a single year when an asset is sold, often pushing the taxpayer into a higher tax bracket. The result is a greater tax burden than would occur if capital gains were taxed as they accrued. The tax treatment of capital gains is one of many challenges for designing an efficient income tax.

EQUITY ISSUES IN INCOME TAXATION

All taxes raise issues of equity, but equity is a bigger issue in income taxation than in taxation of consumption or wealth. Why? Because it is possible to fine-tune the distribution of the burden of the income tax more closely than most other taxes, and because it is one of the few taxes that lends itself to progressivity.

Both horizontal and vertical equity are important issues in income tax design. Recall from Chapters 6 and 8 that horizontal equity means treating people equally when they are in equal economic situations. The definition of equal economic situations is closely linked to equal annual income flow. However, the income flow is only a starting point in defining equal situations, because other factors affect the relative taxpaying ability of two households with the same income flows. There may be a difference in wealth, or household size, or other obligations (medical expenses, caring for aging parents, child care expenses, etc.) that should be taken into account. Such equity concerns account for a significant amount of the volume and complexity of the current federal income tax code.

Vertical equity means treating people with an appropriate degree of difference based on differences in their economic situation or ability to pay. In the case of the income tax, some would argue that proportional taxation constitutes vertical equity (see the box feature later in this chapter on the flat tax). Others would argue, however, that vertical equity should be viewed as a function of the tax system as a whole, not just one particular tax. Because many other taxes in the system are regressive, a progressive income tax serves as a counterweight in the overall system, moving it toward proportionality.

Progressivity can be built into an income tax in two different ways. One way, as was discussed in Chapter 8, is to exclude a certain base amount of income from tax through exemptions, exclusions, or deductions. The second way is to have a graduated series of tax rates that apply to increments of income. The first method increases equity at the expense of complexity, which means higher collection/compliance costs. The second method, progressive rates, may improve equity at the expense of efficiency. Progressive rate structures increase the distortions in people's decisions and also cause them to accelerate or postpone some of those actions on the basis of the tax bracket they would find themselves in one year versus another. End-of-year charitable contributions, bunching of medical expenses in a single year, and postponing or accelerating receipt of certain kinds of income are all "inspired" by the tax consequences under a system with progressive rates. Table 10–2 shows the progressivity of the U.S. federal income tax, measuring taxes as a percentage of adjusted gross income.

COLLECTION AND COMPLIANCE COST ISSUES

The area of compliance and collection costs is the most contentious one in income taxation. Creating a broad tax base for efficiency reasons requires more effort by both tax collectors and taxpayers to keep track of a variety of income flows, increasing both collection and compliance costs. On the other hand, making adjustments in the tax base to accommodate horizontal equity concerns makes the tax law more difficult to administer and more confusing for the taxpayer to comply with. A progressive rate structure, which was put in place in the interest of vertical equity, makes the tax liability more difficult to compute.

The expense of administering the federal income tax is fairly low as a percentage of revenue collected. However, the low collection cost is largely because much of the cost is shifted to the taxpayer and the taxpayer's employer, who must maintain records and fill out various forms in order to comply with the tax. Other forms of income taxes, such as payroll taxes and many state and local income taxes, are simpler to administer and to comply with for a variety of reasons. In some cases, particularly local income taxes and Social Security taxes, a single flat rate applies, and most of the collection is through payroll withholding, often without a need to file a return. In the case of many (but not all) state income taxes, once the federal return is complete, the additional effort required to file a state return is very small.

Table 10–2 Federal Income as a Percentage of Adjusted Gross Income for a Family of Four, Standard Deduction, 2000	Income Range ($)	Taxes as Percentage of Adjusted Gross Income (%)
	10,000	0
	20,000	1.1
	30,000	5.7
	40,000	8.0
	50,000	12.4
	100,000	17.1
	200,000	23.9
	500,000	31.8

U.S. FEDERAL INCOME TAX

The United States has had a federal income tax since the Sixteenth Amendment to the Constitution was ratified in 1913. Initially the tax rate was very low with large exclusions, so that only the wealthiest households paid the tax. By the end of World War II, however, the pressing demands of war finance had driven the top marginal rate to 98%, and a much larger proportion of households was paying income tax. A series of major tax reforms 1954, 1964, 1981, and 1986 reduced those marginal rates, so that by the 1990s tax rates ranged from 15% to 39.6%. In 2001, Congress passed a tax bill that reduced the lowest bracket to 10%, and the top bracket to 35%.

Defining Taxable Income

The process of determining federal income tax liability is conceptually simple, even though the actual process may be very time consuming. The steps are outlined in Table 10–3. The first step is to determine gross income—income from all sources, including wages, salary, rents, royalties, pensions, interest, dividends, self-employment earnings, gifts, and scholarships. (The largest single source of income is wages and salaries; in 1996, they accounted for three-quarters of adjusted gross income.) The taxpayer must then determine which of these income sources need to be reported as income and which do not. Those kinds of income that are not included in gross income are referred to as **exclusions.**

Exclusions can be total or partial. Among the income sources that typically do not have to be reported at all are insurance claims income, most employee fringe benefits, scholarships, gifts received, and interest on state and local bonds. Partial exclusions include a portion of Social Security benefits for higher income households (lower income households get to exclude all Social Security benefits).

From gross income to taxable income there is a series of steps called adjustments, exemptions, and deductions. **Adjustments** are those additions or subtractions that are made to get from gross income to **adjusted gross income.** Adjusted gross income is not yet the basis for tax computations, but this figure is important, because it is used to determine various limitations on exclusions and tax credits and ceilings on certain deductions. Among the adjustments made at this point are subtractions from gross income of contributions to various kinds of retirement saving plans, part of health insurance premiums, job-related moving expenses, rent and royalty expenses, self-employment health insurance and half of self-employment tax, and alimony payments.

For people whose income is modest and comes almost entirely from wages or salary, and who have no self-employment income or other complications, the determination of adjusted gross income is very easy. They can use one of two short, simple tax forms, 1040A or 1040EZ. For others, particularly those with higher incomes, or with self-employment income (and expenses related to earning that income), extensive investments, job changes, or multiple income sources, determining adjusted gross income is the most difficult and demanding part of the whole process.

Determining Taxable Income

The next step in the process is to convert adjusted gross income to **taxable income,** which is the income figure used to compute tax liability. At this point the **filing status** of the taxpayer becomes a factor in determining how much is subtracted from adjustable gross income to arrive at taxable income. Filing status options are joint (a married couple filing a combined return, whether both or just one had income), head of household (a person who has at least one dependent child living with him or her), single, or married filing separately. The marriage tax described in Chapter 8 was a consequence of different treatment of single taxpayers and married taxpayers filing separately. Filing status affects the standard deduction, the adjusted gross income used to calculate phaseout of exemptions and deductions, and the tax rates or table used to compute tax liability.

The two components of the difference between adjusted gross income and taxable income are **personal exemptions** and either **standard or itemized deductions.** These two components, which are available to every taxpayer, exclude a base amount of income from taxation. Exemptions and deductions would make the income tax progressive even without a series of graduated tax rates, as was discussed in Chapters 8 and 9. Taxpayers are entitled to one personal exemption ($2,900 in 2001) for each member of the household. Special rules govern children with earnings of their own, college students, dependent parents, children of divorced parents, and unrelated dependents. For most households, it is pretty easy to figure out how many exemptions to claim, multiply by $2,900, and subtract. For households with

Table 10–3
A Flowchart for
Calculating Federal
Income Tax

Start with sources of income
− Exclusions
= Gross income
± Adjustments
= Adjusted gross income
− Exemptions and deductions
= Taxable income
STOP! COMPUTE TAX LIABILITY HERE!
Tax Liability
− Withholding
− Other credits
+ Other taxes due
= Tax due or refund

higher adjusted gross incomes (above $199,450 for a joint return in 2001), there is a reduction in the amount of the personal exemption that can be claimed that requires some complicated calculations. This provision increases the degree of progressivity of the tax but also adds to the compliance cost for taxpayers. It is scheduled to be phased out starting in 2006 under the provisions of the 2001 tax bill.

Standard and itemized deductions serve several important public policy purposes. Itemized deductions consist of various taxpayer expenditures that Congress has favored with special tax treatment. The major categories are health expenses over a certain percent of income, state and local taxes paid (mostly income and property taxes, but not sales taxes), interest on mortgages and student loans, charitable contributions, and unreimbursed employee business expenses over a certain percentage of income. The deduction for state and local taxes amounts to a limited indirect subsidy of state and local government. The home mortgage and student loan interest deductions are intended to encourage home ownership and investment in education. The charitable deduction reflects a belief that private charities create substantial positive externalities and sometimes even local public goods, and that it may be cheaper or more efficient to subsidize such activities indirectly through the deduction than to provide them directly through government. The unreimbursed business expenses are a cost of earning income, and are somewhat out of place in itemized deductions; they would more logically belong in adjustments to gross income.

Taxpayers may choose to *itemize,* that is, list all the deductible expenditures that they made during the tax year, and subtract them from adjusted gross income, or they may elect to take the standard deduction, which was $4,500 for singles and $7,600 for married taxpayers filing jointly in 2001. The standard deduction is often more than the taxpayer could claim by listing deductions separately, and also saves considerable headaches in terms of record keeping for taxpayers. Only one taxpayer in four itemizes deductions. Mortgage interest, charitable contributions, and state and local taxes are the most important itemized deductions for most households that itemize.

As with personal exemptions, higher income taxpayers encounter a phasing out of their standard or itemized deductions if their income exceeds a certain threshold level. In 2001, the adjusted gross income threshold for phasing out standard or itemized deductions was $132,950. Beyond that income level, taxpayers forfeit itemized deductions in the amount of 3% of excess income (with a few special exceptions). For example, if a household had an income of $150,000, then $511.50 (3% of the difference between $150,000 and $132,950) would be subtracted from their itemized deductions. For very high income households, the itemized deductions disappear entirely. These limits are scheduled to be increased under the 2001 tax legislation.

Computing Tax Liability

Having arrived at taxable income, the next step is to determine taxes owed. Here filing status becomes very important, because there are different tax rates and schedules for married filing separately, single, married filing jointly, and heads of households, again reflecting some difficult equity decisions in designing the tax structure. For incomes up to $100,000, taxpayers can use a table to determine their tax liability. For incomes above that level, taxpayers must use a tax rate schedule. In 2001, rates ranged from 10% on the first $6,000 to 35% on taxable income above $297,350 for single persons.

One of the most common sources of confusion in the federal income tax is the difference between the average rate and the marginal rate. The marginal rate is the tax rate applied to the last dollar of taxable income, while the average rate is simply the tax due as a fraction or percentage of taxable income. For example, a married couple filing jointly in 2001 with a taxable income of $120,000 would have a marginal rate of 31% that applied to the portion of their income that fell between $105,950 and $120,000. But the first $105,950 would have been taxed at the lower rates of 10%, 15% and 28%. Their total tax liability of $27,124 is the result of applying four different marginal rates to four different parts of their income; the average tax rate comes to 22.6% of their taxable income.

For some taxpayers, a second computation, called the alternative minimum tax, is necessary. Some taxpayers, generally high income, manage to reduce their taxable income through extensive use of itemized deductions or other tax preferences such as tax exempt interest income, tax-sheltered business losses, and accelerated depreciation. The alternative minimum tax was designed to increase equity by ensuring a fair contribution from these higher income taxpayers, but it also increased the complexity of the tax system considerably from the standpoint of both collection and compliance costs.

The Last Step: Who Owes Whom?

Finally, the tax form asks the filer to figure out how much has already been paid, what other kinds of taxes need to be figured in, and what credits might apply. The difference will be either the amount owed, (in which case the taxpayer will write a check and attach it to the return or arrange to pay via a credit card) or the amount due as a refund, which will probably take six to eight weeks to arrive if everything was done correctly. Electronic filing, which is becoming increasingly popular, speeds up that process a little.

Most taxpayers who have any tax liability have already paid a part of their taxes either through payroll withholding (the most common method), or through quarterly filings of estimated tax, or both. Payroll withholding not only guarantees the government a steady flow of revenue but also reduces the visibility and the pain of the annual ritual of settling accounts with the federal government. Taxpayers who are self-employed or who have other kinds of income not subject to payroll withholding (interest, dividends, rents, royalties, consulting, taxable pensions, etc.) usually find it necessary to file an estimated tax form each quarter and send in a payment. Taxpayers whose withholding and estimated tax payments are less than 90% of their tax liability may face a penalty for underpayment. That penalty is a strong incentive to make sure that advance payments cover most of the bill.

Taxpayers may also owe other kinds of taxes that are collected through the Internal Revenue Service and that have their own lines on Form 1040. Self-employment taxes for Social Security are the biggest item, along with a few specialty taxes such as environmental excise taxes related to oil spills and soil-depleting chemicals. These additional taxes are added to the tax liability computed on the basis of taxable income and filing status.

Finally, there are credits. **Tax credits** are different from deductions because the value of a tax credit is closer to being equal for all taxpayers, whereas the value of an itemized deduction is greater to a person in a 35% tax bracket than to one in a 15% tax bracket. One hundred dollars spent on child care would save $35 in taxes owed for the first person and only $15 for the second person if it were an itemized deduction. Originally the child care credit was a flat 20% of allowable expenses for children under age 15. Now it ranges from 20% to 30% of expenses, with a ceiling of $2,400 for one child and $4,800 for two or more. The higher credit rates are provided for lower income households, adding a bit of progressivity to the credit in order to encourage lower income families to seek out and use quality child care services.

The child care credit is one of the larger individual income tax credits, amounting to a $2.6 billion tax expenditure in 1998 to 6.1 million households. The child care credit, which was expanded in the 2001 tax cut legislation, covers children with two working parents, for whom child care is a cost of earning income. The most significant credit, however, is the **Earned Income Tax Credit** or **EITC,** which shared $30.4 billion among 19.4 million tax filers in 1998. The EITC represents a step in the direction of a **negative income tax,** an idea that was popularized by economist Milton Friedman in the 1970s.[3]

A negative income tax was originally proposed as an alternative to welfare that would be much less costly to administer and that would gradually reduce the subsidy to lower income households as income increased, rather than facing an abrupt cutoff. Up to a certain income level, households would receive a payment from the government that diminished as their income rose. At a certain threshold level (such as $20,000 for a family of four), the subsidy would become zero, and dollars earned above that amount would be subject to taxation.

The EITC is considerably more modest than Milton Friedman's comprehensive vision for replacing welfare with a combined positive and negative income tax system. Instead, it offers tax relief or cash payments to working households up to an income ceiling, phasing the credits out as income rises. Reforms in the early 1990s expanded its size and scope as an important program for the working poor that has helped to make working more financially attractive than being on welfare. The relationship of this tax provision to public welfare is described in Chapter 18.

Finally, the bottom line: Tax liability plus other taxes owed less withholding less estimated taxes paid less credits equals balance due or refund. Sign it, mail it, add a check if needed, and the taxpayer's work is done for another year.

Tax Evasion, Avoidance, and Audits

Tax evasion is illegal. Tax evasion means falsifying information on your tax return in order to reduce your tax liability, or even not filing at all. Tax evasion can result in financial penalties or even prison sentences. **Tax avoidance** is legal. Tax avoidance means arranging your affairs so as to minimize your tax burden by incurring deductible expenses, investing in tax-exempt bonds, putting money in tax-deferred retirement savings, or other legal techniques. There are also activities that fall in the gray area, sometimes called "tax avoision." Many of the tax shelters that were set up in the 1980s to create large deductible losses have since been disallowed by the IRS.

The probability a taxpayer will have to undergo an **audit** (*examination* is the preferred IRS term) is low, particularly for taxpayers with moderate income and few deductions, credits, or exclusions. The IRS will review your return, check your arithmetic, compare it with reports received from others on your income sources and some deductible items, and notify you by mail if they find discrepancies. Sometimes they may send an unexpected refund! Some returns, however, are selected randomly for a more complete review and

---

3. An excellent history of the evolution of the EITC from the earlier negative income tax discussions can be found in Dennis J. Ventry, Jr., "The Collision of Tax and Welfare Politics: The Political History of the Earned Income Tax Credit, 1969–99," *National Tax Journal* LI:4 (Part 2) (December 2000): pp. 983–1026.

HOW TO COMPLICATE YOUR TAX RETURN

Some people lead relatively uncomplicated lives and can fill out Form 1040EZ or 1040A quickly and put the dreaded annual income tax experience behind them. But others spend hours trying to make sense out of complex provisions. According to the American Institute of Certified Public Accountants, these are the 10 most complicated tax laws for individuals and small businesses to understand and comply with[1]:

1. Alternative minimum tax (a second computation for people with numberous credits and deductions),
2. Earned income credit (a sort of negative income tax for low-income households),
3. Income phaseouts (reducing credits and deductions as income rises),

4. Marriage penalty (differential treatment of two-earner couples and two single persons),
5. Independent contractor (determining whether a worker is an employee or independent contractor),
6. Kiddie tax (on unearned income for children under age 14),
7. Estimated taxes (advance payments to offset underwithholding),
8. Child credit (per-child credit tied to income),
9. Transfer tax (on trusts given to grandchildren), and
10. Half-year rules (on avoiding penalties on half-year withdrawals).

1. "A Top 10 List of Most Complicated Tax Laws," *The Greenville News*, June 1, 1999, p. 7B.

verification. Others are selected because of certain "flags" that call your return to the attention of the IRS. Among the most common flags are exceptionally high itemized deductions (especially for charitable contributions) relative to your income, tax-shelter losses, occupations that lend themselves to significant cash payments, large business expenses relative to income, or having been called in for a prior audit.

Directions for Reform

The U.S. federal income tax undergoes frequent changes and occasional major reforms. The last truly major overhaul of the income tax took place in 1986, which provided a trade-off of base broadening (also known as eliminating loopholes or tax preferences) for a reduction in marginal rates. Since that time, numerous small changes have been made, most of them (except for 1990 and 1993) rate reductions or expansion of exclusions, deductions, and credits. In 2001, Congress again reduced rates and made other changes affecting taxation of capital gains and the treatment of joint returns (marriage penalty).

The gradualist/marginal school of tax reformers always has a laundry list of improvements in the income tax code to increase efficiency, improve equity, and reduce collection or compliance costs while maintaining adequate revenue. High on the list have been eliminating the marriage tax penalty, more tax relief for parents of small children or college students, and stronger incentives for saving, especially for retirement. Exempting labor income in the form of employee fringe benefits such as health insurance, health services, employer contributions to pension plans, company recreation programs, and subsidized cafeteria meals is a major tax expenditure that is frequently a target for reformers who seek to raise more revenue without higher tax rates.

Taxation of capital gains is a perennial issue. Capital gains are taxed at a lower effective rate than income from other sources. Some tax reformers would like to eliminate the tax on capital gains altogether. Proponents of both special treatment and elimination argue that capital gains consist largely of inflation rather than real increases in income. While the same can be said for other sources of income (your salary increase each year is at least partly compensation for inflation), the bunching of capital gains at the time an asset is sold can kick the taxpayer into a higher tax bracket. This bunching effect is part of the rationale for a lower marginal tax rate on capital gains. Proponents of special treatment for capital gains income also argue that encouraging investment in assets that are likely to create capital gains constitutes an incentive to invest, which encourages economic growth. This argument may have some validity, but the current special treatment also applies to antique cars, works of art, and other financial assets that do not affect economic growth.

The alternative approach to gradualism or piecemeal tax reform is a truly major overhaul of the tax code, some going so far as to replace the existing system with either a flat tax (see accompanying boxed feature) or a national value-added tax (see Chapter 11). Some advocates of a major overhaul would like to shift to a tax on consumption, modeled on the one developed by British economist Nicholas Kaldor in the 1950s and tried briefly in India and Sri Lanka.[4] The amount consumed would be measured as the household's assets at the beginning of the year, plus borrowing, less investment, less the end-of-year value of assets. Saving and (financial) investment would not be taxed. Unlike most kinds of taxes on consumption or sales (see Chapter 11), an expenditure tax could be designed to be progressive.

The reality of public choice, however, suggests that there are too many interests vested in the present system and that the adjustment costs of major change may be too high relative to the benefits. The United States is likely to continue its uneasy relationship with the Internal Revenue Service and the federal income tax code with periodic tinkering to respond to complaints about efficiency, equity, and compliance costs.

STATE AND LOCAL INCOME TAXES

Forty-one states, the District of Columbia, and more than 4,000 local governments (about two-thirds of them in Pennsylvania) imposed broad-based individual income taxes in 1994. Among the remaining nine states, two imposed limited income taxes on interest and dividend income. Four of those states—

4. Nicholas Kaldor, *An Expenditure Tax* (London: G. Allen, 1955).

IS THERE A FLAT TAX IN OUR FUTURE?

One of the hot issues in the 1990s, particularly in the 1996 presidential primaries, was the notion of replacing the current federal income tax with a simplified income tax at a single (nonprogressive) rate. Proposed rates during that discussion ranged from 17% to 21%, which are higher than the lowest bracket rate for the current income tax but lower than the average rate for many taxpayers in the current system. The best known version, which combined tax reform with a tax cut, was the Armey–Shelby proposal, which had an initial 20% tax rate and a $31,400 exemption for a family of four.

Developed in the 1980s by economist Robert Hall and political scientist Alvin Rabushka, and promoted in the 1990s by presidential candidate Steve Forbes and House Ways and Means Committee Chair Dick Armey, among others, the notion of a flat (and simple) federal income tax has caught the public imagination. In one typical version, the flat tax on individual wage earners (including deferred wages in the form of retirement earnings) would be combined with a large basic exempt amount per taxpayer or household that would replace personal exemptions and standard or itemized deductions. The business tax would be imposed on all businesses, not just corporations, so taxes on self-employment earnings would be separated from the individual income tax and grouped with income of partnerships and corporations. The elimination of personal exemptions, itemized or standard deductions, tax credits, and many current adjustments to gross income would broaden the tax base. This broader base, together with an expected stimulus to private sector eco-

nomic activity from the lower (and single) tax rate, is expected to offset any revenue loss from the large flat exemption and the lower flat rate.

The flat tax proposal, which has many variations, has generated heated debate and numerous studies about its revenue potential and its impact on horizontal and vertical equity and on compliance and collection costs. Proponents argue that the current system wastes too many resources in compliance costs, a problem that could be resolved by a simple flat tax. On the equity front, one study of a fairly typical variant of a flat tax proposal finds that senior citizens, one-income families, and single parents gain at the expense of nonseniors and two-income households. There is also a decided shift of the tax burden away from higher income households to lower income households, a conclusion affirmed in other research as well.[1]

The biggest challenge to a flat tax is the entrenched interests in certain provisions of the federal tax code, ranging from deductions for mortgage interest and charitable deductions to the special treatment of employee fringe benefits and various kinds of retirement savings plans. Elimination of those provisions would be costly to people who made long-term financial decisions on the basis of those tax rules, and might have a significant negative impact on related industries—home building, nonprofits, and financial services, for example.

1. Maxime Fougere and Guiseppe C. Ruggeri, "Flat Taxes and Distributional Justice," *Review of Social Economy*, 56(3) (Fall 1998): pp. 277–286; Amy Dunbar and Thomas Pogue, "Estimating Flat Tax Incidence and Yield: A Sensitivity Analysis," *National Tax Journal*, 51(2) (June 1998): pp. 303–324.

New Hampshire, Alaska, Tennessee, and Wyoming—considered but rejected a broad-based state income tax in 2001. Florida, Nevada, South Dakota, Texas, and Washington also do not use a broad-based income tax.

Income taxes have a longer history than sales taxes as a state revenue source, beginning with Hawaii, which adopted its income tax in 1901. Nineteen states had individual income taxes in place before the first state retail sales taxes appeared on the scene in 1933. Part of the appeal of this tax to states is its sensitivity to growth. The short-run elasticity of the taxable personal income base, estimated at 1.215, is the highest of all the major state and local tax bases, and the long-run elasticity of 1.195, while not the highest, still indicates a base with a faster growth rate than personal income as a whole.[5]

Except for school districts in Louisiana, counties in Maryland, and multiple local governments in Pennsylvania, most local income taxes are levied by large cities. Some cities levy their income taxes on residents, but the most common form of municipal income tax is a payroll tax at a single rate on employees, some of whom reside in the city while others commute into the city from the suburbs. This kind of tax is somewhat regressive, since the base is limited to wages and salaries, but it is very easy to administer.

Structure of State Income Taxes

State income taxes are somewhat more diverse. To simplify compliance by taxpayers, and provide an opportunity for cross-verification between federal and state governments, most state income taxes are connected to the federal income tax in some way. They may choose as a starting point either federal adjusted gross income, federal taxable income, or tederal tax liability. The approach with the lowest compliance and collection cost is to direct the taxpayer to send in some percentage of federal tax liability, the method used in Rhode Island, Vermont, and North Dakota.

Most states like to differentiate their individual income tax codes to a greater degree than this method provides. Thus, a second approach is to start with federal taxable income and make certain additions and subtractions. This method is used in eight states. Here are some common adjustments:

- Add back in any itemized deduction for state income taxes paid.
- Allow an adjustment for interest earned on federal government bonds.
- Treat retirement income, including Social Security, differently.
- Treat two-earner households differently.

The third approach, used in 27 states, is to start with federal adjusted gross income and then approach personal exemptions and itemized or standard deductions differently. One advantage of this approach is that it makes it possible for those states that do not have community property laws to treat husbands and wives as separate taxpaying entities and thus eliminate any marriage penalty. It does, however, increase the compliance cost for the taxpayer and the collection cost for the state.

The fourth approach, used in five states, is to completely separate the state income tax from the federal income tax. Taxpayers must start over to compute their state tax liability.

In all three of the approaches just discussed, most states (34) opt for a progressive rate structure, with 11% as the highest state marginal rate (Montana and California).

5. Russell S. Sobel and Randall G. Holcombe, "Measuring the Growth and Variability of Tax Bases over the Business Cycle," *National Tax Journal,* XLIX(4) (December 1998): pp. 535–552.

Competitive Issues in State Income Taxation

Although the federal government is somewhat (but not entirely) insulated from the pressures of competition in designing its tax system, interstate competition for higher income residents and business locations is a factor in all major tax decisions, including the issue of whether or not to have an income tax. There are advocates in several of the nine states without a broad-based income tax to adopt one in order to reduce dependence on sales and property taxes. But for several of those states—particularly Texas, Florida, and New Hampshire—the absence of a state income tax has been a "draw" to attract certain kinds of residents and firms.

Noncorporate business firms (partnerships and proprietorships) may find a state without an income tax an attractive place if other locational factors are not significant. Higher income retirees have moved to states like Florida and Texas at least in part because of the absence of an income tax. In response, other states have fine-tuned their income tax systems in order to compete for wealthy retirees by offering special exemptions either based on age or targeted at retirement income (pensions or Social Security).

Competition among states also tends to put downward pressure on income tax rates and particularly on the degree of progressivity. Many states have a flat rate, while even those that are progressive have top bracket rates that are under 10% with only a few exceptions. At the local level, individual income tax rates are almost always flat and generally very low, 1% to 2%, because of competition for location of commercial facilities and residents with other local governments in the area that do not impose income taxes.

Another competitive dimension of any state or local tax is deductibility. Unlike retail sales taxes, state and local individual income taxes qualify as an itemized deduction for taxpayers who do not take the standard deduction. Deductibility reduces the effective state income tax rate for those taxpayers who tend to be in higher tax brackets at both the state and federal levels. For example, a taxpayer whose average state tax rate was 7% and whose marginal federal tax rate was 31% would be able to claim a deduction that reduced his or her effective state tax burden from 7% to $7\% \times (1 - 0.31)$, or 4.83%. Because the federal tax is progressive and because itemizing is more common among higher earning households, deductibility of state and local income taxes tends to reduce the progressivity of the total income tax system, but it also blunts some of the competitive pressures on states to hold their top bracket rates down.

CORPORATE INCOME TAXES

The federal government, 45 states, and the District of Columbia impose a corporate income tax, corporate profits tax, or franchise tax on incorporated business enterprises. Unincorporated enterprises, whether partnerships or proprietorships, are taxed as part of the individual income tax, although some of these enterprises are also subject to a franchise fee or other form of business tax at the state level. The federal corporate income tax is levied on income after expenses (the bottom line on the income statement) at rates ranging from 15% up to 35% on corporate net income of more than $10 million. Most state corporate income tax rates are in the 5% to 7% range, with 15 states using progressive rates. The base of the corporate income tax (corporate net income) is the most cyclically sensitive of all the major tax bases, with an income elasticity of 3.369.[6]

The federal corporate income tax is very complicated to administer because of the problems in defining allowable expenses that can be deducted. These definitional issues also have the potential to distort firms' decisions. There is relatively little difficulty in identifying and deducting firms' expenditures for labor, utilities, supplies or raw materials, capital equipment, land, buildings or rented property, and interest on borrowed money. However, some other expenses fall into a gray area that looks like tax avoidance or even tax evasion. And some questionable provisions have been inserted into the tax code that inflate deductible expenses beyond what normal cost accounting would suggest is appropriate. Three particular areas of controversy in relation to these allowable expenses are (1) depreciation of capital equipment, (2) consumption-type expenditures, and (3) the incentive to borrow rather than to finance new or expanding firms with equity (stock).

Depreciation

Capital equipment that has a useful lifetime of more than one year must be depreciated over several years. The rules on the timing of depreciation can affect the amount of tax owed and favor some kinds of capital over others, or capital over other inputs. Allowing a firm to write off the cost of capital equipment much more rapidly than the actual decline in its economic value (**accelerated depreciation**) is regarded as an incentive to invest in new equipment. Accelerated depreciation was introduced in the federal tax code in 1981 and modified in the 1986 tax reforms. This tax expenditure, which is one of the more costly tax breaks in revenue terms, also distorts the firm's decisions between buying new equipment and repairing old equipment, and discriminates in favor of capital-intensive firms compared to other kinds of corporations.

Disguised Consumption

A second area of long-standing controversy is that of distinguishing between expenditures made in order to produce the firm's product or service and those that are disguised consumption, particularly for the owners of privately held corporations or the stockholders in closely held corporations. Where stock-

6. Sobel and Holcombe, "Measuring the Growth," p. 543.

holders are ineffective at making management accountable, management may enjoy a variety of "perks" that are actually consumption disguised as allowable business expenses. From the three-martini lunch and the corporate management retreat in the Caribbean to the on-site health club, fancy furnishings, and subsidized executive cafeteria, the possibilities for providing tax-free in-kind income to owners and managers are almost endless. Some efforts have been made to crack down on the most flagrant abuses, particularly in the 1986 tax reform, but it is virtually impossible to monitor and require justification for all of a firm's outlays.

Debt versus Equity Financing

The third distortion that arises from the treatment of allowable expenses is the deduction for interest paid on borrowed funds. When firms need additional capital, they have three possible sources: borrowing (debt), issuing stock (equity), or using retained earnings. If there were no tax distortions, market forces would establish an appropriate balance between these three methods. Using retained earnings means forgoing what those funds could earn in a competitive marketplace, so the opportunity cost of using internal capital for investment should be the same as external borrowing. If additional shares of stock are issued, those added shares dilute the value of existing equity (stock), reducing the value of each outstanding share. Pressure from stockholders to maintain the value of their holdings will discourage management from over-using equity rather than debt financing.

The effect of the corporate income tax, however, is to tilt the balance in favor of issuing bonds (borrowing or debt financing) rather than stock (equity financing), because interest paid to borrowers is deductible from the corporate income tax base, but dividends paid to stockholders are not. Corporations put themselves in a riskier financial position with a high debt-to-equity ratio, because stockholders have no choice during bad times but to wait it out, while bondholders have an enforceable claim to payment that could drive a firm into bankruptcy.

Who Pays the Corporate Income Tax?

The incidence of the corporate income tax has been a source of debate among economists for years. The burden must fall in some combination on owners (stockholders), workers, and consumers of the firm's product, because those constitute all the possible parties to any activities in which the burden can be shifted. If (1) all firms were corporations, (2) all owners were individual tax-payers, and (3) all relevant markets were highly competitive, then the corporate income tax would become a tax on capital. Like a tax on raw land, such a tax could not be shifted. In the short run, all of the burden of the tax would fall on the owners of the fixed supply of capital, or the shareholders, who would receive a reduced return on their investment, much like owners of land who are faced with a property tax.

In the long run, however, the supply of financial capital is highly elastic and also flows freely between countries and between business firms and other borrowers, such as government and consumers. To offer the same rate of return as others who are competing for funds, corporations would require a higher pretax return in order to generate the same after-tax return. They would move up their demand curve for capital, acquiring less capital by only choosing those investment projects with much higher rates of return. Corporations may invest less in capital per worker than they would otherwise. Capital is both a substitute and a complement to workers. Less capital investment may mean more workers, but less productive ones (since each worker has less capital to work with), and hence lower wages. In this way some of the burden of the corporate income tax may fall on workers in the long run.

This theoretical analysis is complicated by the fact that corporations compete for funds, for workers, and for customers with other types of firms that are not corporations. While corporations produce most of the output in the U.S. economy, most of the firms in sheer numbers are organized as partnerships or proprietorships. Partnerships and proprietorships lack some of the special advantages of corporations, like limited liability and unlimited lifetimes, but they are generally more attractive from a tax perspective, because their net income is taxed to the owner or partners as individual income. Consequently, one effect of the corporate income tax may be to encourage firms to be organized as partnerships or proprietorships (or one of the special forms of corporations provided for in the tax law) in order to reduce their tax burdens. The result is a less efficient mix of kinds of business organizations than would otherwise occur. A second effect may be that the higher cost of capital to corporations translates into higher prices for their products relative to those of noncorporate firms, shifting some of the burden of the corporate income tax to buyers of products produced by the corporate sector.

Corporations increasingly compete not just with noncorporate firms but also with corporations in other parts of the world that do not pay their governments corporate income tax. In the majority of countries, the primary source of government revenue is taxes imposed on sales, most commonly a value-added tax. These foreign firms will find it easier to attract investors, will have to borrow less, will have a lower cost of capital, and may be able to pass on some of those savings to consumers in the form of lower prices. As a result, U.S. corporations that compete heavily in global markets will be less able to raise their prices. If they also hire labor in highly competitive markets, the ability to shift some of the tax burden to their workers will also be limited, so that shareholders will bear the burden of the corporate income tax.

As you can see, the analysis of the incidence of the corporate income tax is quite complex, particularly when it is considered in the context of the U.S. individual income tax and its treatment of dividends and capital gains. Nevertheless, as long as markets are competitive on both a national and international scale, the main burden of the tax falls on shareholders.

Case Against the Corporate Income Tax

The analysis of incidence leads directly into the major criticism of the corporate income tax. Corporations are owned by their shareholders. Their net income, or profit, belongs to their shareholders. When the shareholders receive part of that income as dividends, it becomes part of their personal income and is subject to individual income tax. When the corporation retains (and reinvests) part or all of its profit or net income, that reinvestment should increase the value of the shares of stock. When the shareholder sells the stock, the capital gain (increase in the value of the stock) is taxable income. The issue for many people, then, involves both efficiency and equity. When dividends and capital gains are both taxed as ordinary income to stockholders, an additional tax on corporate net income amounts to double taxation. It is for this reason that there has been at times (but not currently) a limited dividend exclusion on the individual income tax, and favorable treatment of capital gains.

The alternative proposal is called full integration of the individual and corporate income tax so that corporate profits are taxed only once. If they are taxed at the source, then any distribution or capital gain from sale of stock should be exempt from individual income taxes, or should only be taxed to the extent that the taxpayer is in a higher tax bracket than the corporation. A variety of ways are available for achieving integration. One of them is the proposed flat tax, which separates individual income tax from all kinds of business income, including proprietorships, partnerships, and corporations, which are taxed separately with a parallel business tax.

Full integration assumes that all stockholders are individual taxpayers. A significant amount of corporate stock is held by entities that either pay no taxes or can defer taxes for very long periods of time. The former group includes schools and colleges with endowments, foundations, and charitable organizations of various kinds. The latter includes pension funds, tax-deferred annuities, and individual retirement accounts. For these stockholders, there is no issue of double taxation of either dividends or capital gains, because they do not pay any individual income tax.

Case For the Corporate Income Tax

There are some valid arguments for taxing corporate net income. One is a matter of convenience. Tax collectors need "tax handles"—visible flows of funds, assets, transactions—to latch onto that provide a measure of ability to pay. Corporate net income, which must be disclosed to stockholders each year, is a good tax handle.

A second reason is that corporations benefit from government services ranging from fire and police protection to transportation systems, educational services, and various kinds of infrastructure. The corporate income tax can be regarded as a way to make corporations pay some or all of the cost of these inputs into production. The problem with this second argument is that here is a weak link between the value of services received and the corporation's net income or profit. Firms that use substantial amounts of public services but generate no profit contribute nothing toward the cost of these services, while highly profitable firms contribute heavily even if they use very few services. Fees for services are often a more equitable and effective way of "billing" firms of all kinds for the services that they consume.

A third argument is that taxation of corporate income or profit adds a degree of progressivity to the overall tax system, because shareholders come from the upper end of the income spectrum. Closely related is the argument that if this tax is indeed a tax on capital, it helps to counterbalance any burden of the Social Security payroll tax (see below) that falls on the employer rather than the employee. Absent a tax on capital, the firm may have an inefficiently strong incentive to substitute capital for labor.

Fourth, opposition to the corporate income tax is based on an unrealistic assumption of highly competitive markets. Many corporations enjoy some degree of market power. Some of their net income may be monopoly profit. Unlike normal profit, which is just enough to keep the owners' capital invested in the business, or temporary profit, which serves as a signal to expand output and a reward for a fast response, monopoly profit serves no socially useful function. Taxing monopoly profit is attractive from the efficiency standpoint (no undesirable changes in economic behavior) as well as equity (since owners of firms with monopoly power are generally owned by higher income individuals).

Finally, although dividends are taxed in the year in which they are distributed, capital gains are another matter. If there were no corporate income tax, then under the present system capital gains that result from reinvesting retained earnings would not be taxed under the individual income tax until they were distributed as dividends (which might never happen) or the shareholder realized the gains by selling the stock. The possibilities are unlimited for deferring this income, perhaps until death, when it might never be taxed unless the estate is very large. The corporate income tax makes sure that a substantial annual flow of income is taxed in the year for which it is earned, rather than after long delays, or in some cases, not at all.

SOCIAL SECURITY TAXES

Social Security taxes are simple, but controversial. Employer and employee each pay 7.65% of wages and salaries up to a maximum ($76,200 in 2000). Self-employed persons pay both parts, but with an income tax adjustment to cover the employer part. Of this amount, 1.45% for both employer and employee goes to the Medicare trust fund, and the remaining 6.2% goes to the OASDI (Old Age, Survivors', and Disability Insurance) trust funds. The Medicare tax also applies to income above the maximum. Self-employed persons pay the combined employer/employee rates but receive certain adjustments on their individual income tax returns. Because the tax is only on wages and cuts off at a maximum, the Social Security tax is moderately regressive. It is not a pure tax, nor is it a pure insurance premium, although a recipient of Social Security does need to make payments for a specified number of quarters to be eligible for benefits, and the value of the benefits is somewhat related to the level of contributions.

The Social Security Trust Funds have been a source of great controversy in the 1990s. For more than a decade these trust funds have been running large surpluses, with taxes and interest earnings greatly outdistancing payments to retirees, workers with disabilities, and survivors. The surplus is invested in Treasury bonds, which finance the deficit in the regular budget. Thus, the surplus that appeared for the first time in more than three decades in the fiscal 1998 budget was the result of a deficit in the operating budget that was more than balanced by the surplus in the trust funds. However, those surpluses are projected to disappear and turn into deficits, so that eventually operating budgets will have to include funds to repay the money that the federal government has been borrowing from the trust funds. At some point in the distant future—currently estimated as 2038—the balance in the trust funds will be exhausted, and the Social Security system will not be able to continue paying benefits at the current (inflation-adjusted) levels. These issues are discussed in some detail in Chapter 18.

SUMMARY

Income taxes account for almost all federal government revenues and a substantial share of state revenues. Income taxes in the United States included individual income taxes, corporate income taxes, and Social Security taxes. Forty-one states and more than 4,000 local governments also use income taxes. Income taxes generate substantial revenues and are very responsive to income growth. Income taxes can be customized to improve equity in income distribution as well as to meet other social goals.

One of the biggest challenges to an income tax is defining what constitutes income and which kinds of income should be subject to the tax. Defining income involves not only equity issues but also trade-offs between a broad base and low rates on the one hand, and costs of collection and compliance on the other.

The primary efficiency issue with a broad-based income tax is distorting the income-leisure choice. Most of the efficiency issues with income taxes are related to distortions that result from adjustments, exemptions, and deductions that encourage taxpayers to rearrange their economic choices so as to minimize their tax burdens.

Attempting to create horizontal equity with equal tax burdens for people in equal economic situations is the source of much of the complexity in income taxes in practice. Vertical equity issues are mainly related to the progressive rate structure and the exclusion of a base amount of income from taxation. The combination of these two features has made the U.S. income tax system moderately progressive in practice, although less so than in early decades.

The U.S. federal income tax has low collection costs but high compliance costs for taxpayers.

Individual income taxes are computed by first defining gross income for tax purposes, which excludes certain categories of income that are not subject to tax. Gross income is then converted to adjusted gross income by subtracting certain items that are considered costs of earning income or are granted special tax preferences. Adjusted gross income less exemptions and itemized or standard deductions is taxable income, which is the basis on which tax liability is computed. This tax liability is then adjusted for tax credits and additional taxes due (e.g., self-employment tax). The difference between this figure and tax already paid through withholding or estimated tax is the tax owed or refund due. One of those credits, the Earned Income Tax Credit, is a limited form of a negative income tax designed to provide greater work incentives as well as more progressivity at the lower end of the income tax scale.

The federal income tax system relies heavily on voluntary compliance, with the "incentive" of being audited if a return shows evidence of misrepresentation. The audit rate is low but the penalties can be substantial.

The gradualist school of tax reform points to such areas for improvement as the marriage tax penalty, the treatment of capital gains, and preferred treatment of employee fringe benefits. The alternative is a major structural change, moving toward the flat tax or some kind of consumption tax.

Forty-one state governments and more than 4,000 local governments also levy income taxes. Most local income taxes are at a single flat rate. Most state income taxes are tied to the federal tax either by using federal adjusted gross income or federal taxable income as a starting point or in calculating state income tax due as a percentage of federal income tax liability. A few states operate completely independent systems. Deductibility of state income taxes on the federal income tax reduces the progressivity of the tax system.

While partnerships and proprietorships are taxed under the individual income tax, corporations pay a separate tax on corporate net income or corporate profits. One of the major problems with the corporate income tax is defining allowable expenses. Treatment of depreciation of capital and expenditures that appear to be consumption spending for managers and employees are particularly challenging. A second problem is the issue of double taxation and integration of the individual and corporate income tax. A third challenge is the incentive for firms to rely more heavily on debt than equity financing because interest expenditures are tax deductible. The corporate income tax is also part of the case for special treatment of income arising from capital gains.

Theory suggests that in the short run the incidence of the corporate income tax is on capital or shareholders, but in the long run part of the burden may fall on workers or consumers of products of the corporate sector. Because of the problem of double taxation, there is strong support for integration of the individual and corporate income taxes or, failing that, special tax treatment of capital gains and corporate dividends. Arguments for the tax include convenience of collection, progressivity, consumption of government services by firms, the existence of monopoly power, and the use of corporations to avoid or defer paying taxes, especially on unrealized capital gains.

Social Security payroll taxes are mildly regressive and a significant revenue source for the Federal government.

KEY TERMS AND CONCEPTS

exclusions, 209
adjustments, 210
adjusted gross income, 210
taxable income, 210
filing status, 210
personal exemptions, 210

standard or itemized
    deductions, 210
tax credits, 213
Earned Income Tax Credit
    (EITC), 213

negative income tax, 214
tax evasion, 214
tax avoidance, 214
audit, 214
accelerated depreciation, 220

DISCUSSION QUESTIONS

1. What steps could be taken to make the federal individual income tax more progressive? Less progressive? What advantages does the income tax have over other taxes in terms of keying in on a desired degree of progressivity?
2. Evaluate the flat tax in terms of efficiency, equity, and compliance/collection costs.
3. Taxes affect not only primary markets but also secondary markets. If the corporate income tax is a tax on capital in the corporate sector, use a diagram to describe the effects on (a) demand for labor in the corporate sector and (b) the cost of capital in the noncorporate sector.
4. Use the standard microeconomic model of monopoly (cost curves, demand, and mar-

ginal revenue) to analyze the effect of a percentage tax on corporate profits on the firm's output level and the price of the product.
5. Suppose that you as an economist are asked to evaluate a new state tax provision that exempts the first $20,000 of retirement income for anyone over age 65 from the state income tax. The estimated revenue loss from this provision is $85 million in the first year. It will rise only with the growth in the elderly population since the $20,000 is not indexed. Evaluate this proposal in terms of equity, efficiency, and other criteria discussed in Chapters 8 and 9.

CHAPTER 11

TAXES ON SALES AND CONSUMPTION

Sales taxes lack the drama of an April 15 deadline or the shock effect of an annual property tax bill. Every trip to the store, every impulse purchase, every stop at the pump to tank up the car generates a few cents of federal or state excise taxes or state and local retail sales taxes. The sales tax is always ranked high in popularity (or, more accurately, low in unpopularity) when compared in polls with the federal income and local property tax.[1] Why? Perhaps because sales taxes are relatively painless; they are extracted on a daily basis in very small sums. Economists may prefer that taxes be visible, but taxpayers seem to prefer those taxes that are less visible.

While income taxes are the mainstay of the federal government, sales and excise taxes are the top-ranking source of state revenue. Federal excise taxes and some limited tariffs on imports contribute less than 10% of federal tax revenue. These taxes (including gasoline, alcoholic beverage, tobacco, air transportation, and telephone taxes) are the remnants of a federal revenue system in the 18th and 19th centuries that relied almost exclusively on excise taxes and public land sales to finance the central government. In the last half of the 20th century, a large number of other countries adopted some form of the value-added tax (discussed later in this chapter) as the primary form of central government revenue, including most of Europe, South America, Canada, and Mexico. So the U.S. system, in which sales taxes are used heavily at the state and

1. U.S. Advisory Commission on Intergovernmental Relations, Changing Public Attitudes on Government and Taxes, 1984, 1987, 1990, 1993. Washington, DC.

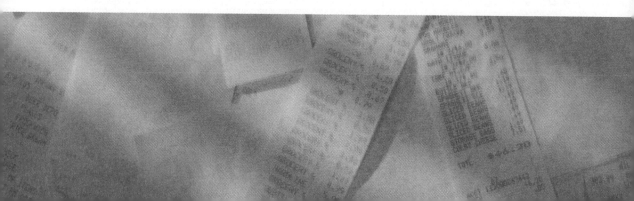

local level but very little at the national level, is quite different from most of the rest of the world.

State sales taxes, including retail sales and gross receipts taxes as well as excise taxes, accounted for 48% of state tax revenue and 38% of state own-source general revenue in 1998. (The share is higher in those states with no broad-based income taxes.) At the local level, retail sales taxes and/or excise taxes are used by more than 7,500 cities and towns, counties, townships and parishes, school districts, and special districts. For these governments, most of which rely heavily on property taxes, sales taxes generated 16% of local tax revenue and 10% of own-source revenue in 1996.

WHY TAX SALES?

Sales or transactions are taxed for both theoretical and practical reasons. The most important practical reason is that transactions provide a "tax handle," consisting of an activity (buying and selling) in which a value is established on which to base the tax, as well as two parties (buyer and seller), each of whom provides a cross-check on the reporting of the other. The oldest form of sales tax is probably the tariff, a tax on goods entering the port or the city from abroad. Where the number of points of entry was limited—airports, docks, city gates—that narrow funnel through which goods must pass created an opportunity for tax collectors to gather and levy the tax with relative ease. As the number of buyers, sellers, and locations grows, however, the sales tax becomes more difficult to administer. The growth of first mail-order and later Internet commerce has posed some serious challenges to state and local retail sales taxes in this country. Most states do not attempt to include all retail transactions in their base because of the compliance and collections costs of extracting revenue from sporadic sellers or very small retailers. However, sales and transactions, with all their limitations, still offer one of the most visible and accessible tax handles.

A second reason for taxing sales is that consumption spending, along with ownership of real property and income, is a measure of ability to pay taxes. The more one spends, presumably, the more taxpaying capacity one has. It is easier to conceal income from the tax collector than it is to conceal purchases. So a sales tax is a way of extracting a contribution to the public treasury from those who are engaging in either legal tax avoidance (by the form in which they get their income) or illegal but undetected tax evasion.

A third reason for taxing sales is particularly important at the state and local level. This tax offers a way of capturing revenue from commuters, tourists, and business travelers who use the public services provided by state and local governments. The sales tax is highly exportable for states that are major travel destinations and for cities that attract large numbers of commuters to work during the day.

Retail sales taxes, the most common form of sales tax in the United States, are relatively responsive to short-run cyclical changes in income, less so to longer term growth. The short-run elasticity of the retail sales tax base is estimated at 1.039 (1.377 if food is excluded), but the long-run elasticities are estimated at only 0.66 and 0.701, respectively.[2] Thus, states that rely heavily on sales taxes need to complement them with other revenue sources that have higher long-run income elasticities.

SALES TAXES, VALUE-ADDED TAXES, AND EXCISE TAXES

The variety of taxes on consumption or transactions is almost endless, but only three basic types are in widespread use in the United States and other countries today: the **retail sales tax** (or sometimes the wholesale tax); the **value-added tax;** and **selective sales taxes** on specific items, such as gasoline, automobile tires, or cigarettes, known as **excise taxes.** Tariffs are a special form of excise tax that apply only to certain imported goods.

We can sort the various kinds of sales taxes in any of several ways. One grouping is to sort them into multistage or single-stage taxes. Tariffs, excise taxes, some kinds of wholesale taxes, and retail sales taxes are single stage. The value-added tax and its predecessor, the cascade tax (*umsatzsteuer* in German), are multistage taxes. A second way to classify the tax is by the breadth of the base. A universal base of all sales or purchases (value-added taxes come close) would represent one extreme, whereas excise taxes or tariffs on specific items would represent the opposite end of the spectrum. Retail sales taxes are closer to the universal end of the spectrum, but the breadth of coverage varies greatly from one jurisdiction to another.

A third classification would be on the basis of who is legally liable to pay the tax, which often bears little relationship to actual economic incidence. Retail sales taxes in the United States are an obligation of the buyer, although in practice they are collected mostly by the seller. Value-added taxes in most countries are an obligation of the seller. When goods are sold to nonresidents, the value-added tax of the sending jurisdiction is rebated at export and the value-added tax of the receiving jurisdiction is imposed at import. This practice not only implements the destination principle (see Chapter 9) but also ensures a level playing field (nondistortion of choice) between domestic and imported goods. Tariffs are generally levied on the importer, excise taxes on the seller in most cases. The distinction is particularly important to tax collectors when there are multiple competing jurisdictions with different rates and coverage, because someone must decide which jurisdiction gets to collect the revenue and impose its tax rules.

2. Russell S. Sobel and Randall G. Holcombe, "Measuring the Growth and Variability of Tax Bases over the Business Cycle," *National Tax Journal*, XLIX(4) (December 1998): pp. 535–552.

EFFICIENCY ISSUES IN SALES TAXATION

A primary objection to sales taxation is that the sales tax tends to erode its own base over time, particularly if the base of the tax is anything less than total consumption or the tax rates are very different in adjacent jurisdictions. People have been creative in finding ways in which to legally avoid the sales tax or reduce the amount paid, particularly in the long run. One is to shop in markets where the tax is lower or nonexistent. Five states in the United States do not have sales taxes, and in other states certain items are exempt that are not widely exempt elsewhere, like clothing in Pennsylvania. Some stores will (legally) waive the state and local sales tax on items being shipped out of state. And, of course, a large volume of mail-order and interstate transactions escape the tax because Congress has not yet addressed the issue of how states can compel out-of-state firms to collect tax on their behalf.

Yet another way to avoid the tax is to shift purchases from taxed to exempt items—more food and less clothing in states where food is exempt and clothing is not, more services and fewer tangible goods in almost every state. Adding to the erosion of the base by the action of buyers is the tendency of state legislatures to add exemptions and exclusions. Among the more popular exclusions for equity reasons are prescription drugs, food (recently removed partially or completely from the tax base in Louisiana, North Carolina, South Carolina, and Georgia), and purchases by charitable organizations. All of these exemptions, and others, may have strong equity justifications, but they must also be evaluated as tax expenditures that reduce revenue and further distort choices.

Shifting between Markets

Figure 11–1 illustrates a simple case of shifting purchases between taxed and untaxed markets as a result of a tax in one market (which might be a state or a city). Remember, another geographic location is a form of substitute just as another local seller or another product can be a substitute. To minimize complications, assume perfectly elastic supply and a tax that is fixed in terms of physical units, such as two cents a gallon for gasoline). The price, P_0, is initially the same in both markets in equilibrium. It is also assumed that some buyers are willing and able to shift to other markets at little or no cost by taking advantage of mail-order, Internet, or travel opportunities, while others lack the information or flexibility to shop outside the local market even with enough time to adjust. Consequently, demand declines in the taxed market but does not shift entirely to the untaxed market.

What is the effect of the tax in the two markets? In the short run, revenue in the first market from a tax per unit of $P_T - P_0$ is rectangle $P_0 P_T ab$. However, once consumers have had the opportunity to adjust, the base of the

Figure 11–1
Tax Base Erosion
with an Excise Tax

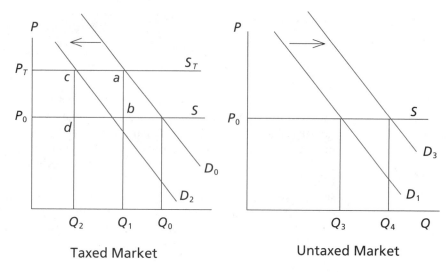

Taxed Market   Untaxed Market

tax declines from Q_1 to Q_2 and revenue drops to rectangle P_0P_Tcd.[3] In the untaxed market, of course, sales increase, although no tax revenue is generated. This ability to shift purchases between taxed and untaxed markets, or between taxed and untaxed consumption, is the primary source of base erosion. The broader the coverage of the tax in terms of both geographic extent and variety of purchases subject to the tax, the less base erosion there will be.

Avoiding Cascading

Another efficiency issue in sales or consumption taxes is ensuring that taxes do not accumulate so that some items are taxed only once and others two or more times, resulting in different tax burdens on different purchases and an unintended distortion of consumer choice. Some earlier forms of sales taxes, still in use in a few less developed countries, collected sales taxes at multiple points during the processing of a good (or service) from one stage of production to another. Wheat sold by the farmer would be taxed, then taxed again as flour when sold by the miller, again as bread when sold by the baker to the retailer, and again when the final customer bought the bread at the grocery store. The tax burden on each good depended less on the tax rate than the number of times it changed hands and caught the attention of the tax collector! For example, assume that in the absence of the tax, the wheat sold for $1, the flour for $2, and the bread for $3 wholesale and $4 retail. Ignoring any reduction in sales that might result from the tax and assuming that all

3. An alternative representation is to draw a long-run demand curve that is more price elastic than the short-run demand curve through the initial, pretax price and quantity combination Q_0, P_0. That curve would, of course, be flatter. Determining the amount of tax revenue raised in the short run versus the long run is left as an exercise for the student.

taxes are shifted forward to the buyer, what would be the effect of a 10% tax? The wheat would sell for $1.10, and the flour for $2.21. The wholesale price of bread would rise to $3.53, and the retail price to $4.98. With no change in the net revenue to sellers, and a 10% tax rate, the price of bread will have risen by almost 25%! An integrated operation, however, that owned its own wheat farm and flour mill and sold directly to consumers would be taxed only once, so that its bread would sell for $4.40, a true 10% tax. Clearly such a tax has the potential to create large and unintended changes in consumer decisions in response to very uneven tax burdens on different goods or different producers/sellers.

Germany and the Netherlands had such **cascade-type taxes** when they joined the European Community back in the late 1950s, but by 1968 they had replaced these taxes with a value-added tax (discussed later). With the support and encouragement of the World Bank, and the example of the European Community's success with the value-added tax (VAT), most of the nations that had been using cascade taxes have replaced them with VATs or some other, less distorting form of sales tax.

The retail sales tax is collected at the point of final sale from retailer or distributor to the final consumer. Ideally, each item would be taxed once and only once. One reason for using a single-stage tax (either wholesale or retail) is to avoid cascading or accumulation of tax on tax, which distorts consumers' choices between different products or services because those that pass through more taxable stages accumulate larger amounts of tax. However, cascading can occur in a single-stage tax if some business purchases at the taxable stage are incorporated into products or services also subject to the tax. One source of this problem is the fact that many items are purchased both by business firms and individuals. When a bakery buys flour, flour should not be taxed, because there will be a tax at retail on the consumer's purchase of the loaf of bread. When a household buys flour with which to bake its own bread, it is truly a final sale and should be subject to tax (unless, of course, food is exempt). Office equipment, tools, office supplies, packaging materials, and software are just a few of the many items that are sold to both business firms and households. If the business firm must pay retail sales tax on its inputs, that tax is reflected in the selling price, and the retail sales tax on the final purchase is compounded by the tax at this earlier stage of processing. If the final product is tax exempt, for example, a lawyer buys software and office supplies, but her services are typically not subject to retail sales tax, then the intent of the tax code to exempt legal services from the retail sales tax is not being fully realized.

How substantial is this problem of cascading with the U.S. retail sales tax? According to economist Raymond Ring, the share of the sales tax falling on business purchases varies greatly from state to state, with an average of 41% and a range from only 11% in West Virginia to 72% in Hawaii where most services (including business services) are subject to sales tax.[4] In states

4. Raymond J. Ring, Jr., Consumers' Share and Producers' Share of the General Sales Tax, *National Tax Journal*, 52 (March 1999): pp. 79ff.

where business purchases are heavily subject to sales tax, cascading can be a significant problem.

On the other hand, a case can be made on both efficiency and equity grounds for some amount of the sales tax in the state of origin being reflected in the price of the good and passed forward to consumers wherever they live. To the extent that such sales taxes are used to pay for public services that benefit producers, these firms are purchasing inputs into the production process that might properly be considered a cost of production—for example, paying for the fire and police service that protects the plant or the roads on which raw materials and final products are transported. Unfortunately, there is rarely any close connection between the amount of sales tax paid on inputs and the amount of public services consumed by the firm.

EQUITY ISSUES IN SALES TAXATION

The primary objection to sales taxes is that they tend to be regressive, except for certain excise taxes on luxury goods. A broad-based tax on sales or consumption, whether a value-added tax, a wholesale tax, or a retail tax, excludes saving by definition. Since saving rises with income (higher income households save a substantially greater fraction of their incomes), consumption and sales tax burden on that consumption becomes a smaller fraction of income as income rises.

Given the popularity of sales taxes (at least in comparison to income and property taxes), what can be done to make them less regressive? The four strategies described here are used in the context of U.S. state retail sales taxes but also applicable to other kinds of broad-based sales taxes:

1. Broaden the base, primarily by including some services, to keep the rate low and include more of the consumption spending of higher income households.
2. Narrow the base by eliminating consumption that represents a large fraction of income for lower income households (especially food and clothing).
3. Fine-tune the retail, wholesale, or value-added sales tax with excise taxes or differential rates on certain items that are consumed more heavily by upper income classes (e.g., luxury taxes, admissions and amusements taxes, travel and tourism taxes).
4. Rebate some of the sales tax through means-tested income tax relief.

Broaden the Base

A few states, most notably Hawaii, New Mexico, and South Dakota, have expanded their sales taxes to cover a substantial number of services. Along with saving, consumption of services tends to rise with increases in income, so that including more services should reduce the regressivity of a sales or value-added tax. Broadening the base also makes it possible to raise the same amount of revenue with a lower tax rate.

Services most commonly taxed include transient housing (motels, hotels, resort villas, etc.), personal services such as massages and hair care, transport services such as auto rentals, and miscellaneous household services such as auto repair, dry cleaning, and lawn care. However, broad coverage of services has been difficult to achieve in most states. In 1995, Florida approved a major expansion of its sales tax base that included legal services, advertising services, and a variety of other personal and business services. Within six months, the governor and the legislature were forced by political pressure to rescind these changes.

Part of the problem in Florida was the power of an organized lobby, led by lawyers and fueled by the power of advertising when both legal services and advertising were targets for taxation. But taxing services faces more fundamental challenges. Services are more likely to be produced and sold by very small firms, greatly increasing the collection costs for the state and compliance costs for firms. Although many states have some services in their retail sales tax bases, the tax still falls primarily on tangible goods.

Narrow the Base

The alternative strategy to make a sales tax less regressive is to exempt certain items. For most low-income families, the biggest item in the budget is housing (rent), which as a service is exempt in most states. Among tangible goods, the most common exemption is food. The food exemption is appealing, but difficult to administer because of the challenge of defining food. Do cat food and dog food qualify? Do the tax writers mean to exempt caviar? What about alcoholic beverages? Does it cover everything purchased in the grocery store, which is likely to include toilet paper, toothpaste, and the *National Enquirer?* Cash registers must be programmed to distinguish between taxable and nontaxable items, which increases both collection and compliance costs. (Some states have resolved this problem by defining food as anything eligible to be purchased with food stamps, for which most cash registers are already programmed.)

The food exemption significantly reduces the base of the tax and makes the revenue less stable. In addition, the food tax exemption suffers the usual problem of tax expenditures in terms of not targeting a particular group very efficiently. Exempting food is a rather inefficient mechanism if the intent is to reach only the poor. Remember that 85% of the population is not poor, yet their food purchases are also exempt!

Despite these drawbacks, two-thirds of the states with sales taxes now exempt food, and there is pressure in the remaining states to follow their example. Georgia, Louisiana, North Carolina, are the most recent states to adopt a partial or total exemption of food. Food is also commonly exempt (*zero rated* is the preferred term) from many value-added taxes in other countries for the same reasons.

Other widely used exemptions that are intended to reduce regressivity are utilities (electricity, gas, water), prescription drugs, and, in a few states, clothing. The clothing exemption (almost always restricted by price or to children's clothing) is somewhat questionable as a technique to make the tax less regressive.

Fine-Tune the Tax

A third tactic for improving the equity of the retail, wholesale, or value-added sales tax is to impose an excise tax or differential tax rate on certain items that are consumed more heavily by upper income households. In the past, these taxes have been used for that purpose at the federal level in the United States, with excise taxes on jewelry and leather goods as well as airline tickets. A brief and disastrous attempt in 1991 to impose a federal luxury tax on yachts was fairly quickly repealed in response to complaints from yacht producers that their business had plummeted dramatically. (Apparently even the very wealthy have elastic ranges to their demand curves!)

Most states have admissions and amusements taxes, sometimes at the same rate as the sales tax, sometimes higher, but in either case the taxes mark a relatively rare expansion into taxing services. The reasonable presumption is that attending concerts, plays, and sporting events is an expenditure of discretionary income more likely to be found in middle to upper income households. Likewise, travel taxes (on airline departures, motel accommodations, and restaurant meals) at rates usually higher than the retail sales tax offer a way to impose taxes on nonresidents (tax exporting) and also an extension of sales taxes into services consumed primarily by higher income households.

Protect the Poor

Seven states operate a rebate program for part of the sales tax, usually subject to an income limit, as a way to provide relief for lower income households. Four states—Hawaii, Idaho, New Mexico, and Vermont—offer a rebate through the personal income tax, while three others (Kansas, South Dakota, and Wyoming) administer the refund separately. In some cases the rebate is only to reimburse for sales taxes on food. This approach has the advantage of giving relief only to low-income households, thus sacrificing less revenue than the tax expenditure approach of exempting food for all state residents. It can be used in combination with the other three strategies to significantly reduce the regressivity of a broad-based retail sales tax, such as that used by most states in the United States.

STATE RETAIL SALES TAX IN THE UNITED STATES

The most important sales tax in the United States in terms of revenue is the state retail sales tax. This tax is a single-stage tax on final sales, primarily to consumers. Although the tax is designed and administered in various ways from state to state, the similarities outweigh the differences, so for practical purposes they can be grouped together in terms of structure, history, and evaluations.

History and Evolution

The retail sales tax as a major source of state revenue arrived in two waves. The first wave, in the 1930s, was a response to revenue challenges during the Great Depression. Prior to that time the property tax was a major source of state as well as local revenue, and states had relatively few demands for services. With dramatic declines in property values, foreclosures, distress sales, and just an inability to collect much of the property tax, state governments had to look to a new revenue source. At the same time, the vastly increased demands for poverty relief filtered upward from overwhelmed local governments first to states and ultimately to the federal level. Twenty-four states adopted retail sales taxes in this first wave from 1933 to 1938.

Pressure to find revenue to improve highways and educate the baby boomers led another 11 states and the District of Columbia to add retail sales taxes in the post–World War II period (1947–1955) and another 11 in the 1960s. The last adoption was Vermont in 1969, leaving only five states with no broad based retail sales taxes: Alaska, Delaware, Montana, New Hampshire, and Oregon.

Why did states turn to sales taxes rather than to other revenue sources? By 1933 the federal government was making fairly heavy use of the individual income tax (used by 26 states at that time), while local governments relied heavily on the property tax. With only three major kinds of broad-based taxes, some form of sales tax (a field largely abandoned at that point by the federal government) seemed the most obvious choice. The value-added tax was not well known at that point and in any case was difficult to administer at the state level because of the needed adjustments at "export" and "import" with other states. It was not even clear that such a process of export and import adjustments would be consistent with the interstate commerce clause of the Constitution. Another alternative might have been a wholesale tax, but this tax has a much narrower base and would therefore have required much higher rates to raise the same revenue. In addition, wholesale activity was spread much more unevenly among states than retail sales. Every town had a Main Street retail sector that could be tapped for state and later local sales tax revenue. Even the arrival of the malls, often outside city limits, still ensured a steady flow of sales tax revenue to the state. So considerations of adequacy and simplicity were important factors in this choice.

Pressure on states to raise revenue was renewed in the 1980s and early 1990s because of declining federal aid to states, the recession of 1990–1992, increased spending demands for corrections and education, and demands for property tax relief through increased state funding of education and other local services. The sales tax was again the favored choice of state governments, either for their own use or for their local governments' use. Between 1978 and 1994, 39 state governments raised their sales tax rates. By 1999, the average combined state–local rate had risen to 8.23%. The median state sales tax rate among states with sales taxes rose from 4% to just over 5%, although the top state rate remained at 7% (Mississippi and Rhode Island). Only Connecticut bucked the upward trend, reducing its sales tax rate from 8% to 6% in the 1990s by instituting an individual income tax. At the local level, the average sales tax was 1.6% each for municipalities and counties. The highest combined state and local rate was in the town of Arab in Alabama, at 11%.

Efficiency Issues

In addition to the general efficiency issues associated with all types of sales taxes, retail sales taxes have their own particular challenges. The retail sales tax can be administered as either an origin principle tax or a destination principle tax, as discussed in Chapter 9. Arguments can be offered for either approach, but the fact that the incidence of a broad-based retail sales tax falls mainly on the consumer supports the choice of a destination principle, so that the person actually paying the tax will be consuming the public services that those taxes support. The U.S. retail sales tax is primarily a destination principle tax with some notable exceptions. Tourists and business travelers pay state and local taxes in the places where they travel, not those of their home states. Many mail-order and Internet purchasers have been able to avoid sales and use taxes altogether because of the difficulty of collecting from the final consumer rather than the retail seller. The gap between taxable sales and actual revenue generated represents not only a revenue loss but an efficiency challenge consumer choice is distorted in favor of those sellers who are able to avoid collecting the tax. This gap, and its growth with the development of e-commerce, represents a serious threat to the revenue base of the retail sales tax in the future. A recent report by the General Accounting Office estimates the revenue loss from these two sources to be in the range of $1.6 to $9.1 billion in 2000, rising to a range of $2.5 to $20.4 billion in 2003.[5]

The fact that the base of the retail sales tax is less than 100% of consumption is also a source of distortion in consumer decisions. The incomplete

---

5. United States General Accounting Office, *Sales Taxes: Electronic Commerce Presents Challenges; Revenue Losses Are Uncertain* (Washington, DC: Government Printing Office, 2000): p. 36.

coverage raises the after-tax price of some items relative to others, encouraging consumers to shift their consumption over time to untaxed items such as food (in about 70% of states) and many services as well as to out-of-state retailers through mail-order and Internet purchases.

Retail sales taxes can also distort locational decisions for not only commercial facilities (often located near state lines to attract buyers from nearby higher tax states) but also industrial firms, because some states tax a wider range of business purchases than others. For firms that buy a large quantity of materials and supplies that are taxable in some states and not in others, there is an incentive to locate their facilities—or at least their purchasing departments—in states that offer the most attractive tax situation.

Equity Issues

Regressivity is the primary equity issue for most kinds of broad-based sales or consumption taxes, but the retail sales tax has some specific equity challenges because of the way it is administered in the United States. The failure to tax most services in most states is an equity as well as an efficiency issue inasmuch as inclusion of services makes the tax less regressive.

The destination principle creates serious challenges for tax administrators in collecting sales or use tax (see Chapter 9 for a discussion of use taxes) on a large share of mail-order and Internet sales, which often escape taxation in either the state of origin or the state of destination. This loophole discriminates among consumers on the basis of the way they choose to shop. Because the Internet and mail-order methods tend to appeal to more sophisticated buyers, it is likely that failure to tax a large share of mail-order and Internet sales makes the sales tax more regressive.

LOCAL SALES TAX IN THE UNITED STATES

The local sales tax has become increasingly popular as a way to take some pressure off the unpopular property tax. Local sales taxes are an important source of revenue for cities, and to a lesser degree other kinds of local governments, providing more than 10% of local tax revenue in 1994. Alaska has local sales taxes at a 6% rate in its boroughs and municipalities, the only state without a state sales tax that authorizes local sales taxes. Nineteen states have local sales taxes in both cities and counties (parishes), four only in counties, two only in municipalities. Louisiana is the only state where all school districts rely on sales tax revenue. Special districts or transit districts also use the tax in eight states, and in South Dakota, three Indian reservations have local sales taxes. While most rates are in the range of 0.5% to 2%, some rates are higher: 5% in New Orleans, for example, 4.25% in New York City, 4.3% combined city–county tax in Denver, and 5% combined city–county tax in

TAXING THE TOURIST

In general, tax exporting to residents of other states or countries as a way of easing the burden of taxation has limited potential for providing one's own citizens with tax relief. One exception is taxing tourists, a practice at which states and nations have become increasingly creative. Just having a local sales taxes in tourist destinations is one technique, but it is more effective to target those activities and services used primarily by travelers in order to shift a share of the burden to out-of-staters or foreigners. Of course, it is impossible to totally exempt a state's or nation's own residents, who do travel within as well as beyond the borders! Taxing transient accommodations (hotels and motels) and rentals, rental cars, airport parking, airport and cruise ship departures, admissions, amusements, downtown parking, restaurant meals, and gambling are all ways to target visitors. Because most of these items (excepting gambling outside casinos) are consumed largely by upper income groups, the part of the tax that does fall on in-state residents contributes to reducing the regressivity of sales taxes within the state.

Some of these taxes can be pretty steep. Visitors to New York City, for example, pay a 12% accommodations tax on their motel rooms. The nation's capital adds 12% to parking and 10% to restaurant meals to take advantage of the many tourists that stop to see the White House, the Washington Monument, and the Smithsonian.

But pushing tourism taxes too hard carries a risk. Like most services, tourist services are in a highly competitive and price-sensitive industry. Taxes can make prices too high relative to other almost equally attractive destinations at home or abroad, so tax officials have to keep an eye on the competition and set their rates accordingly. Over time, travelers may respond to the higher total cost including tax by shifting to cheaper ways of getting around. They may drive their own cars instead of flying and renting, stay with friends and relatives, camp or stay in places with cooking facilities to avoid eating out, or find other economical methods that reduce the yield of the tax. But some localities provide access to unique desirable features, such as breathtaking scenery, long stretches of unspoiled ocean beaches, tropical forests, or whitewater rivers for rafters. These communities may enjoy enough monopoly power in the possession of their unique tourism assets to make demand relatively price inelastic. In that case, tourism taxes could be somewhat higher than those of the nearest imperfect substitute destination without substantially eroding the base.

Although tourism taxes get fairly high marks for equity and moderate to low ratings on efficiency, they have other drawbacks. Tourism is a very cyclically sensitive industry, so tourism taxes fluctuate much more than total economic activity, which makes them a rather undependable revenue source. As a local tax (a fairly common assignment), the revenue potential is distributed very unevenly among counties and municipalities within a given state, and often it is the wealthier communities in resort areas that have the most revenue potential even though the revenue needs are greater in other parts of the state.

The tourism industry (owners of tourist accommodations and facilities and providers of travel services) has lobbied heavily to either limit tourism taxes or earmark the revenue for tourism promotion and tourism-related services. Although economists are generally skeptical about earmarking revenues, this practice is often the only way to overcome the opposition of the affected business interests. Beyond the public choice aspects of earmarking, however, are some equity and efficiency considerations that might make earmarking less harmful. First, the use of the revenue to provide the additional local services (garbage pickup, police and fire protection, park facilities, parking, local transportation, etc.) can convert tourism taxes into benefit taxes and thus avoid distributing some of the additional cost of accommodating tourists to the local permanent population, especially those not employed in the tourism industry. Second, the use of some of the revenue for tourism promotion may help to offset base erosion and maintain revenue in the face of competition for visitors.

Mobile, Alabama. In some states the tax is uniform statewide, while other states allow local option.

The efficiency and collection/compliance cost problems associated with state retail sales taxes are many times magnified in the case of a local sales tax, particularly if the tax is adopted by local option or if rate differences are allowed. It is much harder to collect local sales taxes on the destination principle. Imagine a San Antonio resident shopping in Dallas. The destination principle would require the retailer to determine where you are from and fill out a form to ensure that you are charged the appropriate rate and that the revenue is sent to San Antonio instead of Dallas! So within states, at least, the destination principle is suspended for the more manageable origin principle for local taxes. Large local tax differentials can also affect marginal locational decisions—outside or inside the municipality, on this side of the county line or the other.

In states where the tax is used, or shared, by both counties and municipalities (or special districts), some formula has to be devised to share the revenue appropriately. One kind of formula uses a mixture of population share and place of origin. Because everyone lives in the county (unless the formula specifies the unincorporated part), while a smaller percentage lives inside municipal boundaries, the first part of the formula would favor the county, but the concentration of retail facilities inside municipalities would tend to tip the sharing in favor of cities. In other states, the law specifies a maximum combined rate that can be used partly by the county and partly by municipalities.

EXCISE TAXES

All 50 states and the District of Columbia have some excise taxes, including those levied on gasoline, cigarettes, and distilled liquor. An excise or selective sales tax is imposed on named goods, such as the tax per gallon of gasoline or pack of cigarettes. Many excise taxes are specific; that is, they are stated in terms of the physical units (so many cents per gallon or pack), while others are *ad valorem,* expressed as a percentage of the price. The drawback of a specific tax is that revenue only grows with population and sometimes income, but not with inflation. *Ad valorem* tax revenue increases not only as more units are sold but also as the price per unit goes up. Recall from Chapter 8 that a specific tax can be represented with a parallel demand or supply curve, while an *ad valorem* tax results in a steeper slope on the shadow demand or supply curve.

Rate and Base

Figure 11–2 shows an excise tax on gasoline that is expressed as a percentage of the price. Demand for gasoline is relatively price inelastic in the short

Figure 11–2
An Excise Tax
on Gasoline

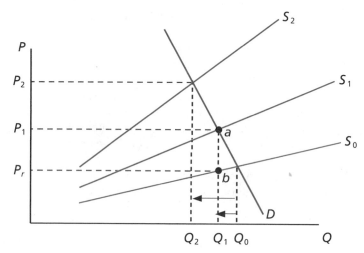

run, since it has few good substitutes for most of its uses (driving cars and trucks and running lawn mowers and motorboats). Supply is moderately elastic since petroleum can be converted among its multiple uses depending on the price that can be obtained for each end product (including gasoline, heating oil, plastics, and fertilizer). In this situation, the tax (the vertical distance between S_0 and S_1) will show up primarily as an increase in the price paid by the buyer, and there will be only a modest reduction in the tax base from Q_0 to Q_1. Tax revenue will be equal to $P_r P_1 ab$. However, further increases in the tax (such as that represented by shadow supply curve S_2) will push buyers into the more elastic range of the demand curve. As the tax rate escalates, both the absolute and percentage decline in Q accelerates (and so does the excess burden or deadweight loss). That is, an increasingly larger increase in the tax rate is required to generate the same increase in revenue (or the same increase in the rate will generate less revenue) because of **base erosion**. Rate and base relationships always offer a challenging trade-off for tax policy of any kind, but particularly so for excise taxes, because the base is already narrowly defined.

Revenue, Equity, and Sumptuary Goals

Excise taxes serve multiple purposes. One is revenue. A second purpose is to tax items consumed more heavily by upper income groups, in order to offset the regressivity of a general sales tax at the wholesale or retail level. A third goal is to discourage consumption of goods or services as a way of reducing negative externalities (**sumptuary taxes**). In fact, many excise taxes are known as "sin" taxes because they are levied on alcohol, cigarettes, and casino games at least in part to discourage drinking, smoking, and gambling. These goals are not always consistent. Revenue and equity goals call for collecting more tax, while sumptuary goals are aimed at shrinking the base. However, governments can regard excise taxes on activities that are socially undesirable as a win–win situation. If people cut back on smoking, drinking, or gambling, they reduce the associated health and social problems related to those activities. If they continue their "bad habits," the government receives more revenue. However, there are limits on the usefulness of taxes as a way to discourage consumption. If the tax rate gets too high, it may be worth it to risk the legal consequences to supply this demand through the black (illegal) market. From bathtub gin to cigarette bootlegging to illegal numbers games, citizens have always found ways to evade excise taxes imposed "for their own good."

Some excise taxes, like the tax on airline tickets, are not intended to discourage the activity. Instead, the tax is levied on a luxury good for which demand is believed to be relatively price inelastic, so that the base will not shrink too much in response to the tax. Recall, however, that demand for most commodities and services is more elastic in the long run than in the short run, so that a tax that is very productive in terms of revenue in the short run may erode the base and reduce tax revenue in the long run.

VALUE-ADDED TAXES

The value-added tax (VAT) emerged from France to become the dominant form of sales tax in the European Community (EC) in the late 1960s. As the EC grew from 6 members to 12 and now 15, new entrants adopted the value-added tax. With the aid and encouragement of the World Bank in many cases, this complex tax was a surprisingly popular revenue tool in South American, Asia, and Africa as well. Most of these countries used the new tax to replace (or integrate) tariffs, excise taxes, cascade-type sales taxes, single-stage taxes at the manufacturer's or wholesaler's level, or other less satisfactory revenue sources in the sales tax category. Because income taxes are used in a much more limited fashion in most other countries, the VAT is not only the predominant form of sales tax but also a major source of central government revenue as well. In most cases it is administered on the destination principle, although some of the formerly communist nations of Eastern Europe apply the origin principle.

The United States' two partners in the North American Free Trade Agreement, Mexico and Canada, both use the value-added tax as an important revenue source. From time to time a VAT has been suggested as a possible replacement for the U.S. federal income tax, which would make the tax system more similar to those of our trading partners and follow recommendations from the World Bank and the International Monetary Fund. The primary obstacle to such a move is that a VAT would compete on the same tax turf as long-established state and local retail sales taxes and would therefore meet considerable political resistance. In a sense, state and local tax authorities have "preempted" the sales tax field and made it less available to the central government.

Basic Features

The VAT is imposed on the value that a producer adds to his raw materials or purchases (other than labor) before selling the product or service. The value added, therefore, consists of labor costs (L) and profit (Π). The VAT can be computed in two different ways:

1. As a tax on labor plus profit, calculated separately or together:

    $$tL + t\Pi \quad \text{or} \quad t(L + \Pi) \ .$$

    If the tax rates are the same on both wages and profits, the choice of a method is based only on relative ease of calculation.

2. As a tax on the difference in the value of output (Q) and the value of purchased inputs (I), which can be calculated separately or together:

    $$tQ - tI \quad \text{or} \quad t(Q - I) \ .$$

The most popular method is $tQ - tI$ because it is the easiest one to compute. The tax rate is simply applied to the value of sales, with a credit for taxes paid on any taxable inputs purchased. Because taxes paid on earlier stages of the production process are always credited against tax due, there is no accumulation or cascading of taxes, and the tax burden on the final product is the same percentage of the price as it was on raw materials and intermediate goods. Some VATs extend to the retail stage, while others end at wholesale.

The multistage feature of the VAT is attractive from the standpoint of international trade, and particularly trade within a free-trade area, customs union, or common market. The VAT can be integrated with customs to ensure that any product arriving in a country with a VAT is subject to the tax of the destination country. Accumulated VAT at export (which is often at the wholesale stage) is rebated at export, and compensating VAT in the importing country is collected when the product is imported. Thus, a skillet or a VCR will have the same amount of VAT accumulated at final sale in Mexico regardless of where it was produced or at what stage of production or distribution it was imported.

Some countries use a single rate, others multiple rates (Belgium has six rates, France and Mexico five), but the central or basic rates range from 6% to 23% with many clustered in the 15% to 20% range. Exemptions are often handled by *zero rating;* charging a tax rate of zero on the final taxable sale, which allows the final seller to receive a rebate for taxes accumulated to

TAXING GAMBLING

An increasingly popular form of state revenue in the 1980s and 1990s was to legalize and tax gambling in various forms. State lotteries had been banished after scandals in the late 19th century and did not reappear until the New Hampshire lottery in 1964, with a slow spread that picked up speed in the 1980s and 1990s. Thirty-eight states had state-run lotteries by 2002. The state's retained from 25% to more than 50% of the gross lottery revenues after paying winners and expenses. However, lotteries are a relatively modest source of state revenue, typically in the range of 1% to 4% of own-source revenues.

Most of the gambling was privately run with state regulation and taxation. Atlantic City and Mississippi, along with a number of native American tribes, have found a gold mine in casino gambling. Indian gambling, authorized under certain rules by 1988 federal legislation, is not a substantial source of state revenue, although some states (notably Connecticut) have negotiated mutually beneficial agreements with recognized Native American tribes for sharing some of the revenue. More often, gambling sponsored by Native Americans has been in competition with other gambling-based sources of state revenue, such as state lotteries, taxes on bingo, casinos, or free-standing video machines, which are found in six states (and were only recently banished from South Carolina).

States along the Mississippi have turned to riverboat gambling. Betting on horse and dog racing is a long-standing source of revenue for states like Florida and Connecticut. Almost every state that has some kind of legal gambling other than a state lottery also has a regulatory authority (typically a gaming commission) responsible for regulating the industry in order to protect consumers, limit access by minors, and generate revenue for the state.

Like other activities with negative externalities that are subject to excise taxes, gambling challenges governments to order their priorities. Is consumer protection the goal of gambling regulation? Or is it to discourage people from gambling, especially minors, because a minority of gamblers become habitual or compulsive or even addicted gamblers? Or is it an easy and somewhat painless source of revenue that makes it possible to fund better services without higher taxes? If it is all three, how are those conflicting goals balanced? Taxes on alcohol and cigarettes may suggest a win–win situation for states—either people continue to use these products and generate revenue or they reduce their consumption and live healthier lives. But gambling is a little different, because it poses no direct risk to physical well-being.

The 38 states that sponsor lotteries are torn between the pressure to restrict an activity that is potentially addictive and socially destructive and the attraction of the revenue that lotteries can provide. Often the flash point for that conflict of goals is the amount of effort the state invests in marketing, advertising, and promotion of the state lottery, crossing the line from permitting gambling to encouraging it. States that allow casinos have used revenues to provide valued public services and relieve pressure on taxes but also recognize that they are not only encouraging undesirable behavior but also attracting an industry with a high proportion of low-wage, dead-end jobs.

There are no easy answers to these questions. The gambling phenomenon is not just American, but worldwide, for lotteries, for traditional forms of gambling (casinos, sports betting, card rooms, slot machines), and for newer electronic forms, including video gambling and Internet casinos. Gambling revenue has a strong appeal to politicians looking to ease the pain of paying for public services, but the social and economic price tag may be higher than they were betting on in the longer term.

that point. Multiple rates are a way of integrating excise taxes into a single system, but they also add greatly to the collection and compliance cost of the system.

Efficiency and Equity Issues

Value-added taxes share the same efficiency and equity attributes as other broad-based sales taxes. In many cases, they are an improvement in efficiency over the kinds of taxes they replaced. Excises and tariffs are more distorting of decisions than broad-based taxes because they single out a few products on which to levy the tax, and usually involve higher rates, increasing the dead-weight loss. Cascade taxes, which VATs have also replaced, create a variety of effective tax rates on different products depending on how many times the inputs, intermediate products, and finished products pass through the market and are taxed. While it is often appropriate on both equity and efficiency grounds to tax different products and services at different rates, the level of tax on any given product is somewhat random rather than reflecting inten-tional distribution of the burden among consumers, elasticity of demand, dis-couraging negative externalities, or other relevant economic and social con-siderations in tax design.

Because the VAT is a sales tax with a fairly high rate compared to the rates for retail sales tax in the United States, it comes under criticism on both equity and efficiency grounds. Like all sales taxes, it is regressive. The high rates increase the deadweight loss or excess burden. It is also criticized in terms of its high collection and compliance costs. VAT both requires and creates an extensive paperwork burden on both tax collectors and taxpayers. However, some countries have found the paper trail useful in attempting to enforce other taxes and regulations, so there may be some benefits as well.

SUMMARY

Taxes on sales are primarily a state and local revenue source in the United States. State re-tail sales and excise taxes accounted for 27% 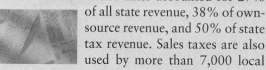 of all state revenue, 38% of own-source revenue, and 50% of state tax revenue. Sales taxes are also used by more than 7,000 local governments.

Sales taxes are appealing because transac-tions offer a convenient tax handle. They also permit tax collectors to tap one of the three measures of ability to pay (consumption) and provide a way of exporting some taxes to vis-itors who use local and state public services. The short-run elasticity of the retail sales tax base is estimated at 1.039 (1.377 if food is ex-cluded), but the long-run elasticities are esti-mated at only 0.66 and 0.701, making revenue vulnerable to economic downturns but rela-tively insensitive to long-term growth.

The types of sales taxes in widespread cur-rent use around the globe are retail sales taxes, selective sales or excise taxes (including tariffs), and value-added taxes. Sales taxes can be grouped by whether they are single- or multi-stage, broad based or narrowly focused, or levied on the buyer or seller.

Sales taxes, particularly selective ones, tend to erode their bases over time as consumers shift their purchases to untaxed forms of consumption or to markets where the tax is not collected. Moving to a state without sales taxes, or making mail-order and Internet purchases are among the major ways of avoiding sales taxes. Distortions of decision making are increased by any compounding or cascading, which can be the result of a multistage tax or even a single-stage tax that also falls at least partly on business inputs into items for further sale.

Sales taxes are regressive. The regressivity can be reduced by broadening the base, primarily by including services; narrowing the base by eliminating consumption that represents a large fraction of income for lower income households (especially food); fine-tuning the retail, wholesale, or value-added sales tax with excise taxes or differential rates on certain items that are consumed more heavily by upper income classes; and rebating some of the sales tax through means-tested income tax relief.

State retail sales taxes came into being in the 1930s, with a second wave enacted after World War II. The average tax rate increased during the 1980s and 1990s. Efficiency issues specific to this tax include the taxation of business inputs and the incomplete coverage of consumption, both of which distort locational choice and allocation of consumer spending among various goods and services. Local sales taxes are more recent in origin and at lower rates, typically 0.5% to 2%.

Excise taxes are used for revenue, to reduce the regressivity of the retail sales tax (or the value-added tax) by imposing higher taxes on luxuries, and to discourage undesirable activities such as drinking alcohol, smoking, and gambling. Excise tax rates tend to be higher than typical retail sales tax rates and thus cause more deadweight loss.

Value-added taxes have come into widespread use in other countries since the 1960s. This tax is levied on the difference between the value of inputs (other than labor) and the value of output or sales, so it is effectively a tax on wages and profits. The most common way of assessing the tax is to levy a tax on sales with a credit for any value-added tax already paid on inputs. Typical rates for a VAT are quite high, in the 15% to 20% rate, and both collection costs and compliance costs are somewhat burdensome. Some VATs are single rate, others multirate, with favored items (such as food) assigned a zero rate and higher than average rates taking the place of excise or selective sales taxes.

KEY TERMS AND CONCEPTS

retail sales tax, 230
value-added tax, 230

excise (selective sales) tax, 230
cascade-type tax, 233

base erosion, 242
sumptuary tax, 242

DISCUSSION QUESTIONS

1. What would be the advantages and drawbacks of replacing the U.S. individual income tax with a value-added tax? What if
the VAT instead replaced the state retail
sales tax?
2. Referring to Figure 11–1, how might the
outcome of imposing a tax in the first market be different if supply were less than
perfectly elastic (i.e., upward sloping) in
both markets? Will there be more or less
deadweight loss and/or base erosion? Why
or why not?
3. Excise taxes are sometimes used for pollution control. Referring back to Chapter
4 and the analysis of taxes to control negative externalities, draw a diagram that involves a tax on textiles in order to incorporate the social costs of water pollution
resulting from the chemicals used in the
textile production process. Assume that
supply is highly but not perfectly elastic
and that demand is moderately elastic. Using the diagram as a starting point, analyze the short-run and possible long-run effects of this tax on the following:
   a. Price of textiles
   b. Quantity of textiles purchased/sold
and tax base
   c. Tax revenue from this particular tax

d. The amount of water pollution
e. Deadweight loss
f. Distribution of the tax burden between customer and supplier
g. Other possible effects (e.g., alternative
production processes)
4. Consider again the issue of base erosion
posed in Figure 11–1. Instead of looking
at two markets, try analyzing the difference between short-run and long-run base
erosion. Draw two demand curves through
the initial, pretax price and quantity combination Q_0, P_0. The original demand
curve is the short-run demand curve. The
second demand curve should be a long-run
demand curve that is more price elastic
(flatter) than the short-run demand curve.
Determine the difference in the amount of
tax revenue raised in the short run versus
the long run. What are the policy implications for tax design?
5. Identify the deadweight loss or excess burden triangles for consumers and producers
when the first tax is imposed in Figure
11–2. By how much do these triangles
grow when the tax increases so that the
shadow supply curve is S_2? What can you
infer about the effects of steadily escalating tax rates on excess burden?

CHAPTER 12

TAXES ON PROPERTY AND WEALTH

The tax everybody loves to hate. The most unfair tax of all. A violation of one's right to be safe from unwarranted intrusions into private property. An attack on the private property foundation of the market economy. These are just a few of the rhetorical attacks on the basic funding source of local governments in the United States and elsewhere, the property tax.

Property taxes are among the oldest taxes in the United States. They are widely used in other countries as well, not only developed industrial countries but also in the urban areas of less developed countries. Even in the formerly communist nations of Eastern Europe prior to the revolutions of the late 1980s and early 1990s, where private property had supposedly been abolished, citizens paid a vestigial property tax on some privately owned shops, homes, land, and other tangible assets. Property, especially "real" property (i.e., land and improvements thereon) is one of the most visible and stationary of tax handles to attract the eye of the tax collector.

Until the Great Depression in the 1930s, state and local governments both relied heavily on the property tax. Beginning in the 1930s, most states shifted to income and/or sales taxes, leaving the property tax largely to local governments as a revenue source, although some state property taxes are still in place. Just because the revenue and the power to set the tax rate was handed over to local government, however, did not mean that state governments were out of the property tax business. States continue to set the rules and oversee the administration of local property taxes.

Property taxes are a significant source of funding for schools as well as for general-purpose local governments (cities, counties, and townships). In fiscal year 1998–1999, property tax collections came to $228 billion. Property taxes accounted for 72% of local government tax revenues, 45% of local own-source revenues, and 27% of all local general revenue.[1]

The property tax is the primary but not the only form of tax on wealth. The poll tax is a very old tax on wealth in the form of human beings, assessed at a flat rate per person or per household. While the poll tax is largely a historical artifact in the United States, it is still in use in other nations, particularly in Africa. Estate and inheritance taxes are also taxes on wealth at the time of transfer to heirs, while gift taxes cover transfers of assets among the living. These other taxes on wealth are also considered in this chapter.

WHY TAX PROPERTY?

Property is singled out as an object of taxation for several reasons, including ability to pay, the benefit principle, and the relative immobility of the tax base.

Like purchases (or consumption) and income, the ownership of property, broadly defined to include all assets, is a measure of ability to pay taxes. Assets produce income, sometimes explicitly (interest, dividends, rent) and sometimes implicitly, in the form of services rendered. Owning a car means that you can consume transportation services without additional payment, rather than renting a car or using public transportation. That reduced expense means that you have more income available for other purposes, including paying taxes, compared to a noncar owner. The same is true of homeowners, who enjoy housing services that have a market value and who would otherwise have to pay explicit rent. The present system of making mortgage payments makes owning and renting seem more similar, so that one might question whether homeowners still can be assumed, on average, to have greater capacity to pay taxes than renters.

Another aspect of the ability to pay argument is that the property tax is a way of ensuring that everyone pays at least some tax. Those who can hide their income and make their purchases largely outside the realm of the tax collector can be compelled to make some contribution to the public treasury with property taxes.

The property tax narrowly defined (on land and improvements) has some elements of a benefit tax, as discussed in Chapter 8. Many of the local services funded with property taxes are services to property, such as roads, fire

---

1. *Census of Governments, 2000* (Washington, DC: U.S. Census Bureau, 2000). Local own-source revenues include fees, charges, licenses, permits, and miscellaneous in addition to tax revenue. General revenue includes intergovernmental aid. The largest figure, revenue, also includes income from local government enterprises such as water and sewer service, transit, electric power, and in some places, liquor stores.

and police protection, streetlights, and garbage pickup. These services enhance or protect property values, so the value of the services could be considered to be roughly proportional to the value of the property being served.

Finally, real property is a much less mobile tax base than income or sales. It may decline in value, but real property is stuck inside the taxing jurisdiction. Because local governments are in a highly competitive situation for attracting higher income residents and business firms, they will be sensitive to keeping their property tax rates somewhat in line with competing jurisdictions, but at least they can count on real property (land and improvements) staying put even if it is subjected to tax.

DRAWBACKS TO TAXING PROPERTY

Taxing property poses four major practical problems: high visibility, the limited base, the problem of valuation, and base erosion. We consider each of these problems in turn.

High Visibility

Although visibility may be considered a good quality in a tax, the property tax is distinctly more visible than other kinds of taxes such at taxes on income and sales. It is often paid once a year in a large lump sum, whereas income taxes are withheld weekly or monthly and sales taxes are paid in small amounts, one purchase at a time. Historically, in a nation of farmers, the annual collection of property taxes in the fall after the harvest made sense, because it was the only time most citizens participated in the cash economy in a large way. Flush with cash from sales of their crops, they would pay their taxes and buy their supplies for the following year. However, that pattern of economic activity is a rarity in a postagricultural, postindustrial society.

This differential visibility may discourage the use of property taxes relative to other kinds of taxes. For homeowners with mortgages, the tax is often paid monthly through an escrow account, which makes their property taxes less visible. Tax collectors are exploring other methods of collection, such as credit card payments and installment payments, to make property tax payments more similar to the payment of other kinds of taxes.

Narrow Base

The use of a limited base that represents only a partial subset of total wealth or assets is the result of the difficulty of locating and valuing many kinds of assets, such as financial assets, commodities, precious metals, and jewelry. In most states, the property tax base consists mainly of land and improvements and vehicles, business equipment, boats, and a few other large, highly visible items that are difficult to conceal from the tax assessor. As a result, the property tax is not a tax on all wealth, just that part of wealth held in these particular forms. By singling out one form of wealth for taxation, the property tax discourages investment in improving land or purchasing items subject to property tax relative to other kinds of assets. This distortion of investment decisions is an undesirable efficiency consequence of property taxation in its present form.

Uncertain Market Value

The third problem is how to establish a credible market value as a basis for taxation. It is easy to establish a value for property that is sold, but many parcels of property rarely change ownership. Some taxable assets remain in family or corporate ownership for decades or even centuries. The value for those properties has to be established by other methods, as discussed below.

Base Erosion

The fourth drawback to taxing property is that this tax suffers to a greater than average degree from the general tendency of a tax to erode its own base over time. In the case of the property tax, this tendency can escalate to deterioration of whole neighborhoods or communities, especially in older cities. As property values decline, a higher rate is necessary to raise the same amount of revenue. As tax rates rise, middle and upper income families move to the suburbs, leaving only the poor and a few wealthy families in enclaves in the city. Costs of social services to an increasingly low-income population rise while the inner city's tax base continues to deteriorate. This pattern was particularly noticeable in the 1960s and 1970s as better highway systems and public transportation made it easier to live in the suburbs while continuing to work in the city.

Many of the older cities of the Northeast and Midwest, however, have experienced a resurgence of development called **gentrification.** As these inner-city properties decline in value, particularly older, well-located and well-constructed buildings, they become attractive for redevelopment, and young professionals are attracted to the convenient location and aesthetic appeal of older buildings. Efforts by older cities to make their downtowns more livable and attractive have also made this kind of "second wave" development financially attractive, rescuing some of the property base of older cities like Baltimore, Portland (both Maine and Oregon), and even parts of New York City.

DEFINING TAXABLE PROPERTY

Three kinds of property are taxed by at least some jurisdictions. **Real property** is the most universal part of the base, consisting of land (developed or undeveloped) and improvements, mainly buildings. Real property is the mainstay of the property tax in just about every jurisdiction. It is sometimes separated into categories such as agricultural, owner-occupied residential, rental, commercial, industrial, and utility.

Personal property consists of other kinds of tangible property besides land and buildings that has been added to the tax base. Automobiles, boats, airplanes, business equipment, farm equipment, railroad rolling stock, and business inventory are the most common categories of taxable personal property, although which ones are subject to tax vary from one jurisdiction to another. In the last few decades, a number of states have reduced personal property taxes by eliminating taxes on merchants' inventory and by reducing or eliminating property taxes on personal vehicles.

Intangibles are the third major category of taxable property. Intangible assets consist of other assets such as stocks, bonds, jewelry, bank accounts, precious metals, art objects, or other financial or physical assets that offer a way to store wealth.

Taxation of intangibles, and to a lesser extent personal property, raises all of the major economic issues about tax design—efficiency, equity, and collection/compliance costs. The efficiency criterion suggests that to tax some forms of wealth and not others will distort consumer decisions about the forms in which they choose to hold wealth, favoring those that are not subject to tax. The equity criterion calls for a broad base of wealth so as not to discriminate against those whose wealth is primarily in the form of real or taxable personal property. Both equity and efficiency, then, would call for a very broad property tax base. Collection and compliance costs, however, can be very high if tax assessors have to track wealth in a large number of forms. Taxes on intangibles and personal property are often easier to evade, and any tax that is easy to evade will eventually erode as more and more taxpayers join the stampede.

CAPITALIZATION OF PROPERTY TAXES

As we discussed in Chapter 7, the level of and changes in property taxes as well as the quality and variety of local public services are reflected in the market value of taxable property. The standard calculation of the present value (PV) of any asset reflects future costs and revenues/benefits according to the following formula:

$$PV = \Sigma \, [B_i - C_i] \, /[1 + r]^i \, ,$$

where i is the particular year in the life of the property (from 1 to n), B is benefits in the ith year (including both the use of the property and any public services), C is the cost in the ith year (including property taxes as well as maintenance, depreciation, etc.), and r is the market rate of discount, or "the" interest rate. If the property has an extremely long lifetime (land, for example, or a well-constructed building that depreciates very slowly), and if the annual benefits and costs are the same in all future years ($B_1 = B_2 = B_3 = \ldots = B_n$) then the formula simplifies to

$$PV = [B - C]/r \ .$$

What does this formula tell us about property taxes? Property taxes are reflected in C. An increase in property taxes that was not matched by increases in services (a part of B) that are equally valued by the present and prospective owners of the property will reduce the present (market) value of the property. Suppose, for example, that a particular property has a present market value of $100,000, and the market rate of interest is 6%. Now increase annual property taxes by $100. What happens to the value of the property? It declines by $C/r = \$1,667$ to $98,333. An enhancement—a sidewalk, a sewer line, regular trash pickup—would likewise increase the value of the property. The quality of a school district often has significant impact on housing prices, not only for parents of school-age children but for other buyers as well, because the value of access to those educational services is reflected in demand for housing in that district.

This process by which changes in taxes or public services are incorporated into the value of houses is called **capitalization.** The effect of capitalization is that changes in taxes and services accrue to the current owners of property in terms of the market value of their property. At least one study of property tax differentials found a significant amount of capitalization of property taxes in real estate prices, although capitalization is often less than the full amount that one might expect on the basis of a simple present value calculation.[2]

EFFICIENCY ISSUES IN PROPERTY TAXATION

Property taxation has two important efficiency issues. One is the incentive to hold wealth in nontaxable form. The second is the impact on location of households and business firms.

Efficiency issues, or distortions of consumer decisions, are particularly significant for the property tax because the effective tax rate is higher than it may appear. As you learned in Chapter 8, the distortions in decisions and the deadweight loss from a tax rise with the square of the tax rate. The property tax is levied on wealth, but it is paid each year out of the income flow from the assets subject to the tax. Typical property tax rates (as a percentage of market value) are in the range of 1% to 2% of the value of the property. Nine of the 10 cities with the lowest property tax rates in the United States are found in Alabama, where rates are in the 0.3% to 0.5% range. Among the top 10 cities, 5 are in New Hampshire, in the 3.4% to 4% range, along with 2 cities each in New Jersey and New York and 1 in Illinois. All of these rates may sound low compared to state income and sales tax rates, but they really are not.

Consider housing, a major component of the property tax base. The income generated by the housing stock is a flow of housing services, which are paid for in rent. If you own a house, you can be viewed as renting it to yourself, in which case the income flow is implicit rather than explicit—the value of the rent you would have to pay for a place to live if you did not own a house. A rule of thumb for rental property is that the rent should be about 1% a month, or 12% a year. After other nontax expenses, such as insurance and repairs, the pretax rate of return on rental housing is probably comparable to other investments of similar risk: 7% to 10% a year. (The risks faced by owners of rental property include periods of vacancy, unexpected major repairs, or decline in the value of property when they decide to sell.) If you think of the property tax as a percentage of the income from the property, then the rate is much higher. A tax rate on the property's value at a rate of 1.5% is paid out of that net return of 10% before property taxes, the effective tax rate on the property income is 1.5%, 10%, or 15%. The same tax with a net return of only 7% would mean an effective tax rate of more than 20%![3]

Distorting Asset Patterns

Households and firms will be influenced in their asset acquisition by property tax considerations. Smaller homes, smaller lots, and a shift of "amenity" assets toward those that are not taxed (such as furnishings) may be a typical household response. Households are often reluctant to make major improvements in their real property because of the property tax consequences. Partly offsetting this effect of the property tax, however, is the federal (and often state) deduction for both property taxes and interest on home mortgages, which make houses more attractive relative to other assets. The United States continues to claim one of the highest rates of owner-occupied property in the developed world, so it appears that the federal income tax advantages more than offset the impact of property taxes on investment in owner-occupied housing. The same may not be true for other types of property, such as rental and commercial property and, where taxed, cars and boats.

Business firms, likewise, must take property taxes into consideration in deciding what mix of assets to use, what kinds of plants to construct, what

3. This calculation is prior to income taxes. The effective tax rate after adjusting for income tax deductibility of property taxes is somewhat lower. For a person in a 35% combined federal and state tax bracket, a 1.25% effective property tax rate is only a 0.81% rate after deducting property taxes for income tax purposes. The after-tax share of income is then 8% to 11% rather than 12.5% to 18%.

size facility to build, how much land to acquire, and so forth. Firms have the choice of alternative production processes that may substitute labor or equipment for floor space and acreage. If a property tax is imposed (or increased), the balance of the cost–benefit calculations will be altered in ways that might not be optimal from the standpoint of resource use.

Distorting Locational Decisions

Far more significant for most public policy makers are the effects of property tax differentials on locational choice by both households and firms. Lower taxes for the same public services, or better public services for the same taxes, will cause decision makers to opt for one location over another (as discussed in Chapter 7). Many times economic efficiency (transportation costs, for example) might call for a different decision than the one that was induced by fiscal surplus calculations.

A community that has some degree of monopoly power—an oceanfront location, spectacular vistas, attractive employment opportunities, good access to highways, or other factors—can levy a higher property tax rate and still be attractive to residents and investors in commercial and industrial firms. Property owners in these communities may be more successful in shifting the burden of the property tax to tenants because they, in turn, have a degree of monopoly power. There are only so many beachfront locations or so many highway interchanges with choice locations for a truck stop. Owners of property in prime locations can continue to earn rents, or above-average returns, because of the very limited supply of such locations. For the average community or the average location, however, property taxes that are higher than in competing locations may induce relocation of residential, commercial, and industrial siting to those nearby lower tax jurisdictions.

EQUITY ISSUES IN PROPERTY TAXATION

The incidence of the property tax is easy to determine for owner-occupied property or for personal property such as motor vehicles, because the "buyer" and "seller" of the services of the property are the same. When it comes to other kinds of property, however, the incidence is more complex. Much residential and commercial property is rented. If you rent an apartment, how much of the property tax falls on you in the form of higher rent and how much is absorbed by the landlord in the form of a lower return on investment? The incidence of property taxes on commercial and industrial property is even more complex. If the commercial or industrial firm owns the property, three possible parties could bear some part of the property tax burden: the owners of the firm (lower profits), the workers (lower wages and benefits), and the customers (higher prices). If the commercial or industrial firm leases the property, the owner of the real property becomes a fourth candidate for bearing some of the burden in the form of lower lease payments received.

Incidence: The Regressive View

Figure 12–1 diagrams the short-run supply and demand for rented apartments in a single city, which has just imposed (or increased) its property tax. In the short run, the supply of apartments is fixed. With demand unchanged, the property tax falls entirely on the owner in the form of lower net rent. Demand is represented by D_0, while the impact of a property tax (or an increase in the property tax) can be represented by shadow demand curve D_1, which represents demand net of tax as seen by the owner of the taxed property. The difference between the unchanged rental price P_0 and the net rent received by the owner P_1 corresponds to the property tax per rental unit. Revenue from the tax is rectangle P_1P_0ba.

However, a lower return to rental property will result in a decrease in the supply, since it may no longer be profitable to maintain older apartment buildings. With some supply elasticity (Figure 12–2), the burden of the property tax will eventually be shared between buyer and seller; the rental price for increasingly scarce apartments rises to P_F, while the rental payment net of tax to the owner falls to P_1. In larger cities, where apartments at desirable locations close to work or to public transportation are scarce, the owner of such properties often possesses a degree of monopoly power that may make it possible to shift more of any change in property taxes forward to buyers.

Figure 12–1
The Market for
Apartments,
Short Run

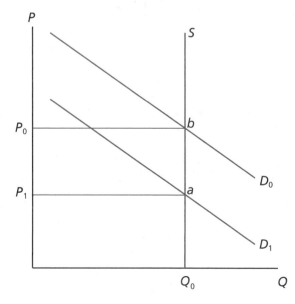

Figure 12–2
The Market for
Apartments,
Longer Term

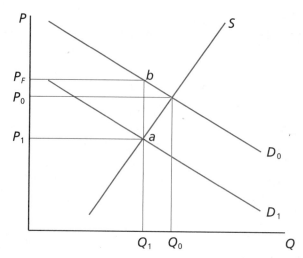

So far, the analysis looks very much like the standard discussion of the effects of an excise tax. because this tax is levied on housing, which everyone consumes, and since spending on housing declines as a percent of income as income rises, one might conclude that the property tax is regressive. A more general property tax on wealth might be expected to be progressive simply because wealth is even more unevenly distributed than income, with a substantial concentration of wealth in the top 5% of households.

Incidence: The Progressive View

However, a widely held alternative view has been supported by empirical studies. This alternative view is based on a broader perspective that looks more carefully at interrelated markets and the flow of resources between them. People who are in the business of constructing rental property must compete in financial markets for loanable funds with other borrowers who are borrowing for purposes that do not involve a property tax obligation, or a smaller property tax obligation. The rate of return on constructing rental property will be lower than could be earned on other uses of the same funds. Resources that would otherwise have been directed toward the production of apartment buildings in Metropolis will now be diverted to other uses, either for building apartments where property taxes are lower or for acquiring other forms of capital not subject to the property tax. Over time, existing properties will be allowed to deteriorate, and some will eventually be torn down. In other words, the supply of rental property may decline, or at least grow more slowly than other kinds of investments not as heavily impacted by the property tax.

Initially, a lower rate of return on rental property compared to other investments implies that at least part of the property tax will fall on owners of rental property, as the previous analysis suggested. But rental property does not exist in isolation. As investors move funds out of rental property into other kinds of assets with smaller tax burdens, the lower rate of return spreads to owners of all kinds of capital. In a world with a property tax, there will be less investment in improvements (mostly buildings) to real estate and more investment in other, nontaxed assets than there would otherwise be. Resources will shift between the two groups of investments until their rates of return are equalized; fewer rental units will earn a higher rate of return than they did when the tax was first imposed (lower, however, than before the tax). Other investments, however, will earn a lower rate of return. According to this view, then, the property tax is a tax on capital. Because ownership of capital is much greater at higher income levels, this view suggests that the property tax is progressive.

Other Considerations

This theoretical description of the incidence of the property tax must be qualified by some real-world considerations. First, real property receives some other tax breaks, particularly in federal and state income tax treatment of depreciation and mortgage interest, which may mitigate the effects of property taxes. Second, markets may not function perfectly in terms of capital being totally fluid or fungible and flowing to more attractive uses. Capital is usually embedded in sites, in buildings, and in equipment. Finally, other factors besides the property tax may affect the return to building, owning, or leasing real property that could offset the negative effect of the property tax.

Empirical evidence may shed some light on this debate. One study, using data from Boston, finds that in the case of rental housing, landlords are only able to shift about 11% to 16% of any increase in property taxes forward to tenants, at least in the short run.[4] A second study, examining the property tax on commercial real estate in the Phoenix area, found similar results, with 60% to 70% of the burden of the tax falling on property owners rather than on consumers of the products and services offered in those establishments.[5] Additional studies would be necessary to confirm these results for other areas and other types of property, but these two studies suggest support for the progressive view.

Is there a firm consensus? No. The older view was compatible with a world of little mobility of individuals among locations or of capital among uses, one of imperfect markets with limited information and slow response. Those circumstances have changed in the last few decades. Information spreads faster and capital markets of all kinds are more closely interconnected. However, improvements to real property (buildings) still represent capital embedded in a particular form and place from which it cannot easily be converted

---

4. Robert J. Carroll, and John Yinger, "Is the Property Tax a Benefit Tax? The Case of Rental Housing," *National Tax Journal* XLVII(2) (June 1994): pp. 295–316.
5. Man, "The Incidence of Differential Commercial Property Taxes."

into a different form of capital in the short run. Buildings can be torn down or allowed to depreciate by not maintaining them, but the opportunity cost may be very high relative to the property tax burden, delaying the market response. Thus, the short-run burden is likely to be distributed differently from the long-term burden.[6]

PROPERTY TAXES AND EDUCATION FUNDING

In most states (Hawaii being the primary exception), the property tax plays a significant role in funding education. Property taxes for education are different from property taxes for the support of other local public services in several respects.

First, a property tax for city or county services has a more direct benefit aspect to it for all residents than the property tax for education, because a significant number of residents may not have children in the public schools. The use of property taxes to fund public education has become particularly controversial with the growth of retirement communities, which generate few if any school pupils, and with the growth of private and home schooling as alternatives to the public schools.

Second, the link between the level of property taxes and the quality of the public schools is often not as direct as that for other local services. In most states (New Hampshire being the chief exception), local school funds are heavily supplemented with equalizing state aid that reduces the differences in per-pupil resources between wealthier and poorer jurisdictions. A series of court decisions have forced states to attempt to more nearly equalize per-pupil resources among school districts in order to ensure that the quality of a child's education is not held hostage to being located in a district with a limited property tax base. Although few states aim for total equality, most do direct more resources to poorer districts than to wealthier districts in order to blunt the impact of differences in local taxable wealth. (Education funding is discussed in more detail in Chapter 16.)

When states undertake to more nearly equalize school resources, then local effort becomes a smaller percentage of school funding. Suppose that state aid is 60% of school funding. Then increasing the local property tax rate in a given district by 20% will only increase total resources available for education by 8% (20% of the 40% local funding), so the increase in relative school quality or school resources is small relative to the size of the tax increase. Some critics of school funding equalization argue that the loss of direct connection between local taxes and school taxes may have been a factor in property tax protests in the 1970s and 1980s.

6. The various views of property tax incidence were summarized in a now-classic work by Henry J. Aaron, *Who Pays the Property Tax?* (Washington, DC: Brookings Institution, 1975).

Finally, school quality is often a significant factor in the price of property, because with a home purchase or a rental lease, a family is buying access to a particular school district or even a particular school. Where school quality is a factor in housing property values, the capitalization process will reflect school quality at least as much as, if not more than, the level of local property taxes. Even households without schoolchildren will take current and expected future school quality into account because it will affect the resale value of their property.

DESIGNING AND ADMINISTERING PROPERTY TAXES

Some of the anger toward the property tax in the last few decades has been directed at the way our taxes are administered rather than the tax rate or size of the property tax bill itself. Property taxation is a two-step process. The first step is to determine the value of the individual taxable properties and then aggregate them into a tax base. The second step is to establish a tax rate, or mill rate, to apply to that base in order to raise the amount of revenue required. Income tax rates and sales tax rates are stable for years at a time while their bases grow at a steady if sometimes uneven pace. For the property tax, however, with infrequent reassessment, the base grows slowly in many years with jumps in reassessment years, while the tax rate or mill rate is changed frequently in order to yield the amount of revenue needed to balance city, county, and school district budgets.

Valuing Property

The first step in levying a property tax is to identify all the taxable properties—land, buildings, and taxable personal property—and to determine a market value for each. This process is known as **assessment.** Some properties, such as automobiles, are relatively easy to value because many similar properties are being bought and sold on a national market and the assessor can determine the values from readily available sales information. The same is true of other kinds of personal property from tractors to office furnishings to railroad rolling stock. Standard rates of depreciation from the Internal Revenue Service code can be applied to the original cost to determine a taxable value.

For land and improvements—houses, stores, warehouses, factories, professional offices—the assessment process is more complex. Assessors generally use a combination of three methods to assess real property: replacement cost, comparative sales prices, and regression analysis.

The first method is to determine the replacement cost of structures on the basis of current building costs per square foot and the size of the structure. For example, if current building costs per square foot are $100 and the assessor is looking at a 2,000-square-foot house, the replacement cost would be $200,000. If the house is not new, depreciation is factored in for age to reduce the value. Land is usually assessed separately based on recent market prices for undeveloped land in the area.

The second method is to look at the sales prices of comparable properties in the neighborhood. For areas with substantial turnover in real property, this market price method is useful, but it is less useful for rural areas, unusual or unique properties, or industrial properties.

The third method, increasingly widely used, is regression analysis. A regression equation for a house might include such variables as land (acreage), square footage, number of bathrooms, basement, garage, and a dummy variable to represent location. The coefficients in the regression equation would be developed by putting in the information for actual property sales in the area. The resulting equation, which represents a combination of the first two methods, would then be applied to valuing property that had not been sold recently.

Most states oversee the assessment process at the local level, providing training and checking to ensure that local valuations are not out of line with the actual market values of properties that are sold. The state may require reassessment at regular intervals. Because a complete revaluation of all taxable property in a jurisdiction is a tedious and expensive process, most local governments reassess less often than annually—typically, assessments are done every three to seven years. More frequent reassessment ensures greater equity among property owners, but the administrative costs usually make annual reassessment impractical.

Classified Tax Systems

Once the market value of a particular property is determined, it is then added to the tax base at some percentage of that value. Some states require 100% assessment; that is, the assessed value and the market value are the same. Others allow or require that the property be added to the tax base at some percentage of its market value. That percentage may be uniform across kinds of property, or it may be different for different kinds of property. If different kinds of property are included in the base at different percentages of their market value, then the state has a **classified property tax system.**

The intent of a classified system is to distribute the property tax burden in a way that is proportional to market value within a classification but not between classifications. For example, owner-occupied residential property may receive a favorable assessment rate, while commercial or industrial property may be added into the tax base at a higher assessment rate. Seventeen states have classified systems, with as few as two classes and as many as eight. Residential property and agricultural property are the classes most likely to receive favored treatment.

Mill Rate

The term **mill rate** reflects the English origins of the property tax in the United States. The *mil,* now more commonly spelled *mill,* was an old English monetary unit that was one-tenth of a cent. A tax rate of 70 mills, then, would be 7% of the market value. The use of this antiquated unit of measure further compounds the aura of mystery and confusion that surrounds the property tax.

The mill rate is usually set by local governments. Because the property tax plays such a central role in funding local governments, the mill rate often becomes the piece of elastic that has to stretch between other revenue sources and expenditure demands to balance the local budget. A first cut at a city, county, or school district budget would estimate expenditures, subtract other revenues (fees and charges, state and federal aid, etc.), and then determine the balance to be raised through property taxes. Given the size of the property tax base, a mill rate can be determined that would raise the needed amount. If that mill rate represents a large jump over previous years, those preparing the budget may need to go back to the drawing boards on the spending side.

Mill rates are not comparable between states because of different assessment methods. A mill rate of 250 on a 6% assessment is equivalent to a mill rate of 15 on a 100% assessment. In both cases, the tax is 1.5% of the value of the property. Because both mill rates and assessment rates enter into determining the tax burden, interstate comparisons are usually made by dividing the dollar tax collections by the market (not assessed) value of the property tax base to calculate property tax burdens as a percentage of property values. Typical values are in the 1% to 3% range for most states, generally lower than average in the Southeast and higher than average in the Northeast.

PROPERTY TAX REVOLT AND ITS AFTERMATH

The term *property tax revolt* refers to a series of events that began in California in the mid-1970s and spread across the nation through the rest of the 20th century. Protests against escalating property tax burdens that came with rapidly increasing housing values led to an initiative in California called Proposition 13 that passed in 1978 (see boxed feature later in this chapter). This initiative reduced property taxes and sharply curbed their growth. Initially, the state picked up a substantial share of lost revenue, but over time, local governments in California have found it increasingly difficult to fund public schools and other local services and have turned to fees and other nonproperty taxes to make up some of the difference. As the movement spread to other states, it took on four different forms: repeal, restraint, relief, and reform.

ENGLISH OR FRANCAIS? TWO WAYS OF IMPLEMENTING A PROPERTY TAX

Most Americans and Canadians are familiar with a particular way of assessing and collecting property tax that is common throughout the English-speaking world. The tax is computed as a percent of the value of the property asset, as a tax on wealth. Whether the value of the property asset is expressed as 100% of market value, as it is in many states, or as some fraction of that value, it is the market value of the asset that is the basis for computing the tax. This system is found wherever the predominant influence has been British. In other parts of the world, however, a different system of property taxation computes the tax on the basis of the income flow rather than the asset value. Because this method of property taxation is used in France, it spread to former French colonies in Africa and is used there as well. This method can be integrated with the income tax, can stand alone where there is not an income tax, or can create a double tax burden on income from real property.

If a real property is leased, rental payments flow from the lessee to the owner and can be taxed. Suppose, for example, you own an office building that has a market value of $1 million and generates rental income of $120,000. An English-style property tax system would base your tax liability on the asset value of $1 million. A mill rate of 25 (2.5%) would generate a tax liability of $25,000. To generate the same tax liability on the gross rental income would require a tax rate of 20.8%. (Some systems tax gross rents, while others tax rents net of expenses.) The nominal rates are higher under a French-style system, but the effects are the same. It is easy to compute a mill rate and a tax rate on rental income that would yield the same revenue out of the same tax base, whether the base is defined as the value of assets or the stream of rental income from those assets.

What about property that is owner occupied and thus generates no income? The French system requires the calculation of a rental equivalent, just as assessors under an English system must estimate a market value for properties that are not sold.

The advantage of the French-type property tax system is that it recognizes that the tax burden must be paid out of the income the property generates, whether that income is explicit (actual rental payments) or implicit (the value of the rental services enjoyed by the owner-occupant). A property with little or no rental value should pay little or no tax. The value of land and buildings as an asset is simply the capitalized sum of future net income streams. A French-style property tax collects revenue on the basis of the annual flow rather than the capitalized sum, and is therefore more flexible in responding to changes in the rental values of taxable properties.

Repeal

Several states, including Arkansas, Michigan, and Utah, attempted to repeal the property tax, that is, to develop some other basis for local government funding, including funding for education. None of these efforts were successful, although in Michigan there was a substantial shift of education funding away from the local property tax toward state funding through a higher sales tax. The failure to repeal the property tax in any state reflects the fact that there are only a limited number of broad-based taxes to provide an adequate and stable revenue source for any government. The property tax is the one tax that has proved most suitable for local use both because property is immobile and because local governments provide services that benefit property owners.

Restraint

Restraint refers to any method of tying the hands of local officials in order to limit growth in taxing and spending, as we discussed in Chapter 3. Many state governments have constrained themselves and sometimes their local governments in terms of overall growth of revenue or spending, limiting it to a particular growth rate or tying it to the growth of personal income. Often restraints (mostly state imposed) are aimed directly at the unpopular property tax. Property tax restraints have included limits on increases in assessments or the use of reassessment to increase revenues (Georgia and South Carolina), limits on the percentage value of the property that can be collected in tax (Proposition 2-1/2 in Massachusetts), restrictions on increases in the mill rates, or in the case of Prince George's County, Maryland, a limit on the dollar amount of property taxes that can be collected. (As we noted in Chapter 3, that last restraint was later repealed.)

Restraint is a rather clumsy tool for containing the growth of government. It has encouraged the growing use of fees and charges (see Chapter 13). For schools, which tend to depend most heavily on the property tax as a local revenue source, it has meant diminished funding and declining educational quality in some areas, particularly California.

Relief

Relief is a difficult political issue. Almost every state has made some effort to provide property tax relief either in general or to specific groups in the last 30 years, often by substituting state funds for local funds in paying for public education, or by providing local governments with access to other revenue sources besides the property tax. Much of the relief, however, has been for designated groups of taxpayers. Groups asking for specific rather than general relief usually represent a category of property (homeowners, new industry, owners of automobiles) or another segment of society that claims injury because of high property tax burdens (the elderly, veterans, etc.).

In states with classified systems, the categories and their assessment rates are prime targets for differential relief. Farmers, owners of undeveloped land, and homeowners tend to receive the most favorable treatment in classified systems. All three of these groups are in a position to make an emotional appeal for special treatment based on the fact that their taxable property may not be yielding much of a cash income stream from which to pay taxes. Legislators are encouraged to envision widows and orphans being evicted from their family homes, or farmers being forced to sell the land that has been in their family for generations in order to pay taxes. While some of these hardship stories are genuine, they also supply political cover for many homeowners and landowners who are not genuine hardship cases. The result, however, is that many states offer favorable tax treatment to these two groups of property owners in one form or another.

Property tax relief also comes in a number of other forms in nonclassified systems. The most common forms of relief are as follows:

- Exempt part or all of the value of property for tax purposes, often called a homestead exemption in the case of owner-occupied housing or a business tax incentive in the case of industry. For homeowners, the exemptions are often categorical, most often over age 65, veterans, disabled, or blind. For business firms, the exemption may be across the board or it may be negotiated as part of a package of incentives for locating in a particular state or a particular location within a state.
- Rebate part of the property tax burden to all taxpayers or to selected taxpayers. The rebates may be funded by the state or by another local tax, such as the local option sales tax in South Carolina.
- Give income tax credits or other direct payments to reduce the property tax burden on housing, usually based on income. The income tax credit is called a **circuit breaker.** At least 30 states have some form of circuit breaker, some of which include renters as well as homeowners.

Reform

Reform of the property tax is a slower, more demanding, and more difficult process of rethinking the property tax so as to make it more equitable, less inefficient, and also less costly to administer. A number of reforms have been implemented in administration to improve the assessment process. California's change in the assessment process was the most radical of all. Residential property is now only reassessed at the time of sale. If it is not sold, its value is increased at a rate of 2% a year. This system, called **acquisition value,** results in substantial inequities in tax burdens between properties of similar market value. Properties that are repeatedly sold at escalating prices will have much higher property tax burdens than properties that remain in the same hands and just see their assessed values rise at a slow and steady 2% a year.

Few other states have copied California's system, but many have put caps on increases in assessments. Others have moved to more frequent assessment. State oversight of local assessors or direct state assessment are often used as a way to improve the accuracy of the assessment process. Other administrative reforms have focused on allowing installment payment of taxes, improving appeals processes, and pooling the property base of smaller jurisdictions to provide more market comparisons. Reform may also involve sweeping re-

FALLOUT FROM PROPOSITION 13

In 1978, voters in California approved an initiative that radically changed not only property taxes but also changed state–local fiscal relations dramatically. The Jarvis–Gann initiative, better known as Proposition 13, was the opening volley in a revolt against the property tax that spread from state to state and continued through the end of the 20th century. This initiative limited property tax rates to 1% of market value, rolled back property taxes to their 1975–1976 value, gave the state responsibility for distributing property tax revenues among jurisdictions, and based assessment on the market price at the time of sale.

Prior to Proposition 13, the average property tax was about 2.7% of market value, so this initiative resulted in a sweeping reduction in property taxes, estimated at $7 billion in the first year. The impact on cities, counties, and school districts was enormous. Since the local property tax was the primary source of revenue for schools, and the property tax rate and revenue were no longer locally controlled, California's school system became the fiscal responsibility of the state, much like Hawaii but unlike most other states. Counties became much more heavily dependent on state aid. Schools in California also saw a decline in per-pupil spending relative to other states over the next two decades. Cities, which generally are least dependent on property taxes (compared to other local governments), shifted more heavily to fees and charges to cover the drop in property tax revenue. By 1996, California cities saw property taxes decline from more than 16% to less than 8% of revenues. So one unintended consequence was "reverse devolution," or shifting responsibility for providing county and educational services up to the state level.

Although many other states have enacted limits on property taxes (such as Massachusetts' Proposition 2-1/2), none have thus far adopted the other radical element of Proposition 13, acquisition value. Taxpayers frequently complain that assessments are arbitrary and unfair, but only California has turned to a system based only on the value at the time of purchase. That value can be increased to account for inflation by up to 2% a year. The result of this system is that there is an actual transaction base for assessment, but it also means that similar properties bear very different tax burdens, depending on how often they are sold.

Local governments have been creative in responding to the challenge, but their options are limited. Cities in California have almost doubled their service charge revenue and increased their enterprise income. Now that new development does not bring a property tax revenue bonanza with it, cities and counties are more inclined to use such revenue tools as impact fees and tax increment financing to ensure that new development does not lead to further declines in services to established residents. With local sales taxes an increasingly important revenue source, cities and counties have been more encouraging to commercial development.

Observers disagree on the overall effects of Proposition 13. Proponents credit it with helping to fuel the boom in California, along with general economic growth, and to contain the growth of government spending. Critics argue that it has not only gutted local control but also seriously damaged the quality of local public services, especially education. For good or for ill, Proposition 13 changed the face of the property tax not only in California but in the rest of the nation as well.[1]

1. See Terri A. Sexton, Steven M. Shiffrin, and Arthur O'Sullivan, "Proposition 13: Unintended Effects and Feasible Reforms," *National Tax Journal,* LII(1) (March 1999): pp. 99–111, for a good summary of the aftereffects of Proposition 13, including inequities in burden distribution, declining public services, shift to nontax revenue sources, and the impact on support for public education.

thinking of decisions about the distribution of the tax burden in systems that have either classified assessments or differential rates for different kinds of property.

OTHER TAXES ON WEALTH

The property tax is the primary form of taxation of wealth in the United States as well as the major source of local government revenue, unlike many other nations. Two other kinds of taxes are classified as taxes on wealth rather than on income or consumption. One is the poll tax. The other is a tax on the transfer of property at death to heirs, known as inheritance or estate taxes.

Poll Taxes

A **poll tax** is a per capita or per household tax that is the same regardless of any measure of ability to pay. It is a specific tax—$10 per head, or per adult, or per household, for example. Because the tax does not vary with income, it is the most regressive of all taxes. Its primary appeal is that it does not distort any decisions, because the only way to avoid the tax is to die or disappear, both actions that are too extreme for most people to consider as a form of tax avoidance! Its other major attraction is simplicity. While it is still labor intensive and prone to corruption, it may be easier to count people than to track and measure income and assets in an economy where a significant amount of production and consumption takes place outside market channels.

The poll tax is rarely used in most industrial countries, although a brief and disastrous attempt was made to use it to replace the property tax in England in the 1980s. It is still used in some less developed nations, particularly in Africa. This tax was used in some parts of the United States at modest levels well into the late 20th century. Its name reflects the fact that proof of payment of the poll tax was sometimes required in order to vote in elections (polls refer to the places where elections are held, or the process of voting).

Estate, Inheritance, and Gift Taxes

When the federal government levies a tax on the transfer of property at the time of death, it is called an **estate tax,** which is a tax on the net worth of the deceased. Fifteen states levy a separate **inheritance tax,** which is a tax on the amount that heirs receive from an estate, which can be credited against the federal estate tax. All states receive a portion of the federal estate tax, so the revenue to states can be substantial—especially states like California, Florida, Nevada, and New York, with higher concentrations of elderly residents.

An estate can avoid tax if it passes to a spouse, but eventually it will come to the attention of the Internal Revenue Service, which effectively taxes estates in excess of $675,000 after expenses, charitable bequests, and payment of debts. The rates are progressive, starting at 18% and rising to 55% on estates in excess of $3 million. These rates are being reduced and the portion of the estate exempt from tax is being increased over a period of nine years, so that by 2010 there will no longer be a federal estate tax, as a result of the 2001 tax cut. However, the bill also contained a "sunset" provision that extends the tax cuts to 2010, after which they must be reenacted. It is possible that the estate tax will be revived at that time.

One of the reasons offered for eliminating the estate tax was that a great deal of effort is invested in methods of avoiding or minimizing estate and inheritance taxes. Wealthier persons can transfer up to $10,000 per recipient ($20,000 if the donors are a married couple) per year without incurring a gift tax. The gift tax, which has the same rate as the estate tax, was instituted to limit this way of avoiding estate taxes. Trusts and other devices take assets out of the estate and reduce the tax burden. The estate and inheritance taxes have also been a major incentive for charitable bequests, which expect to suffer a decline in revenue as the estate tax is phased out.[7]

The estate and inheritance taxes are not a major source of government revenue (about 1.5% of federal revenue), and in practice are paid by only a very small fraction of the population. However, they have been very controversial. One school of thought sees these taxes as an appropriate redistribution of wealth that somewhat levels the economic playing field within generations, as well as a potentially significant source of revenue as estates accumulated during the prosperous years of the 20th century are passed on to heirs. Critics, who won the debate in Congress in 2001, claim that the estate tax is a confiscation of the result of a lifetime of hard work and wise management of resources, and a disincentive to save and invest in order to pass wealth on to one's heirs.

7. A useful discussion of the equity and efficiency issues surrounding the estate and gift taxes can be found in William G. Gale and Joel Slemrod, "Life and Death Questions about the Estate and Gift Tax," *National Tax Journal*, L111(4) (December 2000): pp. 889–912.

SUMMARY

The property tax is a significant source of funding for local governments in the United States, raising more than $228 billion in 1998–1999  and accounting for 72% of local tax revenue. The property tax is the primary form of taxation of wealth; other (minor) taxes on wealth are poll taxes, which are seldom used, and estate and inheritance taxes, which generate relatively little revenue.

Three reasons for using a property tax as a local government revenue source are (1) property ownership is one indicator of ability to pay, (2) most local public services benefit property owners, and (3) real property is less mobile and likely to relocate in response to a tax than other possible tax bases such as consumption spending or income. The chief disadvantages of using this tax are (1) the practical requirement of limiting the base to real and a few kinds of personal property rather than all wealth, (2) the difficulty of establishing the market value of many kinds of taxable property, and (3) the tendency of this tax to erode its base over time by discouraging improvements and maintenance of highly taxed property.

Property taxes are imposed on real property (land and buildings), personal property (tangible assets such as cars, boats, and business equipment), and sometimes intangibles (mostly financial assets). Equity considerations suggest that the base of this tax on wealth should be as broadly inclusive as possible, but practical problems of locating and valuing some kinds of property wealth have resulted in a relatively narrow base. Property taxes, as well as local public services, are reflected in the market value of property through the process of capitalization. Capitalization means that the present value of future benefits (services) and costs (taxes) is added to or subtracted from the present value of the property.

Efficiency issues are particularly important to property taxes because the tax is levied on the value of the asset rather than the annual income stream from the asset and is, in consequence, relatively high if calculated as a percentage of the income stream. Property taxes will influence choices about the forms in which wealth is held and the location of households and firms.

Economists find it difficult to assess the equity impact of this tax, because they have no consensus about the incidence of the tax. If it is analyzed as an excise tax on rentals, then it would appear to be somewhat regressive. If it is analyzed as a tax on capital, then it appears to be progressive. Empirical evidence lends some support to the view of the property tax as a tax on capital.

Property taxes are a major source of funding for public schools in most states. States have had to balance this local funding source with redistributive state aid in order to ensure adequate educational resources for school districts with more limited property tax bases. Because schools are an important local public service and because the bulk of the property tax revenue in most states goes to public schools, both school taxes and the quality of public schools are capitalized into the value of residential property.

Real property is valued, or assessed, for tax purposes by a combination of methods, including market comparisons, adjusted replacement cost, and regression analysis. Personal property is usually valued by adjusting original or replacement cost for depreciation. Assessment is one of the most controversial aspects of the property tax. Some states value all property at market value or at a uniform percentage of market value. Other states apply different percentages to different classes of property, such as owner occupied, industrial, and commercial, in what is called a classified system. The assessed value is then multiplied by the mill rate (one-tenth of a cent per dollar of assessed valuation) to determine the property tax liability. Because of different assessment systems, interstate comparisons compute the property tax as a percentage of market value of taxable property rather than comparing mill rates.

The property tax revolt of the late 20th century has resulted in a number of changes in the property tax system. Attempts to repeal the property tax have failed, but its role has been reduced in many states by allowing local governments to tap other resources or increase the state's share of funding for local services, especially education. Many states have adopted restraints of various kinds on property taxes, including limits on increases in assessments, caps on the mill rate, or even limits on the growth of revenue from the property tax. Property tax relief targeted at specific groups has also been popular, ranging from homestead exemptions and circuit breakers to tax incentives for industry.

The poll tax is a tax levied at a flat rate per person or per household. It is nondistorting but highly regressive and is not widely used in industrial countries. Estate taxes are levied by the federal government on the transfer of property at death. States also levy a tax on the inheritance of property. Because of large exemptions, relatively few people actually pay the tax, and the amount or revenue generated is modest.

KEY TERMS AND CONCEPTS

gentrification, 252
real property, 252
personal property, 253
intangibles, 253
capitalization, 254

assessment, 261
classified property tax system, 262
mill rate, 263
circuit breaker, 266

acquisition value, 266
poll tax, 268
estate tax, 268
inheritance tax, 268

DISCUSSION QUESTIONS

1. What are the costs and benefits of limiting a property tax to real property (land and buildings) instead of expanding it to include other forms of wealth?

2. Suppose that a state has a classified system of property in which owner-occupied property is assessed at 10%, farm property and undeveloped land at 5%, and all other property (including rental, commercial, and industrial) at 15%. What kinds of incentives do individuals face in trying to reduce their tax burdens? Why would it be difficult to compare tax burdens between this state and another one with a nonclassified system?

3. Summarize the arguments about the regressivity or progressivity of the property tax. How might you attempt to verify which view is correct? What factors might make either of the two simple models, the excise tax on rentals or the tax on capital, less likely to predict the distribution of the tax burden in the real world?

4. Suppose that a particular piece of property had a market value of $100,000. Now the local government finds that it must increase taxes by $200 a year on this (and other) properties just to maintain the current level of public services. At an interest rate of 6%, how would this tax increase affect the market value of this property?

5. What are the incentive and disincentive effects of an estate or inheritance tax on work, saving, consumption, and investment? How, in your view, do those considerations weigh against the notion of equality of opportunity discussed in Chapter 6?

CHAPTER 13

FEES AND CHARGES AS A REVENUE SOURCE

Critics of government are fond of saying that government should be run more like a business. By now you have enough familiarity with what government does to understand that some of the techniques used in the private sector are not readily adaptable to situations where externalities or public goods are involved, making it infeasible to supply services on a pure payment basis. However, governments do rely heavily on various kinds of fees and charges to help finance services at all levels of government, from grazing fees on federal lands to dog licenses issued at your local city hall. In many of these cases, a part of government is being run like a business, with signals about demand conveyed through the prices people are willing to pay for services ranging from garbage pickup to airport landing fees.

In 2000, the federal government collected $92 billion in "other" revenue, mostly fees and charges which supplied about 5% of general revenues. Included in that figure was revenue from such government enterprises as the postal service, the Tennessee Valley Authority, and the Commodity Credit Corporation. State and local governments, likewise, raised significant amounts of funds from various kinds of fees and charges, which provided $211 billion in 1998–1999 (about 18% of own-source revenue). About 63% of that amount was collected at the local level, which relies more heavily on fees and charges. State and local governments also reported gross revenue of $75 billion from utilities (water, electric, gas, transit) and state-operated liquor stores, but

FEDERAL BUILDING

while these enterprises produced surpluses for some individual governments, in total they generated a net loss.

The use of fees and charges for generating revenue has grown rapidly in the last two decades in response to a number of factors. Expanded use of fees at the federal level was one of the tools used to reduce the budget deficit in the 1980s and 1990s. At the local level, fees and charges have proven to be a productive substitute revenue source in response to the property tax revolt, especially in California. State governments have found that fees and charges are a useful supplement to their two primary revenue sources, income and sales taxes. Some of the 12 states that do not use either or both of these primary revenue sources rely even more heavily on fees and charges, as Table 13–1 indicates. While Alaska has other resources (mineral royalties and federal payments), all of the other states in this group except New Hampshire place above-average reliance on fees and charges as a revenue source, especially Tennessee and Texas, neither of which has a broad-based income tax.

It is difficult to get a clear measure of growth in fees and charges, because in earlier reporting years they were mixed in with "other," which includes interest, asset sales, and other miscellaneous revenue sources. With that caveat, it is worth noting that between 1974 (prior to the property tax revolt) and 1994, fees and charges and miscellaneous fell as a federal revenue source from 14.3% to 11.8% of general revenue, but at the same time, this category rose as a share of own-source revenue; from 20.1% to 30.1% for states, and from 28.6% to 57.5% for local governments.

Table 13–1
Fees and Charges as Percent of Own-Source Revenue for Selected States, 1998–1999

	Percent
U.S. Average	18.1
Alaska	11.5
Delaware	18.8
Florida	20.0
Montana	19.1
Nevada	20.3
New Hampshire	16.3
Oregon	22.5
South Dakota	16.7
Tennessee	25.3
Texas	18.4
Washington	21.2
Wyoming	24.0

Source: Bureau of the Census.

FEES OR TAXES?

What is a fee, and what is a tax? Both are sums of money paid by citizens to governments to support services—but there are some important distinctions. First, a tax is involuntary, whereas a fee is paid as a result of a voluntary purchase of services by the payer. Second, a tax normally produces general revenue that can be used for any public purpose, whereas revenue from a fee is supposed to be used to cover the cost of providing a specific service.

In practice, the dividing line between taxes and various kinds of fees and charges is often not that clear-cut. Rather, a continuum runs from a pure tax, not linked to a particular service and just providing general revenue, to a pure fee in which payment is made for services rendered. At the tax end of the spectrum are general sales and income taxes, which are involuntary and are used primarily for support of general government. At the fee end of the spectrum are the operations of government enterprises, such as purchasing stamps from the U.S. Postal Service, a token to ride a public subway, or a bottle of wine from a state-operated liquor store, all of which are voluntary and related to the provision of specific services.

In between, toward the tax end of the spectrum, are benefit taxes (property, gasoline) and earmarked taxes. **Earmarked taxes** go into special funds or are spent for special purposes (see boxed feature). For example, part of the revenue from taxes on alcoholic beverages may be earmarked for alcohol treatment, or taxes on accommodations and admissions (movie theatres, sporting events, concerts) may be earmarked for tourism promotion or tourism-related expenses. Crossing the line, business licenses (usually imposed by local governments) are often assessed on the basis of gross revenue and involve no specific services in return, so that even though they are classed as fees and charges they are more like a business income tax. Likewise, permits (for hunting, fishing, marriage, building, etc.) and franchise fees are usually sources of general fund revenue in which there is a charge for permission that may or may not be related to services provided. Law enforcement fines and charges, such as speeding fines, also fall into this middle category, and may be considered more like a tax on undesirable behavior. Revenue from fines and law enforcement charges may go into the general fund or may be used to cover some of the cost of public safety services.

Franchise fees are payments for the privilege of being the exclusive provider of a service for a given area. Used heavily by local governments, these fees determine which cable service or electricity supplier will serve a given area. Revenue from franchise fees for these grants of monopoly privilege is being eroded by deregulation and increased competition in formerly monopolistic industries such as electricity distribution and telecommunications. States also charge franchise fees that range from the highly general (equivalent to a business license fee) to the highly specific (franchises for service providers or

TO EARMARK OR NOT TO EARMARK?

Earmarked revenues are dedicated to a particular use and are not available for general spending purposes. Earmarked revenues are a common practice at all levels of government in the United States. The arguments for earmarking are three. The first argument, suggested in the text, is that there is an element of *quid pro quo,* or a market-like exchange. For taxes, some earmarking is related to the benefit principle—the gasoline tax being the most obvious case. For fees and charges, as indicated in the text, some of these fees are payment for a service, much like private sales, and good accounting practice suggests that these enterprise activities should segregate their revenue and spending streams from the general public budget. Second, there is an equity argument. The impact fee, discussed below, as well as tax increment financing and other ways of funding improvements in public capital to benefit a particular neighborhood or area, is a way of ensuring that the cost falls on those who demand the additional services, rather than on taxpayers in general.

Finally, the third and most important argument is political; earmarking may make a tax or other revenue stream more acceptable to the public if they know it will all be spent on some desirable purpose. For example, states that have adopted lotteries have almost always done so by referendum, because most states had antilottery provisions in their constitutions. To make a lottery more attractive, legislators promised to use the revenue for specific desirable purposes, such as education, economic development, local government, or senior citizen programs. If citizens have to vote on any kind of tax or revenue increase, earmarking increases the chances for approval.

Most economists would support the limited kinds of earmarking associated with fees for service or a clear benefit principle relationship between the revenue source and the object of the earmarking. (This author's personal favorite is the tax on alcoholic beverages in South Carolina, a portion of which is earmarked for alcohol and drug abuse programs!) However, earmarking usually extends far beyond the fee for service or benefit prin-

ciple to ensure preferential treatment for certain groups in the budgetary process. Sometimes it is schools or local governments that are guaranteed the proceeds of a particular revenue source regardless of the competing demands on the state budget. At other times it is parks, or highways, or some other vocal and effective lobbying group within or outside of government that is successful in obtaining an earmarked revenue source. When earmarking is not clearly justified in terms of some kind of "user pays" principle, then the practice needs to be reexamined.

The arguments against earmarking are powerful because they are grounded in fundamental economic principles about choice, trade-offs, and equating at the margin (marginal benefit = marginal cost). When revenues are earmarked, they are removed from that process of weighing one expenditure against another that lies at the heart of good budgetary practice (see Chapter 15). The amount of revenue going to a particular purpose, such as gasoline taxes for highways, may be too much or too little relative to how much would be spent if highways were funded through the general budgetary process. If it is too much, the surplus is not available for other uses. If it is too little, that spending category may find it difficult to compete for additional funding out of general revenue because it already has preferential access to its "own" funds. For example, lottery funding for education has made it more difficult for public education to get increased funds from general revenue sources, even though most state lotteries generate only a modest portion of the funding needed to provide for public education. At the other end of the spectrum, tourism destination states have been involved in a costly and escalating advertising war simply because state tourism departments had preferential access to dedicated revenues from accommodations and admissions taxes.

One last argument is that earmarking can worsen a budget crunch in a revenue downturn. It is often easy to persuade elected officials to earmark certain revenue sources for pet programs

(continues)

TO EARMARK OR NOT TO EARMARK? (CONTINUED)

when revenue is rising and competition for public resources is not too severe. But with a revenue downturn, legislators may find that a substantial part of their revenue stream has been taken off budget, so that preferred projects cannot be cut because their revenues are protected. The burden of budget cuts then falls disproportionately on those public programs and services that do not have access to earmarked revenues. In the next budget upswing, there will be increased pressure to earmark revenue for some of these programs

and services, further reducing the ability of legislators to make the kinds of budgetary trade-offs that are needed.

Despite its political popularity, the weight of good economic reasoning is against earmarking. The case for earmarking needs to be made carefully on the basis of efficiency and equity considerations, and the bulk of the revenue stream at any level of government needs to remain available to the general fund where the important trade-offs are made among spending priorities.

concessions at state parks or on major highways and airports). In the latter case, the state is using its power to create a monopoly privilege just like that created when local governments award cable TV franchises.

Some reporting governments draw a distinction between licenses and permits and fees and charges, with the latter being linked to specific services, such as use of highways or parking garages, garbage pickup, or access to parks, grazing lands, swimming pools, or tennis courts, all of which lie at the fee end of the continuum.

A relatively new category of fees is that associated with growth management, most commonly an **impact fee.**[1] New development requires additional infrastructure and may increase the average cost of providing certain services, such as police and fire protection. The cost of serving new developments depends on such factors as contiguity (how close they are to existing developments) and density (number of houses or dwelling units per acre). Close-in and dense developments are generally less costly to service. The impact fee, which is discussed in more detail below, is used to ensure that new developments pay an appropriate share of the cost of additional infrastructure and services.

To further complicate the task of distinguishing between taxes and fees, many services in the public sector are funded with a combination of general tax revenue and user fees. A transit system or a recreation program may charge a modest fee but operate at a loss, with the difference made up from general

---

1. An alternative approach with similar results is tax increment financing. Here a neighborhood or industrial or commercial area is identified as in need of new public capital or improvements—drainage, sidewalks, new water pipes, etc. The property tax assessor values the property prior to the improvements. After the improvements, the property is valued again. The increase in tax revenue that results from the enhanced property values from investing in capital improvements is used to pay the interest and principal on the bonds used to pay for them. This approach simulates a market mechanism for providing improvements that benefit a clearly defined subset of the population.

tax revenues. We will examine some of the questions about how to balance the roles of taxes and fees in providing some particular kinds of services later in this chapter.

TYPES OF FEES AND CHARGES

Fees and charges fall into three different categories with very different structures, efficiency effects, and distributional impact. *Licenses and permits* are government permissions to engage in certain kinds of activities ranging from hunting and fishing to operating a business. *Fees for services* are charges incurred by citizens or firms who wish to use a particular publicly provided service such as garbage pickup, tennis courts, highways (tolls), building inspection, and health clinics. Both of these revenue sources normally accrue to the general operating fund of the government imposing the charge. *Payments for the services of government enterprises* are services provided by quasi-business

Table 13–2
Major Types of Fees
and Charges

Licenses and permits
  Business licenses (primarily local)
  Drivers' licenses
  Marriage licenses
  Hunting, fishing, camping, and dog licenses
  Building permits
  Automobile license/registration
  Franchise fees (e.g., cable television, electric and gas service)
Fees for service
  Grazing fees (primarily federal)
  Landing fees (airports)
  Park entry fees
  Recreation fees
  Highway tolls
  Solid waste collection and disposal fees
Government enterprises
  Postal service
  Water and sewer
  State liquor stores
  Transit services (bus, subway, etc.)
  Electric and gas utilities operated by state or local governments
Difficult to classify
  Law enforcement fees and fines
  Impact fees

entities within governments with separate fund accounting from the general fund. Surpluses may be transferred to the general fund, however, or deficits may have to be made up out of the general fund, so even government enterprises are not entirely autonomous from their sponsoring governments. Table 13–2 lists some of the more common kinds of payments in each category.

Because of differences in these revenue-creating categories, most of the discussion in this chapter will focus on the second and third categories, fees for service and government enterprises. Many of the items that fall into the category of licenses and permits are more like excise taxes on certain activities (hunting, fishing, marriage, building). Franchise fees and impact fees are discussed separately in the efficiency section because the pricing elements in both are quite different from those involved in setting other kinds of fees and charges—granting monopoly privileges in the case of franchise fees and using fees as a tool to manage growth in the case of impact fees.

EQUITY ISSUES IN FEES AND CHARGES

Equity issues in fees and charges are just as contentious as they are in taxation, but they take different forms. It can be argued that equity calls for users of services to pay for them, but it can also be argued that equity implies that citizens should have access to public services regardless of ability to pay. Fees and charges in combination with taxes and other revenue sources have to balance these two conflicting equity criteria. Until the last few decades, the access argument tended to dominate, and it was common practice to provide a wide range of services through government with little or no payment by users. However, budgetary pressures in the 1980s at all levels, changing philosophies about the appropriate role of government, and recognition of some efficiency values in requiring at least partial payment by at least some users have changed the way policy makers and citizens think about fees and charges for a wide range of public services.

Protecting the Poor

One of the risks of using access for low-income households as a justification for any kind of blanket policy, whether it is eliminating sales tax on food or free tuition at public colleges, is that the revenue loss or expenditure demand can be excessive relative to the amount of the goods or services that actually get to the target low-income population. A sales tax exemption for food not only benefits the 15% of the population that might be considered poor, but also the 85% who are not, with substantial loss of revenue. Free tuition rains on the rich and poor alike. At a zero price, there will be a large and growing demand for services that would be moderated in the face of some fee or charge (see below).

The middle ground between free and unlimited access to protect the poor and ensuring that users pay can be attained by a variety of techniques. One technique is vouchers or other methods of allowing the poor to have free or reduced cost access while others pay a larger share of the cost. Price discrimination based on some easily verifiable characteristic is another technique, including some instances of **cross-subsidies** in which one group pays a price that exceeds marginal cost in order to help fund the service for another group that pays a price below marginal cost.

Vouchers

Vouchers consist of some kind of coupon redeemable for goods and services. The most familiar kinds of vouchers currently are food stamps, housing vouchers, vouchers for K–12 education, and chits redeemable for child care for working mothers coming off public welfare. In all of these cases, government funds allow low-income families to purchase services from private commercial sources. But the same voucher concept appears under other names for services provided in the public sector. Low-income children are eligible for free or reduced-price school lunches, while their classmates pay the full cost. The same children often receive reduced prices or scholarships to local public recreation programs. The drawback of using such a system, which provides subsidies for the poor but not the nonpoor, is the need to verify eligibility based on family income, size, and assets. However, once a system is in place for one service, it can easily be extended to others. Often proof of eligibility for food stamps or free school lunches is used by other government agencies as sufficient validation for free or reduced-fee access to other services.

Price Discrimination

Many goods and services are available at reduced prices for senior citizens, with the age minimum ranging from 55 to 65. In the private sector, senior citizen discounts on airline tickets, movie theaters, restaurants, and other places are simply a form of price discrimination based on different elasticities of demand. Senior citizens are assumed to have not only lower incomes but also more time for comparison shopping and are consequently assumed to be more sensitive to differences in price. In the public sector, the rationale for special treatment of elderly citizens in assessing fees for services is not as clear. Historically senior citizens have, on average, had lower incomes than the rest of the population, but poverty among the elderly has dropped dramatically in the last 30 years, and they are now less likely to be poor than younger families. Some of the favoritism for senior citizens, ranging from reduced rates on public buses to Golden Eagle passes for access to national parks, monuments, and historic sites, may simply reflect a lag in awareness of the improved income position of most seniors. In public choice terms, one might also consider the greater tendency of older citizens to vote and to participate in public affairs as a reason for favoring this group.

Cross-subsidies are often used in public enterprises such as water, sewer, solid waste collection, and public transit. Different users are charged different prices per unit, or different flat rates, based on easily identified categories such as residential or commercial/industrial, with the latter often subsidizing the former. In this way, households are ensured access to public services at a subsidized rate, while higher charges for business users reduce the amount of tax financing that needs to be devoted to providing these essential basic services. In public transit, the charge may be the same for all users even when the cost of providing the service may be higher to some areas than others, which means that those in low-cost, easy-to-serve areas are subsidizing others living in places that are more remote, less dense, or in some other way more costly to serve.

Collecting from Nonresidents

When public services are available to residents and nonresidents alike, tax financing would put too much of a burden on residents alone. A museum, park, or library fee will ensure that even people who do not pay local taxes but use the service will contribute to its cost. Fees are generally a better way to internalize these kinds of positive externalities, especially at the local government level. Sometimes the users live in the county while the service is provided by the city. County residents enjoy lower taxes while obtaining the benefits of the nearby city. The same principle applies to interstate equity, especially in the case of tourists who use state roads and state parks and create burdens on local trash collection and public safety. Tourism taxes are one mechanism for shifting the burden, but so are admission fees to state parks, tolls on state roads, and various kinds of local fees for tourism-related services.

EFFICIENCY ISSUES IN FEES AND CHARGES

The efficiency issues related to fees and charges and the services of government enterprises are different from those that arise from taxation, and more similar to the kinds of questions addressed in the theory of the firm in microeconomics, because these enterprises operate somewhat like autonomous business firms. In taxation, there is a concern about taxes distorting decisions, which is not the case with fees. In fact, fees are often intended to influence people's decisions about how much to use a particular service such as public parking, public transit, public recreation, or solid waste collection. Taxation is concerned with developing appropriate rules about the distribution of the tax burden, while fees are designed to ensure that the burden falls on the user who can rely on the usual decision-making rules; for instance, is the service worth the price?

Fees and charges have five major purposes: to measure and control demand for certain kinds of services, to implement the benefit principle (user pays), to reduce negative externalities, to reduce the pressure on taxes where feasible, and to capture monopoly profits (in the case of franchise fees or government enterprises). In addition, some specialized fees, in conjunction with other tools such as zoning, enable governments to address growth management issues, which is an aspect of intertemporal efficiency.

Measuring and Controlling Demand

While funding through taxes is an appropriate method for pure public goods, a great many goods or services provided through the public sector are not pure public goods. They may be goods or services with substantial positive externalities, or something that the local community has chosen to provide through government rather than the market for reasons such as ensuring access for low-income citizens. Government-provided services with a strong element of rivalry and excludability in consumption is particularly common at the local level, somewhat less so for state and central governments. Examples of such local services with strong private goods characteristics include street maintenance, solid waste collection, fire and police protection, recreation and parks, and, of course, education.

Figure 13–1 describes the demand and supply (marginal cost) for solid waste collection. Positive externalities are associated with solid waste collection. Most of us would prefer not only to have our garbage collected and disposed of properly but also benefit from our neighbors having the same service! The "full" demand curve, reflecting both private and social demand is D_T, which is the sum of private demand D_P and social benefits D_S. The socially optimal price and level of output is P_0 and Q_0.

Figure 13–1
Demand and Supply
for Solid Waste
Collection

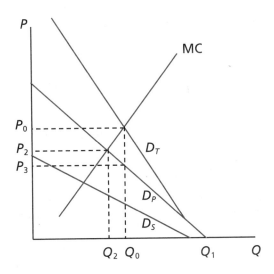

If a good or service with strong positive externalities is provided by the public sector and funded through general taxes, such as sales or income taxes, then citizens respond as if it were free, because their personal tax cost for an additional unit is essentially zero. They will consume, in Figure 13–1, a quantity Q_1, because the marginal benefit of the last unit is equal to the price of zero. That is, they will demand a quantity of service beyond the social optimum—daily pickups, perhaps, or backyard instead of curbside collection. On the other hand, if solid waste pickup is left to the private market to provide, too little will be consumed—Q_2 at a price of P_2. Some consumers will choose not to have their garbage picked up, or picked up as often, creating problems of odor, appearance, and even health risks.

This service is a prime candidate for using a mixture of tax and fee financing. Ideally, the fee would cover the private benefits and the tax funding would cover the social benefits, so the average household should pay a fee of P_3, with the difference $P_0 - P_3$ paid out of general tax revenue. This funding mix will set private marginal benefit plus social marginal benefit equal to the marginal cost of providing additional services.

Note that the margin at which additional units of the service are provided can be either extensive or intensive. At the extensive margin, the city can extend the service to more remote or more scattered customers at the fringes of the service, incurring a higher marginal cost for serving these households. These costs considerations are reflected in annexation and other growth-related issues, discussed below. At the intensive margin, the city could increase the quantity of service provided per household by offering backyard pickup, separate recycling pickups, or more frequent pickups.

In either case, however, the city has accomplished two important goals with this pricing scheme. It has reduced the quantity of services demanded from the quantity at a zero price to the socially optimal amount by requiring people to pay something toward the cost of the service. It has also made a crude measure of demand. If the initial price is too high, people would be likely to opt out, taking their own trash to the landfill or using private providers, as has happened, for example, in Durham, North Carolina. City government could read that signal (or more direct complaints about the high cost!) as an indicator that they had overestimated the private benefits of solid waste collection. If everyone uses the city service, and there are demands for more service at that price, then the initial price is too low. Like a private firm, the city will learn how much to charge by trial and error with the help of customer feedback.

Addressing Externalities

A blend of tax and fee financing is common for many services that are judged to have positive externalities. Public higher education is financed partly by tuition and partly by state and local governments, reflecting a mix of private benefits and positive externalities. K–12 education is generally regarded as consisting more of social benefits relative to private benefits and is therefore funded much more heavily out of taxes than fees. (Education is discussed in detail in Chapter 16.) The use of public transit, which reduces congestion, air pollution, and demand for parking, is generally subsidized so that the fee charged is less than the marginal cost of service. Such a blend of tax and fee financing rather than purely fee-based financing also helps to ensure access to certain services regardless of ability to pay, as discussed earlier.

A related use of fees in order to influence demand is the use of **congestion charges** or **peak-load pricing.** For example, tolls on highways or fees on subways, such as the Washington (D.C.) metro, may vary by time of day. The intended result is to shift some users from peak-demand to off-peak times. If users can shift between times, then there is less pressure to add extra lanes on highways or extra cars or more frequent runs on the subway to accommodate a peak load during a few rush hour periods, with much idle capacity sitting around unused during the off-peak periods. Many federal agencies offer employees flextime, so they can come in very early and leave early or come in after the morning rush and leave after the evening rush. This practice reduces the problems of highway congestion and air pollution and also reduces stress on Washington's public transit. Figure 13–2 illustrates congestion pricing. Off-peak demand is represented by D_A and peak (rush hour) demand by D_B. The marginal cost of serving an additional user during off-peak periods is essentially zero, but once capacity is reached, marginal cost rises quite sharply.

To simplify matters, assume that the subway is free. Then consumers will demand a quantity of service Q_0 at which the marginal benefit is zero, far less than marginal cost. Charging peak-period prices to rush hour customers will reduce quantity demanded to Q_1. Some of those customers may switch to off-

Figure 13–2
Congestion Pricing
on the Subway

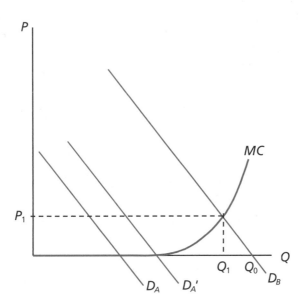

peak hours, increasing off-peak demand to D_A', which makes better use of idle equipment during the off-peak hours. In practice, because marginal costs are not exactly zero, the subway will charge a low rate during off-peak periods and a higher rate during peak periods, but the effect is the same.

There are many applications of congestion charges and peak-load pricing in the public sector. Many public recreation areas collect fees only during the season, in part because the cost of paying a gatekeeper in the off-season would exceed the revenue that it would generate, and the marginal congestion cost of another visitor to a lakefront park in the winter is essentially zero. Only when demand for the service by one user begins to limit the amount available to another or to create additional costs of provision is there any reason to charge a fee.

Elasticity and Fees

Like excise taxes, fees both reduce quantity demanded and generate public revenue. The mix of quantity change and revenue outcomes depends on the height of the fee and the price elasticity of demand. Some publicly provided services, such as parking, may have very inelastic demand because there are no good substitutes. A higher fee in an area without adequate parking can generate substantial revenue without much of a reduction in quantity. Other services, such as recreation, may be very sensitive to price. If a fee is charged for a service with highly elastic demand, it will accomplish the goal of restricting the amount people demand, but it will raise little revenue as they shift to substitutes.

Elasticity and substitution are of particular concern in solid waste pickup in places that have adopted "pay as you throw" policies based on the volume of waste collected. If the fee is too high, people may resort to less desirable alternatives such as burning their trash or burying it in the backyard. If demand is inelastic, the fee will not be very effective as a way to control demand, but it will have the potential to raise a great deal of revenue.

Fees and the Benefit Principle

The primary justification offered for the use of fees for publicly provided services is that many services provided in the public sector do not meet either of the criteria for public goods, nonrivalry or nonexclusion. One might question why the service is being provided in the public sector in that case, or whether it should be privatized. Sometimes privatization is an appropriate answer. In other cases, providing the service through the public sector is justified on some other basis. Perhaps public involvement is the only way to provide access for all citizens regardless of ability to pay. In other cases, there may be a desire to respond to externalities, or the market may be too small to support more than one supplier, which creates a monopoly situation. There may be no private supplier willing and able to provide a service that is not profitable on private grounds but desirable when social benefits are included. In these cases, where the private beneficiaries can be identified and charged, a fee can approximate the goal of Lindahl prices for public goods, which would mean assigning the cost in proportion to benefits received to the extent possible.

Fees and Negative Externalities

Either a fee or a tax is one appropriate way of discouraging the production of negative externalities, such as noise, particulate matter in the air, or effluents into public waters. Such charges, discussed in Chapter 4, fall in the gray area that marks the dividing space between taxes and fees. Such a charge can be regarded as payment for a permit to create negative externalities, much like a building or hunting permit, or as an excise tax on an undesirable activity with the goal of reducing it, like taxes on cigarettes, alcohol, or gambling. Charges on the production of negative externalities are sometimes labeled as taxes and other times as fees, but more often are fees. The term **effluent charge** is used to describe a tax or fee based on the volume of emission of either airborne or waterborne pollutants.[2]

The revenue from such fees may go into the general fund or may be earmarked for specific environmental uses. From an economic perspective, earmarking either fees or taxes on negative externalities for further reduction in the activity generating the externalities is unnecessary. The important issue is that the tax or fee should be set so as to reduce the level of pollution activity to the socially optimal level, as in Figure 4–6 in Chapter 4. If the resulting revenue is then used to further reduce emissions, then the level of pollution could be below the optimal level; that is, more resources would be devoted to reducing externalities than is justified by the social costs they create.

Fees as Tax Relief

Much of the growth in fees at the local government level in the past two decades, especially in California, is not based on theoretical considerations as much as on a need to find some alternative local revenue source to replace part of the property tax revenues. The property tax revolt, discussed in the last chapter, led to substantial reductions in property tax revenues in a number of states, including California, Michigan, and Massachusetts. State aid filled some of the gap, especially for schools, but cities and counties had to look elsewhere. Although the use of local sales and excise taxes has increased, much of the slack has been taken up by fees, charges, licenses, and permits.

---

2. Fees and charges are only one of many tools for regulating externalities. Other approaches range from the regulatory approach to the creation of markets in pollution rights.

SPEED TRAPS, TOLL ROADS, AND THE COST OF DRIVING

One of the more widespread additions to the revenue toolbox in the 1990s was the increased use of toll roads, with permission from the federal government to charge tolls on interstate highways as long as the funds were earmarked for maintenance and improvements. Part of the appeal of charging tolls on interstate highways is that a large part of the cost falls on out-of-state residents, so that tolls are a form of tax exporting. This tax exporting is justified to some degree by the fact that out-of-state residents are using highways paid for at least in part by taxes on local residents. Tolls can also be used effectively to reduce congestion by encouraging motorists to avoid the toll by taking alternative routes.

At the local level, tolls are rarely an option, but there is another way to generate revenue from motorists passing through the city or county—speeding fines. Fines for exceeding the speed limit as a deterrent to excessive or dangerous speeds that create hazards for others on the road are appropriate public policy. When deciding how fast to drive, each motorist must weigh the benefits of getting there faster against the likely fine and the probability of being stopped. But every state has at least a few small communities that rely heavily on speeding fines as a source of local revenue. Sudden changes in speed limits, speed limits that are unrealistically low for the number of lanes or interchanges, and low-visibility speed limit signs are just a few of the techniques to catch unwary motorists. Southern states in particular have a reputation for speed traps, which are well known to locals but not to infrequent visitors.

Speed traps are not only pure opportunism, but are also ultimately self-defeating as word gets around and motorists take other routes or learn where to slow down and watch for smokies. While speeding fines in small towns are, like tolls, a cost of driving, they do little to increase public safety and distribute the revenue burden somewhat randomly among drivers.

It is difficult to determine exactly how much of a total burden should be imposed on cars and trucks in exchange for the privilege of having highways built, maintained, and patrolled for their use (as opposed to trains and subways, which have to build and maintain their own "highways"). Drivers of automobiles already contribute to the public coffers in significant ways. They pay sales taxes on cars when they buy them, property taxes in many states, annual registration or license fees, and taxes on the gasoline needed to keep them running, as well as tolls and speeding fines. Because these taxes and fees are collected by different entities at different times, it is hard to know exactly what the burden on owners and drivers is relative to the costs they impose. There is, however, one interesting indicator. The ratio of the number of cars owned and miles driven to the number of adults or households in the United States continues to rise, while the use of other forms of transit (rail, bus, public transit) has not really caught on. If taxes, tolls, fees, and fines are intended to curtail auto mileage in favor of other means of transportation, the costs of driving may still be too low rather than too high.

Setting Franchise Fees

All levels of governments derive revenue from franchise fees, which are payments in exchange for a grant of exclusive privilege. There are activities or privileges for which franchise fees would be appropriate, such as radio and TV licenses, that are not used or not used very heavily. Local governments have taken advantage of many quasi-monopoly business services to generate franchise revenue. Cable TV companies generally pay a negotiable franchise fee to counties or municipalities in exchange for the exclusive right to serve customers in a given area. The same is often true of telephone, gas, electric, and other utility services. Service areas on some major highways, such as the New Jersey turnpike, are operated by private firms under franchise agreements with payments to the state. Publicly owned airports have the opportunity to grant a variety of privileges ranging from landing slots to restaurants to parking management, for which they normally extract a fee.

Franchise fees are an effort to capture some of the monopoly profits that result from the grant of an exclusive privilege to provide commercial services in a given area. They are also used by private firms; baseball parks, for example, grant franchises (for a price) to vendors of food, drink, souvenirs, and programs. Because it is difficult to determine the exact amount of monopoly profit that will result from a given franchise, the city, county, state, or federal agency has to estimate how much it can charge while still attracting enough competing prospective franchise holders to be able to select for desirable characteristics. Figure 13–3 illustrates the effect of a flat franchise fee on the profits of a monopolistic firm in the short run. Note that, because the franchise fee increases fixed cost but not variable or marginal cost, it has no effect on price or output. It does, however, reduce profits from $AC_0 P_0 ac$ to $AC_1 P_0 ac$, with the difference transferred to the government as general revenue. Franchise fees can also be based on gross or net revenue, in which case they are more like a business income tax. Because such a fee affects marginal cost, it would raise prices and reduce quantity.

Pricing for Public Enterprises

Public enterprises are operations that are run separately from the general fund, with the accounts kept in an enterprise fund, which receives revenues and pays

Figure 13–3
Effect of a Franchise
Fee

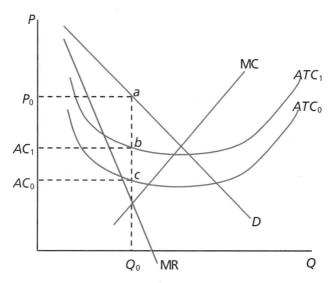

the costs of providing the service. As with any business activity, there is an appropriate price at which marginal revenue equals marginal cost, but these enterprises are not-for-profit monopolists. They have some discretion in setting prices, since their objective is likely to be other than profit maximization.

A public enterprise may set price rather than marginal revenue equal to marginal cost, or operate somewhere in between. Depending on average cost, this pricing strategy could result in a deficit, which will be made up out of the general fund. At this lower price, more use will be made of the service. If the service, such as garbage pickup or public transit, has important positive externalities, then this pricing strategy will move output closer to the socially optimal level at which price (including social benefits) equals marginal cost. It may be difficult for the public enterprise to determine that price and output level precisely, and the public enterprise may be constrained by the amount of subsidy its parent government is willing to provide out of general revenues, but conceptually such a pricing strategy could increase efficiency in the allocation of resources. Many public transit services operate at an intentional deficit in order to subsidize the use of public transit by citizens for both efficiency and equity reasons.

Other public enterprises may intentionally set prices in order to run a surplus (which would be known as a profit in a private firm), which is then transferred to the general fund to provide tax relief for all citizens, regardless of the extent to which they use the service. These enterprises use their monopoly position in much the same way as a private monopoly, except that the surplus is used for public purposes. In South Carolina, 21 municipalities operate retail electricity service enterprises, and many of these municipalities transfer surplus funds each year to their regular budgets. As a result, their citizens enjoy lower taxes and/or better services at the expense of electricity customers. Many of these people are the same (citizens and electricity customers), but some are not. Municipalities may have service areas that extend beyond their corporate limits to include households and business firms who enjoy the benefits of convenient access to the municipality and benefit from some of its services but pay no taxes. Higher electric rates are one way of making these "free riders" contribute to the cost of maintaining the city. There are also non-taxpaying entities inside and outside the city—churches, other nonprofit entities, and state government facilities—that use some city services but are exempt from property taxes. The electric utility enterprise is a way of generating some general revenue from these sources to relieve the burden on tax-paying residents.

Another strategy in pricing public enterprises is to charge a flat rate rather than a fee based on usage, or a combination of a flat fee and a per-unit fee. Students on college campuses often find a transportation fee on their tuition bill, which covers part of the cost of shuttle buses. Students pay this fee regardless of whether they never use the shuttle bus, use it occasionally, or use it regularly. The fee has no impact on their decision on how often to ride the shuttle, because the marginal cost is still zero. By encouraging students to make more use of the shuttle buses at a marginal price of zero, school authorities reduce congestion and demand for on-campus parking, and save themselves the cost of collecting from each passenger.

Water is an example of an enterprise that often makes use of a combination of a flat fee and a per-unit fee. The flat fee may include a certain amount of "free water," such as 1,000 gallons per household per month, with water beyond that amount charged for by the gallon. The per-gallon fee may be flat ($2 per 1,000 gallons) or it may rise with higher usage.

What objectives are served by such a pricing structure? One objective is to ensure access to a certain basic amount of water to all households regardless of ability to pay. A low flat fee will address that objective, while covering some of the infrastructure costs and administrative costs of connecting to the system and measuring usage. (A pure per-household flat fee would have the additional advantage of no expenditures for metering usage, but has other drawbacks.) Lower income households may find that the amount of water permitted under the flat fee is adequate for their needs. Higher income households may use more water for cleaning or gardening, and will pay more for their water use, making the payment system more progressive or at least less regressive than a flat fee per household. The fee for additional use also serves to control demand. Water is not free; it must be pumped, purified, and stored, all of which incur marginal costs. By charging by the unit, marginal units will not be free beyond the basic amount, and households will have an incentive to conserve water, reducing pressure to provide capacity that is based on high peak loads rather than lower average use. Charging per gallon also offers a useful incentive mechanism in times of drought or other water shortage, when rates can be raised to control usage.

FEES AND CHARGES AS GROWTH MANAGEMENT TOOLS

Local governments have increasingly begun to use fees to influence the pattern of growth in order to minimize the cost of servicing a growing population. Land development can follow many alternative patterns even when accommodating the same amount of population. One pattern has been described as "ranchette"—large lots with scattered housing. Another pattern is dense development that may or may not be surrounded by open space. A third is a random distribution with patchwork developments on moderate-sized lots separated by undeveloped land. A fourth pattern is infill development, making use of scattered lots within the developed urban and suburban areas. These alternative land use patterns have very different implications not only for the loss of prime lands to other uses but also for local government service costs.

Land use patterns are the result of individual choices, influenced heavily by both market forces and constraints imposed and incentives offered by governments at all levels. Left to the individual buyer and seller, the ownership and use of land would be determined by the highest present value in terms of projected future revenues and costs, discounted at prevailing private market rates of interest. In some instances, leaving land "idle" while awaiting a future, more attractive use may be the most attractive alternative, an outcome familiar to those who are aware of the workings of futures markets. The actual pattern of land use may be different from the socially optimal pattern for several reasons. Among the major sources of distortions in land use choice are imperfect information, overdiscounting future costs and benefits where benefits are immediate and costs are delayed, spillover effects (externalities), and public policies that create perverse incentives (such as the tax favoritism for owner-occupied residential property in both income and property taxes).

Established residents and local public officials are persuaded that growth will reduce their tax burdens through sharing the cost of public services among more citizens. That expectation is rarely fulfilled in practice. Residential development in particular tends to add more to the cost than the revenue side of local government budgets. Loudon County in Virginia, just outside Washington, D.C., offers one good example:

In Loudon County, Virginia, officials in 1994 estimated that a new home must sell for at least $400,000 to bring in sufficient property taxes to cover the cost of all the services the county provides. By contrast, the average home sold that year for less than $200,000. The fastest selling properties in 1995 were town homes averaging between $120,000 and $160,000.[3]

This estimate confirmed an earlier study in Culpepper County, Virginia, which found that residential development cost $1.25 in county services for every $1 of revenue, while service costs were only 19 cents per dollar of revenue generated for industrial, commercial, or agricultural land.[4] Likewise, Benfield *et al.* cite an earlier study by the American Farmland Trust, which found a revenue-to-cost ratio for residential property of 1:1.11, whereas the ratios were 1:0.29 for commercial and industrial property and 1:0.31 for farmland, forests, and open space.[5] However, as Benfield *et al.* note, these ratios may overstate the benefits of nonresidential development:

A 1991 study by the DuPage County, Illinois Development Department found that, between 1986 and 1989, areas of the county with significant nonresidential development experienced a greater increase in taxes than did areas without nonresidential development . . . commercial development may create a demand for additional nearby residential development which . . . brings a fiscal drain that offsets the benefits.[6]

---

3. Henry L. Diamond and Patrick F. Noonan, *Land Use in America,* (Cambridge, MA: Lincoln Institute of Land Policy, 1996), p. 35.
4. *Ibid*, p. 36.
5. F. Kaid Benfield, Mathew D. Raimi, and Donald D. T. Chen, *Once There Were Greenfields: How Urban Sprawl is Undermining America's Environment, Economy, and Social Fabric* (New York: Natural Resources Defense Council, 1999), p. 107.
6. *Ibid*, p. 113.

GRAZING FEES ON FEDERAL LANDS

Among the many assets owned by the federal government are millions of acres of public lands, most of them in the West. The federal government owns and manages approximately 650 million acres of land, or 28% of the land area of the United States. Four federal agencies manage these lands for various purposes, which include conservation, preservation, and development of natural resources. The Bureau of Land Management and the Forest Service are the two agencies that have responsibility for grazing rangelands totaling about 260 million acres.

In the 19th century, access to public lands was free, but in 1906 the Forest Service began to charge grazing fees on land under its control, although much other public land was still available for use without regulation or fees until 1934. Today, the grazing fees on federal lands are still substantially lower than the rates charged on comparable private lands. In 1993, the monthly fee on federal lands was $1.86 per head of livestock, while fees on state lands averaged $4.58 and on private lands, $9.80. As a result of this history of free (or subsidized) and largely unregulated access, Western ranchers have come to think of grazing on public lands as a property right, and oppose any restrictions on that perceived right as an action that reduces the value of their assets invested in livestock and equipment. On the other hand, public land is not an unlimited resource. It has competing uses. Not only do ranchers compete for a limited supply of grazing land, which will deteriorate in quality over time if overused, but grazing also competes with other uses of the land, such as for recreation or as fish and wildlife habitats.

Grazing rights fees are appropriate for several reasons. First, private firms are using a scarce resource as a production input to a product to be sold in the marketplace. In the absence of a fee, consumers will pay too little for beef or land and will consume more of it than they would if they had to pay the full cost, including the value of the input of grazing land. Second, grazing land requires maintenance and controlled grazing to prevent deterioration. A fee is a way of controlling demand to prevent overuse. Third, public lands are in competition with private lands, on which a fee for grazing is routinely charged. Owners of cattle and sheep are being encouraged to overuse the public resource and underuse the private resource because of the price differential. Livestock owners with federal grazing permits are being subsidized relative to their competitors who must pay full market value for private land grazing rights. The estimated revenue loss to the Treasury is between $20 and $150 million a year.

In the 1990s, the battle between the Department of the Interior and Western ranching interests represented in Congress focused on the proposal to more than double grazing fees over a three-year period and to change rangeland rules to allow more public participation in decisions, greater efforts to protect ecosystems, and reductions in the number of livestock allowed to graze. The increase in the fee was deferred after protests from Congress, but the other regulations were put into effect.

There is little dispute among economists that it is appropriate for the government to charge grazing fees for public land that are comparable to those charged by private landowners. Such fees should cover the cost of managing the program (at present, administrative costs exceed revenue by a substantial amount) as well as the environmental impact, and should also serve to ration a scarce resource among competing uses. But, like many policies that benefit a small number of citizens, it is not easy to gather the political will or critical mass to make a change. Arrayed on one side are the ranching interests, wishing to preserve access to a low-cost source of grazing land. On the other side are environmentalist and recreation interests. For the average citizen, who feels little impact from the revenue loss, the loss of wildlife habitat, or even the price of beef, grazing fees are never going to make it to the top of the political agenda.

Sources: Betsy A. Cody, "Grazing Fees: An Overview," *Congressional Research Service,* May 21, 1996; Betsy Cody and Pamela Baldwin, "Grazing Fees and Rangeland Management," *Congressional Research Service,* December 4, 1998.

Local governments have several nonrevenue tools at their disposal to attempt to direct growth into patterns that are less costly to serve and make better use of existing infrastructure, including zoning and land use plans. One of the most widely used revenue tools, however, is the development impact fee. A charge is assessed against each lot developed to cover some part of the additional costs attributed to the new occupants, which may include building additional water and sewer capacity, police and fire substations, staff and equipment, additional garbage trucks, new landfill capacity, more street maintenance, and construction and operation of additional schools. The rationale behind an impact fee is, once again, user pays. If established residents are not going to benefit from lower taxes as a result of sharing costs with new neighbors, they can at least be shielded from seeing their tax and fee burdens rise with no increase in services just because the city or county must now extend services to new residents. Impact fees, then, serve both equity and efficiency goals. The equity is between new and established residents. The efficiency goal is to constrain growth to what can be effectively serviced and to make sure that the additional costs created by new development are internalized, that is, they fall on those who create the costs.

SUMMARY

Fees and charges are a large and growing component of government revenue in the United States, particularly at the local level. The major types of fees and charges are licenses and permits, fees for public services, and payments for the output of government enterprises.

Fees and charges differ from taxes in that fees and charges result from voluntary decisions by individuals to use particular services, and in that fees and charges are often (but not always) dedicated to covering the cost of the services for which they are charged. In practice, a continuum ranges from a pure tax, charged regardless of the consumption of service and used to generate revenue for the general fund, through earmarked taxes, franchise fees, and permits, to pure exchange of payment for services such as water and sewer utilities. Specialized kinds of fees for specific purposes include franchise fees to capture monopoly profits and impact fees to channel growth in desired directions and ensure that those who cause increased service demands bear a proportionate share of the cost.

Equity in the use of fees and charges must balance the conflicting demands that those who use a service should pay for it with the equally compelling requirement that citizens should have access to basic public services regardless of ability to pay. In the past, the latter argument led to more tax financing than fee financing of services without substantial public good characteristics. Techniques for ensuring access while using fees include vouchers and price discrimination.

Fees and charges are used to measure and control demand for certain kinds of services, to implement the benefit principle (user pays), to reduce negative externalities, to reduce the pressure on taxes where feasible, and to capture monopoly profits. In the absence of a fee, the price to the consumer for another unit of a public good would be zero, so he or she would consume until the marginal benefit was zero, or less than the marginal cost. Fees make it possible both to measure demand and to restrict demand to the socially optimal level. For goods with positive externalities, the fee should cover the private benefit with the social benefits aspects funded through general taxes.

Congestion charges can be used not only to restrict demand but also to shift demand from one time period or location to another, making better use of existing facilities and reducing demand to create additional capacity.

Franchise fees are charged when a government grants an exclusive right to market a good or service in a given jurisdiction, such as cable TV, concessions in state or national parks, or airport landing rights. Franchise fees enable the government to capture some of the monopoly profits that result from the grant of exclusive privileges.

Public enterprises ranging from the Postal Service to your local municipal water service face many of the same pricing challenges as private firms, with the added complication of having to serve the entire population. Some public enterprises are subsidized out of general tax revenues to provide for social benefits or to ensure access to services for low-income households. Others run surpluses that are then transferred to general fund budgets to help pay the cost of other public services.

Impact fees are a useful tool for local governments attempting to address the needs for infrastructure and services in response to population growth by ensuring that the additional costs fall on the owners of the newly developed property rather than burdening existing residents with higher costs but no improved levels of public services.

KEY TERMS AND CONCEPTS

earmarked taxes, 274
franchise fee, 274
impact fee, 276

cross-subsidy, 279
voucher, 279
congestion charge, 283

peak-load pricing, 283
effluent charge, 285

DISCUSSION QUESTIONS

1. Fees for services work much like excise taxes. Review Figure 11–1 in Chapter 11 and draw a diagram that describes the impact of a flat per-household fee on the demand for solid waste collection. Identify the revenue collected and the reduction in the quantity of service demanded. How would your answer be different if the fee were based on the volume of solid waste? How might elasticity of demand affect your answer? Why might the local government choose to use a combination of a flat fee and a per-unit charge for solid waste beyond some minimum amount?

2. Copy Figure 13–3, but change the franchise fee from a flat fee that shifts total cost up parallel without changing marginal cost to one that increases with volume (quantity). Demonstrate that not only profits but also quantity will fall. (*Hint:* MC shifts up and rotates clockwise; *ATC* shifts up, but by increasing amounts as Q increases.)

3. How should the cost of each of the following services be distributed? What role

can fees and charges play in each instance? What part should be played by general tax revenues? Justify your answers in both efficiency and equity terms.

City streets
Sewer service
Solid waste disposal
Fire protection
National defense
City summer recreation for children
State highways
Public libraries
Local bus service
Public parking
Higher education
Streetlights

4. Suppose you are in charge of the municipal water system of Smallville. A drought is threatening your water supply just as the city council has asked you to develop a new water fee schedule. What kind of fee schedule would you develop, taking into account the need to restrict demand, differences in elasticities of demand and ability to pay, and other considerations?

5. You are a Senate committee staffer charged with analyzing the impact of a substantial increase in grazing fees on federal lands, with the proceeds to be used for erosion control and for animal health services for owners of livestock. Evaluate this proposal from both an efficiency and an equity perspective. How would you decide how much to increase the fee?

CHAPTER 14

INTERGOVERNMENTAL GRANTS IN THEORY AND PRACTICE

Whether a government is federal or unitary, there are always some fiscal links between levels of government. Many of those fiscal links are explored in Chapters 2 and 3, which described the basic structure and fiscal operations of federal, state, and local governments in the United States and elsewhere.

Often these fiscal links take the form of shared responsibilities. In the United States, for instance, the National Guard is a shared federal and state responsibility, and the responsibility for providing K–12 education is shared primarily between state and local governments, with some limited federal role. Usually that sharing involves a transfer of funds from one level of government to another that is primarily responsible for providing the service. Such transfers are called **intergovernmental grants.**

The existence of intergovernmental grants means that state and local governments do not have to raise by themselves all the revenue required to fund their programs and services. In fact, intergovernmental grants are a large component of revenue for both state and local governments in a federal system. From the federal perspective, grants are a significant budgetary outlay. In 2000, $292 billion in grants accounted for more than one-fifth of all on-budget outlays, with the four largest categories being Medicaid ($120 billion), highways ($25 billion), welfare (Aid to Families with Dependent Children and Temporary Assistance to Needy Families, $17 billion), and elementary and secondary education ($134 billion).

For local governments, grants from their state government are an even more important source of revenue than those from the federal government. In 1998–99, local governments received $328 billion in intergovernmental aid, about 10% from the federal government and the remaining 90% from their states. Intergovernmental revenue was 38% of local government revenue, slightly more than the total value of tax revenue collected by local government.

For states, federal aid of $254 billion accounted for 27% of general revenue funds,[1] or slightly more than the total of all state sales and gross receipts tax collections. Medicaid, highway funds, and welfare account for about half of federal aid to states, with the rest scattered among a variety of smaller grants. Clearly grants are a significant expenditure for the federal government and a very important source of revenue for state and local governments.

GROWTH AND DECLINE OF FEDERAL GRANTS

The earliest federal grants were made in the 1830s, when land sales and tariffs were generating embarrassing surpluses to the federal treasury. Rejecting proposals to spend the surplus on public works, Congress instead sent the funds back to the states, which used them for a variety of purposes. The 19th century marked the creation of the *categorical grant*, which was intended to involve the states in a partnership with the federal government to carry out a purpose that was identified as important at the federal level. The most significant categorical grant in the 19th century was probably the Morrill Land Grant College Act of 1862, which granted land or equivalent sums to each state to establish colleges with an agricultural and public service mission (see boxed feature).

During the Depression, the federal role in the economy grew substantially in many respects, including its grants program. The nature of grants shifted toward programs that provided relief to the poor and assistance with developing infrastructure. Together with Social Security, the growing regulatory authority of the federal government, and the sharp increase in national defense spending, the federal government experienced two decades of rapid growth. By the 1950s a search was under way for effective ways to turn some of the growing federal responsibilities back to the states, which had lost the status they had enjoyed as the senior partners in the federal system for the first 150 years. With the Kennedy and Johnson administrations and the war on poverty, however, grants began to increase again. The Johnson years saw growth in grants to large cities that were experiencing serious problems with poverty, violence, and decay. These types of problems were not being addressed by rural-dominated state legislatures.

1. Some transfers are also made from local to state governments, about $13 billion in fiscal year 1998–1999.

THE FEDERAL GOVERNMENT AND THE LAND GRANT COLLEGES

Perhaps you attend a major public university. If you do, there is a pretty good chance that the words *land grant* appear in its description somewhere. Every state and the District of Columbia has one or more institutions that were either established or strengthened by federal grants resulting from two pieces of legislation, the 1862 Morrill Land Grant College Act and the Second Morrill Act passed in 1890 to provide for higher education for African-American students. The land grant colleges are unique among federal grants in a number of respects, but they also established a pattern that was followed in later legislation: providing funds for a particular purpose deemed important by the federal government, and doing it in a way that required some long-term commitment to the project by state governments.

The 1862 act granted each state public land in the amount of 30,000 acres for each member of Congress, or a minimum of 90,000 acres for a state with two senators and one representative. States that did not have that much unsold public land were given claims to public lands in states and territories with excess acreage. The funds were used to create a trust fund to endow a college in each state that would emphasize practical education in agriculture and engineering (as well as military training). Later legislation assigned

some specific federal functions to these colleges: the creation of agricultural experiment stations to do research in agriculture and extension services to bring new developments in agriculture to farmers. The idea of extension was imported from England and gradually expanded far beyond agriculture to a broader notion of a public service mission for the nation's land grant institutions. The experiment station and extension service programs continue to receive annual federal support.

Today some of the best known public universities in the nation are land grant colleges. Many of them have the word "state" in their name to distinguish them from other major but non–land grant institutions in the same state (North Carolina State University versus the University of North Carolina, Iowa State, Michigan State). Others have the designation of A&M (agricultural and military), of which the best known is probably Texas A&M. Still others have names that do not make it clear that they are either land grant or public, such as Rutgers University in New Jersey and Clemson University in South Carolina. Whatever they are called, however, they are a living testimony to the power of federal grants to create new institutions and persuade states to become partners in the enterprise.

From 1960 to 2000, federal grants to state and local governments combined grew from $4 billion to $292 billion. Adjusted for inflation, federal grants were almost 9 times larger in 2000 than in 1960. They have also doubled as a share of combined state and local revenues, from 9.4% in 1960 to 19.6% in 1998–1999.[2] However, that growth took place in several spurts, with some peaks and valleys. Even after adjusting for inflation, federal aid tripled in the 1960s as a result of President Johnson's Great Society programs. Grants peaked in real (inflation-adjusted) terms in 1978 during the Carter administration and continued to decline to a 1983 low of $107 million (in 1996 dollars). Federal aid did not get back to the 1978 level in constant dollars until 1991, and has continued to grow at a modest rate through the 1990s. Figure 14–1 shows

2. The 1999 data for local governments was not available at press time.

Figure 14–1
Federal Grants as
Share of Federal
Expenditures,
1960–2000

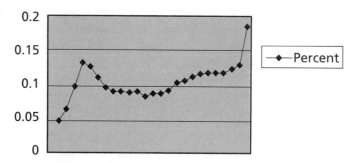

the growth of federal aid to state and local governments as a percentage of total federal spending from 1960 to 2000. Even after expressing grants as a percentage of total federal outlays, the growth spurt of the 1960s and early 1970s, the cutbacks of the Reagan years, and the gradual reinstatement of earlier patterns are clearly shown in the graph.

PURPOSES OF GRANTS

Grants may serve a single purpose or multiple purposes. Among these purposes are equalizing vertically and horizontally, correcting spatial externalities, redirecting priorities, and experimenting with new ideas and approaches. Sometimes a grant serves only one of these purposes, while other grants may serve multiple purposes.

Equalizing Grants

One important function of grants is to balance revenue with service responsibilities both by levels of government and across governments at the same level. In the 1960s, the federal government was widely believed to have a greater ability than state or local governments to raise revenue because it had more "monopoly" power. That is, people might move from city to city or state to state in search of a lower tax burden, but they were unlikely to move to another country just to reduce their taxes. The conclusion drawn from this argument was that it would be appropriate for the federal government to raise money for state and local governments to spend, without specifying the uses except in very broad terms.

Thus was born General Revenue Sharing, which lasted from the mid-1960s until the mid-1980s. General Revenue Sharing to states ended in 1982 and to local governments in 1986. General Revenue Sharing was an example of **vertical equalization,** which attempts to correct the difference between the amount of revenue that a government can raise and the amount of responsibility that appropriately falls to that level in a multilevel or federal system.

State aid to schools and local governments also falls at least partly in this category, because states have greater ability than local governments to raise revenue without driving away households and firms than local governments. Local governments exist in a highly competitive Tiebout situation and must always be mindful of the effect of their tax rates on location decisions. As a consequence, every state but New Hampshire engages in a substantial amount of state aid to local governments, which averaged 34.4% of local government revenue in 1996.[3]

The imbalance between revenue needs and the ability to raise revenue has a horizontal dimension as well. Cities, counties, and school districts vary greatly within and among states in their taxable wealth, that is, the income and property wealth of their residents. The same tax rate will raise very different amounts of revenue per person in different jurisdictions. The federal government addresses this disparity in some of its grants with formulas that favor states and local governments with greater indexes of "need" (poverty rates, per capita income, etc.). Most state education funding formulas also have a need or ability-to-pay index as part of the distribution plan. Per capita grants also address this problem, because more revenue will be collected from higher income/wealth areas than lower income/wealth areas, but each will receive back the same amount per resident. All of these grants are designed to promote **horizontal equalization,** or reduction in the disparities in resources among governments of the same level or type (between cities, or counties, or states, or school districts). Many grants incorporate both vertical and horizontal equalization, particularly at the state-to-local level.

Correcting Spatial Externalities

A second purpose of grants is to offset the spillovers that occur because the service provided by a local or state government may generate benefits to those who live outside that government's boundaries and do not contribute to its support, an issue addressed in Chapter 2. Washington, D.C., provides valued services and a significant employment destination for three adjacent counties in Virginia and two in Maryland. If the social benefits to nonresidents are not taken into account, then the local government in charge will produce less than the socially optimal level of the service. Chapters 9 and 13 explored the use of exportable taxes and fees and charges as mechanisms for correcting such externalities.

Intergovernmental grants can also play a role. If, for example, having well-paved and well-lighted streets benefits not only the residents of Lincoln, Nebraska, but also people who are just visiting or driving through, most of them from other parts of Nebraska, then state aid to street maintenance and lighting

---

3. New Hampshire has been wrestling with the problems posed for both equalization and adequate school funding that arise from relying primarily on property taxes to fund public schools. As of the end of the 2001 legislative session, no broad and lasting solution had been found acceptable.

IN CHINA THE FUNDS FLOWED UPWARD

The notion that the central government has greater revenue-raising power because of its quasi-monopoly position is not universally shared. In many parts of Africa and Asia, it is considered easier to collect most or all taxes at the local level and send them to the central government, which keeps a large share and sends the rest back with instructions about how to spend it. A somewhat similar system existed until the 1990s in Eastern Europe prior to the end of communism and in China.[1] Because the levels of government were more closely integrated, with tight central control, these systems were not federal in the sense that the United States, Canada, Germany, and Australia are federal. Consequently, the concept of intergovernmental grants that take place at "arms length" between somewhat autonomous governments does not apply to these situations.

Why did it make sense in the United States to collect centrally, yet spend locally (through General Revenue Sharing and other intergovernmental grants), while in large parts of the rest of the world, the opposite has been true? The key differences are probably mobility and information systems. In a society where workers and firms are highly mobile, which is true of the Western industrial world, it is difficult to collect taxes at the local level because tax differences between cities, school districts, or states are likely to induce those mobile taxpayers to relocate to a more kindly jurisdiction. Likewise, in a society where workers and firms are highly mobile, they do not stay put long enough for the local tax collector to get a handle on their income, assets, and ability to pay taxes. Only the property itself, which cannot move, lends itself to local assessment and collection of taxes. And the existence of information networks that do track that information on income, assets, and ability to pay creates some economies of scale in centralizing collection.

But consider a society of stable rural villages, where people live for many generations. Tax differences would not be a factor in mobility, partly because of lack of information about alternatives and because the culture discourages mobility. Without complex computer-based information systems, the local tax collector is in a much better position to determine ability to pay and extract revenue than the distant central government.

Many of the features of our revenue system that we take for granted are culturally conditioned. The logic of intergovernmental grants in a Western, industrial, market-based economy is turned on its head when transplanted to a very different historical, cultural, and institutional environment.

1. Recent changes in China and Eastern Europe have shifted toward a more centralized revenue collection system.

will use tax revenues from non-Lincoln residents to improve the quality and quantity of such services. Because the residents of Lincoln are the primary beneficiaries, they should bear most of the cost, but they are not the only beneficiaries.

Recall the analysis of public goods in Chapter 4 (Figure 4–3), reproduced here as Figure 14–2. Now we are reinterpreting that analysis of tax price for two voters by recasting the two demand curves as those of residents (D_A) and nonresidents (D_B). If only the demands of residents are considered, the amount of service provided will be too low. One solution is a subsidy by the state on behalf of nonresident users. The appropriate tax price to be funded by the state is the nonresidents' share of the benefits, or the difference between P_1 and P_B. While such a share may be difficult to pinpoint in practice, it is at

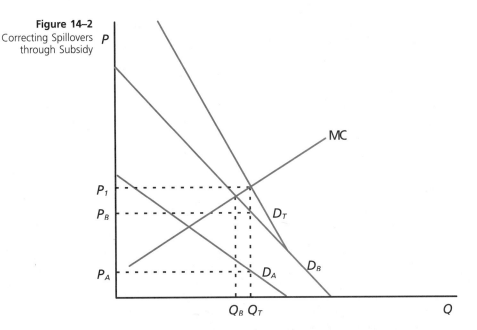

Figure 14–2
Correcting Spillovers through Subsidy

least conceptually clear that some local services have spillover benefits for which state subsidy through statewide general tax revenue is appropriate.

The same is true of spillovers between states. Charlotte, North Carolina, is an urban center for upstate South Carolina, as Memphis is for northern Mississippi and New York City is for two adjacent states, in services ranging from airports to museums to regional health centers. State watershed management creates literal spillovers from the many rivers that serve as state boundaries! The federal government can intervene constructively by providing grants that subsidize activities that also benefit residents of adjacent states.

Redirecting Priorities

Each level of government has its own priorities in terms of the variety and quality of public services to be provided and the externalities to be corrected. Sometimes higher levels of government attempt to override those priorities by mandating local governments to provide certain services. The federal government, for example, mandates certain drinking water standards that local governments must meet. Affirmative action to reduce education and employment discrimination and the Americans with Disabilities Act that regulates access to buildings have generated major complaints from state and local governments about the cost of compliance. State governments exert considerable control over local public schools, even when schools are nominally controlled by local school boards or city or county governments. States also have a great deal of authority over how the property tax is structured and administered in most states even though the property tax is primarily a local revenue source.

When the higher level of government simply orders a state or local government to perform certain functions or meet certain standards without offering to pay some of the cost, that order is known as an **unfunded mandate.** Unfunded mandates have been a source of considerable dissension between state governments and the federal government, almost starting a resurgence of the states' rights arguments that go back to the 1780s. Unfunded mandates are usually a bone of contention between local and state public officials as well.

A less contentious and more incentive-based way of imposing the preferences of a higher level of government on a lower one is through an intergovernmental grant that is earmarked for a particular service. When the services are largely funded and provided by a different level of government, grants can be a tool of persuasion for redirecting priorities. For example, the federal government in the United States has a cabinet-level Department of Education, but in fact both K–12 education and higher education are largely a function of state and local governments. If the federal government wants to be a "player" in public education, it must persuade state and local governments to adopt its priorities and values. The federal government may want to see more emphasis on health education, or school readiness for preschoolers, or vocational training, or computers in schools. Grants are a tool for persuading states and school districts to refashion their priorities in order to receive federal aid.

Experimenting with New Ideas

Grants are a particularly useful device in a federal system because new ideas and programs can be tried out in one or more states or local areas on an experimental basis before being spread to other states if they are successful. The states had a long history of welfare reform and income maintenance experiments, many carried out with federal aid, before welfare reform was finally undertaken in 1995.

States and local governments make useful laboratories of federalism to carry out new ideas and test new approaches on a less than national scale. Usually grants for this purpose are project grants that invite proposals and select the most promising ones for funding, those that might offer useful information for designing broader programs or for implementing them in other places.

CHOICE OF TOOLS

When the central government or a state or provincial government wants to accomplish any of the objectives discussed thus far, a grant is not the only tool and often not the most desirable one. Direct expenditures are another tool. The federal government made this choice in 1965 when Medicare for those over 65 made health care for most of the nation's elderly a direct federal responsibility. (Some health care costs for the elderly, mostly nursing home care, come under Medicaid, a federal–state shared responsibility.) Pell grants and subsidized student loans are federal programs that encourage students to take advantage of higher education, which states may choose to supplement, but no intergovernmental grants are involved. Instead, federal funds flow directly to individuals rather than to other levels of governments.

Tax expenditures in the form of tax credits, adjustments, or deductions are another tool to promote specific goals, such as encouraging private forms of welfare supported by charitable donations or seeking higher education with the aid of various tuition tax credits. State governments also have the options of direct spending and tax expenditures as alternatives to grants. Much of the property tax relief enacted in the last twenty years (and funded) by state governments is an indirect form of aid to public schools, a move that has been more politically popular although perhaps less effective in improving public education than direct grants would have been.

TYPES OF GRANTS

The two basic kinds of grants in terms of use of funds are **general-purpose grants** and **categorical grants.** Distribution of funds also comes in two different types, **formula grants** and **project grants,** depending on whether the money is automatically distributed according to some preset criteria or whether the recipient government must apply and sometimes compete with other applicants for a limited pool of funds. Other project grants are assigned to particular places by legislative action. Within all of these types, the revenue may be given as a **lump-sum grant** or may require a **matching grant** (e.g., one local dollar for every five federal dollars). Finally, a grant may be a **closed-ended grant** (a limited pool of available funds) or an **open-ended grant** (everyone who qualifies or submits an appropriate request is automatically funded). As a rule, general-purpose grants are distributed by formula on a lump-sum basis, while categorical grants may be formula, project, or some of each, and may be either lump sum or matching. Both types can be either closed ended or open ended.

General Purpose or Categorical?

The structure or form of a grant is often dictated by its purpose. A pure equalization grant, such as General Revenue Sharing or many kinds of state aid to local governments, does not put many constraints on how the funds may be spent. A categorical grant, in contrast, must be spent for a designated use, such as putting more police patrols on the street or providing free or reduced-price lunches to schoolchildren.

In practice, even categorical grants have the effect of giving recipient governments some flexibility in the use of their funds. If a local government had planned to put additional police patrols on the streets and federal funds became available for that purpose, then that government could redirect some of its own-source revenues to other priorities, such as more frequent garbage pickup or more streetlights. The ability to shift dollars to other purposes in response to grants is called **fungibility.** Higher levels of government are aware of this possibility and often take safeguards to prevent such shifting of funds, because their goal is to ensure more police patrols or more free lunches than there would have been in the absence of the grant money. Many grants contain **maintenance of effort** requirements, which make continuation of the grantee's current level of spending on the designated purpose a condition for funding.

In the 1970s, the federal government began to use a hybrid type of grant, which has seen even more use in the 1980s and 1990s, called a block grant. A **block grant** consists of funds that must be used within a broad category, such as law enforcement or secondary education or community development, but the recipient government has a great deal of flexibility about exactly how to spend the funds within that category. Many block grants, particularly in the 1980s, were used to consolidate the proliferating categorical grants, with the trade-off that state and local governments received less funding but with more flexibility. In 1999, block grants of $2.6 billion accounted for only about 1% of federal grants to state and local governments, which totaled $277 billion.

Formula or Project?

A second issue in designing intergovernmental grants is how they should be distributed among recipients. A formula grant is distributed according to some set of criteria, while a project grant is usually received in response to competitive applications (or sometimes competition among legislators to provide for their own districts). The formula may be as simple as so many dollars per capita, or may include other factors such as the poverty rate, the number of school pupils, the number of miles of highway, the percent of the population that is elderly, or the relative amount of substandard housing. Much of the state aid to local schools is distributed on the basis of complex formulas that are described in Chapter 16. A formula-type grant can be used for either general-purpose grants or for categorical grants (including block grants) that specify the use to which the funds must be directed. In 1999, about 71% of all federal grants to state and local governments were based on formula distribution.

Project grants often invite state or local governments to compete for a limited pool of funds by submitting proposals to the agency dispensing the funds. At both the state and federal levels, project grants are often noncompetitive. Pork-barrel politics (along with "bringing home the bacon") is the colorful term used to describe the political wheeling and dealing by which representatives ensure that their districts receive funds for special purposes ranging from railroad museums to wetlands conservation to highway construction. Project grants of both a competitive and a noncompetitive nature to state and local governments accounted for about 38% of federal grants in 2000.

Lump Sum or Matching?

A third issue in grant design is whether to provide the funds with or without requiring the recipient government to pay a fair share. A lump-sum grant provides a certain number of dollars to the recipient, which may be available for general use or restricted use, without condition or with a requirement of maintenance of effort. Most of the block grants that have become popular in the last two decades, such as Job Training and Partnership Act (JTPA) grants or community development block grants (CDBG) are lump sum. A matching grant, which is almost always tied to a specific purpose such as highway construction or increased law enforcement effort, changes the relative price of additional units of that particular kind of service. With a matching grant, an extra dollar's worth of highway or police patrol may only cost 50 cents in local funds, while an extra dollar's worth of any other service will cost an entire locally raised dollar. Matching grants use the persuasion of relative price in the marketplace to induce recipients to change their spending patterns in ways preferred by the donor level of government.

Open Ended or Closed Ended?

An open-ended grant obligates the grantor government to fund as many projects, recipients, or governments as meet the stated qualifications. Open-ended grants create challenges for budget-makers, who must estimate how many recipients will qualify for how much in the way of funds. Until welfare reform, the principal welfare program, Aid to Families with Dependent Children (AFDC), was an open-ended program. Since reform in 1995, federal aid to states for welfare-type programs, now known as Temporary Assistance to Needy Families (TANF), has become a closed-ended program with specific dollar amounts. Medicaid, which provides funds for the medically indigent, is another open-ended program that has seen rapid growth in costs in the last 20 years. Closed-ended grants have a specific budgeted amount that must be rationed among competing claimants through a grant application process, a formula, or some other distribution mechanism.

EFFICIENCY AND EQUITY EFFECTS OF GRANTS

Grants have both equity and efficiency purposes. Equity is served by collecting from citizens in both rich and poor jurisdictions (with more usually coming from richer citizens or richer jurisdictions) and redistributing a larger share of the funds to jurisdictions with higher concentrations of low-income citizens. For example, the federal government collects more income tax per capita from residents of Washington, Michigan, and New York, which enjoy higher average incomes than other states. Within those states, more of the tax payments come from their wealthier citizens. When the federal government gives grants for school lunches, community development, welfare, or other programs that are targeted at lower income areas, more of those funds are directed on a per capita basis to states such as South Carolina, Arkansas, and Mississippi, which have lower average incomes and more residents below the poverty line. Other equity indicators are factored into this distribution as well, but poverty rates figure strongly in many grants. Note, however, that even if the grants were distributed purely on a per capita basis, there would still be some redistribution, because a larger share of the funds being redistributed was collected from higher income households.

Efficiency purposes of grants are much more complicated to analyze. Sometimes the purpose of grants is pure equalization; that is, the higher level of government wants to ensure that a minimum amount of publicly funded services is available to citizens regardless of the tax wealth of the place where they live. Lump-sum general-purpose grants are nondistorting within the public sector in much the same way that a poll tax is nondistorting. A lump-sum general-purpose grant does not distort decisions by local public officials about how to spend the funds available to them because the amount of revenue they receive is independent of the actions that they take.

As soon as conditions are attached, however—maintenance of effort, management, specification of how the funds must be used—then local decisions are affected. Some of these distortions are intentional, in order to impose the preferences of a higher level of government on a local government that would not spend in the same way without the carrot and stick of conditional grants. Other distortions are not intended. Sometimes the link between condition and grant is tenuous. The federal government has withheld highway funds from states that did not conform to its desires for higher minimum ages for drinking alcohol or mandatory helmet laws for motorcyclists.

The challenge facing the donor government is to ensure that an additional dollar of funds made available to a recipient government results in increased spending on the intended purpose, rather than reduced local tax effort or a shifting of funds to other purposes. The challenge facing the recipient government is to continue to honor its own priorities and preferences in the spending mix and the level of taxation while taking advantage of the availability of additional funds.

From a larger perspective, these grant funds are not "free." If more grant dollars are returning to Chicago or Dallas from their state or federal government, some of those extra dollars came from the citizens of Chicago or Dallas. But from the local perspective, each community and even each state is almost a pure competitor. If these recipient governments provided no additional tax revenue from which the state or federal government could make grants, the loss of their contribution would be too small to make a difference in the size of the pot available. Consequently, at the margin, local and even state governments often separate the desirability of having the grant program at all and its cost to their citizens from any decisions about whether to accept or apply for funds and how to use them.

Indifference Analysis of Grants

Each type of grant presents different challenges of analysis. Three kinds of grants are analyzed here. The first is a simple lump-sum grant with no maintenance of effort and no spending restrictions. The second is a lump-sum grant that must be used for public safety, broadly defined, with a maintenance-of-effort requirement. The third is a matching grant for additional police patrols in local communities. These three types do not exhaust the possibilities, but they represent most of the challenges faced by donor governments in designing grants and by recipient governments in responding to grants.

Note that efficiency is more difficult to define when the parties have different objectives. From the standpoint of the donor government, a grant is more efficient if it directs more resources toward the desired objective. From the standpoint of the recipient government, however, efficiency means having the freedom to allocate resources in the way that will satisfy the desires of the citizens to whom it is accountable. As the analysis that follows bears out, efficiency from the donor standpoint means lots of "strings" attached, while for recipient governments efficiency means as few strings as possible.

The basic technique of analysis is the same for all kinds of grants. Indifference maps represent the preferences of decision makers, who may be elected officials, appointed officials, or voters. The axes represent alternative bundles of goods. Sometimes the choices on the axes are publicly produced goods and private goods, as in Figure 14–3, while at other times one axis will represent a particular publicly produced good (such as public safety) and all other publicly produced goods (and services). The shape of the indifference curve reflects diminishing marginal utility of both bundles of services. A higher indifference curve (one above and to the right of another) represents more of one or both bundles of services and therefore a higher level of satisfaction at any point on that curve compared to any point on a lower curve.

The budget constraint (the straight line in Figure 14-3) represents available budgetary resources and the prices of each of the two bundles. If the axes are publicly versus privately produced goods, the budgetary resources to be allocated are all the community's income (Y_C). If the axes both represent bundles of publicly produced goods, the budget constraint represents the revenue available to the public sector to allocate. The budget constraint shows the various combinations of the two bundles of goods that can be purchased out of that revenue at the given prices of the two bundles. If the entire budget were spent on public goods, with a price of P_A for each unit, then it would be possible to purchase Y_C/P_A units of public goods. Likewise, if the entire budget

Figure 14–3
Indifference Analysis
of Community
Choice

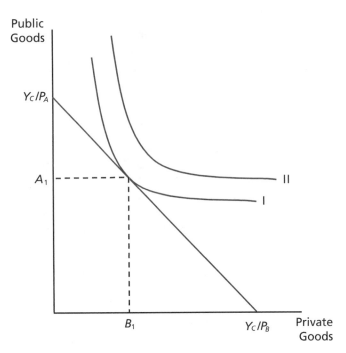

were spent on private goods, with a price of P_B for each unit, then it would be possible to purchase Y_C/P_A units of public goods.

The budget line $(Y_C/P_A - Y_C/P_B)$ is where the effects of the grant are translated into the diagram. An increase in available revenue will shift the budget constraint outward in parallel fashion. A change in the price of one bundle or good but not the other will cause the budget line to rotate. For example, a decrease in the price of a unit of public goods means that more of it can be purchased in combination with any given amount of all private goods. The budget constraint would rotate upward on the vertical axis while going through the same intercept on the horizontal axis, and the community would be able to attain a higher indifference curve.

Lump-Sum Grants

Figure 14–3 represents the choices of a local public sector prior to receiving a lump-sum grant. The price for one unit of a bundle of public goods is P_A and the price for one unit of a bundle of private goods is P_B. Total income in the community is Y_C. If all resources are devoted to public services, the maximum number of units that can be purchased is Y_C/P_A; if all resources are devoted to private services, the maximum number of units that can be purchased is Y_C/P_B. Given the community's (or decision makers') preferences as expressed in the indifference map, this community has chosen to consume A_1

of publicly produced services and B_1 of privately produced goods and services on indifference curve I.

Now the community receives a lump-sum grant to be used for any public purpose, as illustrated in Figure 14–4. The amount of the grant is measured by the vertical distance between the two budget lines, A_3 minus A_1. The community, or its decision makers, responds to this increase in income by choosing a new combination of publicly and privately produced goods and services, A_2 and B_2 on indifference curve II. Citizens have increased their consumption of publicly produced goods and services, but not by the full amount of the grant. Some of the increased revenue has come in the form of a reduction in taxes or other local revenue, leaving consumers more after-tax income to spend on private consumption.

This analysis of the simplest kind of intergovernmental grant has some profound policy implications. One implication is that donor governments may find it difficult to impose preferences on recipient governments. The other implication comes from empirical research on responses to different kinds of funding, known as the flypaper effect, which is discussed in more detail later in this chapter.

Fungibility and Maintenance of Effort

If the intent of the grant illustrated in Figure 14–4 was to increase funds available to the public sector, it was only partially successful. Some of the funds

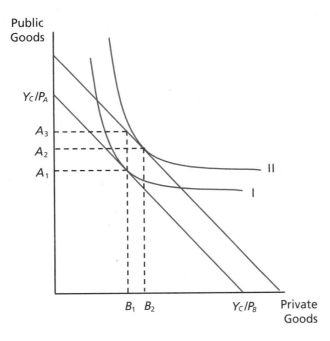

Figure 14–4
Lump Sum Grant

LOTTERIES AND FUNGIBILITY

Nowhere in the public sector has the issue of fungibility come to people's attention as clearly as with state-run lotteries. Lotteries are state-sponsored monopolies that generate revenue for public use. In the 19th century, most states wrote into their constitutions a prohibition on state-sponsored lotteries in response to widespread scandals. When lotteries again became popular in the United States, a referendum was required in order to change that constitutional prohibition. As of 2001, 38 states had state-run lotteries.

To increase the likelihood that the lottery would be approved, state governments adopted a practice of earmarking lottery revenues for some designated public purpose. Education has been the most common purpose, but economic development and senior citizen services are also beneficiaries of lottery revenues in some states. However, some states, including Florida, Illinois, and New York, used part of the additional revenue from the lottery as a substitute for existing education funding rather than increasing the total pool of funds for that purpose. Many citizens felt misled.

Lotteries adopted more recently have addressed that citizen concern by safeguarding lottery funds from the general budget in a number of ways. Georgia is one of several states that segregates lottery funds from general fund revenue and uses the proceeds for some specific programs that receive all of their funds from the lottery. These programs include a college scholarship program for Georgia high school graduates and newly created programs for early childhood education.

While economists generally are critical of earmarking funds for specific uses because it reduces budget flexibility, citizens often feel differently. When they discover that fungibility offers a way

to assert legislators' preferences over voter preferences, it increases their distrust of government because they feel legislators are not responding to their preferences about how additional funds should be spent.

The problem of fungibility is not limited to general-purpose grants. Figure 14–A is exactly the same as Figure 14–4 except that the axes are relabeled "Public Safety" and "All Other Public Goods." Suppose that this community received, instead of a general-purpose grant, a block grant to use for providing public safety services (police and fire protections, jails, emergency medical services, etc.) All of the grant funds are expended on public safety, but some of the locally raised funds are diverted to other uses, such as recreation or libraries or public health. The intent of the donor government to increase the level of public safety spending is met, but not by the full amount of the grant.

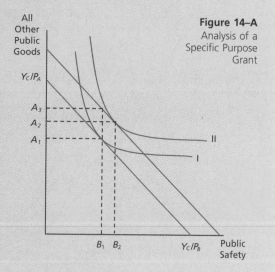

Figure 14–A
Analysis of a Specific Purpose Grant

were diverted into private consumption by substituting intergovernmental funds for locally raised revenues. This is a graphic illustration of the notion of fungibility, or the ability to shift funds between uses in response to changing needs and opportunities. Fungibility is generally regarded by those who spend the money as a good thing, because it gives them more flexibility. But the donor government, or sometimes the citizens (boxed feature), may feel differently about giving them that kind of flexibility.

The most common solution to the fungibility problem for donor governments is to impose a maintenance-of-effort requirement. Such a requirement means that the recipient government cannot reduce its own-source expenditures on the specified service in response to a grant. In Figure 14–5, there is a break in the grant line. If the local government does not continue to maintain its prior spending of B_1 on public safety, the grant will be withdrawn. This constraint forces the local government to choose a different combination of services than it would otherwise have chosen, so that all the grant funds are expended on increased public safety services.

The highest indifference curve that this community can reach with the maintenance of effort requirement is curve II instead of III. Curve II represents an improvement over the no-grant situation, but a lower level of satisfaction with the spending mix compared to what would have been chosen in the absence of a maintenance-of-effort requirement. Of course, this outcome is much more satisfying for the donor government!

Maintenance of effort is conceptually simple but difficult to administer in practice, particularly for continuous funding rather than a one-time grant. With annual funding, the local effort to be maintained has to be adjusted from year to year by some kind of index or formula. Some of the problems associated

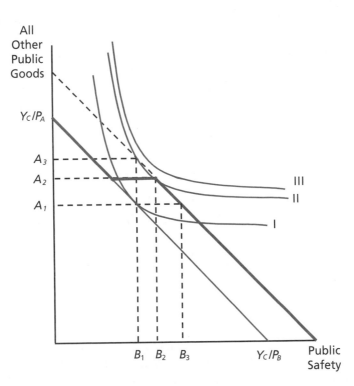

Figure 14–5
A Maintenance-of-Effort Requirement

with implementing a maintenance of effort requirement are discussed in more detail in Chapter 16 on public education.

Flypaper Effect

The second interesting consequence of this analysis of grants is an empirical finding known by the colorful name of the **flypaper effect,** which is shorthand for "money sticks where it lands." If Figure 14–4 represented a tax cut to citizens instead of a lump-sum grant to a local government, the analysis implies that the resulting spending mix would be the same, that is, the same relative increases in spending on public and private goods and services. In other words, a simple application of the theoretical model would predict that public officials will be merely passive translators of the preferences of the median voter expressed in the community indifference map.

In reality, however, the effects are quite different. Even though an increase in private incomes and an intergovernmental lump-sum grant represent the same shift in the budget line and the same increase in total community resources, a grant will increase public spending by about 40% of the amount of the grant, while an increase in private income (including through tax cuts) will only increase public spending by about 10%.[4] Clearly, a larger share of the money seems to stick in the sector where it lands!

A number of explanations have been offered, but the simplest one seems to be that decision makers have their own preferences for how resources shall be used. Those preferences may not exactly coincide with those of the voters. The voting process is an imperfect control mechanism for forcing these public officials to determine and respond precisely to what voters want.

MATCHING GRANTS

Matching grants are designed to encourage specific kinds of spending. Instead of a maintenance-of-effort requirement, matching grants require that additional dollars from the donor government must be matched in some proportion by additional local dollars spent for that particular purpose. The match may be as high as 1:1 but more commonly is an 80–20, 90–10, or 70–30 match, which would mean that an additional $80 (or $90 or $70) dollars of federal or state money requires that the local government also spend an additional $20 (or $10 or $30) on the specified purpose as a condition of receiving the grant. From the standpoint of the recipient government, a match is the equivalent of a steep price cut for one particular service. Whereas a lumpsum grant has only an income effect, a matching grant has both an in-

---

4. James R. Hines and Richard H. Thaler, "Anomalies: The Flypaper Effect," *Journal of Economic Perspectives,* 9 (Fall 1995): pp. 217–226.

come and a substitution effect toward that particular service because it becomes relatively cheaper than other services being provided.

   In the Clinton administration, one of the matching grant programs that
was very popular was for community policing. Figure 14–6 shows community policing (the purpose of the grants) on the horizontal axis and all other
public services on the vertical axis. Before the grant, this community was
spending A_1 on all other public services and B_1 on community policing. Now
the budget line rotates to reflect the fact that the same amount of community
resources will now buy much more community policing because a large share
of the additional cost comes from a federal matching grant. The community
changes its spending mix so that it is now spending A_2 on all other public services and B_2 on community policing.

   How does this compare to the choices they would have made if there were
not a match? If the grant were large enough to get them from indifference curve
I to indifference curve II, but had no match, it would have been a parallel budget line that resulted in a choice of combination A_3, B_3 at point X. This change
from A_1, B_1 is called the *income effect* of the grant. The change in the spending mix along the same indifference curve to A_2, B_2 at point Y—a combination
that represents relatively more spending on community policing—represents
the substitution effect of the grant because of the change in relative prices of
community policing versus other public services. Clearly matching grants are
a powerful tool for imposing donor preferences on recipient governments.

   Grants are the last of the revenue sources available to governments to be
explored. In the remaining chapters, we turn our attention to the expenditure

Figure 14–6
Effects of a
Matching Grant

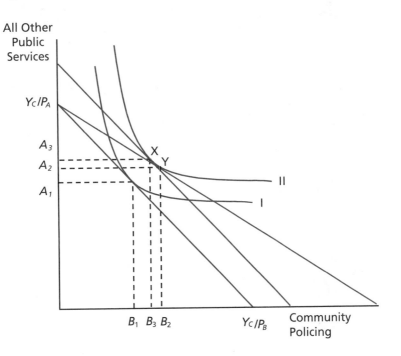

side of the budget, beginning with the budget process itself and then examining some of the major areas of public expenditure.

SUMMARY

Federal grants are an important source of revenue to state and local governments, although less important now than in earlier periods.  State aid to local governments, especially for education, continues to be a major local revenue source in most states. Federal aid has a history of almost two centuries, with major growth occurring in the 1930s and the 1960s followed by some retrenchment in the 1980s and 1990s.

Among the purposes of intergovernmental grants are vertical and horizontal equalization, correcting spatial externalities, redirecting priorities, and experimenting with new ideas and approaches.

Equalizing grants can address either vertical equalization (the ability of governments at different levels to raise revenue commensurate with their expenditure demands) or horizontal equalization (redirecting fiscal resources from wealthier to poorer jurisdictions of the same type, e.g., state to state, county to county).

The existence of spatial externalities can lead to spending less than the optimal amount by a state or local government if a significant part of the benefits spill over to an adjacent jurisdiction. Grants from a higher level of government to encourage the provision of more of such services can correct for this problem.

Grants can also be used to redirect priorities. Although priorities are sometimes redirected by mandates from higher to lower levels of government, a grant can offer an incentive to a state or local government to provide a new service or expand provision of a particular service so as to implement the priorities of the higher level of government without being as coercive as a mandate or regulation. Grants for this purpose are usually quite constrained in the ways that funds can be used.

Grants can be used to try new ideas, approaches, or programs on a limited basis before trying them on a national scale. Other communities or states can learn from these experiments in the laboratories of federalism that grants can encourage.

Grants are just one way of accomplishing the objectives of a higher level of government through partnership with other governments. Sometimes direct expenditures are a good alternative, as with student loans and Medicare to provide health services for the elderly. At other times, the incentives can be offered to individuals instead of other governments through tax expenditures. The best choice of a tool depends on the nature of the objective being sought.

Grants can be classified in many ways. They may be general-purpose grants, with the receiving government free to spend the funds on any public purpose, or categorical grants, which must be spent on a specific use. The revenue may be distributed automatically according to some preset criteria (formula grants, which are about 71% of all federal grants) or only to designated recipients based on competitive applications or legislative discretion. Grants may be given as a lump sum or may require matching contributions by the recipient government. Matching grants change relative prices and generally have a stronger incentive effect toward the target objective than a lump-sum grant for the same purpose.

Finally, a grant may be closed ended (a limited pool of available funds) or open ended (everyone who qualifies or submits an appropriate request is automatically funded). Closed-ended grants provide some budgetary predictability, but at the expense of meeting the needs of all the targeted recipients determined by the grant criteria. If the grant is directed toward a specific purpose, the donor government may have to attach maintenance-of-effort requirements to avoid the substitution of donor funds for local funds with no significant increase in spending on the designated purpose.

Block grants have been used in the last 20 years to reduce the number of categorical grants and provide more flexibility in the use of funds by recipient governments. A block grant is designated toward a broad area of public expenditure, such as community development, but allows recipients broad latitude in adapting the program to local needs and conditions.

Grants have both equity and efficiency effects. Equity effects can be measured by how well grants meet redistributional goals. Efficiency effects are analyzed with the aid of indifference analysis, using indifference curves to represent the preferences of the recipient government or community and budget constraints to represent resources available from both local and grant sources.

A simple lump-sum grant with no maintenance-of-effort requirement and no spending restrictions will increase spending both on public purposes and on private purposes as fungible resources are reallocated in response to an increase in total resources available to the local community. Because such grants usually increase spending on the designated purpose by less than the amount of the grant, donor governments often impose maintenance of effort requirements to ensure that local spending on the target purpose does not decline. Such requirements satisfy the preferences of the donor government but limit the ability of the recipient government/community to maximize the satisfaction obtained out of the total post-grant available resources. The same conclusions apply to a lump-sum grant designated for a specific purpose.

This analysis has been criticized based on empirical research on the impact of grants versus the impact of tax reductions, for which the additional resources accrue directly to citizens rather than to the recipient government's public sector. The flypaper effect finds that "money sticks where it lands"; that is funds that are sent to the local public sector are spent there while funds that are sent to private citizens via tax relief are largely spent for private purposes, with only a limited amount finding its way into increased local public spending.

A matching grant for a particular purpose will change the slope of the budget constraint, because available resources will now support more spending on the target purpose. Such a grant has both income and substitution effects and will have more impact in increasing spending on the target purpose than a lump-sum grant without a maintenance-of-effort requirement.

KEY TERMS AND CONCEPTS

intergovernmental grant, 295
vertical equalization, 298
horizontal equalization, 299
unfunded mandate, 302
general-purpose grant, 303
categorical grant, 303

formula grant, 303
project grant, 303
lump-sum grant, 303
matching grant, 303
closed-ended grant, 303
open-ended grant, 303

fungibility, 304
maintenance of effort, 304
block grant, 304
flypaper effect, 312

DISCUSSION QUESTIONS

1. If you were running the donor government, and wanted to encourage more local spending on immunizations for children, what kind of grant would you devise? Why? How might your answer be different from the perspective of recipient governments?

2. Suppose you are in charge of grants from the state to local governments in order to reduce inequality in the amount of resources that counties have to provide certain basic services such as roads, sheriff's offices, emergency medical services, libraries, and health clinics. Your state has a few large urban areas with some poverty but also a lot of taxable commercial and industrial wealth, prosperous suburban areas, and a lot of rural areas with limited job opportunities and low population density. It is your job to come up with a distribution formula for state aid to counties. What factors might you include in your formula? Why?

3. Residents of Central City are resentful that people from outside the city use their sidewalks, trash pickup, streets, museum, library, and other services but do not pay city taxes. Drawing on Chapters 8 and 13 as well as this chapter, identify at least three ways in which residents of Central City might respond to this concern, including appealing for appropriate action by state government. Which kind of response do you think is most efficient? Most equitable? What problems does each solution involve?

4. Using the same analytical techniques as those developed in this chapter, develop a diagrammatic analysis of a matching grant with a maximum amount available. (*Hint:* When the maximum is reached, the rest of the budget line becomes vertical or horizontal.) How are the effects different from those of a simple matching grant? Does it depend on the size of the maximum? On the shape/position of the indifference map? Are there circumstances in which the ceiling on available funds might have no effect on the mix of services provided?

5. What role might grants play in correcting negative externalities, such as air pollution? Under what circumstances might they be preferred on equity or efficiency grounds to taxes on emissions or regulatory approaches?

GOVERNMENT SPENDING

For much of the history of public sector economics, the focus of attention has been on taxation and revenue. What little attention was given to the expenditure side concentrated on the rationale for public intervention in terms of producing public goods or goods with positive externalities and controlling negative externalities. It is only in the last 30 years that significant attention has been paid to the expenditure side of the equation.

We have already explored some of the broader issues on the expenditure side in Chapters 3 through 6, which examined such expenditure-related questions as the appropriate size of government, the production of public goods and correcting externalities, processes for decision making in the public sector, income inequality, and transfer payments. Part 4 now addresses some of the applied issues in public expenditure, beginning with the budgeting process in Chapter 15.

Any textbook will reflect the experience and preferences of its author in the selection of expenditure categories to use to illustrate the decision-making process within and among budget categories. But that selection will also represent some systematic choices based on specific criteria. Chapters 16 through 19 explore four major kinds of public expenditure in the United States and most other industrial countries: education, infrastructure, Social Security and welfare, and health care. Although these four areas do not exhaust the expenditure activities of governments, they were chosen on the basis of five criteria:

1. Each represents a major component of expenditure.
2. Each involves both federal and state–local roles.

3. Each impacts large numbers of households.
4. Each poses some important policy challenges.
5. Each has been at the forefront of the public policy agenda for the last two decades.

Every one of these four expenditure categories constitutes a significant specialized field in economics that lies beyond the scope of this text. Our interest lies in addressing some basic questions that are central to public finance in each case. Why is this service provided through the public sector rather than the private sector (or in addition to that part supplied by the private sector)? What is the appropriate role of the public sector in providing this service? How is responsibility shared among levels of governments? How is the service financed, and what are the efficiency and equity issues to be addressed in provision and financing? To what extent is it possible to answer the questions raised in Chapter 5 about measuring and valuing output in each of these areas? These are the questions that lie at the heart of public finance as a distinct discipline.

CHAPTER 15

BUDGETING IN THE PUBLIC SECTOR: FORECASTING, COST–BENEFIT ANALYSIS, AND DEBT MANAGEMENT

Every January, the president sends Congress a proposed budget. Congress then parcels it out among various committees, holds hearings, offers amendments, engages in debate, and in good years, actually manages to pass a budget that the president signs in time for the beginning of the new fiscal year on October 1. (Until 1977, the fiscal year began July 1, but Congress found it increasingly difficult to develop a budget in that time frame.) In bad years, Congress passes continuing authorizations and the government manages to continue to function until the budget is finally completed sometime before the Christmas recess. In really bad years, the government shuts down for a few hours or days while Congress and the president try to finalize a budget. It is not a pretty process.

As a general rule, the 50 state governments and the District of Columbia operate on a fiscal year basis that runs from July 1 to June 30, which means that legislatures have to move a little faster than Congress and are generally able to put a budget together before the beginning of the next fiscal year. The thousands of local governments do the same, some on a calendar year, some on a July–June fiscal year, and some on a schedule all their own. Regardless of the level of government, no spending can take place without a budget authorization and an appropriation of funds to cover those expenditures. Once the budget is in place, it is very difficult to initiate any new spending program until the next budget cycle.

BUDGETING PROCESS

A **budget,** whether for a school district, the U.S. government, or a household, is a spending plan that is based on expected revenue and the setting of priorities for the quantity and quality of services to be provided and the transfers to be made. The development of budgets involves three elements:

1. A revenue plan, including a forecast of revenues available from existing sources and any proposed changes to the revenue system;
2. Expenditure forecasts and requests from the various agencies and departments for continuing funding and new projects, which must be evaluated and prioritized in some fashion, including the use of cost–benefit analysis and related techniques; and
3. A procedure for dealing with any gap between revenues and expenditures, how best to use any surplus or how to address any projected deficit.

REVENUE FORECASTING

For a government with a relatively stable tax structure, the first element in developing a budget is to determine how much revenue will be available. The primary sources of revenue for the federal government are income taxes and Social Security taxes. The primary revenue sources for most state governments are income taxes and retail sales taxes. For local governments, the primary revenue source is still the property tax, although local revenue sources are becoming increasingly diversified.

Revenue forecasting is an art, not a science. Revenue forecasting is also very politically sensitive, because revenue forecasters are telling legislators how much money they will have to spend. Forecasters may be pressured into upping the estimates to make pet projects feasible, or estimating conservatively so that legislators can later enjoy the pleasure of allocating the surplus. Politicians who have been burned by having to approve midyear budget cuts when revenue did not meet projections are apt to prefer caution in making forecasts. Revenue forecasters are often public employees who must respond to the political climate as well as their own best judgment and experience in making forecasts.

At the federal level, revenue forecasts are made at least twice a year by both the Congressional Budget Office (CBO) and the Office of Management and Budget (OMB), which is an executive agency. One forecast is released at about the time the budget is sent to Congress in January or February, and the second is released in August as Congress nears the end of the budgeting process. These budgets are revised periodically between the two major forecasts based on changes in economic conditions, proposed policy changes that will affect revenue, and technical adjustments.

By the end of the 20th century, forecasts emerged that predicted growing budget surpluses, based on the expectations of the continued healthy economic conditions of steady growth, full employment, and low inflation that had been experienced for almost a decade. These optimistic forecasts not only affected the approved budgets but also the dialogue about the tax structure, new and expanded expenditure programs, and the future of the Social Security program. Clearly, revenue forecasting plays an important role in making economic policy, even though critics point out that revenue forecasting at the federal level has not been exceptionally accurate.[1]

Economic Forecasts

Any revenue forecast begins with an economic forecast that projects the next few years in terms of income, output, employment, and inflation. The three major sources of federal and state revenue—income taxes, sales taxes, and Social Security taxes—are all closely linked to the performance of the economy. If personal income rises or falls, income tax revenue will rise or fall more than in proportion to the change in personal income, because the federal income tax and the majority of state income taxes are somewhat progressive. If personal income rises or falls, taxable retail sales will also rise or fall in the same direction, although these sales are less volatile than income, so the tax base is more stable. If employment rises or falls, revenue from Social Security taxes will track that change very closely. Many revenue forecasters, particularly at the state level, do not develop their own economic forecasters but instead purchase the services of professional forecasters such as DRI and McGraw-Hill, as well as using forecasts provided by the regional federal reserve banks.

From Economic Forecast to the Tax Base

The next step in revenue forecasting is to link the economic forecast with what is happening to the tax base; that is, how does the forecast for the U.S. economy translate into taxable personal income, taxable corporate income, and payroll subject to Social Security taxes? Or at the state level, how does the forecast for Missouri's or Nebraska's economic growth translate into changes in taxable personal income and taxable retail sales? Each state's answer will be different, because each state defines the base of its major taxes a little differently, as you learned in Chapters 10 and 11.

Table 15–1 shows some recent estimates[2] of the relationship between personal income and the tax bases for income and sales taxes. The property tax base is not as closely tied to economic performance as the other tax bases, but such estimates are less important for forecasting purposes. Because of the

1. Alan J. Auerbach, "Measuring the Impact of Tax Reform," *National Tax Journal*, XLIX(4) (December 1996): pp. 665–674.
2. Russell S. Sobel and Randall G. Holcombe, "Measuring the Growth and Variability of Tax Bases over the Business Cycle," *National Tax Journal*, XLIX(4) (December 1996): pp. 535–552.

Tax Base	Long-Term Elasticity	Short-Term Elasticity
Taxable personal income	1.22	1.16
Taxable corporate income	0.670	3.37
Retail sales	0.660	1.04

time lag between assessment of property and imposition of taxes, local governments generally know the size of the property tax base and can determine expected revenue before preparing their budgets.

In the short term the retail sales tax base grows slightly faster than personal income, but over the longer term, it lags substantially. Retail sales are very sensitive to short-term fluctuations in economic activity. People cut down on big-ticket items whenever they become concerned about their immediate financial future, and respond to good economic times by splurging on cars, boats, appliances, electronics, and home furnishings. But in the long term, the base of the retail sales tax lags behind the growth of personal income, because much of the growth in income goes into the purchase of services (including housing services) not subject to retail sales tax.

Because corporate net income is roughly the same as corporate profits, which are very volatile in the short run, corporate income is also extremely sensitive to short-run fluctuations. Like the retail sales tax base, the corporate income tax tends to lag behind overall growth over the longer term. The best performer is the individual income tax; with personal exemptions and standard deductions changing slowly, any change in personal income in the short or long run will result in a larger change in taxable personal income than in gross income.

From Tax Base to Revenue

The final step in forecasting revenue is to convert expected changes in the tax base into expected changes in revenue. This last step can be carried out in any of several ways. Some forecasters use a moving average of the relationship between tax base and tax revenue over earlier years to make a simple linear projection, after taking into account any changes in the tax structure. Often a board of advisers is involved in fine-tuning revenue projections to take into account other information or influences. Many forecasters use econometric forecasting techniques that develop a statistical relationship between base changes and changes in revenue yield.

Tax Expenditures

An important downward adjustment to the revenue forecast must be made for any changes in tax expenditures. Tax expenditures, described in Chapter 9, consist largely of revenue foregone in order to encourage or promote certain kinds of expenditures in the private sector. The purpose of the tax expenditure may be soup kitchens, land preservation, preventive health care, or enrolling in college. Once these programs are in place and have some history, they can be incorporated into the revenue forecasting techniques described above. But the effects of relatively new programs may be hard to predict, because it is difficult to anticipate how many taxpayers will respond to the incentive and how much they will spend. Most tax expenditures are open ended, like some grant programs. Reductions in your tax bill because you put money into an individual retirement account, sent your child to college, or made your house more energy efficient are all opportunities open to whoever chooses to respond, and the revenue drain from some of these programs can be substantial.

OFF-BUDGET AND ON-BUDGET FUNDS

How big is the government budget? It depends on what you count. The figures reported for the federal, state, and local governments rarely include all the funds that pass through those governments or all the expenditures they make. Rather, there is an operating or general fund budget that covers regular operations and a variety of **off-budget accounts** that do not pass through the legislative budget process on an annual basis.

Social Security, Medicare, and the Combined Budget

At the federal level, the most important off-budget accounts are those of the Social Security and Medicare Trust Funds, which operate independently. Although Congress can change the rules under which these trust funds operate (i.e., changing tax rates and benefit structures), the budgets of these trust funds are not part of the legislative package that must be passed by October 1 each year. Many government enterprises that provide services for payment, such as the Postal Service, are also operated outside of the regular budget, but the largest off-budget sums of money are those that pass through the Social Security and Medicare Trust Funds.

To further confuse the reader of government statistics, the budget deficit or surplus is usually reported as the sum of the on-budget and off-budget accounts, so that a deficit in the regular budget may be offset by a surplus in the off-budget accounts. For example, the 1999 federal budget called for a combined surplus of $124 billion, but only $724 million of that was in the operating budget, while the off-budget accounts had a surplus of more than $123 billion. The surplus in the trust funds has been invested in the bonds that fund the operating deficit, resulting in the appearance of a smaller budget deficit or larger surplus than would actually be the case if the trust funds were truly independent. Figure 15–1 and Table 15–2 show the relationship between the on-budget and off-budget outlays for the federal government from 1960 to 2000.

Figure 15–1
Off-Budget Federal
Outlays as Percent
of Total, 1960–2000

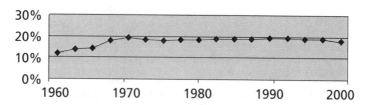

Table 15-2
On-Budget and
Off-Budget
Expenditures,
Federal
Government,
1960–2000

Year	On-Budget Dollars (in billions)	Off-Budget Dollars (in billions)
1960	81.3	10.9
1965	101.7	16.5
1970	168.0	27.6
1975	271.9	60.4
1980	476.6	114.3
1985	769.6	176.8
1990	1028.1	225.1
1991	1082.7	241.7
1992	1129.3	252.3
1993	1142.9	266.6
1994	1182.5	279.4
1995	1227.2	288.7
1996	1259.7	300.9
1997	1290.7	310.5
1998	1336.0	316.5
1999	1382.3	320.8
2000	1457.3	330.8

State and Local Special Funds

State and local governments also have a number of off-budget accounts. Unlike the federal government, they generally have a separate capital account in which purchases of capital assets are funded by a combination of current appropriations and issuance of bonds. Another large group of special funds is the retirement funds for state and local employees, which are managed separately from the operating budget. Retirement funds receive contributions from workers and from the state or local government as employers, make investments, earn income from investments, and disburse pension payments to retired workers. These retirement funds are quite large; state pension funds, in particular, are major institutional investors in the stock and bond markets.

Finally, state and local governments, like the federal government, have enterprise funds for those services that are not primarily tax financed. These enterprise funds include water and sewer funds, locally operated electric and gas utilities, public transit services, and at the state level, higher education

DOES THE UNITED STATES NEED A CAPITAL BUDGET?

State and local governments usually budget separately for operating expenditures and for capital projects. So do most national governments in other countries. The separation of budgets into these two components is considered a good accounting practice. It is also good economics. Just as economists distinguish between stocks and flows, assets and income, debt and debt service, so do both accountants and economists distinguish between the year-to-year recurrent expenditures for providing services and the intermittent acquisition of public capital assets.

The operating budget will probably include appropriations for debt service incurred to acquire assets such as buildings, dams, highways, airports, and land, although some assets are acquired through separate accounts by the issuance of revenue bonds (see below). But those assets are usually paid for over their long useful lifetimes just as households (and business firms) acquire homes, cars, factories, and office buildings by paying for them over their useful lifetime rather than up front and all at once. There may be an initial appropriation of some part of the cost, but borrowing is considered the norm for the bulk of asset acquisition in the public sector as in the private sector.

In the case of public assets, this method of payment has the additional advantage of spreading the cost among all of the taxpayers who benefit from the asset, a group of people that changes from year to year. Having a capital budget and financing assets at least partly by borrowing means that you, as a mobile worker, will not have to pay up front for the full cost of a recreational facility with a 30-year lifetime for a community that you may only live in for 3 or 4 years. Some of the cost will be shifted to the next person to move into town, use the facilities, and pay taxes or fees for debt service.

Although U.S. expenditures are reported in the GDP statistics as government investment or government consumption, the budget that is approved by Congress does not distinguish between ordinary operating expenses, debt service, and ac-

quisition of capital assets. A federal prison or office building is treated as a line-item expenditure just like the payroll for the White House staff or the upkeep of a courthouse or payments for veterans' medical expenses. When debt is incurred, it is simply to provide enough resources to fund the budget and is not tied to any particular capital expense.

Why does the U.S. government not have a similar division into operating and capital budgets? There doesn't seem to be any good answer to that question. Relative to a budget of close to $2 trillion, annual capital expenditures are probably moderate enough to be treated as an operating expense. That is, large capital expenditures will be made every year, and the budgetary impact is going to be about the same whether they are "expensed" (treated as operating rather than capital expenses) or segregated into a capital account and funded through a combination of borrowing and current appropriations. Lumpiness of capital expenditures relative to the total budget—years with large capital outlays and years with relatively few big asset acquisitions—is much more likely to happen at the state and local level. In addition, the pool of taxpayers supporting the capital expenditures is much more stable at the national level than at the state or local level. Finally, most state and local governments are required to balance their budgets, but the budget that has to be balanced is the operating budget, which includes annual debt service but does not include capital projects funded by new borrowing. Having a capital budget gives state and local governments more budgetary flexibility than they would have with a combined budget. Because the federal government does not have to balance its budget, this reason for a capital budget is not an issue.

The drawback of not having a capital budget at the national level is that there is not much careful thought given to how much federal borrowing is appropriate. Federal borrowing in the past has been justified on the basis of macroeconomic

(continues)

DOES THE UNITED STATES NEED A CAPITAL BUDGET? (CONTINUED)

policy, but much of the borrowing from the early 1980s to the late 1990s took place under conditions of relatively full employment when deficits were not needed to stimulate economic activity and federal borrowing drove up the interest rates that private borrowers had to pay. During periods of relative economic prosperity, a balanced or surplus budget is the appropriate macroeconomic policy. Separate capital budgeting would make it clearer when borrowing was being done for capital purposes or for purposes of stimulatory fiscal policy. Without either of these justifications for budget deficits, Congress would have to work harder to balance the operating budget and set clear spending priorities.

institutions. Although state-supported colleges receive annual budget appropriations, they also depend heavily on tuition and contributions and have independent budgets approved by their boards. The only part of their budgets that appears in the state budget are the appropriations, which have varying amounts of detail that direct spending to specific uses.

Government enterprises have been far more numerous in developing nations in the last half century. Many of them were manufacturing firms or services that are normally found in the private sector producing for profit. As part of its program of structural adjustment in the 1980s and 1990s, the World Bank encouraged nations to privatize many public enterprises so that governments can focus on their core businesses such as education, infrastructure, defense, and health care.

BUDGETING EXPENDITURES

The expenditure side of the budget has to address both ongoing programs and proposed new programs. Some kinds of expenditures are forecast in ways similar to revenue forecasting, while others are budgeted and limited to the budgeted amount. Unexpended budget funds in the operating budget normally expire at the end of the fiscal year, giving agencies an incentive to "spend it or lose it" toward the end of the fiscal year. If an agency fails to spend most of its budget, not only does it lose the unexpended funds, but there is also a good chance that next year's budget will be reduced. As a result, federal agencies often engage in spending frenzies in August and September (May and June in state agencies) in order to use up their budgeted funds and protect their budgets for future years.

Expenditure Forecasting

Some expenditures are predetermined because they result from programs that are set by previous congressional or legislative action. These programs

HOW THE FEDERAL BUDGET PROCESS CAME TO BE

In the early days of the United States, the creation of a federal budget was considered a legislative responsibility, with some support and assistance from the Department of the Treasury in compiling expenditure requests from the various agencies. Once the nation recovered from the costs of the Revolutionary War, revenue from customs (tariffs) and land sales was generally more than sufficient to meet expenditure needs, a pattern that lasted for most of the time up to the Civil War. The House Ways and Means Committee exerted great power over both revenue and expenditures until 1865 when a separate House Appropriations Committee was created to deal with the expenditure side of the budget. By the early 1900s, reforms in local government management and a shortfall of federal revenue led policy analysts to turn their attention to reforming the federal budget process. Enactment of the income tax addressed the immediate revenue need, but a report from the Taft administration called for a unified executive budget to be presented to Congress. President Taft failed to get his reforms during his tenure, but they were later reflected in the Budgeting and Accounting Act of 1921, which created the Bureau of the Budget. Agencies requesting funds now presented them to Congress through the Bureau of the Budget rather than directly. The Bureau of the Budget has since evolved into the Office of Management and Budget, an agency of the executive branch.

The period after World War II saw a number of innovations in federal budgeting, many of them short lived. Progress was made toward program and performance budgeting in the 1940s, later to be succeeded by the planning–programming–budgeting system (PPBS) in the 1960s as a comprehensive and policy-based approach to developing a budget. This approach is highly rational but very complex to implement. Although it is still used in the Department of Defense, in other parts of government PPBS was succeeded in the 1970s by another of the waves of budgetary techniques coming from the business community, management by objectives, which was short lived.

President Carter (1977–1981) attempted to introduce the notion of zero-based budgeting (ZBB), which like PPBS is policy based and thorough in its approach to expenditure development and management, but complex to implement and administer. This idea, too, did not survive the term of the president who proposed it.

During the 1970s, congressional frustration over the shifting balance of budget-making power to the executive branch led to the creation of the Congressional Budget Office (CBO), which provides Congress with its own research arm for forecasting and evaluation of revenue and expenditure proposals. This entity is not an alternative budget-maker but rather a nonpartisan source of expert research and analysis. Its forecasts are often more accurate than those of OMB, and its work is widely respected within and outside government.

By 1974, most of the methods and agencies involved in developing the budget were in place. Among the more recent reforms were the Chief Finance Officers Act of 1990 and the Government Performance and Results Act of 1993. The former act required each federal agency to have a chief financial officer (CFO), now standard in most large corporate and nonprofit agencies, and an audited financial statement. The 1993 act requires agencies to submit performance plans and reports to Congress, a partial move toward performance budgeting.

Today the process starts with the budget developed by the president's Office of Management and Budget, which is transmitted to Congress to be parceled out among the relevant committees, analyzed by the CBO, and ultimately shaped by the House Ways and Means Committee and the House Appropriations Committee before being sent to the Senate for its revisions, then to a conference committee, and finally back to the president. In good years, this process ends before October 1—just in time to authorize spending for the new fiscal year.

Source: This brief summary is adapted from Thomas D. Lynch, *Public Budgeting in America, 4th ed.* (Upper Saddle River, NJ: Prentice-Hall, 1995), pp. 35–45.

automatically include every household, firm, or other entity that meets certain criteria. Food stamps, Medicare, Medicaid, Social Security, and other entitlement programs fall into this category. So do prisons, public education, and health clinics, where the number of participants is tied to the crime and enforcement rate, the growth and age distribution of the population, and the number choosing or needing to use public health clinics. Strictly speaking, these outlays are forecast rather than budgeted, because additional expenditures will normally be made even if the amount that must be spent on all those who qualify exceeds the budgeted amount. (There may be ways to economize at the margin with crowded prison cells, crowded classrooms, or long lines at health clinics that deter people from coming, but there is still some additional spending that must be made to accommodate these clients of the system.) Because state and local governments are constrained to balance their operating budgets, they tend to be much more cautious about creating entitlements than the federal government, but they also supply a larger share of the population-driven specific services which affects their budgets in much the same way. Entitlement programs and population-driven services are a major reason for the continuous adjustments in the federal budget surplus or deficit forecast—and it still turns out to be a surprise at the end of the fiscal year!

Expenditure forecasting, like revenue forecasting, lends itself to the development of econometric models and other statistical forecasting techniques. Among the major variables in most forecasting models are expected inflation rates (using some specialized indicator such as the GDP deflator for the federal or state and local government component of GDP) and expected population growth, both in general and in specific age categories. For public schools, the relevant age category is ages 5–18; for prisons, about 18–30 (the prime crime ages); for Medicare, over 65 and especially over 85. Particular categories of expenditures may have other forecasting elements as well, such as heating and cooling costs, construction costs, or even hurricane forecasts for coastal states.

Changes in Planned Spending

A simple projection of present spending into the future to accommodate inflation and population growth does not require a legislative body, only some good accountants and a few economists. The policy part of the budgeting process has two important components. One component is reexamining existing spending patterns and making decisions about reallocating resources or accommodating new needs. Among the techniques for doing that are program budgeting, performance budgeting, and zero-based budgeting. The second component is evaluating new programs and projects using an applied form of marginal analysis called cost–benefit analysis. These policy components of budgeting are discussed next.

PROGRAM, PERFORMANCE, AND ZERO-BASED BUDGETING

Prior to the 1950s, many public budgets were **line-item budgets.** A line-item budget sorts spending into categories of the kinds of goods and services that were purchased. Salaries and wages, utilities, office supplies, recreational equipment, and auto repair services to public vehicles all have line-item entries. Line-item budgets are sorted into the governmental units that are responsible for providing the service. At the local level, for example, there might be a recreation department line-item budget, a garbage collection and disposal line-item budget, and a financial administration line-item budget. Line-item budgets are convenient for accounting purposes, but they only measure inputs. What citizens and public officials need for evaluation purposes is not just a measure of inputs but also intermediate and final outputs. Program and performance budgeting were developed for that purpose.

A **program budget** defines a group of related governmental activities and specifies the funds to be allocated to those activities. For a recreation department, these activities might include a youth sports program, summer camp, outdoor concerts, and water-safety programs. Each of these activities would have its own budget in addition to an overall administrative budget that covers general management and maintenance of facilities and equipment for these individual programs. A program budget makes more sense to an economist because the value of the program can be compared to the cost in making decisions about continuing, expanding, or reducing the budget for the program in future years. Program budgets may also give managers more flexibility about the allocation of funds within the program than a line-item budget.

Performance budgeting goes a step further and attempts to define outcomes, such as the number of children participating in a recreation program or the number of meals served at a senior center. These outcomes are then linked to the budget allocation to attempt to achieve those objectives. Performance budgeting is more difficult and more complex and therefore not used as often as program budgeting.

Zero-based budgeting was an idea that was popular during the Carter administration in the 1970s. The normal practice is incremental budgeting, which starts with the previous year's budget for each agency or program and makes a decision about what to increase and what to leave the same. In zero-based budgeting, each agency or program prepares several "decision packages" with different levels of services and spending, which are then collected and prioritized by those who prepare the budget. Because of the enormous amount of documentation required, zero-based budgeting has not been used very much in the public sector.

BUDGETING AND PUBLIC CHOICE

In Chapter 5 we explored some of the demand side implications of public choice theory, which examines decision making in the public sector under the assumption that not only voters but also elected officials and public administrators engage in self-interested, maximizing behavior. That model of behavior also has some implications for the supply responses of the public sector that are reflected in budget making. The best known models of agency budget making are those of William Niskanen, first developed in his 1971 book, *Bureaucracy and Representative Government.*[3]

Niskanen and others point to the difficulty of evaluating performance and the multiplicity of objectives for public agencies that gives their administrators considerable discretion in making trade-offs within their budgets and in persuading elected officials of the need for additional funding. They also point to incentive structures in the public sector that make it unlikely that the interests and preferences of citizens and voters will be clearly aligned with the interests of those who are assigned the task of addressing those interests and preferences. Those desires are transmitted through the voting process to elected officials (executive and legislative) who, in turn, must translate them to appointed officials, including agency heads. The principal-agent problem in the private sector, wherein stockholders direct boards and boards are supposed to oversee management as the agent of the owners, has an even less effective counterpart in the public sector in ensuring that the ultimate "owners" (citizens) are well served by their agents.

Niskanen's model of the bureaucrat, or agency director, was one of a self-interested maximizer whose goals include salary, power, and reputation, all of which are enhanced by increasing the size of the agency. Competition in the public sector takes place between bureaucrats trying to get more funds for their respective agencies. Bureaucrats are aided in their budget-maximizing task by the fact that they have superior access to information about costs and alternatives compared to either legislators or citizens. As a result, there is constant upward pressure on public expenditures that is driven, not by voters' demand for more or better public services, but by the desire of bureaucrats to increase their own well-being and the ability to use their greater information to persuade legislators to grant the desired budgetary increases.

Public choice theorists have suggested several possible policy responses to the challenge of this kind of bureaucracy-driven budgetary growth. Forcing government agencies to compete with suppliers in the private market has been one response, particularly at the state and local level, where public fire protection, solid waste collection, and even schools have had to demonstrate the quality of services and level of costs in competition with private providers.

3. William Niskanen, *Bureaucracy and Representative Government* (Chicago: Aldine, 1971).

Constraints on the rate of growth of government (the tax and expenditure limitations discussed in Chapter 3) are another form of response, which forces bureaucrats to compete with one another for a slow-growing pot of resources rather than to attempt to increase total resources in the form of a rapidly growing budget.

COST–BENEFIT ANALYSIS

Cost–benefit analysis is a technique for evaluating proposed programs or projects to determine whether the anticipated benefits exceed the anticipated costs over the lifetime of the program or project. Both costs and benefits should include both monetary and nonmonetary costs (e.g., increases or decreases in travel time as a result of a road project). A project may be evaluated in isolation or in comparison to other, competing projects to set priorities for the programs that offer the greatest benefits relative to the costs. Cost–benefit analysis is a complex subject that we cannot do justice to in the space of a few pages, but it is helpful to have a general idea of how the process works.

The Decision Rule

Recall from your microeconomics class how individuals and firms make decisions about allocating scarce resources among competing uses. For any given outlay, the decision maker compares the marginal revenue, marginal utility, or marginal benefit (MB) to the price, or marginal cost (MC). Marginal benefit and marginal utility are closely related, but the preferred measure of the value or satisfaction to the user in cost–benefit analysis is marginal benefit. As long as the increase in benefit is greater than the price or cost, the expenditure will increase total profit for the firm, utility for the individual, or benefit for the organization. So the first form of the decision rule is to purchase a particular good or service up to the point where

$$MB = MC .$$

This decision rule is fine for smaller decisions or decisions where resources are plentiful. Most of the time, however, the decision must be made among competing alternatives, because available resources are limited. Consider a household with a budget constraint B, trying to decide how much to purchase of goods X, Y, and Z, with prices of P_x, P_y, and P_z, respectively. If budget B is sufficiently large so that this household can purchase quantities of X, Y, and Z each up to the point where marginal utility (MU) equals price, then there is no problem. But what if the budget is inadequate to get to that point? Then at least for some of these goods, the household will have to buy less than the optimal amount. If marginal benefit (utility) diminishes with more purchases while price is constant (or in some cases, marginal cost is increasing), buying less than the optimal amount means that

$$MB > P \quad \text{or} \quad MB > MC$$

for at least some goods. For simplicity, we will treat price and marginal cost as the same in order to address the question of how the household allocates its resources so as to maximize its utility under a budget constraint.

The rule that you should recall is that, in order to maximize utility (or profit, or benefit), resources should be allocated among competing uses so that MU/P or MB/P is the same for X, Y, and Z; that is,

$$MB_x/P_x = MB_y/P_y = MB_z/P_z \; ,$$

where the budget constraint, B, is equal to the total spent:

$$B = X \times P_x + Y \times P_y + Z \times P_z \; .$$

The easiest way to demonstrate that this rule maximizes benefit or utility is to consider what would happen if

$$MB_x/P_x > MB_y/P_y \; .$$

If the next dollar spent on X yields more benefit or utility than the last dollar spent on Y, then total benefit could be increased by reducing spending on Y by one dollar and using that dollar to purchase more X instead. Only when the marginal benefit per dollar spent is equal across all three goods is total benefit maximized within the budget constraint.

This simplified budget model is the foundation for the technique of decision making known as cost–benefit analysis. Some projects are evaluated simply to determine whether or not the benefits exceed the costs (is MB greater than or equal to MC?). More often, proposed projects are evaluated comparatively in terms of the excess of benefits over costs or the ratio of benefits to costs or costs to benefits.

Kinds of Cost–Benefit Analyis

There are two important subgroups of comparative cost–benefit analyses. One kind of analysis begins with a predetermined objective, such as a new elementary school, and evaluates the relative costs and benefits of various locations, sizes, and types of construction. Or the objective may be a certain level of public transportation, where the comparative analyses look at bus systems, subways, and other alternatives to find the least-cost method of achieving a particular objective.

The other kind of comparative cost–benefit analysis examines different kinds of projects as a way to set priorities for spending. For example, a local government may have limited borrowing and debt service capacity for capital projects. Perhaps the most it can borrow for the next five years is $10 million. The policy analysts would be assigned to evaluate a number of proposed projects, such as a new library, another fire truck, additional neighborhood parks, and a recycling facility and solid waste transfer station. Because the total cost of these projects is likely to exceed $10 million, a cost–benefit analysis would be helpful in ranking these projects from lowest to highest (cost–benefit) or highest to lowest (benefit–cost) to determine which ones will be funded.

Present Value and Cost–Benefit Analysis

In either case, both the costs and the benefits of a project or program that has a multiyear lifetime must be expressed in terms of present value in order to compare costs to benefits or in order to develop benefit–cost ratios to compare among alternative solutions to a single problem or alternative projects competing for funding. Recall from Chapter 7 the present value formula. If a future value FV is the present value PV plus the interest earned on PV at rate r for i years,

$$PV \times (1 + r)^i = FV \ ,$$

then this equation can be rewritten to express present value in terms of future value:

$$PV = FV/(1 + r)^i \ .$$

If the future value is a series of benefits or costs rather than a single future amount, then the present value of that stream of payments can be written as

$$PV = \Sigma FV_i/(1 + r)^i \text{ for a period of } i \text{ years} \ .$$

This computation is made for both future costs and future benefits, so that there are two present values, one for costs, and one for benefits:

$$PVB = \Sigma FB_i/(1 + r)^i \text{ for a period of } i \text{ years} \ ,$$

$$PVC = \Sigma FC_i/(1 + r)^i \text{ for a period of } i \text{ years} \ .$$

The difference between PVB and PVC is the net present benefits of the project, which can be positive or negative. The ratio PVC/PVB is called the **cost–benefit ratio**. Projects with lower cost–benefit ratios (or higher benefit–cost ratios) are usually given greater priority than those with higher cost–benefit ratios, and projects with a cost–benefit ratio greater than one would not be considered, because their benefits would be less than their costs.

For example, suppose you were performing a cost–benefit analysis for getting a college education. You would compute the present value of the four-

or five-year expenditure you were making, including tuition and books and the opportunity cost of your time but not the cost of food and housing (because you would have to have food and housing even if you didn't go to college), and discount those costs to the present. To make it simple, suppose your cost comes to $15,000 a year for four years and you use a discount rate of 6%. If your first payment is a year away, then the present value of your costs would be

$$\$15,000/1.06 + \$15,000/(1.06)^2 + \$15,000/(1.06)^3 + \$15,000/(1.06)^4 = \$57,960 .$$

What about the benefits? Suppose that you expect your future earnings to increase by $12,000 a year after college for the rest of your life. There is a simple formula for such long periods, which is FV/r, or $200,000, from which we must subtract present value of that extra income for the first five years ($55,335) when you are earning nothing. So the present value of the increased future income stream is $200,000–$55,335, or $144, 665. The present value of the benefits exceeds the present value of the costs by $86,705. The cost–benefit ratio is only about 0.4 ($57,960/$144,665).

Technical Issues

This simple example should have alerted you to the fact that cost–benefit analysis is complicated by a number of technical issues that must be addressed. Surely, you think, there is more to college than dollars. There is football, and friendships, and postponing adult responsibility. There is culture and recreation and time to experiment. There may be missing the family or the annoyance of commuting. Where do these considerations figure in? And why 6%? Where did that number come from? Nonmonetary costs and benefits and the discount rate are the major additional issues for individuals. For public projects, additional factors must be considered.

The important issues in carrying out a public sector cost–benefit analysis are as follows:

1. Counting and assigning values to all the costs and benefits, both monetary and nonmonetary,
2. Choosing an appropriate rate of discount for costs and benefits that occur in the future, and
3. Taking distributional and political considerations into account.

Counting All Costs and Benefits

The easiest costs to count are the explicit costs of construction and annual operation and maintenance for a capital project, or the outlays each year for the life of a program for a new service. The cost calculations may extend for the entire life of the facility or program, or just for some predetermined number of years, after which the facility or program will be reevaluated for continuation. Future costs must, of course, be discounted to determine the present value of those costs.

More difficult to incorporate in the cost–benefit analysis are the nonmonetary costs of a project. Some of these costs may be easy to overlook. The political process can be useful in ferreting out some of these perceived costs through public hearings where neighbors complain about noise and traffic and other drawbacks of having a public facility built in their backyard, or when users of the facilities complain that they are too far away. Many of these costs can be converted to dollar values and incorporated into the cost–benefit analysis.

Shadow Prices

Economists and others have been creative in developing methods by which many of these types of costs can be estimated as **shadow prices.** Shadow prices are estimates of the value of an output or an input to the economy measured by the marginal willingness to pay (for output) or the marginal opportunity cost (for input), that is, the value of the next best alternative sacrificed. The shadow price may be different from the market price because of externalities, because of monopoly distortions, or because the production uses resources for which no charge is made.

Three important techniques that are commonly used in cost–benefit analysis to develop shadow prices are property valuation, value of human life calculations, and estimates of the value of travel time. These three examples do not exhaust the possibilities, but they do represent some significant elements of costs that might otherwise fail to be counted.

Locating an elementary school, a landfill, or a recreational facility near residential property affects property values in ways that can be measured. In an area with frequent turnover in real estate, changes in selling prices will reflect increases or decreases in the value of adjacent property according to whether the new facility increased property values (as a school might do) or decreased property values (as a landfill is likely to do). Unlike many of the annual costs in a cost–benefit calculation, any changes in present property values reflect the owner's and prospective buyer's valuation of how the facility will change the total future costs and benefits of living nearby; that is, they are capitalized in the price of the property. Thus, changes in property values are already discounted and can just be added to the present value of benefits (if positive) or costs (if negative).

The value of human life is often a factor in decisions about allocating public resources. How many lives would be saved or lost if this road were or were not built, if this vaccine was not tested and made available? How many people might suffer illness or death in the absence of a water-testing program? (Remember, cost–benefit analyses can also be used to terminate programs!) Economists have developed some ingenious techniques to determine the value people place on reducing the risks to their own lives in their daily actions, especially in choosing safer or riskier occupations. Most riskier occupations carry a wage premium, and that wage premium offers at least some indication of the value the worker places on his or her life in terms of the risks assumed. An annualized value of the "price" of risk can then be incorporated numerically into a cost–benefit calculation of any project that increases or reduces risk to human life in a measurable way.

Travel expense is another way to infer a measurement of either costs of benefits. This approach was originally developed as a way of valuing recreation benefits by the travel cost people were willing to incur (including the value of time) in order to reach a recreational site. Time is usually valued at the prevailing wage, sometimes at the minimum wage. Travel expense not only offers an indirect measure of benefits but is also an important factor on the cost side in siting decisions. It may, for example, be cheaper to build a new school farther out, but the value of the travel time for students (as well as the busing costs!) must be taken into account. Students presumably place a positive value on their time and have a measurable preference for less travel time over more travel time.

These techniques do not exhaust the highly complex subject of incorporating all the costs and benefits into the calculation, but they offer some suggestions of the more common challenges and some of the techniques used to address them.

Choosing a Discount Rate

There is nothing magical about 6%. The discount rate is a measure of the difference between how an asset or a benefit is valued at the present moment compared to the same asset or benefit a year hence. How much money would you accept now in preference to $1,000 a year from now? How much money would you be willing to postpone spending in order to have $1,000 a year from now? If your answers were $926 to both questions, your personal rate of discount is 8%. Different people have different time preferences just as they have different preferences in other kinds of consumption activities. The rate of discount reflects the sum of all of these preferences expressed in markets where borrowing and lending take place, adjusted for differences in risk between different borrowers. That rate changes from year to year and even month to month. Most cost–benefit analyses use some generally accepted rate of interest such as the yield on 10-year corporate AAA bonds, which are relatively risk free.

The choice of a discount rate will have an important impact on the calculation of costs and benefits. If the costs come early and the benefits are delayed, a lower discount rate will make such a project look a little better relative to another project where total benefits are smaller relative to costs, but the costs and benefits are spread more evenly. If the benefits come soon and the costs come later, a high rate of discount will shrink the deferred costs and make that kind of project look more attractive.

Uncertainty

The numbers that go into the cost–benefit analysis may be contingent on both sides of the equation. Costs can be higher if the project runs into technical difficulties. Benefits may be less if fewer people use a new park or recreational facility than projected. For this reason, cost–benefit analysts often develop a range of estimates rather than a single point estimate.

Distributional and Political Considerations

No matter how carefully and "objectively" a cost–benefit analysis is developed, at some point other considerations almost always come into play. Benefits to higher income people may be weighted differently from those to lower income people, or between single persons and married people, families with and without children, people in states with a lot of political clout and people in states with little influence. Income distributional effects are a legitimate economic and political concern, but one that is difficult to incorporate statistically into a cost–benefit analysis. Pork-barrel projects that make influential politicians look good before reelection time are likely to outweigh the most impressive analysis of costs and benefits. Quick benefits and delayed payoffs may be important for the election cycle even if they force analysts to use inappropriately high rates of discount in order to make certain projects look better. Like any other technique of analysis, cost–benefit analysis is only a tool. The ultimate decisions are in the hands of voters, bureaucrats, and elected officials.

BALANCED BUDGETS, DEFICITS, AND DEBT

The issue of balanced budgets, deficits, and debt is usually addressed in courses in macroeconomics. For the most part, courses in public sector economics leave macroeconomic issues to be addressed elsewhere. But the issue of budget balance and borrowing does have some important implications for the budget process and the choice of what expenditures to fund and whether to make changes in the tax system. It is in that budgeting context that this section gives at least cursory attention to borrowing at the state and local as well as the national level.

State and Local Borrowing

Most state and local governments have to balance their operating budgets. They are able to borrow for capital expenditures, and often borrow to cover temporary shortfalls when expenditures have to be made before some of the revenue is collected. This latter problem is particularly true for local governments that depend on the property tax, because much of that revenue comes in all at once, while expenditures come throughout the year.

When state and local governments borrow for capital projects, they issue debt in a variety of forms, but the two most common forms are **general obligation bonds** and **revenue bonds.** (All this borrowing is lumped together in general discussions of financial markets under the single header of **municipal bonds,** which refers to any debt of states or their political subdivisions, the interest on which is exempt from federal income tax.) General obligation bonds are backed by the general taxing power of the issuing government, and meeting the payment on interest and principal is a priority obligation for that government. These bonds are valued by securities dealers based on the fiscal health and past performance of the issuing government, with lower interest rates on higher rated bonds. Revenue bonds are issued for many capital projects that will generate some kinds of fees or other income, such as dormitories, public transit systems, parking garages, and recreational facilities. These bonds are not backed by the full faith and credit of the issuing government, but the revenue from the project is earmarked for payment of interest and principal on the bonds.

Municipal bonds pay lower than average interest rates (compared to federal government and corporate bonds of similar ratings) because of the federal income tax exemption of the interest income. These bonds are particularly attractive to higher income bondholders, because the higher one's marginal tax rate, the greater the after-tax return is on a given municipal bond. The investor has to calculate the **taxable equivalent yield** (TEY) in order to determine whether or not the bond is a good buy:

$$TEY = r_n / (1 - t) \ ,$$

Where r_n is the yield on a municipal bond and t is the marginal tax rate for the bondholder. For example, if r_n is 5% and the bondholder is in the 36% tax bracket, the taxable equivalent yield would be $(5\%) / (1 - 0.36)$, or 7.8%. This feature makes municipal bonds attractive to higher income taxpayers even at a lower market rate of interest, and gives local borrowing the equivalent of a federal subsidy in the form of a tax expenditure. The policy implications of this subsidy have been hotly debated. Supporters see this tax exemption of municipal bonds as an appropriate transfer of resources to local government to help them develop infrastructure. Critics see it as an incentive to excessive local borrowing, often for inappropriate purposes, such as subsidizing questionable private investments through this preferential access to capital markets.

Federal Surpluses/Deficits, Debt, and Borrowing

The lack of a balanced budget constraint at the federal level has meant that decisions about spending have often been made without reference to the opportunity cost. With a balanced budget constraint, the opportunity cost of a new program or project is either other spending foregone, or additional tax burdens on citizens to fund the program or project. Those explicit costs provide both a challenge and an opportunity to weigh marginal costs and benefits and allocate resources efficiently. Although the federal government needs to have the ability to run deficits during economic downturns, that budget flexibility has often resulted in running deficits during periods when macroeconomic justification was not present. It is only in recent years that the federal budget has returned to balance and even experienced some surpluses.

Federal borrowing has important impacts on many other players in both the public sector and the private sector. High levels of federal borrowing drive up interest rates and make it more expensive for both state and local governments and private firms and households to borrow (crowding out). Using the projected surplus to pay down part of the accumulated national debt will have the opposite effect, putting downward pressure on interest rates and making it easier for households, firms, and state and local governments to borrow. Lower interest rates might help to prolong the unprecedented expansion of the 1990s. Lower interest rates will also reduce the part of federal spending that goes to pay interest on the accumulated national debt, which currently accounts for about 11% of all federal spending.

In the past two decades, a large part of the federal government bonds issued to finance deficits in the operating budget have been purchased by the social insurance trust funds (Social Security and Medicare) which have been running surpluses. Chapter 18 explores the implications of that intragovernmental financing for the future of Social Security.

SUMMARY

A budget is a spending plan based on expected revenue that sets priorities for the quantity and quality of services to be provided or the transfers to be made. It includes a revenue forecast, expenditure forecasts and appropriations for continuing funding of existing projects and outlays for new projects, and a procedure for funding any deficit or allocating any projected surplus.

The revenue forecast is based on anticipated economic conditions, which are then incorporated into formal or informal models that relate the economic forecast to the tax base and, using an elasticity relationship, from the tax base to revenue. These forecasts also reflect any changes in the tax structure including rates and tax expenditures.

The budget of any government does not usually include all revenue and expenditures. Some revenue and expenditures are recorded separately in off-budget accounts that do not pass through the legislative budget process on an annual basis. Social Security and Medicare are the most important federal off-budget accounts, and state employee retirement systems are the largest state off-budget account. There are also separate enterprise funds at the federal as well as the state and local level for many fee-financed services such as water and sewer.

Expenditure budgeting also involves forecasts that are based primarily on inflation projections and population growth. New or expanded programs or projects go through a variety of evaluative processes. Some budgetary processes also periodically apply such scrutiny to existing budgets. The form of the expenditure budget may be a line-item budget, which looks at the recipients of payments (e.g., wages, services purchased), or more likely a program budget, which allocates funds to agencies or programs so that the cost of a program can be related to its benefits. More sophisticated form of developing expenditure budgets are performance budgeting or zero-based budgeting, but both require a great deal of paperwork and are time consuming and expensive to implement.

Public choice theory argues that bureaucrats who develop budget proposals are self-interested maximizers of salary, prestige, and power, which results in continuous demands for budget increases that are difficult for voters or legislators to restrain effectively. Responses to this upward pressure on government spending include encouraging competition between public and private providers of services and various forms of tax and expenditure limitations.

Cost–benefit analysis is a technique of evaluation used in making choices in both the public and private sector that is based on equating marginal benefit to marginal cost, or to maximizing "utility" in allocating resources among competing uses subject to a budget constraint. Cost–benefit analysis attempts to quantify all the benefits and costs of a proposed project, both monetary and nonmonetary. Nonmonetary costs and benefits are quantified using such techniques as changes in property values, human life valuation, and development of shadow prices. The present value of future costs and future benefits is then computed by applying an appropriate discount rate, and the costs and benefits are compared.

When they are compared using a benefit–cost ratio, different projects can be ranked according to the size of the benefit–cost ratio.

State and local governments generally have to balance their operating budgets, which forces trade-offs within the budget. Capital projects are often financed by the issuance of debt or municipal bonds, which may be general obligation bonds (backed by the full faith and credit of the issuing government) or revenue bonds (with revenue from fees or other income from the project earmarked for payments of interest and principal). Because the interest on municipal bonds is exempt from federal income taxes, they are attractive to higher income individuals even at lower interest rates. This tax exemption is a form of federal subsidy for state and local capital spending.

The federal government does not have the same budget constraint and has been able to run large deficits in the past, although recently the federal budget has had smaller deficits and occasional surpluses. This lack of a budget constraint has been blamed for escalations in government spending and for failing to prioritize clearly when considering new or expanding programs. Tax and expenditure limitations that limit growth of spending at all levels have been a frequent response to concerns about uncontrolled growth of government as a result of the ability to run deficits. The current reduction in both borrowing and the national debt should reduce both the budgetary burden of interest payments and the interest rates charged to nonfederal borrowers in capital markets, stimulating both private and public (state and local) capital spending.

KEY TERMS AND CONCEPTS

budget, 320
revenue forecasting, 320
off-budget accounts, 323
line-item budget, 329
program budget, 329

performance budgeting, 329
zero-based budgeting, 329
cost–benefit analysis, 331
cost–benefit ratio, 333
shadow prices, 335

general obligation bond, 338
revenue bond, 338
municipal bond, 338
taxable equivalent yield, 338

DISCUSSION QUESTIONS

1. Many states exempt interest on municipal bonds from state income taxes if those bonds are issued by that state or its local governments. Suppose that you buy municipal bonds issued in your state, and your federal marginal tax rate is 28% and your state marginal tax rate is 6%. If the yield on the bonds is 6.5%, what is the taxable equivalent yield?

2. Suppose that you are hired, with your economics degree, to forecast revenue and expenditures for a large city in your state. Describe the process by which you would go about developing those forecasts.

3. Your assignment is to carry out a cost–benefit analysis for a new parking lot. The cost of the parking lot is $3,000,000. Annual maintenance and operating expenses are $60,000. The revenue from users, including the estimated value of "free" parking for city employees, is $200,000 a year, and the parking lot has an estimated useful lifetime of 15 years. At a 5% rate of discount, what is the cost–benefit ratio for this project? What other factors might you want to take into account? How would your answer be different if the interest rate was 8%?

4. Why are the incentives facing bureaucrats inconsistent with addressing the desires and preferences of voters? How might they be better aligned?

CHAPTER 16

PUBLIC EDUCATION

Providing public education, from preschool through higher education, is a major activity of government at all levels, but in the United States the primary responsibility lies at the state and local levels. The share of financing at the federal level has declined during the last two decades. At the same time, in many states responsibility has been reallocated away from local governments toward the state, at least partly to provide property tax relief.

Few other functions of government touch so many lives so directly. Almost everyone in the country has had some link to a public school or college as a student, teacher, administrator, public official, or community volunteer—not to mention citizen/taxpayer. Public schools are expected to educate young people so they learn the basic skills of a modern industrial society, including work and citizenship skills, and to instill in them a desire for lifelong learning. They are also called on to provide ancillary services, including social services, mental and physical health assistance, and recreation. Public schools provide meeting space for a variety of community activities. At the same time no public function is subjected to greater scrutiny and complaint, with taxpayers and parents demanding better performance for fewer dollars of inputs.

Table 16–1 summarizes the size and scope of elementary and secondary education activities in the United States, including public and private sectors, and federal, state, and local financing. As you can see, elementary and secondary education is a direct and important part of life for

Table 16–1
Education in the
United States, 1999

Education in the United States, 1999	
PreK–12	
Number of public schools	89,508 (1997–1998)
Number of students	48.7 mil (1998–1999)
Public 42.7 million	
Private 6.0 million	
Number of teachers—public schools	3.1 mil (1998–1999)
Total public spending (in millions of dollars)	$305,052 (1996–1997)
Federal 20,081 (6.6%)	
State 146,434 (48%)	
Local 138,537 (45.3%)	
Average per pupil spending (public schools)	$6,915 (1998–1999)

Source: *Digest of Educational Statistics, 1999* (Washington, DC: U.S. Department of Education, 1999).

more than 50 million Americans as teachers and students, or almost one person in five.

WHY PUBLIC EDUCATION?

Although societies have provided for formal education for children and youth for thousands of years, it is only recently that education has been perceived as a function of government. In ancient Rome and Greece, education was provided by the family, with tutors educating the sons (and sometimes even daughters) of wealthier families. For those who were not wealthy, education was more likely to be an apprenticeship to learn a trade or skill, a pattern that has continued well into modern times. In much of Western society, religion offered another path to education. Judaism placed great emphasis on learning to read for religious purposes, and monasteries and convents were havens for education and scholarship throughout the Middle Ages. Even today, private education for the children of the wealthy and church-related schools from preschool through higher education play an important role in the provision of education. But the important difference between earlier societies and modern industrial economies is that education is expected to be both available to and required of everyone, regardless of ability to pay and even to some extent regardless of ability or willingness to learn. The collective judgment is that the costs of ignorance are higher than the price society must pay to provide universal access to education.

Education does not meet the standard tests for a pure public good, because it is neither truly nonrival in consumption nor nonexcludable. Some consumption is collective (hundreds of people can listen to a lecture), but particularly at younger ages, consumption of education services is also competitive. More time and attention given to one student means less for another. There is the benefit of shared learning, so that the optimum class size for learning purposes is not necessarily one, but congestion sets in quickly, which is the reason for all the pressure to reduce class sizes. Exclusion is easy, as those who have been sent away because their names were not on class rolls can testify. So education is excludable and at least somewhat rival in consumption. The justification for public involvement in education, then, must rest on other grounds besides public goods. The efficiency rationale is externalities, both civic and economic. The equity rationale is equality of opportunity rather than equality of results.

Private Benefits

Education is an investment in human capital that pays significant lifetime dividends. The *Monthly Labor Review,* published by the U.S. Department of Labor, does periodic studies of the relationship between earnings and level of educational attainment. Table 16–2 summarizes the earnings comparisons for men and women for selected years from 1972 to 1990. This table is very informative. The male–female earnings gap declined but did not disappear. Within each gender, however, there are some interesting patterns of what happened to

Table 16–2
Education and Earnings, 1972–1990

Median Annual Income for Full-Time Workers Age 25 and Over (1991 dollars)			
Less than 4 Years of High School	4 Years of High School	1–3 Years of College	4+ Years of College
Men			
1972 $26,462	$33,961	$36,117	$48,229
1975 $25,630	$32,812	$36,318	$44,704
1980 $24,380	$32,202	$34,583	$42,754
1985 $22,657	$30,174	$34,104	$45,454
1990 $20,306	$27,629	$32,892	$44,310
Women			
1972 $15,117	$16,911	$21,530	$28,971
1975 $14,548	$18,844	$22,112	$27,523
1980 $15,103	$19,082	$21,393	$27,063
1985 $14,443	$19,583	$22,756	$29,246
1990 $14,338	$19,093	$23,161	$31,666

Source: Alan Eck, "Job-Related Education and Training; Their Impact on Earnings," *Monthly Labor Review* (October 1993): pp. 21–38.

earnings by level of education. Inflation-adjusted earnings for men fell between 1972 and 1990 for all levels of educational attainment, but both the total decline and the percentage decline were much larger for men with less education. Men with less than a high school diploma saw their real earnings fall by more than 23%, while for men with four or more years of college the decline was only about 9%. Women with less than a high school education saw a more modest drop (5.2%), while women with high school diplomas or more all saw some increase in earnings from 1972 to 1990, with the largest gains in absolute dollars ($2,695) going to women with four or more years of college and the largest percentage gain among women with some college.

Within each year, there is a substantial wage differential by level of education. In 1990, for example, both men and women with at least four years of college earned on average 2.2 times as much as a worker of the same gender with only some high school. Even after allowing for the loss of earnings while in school, the return on investing in education is pretty impressive. So it is reasonable to ask why private decisions might result in less than optimal provision of education. For the answer, we turn primarily to externality arguments, secondarily to missing market and equity arguments.

The Efficiency Rationale: Social Benefits

Suppose that you live in a subdivision and have no children, but your neighbors do. Why should you contribute to their education? Shouldn't that be the responsibility of their parents, who chose to bring them into the world and thereby assumed the responsibility for providing them with diapers, formula, toys, pets, transportation, braces, and bicycles? This argument is not just hypothetical. It is one of the reasons why retirement communities sometimes attempt to withdraw from their school districts, arguing that their neighborhood produces no education demands and therefore should not have to contribute to paying for it. Senior citizens have been quoted as saying, "I educated my children, let them educate theirs." The problem with this argument, of course, is that the now-senior citizens are unlikely to have contributed enough tax dollars to cover the cost of educating their own children. Because their children's education was subsidized by others, one could argue that intergenerational equity requires them to contribute in turn (based on their ability to pay) to the cost of educating other children—including their own grandchildren. But the primary rationale for asking all taxpayers to contribute to the cost of public education whether or not they now have or ever have had children in the public schools is the argument that the education of all children creates social benefits.

Types of Social Benefits

There are at least three benefits that correspond to the three functions of individuals in a market democracy as citizens, consumers, and workers. The first benefit is civic in nature. A democratic society can only function with an educated citizenry that understands their civic duties and can carry them out, watchdogging the political process so that it does not generate into the purely self-interested morass that public choice theorists warn us about. The ability to locate, absorb, and interpret information is an essential part of civic participation. Beyond that basic skill, students are trained in the arts of citizenship, including participation in civic affairs and learning how the political system works and how to engage it. The rest of us should benefit from their active and informed participation in the political process by enjoying a more responsive and accountable government at all levels.

The same kinds of skills are essential to participating in the marketplace as an informed consumer, the second form of social benefit. Economists assume that information is available and utilized; rational expectations theory assumes that this process is continuous and rapid, weeding out inferior products and services and ensuring a good match between consumer and product, worker and employer. But that process of acquiring, disseminating, and acting on information assumes that consumers are educated, that they are literate, that they have basic skills in critical interpretation of information. The same kind of watchdogging that works to keep government more honest and accountable is important in the market for consumer goods and services. Everyone as a consumer is protected and benefited by the presence of other informed, articulate consumers in the marketplace, spreading and acting on information to widen the range of informed choice.

The third role through which individuals participate in a market democracy is as producer—as worker or entrepreneur or some combination of the two. As the economy has become more technologically sophisticated, the level of basic skills in reading, math, writing, and analysis required for even entry-level jobs has also increased. While it was once possible to get a few years of education to learn basic writing and arithmetic and then go to work on the farm or in the mill, those options are no longer open. These benefits are those most often emphasized in promoting and supporting public education, but the person being educated actually captures a larger share of the work-related benefits of investing in human capital than civic or consumption effects, because of the gains in lifetime income that may result. However, the worker training component of public education still generates social benefits. An educated workforce is an essential precondition for economic development and a continuing requirement to sustain a growing and increasingly sophisticated economy.

A more subtle benefit to public schools that is not entirely captured in these three roles is the exposure to diversity and the recognition and acceptance of legitimate differences in the values, behaviors, attitudes, and practices of people from different religious or cultural backgrounds. In a culturally heterogeneous society such as the United States, public education that brings people together at a young age can promote an understanding and acceptance of diversity that may contribute significantly to the reduction of social tensions and social conflicts.

Market Failure and Human Capital

One might expect that in well-functioning markets, it would be possible to borrow to pay for education and repay the loan with interest while still having a larger income than one would have had without the education. That strategy for converting financial capital into human capital has become commonplace in financing higher education, both undergraduate and graduate. There is a well-developed market, largely private with public subsidy to hold down interest rates, in providing loans to college students. But such a market would be harder to develop for K–12 students because of the longer period of study and the greater difficulty in "picking winners." By the time students arrive at college, there are already clear indications of their learning and earning potential and thus their ability to repay a loan. College students are also of legal age, so that they can borrow on their own accounts, which is not true of children under the age of 18. The parents of younger children may not be willing to commit themselves to repaying a loan and are not legally able to bind their underage children to a loan obligation. While the market works reasonably well at the post–high school level, these market imperfections would lead to underinvestment in human capital at the precollege level in the absence of public subsidy of some kind.

The Equity Rationale: Equality of Opportunity

From an equity perspective, education is sometimes classified as a merit good— something to which one is entitled by virtue of membership in society, regardless of ability to pay. Like housing vouchers, food stamps and Medicaid, education can be viewed as an in-kind transfer designed so that the children of the poor get the benefits rather than relying on their parents to make sure that they get what they need.

But there is an important difference between education and other services to children in low-income households. Many other countries provide both universal health insurance and universal children's allowances (cash aid) to children without regard to need, with some of the cash aid recaptured through the income tax system. The United States dispenses both health care for children (Medicaid) and cash support, including TANF,[1] food stamps, and housing assistance, on a needs basis, carefully distinguishing between those who pay their own way and those who receive public subsidy. K–12 education is one of the few forms of in-kind redistribution where the same service is offered to all without requiring payment, regardless of ability to pay. Because the public schools are supported by taxes, the wealthy contribute the largest share of the cost and the poor contribute little or nothing, but the only place where any distinction is seen between rich and poor is in the free and reduced-price lunch program.

1. See Chapter 18.

An important part of the equity rationale for providing education at no cost, and the reason that it is generally provided at no charge or only nominal cost to the child's family, is that education is an investment in human capital that will make these children able to become productive and self-supporting adult members of society. Without such an investment, they could easily become trapped in an endless cycle of generations of poverty, with families too poor to invest in their children even when the return is very high. Social benefits by themselves justify some degree of subsidy, but because private benefits accrue to the child and his or her family in terms of increased productivity, economic efficiency suggests that the household should pay for those private benefits. It is only when education is seen as a poverty-preventing, productivity-enhancing strategy that it might be possible to justify a 100% subsidy.

THE EDUCATION PRODUCTION FUNCTION

Economists and educational researchers have devoted considerable attention to measuring the effects of various levels and combinations of educational inputs on student performance both on standardized tests and in the job market (measured by earnings). This relationship is the **education production function,** which shows the amount of "output" (learning or increased productivity) that results from a given mix or level of inputs. It is much easier to define a production function for wheat, or steel, or haircuts in terms of the labor, capital, and raw materials inputs needed to produce a given quantity of output because these products and services have clearly measurable outputs. Although we can indeed measure educational inputs, it is harder to arrive at clear agreement about the appropriate measure of educational output.

This issue is important because policy makers face conflicting pressures; parents and employers are anxious to improve school quality while taxpayers (including some of the same people) want to contain or reduce the amount of tax resources devoted to public education. Hanushek, who has done extensive research in this area, summarized more than 300 such studies. He finds that results are generally inconclusive[2]; some find a statistically significant link between certain inputs (such as the teacher–student ratio) and test scores, while others find little relationship, and others find that the sign is sometimes negative rather than positive. Studies by Card and Krueger did find a positive relationship between educational inputs, specifically expenditures per pupil and the teacher–pupil ratio, and later earnings across a broad spectrum of age groups[3]. More recent studies by Pogue, Maxey, and Lu and by Taylor

2. Erik A. Hanushek, "Measuring Investment in Education," *Journal of Economic Perspectives,* 10(4), Fall 1996, pp. 9–30.
3. David Card and Alan B. Krueger, "School Resources and Student Outcomes: An Overview of the Literature and New Evidence from North and South Carolina," *Journal of Economic Perspectives* 10:4 (Fall 1996): pp. 31–40.

control for family and community backgrounds and other factors so that they can measure the schools' "value-added"; that is, they can separate the effect of schools from other influences on performance. In both cases, these researchers find stronger and positive effects of additional resources on outcomes as measured by student performance.[4] Neither side of the debate can demonstrate conclusively, however, that a clear and direct relationship exists between inputs and outputs in education.

More recently, considerable controversy has arisen about output measures, particularly excessive reliance on standardized tests. Standardized tests are not necessarily either an adequate measure of learning or a predictor of future success as a worker, consumer, and citizen, which are presumably the primary objectives of education. Heavy reliance on test scores to measure the performance of not only students but teachers and individual schools has created a perverse incentive system that encourages teachers to focus on "teaching to the test" at the expense of developing skills and abilities that take longer to acquire and are not directly reflected on the tests.

FINANCING EDUCATION

Paying for education is a big part of the budgets of state and local governments in the United States, with some limited (and declining) targeted federal aid. Table 16–3 summarizes public expenditures for education for the 47 million K–12 students in public schools and the 14.6 million higher education students in the United States in 2000. (Another 6 million students K–12 were in private schools.) Several important facts stand out. Elementary and secondary education is primarily a state and local responsibility, with only about 6.8% of the funding coming from the federal government in 1997–98. Much of that federal aid is in the form of school lunch funds and other kinds of aid to schools or students with special needs; that is, it is primarily categorical aid.

What the table does not indicate is the decline in the federal share of funding K–12 education from 9.8% in 1980 to 6.8% in 1999. State and local governments have had to pick up the slack. Other funding sources—fees, tuition, grants, donations, and so on—provide an important component of the total, although most of it is directed at private education at all levels.

The rationale for supporting education in the public sector needs to be more finely tuned in a federal system, because decisions need to be made not only about the overall level of expenditures but also about how to allocate responsibility among levels of government. How localized are the social benefits of education? To what extent are these benefits, measured in educational

4. Thomas F. Pogue, James Maxey, and Chia-Hsing Lu, "Outcomes of Public Education: Weighing the Effects of Dollars, Family, Peers, and Community," *National Tax Association Proceedings 1999*, (Washington, DC: National Tax Association, 1999), pp. 222–230; and Corinne Taylor, "Challenges in Linking Student Outcomes and School Expenditures," *National Tax Association Proceedings 1999*, (Washington, DC: National Tax Association, 1999), pp. 231–235.

(Dollars in billions)
K–12 education, total	377
Higher education, total	246
Public spending for elementary	
and secondary education:	226.0
Federal	22.2
State	157.6
Local	146.1

Source: National Center for Education Statistics, *Digest of Education Statistics, 2000.*

quality, captured in housing prices? To the extent that the major benefits from education, and from quality education, accrue to local residents, they should have responsibility for financing and overseeing or providing K–12 education. There may be some spillovers within a state and more limited spillovers across state lines from mobile workers, citizens, and consumers that might justify more involvement by higher levels of government.

The primary rationale for a state and national role in financing for K–12 education, however, comes from the equity side. School districts or other local governments responsible for providing education have very different tax resources, and the only way to provide any degree of equalization of access to educational resources is through redistribution of school funds at the state or federal level. Federal funds target specific programs aimed at children who are disadvantaged in terms of household income or other characteristics—children with special needs, feeding programs, and other categorical grant programs that single out schools with a high proportion of students with special needs that may range from a free breakfast to disability access to special education. States play the primary role in equalization of educational funding resources between their school districts or cities and counties.

State Formula Funding and Equalization

A number of court cases during the past few decades have challenged the way schools are funded. One of the most famous cases was a California decision in 1978, *Serrano v. Priest,* in which the state Supreme Court agreed with the complaining parent that the quality of a child's education should not depend on the taxable wealth of the district in which the child's family resides. This case resulted in a significant shifting of responsibility for school funding from the local to the state level in California in order to reduce disparities that resulted from differences in property tax resources. The challenge to states in devising a suitable formula for redistribution of funds among school districts is to ensure adequate funds for each child while ensuring that local officials do not respond to increased state aid by reducing local tax effort. One way to resolve that problem is to fund education primarily through the state, as is true of Hawaii, where 91% of education funding is state supplied (most of the rest is federal). Most states are not willing to assume that large a share of education funding or control and prefer to leave a large share of the responsibility for funding and overseeing schools to the local government, who on average bear 45% of the cost of K–12 education. But a number of states have moved toward assuming a larger share of funding by the state, including Connecticut, Michigan, and New Jersey.

In many states, the bulk of state aid for education is distributed through some kind of formula that incorporates such factors as the number of students, adjusted for different costs for elementary, secondary, special education, vocational, and other groups; the estimated cost of educating a student; the tax base of the local district, reflecting local ability to pay; and the legislatively determined division of effort between state and local governments. For example, the formula in South Carolina is based on a minimum standard of support per student, the basic student cost (BSC) multiplied by the adjusted number of students (ST).

The word *adjusted* here means that there is a factor in the formula that reflects the difference in cost per student for different levels of education or different special student needs. High school students are more expensive to educate than elementary students. Special education students have much lower student–teacher ratios, and vocational education students require a lot of equipment, so both groups cost more to educate. The adjusted number of students is computed by multiplying the various groups of students (measured by average daily attendance the previous year) by a set of state-determined weights that reflect differences in the cost of educating each group. Table 16–4 gives an example of the computation of the adjusted number of students for a hypothetical South Carolina school district.

The required local share (LS) is 30% of the basic student cost times the adjusted number of students, multiplied by an index of ability to pay (AP) that reflects the taxable wealth of the district (the property tax base):

$$LS = 0.3 \times BSC \times ST \times AP$$

Table 16–4
Computing the
Adjusted Number
of Students

Category	Number of Students	Weight	Adjusted Number
Elementary	500	0.84	420
Middle school	300	1.02	306
High school	400	1.25	500
Vocational education	80	1.75	140
Special education	30	2.50	45
TOTAL	1,310		1,411

The index of taxpaying ability is set so that the district with a tax base per pupil that is the same as the state average has an AP of 1. A district that has a tax base per pupil that is 20% above the state average would have an index of 1.2, whereas one with a base that is only 75% of the state average would have an index of 0.75. A high index means a higher expected local share and less state aid. The index of taxpaying ability is the key factor in the equalizing aspect of state aid.

School districts must meet the local share requirement in order to qualify for state aid. The state then pays the difference between the total cost of education BSC × ST and the required local share LS:

$$\text{State aid} = BSC \times ST - LS = BSC \times ST \times (1 - 0.3 \times AP)$$

Table 16–5 computes state aid for the hypothetical district in Table 16–4, which is assumed to have an index of taxpaying ability of 0.9.

This formula is a fairly typical way of distributing state aid to education, but other formulas are also used. In some cases, local governments are required to charge a certain millage or mill rate set by the state to support education, and the state makes up the difference between what that mill rate raises and the state average. This method is called **district power equalization,** implying that one mill should provide the same amount of support per student in every district. School districts (or cities and counties, if they are responsible for education) are usually free to charge a higher school mill rate than the state minimum requirement, but may not charge less.

The diversity of ways in which to equalize state aid is almost as great as the number of states. Texas at one time proposed a method of equalization that simply required the wealthiest districts to send funds to the poorest districts, bypassing any direct state funding. Both California and Michigan responded to school funding crises combined with property tax revolts by shifting a substantially larger share of funding to the state in trade for lower residential property taxes. A larger state share of funding should almost al-

Table 16–5
Computing State Aid and Local Share for a Hypothetical South Carolina School District

(A)	Adjusted number of pupils	1,411
(B)	Basic student cost*	$4,000
(C)	Total outlay for operating expenditures	$5,644,000 (A × B)
(D)	Index of taxpaying ability for this district	0.90
(E)	Local share	$1,523,880 (0.3 × C × D)
(F)	State aid	$4,120,120 (C − E)

*This figure assumes that the formula reflects the full operating cost per pupil. The formula may or may not be based on that actual cost.

ways result in greater equalization of resources per pupil among districts, because states tend to distribute a large share of their support on a formula basis that has some similarities to the one described above.

State equalization aid to public schools is rarely as simple as this example implies. In this particular formulation, the basic student cost may or may not reflect the full cost of education. Formula-driven state aid is usually provided for operational purposes, not for capital expenditures for school buildings, equipment, and buses, which must be funded separately. Grants for special purposes and various kinds of remedial and enrichment programs are an additional component of most state aid programs.

A key figure in this particular kind of formula is the percentage division of responsibility between the state and local governments. If the basic student cost reflected full costs of operation, this 70%–30% state–local division would result in a much larger state share than the U.S. average, which is about 48%, with a wide range from New Hampshire at the low end (13%) to Hawaii at the high end (91%). Because this formula uses a dollar figure for basic student cost that is only about 40% of the actual per pupil expenditure, and distributes other education funds through other channels, South Carolina only provides about 44% of the total cost of K–12 education at the state level.

Interstate Inequality

Because federal aid is a relatively modest component of K–12 education spending, and because different states have not only different resources but also different attitudes and values about public education, educational spending per pupil, educational resources, and educational outcomes vary considerably not only within states but also between states. Spending per pupil in 1995 for current operations ranged from $9,994 in Alaska to $3,888 in Utah, with an average of $5,907. Except for Alaska, spending per pupil was highest in the Northeast (even thrifty New Hampshire ranked 18th!) and the upper Midwest. This pattern reflects a combination of regional values, higher cost of living in some states, and perhaps unionization of school personnel. Low spending (less than $5,000 per pupil) was concentrated in the Southeast and the West, including California.

Downside of Equalization

Equalization of educational inputs is intended to create more equality of opportunity for students who would arrive at the labor market not artificially advantaged or disadvantaged by the quality of the public schools they had attended. However, some issues have been raised by parents, politicians, and economic researchers about the negative impact of equalization, particularly in those states where equalization puts limits on maximum spending rather than concentrating on guaranteeing a minimum. In California, an increased state funding role and the effects of Proposition 13 on property tax revenue have reduced variations in spending per district, but per-pupil spending has steadily fallen behind the national average. In 1995, California ranked 41st in spending per pupil.

Critics argue that the leveling of school quality has limited parental choice and encouraged flight from the public schools to private schools and home schooling as more affluent parents seek a higher quality education for their children than the public schools offer. With state aid and state requirements tending toward greater uniformity in school quality, households can no longer as readily make clear trade-offs in fiscal packages of tax rates, house prices, and the mix of public services offered (including schools). Should households be free to choose a package of lower school quality that comes with lower house prices, lower tax rates, and better nonschool local public services? Or do the interests of children, which may not be fully expressed in the preferences of their parents, take precedence?

Role of the Property Tax

Another group of proposals for school funding reform calls for divorcing school funding from the property tax. Recall from Chapter 12 that the original purpose and rationale for the property tax was that it paid for services that benefited property owners—roads, streetlights, police and fire protection, and so on. The value of those benefits is roughly proportional to the value of property. The benefits of education, however, are not distributed in proportion to property values. Because education consumes increasing shares of property tax revenue, those who perceive that this tax is a benefit tax and that their benefits are low in proportion to their tax burdens will agitate for property tax relief. Those who argue to reduce or eliminate the link between local property taxes and school funding believe that this attitude has been a significant factor in the property tax revolts of the last 25 years of the 20th century.[5]

PUBLIC PRODUCTION, PUBLIC PROVISION, OR PUBLIC SUBSIDY?

The argument that ensuring an adequate K–12 education for all children has important social benefit and equity aspects does not necessarily imply that education should be produced in the public sector. Right now, in the United States, the vast majority of children attend public schools. The school buildings are owned by state or local governments, and the teachers are public

5. Terri A. Sexton, Steven M. Sheffrin, and Arthur O'Sullivan, "Proposition 13: Unintended Effects and Feasible Reforms," *National Tax Journal*, LII(1) (March 1999):99–112.

employees. Decisions about hiring teachers and administrators, class sizes, curriculum, and other matters are made by public officials ranging from state departments of education to local school boards.

At the same time, there are a few places where public schools are run under contract by private for-profit entities, whose earnings depend on the performance of students on standardized tests. There are also children in private schools who are receiving some degree of public assistance in the form of vouchers to pay their tuition, as well as children whose parents pay both taxes to support the public schools and tuition to send their children to private schools. Finally, there is a modest but growing number of children who are educated at home by their parents, usually their mothers—the home schooling movement. Although the government can and does require that children receive a basic education, children are not compelled to attend public schools as long as they are receiving a reasonably comparable and adequate education in some other venue.

Competition and School Quality

Critics of the public school system argue that it has all the drawbacks of any monopoly. Without competition from other suppliers of educational services, this tax-supported exclusive provider can be inefficient and unresponsive to consumers without risking a loss of "customers" or revenue. These critics argue that we cannot evaluate the performance of the public school system without the existence of some nonpublic entity to which it can be compared. While there may well be a public interest in ensuring that children receive an education, that goal can be accomplished in other ways.

Defenders of public education disagree, pointing out the competitive effect of residential mobility on school quality. Recall from Chapter 7 that households choose their residential location based on the package of taxes and services offered by each locality (the Tiebout model). For families with children, schools and school quality are a major factor in that decision. School quality is incorporated in the price of housing in those places where attendance zones are clearly defined so that each house is associated with the right to attend a particular school or set of schools. School quality is reflected in higher housing prices; buyers are willing to pay for school quality, and even buyers who do not have school-age children are aware that the quality of the schools will affect the resale value of their homes.

Real tension exists in public policy between the desire to provide equality of opportunity for all children through education and the advantages of local control, consumer choice, competition within the public sector, and diversity. Inner-city schools in particular, with a declining tax base and an increasing number of "challenge" students (students from backgrounds of poverty or abuse, students from other cultures whose primary language is not

GROWTH, DEVELOPMENT, AND EDUCATION FUNDING

Recall from Chapters 12 and 13 that funding education is an important issue in the area of both property taxes and growth-related fees. Funding the public schools in communities experiencing rapid residential growth is a challenge that can be met in a variety of ways. Rarely do residential property taxes cover the cost of educating the community's children; commercial and industrial property is an important part of the tax base for education as well as other local public services. When growth is primarily residential, there is often a lag between the new development and the collection of property taxes a year or two later, but the children show up in school immediately, and often new schools must be built in advance of their arrival. So local property tax revenues from new residential development are too little, too late in terms of building and operating new schools. Some states offer state aid for school construction in areas of rapid growth, but in many states the challenge of providing enough classrooms falls to the city, county, or school district, and that means it falls on property taxpayers for the most part.

Florida, looking at an estimated $300 million needed for school construction between 2000 and 2005, has been one of a handful of states that has attempted to resolve this problem with a school impact fee. Development impact fees are designed to put the burden of paying for additional public infrastructure on the newly developed property that has generated the demand for that new infrastructure. For most communities, school buildings, school buses, and other education facilities represent a major part of their infrastructure investment. The impact fee, assessed on a per-property basis, is intended to shift the cost of creating new schools to those who created the need. In Orange County, the school impact fee—

which becomes part of the price of a new house—is more than $2,000 for a single-family dwelling.

While Florida is experiencing rapid population growth, not all of those new homes have children. Florida has long been a magnet for retirees, and many of Florida's residential developments are age restricted. No children under 18 may live in many housing subdivisions, apartment or condo complexes, or mobile home parks. Developers and residents of these age-restricted developments have gone to court to demand exemption from the school impact fee on the very reasonable grounds that they do not generate demand for additional schools.

The issue, which came to a head in 2000 with a court case in Volusia County, raises some important questions about equity in paying for public schools. If the spillover benefits from education are concentrated in the local community, then shouldn't everyone contribute, even if they live in an age-restricted development? As Volusia County's attorneys argue, doesn't exempting these communities and putting the burden on homeowners and renters violate the state constitution's guarantee of free access to public education? With a flat fee per housing unit, regardless of whether it is a mobile home or a mansion, isn't a school impact fee a highly regressive way of funding school construction?

Other states are considering the use of school impact fees as a way to distribute the burden of building new schools more fairly among existing and new residents. But the court case in Volusia County, Florida, suggests that school impact fees raise some important new equity questions in the process of resolving this particular dispute between those who were already there and those whose arrival calls for more school construction.

Source: Lori Horvitz and John Kennedy, "Impact Fees," *The Orlando Sentinel*, May 19, 2000.

English), are unable to compete with suburban schools with supportive parents, well-prepared students, and a stronger local tax base. These schools need state equalization in order to meet the basic needs of their students. On the other hand, the recent trend toward increased state funding of education in a number of states that has leveled the playing field in terms of educational quality has also in some cases limited the ability of a local community to voluntarily tax itself to provide better than average schools.

Vouchers

Critics of public schools want to go beyond the Tiebout-type competition that forces schools to be accountable and allow parents to make choices about where to educate their children. **School vouchers** allow parents to "buy" education for their children at any accredited school, public or private, up to a certain sum per child. A voucher for the full amount of the cost of educating the student at some basic level in a private school would be public provision of education. Vouchers that covered less than the full cost of that basic education would be equivalent to a public subsidy. The debate over vouchers has brought to the forefront the question of whether public education requires public production or just public funding with partial or complete private production.

Under a system of vouchers that retained public schools, failing public schools would lose students, while successful schools would attract students, and market forces would force standards of quality upward. Some voucher proponents would limit the use of vouchers to public schools, a program also known as school choice. Most voucher proposals would extend the use of vouchers to private schools as well, although in many cases the voucher is likely to need supplementing by additional payments from the family in order to cover the tuition at a private school.

Supporters of vouchers argue that they are more equitable and more efficient than the present system. They are more equitable because everyone has the same choice and every child receives the same amount of tax support for their education, regardless of what school they attend or what district they live in. They are more efficient because they force schools to compete to attract students, thus mitigating the unresponsiveness of poorly managed schools. In addition, one researcher has pointed out that vouchers decouple the normal relationship between housing, taxes, and school quality. Higher income families might be more willing to live in low-income communities when they can use vouchers to send their children to a more satisfactory school than the local tax base would provide, resulting in a more equal distribution of tax resources for nonschool purposes.[6]

How might a voucher work in practice? Whether the voucher is used to allow a student to transfer from one public school to another, or from a public to a private school (including religious schools), the principle is the same. A figure that represents the average cost of educating a student is transferred

---

6. Thomas J. Nechyba, "Public School Finance and Vouchers in a General Equilibrium Tiebout World," *National Tax Association Proceedings 1997*, (Washington, DC: National Tax Association, 1997), pp. 119–125.

from the school being left to the newly chosen school, coming out of the former school's income from state aid and local taxes. However, the household of the pupil is paying taxes to its district of residence, and equity would require that if the pupil is attending elsewhere, its school taxes should be adjusted upward to reflect those of the receiving district. So the voucher would consist of revenue from the former school based on average per-pupil spending and the household based on any difference in property tax rates if the student is attending a public school. If the student is attending a private school, the voucher would reflect the average cost of public school education in the district of residence and the parents would have to make up any difference in cost.

Experiments with Vouchers: What Is the Evidence?

Vouchers have been used by states to support students in private schools in Milwaukee since 1990–1991, in Cleveland since 1995, and more recently, statewide in Florida. The Milwaukee experience has appealed most to researchers because of the long time period. Vouchers were provided by lottery to low-income applicants to be used in secular private schools. Initially the vouchers were for one-half the cost of public education ($2,500) and five private schools agreed to accept the students and vouchers. The amount of the voucher was later increased. Of the initial voucher-takers, however, more than one-third had left the private schools by the end of the fourth year.

Three separate studies were conducted of the Milwaukee experience. The Witte study found no significant difference in math and reading performance between pupils in the private schools and similar students remaining in public schools. The Peterson study found gains in math but not reading. The Rouse study found similar results, but a follow-up study found that gains for low-income public school students in smaller classes were higher than the gains of voucher students in private schools.[7]

Cleveland's vouchers included religious schools, an issue that has been challenged in court. Again, evaluations of student performance in Cleveland resulted in conflicting evidence. Other voucher experiments in Dayton, New York, Washington (D.C.), and Charlotte provide mixed results with some scattered gains. Florida is the only state currently to go statewide, although vouchers are limited to students at public schools that fail standardized tests twice in four years. These vouchers are the lesser of the per-pupil cost of the failing public school or the private school's tuition, about $3,400 on average, and can be used at any school public or private, religious or secular. So far the number of students is very small, but the potential for expansion is enormous.[8]

7. Martin Canoy and Richard Rothstein, "Do School Vouchers Improve Student Performance?" *The American Prospect* 12(1) (January 1–15, 2001): 42–46.
8. Amy Gutmann, "What Does School Choice Mean?" *Dissent,* 47(3) (Summer 2000): 19–24.

Equity and Vouchers

The equity issues in vouchers are not limited to ensuring a decent education to low-income children in inadequate public schools, although that is the issue voiced most often. A second issue is the perceived inequity of paying taxes to support public schools and then also paying tuition to support one's children in private schools, either because of dissatisfaction with the public schools or because of a preference for a religious or other kind of private school education. If vouchers were universal, as they have the potential to be in Florida, rather than targeted at disadvantaged children as they have been up until now, then a significant amount of public education funding would be diverted to assisting more affluent families with their private school education, and the remaining public schools will have fewer resources with which to educate remaining students.

Vouchers and Higher Education

While vouchers for K–12 education are controversial, vouchers in postsecondary education (better known as merit-based or needs-based scholarships) have been a significant part of education funding for many decades. Georgia dedicates much of the proceeds of its state lottery, initiated in 1993, to scholarships that have relatively modest restrictions on income or scholastic achievement qualifications (graduate from a Georgia high school with a B average, and retain a B average in college). Students can use these scholarships to purchase higher education at public or private institutions within the state. A number of other states have created programs that draw on the Georgia model. Funding students through scholarships rather than funding the general operations of the educational institutions appeals not only to voters and politicians but also to donors to both private and public colleges.

VOCATIONAL EDUCATION AND TRAINING

Vocational education and training take place in a variety of settings from "vo-tech" high schools and "tech-prep" public school programs to community colleges, for-profit training institutes, colleges, short courses and workshops, and on-the-job training. Three sources of funding are possible for such investments in human capital: the worker, the present or future employer, and the public sector. Each of these three groups does contribute to some degree in investing in human capital, but each one by itself will tend to underinvest for different reasons.

Vocational and technical training comes in three forms: general, job specific, and employer specific. General skills refer to such knowledge as the ability to communicate, collaborate, and calculate, to operate basic equipment, and to follow and give instructions. This kind of skill is acquired to some

EDUCATION IN OTHER INDUSTRIAL COUNTRIES

Critics of U.S. public education are fond of pointing to numerous studies of how American pupils compare with their peers in other countries on various kinds of standardized tests. Tests of achievement in science and mathematics for students on the 4th, 8th, and 12th grades were undertaken in 1994–1995 for half a million students in 26 countries. American students ranked 8th (well above average) in mathematics at the 4th-grade level but below the international average at the 8th-grade level and near the bottom at the 12th-grade level. For science, American 4th and 8th graders were above the international average but 12th graders were below average.[1]

What about inputs? The two most widely used measures of educational inputs are expenditures per pupil and teacher–pupil ratios. Expenditures per pupil are not considered an ideal single measure because schools vary in their outlays for expenses not directly related to instruction such as facilities and administration. In addition, high expenditures sometimes reflect a more difficult population to educate, such as children from difficult home situations or non–English-speaking students. In 1994–1995, the United States spent $4,772 per elementary pupil and $8,039 per secondary pupil. The United States ranked behind Luxembourg, Norway, Switzerland, Sweden, and Denmark in spending per elementary pupil but ahead of 14 other countries (data were not available for some countries). For secondary education, the United States ranked ninth out of 19 countries, with five countries spending more than $10,000 per secondary pupil and Luxembourg spending more than twice the U.S. figure.[2]

Some researchers have found a positive and significant relationship between teacher–pupil ratios and student performance.[3] (Remember, a high teacher–pupil ratio is the same as a low pupil–teacher ratio: both indicate more teaching resources per pupil, or more educational input.) For convenience, most measures are pupil–teacher rather than teacher–pupil ratios.) Between 1985 and 1996, the U.S. ratio of pupils to teachers held steady (16.9 in 1996 compared to 17.0 in 1985). Among the 14 other industrial countries for which

degree as part of the general education curriculum in K–12, although some people finish high school lacking in some or all of these skills, which are also emphasized in technical schools, community colleges, and four-year colleges. Because these skills are highly generalized (applicable to a great variety of jobs), they have a value to the worker, to society as a whole, and to the employer, but the employer will simply discriminate in hiring by using tests to evaluate whether a prospective employee has these basic general skills. For this reason, the same arguments that apply to shared responsibility for the individual and the public sector for K–12 and higher education also apply to ensuring that all labor force entrants be equipped with these basic skills.

Other countries invest heavily in job training of various kinds, including a highly regarded apprenticeship program in Germany. In the United States, the **Job Training and Partnership Act (JTPA)** has been a major source of federal funding for training for unemployed workers, housewives reentering the labor force, and others in need of remedial or expanded skills to become employable. Most of the training takes place at community colleges. Studies that attempt to measure the increase in earnings and other effects of JTPA data were available in 1996, the range of ratios was from 11.2 in Italy and Denmark to 22.0 in New Zealand and 22.6 in Ireland. The United States had the fifth lowest ratio.

These measures of performance and inputs are at best suggestive; they are the stuff of headlines, not the products of careful development of models of educational production functions that link outcomes to inputs in any systematic way. Critics of the U.S. educational system point to the outcomes, but fail to address the question of whether performance in mathematics and science is an appropriate or adequate measure of what the schools are being asked to do. Supporters of the public school system focus on the inputs, in particular the comparisons of spending per pupil, and suggest that the United States is underinvesting in its children relative to other countries, even though the pupil–teacher ratios are quite good in comparison to other countries.

Education, more than any other area of public sector activity, offers a real challenge to measuring and valuing inputs, intermediate outcomes, and final outputs even within a single country, let alone between countries. Some of the interstate comparisons within the United States, such as the Card and Krueger study cited earlier, yield useful information about the effects of inputs on outcomes because they are operating within similar institutional frameworks and are therefore less vulnerable to the effects of omitted variables on measuring the educational production function. If there is any single lesson from international comparisons it is not that the United States is performing poorly, or that this country is getting fewer results per teacher-hour or educational dollar, but rather that we are not profoundly different from peer nations in the input and outcome of our elementary and educational systems by the admittedly inadequate available measures.

1. *Digest of Educational Statistics 1999* (Washington, DC: U.S. Department of Education, 1999).
2. *Ibid.*
3. David Card and Alan B. Krueger, "School Resources and Student Outcomes: An Overview of the Literature and New Evidence from North and South Carolina," *Journal of Economic Perspectives,* 10(4) (Fall 1996): pp. 31–40.

training indicate a positive return to the individual, along with relatively weak social benefits.[9]

The second kind of vocational training prepares a worker for a particular kind of skill that would be useful to a number of prospective employers, such as computer skills, auto repair, truck driving, or retail management. Individual employers are hesitant to make such an investment in a particular worker because workers are mobile, and some other future employer, perhaps even a rival firm, may reap the benefits of that training. This investment in vocational training is made in some combination by the present or future worker and the public sector. It is difficult to determine the appropriate balance between public spending and private responsibility in this area, just as it is for higher education.

9. James Heckman, *et al.,* "Substitution and Drop Out Bias in Social Experiments: A Study of an Influential Social Experiment," University of Chicago Working Paper, August 1997, cited in Thomas J. Kane and Cecilia Elena Rice, "The Community College; Educating Students at the Margins between College and Work," *Journal of Economic Perspectives* 13(1) (Winter 1999): 63–64.

Finally, there is on-the-job training. Historically this kind of training has been paid for by the employer, because much (but not all) of it is employer-specific and not readily transferable to another employer. Increasingly, however, with the greater job mobility of workers and more contingent and temporary employment, workers have had to invest in maintaining, upgrading, and expanding their skills in order to remain attractive to future employers.

PUBLIC SUPPORT FOR HIGHER EDUCATION

Higher education is quite different from K–12 education in several respects. First, there is general agreement that more of the benefits of higher education accrue to the student and less to society as a whole in the form of higher lifetime earnings and, as a consequence, the appropriate subsidy is a smaller share of the total cost. Second, college students are of a legal age to assume responsibility for loans to pay for their education; the argument of capital market imperfections has been demonstrated to be less relevant to post-secondary education as student loans become an option for paying for college.

Higher education, public and private, is big business in the United States. Table 16–6 provides a basic description of the size and scope of U.S. higher education. This table points out several important features of U.S. higher education. First, only about 5% to 6% of the population is enrolled in higher education at any given time. Second, tuition and fees paid by the person being educated account for only about 27% of the cost of education. State and federal aid picks up another 36%, with the rest coming from auxiliary enterprises that include recreational facilities, dormitory rentals, food service, and other quasi-commercial enterprises that are a staple feature of college life. If auxiliary enterprises are excluded, then the division of funding responsibility

Table 16–6
Higher Education in the United States, 1993

Number of institutions	3,632
Total enrollment	14,305,000
Two-year institutions	1,442
Total enrollment	5,566,000
Current revenues, all institutions	$170,881,000
Tuition and fees	45,346,000
Federal government	21,015,000
State government	41,248,000
Auxiliary enterprises	16,663,000

Source: *U.S. Statistical Abstract* (Washington, DC: Government Printing Office), p. 183.

between students and government is 42%/58%, respectively. In publicly supported colleges and universities, the student's share is usually much smaller, although still much larger than for K–12 education.

What is the rationale for public support for higher education, which dates back to the Land Grant Act of 1863 for the federal government and much earlier for states that chartered institutions of higher education supported with public funds? Where do the efficiency and equity arguments lie for supporting the acquisition of human capital that clearly yields major future income benefits to those who attend these institutions? The arguments about the value of educated consumers and citizens are much weaker for extending education beyond 12th grade. Certainly private institutions, both nonprofit and for-profit, play a much greater role in higher education than in K–12 education, but publicly supported or publicly assisted institutions still dominate and, as indicated above, the public share is quite large.

Four arguments are offered for publicly supported higher education, although all of them can be challenged. The first is an equity argument. Children of higher income families historically had much greater access to higher education and the resulting greater earnings and opportunities than children from working and middle-class families, a pattern that changed sharply with the growth of state-supported universities and, later, community colleges. In an increasingly technically sophisticated world, equality of opportunity requires access to higher education.

The second argument relates to the ancillary functions of public colleges in terms of research and public service, especially land grant colleges. Some of the public funding goes for those functions which benefit the state in terms of quality of life, economic development, or availability of research and knowledge on public issues that must come from a reasonably objective outside source. Some of the public support for higher education pays for these functions, which are closely intermingled with the educational function, especially graduate education where industry, government, and the nonprofit sector offer training grounds for graduate students in exchange for the benefits they receive from their research and public service involvement.

The third argument, somewhat related, is that higher education is an essential component of an economic development strategy to attract industry that is more technologically sophisticated. Research Triangle Park in North Carolina is often cited as an example of the role of colleges (two public, one private) in attracting sophisticated industry because of the benefits of "agglomeration" in locating near the scientific, technical, and intellectual resources and the potential workers and managers that such industry will need. Colleges also attract retirement communities and commercial facilities because of the intellectual and cultural resources they offer to their surrounding communities.

Finally, for a long time public support for higher education reflected the imperfect capital markets that did not make it feasible for poor but bright students to borrow to pay for their education and repay the loan out of future higher earnings. Such loans are relatively new to the educational financing scene and may justify less public support of higher education in the future. In addition, not all degree programs enhance earnings equally; some generate more cultural or consumption benefits than earnings opportunities. Students who have to repay borrowings out of future earnings may be misdirected into career choices that are less suited to their talents and abilities based on current market prospects for those careers, which can change rapidly. Public support for education may deflect some career choices that are based purely on short-term financial calculations.

SUMMARY

Education is a major function of government and is funded mainly by state and local governments in the United States. Education does  not meet the standard tests of nonrivalry in consumption and nonexcludability for a pure public good. The public role in providing K–12 education is justified in terms of social benefits and equity. The social benefits consist of spillover effects from having better educated citizens, consumers, and workers to make government and producers more responsive and to improve productivity in ways that benefit everyone. Additional social benefits may come from exposure to and acceptance of diversity as a way to reduce social tensions in a culturally heterogeneous society. The equity argument for public funding of education is that education is a merit good that creates equality of opportunity. Public education is also justified by the argument that imperfect capital markets lead to underinvestment in human capital in the absence of government intervention.

Researchers find diverse results about the relationship between educational inputs and outcomes. Some studies find that such factors as teacher–student ratios or per-pupil spending have a significant effect on student perfor-mance on standardized tests, while others are not able to confirm such results.

State and local governments share most of the responsibility for paying for K–12 education. The state's role is partly to ensure a basic minimum standard by sending more funds per pupil to districts with more limited resources than to wealthier school districts. Formulas for distribution consider such factors as the cost per student, the number of students (adjusted for differences in costs for different ages, curricular, or special needs), and the taxable wealth of the district. In some states, the local government must meet a minimum requirement for its own effort to fund education in order to receive state aid. Critics of formula-type equalization argue that it offsets the beneficial effects of the capitalization of the quality of schools as well as taxes in housing prices that allow households to make location decisions on the basis of such competitive factors. On the other hand, there is some evidence that breaking the link between property taxes and schools may weaken local support for education.

Even with public benefits to education, it is not necessary that education be publicly produced, only that it be publicly provided. Critics of public education argue that it has all the drawbacks of a monopoly and that its performance would be improved if schools had to compete to attract and retain students. Vouchers are one of the currently popular proposals, allowing students (or their parents) to use public funds to purchase education, sometimes from competing public schools or school districts, other times from private schools. However, vouchers for private schools raise important questions about the equity effects of widespread, non-means-tested vouchers on those students remaining in public schools. In addition, studies of student performance in voucher experiments are inconclusive about whether students actually experience significant gains from shifting to private schools.

Vocational education takes place in many contexts, including public schools, vocational schools, technical colleges, and higher education in general, as well as in short courses and on-the-job training. Public support for acquiring general skills is based on the same arguments as public support for K–12 education. When the skills become more specific, however (related to a particular job for a particular employer), the benefits are largely privatized. Equity considerations argue that those costs should be borne by the worker and the employee in some proportion. Firms are unwilling to invest heavily in skill development that can be transferred to another employer because workers are mobile and they cannot recoup their investment if the worker receives training and then leaves the firm.

The arguments for public support for higher education are weaker than those for public education because more of the benefits of higher education accrue to the person being educated and because capital markets now function more effectively in making loans available for higher education, a relatively recent development. The rationale for a public role in higher education draws on equity arguments (equality of opportunity), the benefits of research and public service, and the importance of higher education institutions as a factor in economic development.

KEY TERMS AND CONCEPTS

education production function, 348

district power equalization, 352
school vouchers, 357

Job Training and Partnership Act (JTPA), 360

DISCUSSION QUESTIONS

1. In the formula given in the text for local share and state share, what are the variables you can adjust to increase or decrease the state share of funding? What variable or variables would allow you to adjust the distribution of state funding between districts? If the basic student cost was $3,000, and your district's adjusted student number was 2,000, how much aid would your district receive with an index of taxpaying ability of 0.80? An index of 1.3? How high would your index have to be to eliminate all state aid to your district?

2. What are the advantages and disadvantages of vouchers as a method of improving equity and school quality? In what ways might they enhance or reduce the social benefits of publicly provided K–12 education?

3. Explain how the Tiebout model results in beneficial competition between school districts for higher income residents and how that outcome would be changed by either a larger state funding share or school vouchers.

4. Why is a larger public subsidy justified for K–12 education than for higher education?

5. How do colleges engage in price discrimination among students? What is the rationale in terms of appropriate public subsidy for each type of student? Consider equity and efficiency issues in your answer. Among the types of discrimination are those based on income (ability to pay or need), ability (SAT scores), and athletic skills.

CHAPTER 17

INFRASTRUCTURE, CAPITAL SPENDING, AND PUBLIC SECTOR BORROWING

No function of government impacts as many people on a daily basis as the infrastructure of water and sewer systems, highways and bridges, school buildings, and dams. The term **infrastructure** has many meanings, but in public sector economics it usually refers specifically to public sector physical capital. The concept of infrastructure as public sector capital is sometimes extended to the intangible. In Central Europe, after the end of communism, people complained about the lack of the "social infrastructure" of a market system, such as banks, laws protecting property rights, and stock exchanges. In the narrow sense, infrastructure is generally understood to consist of public physical capital—roads, airports, school buildings, water and sewer systems, and parks. However, none of these assets has to be provided solely in or by the public sector; all of these can be, have been, or are provided in some places by either private for-profit or private nonprofit entities. Private toll roads preceded public highways; citizens may obtain water from a municipal water system or a for-profit water supplier; and electric power may be delivered by a public entity, a profit-making firm, or in many rural areas, a rural electrical cooperative. Even if the capital is owned and operated by a government, it was almost certainly constructed by a private commercial contractor.

Public infrastructure as a share of total physical capital in the United States has declined from almost 50% in 1970 to about 40% in the 1990s.[1] The largest share of public infrastructure is

1. *Economic Report of the President 1995* (Washington, DC: U.S. Government Printing Office, 1995), p. 105.

in the state and local public sector, including offices, courthouses, schools, roads and bridges, parks, jails, hospitals, and water and sewer systems. Federal infrastructure includes national parks, post offices, the interstate highway system, prisons, veterans' hospitals, office buildings, and military bases.

Because most state and local public sector capital is financed by borrowing, it is impossible to adequately discuss infrastructure without addressing borrowing and other methods of financing. Both state and local governments issue bonds (municipal bonds) as a major source of revenue for new capital projects. Thus, the financing of public sector capital is an important issue in this chapter.

To make some of the issues in capital projects clearer, this chapter takes a close look at two major areas of public infrastructure spending in the United States that are the same as those of the ancient Roman empire: roads, and water and sewer facilities. The term *roads* is extended to the broader category of transportation facilities, which includes not only highways, but also airports and parking facilities for private transportation as well as various kinds of mass transit such as buses, subways, and light rail. Transportation issues capture such critical issues in public sector expenditure analysis as user pay financing, internalizing externalities, private–public division of responsibility, federal–state–local sharing of responsibility, and, of course, efficiency and equity. Water and sewer infrastructure are provided primarily at the local level, but with federal and state assistance. The major issues related to water and sewer systems that we will explore are those of capital financing and pricing services.

EFFICIENCY ISSUES: WHY PUBLIC CAPITAL?

In a market system, the market is the default provider of goods and services. If public provision is to be justified on efficiency grounds, the argument must rely on some form of market failure. For public infrastructure, or physical capital, several kinds of market failure may be at work. The nature of the market failure often influences the method of financing. The role of the public sector in providing and paying for infrastructure reflects both equity and efficiency concerns.

Public sector capital may be an integral component of a larger program of public service that is justified on the usual grounds of public goods (justice/corrections and jails or prisons), merit goods (health clinics), or substantial positive externalities (school and college buildings). Governments could lease rather than build such facilities, but for some types of buildings and some locations, a publicly owned building is the only or most feasible option.

Often public sector physical capital has some of the essential nonrival, nonexcludability attributes of a public or at least quasi-public good in that the marginal cost of serving an additional user is low to nonexistent. Up to some congestion level, the services of the physical capital can be nonrival in consumption. In addition, the cost of enforcing exclusion of nonpayers may exceed the benefits. Roads and parks, up to the point of congestion (see Chapter 13), have such characteristics.

Some types of public sector capital may have significant positive externalities, even if they also create capturable private benefits. Often those externalities accrue to adjacent landowners. The value of a house adjacent to an attractive park, for example, may increase even if the current owner has no interest in the park. These kinds of benefits can be measured and the beneficiary charged more effectively through property taxes (including tax increment financing or special assessments) than through traditional private market prices.

Public infrastructure is generally used to provide services for which most of the cost is in the capital investment, with relatively low operating costs. (School buildings used to provide education services are a notable exception.) This kind of cost structure makes it unlikely that the market would support more than one supplier in a given area, making the sole supplier a monopolist. Because monopolies usually produce less service at a higher price and are unresponsive to consumer demands, many countries choose to place such activities in the public sector. Municipal water and sewer systems are an application of this rationale for public provision.

Finally, in some cases, private financing may be difficult to arrange for new or risky ventures, or when capital is built in anticipation of growth that may not occur. Government backing of such projects, either directly as owner or indirectly as guarantor, can make it easier to raise the needed funds. This role of government as financial guarantor goes far back into U.S. history. The Erie Canal was the most notable of many such 19th-century state-guaranteed infrastructure projects that proved to be quite profitable. Such a rationale is still valid today in many developing countries, but much less relevant to modern industrial economies such as those of Western Europe and North America.

EQUITY ISSUES: FINANCING INFRASTRUCTURE

Although the federal government does not have a separate capital budget, state and local governments usually separate their capital spending from their operating budgets and borrow for part or all of their capital spending. In addition, states and especially local governments often operate their capital-intensive operations that sell services to citizens as separate **enterprise funds,** so that there is no cross-subsidy in either direction between the enterprise activity and the general fund. For this reason, the primary discussion of financing infrastructure is connected to the state and local sector, although the role of fees and charges is also relevant to federal government infrastructure in some cases (especially parks and museums).

If the primary beneficiaries of new public capital are the residents of the state, county, city, or special district, then equity considerations suggest that those citizens should have primary responsibility for the financing of that capital. However, citizens are mobile, and the citizens who are in a county or school district today are different from those who may be using the facilities in 5 or 10 years. Intergenerational and interpersonal equity considerations suggest that such capital should be financed over its useful lifetime rather than on a pay-as-you-go basis so that future residents who use the capital will also have some responsibility for paying for it. Another alternative to ensure that all users, present and future, pay a fair share of the cost is to institute impact fees, discussed in Chapter 13 and again below.

The trend toward greater reliance on user charges and fees for many public services has also appeared in public sector infrastructure financing. There has been a trend away from general tax financing of infrastructure in favor of identifying beneficiaries and making them pay a reasonable share of the cost. This trend is especially pronounced at the local level because of the property tax revolt.

Many public services that involve infrastructure, such as the police and fire stations and equipment needed to provide fire and police protection, create general benefits in that they meet public option demand. The term **option demand** refers to paying for a service so that it will be there if needed, even if the payer never actually has to use it—somewhat akin to insurance of various kinds. For such services, general tax financing, or debt financing that is repaid out of general tax revenues, is reasonable on both efficiency (controlling demand) and equity (users pay) grounds. Other kinds of services primarily benefit identifiable users (park and recreation facilities) or adjacent landowners (road improvements). Both equity and efficiency considerations support the notion that these direct beneficiaries of services should pay to the extent feasible.

One technique for assigning costs to beneficiaries is by means of special districts whose sole purpose is to fund (and in some cases, maintain or operate) particular kinds of infrastructure. Water and sewer districts have been commonplace for many years, but other kinds have increasingly appeared on the scene in recent decades. Texas has pioneered the use of road districts. Montana uses neighborhood rural special improvement districts. The Denver metropolitan area has a special toll road authority.[2] Such special districts serve some combination of three purposes. First, they can provide residents with some of the benefits, including infrastructure, that come with living in a municipality, without all the additional costs and restrictions. Second, they can allow additional borrowing, and added tax levies to repay that borrowing, when general-purpose local governments have exhausted their borrowing or taxing capabilities.

Finally, special districts can ensure that the cost falls on the primary beneficiaries. Special districts are highly diverse in both purpose and financing.

2. *Financing Infrastructure: Innovations at the Local Level* (Washington, DC: National League of Cities, 1987).

Some are entirely tax financed (typically districts providing roads, neighborhood parks, streetlights, and beautification), while others are almost entirely financed by user fees (districts providing water and sewer) as well as intermediate cases that use multiple financing sources. What these special districts have in common is a responsibility for providing a particular kind of infrastructure to serve a defined area.

Impact fees on developers, special assessments for improvements, and tax increment financing are increasingly commonplace ways to finance improvements that benefit a particular property, neighborhood, or other defined area. New residents require not only extension of water and sewer lines but also more police cars, fire substations, and public parks. Impact fees cover the additional capital costs imposed by developing vacant lots or adjacent tracts. Special assessments are more likely to pay for infrastructure improvements to serve already developed lots. Tax increment financing seeks to capture the additional property tax revenue from the increase in property value that results from infrastructure improvements and then dedicates that revenue stream to paying the capital costs.

Financing infrastructure through such methods that assign costs to beneficiaries offers at least a partial solution to the problem of measuring and valuing the output of public sector capital, at least that part of the value that is attributable to capturable private benefits. Social benefits must be measured in other ways, such as reduction in congestion or air pollution as a result of an additional investment in public transportation.

In the 1960s and 1970s, a significant source of funding for state and local infrastructure was the federal government in the form of grants, especially for water and sewer projects and public housing. Today that source of revenue is greatly diminished. Although federal aid for infrastructure could be defended as a form of fiscal equalization, it has not been a very efficient method. Fiscal equalization can be achieved by other methods that more effectively target poor states and poor individuals.

Innovations in Infrastructure Financing

The 1980s and 1990s saw a great deal of innovation and experimentation in financing infrastructure. The search for new ways to finance infrastructure was driven by high interest rates in the 1980s, declining federal grants, and pressures of growth on existing infrastructure. Currently popular innovations include public–private partnerships; state guarantees, intermediation, and debt subsidies; and the creation of new quasi-governmental bodies for the sole purpose of developing and financing infrastructure.

Public–private partnerships take many forms. Local governments may contract out a service, letting the contractor finance the infrastructure. Solid waste collection is often provided on this basis. In the 1980s, there was a brief flurry of sale-leaseback arrangements for public sector capital, stimulated by tax loopholes that took advantage of tax-exempt municipal borrowing.[3] That option has become less attractive since federal tax reform limited the tax benefits of such arrangements. Limited use has also been made of equity financing (complete or partial ownership by a publicly traded private corporation) of public sector capital that generates a revenue stream from user fees, such as sewage treatment plants and landfills.

States have assumed some responsibility for helping local governments finance infrastructure, sometimes with grants but sometimes with help in obtaining loans or issuing bonds at more favorable interest rates. State bond banks and revolving state loan funds are two widely used methods. State guarantees can make it possible for local governments to borrow on more favorable terms. States can pool borrowing requests from many small communities, with or without a state guarantee, to get to a critical mass that reduces borrowing costs. Some states borrow on their own credit and use the proceeds to create credit infrastructure banks that lend to local governments.

Infrastructure and Growth Management

During the 1990s, the population of the United States increased 13.2%. Accompanying that growth was a demand for additional public services and infrastructure to serve that increased population. Unfortunately, most of those additional 33 million people did not conveniently locate themselves in areas with unused capacity in sewer treatment, water purification and distribution, landfills, schools, highway transportation, recreation facilities, and other public amenities. Some areas lost population and found themselves with excess capacity in public sector capital (schools, jails, sewer systems) and without the population and revenue base with which to service the debt incurred to acquire that capital. But growing areas also found that more people, more jobs, and more development were not an unmixed blessing. Population growth puts pressure on existing infrastructure and creates demand for more infrastructure as well as more spending for operation and maintenance of existing infrastructure. Population growth also should generate more revenue to pay for capital spending and operations and maintenance, but there is not necessarily a one-to-one correspondence between the revenue and expenditure streams. And congestion, with increasing average and marginal costs, can make the challenge even harder.

The first challenge posed by growth is that the local revenue system may not be well suited to generating the additional revenue to support the costs of additional local public services. Many local governments still rely on the property tax as their main source of revenue. Infrastructure must be in place before it is possible to build commercial facilities, apartments, and housing

---

3. In a sale-leaseback arrangement, a local government sells a public building to a private firm and then leases it back. Some of the income tax deductions associated with the building, which had no value to the local government, were then available to the private firm to reduce the overall cost.

subdivisions, but there is often a lengthy lag before the new construction actually contributes to the property tax.[4]

The second challenge posed by growth is congestion, an issue addressed earlier in Chapter 13. Although some of the population has dispersed to less densely populated areas that still have unused capacity in water, sewer, highways, and schools, the tendency is for people to cluster in growing areas where the marginal cost of serving additional people is rising more sharply. Because locational decisions are made by citizens (and developers) without reference to such external costs, the population is distributed in ways that are economically inefficient for purposes of public service delivery. This distribution is not merely a question of clustering in urban centers and along the coasts, but also a matter of optimum density to make the best use of public transportation, schools, roads, garbage pickup routes, police and fire protection, and other services that require an investment in public sector capital.

Neither of these problems is insurmountable. Special assessments, impact fees, and other growth management tools can help to ensure that revenue is adequate.[5] Those tools are often complemented by various regulatory tools (subdivision regulations, zoning, etc.) in an attempt to steer developers and new residents into patterns of location and density that are easier to serve and that minimize the congestion impact on existing facilities.

The methods used to finance infrastructure have an important role to play in growth management as well as in ensuring intergenerational and interpersonal equity. An optimal financing mixture will not only distribute the burden fairly among current users but also between current and future users, while at the same time offering positive and negative incentives to different types of development and choices of locations that minimize the congestion externalities that new residents impose on existing residents and on one another.

State and Local Borrowing

State and local governments borrow for three primary purposes: capital financing, short-term needs, and emergencies. Long-term borrowing for capital financing spreads the cost of acquiring land, buildings, and facilities over the useful lifetime of the capital project. Borrowing also distributes the burden of payment among taxpayers more equitably than putting the entire burden on those who happen to live there at the time the facility is acquired or constructed. At the local level, short-term borrowing is often used to adjust revenue, which comes in unevenly, to expenditure demands, which are more likely to be a level flow throughout the year. Emergency borrowing addresses natural disasters and other unforeseen contingencies. The emphasis in this section is on long-term borrowing for capital purposes.

---

4. Henry L. Diamond and Patrick F. Noonan, *Land Use in America*, (Cambridge, MA: Lincoln Institute of Land Policy, 1996), p. 35.
5. See Chapter 13.

Public sector capital is most often financed through capital markets by the issuance of bonds, which are a way to borrow. A bond is a transferable claim to repayment of the principal with interest at a time and interest rate stated on its face. State and local governments enjoy the advantage of offering bonds whose interest is exempt from federal income taxes.

Some bonds are **general obligation bonds,** backed by the full faith and credit of the issuing government, while others are **revenue bonds,** with the revenue from the sale of services pledged to service the debt. Historically, the former type of debt instrument has been used for public infrastructure that does not generate a revenue stream and the latter for those that do. School buildings, jails, police stations, and city halls do not directly generate revenue, but an identifiable revenue stream from college dormitories, stadiums, toll roads, water and sewer systems, and parking garages can be pledged to service the debt.

States, cities, counties, and school districts borrow in the municipal bond market at favorable rates because the interest income on these bonds is exempt from federal income taxes (and usually from state income taxes in the issuing state as well). For bondholders in higher income tax brackets, the after-tax return on a municipal bond can be very attractive relative to other forms of investment. Demand for such bonds drives their prices up and their yields down so that after-tax yields are roughly equivalent across all financial instruments. After the dust has settled, most municipal bonds will be held by higher income individuals attracted by the tax break, while nonprofit organizations, lower income households, pension funds, and other institutional investors for whom the tax break has no value will concentrate their holdings in other kinds of financial investments.

The **taxable equivalent yield** on a municipal bond is a fairly simple calculation. If R_m is the annual interest rate in percent on a municipal bond, and t is the marginal tax rate facing the bondholder, then to provide an equivalent after-tax yield, a corporate bond whose interest is not tax exempt would have to offer an interest rate of R_c:

$$R_c = R_m \times (1 + t) \ .$$

Alternatively, the taxable equivalent yield on a municipal bond relative to a corporate bond of equal risk rating and maturity would be

$$R_m = R_c / (1 + t) \ .$$

For example, if the current rate on a corporate bond of similar maturity and risk was 8%, and the bondholder was in a combined federal and state tax bracket of 38%, the taxable equivalent yield would be 0.08/1.38 = 0.058 or 5.8%. Any municipal bond yielding more than 5.8% would be attractive to this bondholder. If, however, the bondholder were only in the 30% bracket,

SPORTS STADIUMS: A CASE STUDY IN PUBLIC CHOICE

The last 15 years have seen an explosion of sports facilities built in large and medium sized cities to accommodate football, baseball, and basketball teams as well as other sports. Most of these stadiums and arenas are built with some infusion of local (and sometimes state) public funds, to the tune of about $10 million per facility per year. Even the federal government is contributing indirectly, because many of these facilities are financed at least in part with municipal bonds, the interest on which is exempt from federal income taxes.

Why do cities contribute so heavily to the support of a private, for-profit enterprise? What are the perceived benefits to the city, and how are citizens who may never go to a ball game persuaded to kick in their share of the cost? The burgeoning field of sports economics has attempted to provide some answers to these questions.

The major sports leagues (baseball, football, and basketball) have monopoly power that is protected by a federal antitrust exemption. These leagues determine how many teams there will be and where new franchises will be granted. Teams can always threaten (and sometimes follow through!) to relocate if the local community is not supporting them satisfactorily with either subsidies or attendance. Municipalities want sports teams for a variety of reasons, some sounder than others. Objective studies that attempt to measure the economic impact of sports teams find that the direct, measurable impact on the local economy's income and jobs is quite modest.[1] The fiscal impact is likely to be negative, in part because of the subsidies that municipalities now routinely provide to construction, in part because many of the stadiums and arenas are built on prime, municipally owned land that is lost to the property tax base. There may be some positive effects that are difficult to quantify. The availability of the park as a recreational opportunity may enhance tourism or may increase citizen satisfaction as a resident of a metropolitan area with a full range of recreational and cultural facilities. The national exposure from televised games may enhance the city's visibility and image. With the seemingly modest benefits, then, why do cities routinely cave into pressure to offer or enhance subsidies to team facilities to attract new teams or retain existing footloose ones?

The answer is a case study in public choice. The immediate public benefits are highly visible: a new stadium, sometimes a new team, usually new economic activity in the area immediately around the stadium (although perhaps at the expense of economic activity elsewhere in the city). The costs are spread over a number of years and a number of citizens. Noll and Zimbalist point out that a stadium with a $250 million construction subsidy and a population of 5 million will incur per capita capital costs of $50 million, or about $5 per resident over the life of the bond financing.[2] The benefits are concentrated, accruing to the owners and the players in the form of profits and higher salaries. It is in the interests of the team's owners and players to take advantage of their monopoly position to extract as many concessions as possible from the local government in order to maximize their own potential economic gain.

In a situation that pits competing local governments against a national sports monopoly, some politicians for federal intervention have called to restore the balance of power. Suggestions have ranged from disallowing the federal tax exemption on local revenue bonds used for financing sports stadiums to federal guidelines on stadium financing. But with the powerful hold of televised team sports on the American public, federal action is not likely. Some municipalities have balked at the demands from sports teams. Cleveland lost the Cleveland Browns to Baltimore when, backed by taxpayer anger, the city refused to comply with the team's demands in the 1990s, although they have since received an NFL expansion team. Some larger communities, mindful that they too have monopoly locational power in terms of the size of their potential attendance and support base, have learned to negotiate more acceptable terms. The increasingly visible difference between promised

(continues)

SPORTS STADIUMS: A CASE STUDY IN PUBLIC CHOICE (CONTINUED)

revenue streams and economic impact and the postconstruction economic reality in other cities has also strengthened the hand of local governments in reducing the subsidy to sports facilities. As long as Americans are hooked on professional sports, however, taxpayers (sports fans or not) can expect to be subsidizing these teams through their tax dollars for the foreseeable future.

1. Roger G. Noll, Roger G. and Andrew Zimbalist, eds., *Sports, Jobs and Taxes: The Economic Impact of Sports Teams and Stadiums* (Washington, DC: Brookings Institution, 1997); see especially Chapters 2 and 3.

2. *Ibid*, p. 58.

then a municipal bond would have to offer 6.15% to be as attractive as a corporate bond of similar maturity and risk (0.08/1.3).

Several factors enter into the interest rate that a government must pay on its bonds. Maturity is one factor; the longer the time period, generally the higher the interest rate. But the most important consideration is the evaluation by a bond rating service of the local government's likelihood of repayment of principal and interest in a timely manner. This rating is based on the local government's past track record with debt service as well as its fiscal practices, its reserves, and its tax base, all of which are evidence of ability to repay. In addition, interest rates are different between the two primary kinds of government debt, general obligation bonds and revenue bonds.

Kinds of Debt

State and local governments issue both general obligation bonds and revenue bonds. In 1996, state and local governments had $1.17 trillion in outstanding debt, of which $1.15 trillion was long-term debt. General obligation debt was about 35% of total state and local government debt, with nonguaranteed debt (mostly revenue bonds) making up the lion's share of state and local borrowing. General obligation debt, normally incurred for capital projects, is funded out of general local revenues, so the cost of such projects is paid by present and future taxpayers over the duration of the borrowing period. Revenue debt is issued for facilities that will generate an income from fees, charges, or memberships, that can be used to repay the debt—for example, a sewer system, a transit system, or a recreational facility. The revenue is pledged to retire the debt, but if the revenue is not sufficient, the general fund is not necessarily at risk for making up any shortfall. Because of this higher risk, revenue debt generally carries higher interest rates than general obligation debt.

Offsetting the drawback of higher interest rates are two significant advantages. First, the use of revenue debt is appealing on equity grounds as a way of shifting to a user-pays basis, but it can be more expensive because of higher interest rates. Second, the use of revenue bonds can create additional capacity to borrow (depending on state law) if a state or local government has run into a statutory debt ceiling with its outstanding general obligation debt.

Interest rates on state and local bonds are closely tied to the general level of interest rates. In 2000, a 20-year, newly issued, highly rated state or local government bond was paying an interest rate of about 6.5%. Interest on debt paid by state and local governments in 1998–99 accounted only for about 4 percent of total outlays.

In the wake of tax and expenditure limitation movements during the last 25 years, many state and local governments are even more limited in their ability to borrow than they were prior to the 1970s. Local governments in particular are often limited by constitutional or statutory law to some maximum amount of general obligation debt. Sometimes the ceiling is absolute; at other times a referendum is required to exceed the statutory or constitutional limit.

Not all government debt is financed by bonds. As noted earlier, one method that is increasingly popular is sale-leaseback or simple leasing agreements for various kinds of public facilities and equipment. Another method is lease-purchase, which is roughly equivalent to the installment-type purchases made by households. Facilities that are leased rather than owned remain on the tax rolls and generate property tax revenue to the local government.

TRANSPORTATION INFRASTRUCTURE

Transportation-related expenditures are one of the oldest activities of government. The success of the Roman Empire was due in no small part to the vast network of roads that the Romans built, maintained, and patrolled in order to link the far-flung empire. Transportation by land, sea, and air has always been a blend of private and public activity throughout most of the world. In the present-day United States, the preferred form of transportation is still the private automobile, but drivers travel almost exclusively on roads that are built and maintained by the federal, state, and local governments and park in both private and public parking lots and garages. Trains run on largely privately-owned rail beds with privately owned rolling stock, but the primary form of passenger transportation, Amtrak, is a public corporation. Privately owned airplanes land and take off at largely publicly owned airports. Municipalities and private companies both operate local bus systems, but most intercity traffic is on privately owned buses. Many major cities in the United States, as well as other parts of the world, have subways or light rail systems to move people around faster and with less congestion and air pollution than private vehicles. Table 17–1 summarizes the major kinds of transportation capital in the United States in 1996.

Transportation is very capital intensive. Roads, airports, parking structures, rail beds, rolling stock, aircraft, port facilities, ships, cars, and trucks are the primary ingredients. Like any capital, they require an initial investment,

Table 17–1
U.S. Transportation
Facilities and Travel,
1996

Type of Transportation	Facilities
Highways	
Total miles	3,919,450
Lane miles	8,177,823*
Interstate	204,740
Noninterstate	7,973,083
Airports	18,345
Public use	5,357
Private use	12,988
Transit	
Commuter rail	6,364
Heavy rail	1,477
Light rail	638
Class I Rail	105,779
Amtrak	25,000

Type of Transportation	Travel Miles
Highway	2,482,000,000
Passenger cars/motorcycles	1,482,000,000
Trucks	182,800,000
Buses	6,500,000
Air	8,335,000
Transit**	3,663,000
Rail	499,000

*Lane miles count a mile for each lane. A mile of two-lane road is two miles; a mile of divided high-
way with four lanes on each side is eight miles.
**Includes motor bus, light rail, heavy rail, commuter rail, trolley, ferry boat, and other commuter or in-
tercity transit.

Source: U.S. Department of Transportation.

they depreciate, and they must be maintained and eventually replaced. For this
reason, transportation provides a useful illustration of the kinds of economic
questions that arise in building and financing public infrastructure.

The government's role in building and maintaining highways and public
transportation is a very large one. In 1999, the federal government spent $43
billion on transportation. In 1996, state and local governments spent $91.7
billion on transportation, including highways, air transportation, ports, parking facilities, and transit subsidies, with almost 90% of that total coming from
state governments. A major source of funding for highways is the gasoline
tax, which provides about 30% of all transportation (highway) funds for state

THE INTERSTATE HIGHWAY SYSTEM

For the private passenger automobile, the most significant change in the last half of the 20th century was the development of the interstate highway system. Approved by Congress in 1944, construction did not begin until 1956, with a target completion date of 1975 and financing to be through the gasoline tax. By 1995, there were more than 42,000 miles of highways, carrying 23% of all roadway traffic, nearly one trillion trip miles a year. New segments are still under construction or in the planning stages. Originally projected to cost $41 billion, the combination of cost overruns and extensions of the system resulted in a total outlay of $329 billion in 1996 dollars over the first 40 years.[1]

The rationale for the interstate highway system was, like many such projects, the benefits in terms of economic growth. National defense was also an important justification, so much so that the system was originally called the National Defense Interstate Highway System. (It was recently renamed the Eisenhower Interstate Highway System in honor of Dwight Eisenhower, who was president when construction began.) The economic benefits consisted of greater mobility of workers, goods, and firms, increased competition and access to resources, and creation of a unified national market. At the time of the system's inception, Europe was in the process of developing its common market, and the interstate highway system was envisioned as strengthening the United States' own internal common market.

At the same time, the creators of the system recognized that the benefits would be spread unevenly among beneficiaries, and attempted to assign the lion's share of the cost to the users through gasoline taxes. Because a larger share of benefits from any given interstate highway accrues to residents of the states where the highways run, state sharing in the cost of operation and maintenance was also an important part of the interstate highway program as it developed. More recently, Congress has given limited authorization to states to use tolls as well as gasoline taxes to collect revenue from users to cover the cost of maintenance and repairs.

Although the interstate highway system has certainly been a contributing factor to a unified national market and to economic growth in general, and has in many instances significantly reduced the opportunity cost of travel in terms of time, some side effects have arisen that were not fully anticipated. The economic growth has been uneven, heavily concentrated along major routes at the expense of other locations that do not have such convenient transportation access. A 1995 *Business Week* cover story identified the 350-mile stretch of I-85 from Atlanta, Georgia, through South Carolina to Greensboro, North Carolina, as the boom belt, a region of those three states with rapid industrial, commercial, and residential growth. Charlotte has become a major financial center, Atlanta is a congested and booming home to a diverse economy, and even the Greenville–Spartanburg area of South Carolina has been able to attract many multinational firms, including BMW. But the benefits of that growth have not spilled over to the poorer regions of the coastal plain of all three states, formerly textile and agricultural regions with large minority populations and more limited interstate access. In urban areas, interstate highway construction has led to the razing of residential and commercial areas downtown and sped the movement to the suburbs of higher income residents and shopping malls. Location incentives have been distorted, resulting in even more unequal access among different groups to transportation to work, shopping, housing, and other amenities.

A second set of impacts fell on alternative forms of transportation. Trucking and bus transportation have largely displaced the railroad as a long-haul passenger and commodity carrier in many industries, in part because truckers get to use public highways at rates that are subsidized even after tolls and gasoline taxes, while railroad companies must maintain (and pay property taxes on) their own roadbeds. Rail transportation might have declined in any case, but it is not clear that efficiency dictated the speed of the decline as

(continues)

THE INTERSTATE HIGHWAY SYSTEM (CONTINUED)

much as the implicit subsidy to road-based transportation.

A final set of issues revolves around the relative efficiency of automobile versus other forms of transportation. The interstate highway system has made private automobiles the least expensive form of transportation for most commuters if they consider only private costs and benefits (including convenience) and ignore such costs as congestion and air pollution (estimated to be as high as three cents per vehicle mile[2]).

Some of the other costs are more difficult to quantify, including the value as time lost due to traffic congestion, public expenditures on traffic control, and the economic and human cost of accidents (motor vehicle accidents are still the ninth leading cause of death). Because drivers consider only private costs, which continue to favor auto-

mobile over public transportation in all but the most congested urban areas (such as New York and Boston), there continues to be an insatiable demand for additional highway construction, as well as more parking facilities, on increasingly valuable urban and suburban land. In response to these concerns, urban and transportation planners have searched for other solutions to urban transportation (including subsidized public transit and ways to internalize more of the externalities caused by private vehicles) that rely less on interstate highways and on private automobiles.

1. Wendell Cox and Jean Love, "40 Years of the US Interstate Highway System: An Analysis of the Best Investment a Nation Ever Made," American Highway Users Alliance, June 1996.

2. Clifford Winston and Chad Shirley, *Alternative Route: Toward Efficient Urban Transportation* (Washington, DC: 1998), Brookings Institution, p. 16.

and local governments. Although expenditures for highway construction and maintenance continue to loom large in government budgets at all levels, in recent years more attention has turned to the use of public transportation systems to alleviate congestion, air pollution, and demand for more costly highways to accommodate growing vehicle traffic.

Urban Mass Transit

Like most aspects of the public sector, urban transportation in the United States does not lend itself to generalizations. The forms of transportation in older, mostly Eastern and upper Midwestern cities, are very different from those of newer cities that developed in the era of the automobile. It is much more difficult to "add" mass transit to an established transport grid (as in the Washington Metro or Atlanta's MARTA system) than to have it develop along with the city, as was more or less the case in Boston's MTA system. Sprawling cities like Dallas, Houston, and Los Angeles lack the concentrations of population and a clearly defined urban center as destination, both of which provide older cities a solid basis on which to design viable public transit systems.

Mass transit, primarily buses and subway or light rail systems, is intended to provide convenient access to various parts of the urban area for those who do not own a private automobile and to encourage those who do own cars to reduce their use of vehicles in the urban area in order to reduce air pollution, congestion, and auto accidents—the three major sources of negative externalities associated with driving cars in urban areas that are not taken into account in drivers' decisions. Mass transit also reduces the pressure to use scarce and valuable urban land for parking lots, making it available for other important uses. A well-designed and heavily used urban transit system can make it easier for workers to get to jobs and consumers to access shopping and other urban amenities, so a transit system can play an important supporting role in urban economic development or redevelopment.

Financing Issues

Because major cities are host to millions of visitors—commuters, business travelers, and tourists from across the nation and the globe—the benefits of their public transportation systems extend far beyond their municipal boundaries and accrue largely to people who are not urban taxpayers. The increasing use of local sales taxes and of payroll taxes based on location of employment rather than residence to finance urban government (including transit) helps to collect some revenue from each of these three groups, especially commuters. But completely local financing of public transportation systems would put too large a share of the cost on city residents, who are not the only primary users of the system and who are often less able to pay than wealthier commuters from the suburbs or travelers from outside the region.

Charging for the use of these transit services is another way to shift the burden to users, but setting appropriate prices is difficult for both efficiency and equity reasons. Setting the price high enough to cover full costs, which might appear to be efficient, will drive many commuters back to their cars, increasing problems of air pollution, congestion, and traffic accidents, because the explicit costs of driving are lower than the full costs including externalities imposed on others. In addition, a high price will reduce ridership on buses, subsidies, and other mass transit, raising the average cost and the fee required to cover that cost—an endless spiral of rising ticket prices and declining use. Setting the price low to encourage ridership, on the other hand, would require a subsidy. In the absence of federal or state aid, low fares would shift the burden of financing the system's operations back to local residents.

Once a desired level of subsidy is determined, based on the perceived external benefits from shifting travelers from private vehicles to public transportation, the issue of what price to charge still remains. Part of the solution to the pricing problem is price discrimination. Private firms use price discrimination as a profit-maximizing tool, setting different prices for different customers based on differences in elasticities of demand by age, income groups, time of day, or other factors that enable them to segregate customers and prevent resale. (The problem of resale means that price discrimination is more common in services than in goods.) But price discrimination has a valid role in public sector pricing as well. Remember that pricing in the public sector can be used to manage demand as well as to redistribute to lower income groups through a higher level of subsidy for their consumption of transportation services. With or without a subsidy to all users, it is possible to provide access for the poor in a fashion similar to that of food stamps—tokens or vouchers could be issued that provide free or reduced-price access to transit).

For public transit, the most important factor in controlling demand is time of day, or the morning and evening rush hours. Charging a higher price for peak periods should encourage users who have some time flexibility to shift to off-peak hours, reducing the number of buses or subway train trips that need to be made to accommodate peak demand and ensuring higher ridership for otherwise low-usage trips. Figure 17–1 shows the demand for services at peak hours and off-peak hours, with rising marginal costs to accommodate peak demand. At a single price P_L, there will be Q_1 riders during nonrush hours and Q_3 riders during rush hour. Charging a peak-load price of P_H will reduce the rush hour demand from Q_3 to Q_2. Presumably some of those riders will find a way to rearrange their schedules, including flextime, so that they can be accommodated in the nonrush hour period at the lower price P_L when there is excess capacity.

Figure 17–1
Peak Period Pricing

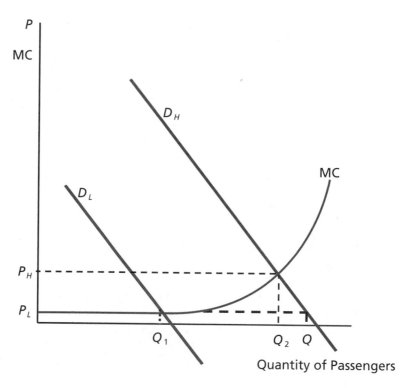

Federal Role

The federal role in providing capital for development of urban transit systems began with enactment of the Urban Mass Transportation Act of 1964. This act led to an increase in publicly owned municipal transit systems from 88 in 1965 to 333 in 1975. This infusion of federal funds slowed the decline in the use of mass transit (bus and light rail) and the inexorable expansion of the number of private cars traveling in or to and from urban areas.[6] Beginning in 1974, federal subsidies were provided for operations as well as for capital assistance. In an effort to encourage ridership through lower fares, aided by federal operating subsidies, urban transit systems began to incur regular operating deficits. By 1997, these systems were generating $10.6 billion in operating revenues against $19 billion in operating expenses (which does not include capital outlays). Buses accounted for 88% ($7.4 billion) of the $8.4 billion operating deficit. Between 1980 and 1997, the federal share of operating costs for urban mass transit fell from 17% to 3%, while the state and local share rose only slightly from 40% to 41%, with the difference made up by increased revenue from fares.[7, 8] This division of responsibility does not necessarily reflect the division of benefits (including externalities) between local residents, state residents, and persons from outside the region, nor does it represent some careful assessment of either interpersonal equity or appropriate sizes of subsidies in order to generate desired levels of usage. The decline in the federal share occurred as part of a more general devolution of responsibilities to state and local governments, spurred by both federal budget deficits and philosophical considerations about constraining growth of government.

WATER AND SEWER SYSTEMS

Most Americans in urban and suburban areas get their water from a public water system. Some still rely on wells, and private water systems exist in many areas; some are for profit, others are organized as cooperatives or as part of a subdivision development. An increasing number of households and business firms are also connected to a sewer system to collect and treat wastewater, rather than the individual septic tanks that were a feature of urban and rural landscapes in the past. Public water and sewer systems are often a municipal responsibility, although they are also operated by counties, special districts, and other government entities. Like transportation, water and sewer systems are capital intensive, and like transportation, water and sewer systems present

---

6. Clifford Winston and Chad Shirley, *Alternate Route: Toward Efficient Urban Transportation* (Washington, DC: Brookings Institution, 1998), pp. 3–4.
7. *Ibid*, pp. 7–11.
8. U. S. Department of Transportation.

pricing and financing challenges. Unlike transportation, however, water and sewer systems tend to benefit primarily local users and are, as a consequence, funded primarily at the state and local level. The federal government had some involvement in developing water and sewer systems in the 1960s and 1970s, but its role today is minimal.

Water and Sewer Financing

States provide assistance to local governments in providing and upgrading water and sewer systems for two reasons. One is that an adequate water and sewer system is an essential precondition for economic development, which is viewed as a state responsibility. Providing poorer regions of the state with the infrastructure needed for economic development is a good long-run fiscal equalization strategy that may make those areas more self-sufficient. The second reason is that the state has a responsibility for water quality that is mandated by the Clean Water Act of 1977. It is easier to monitor and assure quality control for centralized water systems than for wells. Sewer systems, likewise, need to be monitored to protect downstream water from contamination.

In 1996, state and local governments spent $25 billion on sewerage, of which $9.3 billion was for capital outlay. Another $29 million was expended on water supply. While most of the expenditures are recorded at the local level, those expenditures include aid from state to local governments. A major difference between transportation and water and sewer, however, is that revenue covers a very large share of the cost; water and sewer revenues in 1996 of $46 million covered 85% of the cost.

Because water treatment facilities, water storage and distribution lines, sewer collection lines, and sewerage treatment plants are very expensive and have a long useful lifetime, they are almost always financed by borrowing, issuing bonds of up to 30 years' maturity. Water and sewer bonds constitute a substantial share of the municipal bond market. By financing these systems over a number of years, local governments can ensure that all users, present and future, pay a fair share of the cost of the facilities that they use.

Enterprise Funds

Where water and sewer systems are operated by general-purpose local governments (cities, towns, counties, or townships), the most accepted accounting procedure is to segregate the revenues and expenditures into an enterprise fund that is separate from the local government's operating budget. Revenues from water and sewer service are paid into this fund and expenditures made for operations, maintenance, and debt service or capital outlays. If there is a shortfall, the local government may have to subsidize water and sewer service from its general fund. Sometimes local governments make a "profit" (surplus) from water and/or sewer operations, which can be transferred to the general fund to finance other activities. Local governments that serve outlying areas beyond their corporate jurisdiction are often tempted to set rates so as to generate a surplus, so that nonresidents subsidize city residents in that the surplus permits better services for the same taxes or the same services at lower tax rates.

Water and Sewer Pricing

Water and sewer pricing raises some of the same issues as transportation pricing. Opportunities exist for price discrimination in the interest of controlling peak demand and ensuring access for the poor, although peak-load demand is less important in water and sewer than in transportation and electricity. Using prices to control demand reduces the amount of capacity that must be built to serve a given number of households. A common pricing strategy is a two-part tariff: a flat rate for a base number of gallons, such as 1,000, and then an additional per-unit cost for usage over the minimum. The flat rate covers capital costs and "option demand," that is, the privilege of being connected to the system and having access to water as needed. The additional marginal rate for usage above the minimum is usually higher than the short-run marginal cost in order to limit growth of demand, which would require expansion of capacity.

Figure 17–2 shows the pricing structure for such a system and the demand responses of high-income (D_H) and low-income (D_L)users. The pricing structure allows users a base number of gallons Q_0 at a flat rate of P_1. The price charged for usage up to Q_0 is P_1. Low-income households consume

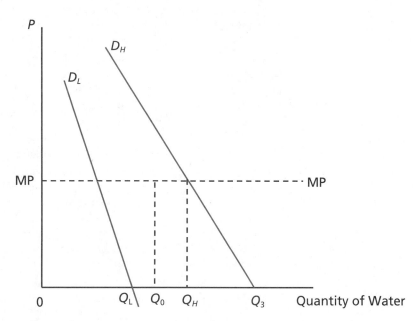

Figure 17–2
Price Discrimination
in Water Supply

quantity Q_L, which is less than Q_0, so they just pay the flat rate. For households consuming more than Q_0, a per-unit charge kicks in at a uniform price MP (some systems use rising prices). Higher income users consume Q_H, where their demand schedule intersects the marginal price. They pay P_1 plus a charge of MP for each gallon over Q_0, and will provide the bulk of the system's revenue. Note that if the flat rate were charged to both sets of both users, high-income households would increase their consumption to Q_3. This pricing scheme ensures access for all households, controls demand, and puts more of the cost on higher income users.

The flat rate for Q_0 may be linked to fixed costs of capital for the system, computed at a per-household level, since the number of households served is a major factor in the treatment capacity and lines invested in by the water authority. With only higher users paying a per-gallon rate, there is a cross-subsidy from higher users (whose demand is likely to be less price elastic) to lower volume users, who may be presumed to be lower income households.

SUMMARY

Infrastructure is public sector physical capital, such as roads, airports, school buildings, water and sewer systems, and parks. Most public sec- tor capital is financed by borrowing, or issuing bonds. Interest on state and local government bonds, called municipal bonds, is generally exempt from federal income taxes.

Much of this capital could be provided by the private sector, so any rationale for public sector capital relies on arguments of market failure. The kinds of market failure cited to justify public sector capital include public goods (low rivalry, low excludability), merit goods, or positive externalities; monopoly characteristics of some kinds of services provided with public infrastructure; or lack of private financing because of risks of various kinds.

Population growth puts pressure on existing infrastructure and creates demand for more infrastructure. Growth does not always generate the necessary revenue to pay for acquiring, operating, and maintaining infrastructure, especially where local governments still rely mainly on the property tax. Growth can also result in congestion, or sharply rising marginal costs, because citizens and developers do not take such external effects into account in making locational decisions. Both of these challenges can be addressed by a combination of regulatory tools and positive and negative tax/fee incentives to distribute population in economically efficient ways.

Financing infrastructure raises issues of interpersonal (rich versus poor, users versus nonusers, etc.) and intergenerational equity (present versus future citizens/users). The federal government has been playing a declining role in financing state and local infrastructure investment, and fees have been of increasing importance. Among recent innovations in financing infrastructure are the use of public–private partnerships, state guarantees and debt subsidies, and the creation of special districts for the sole purpose of developing and financing infrastructure. Impact fees on developers, special assessments for improvements, and tax increment financing are also increasingly used to finance improvements that benefit a particular property, neighborhood, or other defined area.

State and local governments use capital financing to spread the cost of acquiring land, buildings, and facilities over the useful lifetime of the capital project and to distribute the burden of payment equitably among present and future taxpayers. This borrowing takes the form of municipal bonds with a specified maturity and interest rate, with interest exempt from federal income taxes. State and local governments issue both general obligation bonds, backed by the full faith and credit of the issuing government, and revenue bonds, with the revenue from the sale of services pledged to service the debt.

Because of the federal income tax exemption, the interest rate on municipal bonds is lower than on comparable corporate bonds. The taxable equivalent yield on a municipal bond is equal to the nominal yield times $1 + t$, where t is the taxpayer's marginal federal income tax rate. Interest rates are also determined by maturity and by risk, or bond rating. Revenue bonds have become increasingly important, along with sale-leaseback agreements, because many state and local governments are limited in their ability to borrow by constitutional or statutory debt ceilings.

Transportation in the United States is a blend of public and private activity, with a substantial governmental role. Providing transportation is very capital intensive, so borrowing plays an important role in financing transportation facilities. Along with building and maintaining highways, governments at all levels subsidize urban public transit (subways, buses, trolleys, etc.) in order to reduce vehicle traffic, which generates substan-

tial externalities in terms of pollution, congestion, accidents, and traffic control costs. State and federal involvement in funding urban mass transit is justified on the basis of spillover effects, because such transit is used by commuters, business travelers, and tourists as well as local residents. Mass transit attempts to set a price high enough to cover a reasonable share of the operating costs but low enough to make public transit attractive relative to private vehicles. Price discrimination is used to make transit more accessible to the poor and to reduce peak-load demand.

Most Americans in urban and suburban areas get water from a public water system and dispose of wastewater through a local (often municipal) sewer system. Unlike transportation, water and sewer systems tend to benefit primarily local users and are, as a consequence, funded primarily at the state and local level. States provide assistance to local government by providing and upgrading water and sewer systems for reasons of interlocal equity, economic development, and protection of water quality. Water and sewer systems are one of the most frequent reasons for local long-term borrowing.

Where water and sewer systems are operated by general-purpose local governments (cities, towns, counties, or townships), the most accepted accounting procedure is to record revenues and expenditures in an enterprise fund separate from the local government's operating budget. Water pricing raises questions similar to those surrounding transit prices, with price discrimination used to control peak demand and ensure access for the poor. A common pricing strategy is a two-part tariff: a flat rate for a base number of gallons, such as 1,000, and then an additional per-unit cost for usage over the minimum.

KEY TERMS AND CONCEPTS

infrastructure, 367
enterprise fund, 369

option demand, 370
general obligation bond, 374

revenue bond, 374
taxable equivalent yield, 374

DISCUSSION QUESTIONS

1. What are the advantages and disadvantages to a local government of issuing general obligation rather than revenue bonds? What about from the buyer's (lender's) perspective?

2. Suppose that you are in a 27% marginal tax bracket and are trying to decide between a municipal bond with a 6% yield and a corporate bond of equal maturity and risk with an 8% yield. Which one is the better deal? Why?

3. Considering the discussion of privatization in earlier chapters, which parts of the public transportation system do you think most lend themselves to private provision? What are the advantages and disadvantages of privatizing bus and light rail in urban areas?

4. Financing public capital should take into consideration both interpersonal and inter-generational equity. Consider how you might want to finance the construction and operation of a public recreational facility with an expected 30-year useful lifetime and a capacity to serve about 2,000 persons a day in a community of 25,000 people. Would the availability of competing private recreational facilities be a factor in your financing plan?

5. Congestion pricing applies to time of year as well as time of day. The National Park Service operates a number of facilities for which a gatekeeper collects admission at certain times of year, while admission is free at other times. If you were in charge of pricing decisions, how would you decide when to charge admission and when to close the gatehouse and let people enter for free?

CHAPTER 18

WELFARE, SOCIAL SECURITY, AND THE SOCIAL SAFETY NET

One of the most controversial functions of government in a modern market economic system is the redistribution of income and wealth. Chapter 6 noted that just about everything the government does—including collecting taxes and fees, making grants, and providing services—redistributes income or wealth between groups in society. These competing groups are not simply rich versus poor; the gaining and losing groups may consist of owners and workers in different industries, consumers of different kinds of goods and services, owners of different types of property, or individuals in different age cohorts or geographic regions. An entire lobbying industry has grown up in Washington, D.C., and state capitals to either promote redistribution to the groups that support them or at least avoid redistribution away from those groups.

Much of that redistribution is indirect, however. A large share of the federal budget is devoted to a category called "income support" that consists of direct redistribution of funds to individuals. States and some local governments also play an important role in redistribution to individuals. Table 18–1 shows the major categories of direct income support to individuals by all levels of government in 1997, as well as some of the important in-kind transfers for health and social services. Together, these expenditures were equal to almost 14% of personal income. In addition, low-income households received cash benefits from the Earned Income Tax Credit of $27 billion in 1997 (see boxed feature, The EITC Story, later in this chapter).

Table 18–1
Income Support
Programs, 1999

	Dollars (in billions)
Federal	
Income security	247.4
Social Security	409.4
Education, training, employment, and social services	58.3
Health	154.2
Medicare	197.1
Total Federal	1,066.4
State and local	
Public welfare	215.2
TOTAL all levels	1,281.6

Sources: *Economic Report of the President* 2000 Census of Governments 1998–99, U.S. Bureau of the Census.

THE SOCIAL SAFETY NET

In a market system, the normal expectation is that a household will earn its income by making its productive resources available in the marketplace and use that income to purchase the goods and services it wishes to consume. That assumption is valid for most but not all households in any market economy. There will always be households that are unable to earn income because of age, disability, lack of skills, lack of opportunities, or other barriers to working. Others are able to work but cannot earn enough to sustain a decent standard of living. Sometimes the problem is temporary and can be addressed by improving the efficiency of labor markets or by providing unemployment insurance and other programs for periods of high unemployment. But even in robust economic times, some households will be in need of support.

The challenge of a market economy is to ensure that those who cannot earn or cannot earn enough are adequately provided for while at the same time retaining strong work incentives and limiting outlays for support for such households to an acceptable level of expenditure. A system that is too restrictive will leave many people undernourished, badly housed, and without access to essential services such as health care, transportation, and education. A system that is too lavish will have to impose high tax burdens on those who do work in order to support those who do not, creating poor work incentives and inadequate work effort at both ends of the spectrum. A well-designed social safety net must be broad enough to catch those who fall in, but not so attractive as to invite people to jump in.

This chapter addresses two major U.S. social welfare programs, one exclusively federal and one primarily state-supported, that account for most federal and state direct redistribution to individuals—the collection of programs known as "welfare" and the social insurance programs that cover retirees and their survivors and persons with disabilities. Health care through Medicare and Medicaid, which is related to these two programs, is addressed in Chapter 19.

THE EVOLVING SOCIAL WELFARE STATE

From the beginning of modern market societies, the market mechanism has been greatly admired for its efficiency at meeting the wants of consumers, generating rapid response to changing circumstances, and promoting economic growth and higher standards of living. Prominent among the criticisms of a purely market system from the beginning, however, were distributional concerns about both inequality (addressed in Chapter 6) and poverty. Most nations have attempted in some way to soften these rough edges of capitalism through income redistribution.

In the 1930s, a worldwide depression and the aftermath of a major conversion from small town, agricultural economies to an industrial age with population concentrated in large urban centers combined to overwhelm the capacity of local governments to take care of the poor, the elderly, the sick, and others who were unable to earn a living in a market system. Central (and in the United States and Canada, state or provincial) governments became increasingly involved in providing a social safety net. In the United States, the two primary underpinnings of that social safety net were created simultaneously in 1935. One was the Social Security system for those who worked, and the other was the welfare system (Aid to Dependent Children, Aid to the Aged, Aid to the Blind, etc.) for those who were unable to work because of age or other disabilities. With many modifications in the intervening years, these two pillars of the social safety net remained intact in the United States until the 1990s.

The enlarged federal role relative to state and local governments may have been a pragmatic response to necessity, but there is some economic justification as well for locating some of that responsibility at the central level in a federal system. Poorer states tend to have larger concentrations of low-income people with a greater need for assistance and fewer tax resources with which to provide that assistance. If they raise benefits, they have to raise taxes, making them less competitive for attracting or retaining industry and higher income residents. Wealthier states that can afford to offer more generous benefits are hesitant to do so for fear of attracting welfare recipients from other states. This kind of competitive environment is likely to produce less support for the poor than a system where welfare benefits are more uniform and less of a burden on the wealthier citizens of poorer states. If the benefits of anti-poverty programs spill over state boundaries to affect nearby states and even the nation as a whole, then the cost should be shared in a similar manner. All of these reasons offer support and economic justification for the ultimately practical decisions of politicians during the Great Depression who designed and implemented both the welfare system and the social insurance system that are still with us in modified form today.

Welfare reform greatly changed the face of the traditional welfare system in the mid-1990s. Proposals continue to be made and evaluated to make some fundamental alterations in the Social Security system as well. Both of these movements reflect two significant changes. One is the demographic change with a higher ratio of retirees to workers, more working women with young children, and more never-married and divorced women with children. The other is the swing of the philosophical pendulum from the more communal attitudes of reciprocal rights and obligations that characterized public policy in the 1930s through 1960s to a greater emphasis on individual or personal opportunity and responsibility, beginning in the 1970s and continuing through the present day.

WELFARE AND WELFARE REFORM

The term *welfare* in the United States has historically included Aid to the Aged (now part of **Supplementary Security Income, or SSI**), Aid to the Disabled/Blind (now also under SSI, as well as Social Security), General Assistance, and Aid to Dependent Children, later renamed **Aid to Families with Dependent Children (AFDC)**. All of these programs date from the New Deal era. While SSI and Social Security for people with disabilities and retirees took up most of the role formerly played by the first two programs mentioned above, and General Assistance has always been small, the centerpiece of welfare in this country for more than half a century has been the AFDC program.

AFDC was based on the expectation that a typical household would consist of a male breadwinner and a wife/mother whose responsibility was to maintain the home and raise the children. If the male breadwinner was absent, this program would provide for the family, largely widows with children and a few divorced women as well. Over the years, however, the number of female-headed households increased dramatically, the result not only of higher divorce rates but also of more unmarried women (especially teens) having children. More and more mothers of children of all ages and from all economic levels were working outside the home, raising questions about supporting some mothers on welfare with tax dollars from other mothers who placed their children in day care or after-school care in order to support their families. Both of these factors began to erode public support even as the cost of providing assistance rose. In 1960, income security accounted for only 8% of the federal budget; by 1990, that figure had risen to almost 12%.

Economic Incentives

Many economists argued that the system offered strong incentives to choose welfare over low-wage work and strong disincentives for those who left welfare for the labor market. Even though most welfare payments were modest (the average monthly payment to a family of four in 1996 at the beginning of reform ranged from $435 in Mississippi to $833 in New York), that payment was accompanied by Medicaid benefits and food stamps. Mothers who stayed at home did not incur the cost of transportation, work clothes, and day care. Many of the single parents on welfare had limited education and skills and could only hope to qualify for minimum-wage jobs. It would make no sense to commit to a 40-hour week of difficult, often boring, low-paying work when the loss of health insurance and the cost of child care and transportation might well leave the family no better off than before.

The challenge of reform was to identify and encourage those who could be prepared for and supported in a transition to work while continuing to provide assistance to those who were unable to work. There were still many people on welfare with health problems or addiction challenges, people in areas where job opportunities were limited or day care or transportation was unavailable. Any reform needed to recognize that no solution would address all situations, and some provision needed to be made for those who would be unable, at least in the short term, to leave welfare and find a place in the labor market.

Temporary Assistance to Needy Families (TANF)

Powered by both the arguments of economists, the change in expectations for women's labor force participation, the changing mix of families, and the rising cost of welfare, the 1990s saw dramatic changes in the form, nature, and level of assistance to the nonelderly, nondisabled poor. President Clinton was elected on a platform of "ending welfare as we know it," and together with a Republican Congress, made dramatic changes in the welfare system starting in 1996. Even the name was changed to **Temporary Assistance to Needy Families (TANF)**. *Temporary* meant maximum time limits on public assistance for a large share of households, with some exceptions and some discretion granted to states.[1] From matching grants to states to encourage more generous levels of public assistance, the form changed to block grants and the emphasis toward supporting the transition from welfare to work with day care, with retaining eligibility for Medicaid and food stamps, and with training and assistance in job placement. At the same time, the **Earned Income Tax Credit (EITC)**, providing a wage supplement to low-income working families, expanded greatly in the 1990s (see boxed feature, The EIC Story, later in this chapter). In a strong economy with low unemployment rates and a relatively

---

1. States were permitted to exempt up to 20% of their welfare cases on an individual basis.

small cohort of new workers coming into the market, conditions were ideal for getting these hard-to-place workers into the labor market. A final element of the comprehensive program emphasized stronger enforcement of child support obligations by absent parents, mostly fathers.

Results and Evaluation

What has been the outcome of this massive experiment in welfare reform? From January 1994 to January 1999, caseloads were cut in half, from 5 million to 2.5 million. As a result, fewer people received cash support through public assistance than in any year since 1971. Labor force participation by widowed, divorced, or separated mothers with young children rose 20% between 1989 and 1999, and 34% among never-married mothers.

Poverty rates also declined in the 1990s, although the fall in poverty is much less dramatic than the fall in welfare caseloads.[2] Economist Rebecca Blank points to three factors that contributed to this dramatic change. One was the strong economy, with tight labor markets and low unemployment rates, which always reduces poverty rates. A second factor was the change in policy that combined limits on the duration of public assistance with retention of some benefits for those transitioning to work, although it is still too early to have concrete measures of the effect of these changes on both labor force participation and poverty rates. A third factor has been increases in the minimum wage combined with substantial increases in the EITC providing wage subsidies to low-income workers. (EITC is a modest version of the negative income tax proposed in the 1970s by economist Milton Friedman and others).[3]

Researchers at the Urban Institute measured the effects of the various incentives in 12 states on the income of a low-income mother who worked either part time or full time at the minimum wage in 1998. Results vary from state to state because the level of benefits and the rate at which benefits are lost differ. They took into consideration the EITC as well as the retention of Medicaid benefits and child care funding. They concluded that a family moving from welfare to part-time work (20 hours a week) would experience an income gain that ranged from 45% in New York (where welfare benefits are relatively high) to 108% in Mississippi. A further transition to full-time work (35 hours) at the minimum wage would result in an average increase in income of 20% in the 12 states surveyed in response to a 75% increase in hours worked. An increase in the hourly wage for that full-time worker from $5.15 (the minimum wage in 1998) to $9, a 75% increase, likewise resulted only in a 20% increase in family income.[4]

2. Rebecca M. Blank, "Fighting Poverty: Lessons from Recent History," *Journal of Economic Perspectives*, 14(2) (Spring 2000): 4–6.
3. *Ibid.*, pp. 5–16.
4. Norma B. Coe, Gregory Acs, Robert I. Lerman, and Keith Watson, "Does Work Pay? A Summary of the Work Incentives Under TANF," *New Federalism, Issues and Options for States*, Number A-28 (Washington, DC: Urban Institute, December 1998).

In 1999, the National Conference of State Legislatures collected and summarized reports from eighteen states that tracked what happened to recipients after they left welfare. Among the findings that emerged from these studies are these[5]:

- Between 50% and 70% of former welfare recipients are working (the lowest rate was Mississippi, at 35%) at jobs paying between $5.50 and $7.00 an hour. In at least some states, it was found that former welfare recipients are staying in jobs and earning higher wages over time.
- Most families who left AFDC or TANF continue to receive food stamps, child care, and Medicaid. About one-fifth to one-third return to welfare within several months.
- Child care and transportation or family members with a disability continue to be major obstacles to working for many families.

These results are considered generally positive. Proponents of this program feel that their expectations about breaking the intergenerational pattern of dependence have been fulfilled. However, the challenges facing former recipients who are not working or who work but remain in poverty remain an issue of concern.

Prospects for the Future

Because this dramatic change in welfare took place under optimal conditions of low unemployment and steady economic growth, some poverty researchers are concerned about whether the gains in employment and poverty reduction can be sustained into the future. Certainly welfare caseloads, already at dramatically reduced levels, are not likely to fall much further, because those who have remained on welfare since TANF are the ones who are most difficult to place in employment. Many of them suffer from various disadvantages—medical, personal, or geographic—that make employment more challenging. Some of the remaining welfare cases are simply not employable at all. Recognition of the fact that there will always be some persons who must remain on welfare was the justification for exempting up to 20% of a state's welfare caseload in the TANF legislation.

A larger concern is what happens if the economy hits a recession. The welfare-to-work employees are the most recently hired and the least skilled and experienced and therefore are those whose new jobs are most vulnerable in a downturn. Some of them are covered by unemployment insurance, another transfer program that is a shared federal–state responsibility financed by a payroll tax, but many are not. Unemployment insurance benefits are usually exhausted long before the end of a recession.

---

5. Jack Tweedie *et al.,* "Tracking Recipients After They Leave Welfare," National Conference of State Legislatures, August 1999.

THE EITC STORY

Even before welfare reform, harking back almost 30 years is a little-known provision of the federal income tax that provides a refundable credit for low-wage workers. Refundable means that workers receive the money even if they pay no federal income taxes. In 1999, a family with two children could qualify for up to $3,816. As income rose above that level, the credit was phased out, disappearing completely at $30,580. Single-person households and childless households were also eligible for more limited benefits. In 1998, the cost of this tax expenditure to the federal government was $2.2 billion. EITC is replacing AFDC/TANF as the primary form of federal aid to low-income households, but it is aimed only at working households rather than households on public assistance. In addition to the federal program, 15 states also offer some form of earned income tax credit.

The EITC is a modified form of the negative income tax, a proposal that was popular among economists in the 1960s and 1970s. The basic design challenge for a negative income tax, which was originally intended to replace welfare entirely, is to set an acceptable rate for minimum income (benefit to those with no earnings), a rate of decline of benefits as household income rises (the marginal tax rate), and the crossover income level at which all benefits are phased out and the recipient becomes a positive taxpayer. When two of these numbers are determined, the third one is automatically set. For example, if the minimum

guaranteed income for a family of four is set at $10,000, and the benefit loss rate is 25% as income rises from zero, then the crossover income level becomes $40,000. Each of these numbers has problems. If the minimum guaranteed income is too low, large numbers of people will remain below the poverty level. If the crossover income is set too high, the government will face a severe revenue drain. If the benefit loss rate is too high, there is a severe disincentive to work and earn more for low-income households.

The EITC addressed several of these issues in its design. By limiting the program to households with earned income, EITC was decidedly less expensive than a broader negative income tax. Instead of losing benefits as members of the household begin to earn income from paid employment, earnings are initially supplemented by additional EITC credits of 40 cents per earned dollar, up to a maximum of $3,816 on earnings up to $9,400 in 1999 for a family with two or more children. Once a family's earnings exceed $12,460, the maximum credit starts to be phased out at a rate of 21 cents per additional dollar, with the credit ending at an earned income of $30,580. Figure 18–A shows the schedule of benefits in 1999.

This credit is designed to relieve poverty, redistribute income, and provide work incentives. Together with TANF, the EITC has made an important contribution to the reduction in welfare rolls and the increased number of labor force par-

SOCIAL SECURITY

Social Security is the basic pension system that covers almost all working Americans and provides them with a pension when they retire at age 62 or later. This system was created during the depths of the Great Depression, in 1935, and the first check was awarded in 1939. Initially Social Security was only a pension system. In 1939, survivor benefits were added to provide income for dependent widows and widowers and children under 18 (or to age 22 if in college, a benefit that has since been eliminated), and the program became known as OASI (Old Age and Survivors' Insurance). In 1950, benefits

(CONTINUED)

Figure 18–A
EITC Credit, 1999

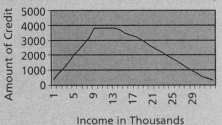

Income in Thousands

ticipants in the last five years. At the same time, the cost of the program to the federal government is expected to increase more slowly than the growth of the economy, including inflation.

While the subsidy range up to an income of $8,900 provides a work incentive, the phaseout period for incomes of $11,600 and higher creates a disincentive, which is the reason why the phaseout rate is lower than the subsidy rate. However, added to Social Security taxes of 7.6% and a federal marginal income tax rate of 15%, a worker in the $12,000 to $30,000 income range would be facing a combined marginal tax rate of 42.6%, not including any state income taxes. In addition, other benefits are phased out at different rates for those transitioning from welfare to work. Fortunately for work incentives, the EITC benefit is increasing over the income range from $0 to $12,000, where benefits to former welfare recipients for food stamps, child care, and

Medicaid begin to be phased out. While the benefit loss is at higher income levels, however, almost 60% of the benefits still go to households in the $10,000 to $20,000 income range.

Research studies confirm that the EITC has been an important incentive for single parents to enter the labor force. It also is a major contributor to reducing poverty among children. EITC is one of the few factors countering the trend toward greater income inequality and toward declining real incomes among families in the lowest two quintiles (fifths) of the income distribution.[1] Work is the ultimate antipoverty strategy for those able and willing to work. Many entry-level workers are paid at the federal minimum wage of $6.15 an hour. For a year-round, full-time worker, that wage translates (at 40 hours a week, or 2,000 hours a year) to an income of $12,300. In 2000, the official poverty threshold for a family of four was $17,050. With EITC, that income would be $15,709, or very close to the poverty threshold. Combined with a wage just moderately higher than the minimum, a four-person household would cross the poverty threshold.

1. Robert Greenstein and Isaac Shapiro, *"New Research Findings on the Effects of the Earned Income Tax Credit,"* Center on Budget and Policy Priorities, March 1998. See also David T. Ellwood, *"The Impact of the Earned Income Tax Credit and Social Policy Reforms on Work, Marriage, and Living Arrangements,"* *National Tax Journal* LIII(4, Part 2) (December 2000): 1063–1105.

for workers with disabilities and at least 40 quarters (10 years) of covered employment were added, and the program became known as OASDI. In 1965, Medicare for those over 65 was added, putting an H into the acronym, so that the program today is known as **OASDHI**—Old Age, Survivors: Disability and Health Insurance. (Medicare is addressed separately in Chapter 19.)

The benefits for these programs are financed by a tax on wages, up to a maximum ($76,200 in 2000). The tax rate is 15.2% of covered wages, which according to law is paid half (7.6%) by the employer and half (7.6%) by the employee. (Self-employed persons pay both halves but receive a deduction for the employer's share.) While this distinction between employer and employee liability is important for federal income tax purposes, the employer's half represents an increase in hourly labor costs. In a competitive market, that increase will be reflected in lower hourly wages and is thus passed on to employees.

As a result, incidence of the Social Security payroll tax in the long run is generally expected to fall almost entirely on the worker. Exactly how the burden of the tax is divided between employer and employee in the short run can vary, depending on the relative elasticities of labor supply and demand in particular markets or occupations. The revenue from the payroll tax (FICA, or Federal Insurance Contributions Act) is deposited in the Social Security Trust Fund, and payments to beneficiaries are paid out of that trust fund rather than the general operating budget of the federal government.

The Trust Fund and the Federal Budget

There is, of course, a connection between the trust fund and the budget. The Social Security Trust Fund has been running surpluses of revenue over expenses and benefits for quite some time. Those surplus revenues are invested in federal government bonds, which is how the U.S. government funds its budget deficits. The trust fund earns interest on those bonds, which is added to the balance of the trust fund. At some point, however, expenses and benefits are expected to exceed revenues for the Social Security Trust Fund, and at that point Congress will have to redeem some of those government bonds in order to provide the resources for Social Security to continue to pay the promised benefits. Such redemption may require higher federal income taxes or other revenues in order to redeem the promises to pay. In the mid-1990s, the surplus was expected to be completely used up by 2029, at which time projected revenue from payroll taxes would be adequate to pay only about 75% of projected benefits. These projections depend on employment, wages, interest rates, and retirement rates over very long periods of time, so they are frequently adjusted. Since that time, a healthy economy and a rising wage base have contributed more revenue than expected, and the projected date of exhaustion has been moved to 2037.

This eventual challenge is made even more complicated by the way in which the federal budget surplus or deficit has been reported since the late 1960s. The reported surplus or deficit is for the unified federal accounts, which includes both the regular operating expenditures and revenues of the federal government and the various off-budget trust funds, of which Social Security is the largest and most significant. For decades the surplus in Social Security has at least partly offset deficits in general government operations, masking the extent to which Congress was authorizing deficit spending. Even the surpluses that have materialized in recent years are overstated, because they include the surplus in the Social Security Trust Fund.

In 2000, the Social Security fund took in revenue of $561 billion, including $60 billion in interest, and paid benefits (including administrative costs) of $402 billion, for a net increase in assets of $152 billion, which was added to the accumulated balance of $550 billion. The system covers 133 million workers and serves 50.8 million beneficiaries, of whom 37.8 million receive retirement and/or survivors' benefits. The ratio of workers to beneficiaries has been declining steadily over the years, and when the large baby boom generation retires starting in 2011 and must be supported by the smaller "baby bust" generation from the 1960s and 1970s, expenditures for retirement benefits will be growing faster than revenues. The worker/retiree ratio is central to the challenge facing Social Security.

Because the Social Security program is so large and impacts so many Americans, it deserves special attention. Most of that attention has been focused on the projections for long-term revenues and expenditures of the social insurance trust funds. Projections in 2000 estimated that by 2022 benefit payments will begin to exceed current taxes and interest, and by 2037 the accumulated surplus will be exhausted. Like any economic projections, these figures are based on assumptions about wage growth (1% a year adjusted for inflation), fertility, longevity, interest rates, marital stability, immigration, labor force participation (especially by women), and unemployment. If wages were to grow at the average rate for the last 50 years (1.7%), for example, then the doomsday scenario is replaced by a system that is in the black for the indefinite future.[6] Other assumptions, likewise, can be wrong. Projections for so long a period and so large a system are very sensitive to even minor adjustments in the assumptions.

What Is Social Security?

Discussions of Social Security often get bogged down in issues relating to Medicare and SSI (Supplementary Security Income), both of which are important; but for the great mass of working Americans, the primary interest right now lies in the old age, survivors, and disability program (OASDI) put in place between 1935 and 1950. This "core business" of Social Security is an intergenerational and interpersonal compact, reflecting both individual and communal values. Every industrial country except Japan has something similar. Japan has a more limited social insurance program and relies more heavily on private savings and families.

The design of the U.S. system reflects the values and the context of the 1930s when it was created. Those values and circumstances include a high value placed on individual responsibility, the importance of earned benefits rather than a "handout," some redistribution, and a labor force in which the norm was that married women did not work outside the home. As a result, OASDI is a hybrid of insurance, pension, and redistribution programs. Like most hybrids, it contains some of the best features of each of those three elements as well as some of the drawbacks of each.

6. Robert Kuttner, "Social Security: If It Ain't Broke, Don't Tinker," *Business Week,* February 22, 1995, p. 22.

The **insurance element** consists of survivors (1939) and disability (1950) programs. Disability is relatively new and much more complex than old age and survivors programs, especially in establishing eligibility. The **pension/ annuity element** is the earliest, and the one most people have in mind when they refer to Social Security. Some of the original discussions when this program was being designed suggest that the system may have been designed so as to protect the middle and upper income classes from the poor. The middle and upper income groups could expect to have to contribute to the support of the elderly poor in their declining years either through charity or through taxes, because this group was not likely to be able or willing to save for their old age out of their meager earnings. So one effect of the Social Security program was to force the working poor to contribute something while they were working.

At the same time, Social Security has a strong **redistribution element** (a much higher ratio of benefits to earnings for lower income earners). The lowest income recipients, or those not covered, receive Supplementary Security Income, a program that replaced Aid to the Aged, some disability, and General Assistance in the 1970s. This program is often confused with Social Security but is in fact a separate program funded by general tax revenues. For workers receiving benefits from Social Security's OA (Old Age) part of the program, workers whose earnings fell at the bottom end of the wage scale receive benefits that replace 90% of preretirement wages.[7] As earnings and social insurance taxes paid rise above the minimum, benefits become a smaller share of the reported earnings base. For the highest income workers, additional dollars earned generate additional benefits of only 15% of the earnings base. From Figure 18–1, it is clear that benefits decline as a percentage of inflation-adjusted average monthly earnings for single workers retiring at the full retirement age, not including any dependent benefits.

An essential feature of the original design of the system was broad coverage, a breadth that has continued to grow as such groups as state and local employees, ministers, self-employed persons, farm workers, and other groups were added to the system over the years. Today there is close to **universal participation** among those employed, a feature that results in two positive benefits: low administrative costs (about 1.5% of benefits paid) and no adverse selection.[8] Those who expect to live to a ripe and healthy old age share the system with those who expect to die young or to be disabled before reaching retirement age.

7. Benefits are 90% of the first $561 of the average monthly wages (indexed for inflation), which are used to compute benefits, plus smaller percentages of average wages over that amount, declining to 15% for the last dollars of average wages for those earning at or near the maximum wage base.

8. Adverse selection occurs when the people who "buy" a particular insurance policy are the ones most likely to have claims. As insurance becomes more expensive, people "self-insure"—they take precautions and do without auto insurance or certain kinds of homeowners' insurance unless required to do so by the state or by mortgage lenders. As these lower cost customers drop out, the average cost rises, making insurance even more expensive for those who remain. Health insurance is particularly careful to avoid adverse selection by refusing to cover preexisting conditions and by emphasizing sales to large groups such as employees of large firms, which are usually a broad mix of low-claims and high-claims clients.

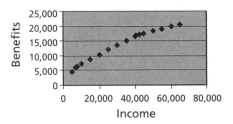

Figure 18–1
Social Security
Benefits versus
Income

PUBLIC PENSIONS IN CANADA AND EUROPE

One advantage enjoyed by Americans is that their demographic challenge in the social insurance system is hitting later than in other parts of the world, especially Canada and Western Europe. Those countries have already had to address the problem of a declining ratio of workers to retirees, combined with much higher unemployment rates than those experienced in the United States in the last decade. Like the United States, the demographic crunch in social insurance in other industrial countries has been combined with budgetary pressures, competitive pressures (the social insurance tax adds to labor costs), and conservative, market-oriented critiques of the existing schemes to pose the question of redesigning the social insurance schemes of 65 years ago for a new era. Some of these countries have implemented various kinds of changes that are being considered for the United States, so it is possible to learn from their experience.

There was a basic similarity between U.S. publicly funded retirement systems and those of other countries prior to recent reforms abroad. Most, like the United States, offer lifetime benefits based on past earnings and are pay-as-you-go rather than actuarially funded programs with benefits based on contributions. Most other countries have had a basic benefit level with some means-tested additions (like SSI) and some earnings-related supplements (like Social Security). However, the U.S. social welfare system differs from those of other industrial countries in some important ways. Compared to Canada and Western Europe, the United States has higher retirement ages, lower benefits relative to past earnings, and lower payroll taxes. Some of these other

systems also give work credit for military service, or for time spent as an unpaid caregiver to children, persons with disabilities, and elderly parents. However, the United States is more generous in one respect. Unlike some other nations, such as Australia, benefits in the United States are an entitlement that is not taken away from the wealthiest citizens (although part of the benefits are taxed for higher income households).

All of these other social insurance systems have undergone some degree of upheaval in the 1990s in response to demographic and economic changes as well as a shift of policies in general to more private sector, market-based solutions to social problems. Policy analyst R. Kent Weaver sorts the responses into program retrenchment, program refinancing, and program restructuring.[1] Program retrenchment has included reducing the indexing of benefits for inflation, increasing retirement ages, restricting eligibility for early retirement, encouraging delayed retirement, reducing benefits to higher income retirees, and recalculating the wage base to include more working years (which reduces the average wage base). These changes are similar to those made in the United States and represent small adjustments that over time can result in substantial costs savings. In addition, a number of countries have taken steps to encourage more use of voluntary private pensions through favorable tax treatment (France, Canada, Australia) or compulsory contributions to private pension plans by employers (Australia, United Kingdom). In the area of refinancing, a few countries have raised their social insurance tax rates, and some countries have begun to invest part of

(continues)

PUBLIC PENSIONS IN CANADA AND EUROPE (CONTINUED)

their social insurance funds in equities to provide faster growth of assets to provide for future beneficiaries (Sweden, Canada). A truly significant change is a trend toward a defined contribution rather than defined benefit plan in Sweden and Germany, which falls under the heading of restructuring.

Relatively few nations have moved far in the direction of an entirely privatized system, in which each person (voluntarily or under mandate) contributes to his or her own pension account, which is managed for his or her retirement and not commingled with the funds of others. Chile has had such a system for 15 years, with mixed reviews, mainly because of the very high administrative cost. Britain has also moved in that direction, as has Australia. Weaver notes that such plans are much more politically acceptable as a supplement to a public pension scheme than as a replacement or substitute.[2] In addition to citizen resistance and administrative cost, there is also a transition challenge of funding those currently retired or approaching retirement who have worked under the existing system while also adequately funding a private, individual account-type system for the current generation of workers.

Britain has made some of the most dramatic reforms, with a three-tier system that offers a standard floor benefit to all financed by a payroll tax, a second tier of benefits that is mandatory but can be provided either through the public sector or approved private programs through the employer or individual retirement accounts, and a third tier of tax-favored retirement savings programs. France and other nations of Western Europe are moving in the same direction with more investment of retirement assets in equities and more emphasis on defined contribution programs.

All of these ideas are being floated in the United States. With a population that is aging more slowly, the United States can take advantage of the experience of other nations to refashion its own public retirement program.

1. R. Kent Weaver, "Insights from Social Security Reform Abroad," in *Framing the Social Security Debate: Values, Politics, and Economics,* R. Douglas Arnold, Michael J. Graetz, and Alicia H. Munnell, eds., (Washington, DC: National Academy of Social Insurance, 1998), pp. 183–283.
2. *Ibid,* p. 225.

Other important design features of OASDHI include the following:

- A **defined benefit program** rather than **defined contribution program.** At one time, most pension plans, public or private, were of the defined benefit form. A defined benefit means that the pension one received after retirement was based on wages and length of service in some combination, and the retiree could expect that same amount—sometimes adjusted for inflation, sometimes not—until death, possibly with some benefit to survivors as well. Public pensions were more likely to have an inflation adjustment than private ones. More recently, many private pension systems and some public ones have shifted to the defined contribution system, where the benefits to the retiree depend on how much is in his or her individual account (contributions plus investment earnings) at the time of retirement and how well that portfolio continues to perform. With a defined benefit program, the risk falls on the employer if the portfolio underperforms, but the employer also gains if the portfolio does well (and many firms have been able to transfer surplus funds from their retirement programs into other uses). With a defined contribution program, the risk of loss and hope of gain are both transferred to the employee/retiree. Many proposals for reforming Social Security would change part or all of the present program from a defined benefit to a defined contribution program.

- The **wage ceiling** or maximum amount subject to Social Security taxes ($80,400 in 2001), which is adjusted annually. The result of having a wage ceiling, combined with covering only wages and not other forms of income, is that this tax is moderately regressive. Figure 18–2 shows the Social Security tax (including the Medicare tax) as a percentage of wages and salaries up to $200,000. Higher earners often also have nonwage income, such as interest and dividends, so that the Social Security tax is an even smaller percentage of their total income.

- The tax rate, which is currently 6.1% for employer and employee for OAS-DHI and another 1.49% each for Medicare. The combined effect is a 15.2% tax on wages, which is relatively high, especially when combined with state and federal income taxes.

- The annual inflation adjustment for benefits, which some critics argue is actually too high (see below).

- The reduction in benefits for retirees who continue to earn above a certain ceiling. The ceiling has been liberalized considerably, so that workers over age 65 are no longer subject to a ceiling. Workers between 62 and 65, however, are subject to a limit ($10,680 in 2001), after which they lose $1 in benefits for every $2 they earn over that limit.

- The marriage penalty for widows and widowers. A widow, for example, who has been collecting 80% of her deceased husband's benefit as a surviving spouse would drop to 50% of her new husband's benefit as a wife rather than a widow if she were to remarry. This last feature is one of several problems related to the differential treatment of spouses (mostly wives) of retired, disabled, or deceased workers versus women who have earned benefits from their own work history. An increasing proportion of women are eligible for either (but not both) types of benefits. As a result, working couples pay more into the system relative to the benefits they may receive than one-earner households.

Figure 18–2
Social Security Taxes as a Percent of Wages

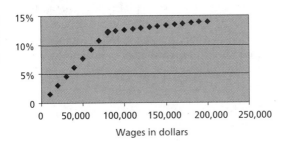

Interpersonal and Intergenerational Equity

Many of the concerns about Social Security can be described as equity issues, relating to interpersonal equity and intergenerational equity. **Interpersonal equity** is often measured as the ratio of lifetime taxes to lifetime benefits. These calculations, which appear in the popular press, are not easy to make; there is no typical earner/recipient, and each person's calculation depends on how long that person lives, his or her earnings pattern, and other factors. A recent issue of the *Social Security Bulletin* reviewed and critiqued various "money's worth" studies that looked at such measures as payback period, benefit/tax ratio, lifetime transfer, and internal rate of return.[9] In making such comparisons it is important to compare apples with apples, considering among other issues the level of risk assumed in the investment mix (it is very low for Social Security Trust Fund investments) and being sure to include administrative costs (also very low for Social Security).

Within age cohorts (people born during the same period), it is estimated that the return is better for couples, women, minorities, and the poor, because women and couples live longer than men and single persons, respectively, and because those with lower average annual wages (including a disproportionate share of minorities) are entitled to benefits that represent a larger percentage of their past earnings. The present value of taxes less benefits is very positive for the lowest income decile, remaining positive up to the middle of the income distribution, and is negative for the top half of the income distribution.[10]

More attention has been paid recently to the issue of **intergenerational equity** in publicly funded retirement. Some critics describe the "pay-as-you-go" nature of Social Security as a sort of Ponzi scheme, with the baby bust generation (1965 onward) subsidizing the generations that preceded them in retirement. Again, looking at age cohorts, researchers found that the earliest cohort examined (1895–1903) earned on average a 12.5% inflation-adjusted return; the 1917–1922 cohort received 5.9%, while the babies born in 1995 are projected to receive a 1.5% inflation-adjusted rate of return. All of these figures compare favorably to a long-term 0.6% inflation-adjusted return on government bonds.[11]

One important consequence of Social Security has been reduced poverty among the elderly. More than half of those current elderly receive more than half of their income from Social Security. Among current workers, about one-half are covered by a pension plan; the others, apparently, are depending on Social Security to provide for their old age. What will happen to the benefits for the elderly and the rates paid by active workers down the road? Again, there is no simple answer: It depends on fertility, longevity, earnings

9. Dean R. Leimer, "A Guide to Social Security's Money's Worth Issues," *Social Security Bulletin* (Summer 1995): 3–14.
10. David Pattison, "The Distribution of OASDI Taxes and Benefits by Income Decile," *Social Security Bulletin*, Spring 1995, p. 21–32.
11. *Ibid.*

growth, interest rates, marital stability, immigration, labor force participation, and unemployment.

Proposals for Reform

The following is a brief summary of some of the reform proposals currently under consideration, most of which focus on the pension component of the program:

1. *Delinking Social Security from the budget.* The reported deficit should not count the net revenue of the Social Security Trust Funds against the operating deficit. This solution makes the challenge of balancing the federal budget much more difficult politically. Recent surpluses have made it a little easier, but if deficits recur, they will be larger and more visible without adding in Social Security Trust Fund surpluses. From the citizens' standpoint, however, such a change will make clearer the extent to which Social Security surpluses are being used for current non-Social Security spending.

2. *Cap the cost of living adjustment (COLA).* There is some evidence that the Consumer Price Index currently used to adjust benefits is overstating inflation, and particularly the impact of inflation on the elderly, because of the strong role of housing and medical costs in the index. Many of the elderly are not affected by the rising costs of buying new homes, because they live in homes that are paid for, and much (but not all) of their medical expense is covered by Medicare. Proposals for change include a lower inflation adjustment or linking the annual adjustment to growth in wages rather than in prices.

3. *Change the assumptions.* Congress and the executive branch of the federal government cannot even agree on what economic assumptions should underlie projections of the budget surplus or deficit over periods of up to 7 years. For Social Security, projections are much longer, and the projected problems in Social Security come in a period some 23 to 33 years hence. These projected revenue shortfalls in the 2020s and 2030s are crucially dependent on assumptions about wage growth, fertility, labor force participation, and immigration. It only takes very small adjustments in some of these assumptions to make the system viable. Perhaps the cries of disaster are premature.

4. *Adjust the age for eligibility.* With longer life spans, retirees are collecting much longer. In addition, more workers are opting to collect reduced benefits (80%) at 62 rather than full benefits at age 65. When Social Security began, the average worker was only expected to collect for a few years after retiring at 65. Recent changes adjusted the age of eligibility for full benefits upward, beginning with the 1940 birth cohort, so that workers born from 1940 on must work past 65 to collect full benefits and will receive less than 80% if they retire at age 62.

5. *Reform or delink other components of the system.* Components to consider include disability eligibility and Medicare. Some argue that Social Security is bearing too many unrelated responsibilities and should be pared back to its "core business"—a form of downsizing or reengineering. Generally, proponents of this reform are not arguing that those other components should be scrapped but that they involve other issues and should be separated and treated differently.

6. *Reconsider treatment of employed versus not employed women.* Because the payroll tax includes payments for survivor benefits, it can be argued that married couples pay twice, but can only collect once. Widows can collect either on their own earnings record or 80% of the benefit that would have been received by their deceased husbands; retired wives, likewise, can collect full benefits on their own records or 50% of their husbands' benefits. This issue will eventually self-correct as women being employed outside the home becomes the norm rather than the exception. In the interim, it is important not to penalize those who got caught in a values revolution.

7. *Increase the wage base.* The wage ceiling has gone up, but the existence of a ceiling means that the fringe benefit cost does not continue to rise beyond a certain point. As a result, the tax is somewhat regressive. In fact, the Social Security payroll tax is the biggest single tax burden for the working poor. Broadening the base would raise more revenue, and make the tax more equitable.

8. *Change the investment mix.* Some reformers would like to see at least part of the trust fund's $550 billion in assets invested in equities, for two reasons. First, the fund should experience greater growth, although at some cost in terms of risk and management expense. Second, this change would help to delink the trust fund from any budget deficit, since the Social Security surplus would no longer be invested entirely in Treasury securities.

9. *Make the system private and/or voluntary.* Republican presidential candidate Barry Goldwater suggested this idea in 1964, and his campaign never recovered from the backlash! Today, a significant number of public figures, including President Bush, are in favor of some degree of privatization, although most advocate partial rather than total privatization. Partial privatization proposals range from investing some of the assets in stocks (above) to allowing individuals to own and manage their own accounts.

If participation remained mandatory, privatization would create a need for monitoring and supervision, in light of a history of private sector problems. Some private pensions did not fulfill their commitment to employees, and many elderly citizens have been victims of unscrupulous investment advisors. Making the system entirely voluntary might also result in many of the poor opting out in order to provide for immediate consumption. Either privatization or voluntarism would reduce or eliminate the insurance and redistribution elements of the Social Security retirement program, limiting its role to being just another pension provider. None of these problems presents insuperable obstacles to making such changes, but they are real concerns that would have to be addressed in some way.

Social Security in Twenty Years

What is the likely future of Social Security? For today's average 30- to 50-year-old worker, benefits are likely to be lower in relation to income than they were for older workers, but the program will be there, still financed largely by a dedicated tax on earnings of some kind, still favoring lower income workers over higher income workers. Part of the trust fund will probably be invested in the economy, in equities and corporate bonds, to provide diversity and growth and to unlink Social Security from the broader question of the budget. The people paying into the system will be different: more women, more minorities, more recent immigrants. Women are more likely to be eligible only on their own accounts, with the few surviving spouses with no earnings of their own shifted to SSI. This change will mean a decline in the survivors' component of the program, in order to focus on the core responsibilities of retirement and disability.

SUMMARY

Market-based economic systems normally make some provision for supporting those who are unable to earn an income because of age, disability, lack of skills or job opportunities, or other factors. Income support or income security programs account for about 14% of federal spending. Expenditures on assistance to needy families have declined in recent years but expenditures for Social Security programs for the elderly, those with disabilities, and survivors of beneficiaries have continued to expand.

Both Social Security and "welfare" (primarily Aid to Families with Dependent Children) originated in the United States in the 1930s as the federal government took over from state and local governments a larger share of the cost of supporting those unable to support themselves through earnings.

Welfare reform and proposals for Social Security reform in the United States in the 1990s were a response to demographic changes (growing numbers of working women with young children and never-married and divorced women, and a higher ratio of retirees to workers). Reforms and proposed reforms also reflected a change in attitudes with greater emphasis on individual or personal opportunity and responsibility.

Historically, welfare has included Aid to the Aged (now part of Supplementary Security Income, or SSI), Aid to the Disabled/Blind (now part of SSI and Social Security), General Assistance, and Aid to Families with Dependent Children (AFDC), which was the largest program, covering single-parent households with children under 18.

AFDC was criticized because the incentives encouraged people to choose welfare over low-wage jobs. The primary challenge of reform was to identify and encourage those who could be prepared for and supported in a transition to work while continuing to provide assistance to those who were unable to work because of health problems, lack of access to day care or transportation, or other factors. In 1996, AFDC was replaced by Temporary Assistance to Needy Families (TANF), with time limits on eligibility for public assistance and support for the transition from welfare to work with day care, continuation of Medicaid and food stamps, and training and assistance in job placement. The Earned Income Tax Credit (EITC) provided an expanded wage supplement to low-income working families. With a healthy economy, welfare rolls dropped dramatically, and the poverty rate also declined.

Social Security provides retirement income for most working Americans retiring at age 62 or later as well as survivors' and disability benefits. The benefits for these programs are financed by a payroll tax. The incidence of both the employer's share (7.6%) and the worker's share (7.6%) of the Social Security payroll tax is believed to fall almost entirely on the worker in the form of lower net wages in the long run. Revenue from the payroll tax is deposited in the Social Security Trust Fund, and payments to beneficiaries are paid out of that trust fund. Presently the trust fund is invested in government bonds, but sometime in the next three decades benefit payments are expected to exceed revenues (including interest) and the trust fund will eventually be exhausted, largely because of a growing ratio of retirees to workers. This projection has led to a number of proposals for reform in order to ensure that benefits can be continued.

The primary Social Security program, retirement pensions, consists of three elements: insurance, pension/annuity, and redistribution. The insurance element provides for dependent survivors, the pension program provides a guaranteed floor or base income for most elderly Americans, and the redistribution gives larger payments relative to past earnings to lower income workers than higher income workers. Nearly universal participation and a simple investment strategy have kept administrative costs very low.

Important features of the present Social Security program include a defined benefit rather than defined contribution plan, a ceiling on the amount of wages subject to the payroll tax, an annual inflation adjustment in benefits, reduced benefits for early retirement, reduced benefits for retirees who earn over a certain amount in wages, and differential treatment of dependent spouses versus those (mostly women) who are entitled to benefits based on their own earnings.

Evaluation and reform of Social Security raise difficult questions of intergenerational equity (benefits relative to taxes paid are higher for current retirees than future retirees) and interpersonal equity (benefits relative to taxes paid for men versus women, low-wage versus high-wage earners, etc.). Social Security has significantly reduced poverty among the elderly.

Proposals for "rescuing" or reforming Social Security include delinking Social Security from the federal operating budget, capping the annual cost of living adjustment, revising the assumptions on which projections are based, increasing the age of eligibility for full benefits, reforming nonretirement elements of the system, rethinking the treatment of employed versus not employed spouses (usually women), increasing the wage base subject to tax, broadening the investment mix to include equities, and making the system partly or completely private and/or voluntary.

KEY TERMS AND CONCEPTS

Supplementary Security
 Income (SSI), 392
Aid to Families with
 Dependent Children
 (AFDC), 392
Temporary Assistance to
 Needy Families (TANF),
 393

Earned Income Tax Credit
 (EITC), 393
OASDHI, 397
insurance element
 (OASDHI), 400
pension/annuity element
 (OASDHI), 400
redistribution element
 (OASDHI), 400

universal participation, 400
defined benefit program,
defined contribution
 program, 402
wage ceiling (OASDHI), 403
interpersonal equity, 404
intergenerational equity, 404

DISCUSSION QUESTIONS

1. If you were an employee, would you prefer a defined benefit or a defined contribution retirement plan? Why?

2. A social welfare system, in order to control expenditures and ensure that all those
who are able to do so work for a living,
must offer both positive and negative incentives to potential welfare recipients.
How did the reforms in the 1990s change
the incentives under TANF (and EITC)
compared to AFDC? What kinds of incentives to work (or not work) are there
for people age 62 and older in the United
States?

3. This chapter identified a number of proposed reforms to the Social Security system in order to ensure that it will be able
to continue to pay benefits into the indefinite future. Evaluate the following proposed reforms to Social Security in terms
of intergenerational equity, cost, risk, free-

dom of choice, and any other criteria that
you think are important:

a. Raising the age for eligibility for retirement benefits

b. Investing the trust fund partially in
equities

c. Adjusting the cost of living adjustment

4. Suppose that the subsidy rate for EITC was
30 percent instead of 40 percent, and the
loss rate was 15 percent instead of 21 percent. On the basis of these numbers, re-
calculate Figure A in the boxed feature titled "The EITC Story."

5. Considering both Figures 18–1 and 18–2
(taxes and benefits of Social Security), do
you think the Social Security system as a
whole is progressive, regressive, or proportional in its effect on the lifetime distribution of earnings? Why?

CHAPTER 19

HEALTH CARE

Perhaps no other debate in public life has gone on so long without some kind of resolution as the discussions going back to the Roosevelt and Truman administrations in the 1930s and 1940s over a federal role in guaranteeing access to health care. While Canada and the nations of Western Europe were creating national health care systems, Americans continued to access health care through a patchwork of public and private hospitals, employer-provided and privately provided health insurance, and private physicians and public health clinics. Many Americans fall through the cracks because they are either without access to adequate health care within a reasonable distance or without the means to pay for it. A major debate in the early 1990s over the shape and future of health care in the first Clinton administration ended with no significant changes to the system. The United States entered the 21st century as the only major industrial nation without some kind of comprehensive health care plan that embraced all citizens.

More than any other basic need, health care has been caught in the no man's land of American ambivalence about expanding the role of government. As a consequence, only two programs of publicly provided health care, one purely federal, one federal–state shared, have evolved since the 1960s and they cover only the elderly and the very poor. **Medicare** is a federal program for those over 65 that provides hospital and physician care. It is funded primarily through a payroll tax and to a lesser degree by premiums deducted from Social Security checks. **Medicaid** is a health

care program for the poor that is means tested, paid for out of general revenue, with costs shared between federal and state budgets.

Health care is in large part produced by the private sector in both for-profit and nonprofit firms, although some services are provided through publicly owned hospitals and clinics. Military personnel, including retired military, have access to health services through military and veterans' hospitals, which is a large component of the public part of the health care system. Aside from the military, however, discussions about the role for the public sector in health care are primarily directed at the financing of health care services, a role that is shared with private insurers and with direct payments by consumers. That public role is carried out through Medicaid and Medicare, which finance health care services to specific groups, and through favorable tax treatment of employer-provided group health insurance to employees. Table 19–1 summarizes spending for health care in the United States in 1997.

INSURABLE RISKS AND THIRD-PARTY PAYMENTS

Any product or service that is paid for at least in part through insurance or other third parties has some unique challenges in using either market or governmental controls to ration the scarce resources involved. Insurance at its

Table 19–1
Health Care
Expenditures in the
United States, 1997

	Dollars (in billions)
By consumers	$535.8
Out of pocket	189.1
Private insurance	346.7
By government	502.2
Other	50.3
TOTAL	1,088.3
Personal health care expenses	$953.6
Hospital care	370.2
Physician services	217.8
Dental services	51.1
Other professional services	61.5
Home health care	30.5
Drugs/medical nondurables	108.6
Nursing home care	84.7
Other health services	29.2
Net cost of insurance and administration	50.3
Government public health	34.6
Medical research	17.9
Medical facilities	16.9

Source: U.S. Statistical Abstract, 2000 (Washington, DC: US Bureau of the Census, 2000).

best is a way of paying for those parts of household spending that are largely beyond our control—natural disasters, automobile accidents, death of a breadwinner, or costly surgery or extended illnesses. Inevitably, the definition of what is a risk appropriate to addressing through insurance gets extended. While health insurance originally focused on major medical insurance—prolonged illnesses and major surgeries—it now commonly covers eye examinations, mental health, routine dental care, some kinds of cosmetic surgery, and other normal and expected or sometimes elective expenditures. As the breadth of coverage has increased, the issues of cost containment have challenged all of the parties involved in paying for health care. These parties include the government, private insurers, providers of health care, employers (who often provide health insurance as a fringe benefit to employees), and, of course, households.

Kinds of Coverage

The original and still primary purpose of any kind of insurance is to cover those kinds of risk that are low probability but very large in amount. Consider a rare disease that might strike one person in a million each year, but if it does, the cost of treating it is $100,000. No one has any way of knowing if he or she will be that one person in a million. In a society of one million people, if each one contributed 10 cents to a fund that provided insurance against that rare disease, then that one person who contracted the disease would at least not suffer major financial injury as well as health injury. The cost per person is small for catastrophic coverage. In practice, of course, the insurer would have some administrative cost and need to create some reserves against the possibility that 2 persons in a million rather than one might contract the disease, so the premium would be more than 10 cents; but even at 50 cents or a dollar the insurance would provide peace of mind for the 999,999 disease-free policyholders and financial relief to the millionth who contracts the disease.

Insurance has been extended in many areas from the catastrophic to the routine. Dental insurance covers routine checkups. Homeowners' insurance protects property from minor as well as major disasters. Auto insurance pays for replacement of window glass. Deductibles have tended to become smaller over time in all kinds of insurance. In effect, many forms of insurance have become a sort of prepayment plan for routine expenditures.

Health insurance is no different. It is possible to buy only catastrophic health insurance, called major medical, while covering routine expenditures out of household budgets. The dominant influence in shifting the "norm" for health insurance in the United States toward broad coverage of routine as well as extraordinary expenditures has been employer-provided health insurance. As Milton Friedman notes, this tax-exempt fringe benefit became a recruiting tool for employers during the tight labor markets of the

1940s.[1] Because employer-provided health insurance is not considered taxable income for purposes of either federal income tax or Social Security taxes, it is an attractive form of supplementary compensation. Consider a worker in a 28% federal income tax bracket and a 7% state income tax bracket who is subject to 7.6% payroll tax (not to mention the other 7.6% paid by the employer). This worker knows that his or her household will incur routine medical expenses of about $1,000 in most years. To pay for them with after-tax dollars earned from employment would require a pretax income of $1,742, to which his employer would have to add $108 for the other half of the Social Security tax, for a total cost of $1,850. Clearly it is in the interest of the employer and employee to convert some part of salary into prepaid health care benefits. Employer-provided health insurance with both routine care and catastrophic health insurance, designed with tax advantages as a primary consideration, later became the model on which Medicare and Medicaid were developed.

Moral Hazard

Employers do have an interest in holding down premium costs in providing health. The biggest challenge in designing any kind of health insurance system, public or private, is the same one that faces any other kind of insurance. If a third party is bearing the cost and if your outlay for insurance is the same regardless of usage, there is no incentive for clients to limit their demand for health care. In insurance, this problem of overuse that ultimately drives up premiums is known as **moral hazard.** To economists, it is a simple matter of following the demand curve down to the horizontal axis to determine how much health care people will demand at a price of zero for the marginal unit.

In medical care, moral hazard has an additional dimension, because many of the decisions about a person's health care—whether to have an operation, whether to remain in the hospital, what prescription to take, whether home health care or skilled nursing or hospice is called for—are made by the doctor as the professional expert without a great deal of consideration about cost. With neither the patient nor the doctor focusing on cost as an element of the decision, any cost containment must be imposed by other parties. Inevitably, such efforts to control costs create considerable resistance on the part of both doctors and patients. Patients find their choices restricted while doctors are subject to limits on the fees they are able to charge. Employers do have an interest in holding down costs, but they have to battle with both the health insurance industry and their own workers in doing so.

The flip side of moral hazard among the insured is selectivity by the insurer. Many people are rejected for health insurance because of preexisting conditions or general high risk. Others are offered individual insurance policies

1. Milton Friedman, "How to Cure Health Care," *Public Interest,* 142 (Winter 2001): 3–30.

only at extremely high premiums, often even for relatively good risks. Group insurance is always cheaper than individual insurance for the same client because a large group contains a mix of persons with very diverse demands for health care services in a given year. The estimated 40 million Americans, almost 15% of the population, without any health insurance are those not poor enough for Medicaid, not old enough for Medicare, not working for an employer who provides health insurance, and not able to afford the high premiums for individual health insurance. Health maintenance organizations, or HMOs, have pulled out of some markets where the higher risk populations they serve require too many services relative to what employers or policy-holders are willing to pay.[2]

DEBATE OVER THE PUBLIC ROLE

Like the continuing debates over Social Security and welfare, arguments over the form and financing of health care in the United States are rooted in the way certain kinds of personal financial risks are managed and shared in a market economy. These risks are a consequence of a market system that puts an emphasis on personal responsibility for earning a living and managing one's income and assets wisely, as opposed to other systems that call for more shared responsibility through government or other cooperative arrangements. Social Security offers protection from outliving one's assets or earning too little to accumulate any assets for the postretirement years. Welfare offers a limited guarantee of protection from starvation for those in temporarily distressed circumstances, although that guarantee is much more limited than it once was. But for many households, the ultimate threat to their financial well-being is a prolonged illness or a very costly accident or surgery that can rapidly deplete their assets and threaten their standard of living both now and in the future.

Health care, like retirement, seems ideally suited for the development of private insurance and payment or prepayment plans. Where does the government come in? Is there a rationale for government production or provision/financing of health care services? Why does it appear that the private sector has failed to deliver socially acceptable outcomes in terms of the quality, cost, and availability of health care services?

Efficiency Issues: Social Benefits of Health Care

The same question that was raised for infrastructure, education, Social Security, and welfare must be addressed for health care. What is the justification for a public role in providing health care? The answers are very similar.

---

2. HMOs are discussed later in the chapter.

Health care is not a public good. It is excludable; it can be rationed by price. There is competition for a limited supply of medical resources that must be allocated among competing users. Clearly health care is rival in consumption. The hour Jones takes with the doctor, and the bed Jones occupies in the hospital are not available to Smith. Like education, a public role in funding health care must be established primarily on the bases of perceived spillover benefits and equity.

Some kinds of health care, particularly preventive, have important positive externalities. Your flu shot protects everyone you come in contact with. Vaccinations have almost wiped out many childhood diseases, protecting everyone else in the process. (There is now a temptation to be a free rider and not get shots for measles, smallpox, and other diseases on the very great odds of never being exposed!) Quick treatment of contagious diseases with antibiotics and other therapies can reduce the spread of the illness to others.

One step removed from these obvious externalities is the effect of health or illness on one's performance as a worker, consumer, and citizen—which is quite similar to the effects of education. Productivity in the workplace is particularly sensitive to health. In addition, deteriorating health can lead to disability. In a social system where public funds are used to support people with disabilities and their families, investing in prevention and cure is almost always cheaper than thrusting more households on Social Security disability or welfare.

Efficiency Issues: Information

Health care services are one area where the consumer is often not in a position to make informed decisions about what services to consume. Instead, consumers rely on medical professionals to make appropriate decisions in their behalf. Thus, it is not only third-party payment but also third-party decision making that makes it difficult for market forces to ensure appropriate allocation of health care resources. For some products where information is difficult to obtain and evaluate, public and private agencies (the Federal Trade Commission or Consumers' Union) attempt to fill the information gap. For example, reading *Consumer Reports* may help a person to avoid buying an unsafe or unreliable car. Required inspections for home loans protect both the home buyer and the lender from buying houses with serious structural defects. But the amount and variety of information needed for good medical decisions is not always accessible to the patient or the patient's family. With medical professionals in the dual role of service provider and decision maker but without the responsibility of paying for the services ordered, other entities must provide some oversight to protect consumers. That role is carried out by both private and public providers of health care payments through various kinds of health insurance.

Equity Issues: Access to Basic Services

For most people, the argument for a public role in either producing or providing health care services is based not on efficiency but on equity. At least some kind of basic health care (no frills!) is widely regarded as a merit good, something to which one is entitled as a member of society along with food, shelter, and some amount of education. Access to such services is presently dependent on a demonstrated ability to pay, either through insurance, Medicare, Medicaid, or personal financial resources. Prior to Medicaid, hospitals took a certain number of "charity" cases among those unable to pay. In fact, many hospitals built with federal funds under the Hill-Burton Act were required to provide a certain amount of charitable services in exchange for those funds.

Free medical services are not exactly abundant, but state and local governments do provide some basic services (vaccinations, well-baby and prenatal checkups, routine tests for blood pressure and cholesterol) through public clinics, and medical personnel often donate some of their time to privately operated free clinics. Hospitals always have and continue to write off some bills as unpayable, a form of free health care services. The existence of such a loose network of free services for those unable to pay is indicative of some widely held belief in basic health services as an entitlement.

With the advent of Medicaid for the poor and Medicare for the elderly, and with the expiration of Hill-Burton obligations for charity cases, the network of health care access for the poor has become somewhat more spotty.[3] The very poor, those on Temporary Assistance to Needy Families (TANF) or those transitioning to work from TANF, have Medicaid. The elderly have either Medicare or Medicaid or sometimes both. Employees of most large firms and public agencies have group health insurance. Individuals not poor enough for Medicaid and not covered by employer-provided health insurance can often pay for routine health care and/or individual health insurance for themselves. But 15% of Americans who do not fit into any of these categories still fall through the cracks of this mixed patchwork of public, private for-profit, and private nonprofit services that constitutes the American health care system. For many states, the issue of those without any insurance is the most pressing one. Arizona and Oregon have been leaders among states in attempting to expand the percentage of citizens with health insurance coverage through either private or publicly funded policies.

Unlike the other kinds of public services described in Chapters 16 through 18 (education, infrastructure, Social Security and welfare), the equity rationale for health care is not solely or even primarily directed at the poor. Because an extended illness or major surgery can threaten the financial stability of even middle-income households, the issue of access to financing for health

---

3. Some hospitals have paid the government to be released from their Hill-Burton obligations so that they can be sold to private, for-profit hospital conglomerates like Humana or Health Corporation of America.

care cuts across most of the income spectrum. Much of the debate over health care at both the state and national levels has centered on the trade-offs between providing more adequate services to those already covered and extending the umbrella of health insurance to those who have no protection. As part of that process, health care policy makers are revisiting the use of employer-provided health insurance as an appropriate model for publicly funded health insurance, where tax benefits are irrelevant but cost containment is at least as important as it is for employers and employees.

Is Privatization the Answer?

If health care were left entirely to the private sector, access to health care would be subject to price rationing. Those who could not afford to pay for health care would not receive any services. While that picture is appalling to contemplate—babies born without medical attention, heart attack or accident victims left to die—it does serve as a reminder of the positive side of using the market to ration services. Some health care services are optional. Some conditions have alternative treatments with vastly different costs, and in a private fee-for-service situation, cost would be more carefully considered. Without third-party payments for prescription drugs, for example, doctors are more likely to prescribe or patients to demand generic instead of brand-name drugs. Optional treatments for conditions ranging from baldness to acne to toenail fungus would be postponed or foregone, or at least weighed against other choices about how to spend one's income.

With entirely private health care, competition among suppliers of health care services would put some downward pressure on prices. In fact, even in the current patchwork situation, buyers of employer-provided health insurance for large groups exert some pressure to keep costs and prices down. Certainly the administrators of the Medicare program have attempted to use their leverage as a major purchaser of health services to hold down medical care costs. But at least partly because of third-party payments by governments and employers, which keep demand high relative to scarce medical service resources, competition has not been very effective in constraining either demand or costs.

HEALTH CARE FOR THE ELDERLY: MEDICARE

Medicare came into being in 1965 after decades of discussion about universal health insurance dating back to 1916. The decision to offer a more limited program only for those over age 65 was a political compromise. The elderly were selected in part because it was politically popular and in part because this age group had so little private health insurance (less than half the elderly at that time). The design of Medicare drew on the private insurance plan for federal workers.

HEALTH CARE IN OTHER INDUSTRIAL COUNTRIES

While American presidential administrations from Roosevelt and Truman to Johnson and Clinton debated expanding the very limited federal role in providing health care, other countries were taking bolder steps. Canada, Australia, and most of the nations of Western Europe have cradle-to-grave health care funded out of tax revenue that is available to all residents at little or no cost. Instead of price rationing, in many countries health care is rationed either by long waiting periods or by restrictions on the kinds of services that can be offered (although in some countries it is possible to engage in traditional fee-for-service medical care as a supplement or alternative to the public system).

Supporters of publicly funded and managed health care argue that these countries provide broad access to basic health care, although often with few "frills." Critics claim that these systems offer fewer services, less high-tech medicine, and less consumer choice.

Economist Uwe Reinhardt, a recognized expert in health care economics, takes issue with this assessment. He argues that in fact Canadian and European health care systems offer equally high quality of care at considerably lower cost.[1] He also takes issue with the definition of the U.S. health care problem as being driven by the elderly. The United States has a lower percentage of people age 65 or older than Japan, Germany, the United Kingdom, France, or Canada, and will still have a lower ratio than those countries 20 years from now.

Reinhardt notes that the United States spends $3,925 per capita on health care (public and private spending) compared to figures ranging from $1,347 in the United Kingdom to $2,339 in Germany. In the United States, health care takes 13.5% of GDP, while in six other industrial nations the cost ranges from 6.7% to 10.4%. But does it buy better results? Are Americans living longer, receiving better care, enjoying healthier lives?[2]

Reinhardt finds that life expectancy for those aged 65 or older is lower in the United States than in New Zealand, Australia, France, and Japan. In consumer satisfaction surveys, Americans express much more dissatisfaction than their counterparts in other countries. One study cited by Reinhardt found that patients in Germany, where per capita spending on health care is $1,000 less, receive more medical inputs (hospital days, prescription drugs, physician visits) than Americans for episodes of the same illness. A major difference between nations is higher prices in the United States for the services of health care professionals. Another important difference is in administrative cost, which is considerably higher in the United States.[3]

These international comparisons raise some significant questions about the peculiarly American system of providing health care through a patchwork of public and private insurance, public and private hospitals, third-party payments, and fragmented oversight that has had limited effectiveness in providing consumers genuine choice while achieving the goal of cost containment. Perhaps health care is an area where Americans could benefit from importing rather than exporting ideas about how to balance public and private roles in the provision of services with social benefits and strong equity dimensions.

1. Uwe Reinhardt, "Health Care for the Aging Baby Boom," *Journal of Economic Perspectives*, 14(2) (Spring 2000): 71–83.
2. *Ibid.*
3. *Ibid.*

For 40 million people over 65 and those with disabilities, Medicare is the primary source of health insurance, although many of them have supplementary health insurance as well. At $220 billion in 2001, Medicare spent more than $5,500 per beneficiary on average—20% of all health care costs and 12% of the federal budget. Spending has grown rapidly in response to cost-increasing changes in medical technology as well as a growing elderly population, although that increased spending has also resulted in improved health and life expectancy among the elderly. Projections call for a continued increase in both beneficiaries and cost per recipient that will greatly exceed the growth of the payroll contributions and payments for Medicare Part B by recipients that together support the Medicare trust fund.[4]

Medicare has two parts. About 60% of the program is hospital insurance, Part A, which pays for hospital care and some limited alternatives (nursing facilities, home health care, hospices), and is funded by a payroll tax of 2.9%, half paid by employers and half by employees. At present this fund is projected to remain solvent until 2025, a much longer time horizon than had previously been expected. The rapid growth and threat of insolvency comes in Part B, which covers doctors, outpatient care, lab tests, medical equipment, and some other services. Part B is funded mainly through general tax revenues. The premium paid by beneficiaries has increased but still accounts for only about 10% of the cost. Medicare does not cover extended nursing home care or prescription drugs outside the hospital.

Medicare adopted many features of private employer-financed health insurance. These policies have provisions to control usage by making sure that the patient bears some share of the cost. One such feature is the **deductible,** the amount the patient must pay out of pocket each year before insurance benefits can be tapped. Another feature is **copayments,** which is the percentage of the bill paid by the patient, typically 20% for physicians' services. A third feature of many private policies is an annual and/or lifetime maximum total payment, which is not a part of Medicare. These provisions play an important incentive role in containing the growth of demand for services, essential to any kind of insurance program, public or private. However, many Medicare clients also have private "Medigap" insurance that covers most of the expenses they would otherwise have to pay, including deductibles and copayments. Consequently, those over age 65 often have little incentive to restrict their use of health care compared to younger persons, and their demands have contributed to a rise in the cost of health care that is faster than the general rate of inflation. In addition, this age group generally has more health care demands in any payment situation as health begins to deteriorate in the aging process.

HEALTH CARE FOR THE POOR: MEDICAID

Health care for low-income families with children and low-income elderly is provided through Medicaid, created in 1965. Medicaid is funded through general tax revenues with cost sharing between the federal and state governments.

---

4. Mark McClellan, "Medicare Reform: Fundamental Problems, Incremental Steps," *Journal of Economic Perspectives,* 14(1) (Spring 2000): 21–44.

Although two-thirds of the enrollees in Medicaid are under 65 (including many children), the largest share of the spending is for the elderly. Unlike Medicare, Medicaid does pay for long-term nursing home care, and elderly persons who have exhausted their financial resources in long-term care often wind up on Medicaid. Medicaid also pays for basic health care services such as hospital stays, physicians' care, and medical equipment. Medicaid, like Medicare, sets the amount it will reimburse for various services, usually at rates less than are customarily charged. Some health care service providers refuse to accept patients who will pay through Medicaid or limit the percentage of their services provided to Medicaid patients because of the relatively low reimbursement rates. Many Medicaid patients have been directed by their states into managed care programs (see below).

Medicaid is administered by the states, with different benefits in different states, although there are federal guidelines about eligible participants and eligible services. Medicaid funds are provided through matching grants, with higher match ratios for lower income states to encourage them to provide more services. Recall from Chapter 14 that a matching grant will normally stimulate more spending by the recipient than a flat grant of an equal dollar amount because a matching grant has both income and substitution effects. As other federal grants to states were reduced in the 1980s, the relative share of Medicaid in federal grants to states grew from 21% in 1985 to 42% by 1992. Over the same period, Medicaid also became the fastest growing item in many states' budgets.

Originally Medicaid for the nonelderly, nondisabled population was limited to families receiving Aid to Families with Dependent Children. In 1987 it was expanded to cover prenatal care for women and health services for children with incomes up to 133% of the poverty level, and states were allowed to expand that eligibility up to 185% of the poverty level and still receive matching federal funds. Not all states adopted the more generous guidelines, however, so eligibility is a continuing bone of contention between the states and the federal government. At least this change permits states to greatly increase Medicaid eligibility among the low-income population and receive their federal matching funds for such expansion.

REFORMS IN MEDICARE AND MEDICAID

Efforts to reform health insurance were a primary focus of the Clinton administration in the 1990s. Despite extensive hearings and discussions, however, few changes were made. Most of the discussions have centered around three issues. The first is the lack of health insurance for about 15% of the population. The second is cost containment. The third is expansion of coverage, particularly for the elderly, to include prescription drugs, which are often a major expense and at the same time can be a preferable alternative to more expensive forms of care that may involve hospitalization or surgery. The

expansion of Medicaid in the 1980s helped to address the lack of health insurance for one segment of the population, but a significant part of the population still does not have health insurance. The Balanced Budget Act of 1997
made some significant changes to Medicare and Medicaid that attempted to
address the first two of these objectives. Some states have taken steps to provide prescription drug coverage for elderly citizens on a means-tested basis,
and prescription coverage with deductibles and copayments is under consideration for Medicare and Medicaid at the federal level. Legislation in 1997
cut Medicare and Medicaid payments over a five-year period to health care
providers treating those with disabilities and elderly patients. This complex
set of changes to reimbursement formulas was intended to reduce combined
Medicare and Medicaid outlays by at least $115 billion over five years.

At the same time, this legislation created the **Child Health Insurance Program (CHIP)** or Title XXI. The intent of CHIP was to expand the number of
insured children in families previously above the income limits for Medicaid.
Congress appropriated about $4 billion a year for approved state programs,
which had to be at least as generous in eligibility as the upper limits of existing Medicaid eligibility, but could go higher in the income scale. A state-
approved CHIP plan also had to meet at least minimum standards for coverage but also could exceed those limits. This initiative put the responsibility on
the states to devise plans in which they would continue to share in the cost,
but would still be assisted with additional federal matching grant funds.

COST CONTAINMENT STRATEGIES

One of the unusual features of Medicare, not generally seen in private health
insurance, is the **Prospective Payment System (PPS)**. Since 1983, hospital reimbursements have been based on a fixed amount per stay for a particular diagnosis rather than actual hospital costs. The payment is based on national
averages for length of stay and adjusted for local conditions (wages, type of
hospital, etc.). This method has succeeded in reducing the length of the average hospital stay, because hospitals have an incentive to discharge patients
sooner. It also encourages health care providers to use more outpatient care,
which is still reimbursed on a cost basis.

Another strategy for keeping costs (and insurance premiums) down is to
enroll households in **health maintenance organizations (HMOs)**. HMOs are
one form of **managed care,** which replaces the traditional fee-for-service payment that encourages providers to offer unnecessary services. An HMO consists of a network of hospitals and physicians, both primary care and specialists, who enroll members on the basis of a per-patient or per-family charge
and provide both primary and acute health care. Pioneered in California,
HMOs and other managed care systems have spread rapidly across the country. Many employer-provided plans specify managed care or HMOs, while
others encourage their members to enroll in such a program as an option.

Some health care consumers are unhappy with the limitations on their choice of doctors or the availability of certain kinds of health care services, but HMOs have been popular with employers because they are often less costly.

An unusual strategy that attempted to balance universal coverage for all citizens with cost containment was tried in Oregon beginning in 1989, which attempted to rank medical diagnoses and treatments. Medicaid coverage would be denied for low-priority services in order to provide funds for all persons living in poverty. This plan was criticized for rationing care for the poor, but it did reduce the percentage of the state's population without health insurance. Savings in practice were modest because the plan as finally implemented did not impose as many restrictions as originally planned.[5]

OTHER PROPOSALS FOR REFORM

Some critics of Medicare would like to shift it from the present defined benefit plan to a system that gives individuals something equivalent to a medical voucher with which to purchase health care services and/or private health insurance. If the voucher was used for insurance (a plan known as premium support), individuals would have the option of supplementing the voucher to buy more extensive coverage or lower deductibles and copayments.

For those not on Medicare or Medicaid, another proposal is for **medical savings accounts,** which would allow households to set aside tax-free funds to purchase health care. Any funds unspent at the end of the year could accrue for future medical expenses or could be converted to ordinary taxable income. At present, employer-provided health care is exempt from income taxes as a fringe benefit, and individuals who purchase their own insurance can deduct health care premiums on their federal income tax. This tax expenditure is a significant public contribution to financing privately purchased health care. Milton Friedman is one of many voices proposing that tax incentives be restructured so as to encourage employer plans that combine major medical (catastrophic) coverage with a medical savings account to allow households to choose how to allocate their medical expenditures and to allow medical expenses to be weighed against other uses of funds in the household budget.

Finally, some proposals for reform would increase the present payroll tax of 1.45% paid by employers and employees in order to strengthen the Medicare trust fund, or shift some or all of the cost of funding Medicare to general tax revenues. A related financing proposal is to increase the premium paid by individuals for Part B. Either of these solutions would provide more financing resources but would not address the issues of cost containment and expanding the number of persons with coverage.

5. Michael Sparer, "Health Policy for Low Income People in Oregon," Urban Institute, September 1999.

SUMMARY

The only major public health care programs in the United States are Medicare for the elderly and people with disabilities and Medicaid for low-income households. Other households rely on private (often employer-provided) health insurance or have no health insurance.

Private employer-provided health insurance combines catastrophic or major medical insurance with payment for routine medical care because of tax advantages, despite the drawbacks in terms of restraining demand. This model was used to develop Medicare and Medicaid where tax advantages are not involved and restraining demand is more important.

The debate over the public role in health care is directed at the financing or provision of health care services, which are largely provided by private health care providers. The challenge in financing health care is that third-party payments create only limited incentives for the consumer or service provider to restrict their demand for services.

The social benefits of health care include the protection extended to others in the case of contagious diseases as well as the more general benefits of a healthy population and the costs of disability that can result from inadequate health care. Health care also is subject to unusually problematical information problems since the provider is generally more knowledgeable than the consumer.

Public provision of health care services is also regarded as an equity issue that cuts across income groups because of the potentially large financial risk from a prolonged illness or other kinds of costly health care needs.

Medicare is the primary source of health insurance for those with disabilities and those over 65. It consists of Part A, funded out of payroll taxes to pay for hospital services, and Part B, funded out of general tax revenues and premiums paid by the insured, to cover physicians' services and other benefits. Like private health insurance, Medicare has some built-in cost containment features such as deductibles and copayments.

Medicaid provides health insurance for low-income households, primarily for children. It is funded out of general tax revenues and is a state program with substantial federal assistance in the form of matching grants.

Cost containment efforts include the Prospective Payment System for Medicare and the use of HMOs and managed care to replace the traditional fee-for-service method of payment. Oregon attempted to generate savings from a rationing system in order to extend coverage to more of the uninsured, but cost savings have been limited.

Current reform proposals include the use of medical insurance vouchers and medical savings accounts, as well as additional funding for Medicare through a higher payroll tax or a shift to general tax revenues.

KEY TERMS AND CONCEPTS

Medicare, 410
Medicaid, 410
moral hazard, 413
deductible, 419
copayment, 419

Child Health Insurance
    Program (CHIP), 421
Prospective Payment System
    (PPS), 421

health maintenance
    organizations (HMO), 421
managed care, 421
medical savings accounts, 422

DISCUSSION QUESTIONS

1. Why is it so difficult to use markets and prices to ration scarce health care resources among consumers compared to other kinds of goods and services?

2. How would a defined contribution plan such as medical savings accounts affect the demand for health care services?

3. What is the justification for a public role in paying for health care?

4. What are the advantages and disadvantages of catastrophic versus routine care insurance for employers? Taxpayers? Health service providers? Sick people?

5. Uwe Reinhardt argues that Canadian and European health care systems are less expensive and give better quality care than the U.S. system. Evaluate his arguments.

EPILOGUE

Like any textbook, this one does not say all there is to say about public sector economics. It does offer the basic analytical tools, the institutional and historical context, and the language and practices of this particular branch of economics. The purpose of a textbook is both to provide a foundation of knowledge and skills and to point the student in the direction of his or her continuing education in that particular field.

Some important issues in public sector economics are not addressed or addressed very lightly in this book. Although taxes and other revenues were given fairly thorough coverage, all of the taxes discussed involve many complex judgments about what constitutes equity, how much efficiency to sacrifice for adequacy, and other detailed matters beyond the scope of a single course or textbook. Most of the areas not addressed, however, are on the expenditure side of the budget. Entire courses are devoted to cost–benefit analysis, rather than the brief introduction offered here.

In the area of specific expenditures, national defense occupies a significant part of the federal budget and raises complex and controversial issues in recruitment, and retention of personnel as well as procurement and deployment of resources. Public safety—fire and police protection, the judicial system, prisons, and counterterrorism—are important public matters. Housing is an area where the public sector plays an important role at all levels. The four chapters in this book that examined specific areas of public expenditure were chosen to reflect the issues that have been most prominent in the past decade and that are expected to be in the forefront of public debate in the near term. They were also chosen because they involve state and local as well as federal participation.

Armed with the skills developed in this course, you should be better able to follow debates on important public sector issues in *The Wall Street Journal* or *Business Week*. You can probably read and interpret many of the professional articles in the *National Tax Journal,* which deals with a broad array of issues, primarily revenue related. The understanding of public sector economics will also spill over into other economics courses, because there is some public role or involvement in all areas of economics.

A better understanding of what government is for and what its responsibilities are in a market system may also be helpful in assessing your own values in a political context. This book does not take a particular political stance, but underlying this book is a perspective that government is a potentially useful tool (with some limitations) for improving economic welfare. That view will be disputed on the right by those who find government a useless burden and those on the left who think it should be much more actively involved in resource allocation and income distribution.

I took my first class in public sector economics (then known as public finance) in 1963, during the administration of President John Kennedy. Those were exciting times. A tax cut was given to stimulate growth, and a novel proposal made for general revenue sharing that materialized later. There was also a general faith in the ability of the United States to do just about anything and for the government to play a leadership role in making that anything happen. At the same time, government almost always meant the federal government. States were dominated by rural legislators and focused most of their attention on schools and roads. Local governments were primarily providers of services to homeowners and businesses like streets and sidewalks and police and fire protection which were financed by the property tax.

Since 1963, the changes in the size and scope of government activity at all levels have been dramatic. The intervening 40 years have seen the birth and death of general revenue sharing, numerous tax cuts and tax reforms, national debates over Social Security and health care, welfare reform, an increased role of government in growth management, the property tax revolt, devolution of responsibilities to lower levels of government, more activist and more responsive state governments, and increasing recognition of the need to provide local services on a regional level.

During your lifetimes, you can expect equally dramatic changes. A textbook and a course can only provide a foundation for encountering and responding to those changes. The rest is up to you.

GLOSSARY

A

ability to pay A basis for equitable taxation determined by one's income or other measure of resources from which taxes could be paid.

accelerated depreciation Type of depreciation that permits the reduction in the value of an asset to take place more rapidly for tax purposes than the actual decline over the asset's useful lifetime.

acquisition value A system of property tax valuation used in California in which properties are only reassessed when sold, and otherwise just increased in taxable value by a set amount each year.

ad valorem tax A tax that is calculated as a percentage of the price or value of the item subject to tax.

adequacy Quality of a tax that measures the amount of revenue it can raise relative to what the government needs.

adjusted gross income (U.S. income tax) Gross income minus certain permitted exclusions and adjustments; an intermediate step toward the determination of taxable income.

adjustments (income tax) Items that are subtracted from gross income to arrive at adjusted gross income.

Aid to Families with Dependent Children (AFDC) Primary welfare program for families until 1995; provided aid to qualifying children and the resident parent.

allocation/distribution/stabilization A sorting of the functions of government developed by economist Richard Musgrave into those that affect the mix of output or the use of resources (allocation), the shares of income and wealth by various groups in the population (distribution), and the macroeconomic impact of government on the level of output, employment, and prices.

B

assessment The process of determining the value of a taxable asset for purposes of imposing property taxes.

base erosion The reduction of the base of a tax either as a result of high rates or as a result of legislative action to exempt some components of the base.

benefit principle The principle that taxes paid should be proportional to benefits received from the government.

benefit tax A tax imposed on those who benefit from the public good or service financed by the revenue from the tax.

block grant Intergovernmental grant that must be spent within a broad category, giving recipient government broad flexibility about exactly how the funds are used.

budget A statement of expected revenues and planned expenditures for a future period.

C

capitalization The process by which changes in expected future benefits or revenues and expected future costs are incorporated into the market value of an asset.

capture theory of regulation The theory that regulatory agencies will develop close relationships with and eventually serve the interests of the industries they are supposed to be regulating in the interests of consumers.

cascade-type tax A tax that is imposed at more than one stage of production and distribution.

categorical grant A grant from one government to another or from a government to a private group that can only be used for a narrowly specified purpose.

centralization Concentration of government activities at the federal rather than state/provincial level or at the state/provincial level rather than the local level.

Child Health Improvement Program (CHIP) A federal program created in 1997 to expand the number of insured children in families previously above the income limits on Medicaid.

circuit breaker A form of property tax relief in which low-income households receive rebates for part or all of their property tax through the state income tax.

classified property tax system A property tax system in which different classes of property (residential, industrial, etc.) are assessed for tax purposes at different percentages of their market value.

clawback Provision in some state laws that requires relocating firms to repay economic incentives (tax breaks, worker training, etc.) if they do not remain in that location for a certain minimum length of time.

closed-ended grant A grant program that has a fixed number of dollars to allocate.

collection cost(s) Costs incurred by the government in order to collect taxes.

compensation principle A test for whether a change improves or worsens economic welfare by answering the question "Could the gainers from the change compensate the losers for their loss and still retain some net gain?"

compliance cost(s) Costs incurred by the taxpayer in determining the amount of tax owed and remitting payment.

congestible goods nonrival in consumption until they reach capacity, after which the consumption by one person reduces the availability to another.

congestion charges Fees charged during periods of peak usage of certain facilities such as roads and parks to reduce congestion.

consumer surplus The difference between the amount that a consumer pays for a purchase and the value or utility derived from that purchase.

copayment In health insurance, the percentage of certain costs that is borne by the patient rather than the insurance provider (typically 20%).

cost–benefit analysis A technique of project evaluation that determines and compares expected future costs and benefits from proposed projects.

cost–benefit ratio The ratio of the present value of future costs to the present value of future benefits, used to evaluate the desirability of a project.

cross-subsidy Using surplus revenues from one activity or customer group to help pay for another.

D

deductible (health insurance) The amount of out-of-pocket expense the policyholder must incur before insurance begins to reimburse.

defined benefit program A pension program that guarantees certain benefits for life based on factors such as length of service and average salary.

defined contribution program A pension program in which benefits are determined by the amount in the pensioner's account resulting from the employee's own contributions, employer contributions, and interest or dividend earnings.

devolution Assignment of responsibilities formerly held by a higher level of government to a lower level (federal to state, state to local).

district power equalization A school funding program in which states provide enough to each school district to make sure that the funds available are equal to the state average for the mill rate charged in the district.

duopoly An oligopoly situation involving only two firms or parties.

E

earmarked taxes Tax revenues that flow into special funds or are set aside for specific uses rather than being part of the general fund.

Earned Income Tax Credit (EITC) A program of redistribution for the working poor that provides income tax rebates for low-income households.

economic efficiency Allocation of resources so as to maximize welfare by making marginal cost equal to marginal benefit..

education production function The relationship between educational resources and educational outcomes or results.

effective tax rate Income tax liability computed as a percentage of gross income.

efficiency Allocating resources to their highest and best uses and distributing output to those who want it most as measured by the prices they are willing to pay.

effluent charges Fees charged for the emission of pollutants based on volume emitted.

enterprise fund A government fund that segregates revenues and costs associated with a particular service (such as water or sewer) that operates independently of the general fund.

equality of opportunity The idea that everyone is ensured equal access to employment and other means of acquiring income and wealth through such means as education and health care.

equality of results The idea that everyone is ensured an equal share of society's income and wealth regardless of their contribution.

estate tax A federal tax on the transfer of accumulated wealth to one's heirs at death.

excess burden/deadweight loss The amount of consumer or producer surplus lost in imposing a tax that is not transferred to the government as revenue.

excise/selective sales tax Tax imposed on a specific item or service, such as gasoline, tobacco, or alcohol.

exclusions (federal income tax) Kinds of income not included in gross income for tax purposes, such as college scholarships.

exemptions (federal income tax) An amount per person or dependent that is subtracted from adjusted gross income before computing tax liability.

externality A cost or benefit falling on a third party who is not directly involved in a transaction as buyer or seller.

F

filing status Classification of a household for income tax purposes based on the membership of the household as a joint return, single, head of household, or married filing separately.

fiscal autonomy The freedom of a lower level of government to make independent decisions about budgets and revenues.

fiscal capitalization The change in the value of taxable property that results from changes in taxes or local public services.

fiscal deficit A shortfall between benefits of services provided by a local, state, or national government to an individual or firm and the value of taxes and fees paid to that government.

fiscal federalism A system of multiple levels of government with some distinct areas of responsibility and sources of revenue as well as some shared revenues and responsibilities.

fiscal impact The effect of a decision or action on the revenues and expenditures of a particular government.

fiscal surplus The excess of benefits from services provided by a local, state, or national government to an individual or firm over the value of taxes and fees paid to that government.

fiscal year Period covered by a government's budget: October 1 to September 30 for the federal government, July 1 to June 30 for many state and local governments.

fiscal zoning Use of local taxes and fees so as to direct land use in particular desired directions.

flypaper effect The tendency of intergovernmental grant funds to "stick where they land"; that is, for funds given to the state or local public sector to increase spending for public purposes and funds given back to taxpayers to increase spending for private purposes.

formula grant A grant based on one or more objective criteria such as population, poverty rate, or miles of highway.

franchise fee A charge made by a government for the exclusive privilege of operating a private enterprise in a given area.

free rider A person who takes advantage of nonexcludability by consuming a public good without contributing to the cost of its production.

fungibility The ability to shift funds from one use to another in response to a grant for a specific purpose.

G

general obligation bonds State or local government debt instruments that are backed by the full faith and credit of the issuing government and are payable out of general revenue.

general-purpose grant A grant from one government to another that may be used for any acceptable public purpose.

general revenue Funds available for general budgetary purposes, excluding off-budget and enterprise funds.

General Revenue Sharing A program of federal grants to state and local governments in the 1970s and 1980s that were not restricted to particular uses.

gentrification Rehabilitation of older urban buildings for use by middle- to upper-income households.

government failure An outcome of government processes that reduces or fails to improve economic efficiency.

H

health maintenance organization (HMO) A network of hospitals and physicians, both primary care and specialists, that enrolls members on the basis of a per-patient or per-family charge and provides both primary and acute health care.

home rule A grant by a state of considerable discretionary authority to local governments.

horizontal equalization Actions to ensure that resources are distributed more equally among governments at the same level so as to ensure that they can provide at least minimal standards of services to their citizens.

horizontal equity Justice or fairness in the distribution of benefits or burdens between people or communities in similar economic circumstances.

I

impact fee A fee charged to developers or builders for construction on vacant lots to cover the additional cost of providing infrastructure and services to new residents or businesses.

incidence The determination of who actually bears the burden of a tax in terms of paying higher prices or receiving less income or a reduction in the value of assets.

infrastructure Physical and other capital assets, usually public, that provide the supporting backdrop for a market system; includes transportation, parks, waterways, public buildings, and water and sewer systems.

inheritance tax A tax imposed by U.S. states on the receipt of wealth from a deceased person.

initiative and referendum Democratic processes that permit citizens to initiate legislation that is then passed or defeated by popular vote.

insurance element (OASDHI) That part of Social Security that protects participants from the risk of disability or loss of a breadwinner (disability and survivors' insurance).

intangibles In property tax, taxable assets other than real property or tangible personal property such as cars and business equipment, primarily financial assets.

intergenerational equity Justice or fairness in the distribution of income, assets, or opportunities between individuals of different generations or cohorts.

intergovernmental grant A sum of money transferred from one government to another, usually from the central government to state or local governments or from state to local governments, with the purpose for which it is to be expended specified by the granting government.

internalizing externalities Actions to make individuals bear the external costs or receive the internal benefits of their own actions so that they will make decisions that are both socially and privately optimal.

interpersonal equity Justice or fairness in the distribution of income, assets, or opportunities among individuals of the same generation or cohort.

J–L

Job Training and Partnership Act (JTPA) A federal program to provide funds for training for unemployed workers, housewives reentering the labor force, and others in need of remedial or expanded skills to become employable.

Laffer curve A diagram showing the relationship between tax rate and tax revenue that implies that higher rates may reduce rather than increase revenue beyond some point.

Leviathan The notion of the government as an uncontrollable monster that devours resources; named after a mythical Babylonian sea monster.

Lindahl prices Prices for a public good that are set equal to the marginal benefit for each user.

line item budget A budget that lists planned expenditures according to items purchased (labor, supplies, etc.) rather than according to the service provided or agency.

local public goods Public goods for which most of the benefits accrue to residents of a particular local area.

lump-sum grant A grant whose amount is not dependent on any matching effort by the recipient.

M

maintenance of effort A condition of a grant that requires the grantee to continue to expend at least the same amount of own funds on the purpose of the grant as before receiving the grant.

managed care An alternative to traditional fee-for-service medical practice that charges clients a flat rate to cover all services and determines what services will be available in a particular case or what provider may be used.

marginal social benefit The increase in positive externalities that results from producing or consuming one more unit of a good or service.

marginal social cost The increase in negative externalities that results from producing or consuming one more unit of a good or service.

marginal tax price The increase in an individual's tax burden required to support the production of a particular public good.

marginal tax rate The additional percent of tax on an additional dollar of income or expenditure.

market failure An outcome of market processes that does not satisfy the criterion of Pareto optimality (Q.V.).

matching grant A grant that requires the grantee to contribute to the purpose of the grant in some fixed ratio for each dollar received.

means testing Limiting distribution of benefits to those whose income does not exceed a certain limit.

median voter model A model of political behavior that assumes that politicians respond to the preferences of the median voter in order to assemble a critical mass of support around the center of the distribution of voters and their preferences.

Medicaid A U.S. health care program that is means tested, paid for out of general revenue, with costs shared between federal and state budgets.

medical savings accounts Tax-free funds set aside by households to purchase health care.

Medicare A U.S. federal health care program for those over 65, providing hospital and physician care and funded primarily through a payroll tax and to a lesser degree by premiums deducted from Social Security checks.

mill rate The (property) tax rate stated as tenths of a cent per $100 of assessed valuation.

moral hazard The risk that people who are insured will become careless because they know they will be reimbursed for losses.

multiplier effects Secondary increases in employment or income resulting from a primary change, such as the location of a governmental facility or a new private industry or commercial development in an area.

municipal bonds Debt instruments issued by state and local governments; the interest income is exempt from federal income taxes.

N

negative income tax An income tax system that collects revenue from taxpayers above a certain income level and pays people whose incomes fall below that level.

nonexcludability The inability to keep nonpayers from consuming a good without incurring a cost greater than the value of the additional revenue.

nonrivalry Characteristic of a public good; consumption by one person does not diminish the amount available to another.

O

OASDHI Initials of the social insurance program of Old Age, Survivors', Disability, and Health Insurance, better known as Social Security.

off-budget accounts Part of a government's accounts that are not included in the general budget, such as trust funds and enterprise funds.

open-ended grant Grant program that does not have a fixed dollar ceiling but is given to all eligible recipients who meet the criteria.

option demand Demand for a service that is primarily a demand for it to be available in case it is needed, for example, a fire station.

own-source revenue (state or local) Funds raised through taxes, fees, charges, and other sources under the control of the particular government; excludes intergovernmental.

P

Pareto optimality A situation in which no change can be made that makes some people better off without making at least one person worse off.

peak-load pricing Setting higher prices for periods of peak demand so as to shift some users to off-peak periods.

pension/annuity element (OASDHI) The part of Social Security that provides retirement income to workers and their dependents who have accumulated enough quarters of coverage and meet the age requirement.

performance budgeting Budgeting based on desired outcomes, with budget allocations set so as to try to attain those objectives.

personal exemptions Amount excluded from income for tax purposes based on the number of qualifying members of a household.

personal property Items other than land and buildings that may also be subject to property tax such as cars or business inventories.

poll tax A per capita or per-household tax of a flat amount; simple to administer but highly regressive.

privatization Transfer of activities from the public to the private sector.

project grant Intergovernmental grant distributed on the basis of invited proposals for particular purposes.

program budget A budget that defines a group of related governmental activities and specifies the funds to be allocated to those activities..

proportional representation Dividing representation in a state or district in proportion to votes received rather than winner takes all.

proportional tax A tax that takes a constant percentage of one's income as income rises.

Prospective Payment System (PPS) Hospital reimbursements based on a fixed amount per stay for a particular diagnosis rather than actual hospital costs, using national averages for length of stay and adjusted for local conditions.

public choice A branch of public sector economics that blends economic theory and political science to examine the behavior of public officials as self-interested individuals and the implications of that approach for public policy.

public finance/public sector economics The field of economics that addresses the revenue and expenditure activities of government.

public goods Goods and services that are nonrival in consumption and not excludable for nonpayers and that would not be produced at all or not in sufficient quantity by the private market.

public provision Policies to ensure that a good or service is available through government support; does not require public production.

R

rational ignorance The choice by individuals not to be informed and active in public decisions because the cost of becoming informed and participating is greater than the benefits they receive.

real property Assets in the form of land or improvements, mainly buildings.

redistribution element (OASDHI) The aspect of Social Security that gives relatively higher benefits to low-wage workers than to higher wage workers in comparison to their preretirement income.

residual claimant The person who is entitled to any surplus or profit, or who is responsible for any deficit or loss, after all the other claimants (workers, suppliers, etc.) have received their due.

retail sales tax A broad-based consumption tax collected only at final sale on most goods and some services in the United States; used by most state and many local governments.

revenue bonds Debt instruments used by state and local governments to build income-generating facilities (dormitories, stadiums, hospitals, etc.) for which revenue from the facilities' sales is pledged to repay the debt.

revenue forecasting The act of predicting government income in future budget years on the basis of past experience and current conditions.

S

severance tax A tax on the extraction of minerals and other natural resources.

shadow demand (supply) curve A second supply or demand curve that reflects the difference in the perceptions of supply or demand by buyer and seller; the difference between the two curves is the amount of the tax.

shadow prices Imputed prices or estimated values for sources of benefit or cost that do not pass through the market, such as the value of travel time.

shifting The process of passing on the burden of the tax from the person who is initially required to pay a tax to a customer, worker, supplier, or owner.

spatial externalities Spillover effects that are experienced by people in proximity to the activity creating the effect.

specific tax A tax that is expressed as a function of some physical measure (quarts, miles, dozens) rather than as a percent of the price.

sumptuary tax A tax intended to discourage consumption of the item taxed.

Supplementary Security Income (SSI) A program that provides income transfers to elderly, blind, and other individuals who do not qualify for either TANF or Social Security; replaced Aid to the Aged, Aid to the Blind, and General Assistance.

T

tax credits Reductions in tax liability for specific kinds of expenditures or circumstances, such as the child care credit for child care expenses for qualifying families.

tax expenditure Revenue foregone from a tax by creating an exemption, deduction, exclusion, or credit.

tax and expenditure limitations (TELs) Ceilings on growth of taxes, government revenue, or government spending enacted by statute or constitutional amendment in order to limit the growth of government.

tax exporting Shifting of part or all of the tax burden to nonresidents.

taxable equivalent yield The percentage return on a municipal (tax-free) bond that is the same as the after-tax return on a taxable corporate bond of the same degree of risk.

taxable income In U.S. income tax, the amount of income on which the computation of tax liability is based after adjustments, exclusions, deductions, and exemptions.

Temporary Assistance to Needy Families (TANF) Assistance for families unable to support themselves on a short-term basis, replaced Aid to Families with Dependent Children in 1996.

Tiebout hypothesis A model that predicts that people will choose to locate in communities based on the fiscal surplus each community offers, resulting in competitive constraints on local governments to hold down taxes and offer attractive service packages.

total revenue Government revenue from all sources, including off-budget and enterprise funds.

transfer payments Payments by government to individuals for whom no services are required in exchange (e.g., welfare, Social Security).

two-part tariff A charge for a service with two components, a flat fee for every user regardless of quantity and an additional charge per unit consumed (flat fee may include some minimum quantity at no additional charge).

U, V

unfunded mandate A requirement imposed by a higher level of government on a lower one to carry out some specific action, without any provision for the higher level of government to pay part or all of the cost.

unified budget A governmental budget that combines all accounts, including off-budget or enterprise funds.

universal participation A program that requires everyone who is eligible to participate; Social Security is one such example.

use tax Tax due from the consumer on purchases out of state that would have been subject to retail sales taxes if purchased in-state.

value-added tax A tax collected at every stage of production and distribution (sometimes exempting retail), with a credit for taxes at the preceding stage so that no accumulation or cascading of taxes occur.

veil of ignorance A thought experiment developed by philosopher John Rawls that asks people to design a set of rules for distribution of wealth, income, or opportunities without knowing where they will fall within that system.

vertical equalization Actions to ensure that resources are distributed among levels of government more in proportion to their expenditure responsibilities through redistribution from one
   level of government to another.
vertical equity Justice or fairness in the distribution of benefits or burdens between people or
   communities in different economic circumstances.
visibility The level of awareness of the public of
   the existence and amount of tax being collected.
voting paradox The possibility that the ranking
   of more than two alternatives is not transitive, so
   that in paired voting A is preferred to B, B is preferred to C, and C is preferred to A.
vouchers Grants from government to individuals
   that can be used to purchase certain specific ser-

vices (such as education) from private or public
suppliers of their choice.

W–Z

wage ceiling (OASDHI) The maximum amount
   of employment earnings on which Social Security
   taxes are collected.
workable competition The existence of enough
   competition among buyers and/or sellers so as to
   give results that are reasonably close to those of
   the perfectly competitive model.
zero-based budgeting A budgetary process that
   starts at a base of zero and requires justification
   of every expenditure instead of making incremental adjustments from the previous year's budget.

INDEX

A

Ability to pay, 172
Ad valorem taxes, 162, 163, 164
Administrative cost
  and efficiency, 121
  and fraud, 121
Adverse selection, 400
Affluent Society, 54
Aid to Families with Dependent Children (AFDC), 34, 305, 392
  administration of, 122
  cost of, 295
Alaska, taxes in, 186
Allocation, government role in, 3
American Canoe Association, and hog farm pollution, 31
Americans with Disabilities Act, 301
Antitrust law, encouragement of competition by, 138
Apartments
  longer-term market for, 258
  short-run market for, 257
Armey-Shelby Proposal, 217
Articles of Confederation, in evolution of fiscal federalism, 32
Assessment
  for infrastructure financing, 371
  of property, 261
Assessment rate, defined, 28

B

Balanced Budget Act of 1997, 421
Bell-shaped curve, 107
Benefit principle, 173
  fees and, 284
Benefit tax, 75
Black market, 243
Block grant, 304
Bonds
  defined, 374
  general obligation, 338, 374
  municipal, 338
  revenue, 338, 374
  for water and sewer systems, 384
Budget
  balanced, 337
  constraints in, 307
  debts and, 337
  deficits in, 323, 337
  defined, 320
  expenditures in, 326
  lack of constraints in, 56
  line of, 308
  line-item, 329
  performance, 329
  planned spending changes in, 328
  program, 329
  revenue-expenditure gap in, 320
  surplus in, 323
  zero-based, 329
Budgeting
  process of, 320
  and public choice, 330
  in public sector, 319–340
Budgeting agency models, 330

Budgeting and Accounting Act of 1921, 327
Burden, excess, 159, 160
  of excise tax on lightbulbs, 161
  and multiple tax bases, 166
  tax rate and, 167
Bureau of Budget, 327
Bureau of Census, 38
Bureau of Land Management, 291
Bureaucracy-driven demand, 55
Bureaucrats, and incentives, 95
Buses, 380
Business travelers, sales taxes and, 229
Businesses, unincorporated, taxes on, 206

C

Calculus of Consent, 99
California Proposition 13, 263
  fallout from, 267
Canada, public pensions in, 401
Capital budget, 325
Capital equipment, depreciation of, 220
Capital gains taxes, 207, 216
Capital spending, 367–388
Capitalization
  defined, 254
  fiscal, 151
Capture theory of regulation, 138

Cascade taxes, 230
  produced by value-added taxes, 246
Categorical grants, 296, 303
Census of Governments 1997, 18, 19
Centralization of governments
  gains from, 19
  losses from, 19
Charges
  and congestion, 283
  efficiency issues in, 280
  effluent, 285
  equity issues in, 278
  externalities in, 282
  as growth management tools, 289
  for infrastructure use, 370
  purposes of, 281
  as revenue source, 272–294
  types of, 277
Charitable organizations, tax expenditures favoring, 193
Chief Finance Officers Act of 1990, 327
Child care credit, on income tax, 213
Child credit, on taxes, 215
Child Health Insurance Program (CHIP), 421
China, upward flow of funds in, 300
Cities
  annexation of, 30
  creation of, 29
  growth of, 29
  income taxes assessed by, 218
  incorporation of, 29

435